International Economics

FIFTH EDITION

The Pearson Series in Economics

Abel/Bernanke/Croushore
Macroeconomics*

Bade/Parkin
Foundations of Economics*

Bierman/Fernandez
Game Theory with Economic Applications

Blanchard
Macroeconomics

Blau / Ferber / Winkler
The Economics of Women, Men and Work

Boardman / Greenberg / Vining / Weimer
Cost-Benefit Analysis

Boyer
Principles of Transportation Economics

Branson
Macroeconomic Theory and Policy

Brock/Adams
The Structure of American Industry

Bruce
Public Finance and the American Economy

Carlton/Perloff
Modern Industrial Organization

Case/Fair/Oster
Principles of Economics*

Caves/Frankel/Jones
World Trade and Payments: An Introduction

Chapman
Environmental Economics: Theory, Application, and Policy

Cooter/Ulen
Law & Economics

Downs
An Economic Theory of Democracy

Ehrenberg/Smith
Modern Labor Economics

Ekelund/Ressler/Tollison
Economics*

Farnham
Economics for Managers

Folland/Goodman/Stano
The Economics of Health and Health Care

Fort
Sports Economics

Froyen
Macroeconomics

Fusfeld
The Age of the Economist

Gerber
International Economics

Gordon
Macroeconomics

Greene
Econometric Analysis

Gregory
Essentials of Economics

Gregory/Stuart
Russian and Soviet Economic Performance and Structure

Hartwick/Olewiler
The Economics of Natural Resource Use

Heilbroner/ Milberg
The Making of the Economic Society

Heyne/ Boettke / Prychitko
The Economic Way of Thinking

Hoffman/Averett
Women and the Economy: Family, Work, and Pay

Holt
Markets, Games and Strategic Behavior

Hubbard
Money, the Financial System, and the Economy

Hubbard/O'Brien
Economics*

Hughes/Cain
American Economic History

Husted/Melvin
International Economics

Jehle/Reny
Advanced Microeconomic Theory

Johnson-Lans
A Health Economics Primer

Keat/Young
Managerial Economics

Klein
Mathematical Methods for Economics

Krugman/Obstfeld
International Economics: Theory & Policy*

Laidler
The Demand for Money

Leeds/von Allmen
The Economics of Sports

Leeds/von Allmen/Schiming
*Economics**

Lipsey/Ragan/Storer
*Economics**

Lynn
Economic Development: Theory and Practice for a Divided World

Melvin
International Money and Finance

Miller
*Economics Today**

Understanding Modern Economics

Miller/Benjamin
The Economics of Macro Issues

Miller/Benjamin/North
The Economics of Public Issues

Mills/Hamilton
Urban Economics

Mishkin
*The Economics of Money, Banking, and Financial Markets**

*The Economics of Money, Banking, and Financial Markets, Business School Edition**

Murray
Econometrics: A Modern Introduction

Nafziger
The Economics of Developing Countries

O'Sullivan/Sheffrin/Perez
*Economics: Principles, Applications and Tools**

Parkin
*Economics**

Perloff
*Microeconomics**

Microeconomics: Theory and Applications with Calculus

Perman/Common/McGilvray/Ma
Natural Resources and Environmental Economics

Phelps
Health Economics

Pindyck/Rubinfeld
*Microeconomics**

Riddell/Shackelford/Stamos/Schneider
Economics: A Tool for Critically Understanding Society

Ritter/Silber/Udell
*Principles of Money, Banking & Financial Markets**

Roberts
The Choice: A Fable of Free Trade and Protection

Rohlf
Introduction to Economic Reasoning

Ruffin/Gregory
Principles of Economics

Sargent
Rational Expectations and Inflation

Sawyer/Sprinkle
International Economics

Scherer
Industry Structure, Strategy, and Public Policy

Schiller
The Economics of Poverty and Discrimination

Sherman
Market Regulation

Silberberg
Principles of Microeconomics

Stock/Watson
Introduction to Econometrics

Introduction to Econometrics, Brief Edition

Studenmund
Using Econometrics: A Practical Guide

Tietenberg/Lewis
Environmental and Natural Resource Economics

Environmental Economics and Policy

Todaro/Smith
Economic Development

Waldman
Microeconomics

Waldman/Jensen
Industrial Organization: Theory and Practice

Weil
Economic Growth

Williamson
Macroeconomics

International Economics

FIFTH EDITION

James Gerber
San Diego State University

Addison-Wesley

Boston Columbus Indianapolis New York San Francisco Upper Saddle River
Amsterdam Cape Town Dubai London Madrid Milan Munich Paris Montreal Toronto
Delhi Mexico City Sao Paulo Sydney Hong Kong Seoul Singapore Taipei Tokyo

For Monica and Elizabeth.

Editor in Chief: Donna Battista
Acquisitions Editor: Noel Kamm Seibert
Editorial Assistant: Carolyn Terbush
Managing Editor: Nancy Fenton
Art Director, Cover: Linda Knowles
Cover Designer: Elena Sidorova
Supplements Editor: Alison Eusden
Media Producer: Angela Lee
Marketing Manager: Elizabeth Averbeck

Marketing Assistant: Ian Gold
Senior Manufacturing Buyer: Carol Melville
Production Coordination, Composition,
  Text Design, and Illustrations: GEX
  Publishing Services
Printer/Binder: Edwards Brothers
Cover Printer: Lehigh Phoenix
Cover Image: Martin Child/Getty Images

Copyright © 2011, 2008, 2005, 2002, 1999 Pearson Education, Inc.

All rights reserved. No part of this publication may be reproduced, stored in a retrieval system, or transmitted, in any form or by any means, electronic, mechanical, photocopying, recording, or otherwise, without the prior written permission of the publisher. Printed in the United States of America. For information on obtaining permission for use of material in this work, please submit a written request to Pearson Education, Inc., Rights and Contracts Department, 501 Boylston Street, Suite 900, Boston, MA 02116, fax your request to 617-671-3447, or e-mail at http://www.pearsoned.com/legal/permissions.htm.

Library of Congress Cataloging-in-Publication Data

Gerber, James.
  International economics / James Gerber.--5th ed.
    p. cm.
  Includes index.
  ISBN 978-0-13-510015-8 (casebound : alk. paper)
  1. International economic relations. 2. International economic integration. 3. International trade.
4. Commercial policy. 5. United States—Foreign economic relations. I. Title.

HF1359.G474 2010
337--dc22

2009046215

10 9 8 7 6 5 4 3 2 1

Addison-Wesley
is an imprint of

www.pearsonhighered.com

ISBN-13: 978-0-13-510015-8
ISBN-10: 0-13-510015-1

BRIEF CONTENTS

Suggested Readings are available on the Companion Website at www.pearsonhighered.com/gerber

CONTENTS

Suggested Readings are available on the Companion Website at
www.pearsonhighered.com/gerber

PREFACE

International Economics is designed for a one-semester course covering both the micro and macro components of international economics. The Fifth Edition continues the approach of the first four editions by offering a principles-level introduction to the core theories, together with policy analysis and the institutional and historical contexts of our world's increasingly international economic integration. My goal is to make economic reasoning about the international economy accessible to a diverse group of students, including both economics majors and nonmajors. Many of the issues covered are contentious, particularly in light of the financial crisis that began in 2008. My intention is to present the consensus of economic opinion, when one exists, and to describe the differences when one does not. I recognize that the presence or absence of consensus is sometimes contentious itself, but in general economists agree more about matters related to trade than they do about matters on the finance side. The text reflects that perspective.

New to the Fifth Edition

This Fifth Edition of *International Economics* preserves the organization and coverage of the Fourth Edition and adds a number of updates and enhancements. New to this edition:

- All tables and graphs have been updated.
- Chapter 1 is reorganized to include a brief introduction to the global economic crisis that began in 2007.
- Chapter 2 incorporates a discussion of regional trade agreements and the WTO, including the concepts of trade diversion and creation.
- Chapter 3 introduces the concept of the resource curse in a case study on petroleum exports and has a new case study on losing comparative advantage and world cotton production.
- Chapter 4 has new material on off-shoring and outsourcing and a new case study on off-shoring by U.S. multinational corporations.
- Chapter 5 presents new material on geography and trade and a new case study on Mexico's export processing industry.
- Chapter 7 has a new case study on traditional knowledge and intellectual property rights.
- Chapter 9 introduces the concept of sudden stops and presents a new case study examining the current crisis and its effects on the balance of payments of the United States.

- Chapter 10 includes a new case study on monetary unions, including the CFA region of West Africa.
- Chapter 11 provides a discussion on the limits of fiscal policy's ability to counteract a crisis through a case study of Argentina's crisis of 2001.
- Chapter 12 leads up to a new case study of the 2007–2008 financial crisis. The new material builds on economic theory and on a comparative analysis of earlier financial meltdowns in Mexico (1994–1995) and Asia (1997–1998).
- Chapter 13 has two new case studies, one on NAFTA and the impact of Mexican agricultural reforms and another on manufacturing in the United States.
- Chapter 14 is updated to include a discussion of reforms under the Lisbon Treaty and student mobility under the Erasmus Program.
- Chapter 15 has a new case study of the Chilean Model.

Hallmarks of International Economics

Several features of *International Economics* distinguish it from the many excellent texts in the field:

- First, the approach is broader than the theoretical apparatus used by economists. Economic theory is covered and its mastery is essential, but it is my belief that most readers grasp theory more completely when it is presented along with real-world applications. To this end, I have supplemented economic theory with case studies and other content ranging from the role of economic institutions and the analysis of international economic policies to the recent history of the world economy.
- Second, the objective of covering both the micro and macro sides in a one-semester course necessitates paring back the coverage of theory in order to focus on the central concepts. As all instructors are aware, many theoretical topics are of secondary or tertiary importance, which can pose a problem for students who may lack the needed breadth and depth of understanding to rank topics by their relative importance.
- Third, *International Economics* provides richer historical and institutional detail than most other texts. This material illuminates the relationships between economic theory and policy, and between economics and the other social sciences.
- Fourth, I have organized Part 4 of the book into five chapters, each focused on a geographic area as follows: North America, the European Union, Latin America, East Asia, and China and India. These chapters offer students the chance to broaden their understanding of world trends and to observe the intellectual power of economic theory in practice.

Flexibility of Organization

A book requires a fixed topical sequence because it must order the chapters one after another. This is a potential problem for some instructors, as there is a wide variety of preferences for the order in which topics are taught. The Fifth Edition strives for flexibility in allowing instructors to find their own preferred sequence.

Part 1 includes two introductory chapters that are designed to build vocabulary, develop historical perspective, and provide background information about the different international organizations and the roles that they play in the world economy. Some instructors prefer to delve into the theory chapters immediately, and reserve this material for later in the course. There is no loss of continuity with this approach.

Part 2 presents the micro side of international economics, while Part 3 covers the macro side. These two parts can easily be reversed in sequence if desired.

Part 2 includes six chapters that cover trade models (Chapters 3–5) and commercial policy (Chapters 6–8). A condensed treatment of this section could focus on the Ricardian model in Chapter 3, and the analysis of tariffs and quotas in Chapters 6 and 7. Chapter 8 on labor and environmental standards can stand on its own, although the preceding chapters deepen student understanding of the trade-offs.

Part 3 covers the balance of payments, exchange rates, open-economy macroeconomics, and international financial crises. Chapter 11 on open economy macroeconomics is optional. It is intended for students and instructors who want a review of macroeconomics, including the concepts of fiscal and monetary policy, in a context that includes current accounts and exchange rates. If Chapter 11 is omitted, Chapter 12 remains accessible as long as students have an understanding of the basic concepts of fiscal and monetary policy. Chapter 12 relies most heavily on Chapters 9 (balance of payments) and 10 (exchange rates and exchange rate systems).

Part 4 presents five chapters, each focused on a geographic area. These chapters use theory presented in Chapters 3–12 in a similar fashion to the economics discussion that students find in the business press, congressional testimonies, speeches, and other sources intended for a broad civic audience. Where necessary, concepts such as the real rate of exchange are briefly reviewed. One or more of these chapters can be moved forward to fit the needs of a particular course.

Supplementary Materials

The following supplementary resources are available to support teaching and learning.

Companion Website: www.pearsonhighered.com/gerber

- David Dieterle of MCEE Walsh College has prepared a Web-based PowerPoint presentation comprising lecture notes and all of the text's tables and figures.
- In recognition of the importance of the Internet as a source of timely information, the Companion Website offers Web links for each chapter of *International Economics*. These links, complete with descriptions of the content available at each site, provide easy access to relevant, current data sources.
- The Companion Website also features multiple choice quizzes for each chapter of the text, written by Deborah Swenson of the University of California, Davis.

Other Supplements

Laura Wolff of Southern Illinois University, Edwardsville, has updated the Study Guide, which offers handy review and study aids as well as practice problems and tests. Laura has also revised and improved the Test Item File and brought it up to date with the text, and Ross vanWassenhove of the University of Houston has accuracy reviewed the Test Item File and the TestGen material, which are available for download on the Instructor's Resource web site. The Instructor's Manual is also available online as an additional resource. Finally, the CourseSmart eTextbook for the text is available through www.coursesmart.com. CourseSmart goes beyond traditional expectations providing instant, online access to the textbooks and course materials you need at a lower cost to students. And, even as students save money, you can save time and hassle with a digital textbook that allows you to search the most relevant content at the very moment you need it. Whether it's evaluating textbooks or creating lecture notes to help students with difficult concepts, CourseSmart can make life a little easier. See how when you visit www.coursesmart.com/instructors.

Acknowledgments

All books are team efforts, even single-authored books. I owe a debt of gratitude to a large number of people. At San Diego State University, I have benefited from the opportunity to teach and converse with a wide range of students. My colleagues in San Diego and across the border in Mexico have been extremely helpful. Their comments, and our conversations, constantly push me to think about the core economic ideas that should be a part of a college student's education, and to search for ways to explain the relevance and importance of those ideas with greater clarity and precision. Any failure in this regard is, of course, mine alone.

I am deeply grateful to Noel Seibert, Carolyn Terbush, Nancy Fenton, Alison Eusden, and Angela Lee.

Finally, my gratitude goes to the numerous reviewers who have played an essential role in the development of *International Economics*. Each of the following individuals reviewed the manuscript, many of them several times, and provided useful commentary. I cannot express how much the text has benefited from their comments.

Mary Acker
Iona College

Jeff Ankrom
Wittenberg University

David Aschauer
Bates College

H. Somnez Atesoglu
Clarkson University

Mohsen Bahmani-Oskooee
University of Wisconsin, Milwaukee

Richard T. Baillie
Michigan State University

Mina Baliamoune-Lutz,
University of North Florida

Eugene Beaulieu
University of Calgary

Ted Black
Towson University

Bruce Blonigen
University of Oregon

Lee Bour
Florida State University

Byron Brown
Southern Oregon University

Laura Brown
University of Manitoba

Albert Callewaert
Walsh College

Tom Carter
Oklahoma City University

Srikanta Chatterjee
Massey University, New Zealand

Jen-Chi Cheng
Wichita State University

Don Clark
University of Tennessee

Raymond Cohn
Illinois State University

Peter Crabb
Northwest Nazarene University

David Crary
Eastern Michigan University

Al Culver
California State University, Chico

Joseph Daniels
Marquette University

Alan Deardorff
University of Michigan

Craig Depken II
University of North Carolina, Charlotte

John Devereaux
University of Miami

K. Doroodian
Ohio University

Carolyn Evans,
Santa Clara University

Noel J. J. Farley
Bryn Mawr College

Lewis R. Gale IV
University of Southwest Louisiana

Kevin Gallagher
Boston University

Ira Gang
Rutgers University

John Gilbert
Utah State University

James Giordano
Villanova University

Amy Jocelyn Glass
Texas A&M University

Joanne Gowa
Princeton University

Gregory Green
Idaho State University

Thomas Grennes
North Carolina State University

Winston Griffith
Bucknell University

Jane Hall
California State University, Fullerton

Seid Hassan
Murray State University

F. Steb Hipple
East Tennessee State University

Paul Jensen
Drexel University

George Karras
University of Illinois at Chicago

Kathy Kelly
University of Texas, Arlington

Abdul Khandker
University of Wisconsin, La Crosse

Jacqueline Khorassani
Marietta College

Sunghyun Henry Kim
Brandeis University

Vani Kotcherlakota
University of Nebraska at Kearney

Corrine Krupp
Michigan State University

Kishore Kulkarni
Metropolitan State College of Denver

Farrokh Langdana
Rutgers University

Daniel Y. Lee
Shippensburg University

Mary Lesser
Iona College

Susan Linz
Michigan State University

Marc Lombard
Macquarie University, Australia

Thomas Lowinger
Washington State University

Nicolas Magud
University of Oregon

Bala Maniam
Sam Houston State University

Mary McGlasson
Arizona State University

Joseph McKinney
Baylor University

Judith McKinney
Hobart & William Smith Colleges

Howard McNier
San Francisco State University

Michael O. Moore
George Washington University

Stephan Norribin
Florida State University

William H. Phillips
University of South Carolina

Frank Raymond
Bellarmine University

Donald Richards
Indiana State University

John Robertson
University of Kentucky Community College System

Jeffrey Rosensweig
Emory University

Marina Rosser
James Madison University

Raj Roy
University of Toledo

Michael Ryan
Western Michigan University

George Samuels
Sam Houston State University

Craig Schulman
University of Arizona

William Seyfried
Winthrop University

Eckhard Siggel
Concordia University

David Spiro
Columbia University

Richard Sprinkle
University of Texas, El Paso

Ann Sternlicht
Virginia Commonwealth University

Leonie Stone
State University of New York at Geneseo

Carolyn Fabian Stumph
Indiana University, Purdue University, Fort Wayne

Rebecca Summary
Southeast Missouri State University

Jack Suyderhoud
University of Hawaii

Kishor Thanawala
Villanova University

Henry Thompson
Auburn University

Cynthia Tori
Valdosta State University

Edward Tower
Duke University

Jose Ventura
Sacred Heart University

Michael Welker
Franciscan University

Jerry Wheat
Indiana State University

Laura Wolff
Southern Illinois University, Edwardsville

Chong K. Yip
Georgia State University

Alina Zapalska
Marshall University

Introduction and Institutions

The United States in a Global Economy

Introduction: International Economic Integration

In August of 2007, a crisis erupted in the housing sector of the United States. At the time, few people realized that the "sub-prime mortgage crisis" would become a demonstration of international economic integration or that it would push the world economy to the brink of collapse. The crisis grew through the remainder of 2007 and into 2008, so that by the summer nearly all high income economies were in deep distress. Contagion from the crisis spread like an epidemic as banks and other financial firms collapsed and solvent firms stopped lending. The scarcity of credit caused difficulties for businesses that could not find financing for their day-to-day operations while, at the same time, consumers cut back on their spending and businesses cut back on their purchases of new investment. By the end of 2008, economies around the world were in recession, with the notable exceptions of China, India, and the major oil producers.

This episode is the most dramatic instance since the Great Depression of the 1930s of a crisis leading to severe economic recession in many countries around the world. It is, however, only one of several recent examples of crises spilling across national borders. The Russian Crisis of 1998–99, the Asian Crisis of 1997–98, the Mexican Crisis of 1994–95, the Latin American Debt Crisis of 1982–89, and a number of others caused major damage to financial systems, businesses, and households, both in the places where they originated and in many other countries.

The international integration of national economies has brought many benefits to nations across the globe, including technological innovation, less expensive products, and greater investment in regions where local capital is scarce, to name a few. But it has also made countries vulnerable to economic problems that have become more easily transmitted from one place to another. Given that the benefits and costs of international economic integration are surrounded by controversy, it is worth clarifying what we mean by the term "international economic integration," or "globalization in the economic sphere." In order to help us understand these forces better, a historical perspective is also useful.

Elements of International Economic Integration

Most people would agree that the major economies of the world are more integrated than at any time in history. Given our instantaneous communications, modern transportation, and relatively open trading systems, most goods can move from one country to another without major obstacles and at relatively low cost. For example, most cars today are made in fifteen or more countries after you consider where each part is made, where the advertising originates, who does the accounting, and who transports the components and the final product. Nevertheless, the proposition that today's economies are more integrated than at any other time in history is not simple to demonstrate. It is clear that our current wave of economic integration began in the 1950s, with the reduction of trade barriers after World War II. In the 1970s, many countries began to encourage financial integration by increasing the openness of their capital markets. The advent of the Internet in the 1990s, along with the other elements of the telecommunications revolution, pushed economic integration to new levels as multinational firms developed international production networks and markets became ever more tightly linked.

Today's global economy is not the first instance of a dramatic growth in economic ties between nations, however, as there was another important period between approximately 1870 and 1913. New technologies such as transatlantic cables, steam powered ships, railroads, and a number of others led the way, much as they do today. For example, when the first transatlantic cable was completed in 1866, the time it took for a New York businessperson to complete a financial transaction in London fell from approximately three weeks to one day, and by 1914 it had fallen to one minute as radio telephony became possible.

We have mostly forgotten about this earlier period of economic integration and that makes it easier to overestimate integration today. Instantaneous communications and rapid transportation, together with the easy availability of foreign products, often cause us to lose sight of the fact that most of what we buy and sell never makes it out of our local or national markets. We rarely pause to think that haircuts, restaurant meals, gardens, health care, education, utilities, and many other goods and services are partially or wholly domestic products. In the United States, for example, about 82.3 percent of goods and services are produced domestically, with imports (17.7 percent) making up the remainder of what we consume (2008). By comparison, in 1890 the United States made about 92 percent of its goods and services, a larger share than today, but not radically different.

The question as to whether we are more economically integrated today or in some period in the past is not only academic. Between the onset of World War I in 1914 and the end of World War II in 1945, the world economy suffered a series of man-made catastrophes that deintegrated national economies. Two world wars and a global depression caused most countries to close their borders to foreign goods, foreign capital, and foreign people. Since the end of World War II, many of the economic linkages between nations have served to repair the damage done during the first half of the twentieth century, but there is no reason to think that events might not cause a similar decoupling in the future.

Understanding international economic integration requires us to define what we mean by the term. Economists usually point to four criteria or measures for judging the degree of integration. These are trade flows, capital flows, people flows, and the similarity of prices in separate markets. The first three points are relatively self-explanatory, while the similarity of prices refers to the fact that integrated economies have price differences that are relatively small and are due mainly to differences in transportation costs. Goods that can move freely from a low-cost to a high-cost region should experience price convergence as goods move from where they are plentiful and cheap to where they are relatively scarcer and more expensive. Each of these indicators—trade flows, factor (labor and capital) movements, and similarity of prices—are measures of the degree of international economic integration.

The Growth of World Trade

Since the end of World War II, world trade has grown much faster than world output. In 1950, total world exports—which are the same as world imports—are estimated to have been 5.5 percent of world **gross domestic product (GDP)**. By 2005, fifty-five years later, they were 20.5 percent of world GDP, nearly four times more important relative to the size of the world economy. One measure of the importance of international trade in a nation's economy is the sum of exports plus imports, divided by the gross domestic product (GDP), where GDP is a measure of total production. Specifically, it is the value of all final goods and services produced inside a nation during some period, usually one year. The ratio of trade to GDP is called the **index of openness**, represented as follows:

$$\text{Index of Openness} = (\text{Exports} + \text{Imports}) \div \text{GDP}$$

Openness does not tell us about a country's trade policies and countries with higher openness measures do not necessarily have lower barriers to trade, although that is one possibility. In general, large countries are less dependent on international trade because their firms can reach an optimal production size without having to sell to foreign markets. Consequently, smaller countries tend to have higher measures of openness.

Figure 1.1 shows the openness index for six countries between 1913 and 2006. The decline in trade between the onset of World War I and 1950 is clearly visible in each country, as is the subsequent increase after 1950. Another pattern shown in Figure 1.1 is the smaller indexes for the United States and Japan, which have the largest populations, and the much higher index for the Netherlands, which has the smallest population in the sample. In general, smaller countries trade more than larger ones since they cannot efficiently produce as wide a range of goods and must depend on trade to a greater extent. For example, if the Netherlands were to produce autos solely for its own market, it would lack economies of scale and could not produce at a competitive cost, whereas the U.S. market can absorb a large share of U.S. output. Hence, the openness index measures the relative importance of international trade in a nation's economy, but it does not provide any direct information about trade policy or trade barriers.

Figure 1.1 gives a historical overview of the decline and subsequent return of international trade after World War II, but it obscures important changes in the composition of trade flows from early in the twentieth century to those at the end of the century. Prior to World War I most trade consisted of agricultural commodities and raw materials, while current trade is primarily manufactured consumer goods and producer goods (machinery and equipment). Consequently, today's manufacturers are much more exposed to international competition than was the case in 1900. In addition, much of the growth of world trade since 1950 has been accomplished by multinational corporations. With production sites in multiple countries and inputs that pass back and forth between affiliates, multinational corporations have become dramatically important. This trend has been supported and encouraged by the telecommunications revolution and transportation improvements that have lowered the costs of coordinating operations that are physically separated by oceans and continents. And finally, it has also become possible to coordinate from a great distance service operations such as accounting and data processing. In sum, trade today is qualitatively different than in 1913, and the growth of the openness index since 1950 cannot tell the whole story.

Capital and Labor Mobility

In addition to exports and imports, factor movements are also an indicator of economic integration. As national economies become more interdependent, labor and capital should move more easily across international boundaries. Labor, however, is less mobile internationally than it was in 1900. Consider, for

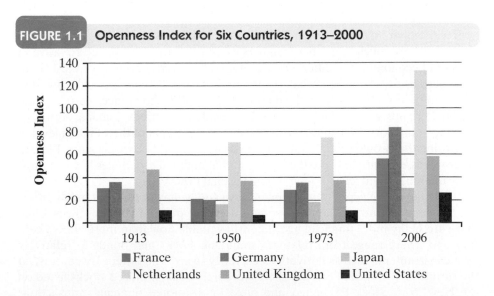

FIGURE 1.1   **Openness Index for Six Countries, 1913–2000**

Source: Maddison, A. (1991). "Dynamic Forces in Capitalist Development" and The World Trade Organization "Statistics Database: Trade Profiles." Note that 2006 is an average of 2005–2007.

example, that in 1890 approximately 14.5 percent of the U.S. population was foreign born, while in 2006, the figure was 12.1 percent. In 1900, many nations had open door immigration policies, and passport controls, immigration visas, and work permits were exceptions rather than rules. In the 1920s, the United States sharply restricted immigration and international labor mobility declined. These restrictions lasted until the 1960s, when changes in immigration laws once again encouraged foreigners to migrate to the United States.

On the capital side, measurement is more difficult, since there are several ways to measure capital flows. The most basic distinction is between flows of financial capital representing paper assets such as stocks, bonds, currencies, and bank accounts, and flows of capital representing physical assets such as real estate, factories, and businesses. The latter type of capital flow is called **foreign direct investment (FDI)**. To some extent, the distinction between the two is immaterial because both types of capital flows represent shifts in wealth across national boundaries and both make one nation's savings available to another.

When we compare international capital flows today to a century ago, there are two points to keep in mind. First, savings and investment are highly correlated. That is, high savings countries tend to have high rates of investment, and low savings is correlated with low investment. If there were a single world market in which capital flowed freely and easily, this would not necessarily be the case. Capital would flow from countries with abundant savings and capital to countries with low savings and capital, where it would find its highest returns. Second, a variety of technological improvements increased capital flows in the 1800s, as they are doing today. Transoceanic cables and radio telephony have already been mentioned, but capital flows also increased in the late 1800s because there were new investment opportunities such as national railroad networks and other infrastructure, both at home and abroad.

If we compare the size of capital flows today to the previous era of globalization, flows today are much larger but mainly because economies are larger. Relative to the size of economies, the differences are not great and may even favor the 1870 to 1913 period, depending on what is measured. Great Britain routinely invested 9 percent of its GDP abroad in the decades before 1913, and France, Germany, and the Netherlands were as high at times. For significant periods, Canada, Australia, and Argentina borrowed amounts that exceeded 10 percent of their GDP, a level of borrowing that would send up danger signals in the world economy since 1950. In other words, it is hard to make the argument that national economies have a historically unprecedented level of international capital flows today.

While the relative quantity of capital flows today may not be that much different for many countries, there are some important qualitative differences. First, there are many more financial instruments available now than there were a century ago. These range from relatively mundane stocks and bonds to relatively exotic instruments such as derivatives, currency swaps, and others. By contrast, at the turn of the twentieth century there were only a few hundred stocks listed on the New York Stock Exchange, and most international financial transactions involved the buying and selling of bonds.

A second difference today is the role of foreign exchange transactions. In 1900, countries had fixed exchange rates and firms in international trade or finance had less day-to-day risk from a sudden change in the value of a foreign currency. Many firms today spend significant resources to protect themselves from sudden shifts in currency values. Consequently, buying and selling assets denominated in foreign currencies is the largest component of international capital movements. For example, according to the Bank for International Settlements in Geneva, Switzerland, *daily* foreign exchange transactions in 2007 were equal to $3.21 *trillion*. In 1973, at the end of the last era of fixed exchange rates, they were $15 billion.

The third major difference in capital flows is that the costs of foreign financial transactions have fallen significantly. Economists refer to the costs of obtaining market information, negotiating an agreement, and enforcing the agreement as **transaction costs**. They are an important part of any business's costs, whether it is a purely domestic enterprise or a company involved in foreign markets. Due to sheer distance, as well as differences in culture, laws, and languages, transaction costs are often higher in international markets than in domestic ones. Today's lower transaction costs for foreign investment means that it is less expensive to move capital across international boundaries.

The volatile movement of financial capital across international boundaries is often mistakenly regarded as a new feature of the international economy. Speculative excesses and overinvestment, followed by capital flight and bankruptcies, have occurred throughout the modern era, going back at least to the 1600s and probably earlier. U.S. history shows a number of such cases. During the fifty years after 1890, at least four episodes of overspeculation and crisis hit the U.S. economy: 1890 to 1893 (speculation in silver stocks), 1907 (coffee futures and trust companies), 1920 to 1921 (agricultural land), and 1929 (U.S. stocks).

One way to read the history of financial crises in the United States and elsewhere is to recognize that today's turmoil in financial markets is not entirely new. The 1930s, for example, produced a crisis of worldwide proportions that resulted in nearly a decade of stagnant growth and contributed to the rise of fascism in Europe.

Three Features of Contemporary International Economic Relations

While international economic integration has been rapid, it does not appear to be historically unprecedented. Trade, as measured by the openness index, is about 50 percent more important to the U.S. economy than it was in 1890, although manufacturers and service providers are more exposed to the international economy. Labor is less mobile than in 1900 due to passport controls and work permits, but capital is more mobile and encompasses a larger variety of financial forms. (It remains to be seen if capital will continue to mobile after the recent crisis. New regulations will undoubtedly affect capital mobility, but it is too early to tell how.) Prices in many U.S. and foreign markets tend to be similar, although there are still significant differences such as the price of a pair of jeans in the United States and Europe. In quantitative terms, the differences between today and 100 years ago may not be as great as many people imagine, but qualitatively, a number of additional features of the world economy separate the first decade of the twenty-first century from the first decade of the twentieth.

Deeper Integration   High-income industrial countries have low barriers to imports of manufactured goods. There are a few exceptions, for example in sectors making processed foodstuffs and apparel, but as a general rule import tariffs are low and other forms of overt protection are uncommon. Low trade barriers are the result of agreements at the end of World War II that set in motion a process to slowly roll back the high levels of protection that were implemented in the 1920s and 1930s. One surprise from lower trade barriers is that various domestic policies have become barriers to trade. These policies are generally not enacted to influence trade flows, but as trade increased, they had that effect. They include sensitive issues such as labor and environmental policies, the rules of fair economic competition, conditions placed on investment, and government support for specific industries.

Negotiations between nations can be difficult in these areas because they represent fundamental elements of a country's domestic policy. By comparison, when nations open their markets symmetrically through simultaneous reductions in import taxes, the change is easily understood by most people and appeals to their sense of fairness. A similar symmetry in changing labor standards or investment rules is more difficult to define. When restrictive investment rules are eliminated, for example, it may seem that there is no reciprocal action, and that foreign influence has undermined national sovereignty.

Economists refer to the elimination of **tariffs** (taxes on imports) and **quotas** (quantitative restrictions on imports) as **shallow integration**, or integration at the border. These changes only directly affect the flow of goods and services coming across national boundaries. By contrast, the elimination or reduction of trade barriers caused by non-trade-related domestic policies is referred to as **deep integration**. Deep integration directly affects more than the flow of goods and services across a nation's boundaries since a variety of domestic policies may be changed, including those in such fundamental areas as business-government relations.

The issues of deep integration take up a sizable part of the dialogue over matters related to foreign trade and investment. Most economists share the opinion that it is not necessary, and is often undesirable, for nations to adopt the same or similar policies in every case where a difference creates trade conflict. For example, countries have a wide variety of safety and consumer protection standards and there is no reason to try to make them all the same for every traded good. Nevertheless, small countries fear that they will be forced to adopt the standards of the United States or some other industrial economy, and large countries such as the United States worry that their domestic policies will be determined by the collective action of small countries. An international dialogue on these issues is a relatively new experience and a key feature of contemporary international economic relations.

Multilateral Organizations   At the end of World War II, the United States, Great Britain, and their allies created a number of international organizations that were given active roles in maintaining international economic and political stability. Although the architects of these organizations could not envision the challenges and issues they would confront over the next fifty years, the organizations were given significant flexibility and they continue to play an important and growing role, in part as a forum for addressing the issues of deep integration.

The International Monetary Fund (IMF), the World Bank, the General Agreement on Tariffs and Trade (GATT), the United Nations (UN), the World Trade Organization (the WTO began operation in 1995, but grew out of the GATT), and a host of smaller organizations have broad international participation. They serve as forums for discussing and establishing rules, as mediators of disputes, and as organizers of actions to resolve problems. All of these organizations are controversial and have come under increasing fire from critics who charge that they promote unsustainable economic policies that often destroy the environment and protect the interests of wealthy elites. Many critics argue that they are also tools of the United States and other rich nations, while critics in the United States sometimes argue that they are unnecessary foreign entanglements that severely limit the scope for national action (Chapter 2 examines this issue in detail). Nevertheless, these organizations are attempts to create internationally acceptable rules for trade and commerce and to deal with potential disputes before they spill across international borders. Without a doubt, they are an entirely new element in the international economy.

Regional Trade Agreements   Agreements between groups of nations are not new. Free-trade agreements and other forms of preferential trade have existed throughout history. What is new is the significant increase in the number of **regional trade agreements** that have been signed in the last twenty years, especially in the 1990s. It is too early to say if this is a new trend or simply a phenomenon that will soon disappear.

The formation of preferential trade agreements is controversial. Trade opponents dislike the provisions that expose more of the national economy to international competition, whereas some trade proponents dislike the preferential nature of these agreements, which invariably favors regions included in the agreement at the expense of regions outside the agreement. The North American Free Trade Agreement (NAFTA), the European Union (EU), the Mercado Común del Sur (MERCOSUR), and the Asia Pacific Economic Cooperation (APEC) are the largest alliances, but they are only the tip of the iceberg of regional economic alliances.

Trade and Economic Growth

It is not surprising that many people are more than a little apprehensive about increased international economic integration. The list of potential problems is a long one. More trade may give consumers lower prices and greater choices, but it also means more competition for firms and workers. Capital flows make more funds available for investment purposes, but they also increase the risk of spreading financial crises internationally. Rising immigration means higher incomes for migrants and lower labor costs for firms, but also it means more competition in labor markets and, inevitably, greater social tensions. International organizations may help resolve disputes, but they may also reduce national sovereignty by putting pressure on countries to make operational changes. Free-trade agreements may increase trade flows, but again, that means more competition and more pressure on domestic workers and firms. Given the pluses and minuses, it seems appropriate to ask whether these changes are worth it.

In general, economists remain firmly convinced that the benefits of trade outweigh the costs. There is disagreement over the best way to achieve different goals (for example, how to protect against the harmful effects of sudden flows of capital), but the general belief that openness to the world economy is a superior policy to closing off a country is quite strong. To support this stance, economists can point to the following kinds of evidence:

- Casual empirical evidence of historical experience
- Evidence based on economic models and deductive reasoning
- Evidence from statistical comparisons of countries

While no one of these is conclusive by itself, together they provide solid support for the idea that open economies generally grow faster and prosper sooner than closed ones.

The historical evidence examines the experiences of countries when they tried to isolate themselves from the world economy. There are the experiences of the 1930s, when most countries tried to protect themselves from world events by shutting out flows of goods, capital, and labor. This did not cause the Great Depression of the 1930s, but worsened it, and ultimately led to the misery and tragedy of World War II. There are also the parallel experiences of countries that were divided by war, with one side becoming closed to the world economy, and the other side open. Germany (East versus West), Korea (North versus South), and China (mainland China versus Taiwan and Hong Kong) are the best examples. There are also the experiences of Latin America and East Asia in the 1960s, 1970s, and 1980s. It is perhaps not too much of a generalization to say that East Asia integrated itself into the world economy and watched growth take off, while Latin America partially closed its doors and realized mediocre growth and a decade of depression and crisis in the 1980s.

Economic theory generally supports these examples by suggesting the causal mechanisms that lead from trade to faster growth. Trade theory also points to cases where the costs of trade may outweigh the benefits (see Chapter 5), but generally, the benefits of increased innovation and access to new technologies and ideas that are fostered by trade are seen as positive factors. On the consumer side, trade provides a greater variety of goods and offers them at lower prices.

The statistical evidence of the benefits of more open economies comes from comparisons of large samples of countries over different periods. While the statistical tests of the relationship between trade policy and economic growth suffer from their own technical shortcomings (usually problems of measuring trade policy), the results consistently show that more open economies grow faster. These results cannot be viewed as absolutely conclusive, but together with trade theory and the casual empirical evidence drawn from historical experiences, the available statistical analysis provides additional support for the notion that trade is usually beneficial.

Twelve Themes in International Economics

Each of the twelve themes below are examined in the chapters that follow. These themes are overlapping, multidimensional, and often go beyond pure economics. International economic analysis cannot claim the final word, but it is hoped that you will find that it provides an analytically powerful and logically consistent approach for thinking about the issues raised by these themes.

The Gains from Trade (Chapters 3, 4, and 5)

Why is international trade desirable? We have briefly addressed this issue, and we will consider additional points as we continue. Given that economic analysis clearly demonstrates that the benefits of international trade outweigh the costs, it is not surprising that virtually all economists support open markets and increased trade. Recent polls of economists put the level of agreement on this issue at around 98 percent, when a general question is asked about the desirability of closed versus open markets. The benefits were first analyzed in the late 1700s, and are perhaps the oldest and strongest finding in all of economics.

Wages, Jobs, and Protection (Chapters 3, 6, 7, and 8)

International trade benefits the majority of people in a national economy, but it does not benefit every member of society. Workers in firms that cannot compete may be forced to find new jobs or take pay cuts. The fact that consumers pay less for the goods they buy, or that exporters hire more workers, may not help them. Increased awareness of the international economy has heightened the fears of people who feel vulnerable to changes in the international economy. They are concerned that wages in high-income countries must fall in order to compete with workers in low-wage countries, and that their jobs may be moved overseas. One of the key issues challenging policymakers is to find the right mix of domestic policies so that the nation benefits from trade without creating a backlash from those individuals and industries that are hurt.

Trade Deficits (Chapters 9, 11, and 12)

In 1980, a comprehensive measure of trade accounts in the United States showed that there was a slight surplus. Since then, only two of the following twenty-eight years had surpluses, and the sum of the deficits since 2000 is more than $5.3 trillion (2001 through 2008). The United States was not the only country running deficits, but each year a country runs a deficit in its trade accounts, it must borrow from abroad, essentially selling a piece of its future output in order to obtain more goods and services today. As the United States and a few other countries borrowed, China, Germany, Japan, and oil producers like Saudi Arabia lent. These large imbalances in lending and borrowing played a key role in the crisis that began in 2007.

Regional Trade Agreements (Chapters 2, 13, and 14)

As the world economy becomes more integrated, some regions are running ahead of the general trend. Western Europeans, for example, have eliminated many of the economic barriers separating their nations, and are creating a broad political and economic union. With implementation of NAFTA in 1994, the United States, Canada, and Mexico became a free-trade area while the largest countries in the Pacific Basin, including China, Japan, and the United States, have agreed to turn the Pacific region into another free-trade area by 2020. The three NAFTA countries each individually signed free trade agreements with most of Central America and the Dominican Republic, and the United States continues to negotiate with countries in South America and Asia. Since 2004, ten central and Eastern European countries have joined the EU, along with two small Mediterranean states. The ten members of the Association of South East Asian Nations (ASEAN) have moved to create a free-trade zone, and China has become an active participant in trade agreements, along with a number of other countries.

The Resolution of Trade Conflicts (Chapters 2, 7, and 8)

Commercial conflicts between nations cover a wide variety of issues and complaints. In one sense these conflicts are routine, as the WTO provides a formal dispute resolution procedure that has the assent of most of the world's nations. The WTO process does not cover all goods and services, however, nor does it say much about a large number of practices that some nations find objectionable. The ability of nations to resolve conflicts without resorting to protectionist measures is one key to maintaining a healthy international economic environment. Disputes can become acrimonious, so it is imperative that differences of opinion are not permitted to escalate into a wider disagreement. Trade wars are not real wars, but they are harmful nonetheless.

The Role of International Institutions (Chapters 2 and 12)

The organization with the greatest responsibility for resolving trade disagreements is the WTO. The WTO came into existence in 1995 and was an adaptation of the GATT, which was created shortly after World War II. Resolving trade disputes is only one of the new roles played by international organizations. Various organizations offer development support, technical economic advice, emergency loans in a crisis situation, and other services and assistance. These organizations perform services that were not offered before World War II (development support), or that were done by a single country (lending in a crisis)—usually the world's greatest military power. They exist today only through the mutual consent and cooperation of participating nations; without that cooperation, they would dissolve. Their abilities are limited, however. They cannot prevent crises, and they cannot make poor countries rich. They are also controversial and are viewed by some as tools of the United States or as a threat to national independence. They are very likely to grow in function, however, as many international problems cannot be solved by individual nations alone.

Exchange Rates and the Macroeconomy (Chapters 10 and 11)

Sixteen of the twenty-seven members of the EU have adopted the euro as a common currency and several more are preparing to join them. Panama, El Salvador, and Ecuador use the U.S. dollar, although Ecuador is questioning whether it should continue to do so. Some members of the U.S. Congress think that China artificially manipulates its currency in order to gain commercial advantages, and China's leaders worry that the United States might let the dollar sink in value in order to depreciate its foreign debt. Exchange rate systems come in a variety of forms and link the domestic economy to the rest of the world. They can help protect a country against harmful developments outside its borders, but they can also magnify and transmit those developments to the domestic economy. Exchange rates play a key role in the international economy.

Financial Crises and Global Contagion (Chapter 12)

As international trade and investment barriers declined, and as new communications and transportation systems developed, increasing quantities of capital flowed across national borders. These flows were encouraged by financial innovation and a general spirit of deregulation that held sway in much of the world from the late 1970s forward. Capital flows brought many desirable things, such as investment, new technology, and higher consumption, but they also often outpaced our ability to monitor and supervise, and were frequently at the root of financial crises, including the severe global crisis that began in 2007. Economists are engaged in a broad discussion today, aimed at finding techniques for reducing the macroeconomic and financial volatility caused by capital flows without hampering the new investment and lending that they provide.

Capital Flows and the Debt of Developing Countries (Chapters 2, 9, and 12)

In 1996, the World Bank and the IMF began a debt relief program for a group of forty-two countries labeled the Highly Indebted Poor Countries (HIPC). Thirty-four of these countries are in Africa. At the same time, non-governmental groups and celebrities, such as Bono, began to lobby successfully for a reduction in the debts of poor countries and for changes in the lending policies of rich countries. In many parts of the world, problems of extreme poverty are compounded by large foreign debts that are unlikely to be repaid and often require a constant supply of new loans to pay interest on the old ones. The search for workable solutions is complicated in the borrowing countries by economic shocks, corruption, and unsustainable economic policies. Common problems in the lending countries include unwise loans to corrupt dictators and loans for some expensive and unnecessary goods sold by rich countries.

Latin America and the World Economy (Chapter 15)

In Latin America, the 1980s are known as the Lost Decade. High levels of debt, deep recessions, and hyperinflation caused the region to lose a decade of growth and development. In response, many countries embarked on a profound shift in their economic policies. They opened markets, allowed increased foreign investment, signed trade agreements, and ended a long period of relative isolation from the world economy. These policy changes became known as the Washington Consensus and helped to bring an end to the Lost Decade, but few economists think the polices were successful. Growth remained relatively low in many places, financial crises continued to undermine economic gains, and traditional issues of economic fairness were largely ignored. Latin American countries have developed a wide variety of new policies and experiments as they try to reduce poverty, generate prosperity, and provide opportunity for all their citizens.

Export-Led Growth in East Asia (Chapter 16)

Throughout the late 1980s and into the 1990s, it was hard to ignore the East Asian "miracle." While some economists point out that it was not really a miracle —just a lot of hard work and sound economic policies—the growth rates of the "high-performance Asian economies" were unique in human history. Rates of growth of real GDP *per person* commonly reached 4 to 5 percent per year, with 6 to 8 percent not unusual. In 1997, an economic and financial crisis hit the region hard. Although there were lingering effects, by 2000 the economies of the region's developing countries were growing at more than 7 percent a year. One of the dominant traits of the countries in East Asia is the extent to which they are outward looking and dependent on the growth of their manufactured exports. An open question is whether these countries can continue to use the same export-led strategy after the global crisis that began in 2007.

The Integration of India and China into the World Economy (Chapter 17)

China and India are the most populous countries in the world. In 2009, China's 1.33 billion people plus India's 1.16 billion accounted for 37 percent of the world's population of 6.77 billion. Throughout most of the twentieth century, both countries had limited economic ties with other nations and made very little impact on the world economy. This began to change in 1978, when China began a dramatic shift away from isolationism. Reforms in China's economy led to an ever-growing presence of foreign investment, more exports and imports, fewer restrictions on privately owned enterprises, and in 2001, membership in the WTO. India's transformation from a relatively closed economy toward greater openness began later, in 1991, and has proceeded at a slower pace. Nevertheless, its sheer population size coupled with the technical excellence of its scientists and engineers and its developing high technology sector have turned it into a growing force in the world economy. Low wages and competitive firms and technologies in China and India have caught the attention of nearly all developing and developed nations, and have generated a variety of fears and opportunities, both realistic and unrealistic.

Vocabulary

deep integration

foreign direct investment (FDI)

gross domestic product (GDP)

index of openness

quotas

regional trade agreement

shallow integration

tariffs

transaction costs

Study Questions

1. How can globalization and international economic integration be measured?

2. In what ways is the U.S. economy more integrated with the world today than it was a century ago? In what ways is it less integrated?

3. What is "openness"? How is it measured? Does a low openness indicator indicate that a country is closed to trade with the outside world?

4. Describe the pattern over the last century shown by the openness index for leading industrial economies.

5. Trade and capital flows were described and measured in relative terms rather than absolute terms. Explain the difference. Which terms seem more valid—relative or absolute? Why?

6. The relative size of international capital flows may not be much greater today than they were 100 years ago, although they are certainly greater than they were 50 years ago. Qualitatively, however, capital flows are different today. Explain.

7. What are the new issues in international trade and investment? In what sense do they expose national economies to outside influences?

8. Describe the three kinds of evidence that economists use to support the assertion that open economies grow faster than economies that are closed to the world economy.

International Economic Institutions since World War II

Introduction: International Institutions and Issues since World War II

As World War II was drawing to a close, representatives from the United States, Great Britain, and other Allied nations met in the small New Hampshire town of Bretton Woods. The outcome of these meetings was a series of agreements that created an exchange rate system (which lasted until 1971); the International Bank for Reconstruction and Development (IBRD), also known as the **World Bank**; and the **International Monetary Fund (IMF)**. In 1946, two years after Bretton Woods, twenty-three nations including the United States and Great Britain began talks on reducing their trade barriers, leading to the **General Agreement on Tariffs and Trade (GATT)**, which began operation in 1948.

This chapter focuses on these global economic institutions, their history, their role in the world economy, and controversies surrounding their activities. Institutions that do not have a primary economic role, such as the General Assembly of the United Nations or the North Atlantic Treaty Organization (NATO), are not included.

International Institutions

International economic institutions are an important feature of the world economy. When social scientists try to explain the increasing integration of national economies after World War II, one of the key explanations must be the increased stability and reduced uncertainty that these institutions help to create. Nevertheless, as international economic integration has increased, these organizations have come under more scrutiny and received much criticism. Before we look at their impact and some of the criticisms levied at them, we should define what we mean by an *institution*.

When most people hear the word **institution**, they probably think of a formal organization. However, economists tend to define institutions more abstractly. For example, the "New Institutionalists," led by economist Douglas North, have argued that organizations are not institutions in themselves, but are rather the rules that govern behavior—telling us what is permissible and what is not and acting as constraints that limit our actions.

Institutions can be formal or informal. A formal institution is a written set of rules that explicitly state what is and is not allowed. The rules may be embodied in a club, an association, or a legal system. An informal institution is a custom or tradition that tells people how to act in the same way that a law does, but without legal enforcement. For example, informal institutions include the rules of socializing, gift exchange, table manners, e-mail etiquette, and so on. In this chapter, the term *institution* refers to rules and organizations.

A Taxonomy of International Economic Institutions

International economic institutions come in many shapes and sizes. They can be lobbying groups for a particular commodity or an international producer's association, the joint management by several nations of a common resource, trade agreements or development funds for a select group of nations, or even global associations. Although this chapter's focus is on global economic institutions, it is useful to look at a taxonomy of international economic institutions, from the most limited and specific, to the most general. Table 2.1 shows five main types.

TABLE 2.1	A Taxonomy of International Economic Institutions, with Examples
Type	**Examples**
Commodity- or industry-specific organizations: These range from Trade Associations to international-standards-setting bodies to powerful cartels	■ Oil Producing and Exporting Countries (OPEC) ■ International Telecommunications Union (ITU) ■ International Sugar Organization ■ International Lead and Zinc Study Group
Commissions and agencies for managing shared resources	■ International Boundary and Water Commission (IBWC) ■ Lake Chad Basin Commission ■ Mekong River Commission
Development funds and banks	■ Inter-American Development Bank (IDB) ■ North American Development Bank (NADBank) ■ Asian Development Bank ■ Islamic Development Bank
International trade agreements involving a few nations (regional trade alliances or trade blocs)	■ North American Free Trade Agreement (NAFTA) ■ US-Israel Free Trade Agreement ■ Mercado Común del Sur (MERCOSUR) ■ Asia-Pacific Economic Cooperation (APEC)
Global organizations for trade, development, and macroeconomic stability	■ International Monetary Fund (IMF) ■ World Bank ■ World Trade Organization (WTO)

The IMF, the World Bank, and the WTO

Three global organizations play a major role in international economic relations and are central to this book: the International Monetary Fund (IMF), the World Bank, and the **World Trade Organization (WTO)**. The IMF and the World Bank date from the end of World War II; the WTO began in 1995 and grew out of the GATT, which it deepens and broadens. Accordingly, it is useful to know the history and function of the GATT as well as the WTO.

The IMF and World Bank

During World War II, the United States and Great Britain (and a few other Allies) held regular discussions about the shape of the postwar international economic order. They wanted to avoid the mistakes of the 1920s and 1930s, when a lack of international cooperation led to the complete collapse of economic relations. The culmination of these talks was the **Bretton Woods conference** held in July 1944, in Bretton Woods, New Hampshire. The agreement was largely a result of negotiations between the United States and the United Kingdom, and led directly to the creation of the IMF and the IBRD. The IBRD later added the International Development Association (IDA) for assisting the poorest countries with their development needs. Together, the IBRD and the IDA comprise the World Bank.

The IMF began operation on December 27, 1945, with a membership of twenty-nine countries. Its success is indicated by the fact that by the year 2003, it had grown to 184 members. The IMF provides loans to its members under different programs for the short, medium, and long term. Each member is charged a fee, or **quota**, as the price of membership. The size of the quota varies with the size of the nation's economy and the importance of its currency in world trade and payments. Important decisions within the IMF are made by vote with the weight of each nation's vote proportional to its quota. This gives the high-income countries of the world a voting power that is disproportionate to their population. For example, the United States alone controls nearly 17 percent of the total votes, and the the seven largest industrial economies (Canada, Italy, France, Germany, Japan, the United Kingdom, and the United States) control almost 45 percent. Some votes on IMF policy require a "super majority" of 85 percent, giving the United States a veto power on those particular issues.

The most visible role for the IMF is to intercede, by invitation, whenever a nation experiences a crisis in its international payments. For example, if a country imports more than it exports, then it may run out of foreign exchange reserves. **Foreign exchange reserves** are dollars, yen, pounds, euros, or another currency (or gold) that is accepted internationally. In addition, the IMF has its own currency, called an SDR, or special drawing right. SDRs are based on a country's quota and are a part of its international reserves. If a country lacks reserves, it cannot pay for its imports, nor can it pay the interest and principal it owes on its international borrowings. This is one scenario that warrants a call to the IMF. The IMF makes loans to its members, but it usually extracts a price above and beyond the interest it charges. The price is an agreement by the borrower to change its policies so that the problem cannot recur. If simple economic reforms such as a cut in the value of the currency, or limits on the central bank's creation of credit, are insufficient to solve the problem permanently, then the IMF usually requires a borrower to make fundamental changes in the relationship between government and markets in order to qualify for IMF funds. These requirements are known as **IMF conditionality**. For example, during the crisis of 1997–1998, the IMF was the main provider of funds and expertise to East Asia, again, with a great deal of controversy over the advice it gave and the conditions it imposed.

The IMF's resources for dealing with crises are limited. When the United States and other large economies experienced the crisis that began in 2007, IMF resources were far from adequate for addressing the issues. In 2009, the largest member countries voted to increase its resources to $750 billion, which is still far below the amount necessary to stem a crisis in the United States or in other large economies. In part this reflects the institution's asymmetry, as high-income countries are generally unwilling to give the IMF either the funds or the power to allow it to intervene effectively in their economies.

The World Bank is the other major organization that emerged from the Bretton Woods Conference. It has the same membership and a similar structure. Members buy shares that convey voting rights on policy proportional to the shares. The original purpose of the World Bank was to provide financing mechanisms for rebuilding Europe at the end of World War II; however, it was soon apparent that its capital reserves were inadequate to the task. In addition, the United States found it politically preferable to have more direct control over the reconstruction funds, rather than routing them through an international organization. Hence the job of reconstruction was directed toward the newly created Marshall Plan, and the World Bank moved toward assisting development in nonindustrial economies.

The GATT, the Uruguay Round, and the WTO

At the end of World War II, a third global economic organization, the International Trade Organization (ITO), was proposed. If it had been implemented, the ITO's job would have been to establish rules relating to world trade, business practices, and international investment. U.S. opposition killed the idea of the ITO, however, and no such organization was created until 1995. Nevertheless, in 1946, while they were still considering the idea of the ITO, twenty-three countries opened negotiations over tariff reductions. These negotiations led to some forty-five thousand tariff reductions affecting $10 billion, or one-fifth of world trade. In addition, a number of agreements were made on rules for trade, with the expectation that the rules would become a part of the ITO. Both the tariff reductions and the rules were implemented in 1948; when the possibility of an ITO died in 1950, the agreements on tariffs and trade rules remained in force as a separate agreement, known as the General Agreement on Tariffs and Trade (GATT). The GATT has been very successful in bringing down trade barriers gradually. One indicator is that international trade has grown over the last fifty years from 5 percent of world GDP to 20 percent.

The GATT functions through a series of **trade rounds** in which countries periodically negotiate a set of incremental tariff reductions. Gradually, through the Kennedy Round in the mid-1960s and the Tokyo Round of the 1970s, trade rules other than tariffs began to be addressed, including the problems of dumping (selling in a foreign market below cost or below a fair price), subsidies to industry, and nontariff barriers to trade. As tariffs came down, these nontariff issues became more prominent.

The GATT intentionally ignored the extremely contentious sectors of agriculture, textiles, and apparel. In addition, trade in services was ignored because it was not important. The accumulation of unresolved issues in these sectors, however, along with the increased importance of nontariff trade barriers, led to the demand for a new, more extensive set of negotiations. These demands culminated in the **Uruguay Round** of trade negotiations that began in 1986 and concluded in 1993. In 1994, the new agreement was signed by 125 countries, and by 2008, its membership had grown to 153 members, with approximately another 30 in the process of negotiating to join.

The WTO continues trade talks and sector-specific discussions between comprehensive rounds of negotiations. For example, in 1997, 69 countries signed an agreement to open their telecommunication sectors, and another 70 agreed to significant opening in their financial services sectors. In addition, every two years, trade ministers from the member countries meet to set the WTO's policy objectives. In 2001, trade ministers meeting in Doha, Qatar, agreed to launch a new round of trade negotiations emphasizing issues of developing countries. The **Doha Round** proposed a **Doha Development Agenda** to consider trade issues of importance to developing countries. The discussions are on and off, with periods of inactivity interspersed around intense negotiations. A key issue is farm subsidies in high-income countries of the European Union, the United States, and Japan, and the desire for greater market access by developing countries and some high-income countries with strong farm sectors, such as Australia. Other issues include trade in services and the problems that poor countries face in implementing the agreement.

The foundations of all WTO and GATT agreements are the principles of **national treatment** and **nondiscrimination**. National treatment is the requirement that foreign goods are treated similarly to the same domestic goods once they enter a nation's markets. Nondiscrimination is embodied in the concept of **most-favored nation (MFN) status**. MFN requires all WTO members to treat each other as well as they treat their most-favored trading partner. In effect, this is a prohibition against discrimination. Somewhat contradictorily, MFN allows trade agreements such as the North American Free Trade Agreement (NAFTA) and the European Union (EU) even though every trade agreement causes countries to discriminate in favor of each other and implicitly against nonmembers. In theory, the WTO permits such agreements as long as they do not harm the overall level of international trade, and in practice, the WTO has never challenged the validity of a trade agreement between member countries.

CASE STUDY

The GATT Rounds

Agreements in the GATT forum to reduce trade barriers take place in rounds of negotiations. Counting the first round, there have been nine rounds of negotiations, with the Doha Round still in progress. Originally, the GATT was an international agreement and not an organization. The failure to create the International Trade Organization in 1950, however, resulted in the gradual conversion of the GATT into a *de facto* organization by 1960, with a permanent secretariat to manage it from Geneva. Table 2.2 lists the various rounds of negotiations.

The first five rounds were organized around product-by-product negotiations. Beginning with the Kennedy Round, negotiations were simplified as countries negotiated an across-the-board percentage reduction in all tariffs for a range of industrial products. One effect is that tariffs have never been uniform across countries. The goal has been to bring them all down, but not necessarily to create the same tariff for all countries.

The Tokyo Round is notable because it was the first round to begin to establish rules regarding subsidies. Subsidies give an industry a competitive advantage, since the national government pays part of the cost of production, either through direct payment or indirectly through subsidized interest rates, artificially cheap access to foreign currency, or some other way. The Tokyo Round began the laborious process of creating rules in this area, one of the most important being the agreement to prohibit subsidies for exports of industrial goods (but not agricultural goods or textiles and apparel).

The subsidy issue of the Tokyo Round was carried forward into the Uruguay Round, where subsidies were defined in greater detail. The Uruguay Round accomplished many other things as well, not the least of which was the creation of the WTO as a formal organization to oversee and administer the GATT. Additional accomplishments are described in Chapter 7, which explores trade policy and trade barriers in more detail.

TABLE 2.2	The GATT Rounds	
Round	Year	Number of Participants
Geneva I	1947	23
Annecy	1949	13
Torquay	1951	38
Geneva II	1956	26
Dillon	1960–1961	26
Kennedy	1964–1967	62
Tokyo	1973–1979	102
Uruguay	1986–1993	105
Doha (WTO)	2001–	153

Regional Trade Agreements

Regional trade agreements (RTAs) between two or more countries are another important institution in the world economy. Many of these have familiar names, such as NAFTA and the EU. Regional agreements can be classified into one of five categories, although they often combine elements from a couple of the categories.

Five Types of Regional Trade Agreements

RTAs are bilateral (two countries) or plurilateral (several countries). The WTO is not an RTA because it is worldwide in scope and not just regional. In trade jargon it is called a multilateral agreement because it includes, potentially, all the countries of the world. Some plurilateral agreements are quite large, such as the EU, which has twenty-seven members, or the Asia Pacific Economic Cooperation group, which has twenty-two. Table 2.3 lists five types of trade agreements and their characteristics.

TABLE 2.3	Five Types of Regional Trade Agreements
Type of agreement	Characteristics
■ Partial trade	■ Free trade in the outputs of one or a few industries
■ Free-trade area	■ Free trade in outputs (goods and services)
■ Customs union	■ Free-trade area plus a common external tariff for nonmembers
■ Common Market	■ Customs union plus free movement of inputs (capital and labor)
■ Economic union	■ Common market plus substantial harmonization of economic policies, including possibly a common currency

CASE STUDY

Prominent Regional Trade Agreements

Each of the four levels of integration is an example of a different kind of **regional trade agreement (RTA)**, or **trade bloc**. The question naturally arises as to how many agreements there are and whether they are beneficial or harmful for the world economy. The simple question of how many is difficult to answer precisely. Many of the agreements do not fit neatly into any of the four categories, so it is not clear they should be counted. That is, should all partial agreements be counted when they are not quite free-trade areas, yet they have elements of free trade, customs unions, and even common markets? In addition, many of the agreements exist either on paper only (have no real effect), or have yet to be fully negotiated and/or implemented. Until there is substantial implementation, there is always the possibility that the agreement will collapse, because opening an economy inevitably generates opposition from uncompetitive sectors.

Countries that have signed the GATT are obligated to notify the GATT secretariat when they form an RTA. According to the WTO, since the implementation of the GATT in 1948 they have been notified about more than 400 RTAs. Some of these are defunct, but over 200 were still operating in 2009. Most of the agreements that are still functioning were started in the 1990s, with 164 agreements entering into force since 1992. Europe accounts for about 65 percent of the RTAs currently in force, and about 78 percent of all RTAs involve developed countries only (43 percent) or developed and developing countries (35 percent).

The answer to the second question above—are they beneficial or harmful?—is even more difficult to ascertain. A 1995 study by the WTO concluded that in most cases "regional and multilateral integration initiatives are complements rather than alternatives." Broadly speaking, the WTO sees these agreements as helping it to further reduce trade barriers. This view is not shared by all economists, however, as any regional agreement must favor the interests of its members over the interests of outsiders. In other words, there is an element of discrimination that goes against the WTO's fundamental principle of equal treatment (most favored nation). Preferential treatment for members of the trade agreement causes most regional trade agreements to destroy some of the trade between their members and nonmembers. The WTO recognizes this problem, but argues that as long as a regional agreement creates more new trade than it destroys, the net result is beneficial. In addition, the WTO sees the regional trade agreements as places where countries can try out new arrangements, some of which will be eventually incorporated into the larger, global agreement.

Nearly all WTO members belong to at least one RTA, and many countries belong to several. For example, Mexico is a member of NAFTA (Canada-Mexico-United States) but in 2000 it entered a free trade agreement with the European Union. It has also signed free trade and other agreements with other countries, including Chile, Japan, Israel, and Costa Rica, among others. Table 2.4

lists some of the RTAs currently in force. Among the best known are the EU, the EFTA, the NAFTA, MERCOSUR in South America, the ASEAN Free Trade Area in Southeast Asia, and COMESA in eastern and southern Africa. There are many more, however, ranging from tariff agreements on a subset of output to common markets and economic unions. The dates in parentheses are the dates of implementation of the agreements.

TABLE 2.4   Prominent Regional Trade Blocs

Region/Trade Bloc	Objective
Africa	
COMESA—Common Market for Eastern and Southern Africa (1993)	Common market
ECCAS—Economic Community of Central African States (1992)	Common market
ECOWAS—Economic Community of West African States (1975)	Common market
Asia	
AFTA—ASEAN Free Trade Arrangement (1992)	Free-trade area
ANZCERTA—Australia–New Zealand Closer Economic Relations (1983)	Free-trade area
APEC—Asia-Pacific Economic Cooperation (1989)	Free-trade area
Europe	
CEFTA—Central European Free Trade Arrangement (1992)	Free-trade area
EEA—European Economic Area (1994)	Common market
EFTA—European Free Trade Association (1960)	Free-trade area
EU—European Union (1957)	Economic union
Middle East	
ACM—Arab Common Market (1964)	Customs union
AMU—Arab-Maghreb Union (1989)	Economic union
GCC—Gulf Cooperation Council (1981)	Common market
Western Hemisphere	
ANCOM—Andean Common Market (1969)	Common market
CACM—Central American Common Market (1961)	Customs union
CARICOM—Caribbean Community (1973)	Common market
MERCOSUR—Southern Cone Common Market (1991)	Common market
NAFTA—North American Free Trade Area (1994)	Free-trade area

Sources: Harmsen, Richard, and Michael Leidy, "Regional Trading Arrangements," in *International Trade Policies: The Uruguay Round and Beyond. Volume II: Background Papers*. Washington, DC: International Monetary Fund, 1994.

The WTO, "Regionalism." Geneva: The World Trade Organization. http://www.wto.org/english/thewto_e/whatis_e/tif_e/ bey3_e.htm. Accessed October 6, 2000.

A **partial trade agreement** is the least comprehensive RTA. It occurs when two or more countries agree to drop trade barriers in one or a few economic sectors, such as steel, autos, or any other line of production. Partial trade agreements are used when countries are reluctant to open all sectors, but they desire free trade for a limited set of goods.

As more goods are included in the partial trade agreement, it begins to look more like a **free-trade area**. One example is NAFTA, but there are many others, such as the European Free Trade Area (EFTA) and the U.S.-Israel Free Trade Agreement. In a free-trade area, nations trade goods and services across international boundaries without paying a tariff and without the limitations imposed by quotas, which are direct limits on imports. In reality, however, most free-trade areas such as NAFTA do not allow completely free trade. Nations usually reserve some restrictions for particularly sensitive items. For example, as part of its efforts to protect its culture, Canada limits the number of U.S. television programs that Canadian television stations may purchase. With a free-trade area, nations usually keep their own health, safety, and technical standards, and may deny entry of imports if they do not meet national standards.

The next level of integration is called a **customs union**. A customs union is a free-trade area plus a **common external tariff** toward nonmembers. Between the mid-1970s and the early 1990s, the EU was a customs union, and in today's economy, MERCOSUR (Brazil, Argentina, Uruguay, Paraguay, and Venezuela) is one. This means that the five members have free trade with each other and the same tariff on imports from nonmembers, for example American computers. As with free-trade areas, many items are usually left out of the agreement. In the European case, each nation retained its own tariffs and quotas with respect to Japanese autos. Common markets are the next level beyond customs unions. A **common market** is a customs union plus an agreement to allow the free mobility of inputs, such as labor and capital. The clearest example is the EU in the 1990s. The three NAFTA countries have elements of a common market (without the common external tariff) because they allow capital to move freely around the region. NAFTA also grants relatively free movement to certain types of white-collar labor, such as architects, business consultants, and others.

The final level of economic integration is an **economic union**. An economic union is a common market with substantial coordination of macroeconomic policies, including a common currency, and harmonization of many standards and regulations. The clearest examples are the states of the United States or the provinces of Canada. The BENELUX Union of Belgium, the Netherlands, and Luxembourg is an example of separate nations that have formed a union, and the EU is in the process of becoming an economic union, with the euro as its common currency, and at some point, with a common defense policy and common citizenship rights.

Regional Trade Agreements and the WTO

When a WTO member signs an RTA, it is obligated to notify the WTO. Since 1948, well over 400 agreements have been listed with the WTO, with about three-fourths of the notifications having occurred since 1995. Not all of these agreements are still active, but more than 225 were considered active in 2008.

RTAs are inherently discriminatory since countries in an RTA discriminate in favor of each other and thereby deny most-favored nation treatment to non-RTA members. Nevertheless, the GATT and the WTO have allowed RTAs under the assumption that they create more new trade than they destroy with their discriminatory practices. In economic terms, **trade creation** must exceed **trade diversion**. An example will clarify these two concepts.

Suppose that the United States imports apparel from a wide variety of locales, including Haiti, among others. Further, suppose the United States has high tariffs on apparel, but the tariffs are nondiscriminatory and therefore in compliance with the WTO rules. If Haiti is a low-cost producer, then after paying the same tariff that all exporters to the United States face, its goods will be competitive in the U.S. market. One last assumption is that Mexico also produces apparel, but its cost are above Haiti's, so most U.S. imports come from Haiti, not Mexico. In this hypothetical example, when the United States signs a free trade agreement with Mexico, Mexican apparel can enter the United States without Mexico paying a tariff, while Haiti continues to pay a tariff on its apparel. As a result, even though Mexico has higher costs of production than Haiti, its goods could become cheaper in the U.S. market. In that case, trade is diverted from Haiti to Mexico, even though Haiti is the low-cost producer. This would be a backward step in world production since resources would be allocated from the lower-cost producer to the higher-cost, and it is precisely this type of change against which the WTO rules are meant to guard.

The GATT/WTO agreement recognizes that most RTAs create some trade diversion, but the goal is to create more new trade, due to the dropping of barriers between trading partners, so that new trade outweighs the value of trade that is diverted. However, something very close to the hypothetical scenario just described occurred throughout many parts of the Caribbean Basin and Central America when the United States, Mexico, and Canada became a free-trade area in 1995. In response, the United States provided financial assistance and relaxed its trade barriers for countries in Central America and the Caribbean.

For and Against RTAs

Both the arguments for and against RTAs involve more than pure economics. Politics, international relations, and national security also play a role. The central economic question is whether they are supportive of a gradual, long run increase in world trade, or whether they tend to become obstacles to further relaxation of trade barriers. In trade jargon, the issue is whether they are building blocks or stumbling blocks.

Proponents of trade agreements view them as building blocks toward freer, more open world trade. They have several arguments on their side. First, it is easier for a few countries to reach agreement than it is for all the countries in the WTO. Therefore, RTAs create conditions where countries can lower their barriers without having to negotiate an agreement with all 153 members. Second, the domestic effects of a reduction of trade barriers are less dramatic since an RTA covers less than the world economy, and thereby limits the sudden surge of competition that might occur if all the WTO nations were allowed in. This also allows members to go further and to potentially open more than they would under a multilateral agreement. Third, RTA member countries can experiment with new agreements that are impossible among a large number, such as the opening of certain types of services that have been traditionally closed. Insurance and telephony are examples. And fourth, RTAs can be used as a political and economic threat to encourage agreements in the WTO forum. For example, some argue that the US-Mexico-Canada agreement helped push countries toward conclusion of the Uruguay Round agreement as they feared the United States might develop its own regional bloc and abandon its multilateral commitments.

Opponents of RTAs question many of these assumptions. Their greatest criticism is that RTAs undermine progress toward multilateral (worldwide) agreements. Pro-trade opponents of RTAs do not believe that they encourage agreements through the WTO, but instead they believe that they polarize countries and draw energy away from the work of reaching agreement. Opponents point out that RTAs are often discriminatory against poor and less-developed countries, particularly when they involve a rich giant like the United States and small, developing countries such as Guatemala and El Salvador. Not only are low-income countries unable to negotiate forcefully, they often lack the resources and infrastructure that will be needed to take advantage of a market opening. Further, in their view, rich countries like the United States have no need of trade barriers against products from small developing countries.

The Role of International Economic Institutions

People rely on institutions to create order and reduce uncertainty. By defining the constraints or limits on economic, political, and social interactions, institutions define the incentive system of a society and help to create stability. The provision of order and the reduction of uncertainty are so important that when they are absent, economies cannot grow. Within a nation, the formal rules of behavior are defined by the various levels of government. In the United States, for example, this includes cities, counties, special districts, states, and the federal government. In the international sphere, however, there are no corresponding sets of government. The establishment of rules for international trade and international macroeconomic relations are dependent on the voluntary associations of nations in international economic organizations.

The primary difference between international economic organizations and the government of a single nation is that the former have limited enforcement power. National and local governments have police powers that they can use to enforce their rules; international organizations have no police power, but they have more subtle powers for encouraging cooperation. For example, the IMF and World Bank can withdraw lines of credit to developing countries. The withdrawal of IMF credit raises a red flag for private lenders and makes it more costly for uncooperative nations to gain access to capital in private markets. Likewise, the WTO can legitimize retaliatory sanctions against nations that fail to honor their trade obligations. Basically, however, international organizations rely on moral suasion and the commitments of individual nations to remain effective. If individual nations choose not to join or decide to withdraw their support, there is nothing the IMF, World Bank, or WTO can do.

The provision of order and the reduction of uncertainty are services that everyone values. This is why we pay police officers, judges, and legislators. Although public order and the lessening of uncertainty are intangibles, they are desired and valued in the same sense as more tangible material objects. Their economic characteristics are different from most goods and services however, and they fall into the category known as **public goods**.

The Definition of Public Goods

By definition, public goods are **nonexcludable** and **nonrival** or **nondiminishable**. Nonexcludability means that the normal price mechanism does not work as a way of regulating access. For example, when a signal is broadcast on the airwaves by a television station, anyone with a TV set who lives in its range can pick it up. (Of course, this is not the case with cable stations, which are granted permission to scramble their signals. Signal scrambling is a clever technological solution to the problem of nonexcludability.)

The second characteristic of public goods is that they are nonrival or nondiminishable. This refers to the attribute of not being diminished by consumption. For example, if I tune in to the broadcast signal of a local TV station, my neighbors will have the same signal amount available to them. Most goods get smaller, or diminish, when they are consumed, but public goods do not.

Private markets often fail to supply optimal levels of public goods because of the problem of **free riding**. Free riding means that there is no incentive to pay for public goods because people cannot be excluded from consumption. Given this characteristic, public goods will not be produced optimally by free markets unless institutional arrangements can somehow overcome the free riding. In most cases, governments step in as providers and use their powers to tax as a means to force people to pay for the goods.

Maintaining Order and Reducing Uncertainty

Two of the most important functions of international economic institutions are to maintain order in international economic relations and to reduce uncertainty. Together, these functions are often instrumental in the avoidance of a global economic crisis. Furthermore, if a national crisis threatens to become global, international institutions often help to bring it to a less costly end and to prevent nations from shifting the cost of national problems to other countries.

The maintenance of order and the reduction of uncertainty are general tasks that require specific rules in a number of areas of international economic interaction, although economists do not completely agree on the specific rules or the specific types of cooperation that should be provided. Nevertheless, the proponents of international institutions, such as economist Charles Kindleberger, have noted several areas where institutions are needed in order to strengthen cooperation and prevent free riding in the provision of international public goods. Among these items are the four public goods listed in Table 2.5.

Kindleberger and others have argued that the absence of a set of rules for providing one or more of these public goods has usually been a key part of the explanation of historical crises such as the worldwide Great Depression of the 1930s. If no international institutions are available to help nations overcome the tendency to free ride, then international economic stability grows more fragile. As an illustration, consider the first item listed in Table 2.5. During recessions, politicians begin to feel enormous pressure to close markets in order to protect jobs at home. During the 1930s, for example, most nations enacted high tariffs and restrictive quotas on imports. This set in motion waves of retaliation as other nations followed suit and imposed their own tariffs and quotas. In the end, no one benefited and international trade collapsed.

In essence, each nation was free riding. In a recession, free riders want to close their markets to reduce imports and create more jobs. At the same time, however, they want all other nations to stay open so that they do not lose any export markets. These motives are inconsistent, and the effect of free riding behavior is that all countries retaliate by closing their markets, international trade collapses, and everyone is worse off than before. Kindleberger shows that the shift in trade policies toward high tariffs and restrictive quotas helped to intensify and spread the Great Depression of the 1930s. In the crisis and world recession that started in 2007, governments and central banks were well aware of the history of the 1930s and struggled not to repeat the same mistakes.

Kindleberger also argues that the sudden decline in capital flows to developing countries in the 1930s and the complete absence of a **lender of last resort** deepened the Great Depression and provides further historical evidence for the importance of international institutions. The lack of a lender of last resort was particularly critical because a number of countries with temporary financial problems soon passed into full-blown financial collapse. As it became impossible

TABLE 2.5	Four Examples of International Public Goods	
Public Good	**Purpose**
Open markets in a recession	To prevent a fall in exports from magnifying the effects of a recession
Capital flows to less-developed countries (LDCs)	To assist economic development in poor countries
International money for settlement of international debts	To maintain a globally accepted system for paying debts
Last-resort lending	To prevent the spread of some types of financial crises

for them to pay their foreign debts, the crisis spread from the indebted nations to the lending nations. In 2009, during the recent crisis, the world's largest economies approved an increase in funding for the IMF so that it would be able to continue its role as a lender of last resort.

No one has tried to measure the frequency of potentially disastrous international economic events. Their occurrence is not infrequent, however, and it is relatively easy to list a number of recent events that have had the potential to turn into major global problems: the debt crisis in many developing countries in the early 1980s, the collapse of the Mexican peso in 1994, the transition to capitalism by socialist countries, the Asian crisis of 1997, Russia's default on its debt in 1998—the list is fairly long.

In each crisis or potential crisis, international institutions play an important role by preventing free riding. Lacking much in the way of formal enforcement mechanisms, they overcome the free rider problem by changing each nation's expectations about every other nation. For example, if all countries are committed to open markets in good times and bad, then during a worldwide recession no country expects its trading partners to close their markets. As another example, if each country pays a share of the IMF's operating funds, then it overcomes the problems that arise when each country waits for the others to make risky loans during a crisis. The effectiveness of international institutions depends on the credible commitment of the world's nations. If a country agrees to a set of rules, but has a reputation for breaking its agreements, then its commitment is not credible. Institutions cannot overcome the free rider problem under those circumstances.

CASE STUDY

Bretton Woods

After World War I, the United States retreated into a relative isolationism under the mistaken belief that noninvolvement in European affairs would protect the country from entanglement in disastrous European conflicts such as World War I. The rise of Hitler, Japanese aggression in the Pacific, and the start of World War II showed that this policy would not work.

The United States began to realize its mistake in the 1930s as it watched Hitler take over a large part of the European continent. U.S. and British cooperation and planning for the postwar era began before the United States entered the war in December 1941, and long before the outcome was known. President Roosevelt and Prime Minister Churchill met on a battleship off the coast of Newfoundland in August 1941. Soon after, they announced the Atlantic Charter, a program for postwar reconstruction that committed both nations to working for the fullest possible economic collaboration among all nations after the war. Concurrent with the Atlantic Charter, the United States and Britain began discussing the kinds of international institutions that might be proposed.

All parties agreed that in any postwar order the United States would have to be the political, military, and economic leader. The United States had surpassed Great Britain in wealth and size several decades earlier, and its leadership during the war gave it prestige and credibility. In addition, the physical infrastructure of the United States was not damaged by the war, and it was the only industrial nation able to provide the financial capital and physical material needed to repair the war damage.

Looking back to the 1920s and 1930s, the postwar planners recognized four serious problems that they should guard against: (1) the worldwide depression; (2) the collapse of international trade; (3) the collapse of the international monetary system; and (4) the collapse of international lending. Discussions during World War II were mainly devoted to rules, agreements, and organizations that could be created to avoid these problems. The following international institutions were viewed as central for the achievement of these goals:

- An international organization to help stabilize exchange rates and to assist nations that are unable to pay their international debts
- Agreements to reduce trade barriers
- An international organization for providing relief to the war-damaged nations, and to assist with reconstruction

Plans for the postwar period were finalized at a conference held in July 1944, in Bretton Woods, New Hampshire. The Bretton Woods institutions include the IMF, the World Bank, and the Bretton Woods exchange rate system. Although it was conceived separately, the GATT is sometimes included because it embodies the goals and ideas of the Bretton Woods planners with respect to international trade. Together, these institutions are a historically unique set of international economic institutions, and each, in its own area, has played a key role in the history of the international economy since 1945.

The founding principles of the Bretton Woods institutions are relatively simple. First, trade should open in all countries, not just in the United States alone, or in the United States and the United Kingdom together. In economic terms, this was a call for multilateral opening, as opposed to unilateralism (one-sided opening) or bilateralism (two-sided opening). Second, nations should not discriminate against other nations. Whatever tariffs and quotas the United Kingdom or the United States might levy against another country, they should be the same ones imposed on everyone. Third, in order to ensure the ability of importers to purchase goods abroad, countries should not limit the buying and selling of currency when its purpose is to pay for imports. Fourth, exchange rates should be fixed but with the possibility for periodic adjustment. These principles formed the cornerstones of the institutions.

Criticism of International Institutions

The World Bank, IMF, WTO, and various regional trade agreements have provided financial resources for development, technical assistance for crisis management, and mechanisms for opening markets. Not everyone agrees that these efforts are positive on balance, however, and even those who view their actions favorably would agree that there is room for improvement. The range of criticism covers a wide spectrum, from public demonstrations against trade ministers meeting under the auspices of the WTO to the well-informed criticisms by leading economists such as Nobel Laureate Joseph Stiglitz. The underlying question is whether the IMF, World Bank, and WTO are fostering development and economic security, or generating greater economic inequality and compounding the risks to vulnerable groups.

   In general, most analysts probably agree that some types of international institutions are necessary due to the international public goods discussed earlier. The IMF, World Bank, and WTO were created in response to real historical events and for the explicit purposes of avoiding crises and promoting growth. Economic changes such as transportation and communication revolutions; the integration of new markets in Europe, East Asia, and Latin America; and technological innovations have increased the need for institutions by reducing the isolation of nations and creating more interactions and spillovers among them. While there is a widely recognized need for a set of agreements covering the international economic policies practiced by individual nations, there is less consensus regarding the content of the agreements and how they should be implemented.

Sovereignty and Transparency

Sovereignty covers the rights of nations to be free from unwanted foreign interference in their affairs. One of the strongest complaints about international institutions is that they violate national sovereignty by imposing unwanted domestic economic policies. For example, when a country experiences a financial crisis, the IMF is often the only potential source of outside help. Once engaged, however, the IMF imposes conditions that sometimes amount to a complete rearrangement of national economic policies. Specific examples include IMF requirements that countries cut government spending, privatize their publicly owned enterprises, and open their financial sector to the free movement of capital. Each of these may go against public preferences. For example, when a country is in the midst of a financial crisis, cuts in government spending can increase the depth of a recession and often have a disproportionately large impact on the middle class and the poor. Aside from the potential benefits or costs, often it appears that governments are coerced by the international financial community. In response to this perception, some argue that if countries avoid financial crises, they do not need to ask for help. Furthermore, it would be harmful to everyone if the IMF lent money unconditionally. Still, the issue of how hard international institutions should be allowed to push countries to change their policies is an open debate.

Closely related to the issue of sovereignty is the issue of transparency. Transparency concerns are based on questions about the decision making that occurs within international institutions. As noted earlier, the IMF and the World Bank have voting structures based on the size of the quotas or dues paid by each country. This gives the United States in particular, and developed country interests in general, control over these bodies and makes it difficult for them to differentiate U.S. or EU interests from the interests of client countries. For example, a client country may be told to open its financial markets because it will increase foreign capital inflows and investment, but the main beneficiaries are banks and financial firms in the United States or the EU. Some critics conclude that IMF and World Bank policies are explicitly designed to benefit special interests in developed countries and do not serve the interests of the world economy.

The governing structure of the WTO is not based on quotas or dues, but the fact that developing countries lack the armies of lawyers, trade association lobbyists, and industry specialists that the United States and the EU can muster during a round of negotiations puts them at a disadvantage. A specific example is the Uruguay Round deal on agriculture and intellectual property rights. Developed countries pushed a comprehensive and strict set of enforcement policies for protecting intellectual property rights (copyrights, trademarks, patents, brand names, and so on). In return, developing countries thought that they would face fewer barriers to selling agricultural products in industrial country markets. In fact, their access to developed country agricultural markets was much less than anticipated, and the costs of enforcing intellectual property rights turned out to be higher than expected.

Ideology

Issues of sovereignty and transparency are compounded by questions about the value of the technical economic advice given by the IMF and other institutions. Some of the sharpest criticisms come from economists who strongly favor international economic integration but argue that the advice and technical assistance provided to developing countries are a reflection of the biases and wishes of developed country interests. For example, critics charge that the IMF views financial sector interests as preeminent, often to the harm and neglect of other sectors. When polled, the vast majority of professional economists favor more open trade over protectionism, but there is no consensus whether developing countries are better off with the free movement of capital. Some economists favor free capital movement as a means of ensuring adequate investment, while others favor limits on capital flows in order to reduce the risk of financial crisis. There are strong arguments on both sides of this debate, but given the costs of the financial crisis that started in 2007, it seems highly likely that the proponents of more controls on capital flows, with more regulations and less open capital markets, will become more influential. This means that the position of the IMF over the last few decades will shift away from completely open capital markets and toward more regulation. As always, the goal will be to find ways to minimize volatility and risk while ensuring that capital is available where it is needed.

Similarly, the IMF and World Bank have been major proponents of privatization. Privatization of publicly owned enterprises can have a number of benefits, but it can also impose high costs. When countries lack regulatory structures or when local institutions are easily captured by powerful economic interests, privatization may trade a public monopoly for a much more predatory private one. Similar criticisms have been voiced about the lending practices of the World Bank. Some critics view its loans and development programs as frequently driven by ideological goals that are out of touch with local conditions and therefore unlikely to achieve the intended development outcomes. These critics share a deep skepticism about grand schemes for "fixing a country" all at once with a universal set of policies that can be applied anywhere. It is important to note that international institutions are often blamed for outcomes that they did not promote. They are easy targets and more than one national government has blamed them as a way to deflect criticisms. "The IMF made me do it" can be an easy way out of a difficult domestic political situation.

Implementation and Adjustment Costs

Trade agreements and the WTO are a major focus of complaints by the critics of economic integration. In particular, when agreements combine developing and developed countries, asymmetries in negotiating skills and the ability to absorb the costs of implementation and adjustment are singled out for criticism. An often cited example is the previously mentioned case of the Uruguay Round agreement on intellectual property rights. In order to implement this part of the agreement, developing countries have to create or improve their patent systems and copyright and trademark enforcement mechanisms. The latter step would entail cutting down on pirated drugs, videos, CDs, software, and so on. The opportunity cost of implementing this part of the agreement is substantial, particularly for a developing country with very limited resources.

Once in place, trade agreements always impose costs in the form of adjustments to the new opportunities and challenges. Some markets will expand while others will contract. In general, the costs of adjusting to the new incentives are less significant than the benefits, but for some developing countries the adjustment costs may be quite large. Developing countries tend to have higher unemployment (often disguised or hidden in the informal sector), so that workers laid off in a contracting industry may spend more time looking for work. Their economies are also less diversified, and sudden shocks such as a surge of imports can have large effects. These problems are made more severe by the lack of social safety nets to protect unemployed workers and their families. In order to take advantage of the opportunities presented by greater access to foreign markets, countries may need to construct new infrastructures, for example, roads and ports for moving fresh produce. The ability of developing countries to build infrastructures is more limited than for developed countries, as is the access to credit.

Issues of sovereignty and transparency, ideological biases, and the costs of implementation and adjustment are only a partial catalog of the concerns raised by the critics of international institutions. In general, however, there is widespread agreement among professional economists that there are theoretical and practical reasons for their existence. Nevertheless, beyond a basic consensus about need, many issues remain subject to debate, particularly issues of governance and the amount of authority that should be vested in international organizations. Still, in spite of these uncertainties, it is safe to say that if these international institutions did not exist, we would create them.

Summary

- Institutions are the "rules of the game." They can be formal, as in a nation's constitution, or informal, as in a custom or tradition. In both cases, we depend on institutions as mechanisms for creating order and reducing uncertainty. Global institutions have played an important role in fostering the growth of international trade and investment during the last fifty years. They have defined a set of rules that have helped avoid trade wars and the problems of the 1930s.

- The "Big 3" of international economic organizations are the International Monetary Fund, the World Bank, and the World Trade Organization. The latter grew out of the General Agreement on Tariffs and Trade. The IMF, World Bank, and the GATT were created at the end of World War II with the purpose of avoiding a return to the destructive economic conditions of the interwar years.

- Regional trade agreements are another important type of international institution, although they are not global in scope. Formally, there are five types of regional trade agreements. In order, from less integrated to more integrated, they are partial trade agreements, free-trade areas, customs unions, common markets, and economic unions. Each level is cumulative and incorporates the features of the previous level. In reality, however, actual trade agreements usually combine features from two or more types.

- Many economists favor regional trade agreements as building blocks for more open world trade, but some pro-free-trade economists are opposed on the grounds that they are harmful to multilateral WTO agreements and are discriminatory. In general, the WTO allows RTAs as long as they create more trade than they divert.

- International economic institutions are an attempt to overcome the problem of free riding by individual nations in the sphere of providing international public goods. The most important public goods are order and a reduction in uncertainty. Some economists believe that these goods are best provided when there are agreements that help keep markets open in recessions and in boom periods, when there is an international lender of last resort, when there are sufficient lenders of capital to developing nations, and when there is an adequate supply of money for international payment.

■ Most analysts agree that some forms of international institutions are necessary as a precaution against crises and to promote growth, but there is significant disagreement over the design of governance structures and the scope of their responsibilities.

■ Primary areas of criticism are in sovereignty, transparency, ideological bias, and implementation and adjustment costs.

Vocabulary

Bretton Woods conference

common external tariff

common market

customs union

Doha Development Agenda

Doha Round

economic union

foreign exchange reserves

free riding

free-trade area

General Agreement on Tariffs and Trade (GATT)

IMF conditionality

institution

International Monetary Fund (IMF)

lender of last resort

most-favored nation (MFN) status

national treatment

nondiminishable

nondiscrimination

nonexcludable

nonrival

partial trade agreement

public goods

quota

regional trade agreement (RTA)

sovereignty

trade bloc

trade creation

trade diversion

trade rounds

Uruguay Round

World Bank

World Trade Organization (WTO)

Study Questions

1. What is an institution? Give examples of formal and informal institutions. Explain how they differ from organizations.

2. What are the arguments in favor of international organizations? What are the arguments against? Which do you think are stronger?

3. Give the arguments for and against free trade agreements. How might the signing of a free trade agreement between the United States, Central America, and the Dominican Republic have harmed Bangladesh?

4. What are public goods and how do they differ from private ones? Give examples of each.

5. What are the main tasks or functions of each of the following:
   - The International Monetary Fund
   - The World Bank
   - The General Agreement on Tariffs and Trade
   - The World Trade Organization

6. When nations sign the GATT, they bind their tariffs at their current level, or lower. Tariff binding means that they agree not to raise the tariffs except under unusual circumstances. Explain how tariff binding in the GATT prevents free riding during a global slowdown.

7. Kindleberger's study of the Great Depression of the 1930s led him to believe that market economies are sometimes unstable and that nations can get locked into prolonged downturns. Other economists are not convinced. Suppose that you disagree with Kindleberger and that you believe that market-based economies are inherently stable. How would you view the need for international institutions to address the provision of each of the public goods listed in Table 2.5?

8. What are the five main types of regional trade agreements and what are their primary characteristics?

9. Critics of the global institutions have a variety of complaints about the WTO, the IMF, and the World Bank. Explain the main categories of complaints.

International Trade

Comparative Advantage and the Gains from Trade

Introduction: The Gains from Trade

This chapter introduces the theory of comparative advantage. A simple model is used to show how nations maximize their material welfare by specializing in goods and services that have the lowest relative costs of production. The improvement in national welfare is known as the **gains from trade**. The concepts of comparative advantage and the gains from trade are two of the oldest and most widely held ideas in all of economics, yet they are often misunderstood and misinterpreted. Therefore, it is worth the effort to develop a clear understanding of both.

Adam Smith and the Attack on Economic Nationalism

The development of modern economic theory is intimately linked to the birth of international economics. In 1776, Adam Smith published *An Inquiry into the Nature and Causes of the Wealth of Nations*, a work that became the first modern statement of economic theory. In the process of laying out the basic ground rules for the efficient allocation of resources, Smith initiated a general attack on **mercantilism**, the system of nationalistic economics that dominated economic thought in the 1700s. Mercantilism stressed exports over imports, primarily as a way to obtain revenues for building armies and national construction projects. Although Smith successfully established modern economics, he did not end mercantilist thinking, which persists today as economic nationalism.

The key mistake in mercantilist thinking was the belief that trade was a **zero sum** activity. In the eighteenth century the term *zero sum* did not exist, but it is a convenient expression for the concept that one nation's gain is another nation's loss. A moment's reflection should be enough to see the mistake in this belief, at least as it applies to voluntary exchange. When a grocery store sells a gallon of milk or a loaf of bread, both the store and the consumer are better off. If that were not the case, the store would not sell and the consumer would not buy. Voluntary exchanges such as this are positive sum, not zero sum. In this sense, sports metaphors that have a winner and a loser are usually not an apt description of trade relations. Trade is more dance than football, more rock climbing than bicycle racing.

No one in the 1770s thought that they were living in the midst of an industrial revolution, but Smith was observant enough to perceive that many improvements in the standard of living had occurred during his lifetime as a result of increasing specialization in production. When he analyzed specialization, he made one of his most important contributions to economics: the discovery that specialization depends on the size of the market.

A contemporary example may be helpful. If a car company were permitted to sell its cars and trucks only in Michigan, it would have much less revenue and would sell many fewer vehicles. It would hire fewer employees, and each person would be less specialized. As it is, the market is so large (essentially, the world) that car companies can hire engineers who are completely specialized in small, even minuscule, parts of a car—door locks, for example. Your door lock engineer will know everything there is to know about the design, production, and assembly of door locks and will be able to put them into cars most efficiently. A firm that was limited to the Michigan market could never afford to hire such specialized skills in every area of vehicle manufacture.

One of the keys to Smith's story of wealth creation is access to foreign markets. If no one is willing to import, then every company is limited by the size of the national market. In some cases, that may be large enough (the United States or China), but in most cases, it is not. Small- and medium-sized countries cannot efficiently produce every item they consume. Holland, for example, has always imported a large share of its goods and has depended on access to foreign markets in order to earn money to pay for imports.

Smith was highly critical of trade barriers because they decrease specialization, technological progress, and wealth creation. He also recognized that imports enable a country to obtain goods that it cannot make or cannot make as cheaply, while exports are made for someone else and are useful only if they lead to imports. The modern view of trade shares Smith's dislike of trade barriers for mostly the same reasons. Although international economists recognize that there are limitations to the application of theory, most economists share a strongly held preference for free and open markets. In Chapters 6 and 7 we will examine trade barriers in greater detail, but at this point we will develop a deeper understanding of the gains from trade by means of a simple algebraic and graphical model.

A Simple Model of Production and Trade

We will begin with one of the simplest models in economics. The conclusion of this analysis is that a policy of free trade maximizes a nation's material well-being. Later, we will examine some of the cases where real-world conditions do not conform to the assumptions of the model and where the optimality of free trade is questionable.

The basic model is often referred to as a Ricardian model, since it first took form in the analysis of David Ricardo. The model begins by assuming that there are only two countries, producing two goods, using one input (labor). More complex models can be built with n countries producing m goods and using k inputs, but other than adding a layer of mathematical sophistication, the final outcome is almost the same. The Ricardian model assumes that firms are price takers, or, in other words, markets are competitive, and no firm has market power. The model is static in the sense that it assumes that technology is constant and there are no learning effects of production that might make firms and industries more productive over time. We will relax both of these assumptions in the coming chapters. Ricardo assumed that labor is perfectly mobile and can easily move back and forth between industries, another simplifying assumption that will be dropped in Chapter 4. In this chapter, we assume that labor is mobile between industries, but not across national boundaries.

Absolute Productivity Advantage and the Gains from Trade

To begin, we define *productivity* in the Ricardian model. Productivity is the amount of output obtained from a unit of input. Since labor is the only input, we can define **labor productivity** as follows:

(units of output)/(hours worked)

If, for example, two loaves of bread can be produced in one hour, then productivity is as follows:

(2 loaves)/(1 hour)

or two loaves per hour. If four loaves are produced in two hours, then productivity is still as follows:

(4 loaves)/(2 hours) = 2 loaves per hour

Suppose that there are two goods, bread and steel, and two countries, the United States and Canada. Suppose also that each produces according to the productivities shown in Table 3.1.

The values in Table 3.1 shows that productivity in the making of bread is greater in Canada than in the United States, and that productivity in steel is

TABLE 3.1	Output per Hour Worked	
	United States	Canada
Bread	2 loaves	3 loaves
Steel	3 tons	1 ton

Canada is more productive than the United States in bread production, but the United States is more productive in steel production.

greater in the United States. Canada has an **absolute productivity advantage** in bread because it produces more loaves per hour worked (three versus two in the United States). Using the same logic, the United States has an absolute productivity advantage in steel production.

The basis of Adam Smith's support for free trade was the belief that every country would have an absolute advantage in something, and that the source of the advantage did not matter. Whether it was due to special skills in the labor force, climate and soil characteristics of the country, or the temperament of its people, there would be goods that each country could manufacture, grow, or dig out of the ground more efficiently than its trading partner. Consequently, every country could benefit from trade.

In the numerical example outlined in Table 3.1, each loaf of bread costs the United States 1.5 tons of steel. Put another way, the **opportunity cost** of bread is 1.5 tons of steel, since each unit of bread produced requires the economy to move labor out of steel production, forfeiting 1.5 tons of steel that it could have produced instead. This follows from the fact that each hour of labor can produce either 2 loaves of bread or 3 tons of steel. We can write this ratio as the barter price of bread as follows:

$$P_{us}^{b} = \frac{3 \text{ tons}}{2 \text{ loaves}} = 1.5 \left(\frac{\text{tons}}{\text{loaves}} \right),$$

where b is bread and us is the country. Similarly, we can write the U.S. price of steel as the inverse as follows:

$$P_{us}^{s} = \frac{2 \text{ loaves}}{3 \text{ tons}} = 0.67 \left(\frac{\text{loaves}}{\text{tons}} \right).$$

You should be able to verify that the Canadian price of bread will be 0.33 (tons/loaf) and that steel will cost 3 (loaves/ton).

If the United States can sell a ton of steel for more than 0.67 loaves of bread, it is better off. Similarly, if Canadians can obtain a ton of steel for fewer than 3 loaves of bread, they are better off. Each country will gain from trade if the United States agrees to sell steel for fewer than 3 loaves of bread but more than 0.67 loaves. Anywhere in that range, both Canadians and Americans will benefit. In the end, trade will occur at a price somewhere between these two limits as follows:

$$3.0 \left(\frac{\text{loaves}}{\text{tons}} \right) > P_{w}^{s} > 0.67 \left(\frac{\text{loaves}}{\text{tons}} \right),$$

where $P_{w}^{s} = $ the world price of steel (the trade price). Without knowing more details about the demand side of the market, it is impossible to say whether the price will settle closer to 3.0 (the Canadian opportunity cost of steel) or 0.67 (the U.S. opportunity cost). The closer the price is to 0.67, the more Canada benefits from trade, and the closer it is to 3.0, the more the United States benefits. Regardless of which country benefits more, as long as the price is between these two limits, both countries benefit from trade.

CASE STUDY

Comparative Advantage in a Single Natural Resource

Natural resources are a source of comparative advantage in many countries. Chile has copper, Botswana has diamonds, and Saudi Arabia has oil. Crude oil is probably the most important geopolitical resource today, and it is certainly the largest resource market. In fact, other than currency trading, international trade in crude oil exceeds the volume and value of any other good or service. According to the U.S. Department of Energy, worldwide daily exports of crude oil in 2008 were 85.5 million barrels. At an average price of around $98 per barrel (prices were inordinately high that year), it is equivalent to more than $8,375 million per day. As large as it is, oil trading is still a fraction of 1 percent of daily trading in the world's currency markets.

Comparative advantage in crude oil production depends largely on a country's endowment of oil, and as everyone is aware, countries in the Middle East have a majority of the world's proven reserves of crude oil. Table 3.2 shows the ten countries with the world's largest reserves and the share of fuel and mining products in their total exports.

Oil is valuable. Consequently, when countries have oil reserves economic forces push them to develop their oil industry. Capital and labor are pulled into the oil sector because it is the most valuable use of inputs and a clear example of following comparative advantage, but one consequence is that it becomes difficult to develop other economic activities. This is evident in Table 3.2 where the proportion of total exports that are oil or its derivatives is extremely high. Most of the economies in Table 3.2 are one-product economies.

The downside of having a single, valuable resource can be significant. Consider the list of countries and ask two questions: Which countries are prosperous and which are genuine democracies? Only three of the ten, Saudi Arabia, Kuwait, and the United Arab Emirates (UAE), qualify as high income. Kuwait and the UAE exceed the level of most of the world's economies and are truly rich. Saudi Arabia has a decent standard of living ($23,000 in 2007), but it is only about two-thirds of the average of the world's high-income economies, which was over $36,000 in 2007. The rest have incomes between $10,000 and $15,000 per person. That is not poverty, but it is less than one-half of the average for high-income economies. The exception is Nigeria, which is only about 5 percent of the level of a high-income country.

The **resource curse** is the name economists give to the negative economic effects that sometimes occur when a country has a single, valuable resource such as oil. The resource curse is not inevitable for economies with large endowments of oil or some other valuable mineral, but it poses a challenge and it should caution us about believing that resources are a path to prosperity. One of the disadvantages of owning a valuable natural resource such as oil is that it raises economic returns to its extraction and production, causing labor and capital to be concentrated in that activity alone. In other words, it is difficult to develop a diversified and highly educated labor force if one activity is dominant. When the price of the dominant commodity fluctuates, as it inevitably will, national income is altered in a very short amount of time. This leads to severe macroeconomic instability and alternating boom and bust cycles.

A further problem of a rich endowment of a single resource is that it often causes political turmoil. There are strong incentives to try to gain control of the resource, leading to factions in leadership and political strife as different groups struggle with each other. The promise of significant wealth can easily lead to corruption in countries with weak governments, as politicians buy the political support they need. In the worse cases, civil war is a possibility.

Not every country with resources suffers from a resource curse. Strong institutions to guard against corruption, and commitment to education, skills, and savings, can develop the human capital and financial capital that a country needs in order to diversify its economy and provide for the inevitable day when the resource is no longer as valuable.

TABLE 3.2   **Ten Largest Oil Reserves**

Country	Reserves*	Trade share**
Saudi Arabia	264.2	88.2
Iran	138.4	87.3
Iraq	115.0	100
Kuwait	101.5	96.4
UAE	97.8	60.4
Venezuela	87.0	92.1
Russia	79.4	72.5
Libya	41.5	97.9
Kazakhstan	39.8	82.8
Nigeria	36.2	97.1

*Billions (thousands of millions) of barrels, given current technology

**Exports of fuels and mining products divided by total exports ($\times$ 100)

FIGURE 3.1   **A Production Possibilities Curve for the United States**

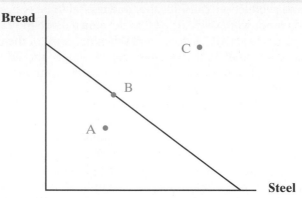

In a model with only two goods, the production possibilities curve shows the trade-offs between them.

Comparative Productivity Advantage and the Gains from Trade

At this point, the obvious question to ask is what happens if a country does not have an absolute productivity advantage in anything. It is not hard to imagine an extremely poor, resource-deficient nation with low literacy and scarce capital. What can these countries produce more efficiently than the United States or Germany? Why would a rich country want to trade with them when they are inefficient at everything? The answer is that even if a country lacks a single good in which it has an absolute productivity advantage, it can still benefit from trade. Perhaps even more surprising, high-income countries also benefit from the trade. In other words, the idea that nations benefit from trade has nothing to do with whether a country has an absolute advantage in producing a particular good. In order to see this, first we must develop a few more basic concepts.

The Production Possibilities Curve

The **production possibilities curve (PPC)** shows the trade-offs a country faces when it chooses its combination of bread and steel output. Figure 3.1 illustrates a hypothetical PPC for the United States. Point B on the PPC is an efficient point of production because it utilizes existing resources to obtain the maximum possible level of output. The assumption of full employment is equivalent to assuming that the United States is operating at a point like B that lies on its PPC. At point A, the economy is inside its production curve and is operating at an inefficient level of output because it is not obtaining the maximum possible output from its available inputs. At point A there is waste in the economy, since a greater quantity of bread and steel could be produced with the existing labor supply. Point C is infeasible because resources do not permit the production of bread and steel in the combination indicated.

The PPC shown in Figure 3.1 is a straight line because it is assumed that the trade-off between bread and steel does not change. This follows from the assumption that labor is homogeneous and that no group of workers is more skilled than another group. The trade-off between bread and steel is another way to refer to the opportunity cost of steel. This follows from the definition of opportunity cost as the best forgone alternative: In order to produce a ton of steel, the United States gives up two-thirds of a loaf of bread. In Figure 3.2, the slope of the PPC is 0.67, the number of loaves of bread forgone (Δbread) divided by the quantity of steel obtained (Δsteel)—written as follows:

$$\text{Slope of the PPC} = (\Delta\text{bread output})/(\Delta\text{steel output})$$

$$= \text{opportunity cost of steel}$$

Relative Prices

Suppose that the slope of the PPC is –0.67, as shown in Figure 3.2. If the United States does not trade, it gives up 0.67 loaves of bread for an additional ton of steel. This trade-off is called the **relative price** of steel or the opportunity cost of steel. The term *relative price* follows from the fact that it is not in monetary units, but rather in units of the other good. If no trade takes place, then the relative price of a good must be equal to its opportunity cost in production.

It is easy to convert the relative price of steel into the relative price of bread: Simply take the inverse of the price of steel. In other words, if 0.67 loaves of

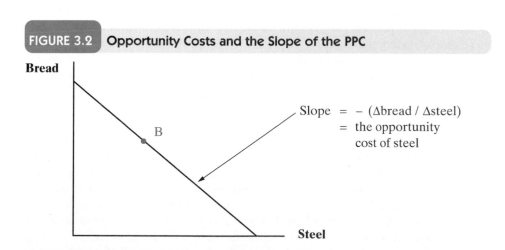

FIGURE 3.2   **Opportunity Costs and the Slope of the PPC**

The slope of the PPC is the opportunity cost of the good on the horizontal axis. This follows from the definition of the slope as the ratio of the vertical change to the horizontal change moving along the PPC.

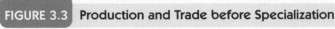

FIGURE 3.3   **Production and Trade before Specialization**

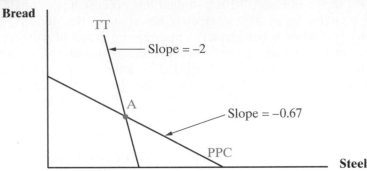

If the United States produces at A and the trade price of steel is 2, then it can trade steel for bread and move its consumption bundle outside its PPC.

bread is the price of 1 ton of steel in the United States, then 1.5 tons of steel is the price of 1 loaf of bread. By the same reasoning, 1.5 tons of steel is the opportunity cost of 1 loaf of bread in the United States when production is at point B or at any other point along the PPC in Figure 3.2.

The Price Line or Trade Line

The complete absence of trade is called **autarky**, and in this situation both the United States and Canada are limited in their consumption to the goods that they produce at home. Suppose that autarky prevails initially and the opportunity cost of steel in Canada is 3 loaves of bread per ton, and in the United States it is 0.67 loaves per ton (as given in Table 3.1). In this case, both countries can raise their consumption levels if they trade. In particular there will be gains from trade if the price settles somewhere between the opportunity costs in Canada and in the United States. That is, the countries benefit if the following is true:

$$3.0 \text{ (loaves/ton)} > P_w^s > 0.67 \text{ (loaves/ton)}$$

Suppose that the price settles at 2 loaves per ton. In the United States, the pre-trade price was 0.67 loaves per ton. This is illustrated in Figure 3.3, where the PPC for the United States is shown with the production point at A. The trading possibilities for the United States are illustrated by line TT, the **price line** or **trade line**. The slope of TT is -2, which is the relative price of steel, or the rate at which bread and steel can be traded for each other. TT passes through point A because this is the combination of steel and bread that is available to trade if the United States produces at A. If the United States chooses to trade, it could move up TT, trading each ton of steel for 2 loaves of bread. This is a better trade-off than it gets if it tries to make more bread, since along its PPC each ton brings only two-thirds more loaves of bread. While it is always impossible to produce outside the PPC, in effect, the United States can consume outside it by trading steel for bread.

The Gains from Trade

You should wonder why the United States would choose to make bread at all, since a ton of steel not produced brings in only two-thirds of a loaf of bread. If the United States were to specialize in steel production and trade for bread, it could do much better, since it would get two loaves for each ton. This possibility is shown in Figure 3.4. Here, the pre-trade production point for the United States is at A. This is also its consumption point, since in the absence of trade, consumption must equal production. Point B in Figure 3.4 represents production that is completely specialized in steel. With the opening of trade, production could occur at B, and the United States could trade up along TT′, which has a slope of −2, the same as TT. If the United States produces at B and moves up TT′, it can reach a point like C, which is unambiguously superior to the consumption bundle available when production is at point A because it represents more of both bread and steel. Similarly, for any combination of bread and steel that is available along the PPC, or along TT if the United States produces at A and trades, there is a consumption bundle on TT′, which represents more of both goods.

The most important thing to note about production point B is that it maximizes U.S. income. This follows from the fact that it makes available the greatest combinations of bread and steel. To see this, consider that no other point of production puts the United States on a price line that lies farther out from the origin. Every other production point on the United States' PPC lies below TT′, and every trade line with a slope of −2 that passes through the PPC at a point other than B also lies below TT′. In other words, given the United States' PPC and a relative steel price of 2, the largest bundle of consumption goods is obtained when the United States specializes in steel and trades for its bread.

The United States benefits from trade, but does Canada? Unequivocally, the answer is yes. Consider Figure 3.5 where point A is Canada's pre-trade production

---

FIGURE 3.4   Production to Maximize Income

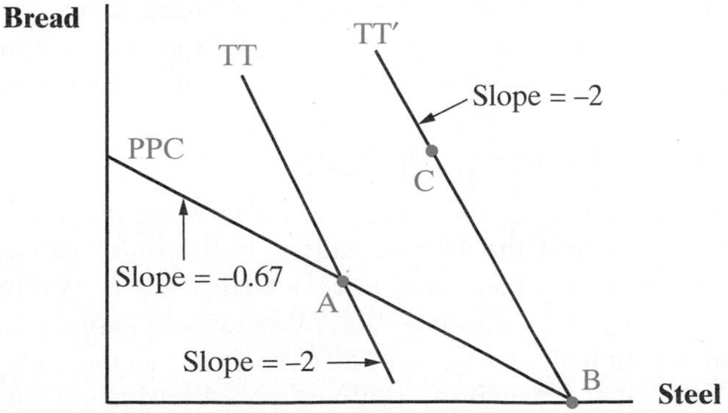

By specializing production at B and trading for bread, the United States obtains the largest possible consumption bundle.

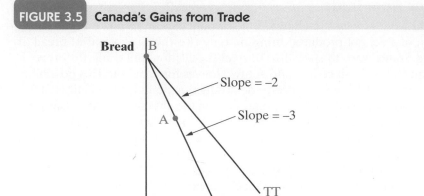

FIGURE 3.5   Canada's Gains from Trade

By specializing production at B and trading for steel, Canada obtains the largest possible consumption bundle.

point. Along Canada's PPC, the opportunity cost of steel is 3 loaves of bread per ton. After trade, the price settles between 0.67 and 3.00, at 2 loaves per ton. With a trade price of 2 (price line TT), Canada maximizes its income by moving along its PPC to where it is completely specialized in bread production. Then it can trade bread for steel at a trade price that is more favorable than its domestic trade-off of 3 loaves per ton. Canada, too, can consume at a point on TT that is outside its PPC and above and to the right of its pre-trade equilibrium at point A. Canada, like the United States, is better off because with trade it gets a larger combination of both goods than it can produce for itself.

A numerical example will help clarify the existence of gains from trade. Suppose the relative price of steel is 2 loaves per ton. When the United States increases its steel output by 1 ton, it gives up 0.67 loaves of bread output, but it can trade the steel for 2 loaves, leaving a net gain of 1.33 loaves (2 − 0.67 = 1.33). In order to meet U.S. demand for 2 more loaves of bread, Canada must give up 0.67 ton of steel production. It trades the 2 loaves for 1 ton of steel, however, leaving a net gain of 0.33 ton (1 − 0.67 = 0.33). Hence, both countries benefit from the trade.

Domestic Prices and the Trade Price

Now we know that as long as the trade price is between the pre-trade domestic prices in Canada and the United States, both countries can gain from trade. What ensures that the trade price actually settles within this range, 3.0 (loaves/ton) $> P_w^s > 0.67$ (loaves/ton)? What would happen if, for example, P_w^s were equal to 4, or 0.5?

Consider the first case when the trade price is 4 loaves per ton of steel. At $P_w^s = 4$, the trade price of steel is greater than the production cost in each country. Clearly, the United States would want to continue to specialize in steel and trade it for bread. Nothing has changed with regard to the U.S. strategy for maximizing its consumption bundle, or income. The only difference now is that the United States gets 4 units of bread for each unit of steel, instead of 2 as before. In Canada's case, the higher price of steel makes it profitable for Canadian producers to switch to steel production. This follows because the production opportunity cost of steel is 3 loaves of bread, but each ton produced can trade for 4 loaves. By specializing in steel production and trading for bread, Canada maximizes its consumption bundle.

Finally, it should be obvious that both countries are specialized in steel production and that no one is producing bread. Both Canada and the United States will bring their excess steel to market looking to trade it for bread, but neither country has any to trade. There is a bread shortage and a glut of steel. Consequently, bread prices rise, and steel prices fall. This goes on at least until the trade price of steel falls below the opportunity cost of production in Canada, the higher-cost country. Once P_w^s is less than 3, Canadian producers switch back to bread, steel production goes down, bread is up, and trade can resume.

In the second case, where P_w^s is less than 0.67, Canada continues to specialize in bread, and the United States switches. Bread is the surplus good, steel is in short supply, and a similar dynamic causes the price to move in order to ensure that both goods are produced. The equilibrium trade price, then, has to be within the range we specified earlier, between the opportunity costs in the two countries. In our case, this is between 0.67 and 3.0 loaves per ton.

At the extreme, the trade price could be equal to the opportunity cost in one country; for example, if the trade price of steel is 0.67 loaves per ton, then the United States is indifferent about trading. It cannot be hurt by trading, but it does not gain either, since all the gains go to Canada. Similarly, if the trade price is equal to Canada's opportunity cost, then Canada is indifferent and all the gains accrue to the United States.

Without more information we cannot say much more about the trade price. Will it be close to 0.67 or to 3.0? The answer depends on the strength of demand for each good in both countries, but we have not explicitly included demand in our model, so we cannot say. We do know that if the price is closer to 0.67, then the gains from trade are larger for Canada, and if it is closer to 3.0, the United States benefits more. Nevertheless, both countries gain as long as the price is between the two opportunity costs, and economic forces determine that the price must be in that range.

Absolute and Comparative Productivity Advantage Contrasted

Absolute productivity advantage is defined as having higher labor productivity. We saw that if each country has an absolute productivity advantage in one of the goods, they can both benefit by specializing in that good and trading it for the other good. Note, however, that the gains from trade did not depend in any way on each country having an absolute advantage. In fact, it was the pre-trade opportunity costs of bread and steel in each country that mattered. Opportunity costs were derived from the productivities, but since they are a ratio, vastly different levels of productivity can lead to the same trade-off.

A country has a **comparative productivity advantage** in a good, or simply a comparative advantage, if its opportunity costs of producing a good are lower than those of its trading partners. The concept of comparative advantage is based on the idea that nations maximize their material well-being when they use their resources where they have their highest value. In order to know the highest-valued usage for any resource, we must compare alternative uses. If, by comparison to that of the United States, Canada's opportunity cost of bread is lower, then it should produce more bread and trade for steel.

The distinction between absolute and comparative productivity advantages is one of the most important in economics. It is also one of the least understood, in spite of the fact that it is relatively simple. For example, it is common to read or hear comments about competitiveness that assume that if a country does not have an absolute advantage, it will not be able to sell its products abroad. Our model explains why this logic is erroneous and why even the least productive nations export some goods.

Gains from Trade with No Absolute Advantage

Consider the case shown in Table 3.3. Japan has an absolute advantage in both cars ($2 > 0.5$) and steel ($2 > 1$), yet it can still gain from trade, as can Malaysia, even though it lacks an absolute advantage in either good. If Japan does not trade, it is limited to its own production possibilities, which require it to give up 1 ton of steel for each car it produces. In Malaysia, each car costs 2 tons of steel. Hence, there is scope for a mutually beneficial exchange.

Japan's opportunity cost of steel production is greater than Malaysia's even though it has a higher absolute rate of productivity in steel. Therefore, if it follows its comparative advantage and maximizes its income, it will specialize in cars, the sector where its opportunity cost is lower than Malaysia's. Once trade opens, the world price of cars will be between 1 and 2 tons of steel per car, the opportunity costs of production in Japan and Malaysia as follows:

$$1\left(\frac{\text{tons}}{\text{car}}\right) < P_w^c < 2\left(\frac{\text{tons}}{\text{car}}\right)$$

TABLE 3.3	Output per Hour Worked	
	Japan	Malaysia
Cars	2	0.5
Steel	2 tons	1 ton

Let the price be 1.5 tons of steel per car. If Japan moves to specialize in cars with the opening of trade, it gives up 1 ton of steel for each additional car it produces. With the additional car, it can trade for 1.5 tons of steel, which is a net gain of 0.5 tons over its own production. Similarly, Malaysia gives up 0.5 cars produced for each additional ton of steel it manufactures, but it gains 0.67 cars from each ton of steel traded. Both countries benefit and both countries are able to consume a greater amount of both goods than they could if they relied on their national production alone.

This is a very simplified example of the gains from trade, but it illustrates a fundamental principle. What matters most for the purposes of trade is not a country's absolute advantage, but rather its comparative advantage. This is a central point of international economics: differences in absolute advantage do not eliminate gains from trade. Furthermore, although both countries gain from trade, it does not imply that their living standards or income are equal. Malaysia's income will be less than Japan's because it produces less per hour. In effect, an hour of work in Malaysia returns the equivalent of 1 ton of steel or, through trade, 0.67 cars. Japanese workers produce 2 cars per hour worked, which is equivalent to 3 tons of steel through trade. As a result of higher absolute productivity, incomes in Japan are quite a bit higher, with or without trade.

CASE STUDY

Changing Comparative Advantage in the Republic of Korea, 1960–2007

Few countries began life with a more limited set of possibilities than the Republic of Korea (South Korea). Liberated from its forty years of colonial status (1905–1945) by the defeat of Japan in World War II, Korea was soon wracked by civil war (1950–1953) and divided into two nations. Many observers were pessimistic about the future of noncommunist South Korea. The industrial capacity of the country was mostly located in communist controlled North Korea, and South Korea had little to offer besides the dedication and hard work of its people. Yet, over the following fifty years, few countries have grown faster. The Republic of Korea is an economic success story that is worth studying.

From 1960 to the present, per capita income in the Republic of Korea grew at the rate of 5.6 percent per year, in real terms (Table 3.4). At this rate, per capita income doubles every twelve years, and over the span of one generation, average incomes increase nearly four times.

Korea's economic strategy for the first few years after the Korean War was to limit imports and concentrate on producing import substitutes, a common strategy for developing countries in the 1950s. Korea was one of the first to

TABLE 3.4	Indicators of the Korean Economy			
	1960	1980	2000	2007
GDP per capita, ($US, 2000)	1,110	3,221	10,884	14,563
Openness	15.8	72.0	78.5	90.4

recognize its limitations and to change its policies. In 1960 and 1961, political changes led to a change in economic policies and a more aggressive engagement with the world economy. Korea removed many of its restrictions on imports and began to promote export-oriented industries. Between 1960 and 2007, its openness index increased from 15.8 to 90.4.

Initially, Korea's export efforts were limited to the commodities on hand, mostly minerals, a few agricultural and marine products (for example, seaweed) and very simple consumer goods. Over several decades after 1960, its export industries evolved several times, from simple products requiring few skills and little capital to products that required more skills and greater capital. After its first few years of exploring its comparative advantage, Korea developed competitive sectors in wigs, textiles, shoes, and plywood. With the increase in income came increases in skills and financial capital. This permitted the development of more skill and capital intensive industries such as steel, shipbuilding, household appliances, and electronic subassemblies. Eventually, these were followed by cars, computers, and electronics. In the first decade of the new millennium, Korea is a high-income industrial economy and is capable of exporting the most technologically advanced products available in several fields. Clearly, its history demonstrates that comparative advantage is not unchangeable, and that it can be a vehicle for raising incomes and promoting development.

An increasing share of Korea's output was sold in world markets. Consequently, production was not limited to the growth in its own domestic market. In addition, its goods had to be competitive in quality and price. Its ability to obtain imports at world prices was also important, but standing behind Korea's competitiveness was its rapid increases in productivity. Without more output per hour of work, incomes could not have risen as fast as they did, and Korea's ability to shift its comparative advantage from low-skill to increasingly higher-skill products could not have gone forward. In turn, productivity increases require a host of complementary changes, ranging from the development of universities and research institutes to organizational changes and the raising of financial capital for investing in new machinery and equipment.

In the process of promoting exports and raising productivity, Korea encountered a number of obstacles including its own bureaucratic inflexibility, problems in marketing to foreign markets that are radically different from Korea, and a shortage of technical management and industrial expertise.

The Korean experience is an example of a country that used its comparative advantage to develop export markets. At the same time, it also used the competitive pressures of foreign competition to raise its own productivity and quality standards, which in turn raised the incomes of its citizens. Korea's success was a joint product of efforts by its government, the private sector, and a number of public-private organizations. The role that each of these played is still hotly debated. Is Korea's success due to the wise guidance of government policies, or did those policies play a secondary (or even negative) role to markets and competition?

Comparative Advantage and "Competitiveness"

The rhetoric of "competitiveness" is so common in our public discourse that it is useful to consider its relationship to comparative advantage. In the analysis so far, comparative advantage resulted from productivity differences between nations in autarky. In our simple model of a barter economy, wages, prices, and exchange rates were omitted. Real businesses do not barter steel for bread, however, and they cannot pay their workers by dividing up the firm's output.

In general, by ignoring money wages, money prices, and exchange rates, we assumed that all goods and labor were correctly priced. In other words, we assumed that the prices of outputs and inputs are an accurate indication of their relative scarcity. In this case, there is no difference between a nation's comparative advantage and the ability of its firms to sell goods at prices that are competitive. That is, if all markets correctly value the price of inputs and outputs, then a nation's commercial advantage is determined by its comparative advantage.

Unfortunately, markets sometimes fail to produce optimal outcomes, and at times, outputs and inputs are incorrectly priced. Sometimes, undervaluation or overvaluation of a good stems from inherent difficulties in measuring its true value or in measuring its true cost of production. For example, we usually ignore the costs of air pollution when we measure the costs of driving a car. Other times, undervaluation or overvaluation may result from government policies, as when prices are maintained at an artificially high or low level. In either case, the fact that a market price may not accurately reflect the economic value of an input or an output means that a wedge is driven between commercial or **competitive advantage** and comparative advantage.

It is often (incorrectly) argued that nations should pursue commercial advantages for their firms even if it means a misallocation of resources. In effect, this means a country follows policies that lower living standards by failing to maximize the value of national output. In terms of Figure 3.4 and Figure 3.5, this is equivalent to asserting that the United States and Canada should each remain at a point like A, where the United States overestimates the value of producing its own bread and Canada overestimates the value of steel. Both countries end up with consumption bundles that are suboptimal from the standpoint of national welfare.

Consider a real-world example. Indonesia tried to develop an aircraft industry in spite of the fact that it lacks a comparative advantage in aircraft production. Nevertheless, through a combination of government policies (some of which paid people to buy the planes!) the price to foreigners was competitive at times. From the perspective of Indonesian national welfare and the optimal use of scarce Indonesian resources, this was a mistake. From the perspective of a business, however, Indonesian policies made it profitable to make airplanes, even though it meant using resources in ways that were suboptimal from the national perspective.

This case illustrates the common mistake of equating nations with business enterprises. Indonesian plane manufacturers care about their subsidies and any other policy that makes them profitable. The national interest, however, is to achieve the most efficient allocation of resources possible within the framework of the nation's laws and values. It is possible to make individual firms highly profitable through subsidies or protection from international competition, while at the same time and through the same policies cause the nation's overall standard of living to be lower than it would be otherwise. Businesses are not designed to ensure that resources are efficiently allocated at the national level. If they can legally tip the playing field in their direction, they will not hesitate.

Another important distinction between nations and business enterprises is that nations do not compete with each other in any normal sense of the word. Economic relations between the United States and Canada, or any pair of nations, are not equivalent to the commercial competition that exists between companies such as Coke and Pepsi. If Canada grows, the United States does not go out of business or suffer in any identifiable way. In fact, Canadian growth would be a stimulus to U.S. growth and would create spillover benefits for Americans. Cola companies fight over a relatively static market size, but nations can all simultaneously increase their incomes.

Economic Restructuring

Economic restructuring refers to changes in the economy that may require some industries to grow and others to shrink or even disappear altogether. For example, the United States has seen a dramatic decrease in the size of its steel industry and, some years later, a rebirth of a new industry based around smaller, more specialized steel mills. Today, the car industry is shrinking, with a long term prospect that is as yet unknown. In any dynamic economy, some types of economic activity will be growing, and others will be scaling back or dying. In some cases, these changes are a direct consequence of increased openness to foreign competition. For example, the influx of Japanese cars has played a major role in the reorganization and restructuring of the U.S. auto industry.

In our simple Ricardian model, after the opening of trade the United States was able to maximize its well-being by shifting workers out of bread production and into steel production. Even though this restructuring of the economy improved overall economic welfare, it does not mean that it benefited every individual—a nation's gains from trade may be divided in different ways, and it is usually the case that some individuals benefit while others are hurt by trade. If there are net gains from opening trade (which are measured by an increase in the consumption bundle), then it means that the economic gains of the winners are greater than the economic losses of the losers, and therefore the nation as a whole is better off. Nevertheless, opening an economy to increased foreign competition is rarely painless and usually generates a number of new problems. In the model used in this chapter, it was assumed that workers can effortlessly and without costs move back and forth between industries as one expands and the other shrinks. In reality this is not an option. While some laid off workers in a declining industry may quickly find new jobs, most do not. They may not know which companies need workers, or their skills may not match those that are in demand.

The model of comparative advantage does not offer a set of policies for addressing the problems of dislocated workers. Those policies have to come from another branch of economic analysis, such as labor economics, and from outside economics. It is widely recognized, however, that changes in trade patterns, whether they are due to trade agreements, a unilateral reduction in trade barriers, technological breakthroughs, or any other cause, will result in some dislocation of firms and workers. Most economists continue to support more open trading arrangements, however, because foreign trade increases our choices as consumers, it lowers the costs of inputs for producers, it increases competition and innovation, and it leads to a greater diffusion of technological change. Nevertheless, it is important to keep in mind that the gains from trade do not mean that every worker or every firm benefits.

To a large extent, political assumptions about the way the world works will color the solutions to the problem of worker dislocation offered by economists, political scientists, and other social scientists. For example, some ardent believers in less government intervention in the economy would argue that government should not have any policies for handling unemployment caused by the rapid growth of imports. They maintain that unemployment is a self-correcting problem; laid-off workers will look for new jobs and will, if necessary, accept lower wages. Others make a value judgment that this sort of social problem should not be a governmental concern and that it should be left up to the private economy and individual initiative.

An alternative to the "do nothing" approach is for the government to look for ways to compensate the losers. The proponents of this view justify it on several grounds. First, the nation as a whole benefits from trade, so there are newly added resources to the economy that make compensation possible. Second, many people believe that they have an ethical obligation to assist people hurt by economic change. And third, compensation reduces the incentives to oppose foreign trade.

The practice of offering **trade adjustment assistance (TAA)** is common in many countries, including the United States. Usually these programs take the form of extended unemployment benefits and worker re-training. For example, the U.S. government created a special program of benefits for workers who are hurt by trade with Mexico due to the signing of the North American Free Trade

Agreement (NAFTA). In 1994, the first year of NAFTA, 17,000 workers qualified for TAA under the NAFTA provision. Generally, in order to qualify for the benefits, workers must demonstrate that they were laid off as a result of imports from Mexico or Canada or because their firm relocated to one of those countries. Needless to say, it is sometimes difficult to establish a direct link between imports and job loss; a poorly managed firm may have been on its way out of business with or without imports.

The important point is that trade creates change, and it may be difficult for some people, industries, or communities to deal with it. When a nation moves along its PPC toward a different mix of industries, there is a period of transition that is painful for some. Economic restructuring does not happen overnight, and although it is desirable for the higher living standard it brings, change and transformation cost time and money.

CASE STUDY

Losing Comparative Advantage

The case study on Korea shows that comparative advantage is not fixed in time but changes as countries develop their economies. Changing comparative advantage cuts two ways, however, and some production stops being an efficient use of a country's capital and labor. In the Korean case, there are products that it exported early in its development that are no longer cost efficient to make.

Agriculture is an area where many countries experience a declining comparative advantage over time. Some agricultural crops tend to be very labor intensive, and the cost of labor rises as an economy develops. Technology may solve some of the problems of rising wages by reducing the need for labor, but other crops resist an efficient technological solution. In an ideal world, workers in industries that lose their comparative advantage would easily and quickly move to an industry where new opportunities appear.

Comparative advantage in agriculture is not the only concern countries have when thinking about their agricultural sector. Issues of food safety, food independence, and support for rural culture and society are all concerns to one degree or another, more in some countries than others.

One of the objectives of the Doha Round of the World Trade Organization (WTO) is to create an economic environment in which low-cost agricultural producers have access to other countries' markets. The goal is to create greater efficiency in the world economy by locating production where the opportunity costs are lowest, while at the same time creating opportunities for developing countries. If a developing country has a comparative advantage in, say, cotton, but foreign markets are not open, it cannot fully obtain the benefits of its comparative advantage.

Cotton is not a food crop and its treatment highlights some of the fundamental difficulties involved in persuading countries to drop trade barriers, as well as the fundamental reasons why it is desirable to see barriers fall. According to the International Cotton Advisory Committee, the highest cost producers in the world include Greece, Spain, and the United States, all of which are countries classified as high-income by the World Bank. Lowest-cost producers are in sub-Saharan western Africa (e.g., Burkina Faso, Mali, Benin) and central Asia (e.g., Uzbekistan and Tajikistan).

Cotton is not a major item in world trade, accounting for only about 0.12 percent of total merchandise trade in 2003. Nevertheless, it is important. As many as one hundred million households depend on income earned growing cotton, and several of the low-cost producers depend on their cotton export earnings to buy essential imports such as grain. Table 3.5 compares cotton production, its share of trade, and income per person in a few of the low-cost and high-cost producers. As shown, low-cost countries produce less but depend more on cotton exports, as their very low levels of income put them close to the edge of survival and they have fewer goods to export. High-cost producers depend much less on their cotton exports and have much higher incomes.

High-cost producers like the United States and Greece depend on a variety of government interventions to keep their cotton producers in business. In Greece,

TABLE 3.5   Low-Cost and High-Cost Cotton Producers

Country	Cotton exports, 2004 (millions $)	Percent of total exports, 2004	Income per person, 2007
Low-cost producers			
Western Africa			
Benin	154.1	27.1	570
Burkina Faso	264.1	55.1	430
Mali	207.0	21.2	500
Central Asia			
Tajikistan	161.6	17.7	460
Uzbekistan	550.7	12.9	730
High-cost producers			
Greece	364.6	2.3	25,740
United States	4,251.2	0.5	46,040

Sources: Food and Agricultural Organization; World Bank; World Trade Organization.

direct and indirect payments, along with tariffs on imports of cotton, are administered through the European Union's Common Agricultural Program. In the United States, the Department of Agriculture administers a number of farm support programs, including payments to farmers, subsidized loans, revenue guarantees, subsidized insurance, marketing and promotion assistance, and others, while the Department of Commerce administers a set of tariffs on foreign cotton entering the U.S. market.

Rich countries that try to keep their high-cost producers in business do more than keep production going where it is less efficient. They also have the potential to harm the living standards of some of the world's poorest countries and to block one of their paths to higher incomes. By using their wealth to subsidize production, high-cost producers increase world supply and limit the ability of low-cost producers to fully exploit their comparative advantage in cotton.

The Doha Round of the WTO and its Doha Development Agenda are an attempt to create a set of rules that would limit the damage done to developing countries by limiting economic subsidies for farmers. High-income countries find it politically difficult, however, to give up their support for older, less efficient sectors.

Summary

- The single most important determinant of trade patterns is the opportunity cost of producing traded goods. Countries that sacrifice the least amount of alternative production when producing a particular good have the lowest opportunity cost, or a comparative advantage. The idea of comparative advantage has been one of the most enduring concepts of economic thought and has been a central theme in international economic policy since the mid-1800s.

- Nations that produce according to their comparative advantage are maximizing the benefits they receive from trade and, consequently, their national welfare. This is the same as maximizing their gains from trade.

- Comparative advantage is often confused with absolute advantage. The latter refers to the advantage a nation has if its absolute productivity in a particular product is greater than its trading partners. It is not necessary to have an absolute advantage in order to have a comparative advantage.

- One common fallacious argument against following comparative advantage is that workers in other countries are paid less than workers at home. This argument neglects the issue of productivity. Developing-country wages are lower because the value of output from one hour of labor is less. Labor productivity is less because workers are generally less skilled, they have less capital on the job, and they have less capital in the surrounding economy to support their on-the-job productivity.

■ Businesspeople look at the issue of trade differently than economists do because they have different objectives in mind. Businesspeople are often concerned about their ability to compete—that is, to sell a particular item in a given market at the lowest price. Their perspective is that of the firm. Economists focus on the efficient use of resources at the national or global level. The perspective is that of all firms taken together.

Vocabulary

absolute productivity advantage	opportunity cost
autarky	price line
comparative productivity advantage	production possibilities curve (PPC)
competitive advantage	relative price
economic restructuring	resource curse
gains from trade	trade adjustment assistance (TAA)
labor productivity	trade line
mercantilism	zero sum

Study Questions

1. Use the information in the following table on labor productivities in France and Germany to answer questions a through f.

Output per hour worked

	France	Germany
Cheese	2 kilograms	1 kilogram
Cars	0.25	0.5

a. Which country has an absolute advantage in cheese? In cars?

b. What is the relative price of cheese in France if it does not trade? In Germany?

c. What is the opportunity cost of cheese in France? In Germany?

d. Which country has a comparative advantage in cheese? In cars? Explain your answer.

e. What are the upper and lower bounds for the trade price of cheese?

f. Draw a hypothetical PPC for France and label its slope. Suppose that France follows its comparative advantage in deciding where to produce on its PPC. Label its production point. If the trade price of cars is five kilograms of cheese per car, draw a trade line showing how France can gain from trade.

2. Suppose that the table in Study Question 1 looks as follows. Use the information to answer questions a through f.

Output per hour worked	France	Germany
Cheese	1 kilogram	2 kilograms
Cars	0.25 car	2 cars

   a. Which country has an absolute advantage in cheese? In cars?
   b. What is the relative price of cheese in France if it does not trade? In Germany?
   c. What is the opportunity cost of cheese in France? In Germany?
   d. Which country has a comparative advantage in cheese? In cars? Explain your answer.
   e. What are the upper and lower bounds for the trade price of cheese?
   f. Draw a hypothetical PPC for France and label its slope. Suppose that France follows its comparative advantage in deciding where to produce on its PPC. Label its production point. If the trade price of cars is five kilograms of cheese per car, draw a trade line showing how France can gain from trade.

3. Explain how a nation can gain from trade even though as a result not everyone is better off. Is this a contradiction?

4. Economic nationalists in developed countries worry that international trade is destroying the national economy. A common complaint is that trade agreements open the economy to increased trade with countries where workers are paid a fraction of what they earn at home. Explain the faulty logic of this argument.

5. Many people believe that the goal of international trade should be to create jobs. Consequently, when they see workers laid off due to a firm's inability to compete against cheaper and better imports, they assume that trade must be bad for the economy. Is this assumption correct? Why, or why not?

6. Suppose that Germany decides to become self sufficient in bananas and even to export them. In order to accomplish these goals, large tax incentives are granted to companies that will invest in banana production. Soon, the German industry is competitive and able to sell bananas at the lowest price anywhere. Does Germany have a comparative advantage? Why, or why not? What are the consequences for the overall economy?

Comparative Advantage and Factor Endowments

Introduction: The Determinants of Comparative Advantage

The theory presented in Chapter 3 assumed that countries had different levels of productivity, but the reasons why one country might be more productive than another in a particular line of production were not analyzed. In this chapter, the idea of comparative advantage is examined in more detail, beginning with the factors that determine it. We will also examine the impact of trade on income distribution. In the simple model discussed in Chapter 3, it was assumed that everyone that wanted a job could find one and that after trade began, anyone laid off from the shrinking industry found employment in the expanding one. The opposition to expanded trade, however, often comes from people who fear that increased trade will downsize their industry, and they do not view themselves as having options for employment in the expanding sectors. We also saw that trade causes the price of the export good to rise and the price of the import good to fall, making the nation as a whole better off. In reality, we consume both export and import goods, and the fact that the nation is better off may not reflect individual circumstances if consumption is heavily weighted toward the export good.

Modern Trade Theory

In Chapter 3, comparative advantage depended on each country's relative productivity, which was given by assumption at the start of the exercise. Smith and Ricardo thought that each country would have its own technology, its own climate, and its own resources, and that differences among nations would give rise to productivity differences. In the twentieth century, several economists developed a more detailed explanation of trade in which the comparative advantage of a country depends on its endowments of the inputs (called factors of production, or simply, factors) that are used to produce each good. The theory has various names: the Heckscher-Ohlin theory (HO), the Heckscher-Ohlin-Samuelson theory, or the Factor Proportions theory. They all refer to the same set of ideas.

TABLE 4.1	An Example of Factor Abundance	
	United States	Canada
Capital	50 machines	2 machines
Labor	150 workers	10 workers

The United States is capital abundant and Canada is labor abundant.

The Heckscher-Ohlin (HO) Trade Model

The HO trade model begins with the observation that nations are endowed with different levels of each input (factors). Furthermore, each output has a different technology for its production and requires different combinations and levels of the various inputs. Steel production, for example, requires a lot of iron ore, coking material, semiskilled labor, and some expensive capital equipment. Clothing production requires unskilled and semiskilled workers with rudimentary capital equipment in the form of sewing machines.

In order to analyze how the availability of inputs creates productivity differences, first we define **factor abundance** and **factor scarcity**. Table 4.1 illustrates the concepts with a numerical example. The capital-labor ratio of the United States (K_{us} / L_{us}) is $^{50}/_{150}$, or $\frac{1}{3}$. Canada's (K_{can} / L_{can}) is $^{2}/_{10}$, or $\frac{1}{5}$. Because the United States' capital-labor ratio is higher than Canada's ($K_{us} / L_{us} > K_{can} / L_{can}$), the United States is the relatively capital-abundant country and Canada is the relatively labor-abundant country. Note that Canada's absolute labor endowment is less than that of the United States, but Canada it is still considered labor-abundant because it has more labor relative to its capital.

Relative abundance of a factor implies that in autarky its relative cost is less than in counties where it is relatively scarcer. Conversely, relatively scarce resources are more expensive. Consequently, capital is relatively cheap in the United States and labor is relatively expensive. It follows that economies have relatively lower costs in the production of goods where the technology calls for greater quantities of the abundant factor and smaller quantities of the scarce factor. In this example, Canada will have a lower opportunity cost in production that uses relatively more labor and relatively less capital, while the United States will have a lower opportunity cost in production that uses relatively more capital and less labor.

The **Heckscher-Ohlin (HO) trade theory** makes this point exactly. It asserts that a country's comparative advantage lies in the production of goods that intensively use relatively abundant factors. In other words, comparative advantage is determined by a nation's factor endowment, and once this is determined, it should be possible to predict the goods a country exports and imports.

To clarify, consider the United States. It is richly endowed with a wide variety of factors. It has natural resources in the form of rich farmland and extensive forests. It has highly skilled labor, such as scientists, engineers, and managers.

Although savings rates are not very high, the wealth of the nation has enabled it to create an abundance of physical capital, both public and private. Its exports, therefore, should include agricultural products, particularly those requiring skilled labor and physical capital, and all sorts of machinery and industrial goods that require intensive input of physical capital and scientific and engineering skills.

One leading U.S. export is commercial jet aircraft—a product that requires a vast array of physical capital and scientific, engineering, and managerial talent. The United States is also a major exporter of grains and grain products, such as vegetable oils. These are produced with relatively small labor inputs, very large capital inputs (combines, tractors, and so on), farmland, and a great deal of scientific research and development that has produced hybrid seeds, pesticides, herbicides, and other agricultural inputs.

Gains from Trade in the HO Model

In the Ricardian model we assumed that each country faced a constant set of trade-offs: two loaves of bread for three tons of steel (United States) or three loaves of bread for one ton of steel (Canada). The constant costs of the Ricardian model stemmed from the fact that there was one homogeneous input: labor. Labor could be used to make bread or steel. Workers did not vary in their skills, and since there was no capital input, each worker was as productive as the next. Consequently, when labor was reallocated from bread to steel, or vice versa, the trade-off was always at a constant rate.

In the HO model, we have a multiplicity of inputs—labor, capital, farmland—so each worker may be equipped with a different quantity of supporting inputs, such as capital. Obviously, at the end of the day a worker with a $5 shovel will have dug a smaller hole than one equipped with a $150,000 earth-moving machine. Furthermore, the quality of labor and capital can vary. Some labor is skilled, and some is unskilled. Certain jobs require scientific or other technical training, while others require basic literacy or even less. Similarly, capital can be low- or high-tech, and resources such as farmland have different fertility and climate characteristics. In effect, each important qualitative difference can be treated as a key characteristic of a separate input, so unskilled and skilled labor can be considered different factors.

If a country has multiple inputs with various suitabilities for different tasks, we can no longer assume a production possibilities curve (PPC) with constant costs. Rather, the economy is assumed to have increasing costs, which implies that each country has a rising opportunity cost for each type of production. Consequently, as the United States or Canada moves labor, capital, and land into bread production, each additional unit of bread leads to a greater loss of steel output than the one before. The reason is straightforward: If more bread is wanted, resources must be taken out of steel. The optimal strategy is to move resources that are relatively good at bread production, but poor at steel production. This leads to the greatest gain in bread with the smallest loss of steel. The next shift in production, toward more bread, cuts deeper into the stock of resources used for steel production, and in all likelihood there will not be resources to move that are as good at bread and as poor at steel as the previous production shift. Consequently, in order to get the same increase in bread, more steel must be given up than before. This result is symmetric, so shifts going the other way, toward more steel, cause the opportunity cost of steel to rise with each shift. Figure 4.1 illustrates a PPC with increasing costs.

As with constant costs, the trade-off between bread and steel is equal to the slope of the PPC. Since the PPC is curved, its slope changes at every point, and we must measure the trade-off at the point of production. For example, in Figure 4.2, if the United States is producing at point A, then the opportunity cost of an additional ton of steel is equivalent to the slope of the PPC at point A. Since the PPC is a curve rather than a straight line, the slope is measured by drawing a tangent line at the point of production and measuring its slope.

Most of the analysis of the gains from trade discussed in Chapter 3 carries over into the HO model. In order to demonstrate this, assume that point A is the U.S. production point in autarky and that at point A the opportunity cost of steel is 0.67 loaves of bread. This means that the slope of the tangent at A is -0.67. Also assume that Canada's opportunity cost of steel is above that of the United States at 3 loaves of bread per ton, the same as before. Also assume that after trade begins, the world price, or trade price, is 2 loaves of bread per ton of steel, the same as the example shown in Chapter 3. After trade opens, the United States can continue to produce at A and not trade, or it can produce at A and trade. Trade line TT shown in Figure 4.3 illustrates the possibilities if the United States stays at point A on its PPC.

FIGURE 4.1   **The United States' Production Possibilities Curve with Increasing Costs**

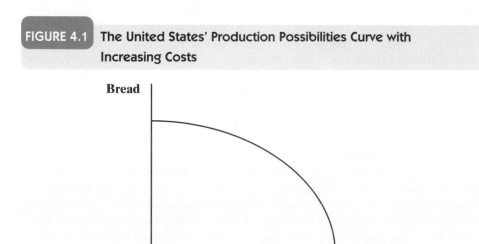

Moving from left to right, the opportunity cost of another unit of steel increases.

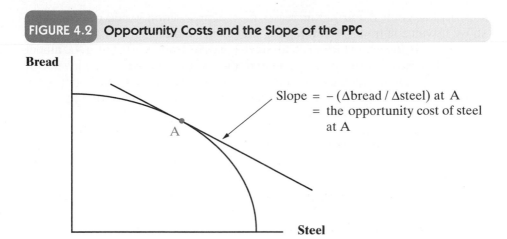

The opportunity cost of steel is measured by the slope of the tangent at the point of production.

TT is the price line with a slope of -2 passing through A and showing the combinations of bread and steel that are available when production is at A and trade is possible. In Figure 4.3, TT′ is a trade line that is tangent to the PPC at point B, an alternative production point to the right of A and closer to the steel axis. If the United States exploits its comparative advantage and shifts toward increased steel production, increasing costs come into play, which is the same as saying that the marginal cost of steel output is rising. As production rises, the gap between the opportunity cost of production and the trade price narrows, until finally, they

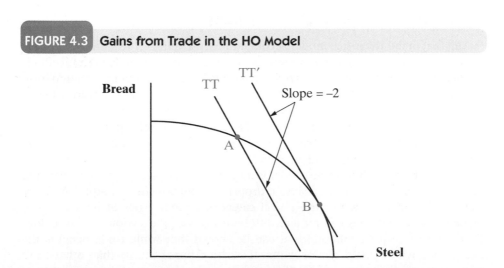

TT is the trade line if production is at A. Production at B maximizes income.

are equal at point B. Further increases in steel production would push the cost above its value in trade; therefore, they are not warranted.

At point B, the opportunity cost of steel equals its trade price. Since the model is symmetric and the opportunity cost and trade price of bread are the inverse of the steel, the same equivalency holds for bread. To the left of B, the opportunity cost of steel (bread) is less (greater) than the trade price, so more (less) production is warranted. To the right of B, the opportunity cost of steel (bread) is greater (less) than the trade price, so less (more) production is warranted. Only at point B does the opportunity cost equal the trade price. Since no other changes can make the United States better off, point B is the production combination that maximizes income.

Graphically, the superiority of point B can be seen by first comparing B to A. Point B is clearly superior to A in terms of the consumption possibilities because for every point along TT there is another point on TT′ that offers more of both goods. That is, TT′ lies above and to the right of TT. Since a greater combination of both goods is available if the United States produces at B and trades, B is superior to A. Furthermore, when the trade price is 2, every other production point along the PPC leads to smaller consumption bundles. That is, at any other production point, a trade line with a slope of −2 that passes through the point will lie below and to the left of TT′, representing smaller combinations of steel and bread. Consequently, point B maximizes income by creating the largest possible consumption bundle.

The notion of gains from trade in the HO model is nearly the same as the Ricardian model. The only significant difference is that specialization is not complete in the HO model. The United States continues to make some bread, and Canada makes some steel.

Trade and Income Distribution

Recall that in the Ricardian model of comparative advantage, the nation as a whole gained from trade, and, by assumption, we ruled out the potentially harmful effects of trade on some members of society. When trade began, the economy shifted from one point on its production frontier to a different point. Workers that were affected by the production shift simply moved out of the declining industry and into the expanding one. Everyone had the same skills, and each type of production required only labor, so everyone had access to a job, and everyone benefited from both the fall in the price of the imported good and the rise in the price of the exported one.

The Heckscher-Ohlin trade model is a more sophisticated way to analyze the gains and losses from trade because it drops these unrealistic assumptions. Labor can be divided into two or more skill categories, other types of inputs can be included, and industries can require different mixes of the various inputs. Under these more realistic assumptions, it can be shown that while trade benefits the nation as a whole, some groups within the nation benefit more than others, and some will actually be harmed. Furthermore, it can be shown that there is a systematic relationship between the factor endowments of a country and the winners and losers from trade. Opening the discussion to an analysis of winners and losers adds an important and necessary element of realism. We are all aware that not everyone favors increased trade, and without an analysis of trade's income distribution effects, we have no basis for understanding the opposition to increased trade.

The Stolper-Samuelson Theorem

The analysis begins by recognizing that everyone's income depends on the inputs that he or she supplies to the economy. Labor earns wages that may be high or low, depending on the skill level; owners of capital earn profits; landowners earn rents. The amount of income earned per unit of input depends on the demand for the inputs as well as their supply. The demand for a particular input is sometimes referred to as a **derived demand** because it is derived indirectly from the demand for the output that it is used to produce. If the output is in high demand, and consequently its price is high, then the inputs that are used to produce it will benefit by receiving higher returns.

In general, any change in the economy that alters the price of outputs will have a direct impact on incomes. We have seen that trade causes output prices to change. Specifically, the price of the export good rises, while the price of the import falls. The movement of prices causes a change in the demand for each factor and leads to a change in the returns paid to each factor. Hence, trade affects income distribution.

When trade begins and output prices change, resources leave the sector that produces imported goods and move into the sector that produces exports. In the HO model, unlike the simple Ricardian model, different goods are produced with different combinations of inputs, so the movement along the production possibilities frontier causes a change in the demand for each input. Factors that are used intensively in the imported goods sector will find that the demand for their services has shrunk—and so has their income. Conversely, factors used intensively in the export sector will experience an increase in the demand for their services and in their incomes. In sum, when trade begins, incomes of the factors used intensively in the import sector fall, and incomes of the factors used intensively in the export sector rise.

These effects are summarized in the **Stolper-Samuelson theorem**, which is derived from the HO theory. The Stolper-Samuelson theorem says that an increase in the price of a good raises the income earned by factors that are used intensively in its production. Conversely, a fall in the price of a good lowers the income of the factors that it uses intensively.

Figure 4.4 illustrates these tendencies. Suppose that the United States and Canada can make bread or steel, using capital and labor. Also suppose that bread is the labor-intensive product, shown as follows:

$$K^b / L^b < K^s / L^s$$

and that the United States is relatively well endowed with capital, compared to Canada, as follows:

$$K_{can} / L_{can} < K_{us} / L_{us}.$$

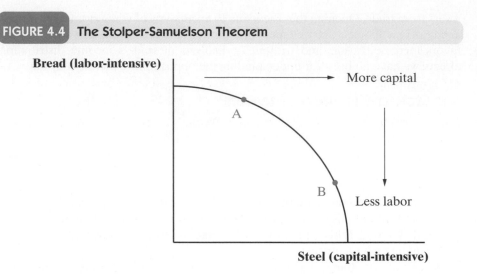

FIGURE 4.4 **The Stolper-Samuelson Theorem**

Movement along the PPC from A to B reduces the economy's demand for labor and increases its demand for capital.

According to the HO theory, the United States will have a comparative advantage in steel, which it will export in return for Canadian bread. In Figure 4.4, after trade begins, the United States moves along its PPC toward the steel axis from point A to point B.

As the United States shifts along its PPC, the change in the mix of goods produced leads to lower demands for labor and higher demands for capital. The steel industry will pick up some of the labor laid off in the bread industry, but since it is not as labor intensive as bread, its increase in labor demand is less than the fall in labor demand in the bread industry. The net result is that labor experiences a fall in demand, leading to a fall in wages and income earned. Note that Stolper-Samuelson does not state that all factors used in the export industries are better off, or that all factors used in the import competing industry get hurt. Rather, the abundant factor that is used to determine comparative advantage and exports is favored, and the scarce factor sees a decline in its income, regardless of industry.

The Stolper-Samuelson theorem is a starting point for understanding the income distribution effects of trade, but it tells only part of the story. An extension of the theorem, called the **magnification effect**, shows that the change in output prices has a magnified effect on factor incomes. For example, if after opening trade bread prices declined by 75 percent, then the fall in labor income will be greater than 75 percent. Similarly, if the price of an export good (steel) rises by 50 percent, for example, incomes earned by the intensively used factors in the export sector (capital) rise more than 50 percent.

The ultimate effects on income of an opening of trade depend on the flexibility of the affected factors. If labor is stuck in bread production and unable to move to the steel sector, it could be hurt much worse than if it were completely flexible to move. Another example illustrates this point: Within the debate over U.S.-Mexico free trade, there is a small, but intense, controversy surrounding avocado production. Mexico has a comparative advantage in avocados because it is well endowed with the necessary inputs (a particular quality of land and climate, together with unskilled labor and a little capital). If free trade were to open in the avocado market, the owners of avocado orchards in California would find their investments in land, equipment, and avocado trees worthless. Why would anyone pay $1 or more per avocado when Mexican ones sell for 25¢ or less? However, many of the California avocado groves are located in the suburbs of sprawling metropolitan regions, and presumably, if the land were worthless for avocado production, it could be put to valuable use in another line of production—for example, as housing developments. Consequently, the income of the landowners may not decline in the long run, although in the short run landowners may be unable to put their land to an alternative use. In order to build these considerations into a trade model, we must turn to a short-run version of the HO model.

The Specific Factors Model

In the short run, the ability of factors to move between different output sectors is more limited. For example, suppose stiffer competition in the world steel industry causes American steelworkers to take pay cuts, and perhaps some to lose their jobs. In the long run, most of the laid-off steelworkers will find jobs outside of the steel sector, but in the short run, they are stuck with cuts in pay and layoffs. Similarly, physical capital is usually dedicated to a particular use and cannot be converted into producing a different product, and, as we have seen, land is usually tied up in a particular use and cannot be switched to something else instantaneously. In the long run, however, plants and equipment can be redirected to a different line of production, land can be put to different uses, and workers find jobs doing something else.

In order to highlight the ability of labor and other factors to find alternative employment in the long run but not in the short run, sometimes economists add conditions to the HO model. Suppose there are three factors—land, labor, and capital—and two goods—steel and bread. Assume that the production of steel takes capital and labor, while bread takes land and labor. In this version of the HO model, labor is the variable factor because its use varies between both goods. Land and capital are the specific factors because their use is specific to bread and steel, respectively.

The model just described is an example of the **specific factors model**, a special case of the HO model. The HO model assumes that factors migrate easily from one sector to another—from steel to bread, for example. In the specific factors model (Table 4.2), each good is produced with a specific factor, whose only use is in the production of that good, and a variable factor, which is used to produce both goods. The specific factors (land and capital) are immobile and cannot move between bread and steel, while the variable factor (labor) is completely mobile between industries.

TABLE 4.2	A Specific Factors Model	
	Outputs	
Inputs	Bread	Steel
Specific factors	Land	Capital
Variable factors	Labor	Labor

The specific factors of land and capital can be used to produce only one good. The variable factor of labor is used in both bread and steel production.

The determinants of comparative advantage with a specific factors model are similar to the analysis with an HO model. As with HO, comparative advantage depends on factor endowments. The main difference in the two models is that the specific factor plays a critical role. Suppose that Canada is relatively well endowed with land and that the United States is relatively well endowed with capital. Then Canada exports bread, and the United States exports steel. The reasoning is the same as with the HO model. Since Canada is well endowed with the specific factor used to make bread, its opportunity cost of bread production is lower than it is in the United States, where land is relatively less abundant. Similarly, steel uses capital, which is abundant in the United States and relatively scarce in Canada.

The analysis of the income distribution effects of trade is straightforward. When trade opens, each country follows its comparative advantage and moves toward greater specialization. The shift in production alters the demand for the specific factor that is used in the industry that shrinks. In each country, the specific factor in the declining industry experiences a fall in income. For example, Canada cuts back on steel production in order to concentrate on bread, which it exports for steel. Canadian owners of capital are hurt, since the structure of the economy changes from the production of capital-intensive steel, while Canadian landowners experience precisely the opposite effect. Their incomes rise as the demand for land to produce bread exports rises. In the United States, landowners lose and capital owners win.

In this example, the income distribution effects of trade on labor, the variable factor, are indeterminate. Since labor is mobile, workers laid off in the declining sector find employment in the expanding sector. Canadian workers find that steel is cheaper, so they are better off to the extent that they consume products that embody steel. On the other hand, the fact that the world price of bread is above the price that Canadians paid in autarky means that they are worse off to the extent that their income goes to buy bread. The net effect on Canadian labor depends on which effect is strongest, rising bread prices or falling steel prices. U.S. workers face rising steel prices and falling bread prices, and, again, the net effect is ambiguous and depends on their consumption patterns.

CASE STUDY

Winners and Losers under NAFTA

The North American Free Trade Agreement (NAFTA) created a free-trade area in Canada, Mexico, and the United States. The agreement was signed and ratified by each government in 1993 and implemented on January 1, 1994. It phased out most tariffs, some immediately and others more gradually. Five years prior, in 1989, the United States and Canada had implemented a free-trade agreement (the Canadian-United States Trade Agreement, or CUSTA), and NAFTA was not expected to cause significant additional effects.

Where the United States and Canada have relatively abundant supplies of capital and skilled labor, including scientists, engineers, and technicians, Mexico has relative shortages of skilled labor and relatively abundant supplies of unskilled and semiskilled labor. Given these simple observations, it was possible to estimate the winners and losers in NAFTA. Mexican industries that were expected to do well were the ones that took advantage of its climate (tropical fruits, vegetables), its natural resources (oil and minerals), and its unskilled and semiskilled labor (standardized manufacturing, such as vehicles). U.S. industries that expected to benefit were those that used its natural resource endowments, particularly when they could be combined with skilled labor and capital (grains, oilseeds), and industries that use science, technology, and capital to produce sophisticated manufactured goods (machinery, chemicals, plastics).

In Table 4.3, products that have done particularly well in the United States include chemicals and plastics and related products, along with industrial machinery and grains. These products combine capital in the form of sophisticated machinery and skilled labor in the form of engineering, science, and design. The lead category in each country's exports are related. Mexico exports oil to the United States, where it is used to fuel vehicles and generate power, but also to manufacture sophisticated fuels, chemicals, and plastics, which the United States exports back to Mexico. This is a clear example of comparative advantage combining Mexico's natural resources with the United States' technology and capital.

Looking at the next three categories in each country's list, comparative advantage is less clear since they are the same goods: electrical machinery (computers, televisions, medical imaging devices, etc.), industrial machinery (pumps, generators, elevators, conveyors, engines, appliances, etc.), and vehicles (cars, trucks, and parts). Here, it helps to know another fact about U.S.-Mexico trade: For many goods, the exporting firm is also the importing firm. For example, a car company might manufacture motors in Ohio or Texas, and then ship them to its plant in Coahuila, Mexico, for assembly into a car or truck. This is intrafirm trade, or trade within a single firm. It is difficult to measure, but in 1999 it is estimated that 66.4 percent of U.S. imports from Mexico and 44.3 percent of exports to Mexico were intrafirm. Comparative advantage matters because modern

TABLE 4.3	Major Products in U.S.-Mexico Trade	
Product	Billions of dollars, 2008	Percent growth, 1994–2008
U.S. Exports		
Chemicals, plastics, and related	26.9	446
Electrical machinery	25.0	142
Industrial machinery, appliances	22.5	196
Vehicles and parts	14.0	148
Grains	4.1	327
Total exports by United States to Mexico	151	198
Mexico Exports		
Petroleum and related	41.9	720
Electrical machinery	53.5	272
Vehicles and parts	32.2	351
Industrial machinery, appliances	24.8	360
Beverages	2.5	644
Total exports by Mexico to United States	215	336

Source: U.S. Department of Commerce, TradeStats Express.

communications allows firms to cut up their production in order to locate different stages in different locations where the combination of labor, capital, and natural resources are best suited.

The process of moving production between the United States and Mexico involves both gains and losses. Some firms are more productive as a result, and may export more to Mexico and to the rest of the world. Other firms may just barely hold on by moving production, or may reduce their U.S. or Mexican presence overall. For example, competition from Asia or another region may cause a U.S. firm to divide its production between the United States and Mexico, thereby reducing the number of jobs in the United States, but staying in business as a result. The laid-off workers in its U.S. plants lose, but without the job shift the losses might have been greater.

The U.S. sectors most affected tend to be low-skilled or semiskilled manufacturing processes that use relatively less capital to make goods that are not specialized. That includes the apparel industry, simple electronic components, some parts and stages of motor vehicle manufacturing, and some kinds of machinery.

The number of workers hurt is highly controversial since it is not always possible to determine if trade with Mexico or Canada is the actual cause of a layoff, or what would have happened to the firm if it did not shift some production to Mexico. Some apparel, for example, moved to Mexico where it flourished for a while, only to be forced out of business as the Chinese apparel industry gained greater access to the United States and other markets. Apparel is an area where the United States has lost much of its historic comparative advantage and it will be difficult to keep in the United States.

Gains and losses from the NAFTA is a politically contentious issue in all three NAFTA countries. Chapter 13 provides some additional discussion.

Empirical Tests of the Theory of Comparative Advantage

All the popular theories of trade are variations on the idea of comparative advantage. In addition, each theory makes predictions about the goods that a country will export and import. Therefore, it should be relatively straightforward to test each theory by holding its predictions up to actual trade flows and seeing if the two match. Unfortunately, empirical tests of trade theories are more difficult to conduct than they are to describe. Part of the problem is that it is difficult to measure variables such as factor endowments and prices in autarky.

The trade theories presented here and in Chapter 3 are the two most widely accepted by economists—the Ricardian theory of trade, based on relative productivities, and the Heckscher-Ohlin theory, based on factor endowments. In the Ricardian theory discussed in Chapter 3, comparative advantage depended on relative productivity. This model is easier to test because it is easier to measure labor productivity than factor endowments. Therefore, it is not surprising that statistical tests of the Ricardian theory have been more successful. In general, they have confirmed the hypothesis that trade patterns between pairs of countries are determined to a significant degree by the relative differences in their labor productivities. More specifically, as labor productivity in a particular industry increases, the greater the likelihood the country becomes a net exporter of the good.

Tests of the Heckscher-Ohlin theory of trade have been mixed. One of the problems for researchers in this area is that it is difficult to obtain a uniform set of measurements of factor endowments. In the presentation of the model in this chapter, only two inputs were considered, although we expanded that to three when we covered the specific factors model. In reality, there are many more than three factors. There are different kinds of labor (unskilled, semiskilled, managerial, technical, and so on), and there are many varieties of natural resources and capital. None of these categories has standardized definitions, and consequently each type of labor, capital, and natural resource is measured differently in each country. As a result, formal statistical analyses of tests of the HO theory have concluded that measurement errors in the data are a major problem.

Nevertheless, the consensus among economists seems to be that endowments matter, although they are far from the whole story. Even if it were possible to measure factor endowments accurately, technological differences between countries would not be captured, and these can be a significant source of productivity differences. In addition to technology, other important determinants of trade patterns not considered by the factor endowment theory are economies of scale, corporate structure, and economic policy.

While the theory of trade based on factor endowments receives mixed empirical support, it nevertheless remains the foundation of most economists' thinking about trade. This may seem curious, but there is actually a good reason for it. While factor endowments cannot explain all of the world's trade patterns, they do explain a significant part of them. Therefore, it is useful to begin with factor endowments and to supplement this view with other ideas. Perhaps most importantly, the factor endowment schema is a useful way to categorize the income distribution effects of trade. For both of these reasons, the HO model and its variations remain at the core of international economics.

Extension of the Heckscher-Ohlin Model

Several alternative trade models are popular in the literature. Both of the models presented next focus on an attribute of production in an industry or group of industries that makes them unlike the simple models assumed by the Ricardian and HO models. Both, however, are elaborations of the theory of comparative advantage. In Chapter 5 we will leave the comparative advantage framework and look at cases where trade is not determined by productivity differences or factor endowments.

The Product Cycle

The **product cycle** model of trade was developed by Raymond Vernon. The model is an insightful analysis that incorporates ideas about the evolution of manufactured goods and technology. One of its greatest strengths is that it can explain exports of sophisticated manufactured goods from countries that have shortages of skilled labor and capital.

Vernon pointed out that many manufactured products, such as automobiles, VCRs, and semiconductors, go through a product cycle in which the inputs change over time. Initially, when these goods are brand new, there is a great deal of experimentation in both the characteristics of the final product and its manufacturing process. For example, when video machines were first developed for the home market, there was a wide variety of different forms to choose from. There were laser discs, Betamax, and VHS, each of which had different sets of options, often even within the same technology. That is, while Betamax differed from VHS, the features on a VHS machine were not standardized either.

In this early stage of production, manufacturers need to be near a high-income market, where consumer feedback is greatest. Experimentation with basic design features requires information about the market's reaction. Consequently, there must be a consumer base with substantial income and skilled marketing to advertise information about the product. In addition, on the input side, experimentation and improvement in design and manufacturing require scientific and engineering inputs, along with capital that is willing to risk failure and an initial period of little or no profits. Both the consumption side and the production side necessitate that product research, development, and initial production take place in industrial countries.

Over time, however, the product begins to leave the early phase of its development and production and enters the middle phase (see Figure 4.5 and Figure 4.6). The product itself begins to be standardized in size, features, and manufacturing process. Experimentation with fundamentally new designs begins to wane as product development shifts toward incremental improvements in a basic design. In the middle phase, production begins to shift to countries with low labor costs. Standardized manufacturing routines are increasingly common, using low-skilled and semiskilled labor in assembly type operations.

Countries reach the late phase of the product cycle when consumption in high-income nations begins to exceed production. At this point, an increasing share of the world's output is moving to developing countries where abundant unskilled and semiskilled labor keeps labor costs low. The pressure on high-income countries in the late phase is to turn toward innovation of new products, which starts the cycle over again.

FIGURE 4.5 **The Product Cycle in High-Income Countries**

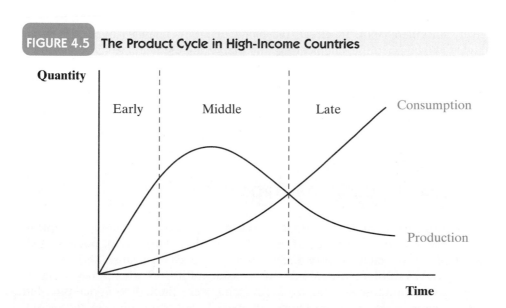

Many manufactured goods experience a product cycle of innovation, stabilization, and standardization.

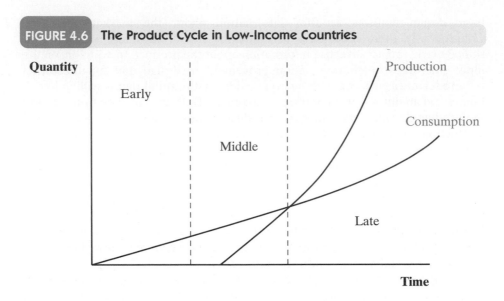

FIGURE 4.6 **The Product Cycle in Low-Income Countries**

Low-income countries begin producing during the middle period when product design and production techniques begin to stabilize.

The product cycle is a more elaborate story about technology than either the Ricardian or HO models. It may seem to differ fundamentally from those models, but in fact it is very similar. At its core is a story about opportunity costs. As manufacturing processes become standardized, they can be performed by relatively unskilled labor. In effect, the blend of inputs changes over time, from highly skilled scientific, engineering, and marketing elements to basic unskilled and semiskilled labor. Consequently, the opportunity cost of production in developing countries becomes lower than the cost in high-income countries. In essence, it's the Ricardian story once again.

CASE STUDY

United States–China Trade

China is the world's most populous nation, with more than 1.33 billion people in mid-2008, according to the U.S. Census Bureau. The World Bank puts its GNP per capita at the equivalent of $2,300 (at market exchange rates, 2007). China's economy was substantially closed to the outside until 1978, when it began significant economic reforms. Initially, the reforms were limited to agriculture, but they quickly incorporated a number of special economic zones in the coastal regions (see Chapter 17). China's proximity to Hong Kong, along with large populations of Chinese in Taiwan, Hong Kong, Singapore, and other regions of East

Asia, enabled it to attract huge amounts of foreign investment once it became receptive to capital inflows. The net result is that its economy and, especially, its exports have grown rapidly over the last two decades.

China's resource endowment includes a huge population of unskilled and semiskilled labor and a relative scarcity of scientific and engineering talent. It is not surprising, therefore, that its exports are heavily weighted toward labor-intensive manufactured goods. Table 4.4 lists the top ten Chinese exports to the United States in 2008. The major items are simple manufactured goods that use China's abundant labor together with a little capital: toys, shoes, plastic items, and so on. In the top ten, items 1, 2, 5, 8, 9, and 10 fall into this category.

Computers and accessories (items 3 and 4) and televisions and telecommunications equipment (items 6 and 7), however, appear to be different. These are high-technology items related to telecommunications and computing. They also illustrate the product cycle since many of the goods originate in assembly operations that have been set up with capital from outside China. A cell phone or computer manufacturer, for example, decides to take advantage of low wages by producing a standardized product in China. Once the assembly plant is built, only a handful of skilled workers are required to keep it running. Most workers can be quickly trained to fasten pieces and to perform simple diagnostic tests on the product. The result is that China exports telecommunications and computing equipment and appears to have a developing high-technology sector.

TABLE 4.4   **Top Ten Chinese Exports to the United States, 2008**

Item	Value, Millions of $US
1. Toys, shooting and sporting goods, and bicycles	29,166
2. Other household goods (clocks, lamps, cleaning, etc.)	27,502
3. Computer accessories, peripherals, and parts	27,007
4. Computers	25,042
5. Apparel and household goods—other textiles	15,294
6. Television receivers, DVDs, and other video equipment	15,097
7. Telecommunications equipment	14,495
8. Apparel and household goods—cotton	13,381
9. Furniture, household items, baskets	13,278
10. Footwear of leather, rubber, or other materials	11,632

China's labor endowment and the product cycle explain its exports to the United States.

Source: US Census Bureau, "End-Use Data," *Country and Product Trade Data, 2008.* Retrieved June 2008, from http://www.census.gov/foreign-trade/statistics/country/index.html.

Foreign Trade versus Foreign Investment

In the product cycle, firms invest abroad instead of exporting, and some of the output may be imported back into the home country. This pattern is very different from the simple Heckscher-Ohlin model where countries export one good and import another. First, it implies that under the conditions outlined in the product cycle, firms prefer to invest abroad rather than to export. That is, they substitute foreign investment for foreign trade. Second, the part of the output that they ship from their foreign operation back into the home country is international trade, but it is handled entirely within a single firm. That is, they engage in **intrafirm trade**: international trade between a parent company and a foreign-owned affiliate.

Intrafirm trade is difficult to measure, but in the mid-1990s, it was estimated that about one-third of U.S. merchandise exports and two-fifths of merchandise imports were intrafirm. Most foreign investment, however, is not for the purpose of exporting, but rather is intended to supply the market where the foreign investment is located. Whether for trade purposes or not, the selection of foreign investment instead of foreign trade poses a number of questions for economists and business scholars. Why do firms sometimes prefer to set up foreign-based operations instead of buying imports directly from a separate company located overseas? Or, if the foreign investment is for the purpose of selling in the foreign market, why don't companies export directly to the market instead of producing there? In essence, the questions are the same because both ask about the circumstances that cause foreign investment rather than foreign trade.

The product cycle provides one answer to these questions, but it is an incomplete answer, because it does not explain why a firm would invest in China instead of in Mexico. If labor costs are the only reason, then Africa would have the most foreign investment instead of the least of any continent. Furthermore, the product cycle is unable to explain why the greatest proportion of foreign investment goes to developed, industrial countries in Europe and North America where the comparative advantages are the same as or similar to those of the countries that supply the most foreign investment. According to World Bank data, developing countries (low- and middle-income) received just 11.4 percent of the world's foreign investment in 2000, with the developed world receiving the other 88.6 percent. While the share of developing countries varies from year to year, it rarely exceeds 30 percent.

Research into the trade-offs between investing abroad versus exporting from a home base acknowledges the importance of both the microeconomic characteristics of firms and the macroeconomic characteristics of countries that attract foreign investment. Microeconomic factors look at the internal constraints and opportunities of individual firms, while macroeconomic factors take into account the conditions inside countries that cause them to be suitable locations for a foreign firm to invest. The analytical framework that combines both sets of characteristics is known as the **OLI theory** of foreign direct investment. Its founder, John Dunning, offered it as an eclectic theory combining many different microeconomic and macroeconomic elements.

OLI is an acronym for *ownership-location-internalization*. In Dunning's analysis, firms investing abroad own an asset that gives them a competitive advantage in the world market (ownership). The asset may be something tangible, such as a patent, an innovation, a blueprint, or a trade secret. Or it may be something intangible, such as a trademark or the firm's reputation. In either case, ownership of a valuable asset confers a potential advantage on the firm. Second, the firm will seek a production location that offers advantages (location). These may be in the form of low input costs, a large customer base, or an ability to produce a better product more efficiently due to the surrounding economic environment. Cheap labor is only one possibility, and if it does not come with a good infrastructure of roads and utilities, does not supply the skills that employers need, or is too far from the product's final market, then the fact that wages are low will not overcome the country's disadvantages.

Third, and most abstractly, the firm that invests abroad tries to capture within itself all the advantages that ownership of its asset confers (internalization). A firm that invests abroad can, if it chooses, simply sell the rights to its asset and let a foreign firm do the production—and in fact, many firms operate this way. That is, as an alternative, the investing firm can sell a license to its technology or its trademark or its trade secrets. Some firms, however, choose to take on the added costs of setting up production in a foreign location. There are many potential reasons for this choice, including the fear of theft or copy of its technology, the problem of monitoring and enforcing a contract with a foreign firm, and the concern that production mistakes by the foreign firm may hurt the reputation or trademark of the home country firm. Whatever the reason, the investing firm decides that it benefits more if it internalizes the advantages of asset ownership within itself rather than sells those advantages to another firm.

Dunning's analysis has been added to and extended by a large number of scholars who have found it to be a robust and adaptable description of the behavior of many firms. It is not a theory of trade, because it describes the circumstances that motivate firms to invest abroad rather than to engage in trade, but it does not contradict trade theory. Rather, it simply states that firms are internationally mobile and will use the comparative advantages they find in different locations. In this sense, it demonstrates how those advantages motivate individual firms to adapt their own behavior.

Off-Shoring and Outsourcing

Off-shoring and **outsourcing** are frequently used terms, but with varying definitions. In this text, off-shoring is defined as the movement of some or all of a firm's activities to a location outside the home country; outsourcing is the reassignment of activities to another firm, either inside or outside the home country. All combinations of off-shoring and outsourcing are possibilities and exist in the world economy. Some firms off-shore but do not outsource, choosing to use a **foreign affiliate**, which is defined as a foreign-based operation owned by the firm in the home country. For example, the case study on winners and losers in NAFTA made the point that a great deal of U.S.-Mexico trade is intrafirm, with car parts and electronic components going back and forth between parent companies in the United States and its foreign affiliates in Mexico. The parent companies have off-shored some production to Mexico, while choosing not to outsource. Others outsource, but do not off-shore, for example, if they subcontract activities with a domestic provider. A car company might decide to buy parts from a local firm rather than make them or to have them made in Mexico. And, finally, a firm may off-shore and outsource when it relocates production to a foreign location and signs a contract for delivery of services or goods with a firm that is not owned by the parent company.

Off-shoring became a concern in the 1980s when modern communications and transportation technology made it possible for firms to relocate production abroad. Initially, off-shoring was of greatest concern to workers in manufacturing industries, but by the 1990s, as advancements continued in information technologies, it became possible to off-shore some services. This created concerns for workers in service sectors outside of manufacturing. Historically, most services have been consumed at the point of production, but more recently it has become possible to relocate some service production away from the point of consumption. For example, a doctor in the United States or Europe might consult a colleague in India who is specialized in reading a particular type of X-ray. The Internet and increased efficiencies in telephony make it possible for doctors in both places to see the same image and to inexpensively communicate with each other.

The effects and extent of off-shoring are not well understood since most countries do not collect the necessary types of data. Nevertheless, the first generation of research and analysis points toward a conclusion that is consistent with our traditional understanding of trade and comparative advantage—there is no obvious reason why trade in services should be different from trade in goods. An import that arrives by truck or ship is not conceptually different from one that arrives over the Internet. Services imports and exports should not be any different in this regard, and specialization and trade should provide the same or similar gains for services as they do for goods.

The main focus of debate about off-shoring, whether in services or manufacturing, is the effect that it has on the home country, and in particular, the issue of job loss. Off-shoring is particularly unsettling for workers who felt immune from international trade, such as service workers, and it seems to be another instance of creeping globalization making life less certain. Research, however, shows that off-shoring has a variety of possible patterns. In some cases it leads to job losses in the home country, while in others it is complementary to home production rather than a substitute, and leads to an expansion of jobs and production rather than a contraction.

CASE STUDY

Off-Shoring by U.S. Multinational Corporations

As technology has made communications easier and as national governments have allowed economies to become more open to foreign investments, firms have responded by shifting production overseas. Data on off-shoring is not routinely gathered, although national statistical agencies, such as the Bureau of Economic Analysis (BEA) in the United States, have increased their efforts over the years so that economists and policymakers might better understand the extent of the phenomenon and the reasons behind it. It still remains difficult to measure how many services have been off-shored, but new efforts in data collection have made it possible to see how much manufacturing has moved abroad and to better understand the motives for off-shoring.

Table 4.5 shows two pictures of U.S. multinational corporations, one in 1977 and the other in 2003, the most recent year of data. The table shows the percent of multinational activities, measured in three ways, which are performed off-shore, through a foreign affiliate. The three measures are value added, capital expenditures, and employment. Value added is a measure of the total value of production minus the value of purchased intermediate inputs. It is a measure of the firm's contribution to production. Capital expenditures include things such as machines, laboratories, and buildings, and employment is the number of workers. As shown in the table, the share of multinational's value added created abroad rose from 25 percent in 1977 to 26 percent in 2003, hardly a change during the period of intense globalization. Employment shows the biggest change, with 22 percent of total workers off-shore in 1977 and 28 percent in 2003. How can multinationals produce nearly the same share of output value added at home with a smaller share of its total employment? Two words: productivity increases.

Several factors motivate firms to locate off-shore or to move some of their production there. Most importantly, firms locate production off-shore in order to obtain access to a market and to produce specialized products that fit a particular

TABLE 4.5 U.S. Multinational Corporations and Production Outside the United States

	1977	2003
Value added	25	26
Capital expenditures	21	26
Employment	22	28

The share of multinational activity outside the United States has not changed dramatically since 1977.

Source: Bureau of Economic Analysis.

market's need. This finding runs counter to the conventional wisdom that says that firms locate abroad in order to find low wages or to escape environmental or labor regulations. The conventional wisdom is not wrong, but describes only a small, unknown share of off-shoring. The reason economists think so is because the vast majority of off-shoring by U.S. multinationals is in high-income, high-wage economies. According to the BEA, about 67 percent of all U.S. off-shoring is in high-income countries, with the figure for manufacturing alone around 80 percent. If the primary motive for locating abroad were to find lower wages or weak environmental regulations, it does not seem likely that a large majority of off-shoring would be in high-wage, industrially developed places such as Europe, Canada, and Australia.

Another finding that runs counter to some of the conventional wisdom is that the bulk of off-shoring is horizontal and not vertical. That is, firms often invest abroad to do activities similar to the ones they do at home, rather than off-shoring some piece of their production process that fits into the overall production chain. Again, this reinforces the idea that off-shoring is to serve a new market, rather than to find low wages.

It should be clear that some firms do indeed move in order to find lower wages and to cut production costs. However, that is less common than supposed and is far from the primary consideration of firms that off-shore.

Migration and Trade

According to the World Bank, in 2005 there were 194.8 million international migrants spread across the globe. Nearly 60 percent were in high-income countries, and over 20 percent were in the United States alone. International migration is not considered a possibility in the HO model. Workers are allowed to move between sectors in the model, but not between countries. This is an important consideration since international migration alters the labor endowments that the model assumes to be fixed.

Economists have long studied migration, as have sociologists, demographers, political scientists, and other social scientists. Each discipline brings its own tools of analysis and contributes another piece to our understanding of the determinants and effects of migration. Sociologists and anthropologists, for example, have helped to clarify that the decision to migrate is often a family decision or, in some cases, a community decision to send one of its members abroad. Political scientists have helped to clarify how migration policies are set and enforced, or not enforced, as the case may be. The economic view of migration tends to understand it in terms of the individual migrant and the underlying incentives to migrate. In this view, economic incentives play a major role by determining the factors that cause migrants to leave and the factors that attract them to a particular destination.

Economists refer to **supply-push factors** as the forces inside a country that cause people to think about leaving. Push factors include recessions, long-run structural changes that cause job dislocations, wars, natural disasters, and anything else that makes life difficult at home. Examples of structural changes include the recent transformations of central European economies, Latin American economic reforms, and industrial development in many parts of the globe. In the near future, we can expect large migrations from changing agricultural patterns and the inundation of coastal areas as a result of climate change.

Demand-pull factors are the forces that pull migrants to a particular country or place within a country. Key factors include the cost of reaching a particular destination, the probability of finding a job, and the wage that will be earned. The wage gap between developed countries and developing countries explains a large share of the flow of migrants, but other factors are important as well. The business cycle in the receiving country, its migration policies, and the overall set of opportunities encountered by foreign workers are all important demand-pull factors.

A third factor determining migration is the existence of **social networks**. Migrants do not scatter randomly around a desirable destination, but instead congregate in certain places. This is partly due to job opportunities, but it also reflects the fact that migration is hard and expensive and the presence of family or community members makes it a little easier. The supply of information about the new locale is better if there are already migrants who can report home on conditions, and who can help newcomers become established with a place to live, a job, and familiar faces to ward off loneliness.

In theory, if the endowment of a particular factor increases, then the relative abundance of the factor and, potentially, its comparative advantage also change. In practice, labor inflows are often used to produce services that are not traded. For example, two countries with large percentages of foreigners in their population are United Arab Emirates (71.4 percent) and Kuwait (62.1 percent). A large share of the foreign workers in those countries are Filipinos, Palestinians, and other migrants who work as domestics, providing cleaning, cooking, day care, and other services that cannot be traded. These migrants do not have a direct impact on the host country's comparative advantage since the labor is not used to produce tradable goods (although they free up citizens to work in the export sector). However, many migrant workers are also engineers and business specialists who provide technical expertise to the oil and gas industry. Without some high-skilled migrant labor, it is possible that production in these oil- and gas-producing countries would be much more limited.

Most international migration is from developing to developed countries. For example, in the 1980s and 1990s, civil wars in Central America produced large outflows of Salvadorian and Guatemalan immigrants to the United States, many of whom settled in California where some found employment in apparel manufacturing. California's apparel sector added over 40,000 jobs between 1983 and 1997 (a growth of almost 50 percent), largely based on the availability of low-wage, unskilled immigrant workers. Given that apparel is a declining sector in the United States, immigrant labor appears to have postponed the decline of the industry in California for about a decade. In the long run, however, apparel continues to decline as the immigrants are assimilated into the U.S. economy. Other U.S. examples of where immigration influences comparative advantage include certain agricultural crops that depend on abundant supplies of immigrant labor and the tourism industry. Over the long run, however, assimilation occurs and the children or grandchildren of migrants (if not the migrants themselves) become similar to non-migrants, both in terms of their skills and their wages.

The Impact of Trade on Wages and Jobs

Since the 1960s, manufacturing in North America and Europe has become a smaller part of the economy when measured as a share of GDP and as a share of overall employment. At the same time, wage inequality has increased, rather slowly at first, then more rapidly in the 1980s. Wage inequality has been particularly severe in the United States and has primarily affected younger workers and workers with less education or fewer skills.

Does trade with low-wage countries cause wages to fall in high-wage countries? Are industrialized countries losing jobs to developing countries? Organized opposition to trade is usually premised on these points. It is probably no surprise that U.S. public opinion about the impact of trade on wages and jobs is divided along educational and skill lines, with more highly educated and more-skilled workers favoring reduced trade barriers, and less-skilled and less-educated workers opposing.

One issue is whether trade has a negative impact on the number of jobs available to workers in high-wage countries. Economic theory offers some evidence on this issue. In the medium-run and long-run, the absolute number of jobs depends mainly on factors such as the age and size of the population, rules governing the hiring and firing of employees (labor market policies), and the generosity of the social safety net (incentives to work). In the short run, one of the primary determinants of the number of jobs is the government's macroeconomic policies, which determine variables such as interest rates, taxes, and overall government expenditures. While trade may have a short-run effect as well, particularly if firms cannot compete against imports, or if sudden opportunities for export expansion appear, these impacts are outweighed by macroeconomic policies affecting the entire domestic economy over the medium and long runs. By comparison, changes in trade flows usually affect one or two manufacturing industries and a small share of overall GDP. Trade will certainly affect the composition of jobs, but it is unlikely to have much impact on the overall number of jobs. The last point is worth emphasizing. Trade definitely causes some firms to shrink. In sectors where competition from imports is particularly intense, it is not unusual to read about factories that close their doors as a result of competition from developing countries.

Many economists think that the reductions in manufacturing employment in all industrial countries appears to have resulted from productivity gains, not trade. Manufacturing is easier to automate than services and as a consequence has much faster rates of productivity growth than services. Many services, on the other hand, have stagnant or very slow rates of productivity growth. Often, the same number of workers is required today as it was centuries ago; one haircut, for example, still takes one barber, and modern musicians are no more "productive" at playing Bach's Brandenburg Concertos than they were in the 1700s. When incomes rise, we consume more services and more manufactured goods, but because the services require more or less the same number of workers per unit made, and manufactured goods can be made with fewer workers per good, a growing share of our total employment ends up in services.

The second issue concerns the impact of trade with less-developed countries (LDCs) on the wages of workers in the advanced industrial economies. This question has been studied by many economists, and the general consensus is that trade may have caused some of the decline in wages for the less skilled (and, hence, some of the increase in wage inequality), but it is responsible for only a small share of the overall changes. The primary culprit seems to be technological changes that have reduced the role of unskilled and semiskilled labor in manufacturing.

The Stolper-Samuelson theorem predicts that if the United States and other industrial countries have relatively scarce supplies of unskilled labor (by comparison to less-developed countries), then trade will cause the wages of unskilled workers to fall. Over the years, however, firms can alter their use of inputs to take advantage of cheaper unskilled labor and to conserve more expensive skilled labor. The key is that the time frame must be sufficiently long so that firms can alter their capital and other inputs. In the case of skilled and unskilled labor the reverse has happened. As skilled labor has become more expensive, firms have used relatively more, and as unskilled labor has become cheaper, they have used less. This trend has gone on for over two decades, so firms have had plenty of time to alter their production technologies if they can. One explanation is that technology has created larger roles for skilled labor and smaller ones for the unskilled.

While it seems the consensus of professional economic opinion is that technological change and not trade is responsible for the lion's share of both the decline in manufactured jobs and the growth of wage inequality, there is also a widespread recognition that economists really aren't sure. A small number of economists continue to argue that trade has played a far larger role in the growth of wage inequality than is generally recognized. If they are correct, the policy conclusions are likely to be the same. In both cases, where trade is responsible for inequality and where it is not, there is a need for education and training programs targeted at the less skilled. Chapters 6 and 7 will show that blocking trade to protect jobs is extraordinarily expensive, and doing so to protect wages will actually make things worse in the long run.

Summary

- The Heckscher-Ohlin (HO) model hypothesizes that comparative advantage is based on national differences in factor endowments. Countries export goods that have production requirements that are intensive in the nation's relatively abundant factors. They import goods that require intensive input from the nation's relatively scarce factors.

- The Heckscher-Ohlin model has implications for the income distribution effects of trade. The opening of trade favors the abundant factor and reduces the use of the scarce factor. Consequently, the income or returns earned by the abundant factor rises, while it falls for the scarce factor. A corollary to the Heckscher-Ohlin model, called the Stolper-Samuelson theorem, describes these effects.

- In the specific factors model, some factors of production are assumed to be immobile between different outputs. Consequently, when trade expands the production of it, the specific factor used to produce it experiences a rise in the demand for its services, and its income increases. The specific factor used to produce the import good experiences a fall in the demand for its services, and its income declines. The specific factors model can be viewed as a short- to medium-run version of the HO model.

- Empirical tests of the theory of comparative advantage give mixed results. While underlying productivity differences explain a significant share of trade, national differences in factor endowments are less successful at explaining trade patterns.

- Several alternative trade models have been hypothesized. Most are elaborations of the theory of comparative advantage. Two of the most popular alternative trade theories are the theory of the product cycle and the theory of intrafirm trade. The product cycle focuses on the speed of technological change and the life history of many manufactured items through periods of innovation, stabilization, and standardization. The theory of intrafirm trade allows a role for comparative advantage but also has industrial organization elements. It is impossible to state a general rule about the determinants of intrafirm trade.

- Off-shoring is the movement of some or all of a firm's activities to another country. Outsourcing is the reassignment of activities to another firm, either in a domestic or foreign location. Off-shoring has been advanced by the telecommunications revolution and is a relatively new phenomenon. Nevertheless, traditional trade models are useful in its analysis.

- International migration can alter a country's comparative advantage, although in practice most countries do not receive enough migrants or a sufficiently long enough flow of migrants to cause long-run changes. Migrants are motivated by supply-push factors in their home country, demand-pull factors in the receiving country, and social networks that provide information and resources for settling in the new country.

- In the medium to long run, trade has little or no effect on the number of jobs in a country. The abundance or scarcity of jobs is a function of labor market policies, incentives to work, and the macroeconomic policies of the central bank and government. In the short run, trade may reduce jobs in an industry that suffers a loss in its competitiveness, just as it may increase jobs in an industry with growing competitiveness.

- The consensus among economists is that trade between developing and high-income countries may have contributed slightly to the decline in real wages for unskilled workers in the industrial economies. This is consistent with the predictions of the Stolper-Samuelson theorem. The main cause of increasing wage inequality is thought to be technological changes that have reduced the demand for unskilled labor and increased it for skilled, highly educated labor. This point is not settled, however, and continues to receive a significant amount of empirical investigation.

Vocabulary

demand-pull factors	off-shoring
derived demand	OLI theory
factor abundance	outsourcing
factor scarcity	product cycle
foreign affiliate	social networks
Heckscher-Ohlin (HO) trade theory	specific factors model
intrafirm trade	Stolper-Samuelson theorem
magnification effect	supply-push factors

Study Questions

1. According to the following table, which country is relatively more labor-abundant? Explain your answer. Which country is relatively capital-abundant?

	United States	Canada
Capital	40 machines	10 machines
Labor	200 workers	60 workers

2. Suppose that the United States and Canada have the factor endowments in the preceding table. Suppose further that the production requirements for a unit of steel are two machines and eight workers, and the requirement for a unit of bread is one machine and eight workers.

    a. Which good, bread or steel, is relatively capital-intensive? Labor-intensive? Explain your answer.

    b. Which country would export bread? Why?

3. Suppose that before trade takes place, the United States is at a point on its PPC where it produces twenty loaves of bread and twenty units of steel. Once trade becomes possible, the price of a unit of steel is two units of bread. In response, the United States moves along its PPC to a new point where it produces thirty units of steel and ten units of bread. Is the country better off? How do you know?

4. Given the information in Study Questions 1 and 2, explain what happens to the returns to capital and labor after trade begins.

5. Suppose that there are three factors: capital, labor, and land. Bread requires inputs of land and labor, and steel requires capital and labor.

    a. Which factors are variable, and which are specific?

    b. Suppose Canada's endowments are 10 capital and 100 land and the United States' are 50 capital and 100 land. Which good does each country export?

    c. How does trade affect the returns to land, labor, and capital in the United States and in Canada?

6. Describe the changes in production requirements and location of production that take place over the three phases of the product cycle.

7. Does intrafirm trade contradict the theory of comparative advantage? Why or why not?

8. General Motors is a U.S.-based multinational, but it is also one of the largest car manufacturers in Europe and South America. How might Dunning's OLI theory explain the trade-offs GM faced as it decided whether to export to those two markets or to produce in them?

9. Many domestically owned apparel manufacturers buy their garments overseas, sew their labels into them, and then sell them abroad or back into the home market. What are some of the considerations that a clothing manufacturer might go through to choose this strategy instead of producing at home and exporting?

10. Suppose Spain were to open its borders to the large number of unskilled Africans seeking to immigrate. In general, what effects would you expect to see in Spain's trade patterns and its comparative advantage?

APPENDIX

Finding Trade Data

U.S. Data

Data on U.S. trade in individual commodities are easy to find. The problem for the first-time user of U.S. data is to make sense of the classifications used to categorize goods and services. Export and import statistics are initially collected and compiled into eight thousand and fourteen thousand commodity classifications, respectively. These classifications conform to a standard for classifying goods known as the Harmonized Commodity Description and Coding System, or the Harmonized System (HS). The HS was developed by the Customs Cooperation Council in Brussels, Belgium, and included participants from the United States, Canada, Western Europe, and Japan. A source of confusion is that the description of U.S. data in HS format bears the names HTSUSA (Harmonized Tariff Schedule for the United States, Annotated) for imports and Schedule B for exports.

A second system of classifying goods is also used by the United States, the United Nations, and many other nations. This is the Standard International Trade Classification (SITC). The SITC is on its third revision, so it is sometimes called the SITC-Rev. 3. The Harmonized System and the SITC are interrelated, and in effect, the SITC scheme is an aggregation of the HS. The SITC system is useful for international comparisons and is the form in which the most commonly available U.S. publications present their data.

Three other commodity classifications are in use, and although they are of lesser importance worldwide, they are relevant for research on the United States. One is another summarization of the HS into what is called the End Use Commodity Category. It consists of 6 principal categories and 140 broad category definitions. Several of the more commonly found U.S. publications use these commodity definitions to summarize reported data. The North American Industrial Classification System (NAICS) is a harmonization of the classification codes of the United States, Mexico, and Canada. It is the primary system for reporting data by industry, rather than by the type of good, which allows comparisons to be made between industries and for trade data to be linked to the characteristics of industries.

Free online data can be obtained from Trade Stats Express at http://tse.export. gov, which offers both state-level and national data, but for merchandise goods only. Exports and imports of services are available in the FT900 publication series, also available online at http://www.census.gov/foreign-trade/Press-Release/current_press_release/.

International Data

Most international data are presented in SITC-Rev. 3 format. As with U.S. data, service exports and imports are sometimes omitted. The following are useful sources:

1. The World Trade Organization has extensive trade and tariff data, including trade profiles of its members. See the WTO Web site at http://www.wto.org, under the resources tab across the top of the homepage.

2. The International Trade Center offers trade data, country trade profiles, and analysis of competitiveness. See its Web site at http://www.intracen.org.

3. *Direction of Trade Statistics (DOTS)* is a regular publication of the International Monetary Fund and is available in most university libraries. It is a good information source on the quantity of merchandise traded between countries, but does not disaggregate trade by commodity.

Beyond Comparative Advantage

Introduction: More Reasons to Trade

Comparative advantage is the foundation of our understanding of the gains from trade and the potential income distribution effects of trade. Unfortunately, trade models built exclusively on the idea of comparative advantage have a mixed record when it comes to predicting a country's trade patterns. This is an important failure since we tend to think that if we accurately measure a country's comparative advantage we should be able to predict import and export patterns. The problem, however, is that it is exceedingly difficult to measure a country's comparative advantage. This problem is compounded by the fact that there are many potential products an economy might export that use the same comparative advantage, and there is no way to determine which specific products will dominate. Furthermore, and perhaps most seriously, a large share of international trade is not based on comparative advantage. This chapter takes up two important exceptions to the models of the previous chapters, and examines how and why many countries try to select and plan the development of their export industries.

The first section tries to make sense of the fact that an important share of world trade consists of countries exporting the same thing they import. Canada and the United States, for example, have the largest trade relationship in the world, and a large share of it is based on both countries exporting cars and car parts to each other. This pattern is clearly at odds with the bread-for-steel examples shown in Chapters 3 and 4. In the second section of the chapter, we examine industrial clustering. Many traded goods and services that are essential parts of a country's exports are produced in regional clusters. For example, the U.S. advantage in entertainment products (music, television programming, and movies) largely reflects the output of a handful of regions such as Hollywood and Nashville. Software reflects clusters in Silicon Valley, Seattle, and a few other spots; biotechnology is in San Francisco, San Diego, and a handful of other places. Surprisingly, international trade can play an important role in this type of clustering and may, under certain conditions, prevent new clusters from forming.

The issue of regional clusters leads directly into a discussion of industrial policies in the third section of the chapter. Industrial policies are used to address the challenge of trying to plan an advantage in a particular industry or a group of products. Can countries pick the items they will export and successfully build a strong export industry? What are the costs and benefits of the policies they follow? Basically, we are asking how nations can use policies to shape their economic development.

Intraindustry Trade

The models of comparative advantage developed in Chapters 3 and 4 are built on the foundation of country differences. In those models, differences in productivity (Chapter 3) or factor endowments (Chapter 4) make it possible for countries to raise their living standards by specializing their production and trading. The point of these models is not to paint a detailed portrait of economic life, but rather to create a simplified abstract model of the economy that is focused on key economic relations in the area of trade. To that end, unnecessary details are omitted, and rare or exceptional cases are ignored.

Sometimes it happens that rare or exceptional cases become more important over time. Such is the case with the increasing importance of **intraindustry trade** (the prefix "intra" means *within*). Intraindustry trade is the international trade of products made within the same industry, for example steel-for-steel or bread-for-bread. The opposite of intraindustry trade is **interindustry trade** (the prefix "inter" means *between*). Interindustry trade is international trade of products between two different industries (for example, bread-for-steel). The growing importance of intraindustry trade has forced economists to develop a new set of models in order to explain the reasons why countries often export the same goods they import, and to explain the benefits from this type of trade.

Measures of Intraindustry Trade

Intraindustry trade between industrial countries is common. Empirical measures of the importance of intraindustry trade vary, however, because of the fundamental problem of defining an industry. For example, if computers are defined as office machinery, then computers and pencil sharpeners are in the same industry and a country that exports computers and imports pencil sharpeners would engage in intraindustry trade. In general, the broader the definition of an industry, the more trade appears to be intraindustry. Conversely, the more detailed the definition, the less trade is defined as intraindustry.

Intraindustry trade is measured for each industry with the following statistic called the **Grubel-Lloyd (GL) index**:

$$GL_i = 1 - \frac{|X_i - M_i|}{X_i + M_i}$$

If exports of a domestic industry are equal to the value of imports from the same industry ($X_i = M_i$), then the numerator in the ratio is equal to 0 and the index equals 1. In that case, all of the industry's trade is intraindustry. Conversely, if a country only exports or only imports, then either X_i or M_i will be 0. In that case, the numerator equals the denominator, the index is 0, and none of the industry's trade is intraindustry. In order to calculate the index for the whole economy and not just for one industry, each industry's index is multiplied by its overall share in total trade, the indexes are added together, and the result is subtracted from 1. It is customary to multiply the GL index by 100.

Many European countries and the United States have a large share of their total trade that is intraindustry. In the late 1990s, the Grubel-Lloyd indexes for Germany, France, the United Kingdom, and the United States were between 68.5 and 77.5 for merchandise trade. Evidence suggests that intraindustry trade is greater in high-technology industries, (where there is more scope for product differentiation), in countries that are more open to trade, and in nations that have received larger amounts of foreign direct investment.

Characteristics of Intraindustry Trade

In the models of comparative advantage-based trade presented in Chapters 3 and 4, production costs are either constant (Chapter 3) or increasing (Chapter 4). Accordingly, each additional unit of bread produced led to the loss of a fixed or increasing amount of steel. The production of many goods, however, is characterized by economies of scale, or decreasing costs, over a relatively large range of output. Economies of scale can be either **internal economies of scale** or **external economies of scale**. Internal economies are defined as falling average costs over a relatively large range of output. In practice, this leads to larger firms because size confers a competitive advantage in the form of lower average costs. One of the distinguishing features of intraindustry trade is the presence of internal economies of scale. In the case of external economies, larger firms have no inherent advantage over smaller firms, but average costs decline for all firms as the size of the industry increases. Unlike internal economies of scale, with external economies the size or scale effects are located in the industry and not in the firm.

Table 5.1 illustrates a firm's cost structure when it experiences increasing returns to scale. In most cases, there is a threshold level of production above which the average cost per good begins to increase, rather than continuing to fall. Increasing returns are usually based on the inherent development, engineering, or marketing aspects of production and are associated with products that have a large fixed cost component. Car companies, software, and popular household brand name products, to name a few, tend to have large fixed costs. These occur for various reasons, such as the cost of constructing a large production plant, large R&D budgets, or large marketing expenditures. Software, for example, requires large up-front expenditures on R&D to develop a product, and the more units a firm can sell, the more it can spread out those fixed R&D costs.

Internal economies of scale have important implications for the type of market that prevails. In Chapters 3 and 4, it is assumed that firms operate in competitive markets where no one firm can influence prices or overall industry output.

TABLE 5.1	Increasing Returns to Scale for a Single Firm	
Output	Total Cost	Average Cost
100	1000	10
200	1400	7
300	1500	5
400	1600	4
500	1650	3.5
600	1950	3.25

As production increases, total costs rise, but the cost per unit falls. Bigger firms are more efficient than smaller firms.

When larger firms are more competitive, however, it reduces the number of firms in a market and leads to one of several types of market structures. In an **oligopoly**, a handful of firms produce the entire market output. In this case, the pattern of production and trade is very difficult to predict because each firm uses predictions about the actions of its competitors as it formulates its own profit-maximizing strategy. This type of response means that each firm alters its output level as it sees what its competitors are doing, and production levels and trade become less predictable. An example is presented later in the chapter when we discuss industrial policies and strategic trade theory.

Often, internal economies lead to the relatively common market structure called **monopolistic competition**. Recall that in a pure monopoly, one firm produces the entire industry output. In monopolistic competition, there is competition among many firms, but their competition is attenuated by the practice of **product differentiation**. With product differentiation, each firm produces a slightly different product. This gives rise to the monopoly element of monopolistic competition, in that each firm is the sole producer of its products. For example, only Ford can sell Ford Explorers. Unlike a pure monopoly, however, every other firm produces a close substitute and this introduces a real element of competition.

In monopolistic competition, the level of competition among firms increases whenever new firms enter the market. This has two effects. On the one hand, heightened competition will lead to lower prices because products are substitutes for each other and in the struggle to capture sales, downward pressure is placed on prices. On the other hand, when more firms divide the market, on average each firm sells fewer units of output, and so costs rise. This follows directly from the internal economies of each firm. As long as prices are above costs, more firms will enter the market, and whenever prices are below costs, firms exit.

The presence of internal economies of scale is the reason why firms want to enter export markets. Any firm that exports has a competitive advantage since it will have higher sales and be able to take advantage of the cost-reducing effects of its internal economies of scale. For any given number of firms, average costs are lower in a larger market. This follows from the economies of scale that each firm experiences and the fact that if the number of firms is held constant, each firm sells more as the size of the market expands.

The Gains from Intraindustry Trade

Intraindustry trade also creates gains from trade. While the increase in the size of the market leads to lower costs through the effect of scale economies, competition among firms forces them to pass on their lower costs to consumers in the form of lower prices. Lower prices for exports and imports stands in marked contrast to the case of comparative advantage-based trade. Recall that in the trade models of Chapters 3 and 4, each country's consumers benefit from a reduction in the price of the good it imports, but at the same time, the price of the export rises. With intraindustry trade, however, prices for imports and exports decline, leading to unambiguous benefits for consumers in both countries. Trade enables firms to produce for a larger market and at a higher level of efficiency. That raises everyone's real income through the reduction in prices.

The expansion of the market that occurs with trade ultimately leads to an increase in the number of firms. This follows from the fact that exports create a situation where costs are below prices, attracting new firms into the market until excess profits are competed away. It is indeterminate if the increase in the number of firms comes about through an increase in domestic or foreign firms, or how the increase might be divided between the two. While it is safe to say that the combined foreign and domestic industry will expand, the location of the expansion is indeterminate. While it is conceivable that foreigners might expand disproportionately and leave the domestic industry smaller than it was initially, intraindustry trade is usually perceived as less threatening to jobs and firms than comparative advantage-based trade. This difference is primarily due to the decline of the import sector in comparative advantage-based trade and the need for some or all of its workers to look for work in the expanding export sector. By contrast, in intraindustry trade there is a significant likelihood that trade expands the number of domestic firms and the quantity of domestic output. At the very least, domestic firms have an opportunity to expand, and it would be expected that well-run firms would take heed of the larger market available to them.

In addition to lower prices (higher real income) and the potential expansion of production, another benefit from intraindustry trade is that it increases consumer choices. Without trade, consumers are limited to the goods produced in the domestic market. This is not necessarily a limitation for some people, but a scan of the highways should be enough to convince anyone that many consumers prefer foreign-made goods over their domestic substitutes. The value of added choices is not easy to measure in dollar terms, but it is clearly a significant benefit for most people.

CASE STUDY

United States and Canada Trade

In 1965, the United States and Canada implemented a free-trade policy that covered autos and auto parts. The results were dramatic, particularly on the Canadian side of the border. Prior to the Auto Pact, Canada required most cars sold domestically to be made inside the country. The relatively small market in Canada meant that only a few different car models were produced, each in small batches that cost more to make since automakers could not take full advantage of economies of scale in production. After the Auto Pact, automakers refocused production on a smaller number of models that were produced for the combined Canadian and U.S. market. Canadian productivity in the automobile industry rose dramatically as the scale of production increased. In addition, as imports from the United States increased, Canadian consumers had many more models from which to choose.

The automobile industry integrated production in the United States and Canada completely. Trade between the two countries rose dramatically, and eventually grew into the largest bilateral trade relationship of any two countries in the world. Table 5.2 illustrates the importance of intraindustry trade.

Three of the top five U.S. exports to Canada and two of the top five imports are motor vehicles or related products. In terms of value, an overwhelming share of the top five exports and imports are car related. Clearly, intraindustry trade is fundamental to the U.S.-Canadian trade pattern.

It is also interesting to note that the top five U.S. imports include a number of Canadian exports that take advantage of its natural resource endowment. This part of the trade relationship illustrates comparative advantage-based trade built around differing factor endowments. As a result, U.S.-Canadian trade is partly intraindustry, partly interindustry comparative advantage-based.

TABLE 5.2	U.S.-Canadian Merchandise Trade, 2008 (Billions of US$)		
Top Five U.S. Exports	Value	Top Five U.S. Imports	Value
Vehicle parts, not engines*	20.4	Crude oil	62.7
Passenger cars*	14.7	Passenger cars*	31.4
Busses, trucks, other vehicles*	10.8	Natural gas	30.7
Industrial machines	7.7	Vehicle parts, not engines*	12.1
Civilian aircraft, incl. parts	6.7	Other petroleum products	8.7

Vehicles and vehicle parts are the largest component of U.S.-Canadian trade.

*Related to motor vehicle manufacturing.

Source: US Census Bureau, "End-Use Data," *Country and Product Trade Data, 2008.* Retrieved June 2008, from http://www.census. gov/foreign-trade/statistics/country/index.html.

Trade and Geography

Paul Krugman, winner of the 2008 Nobel Prize in Economics has stated that international trade is really about geography and the decision every firm must make about the location of its activities. Produce at home or abroad? If abroad, then in which country? If at home, in what part of the country? Produce close to a city, or in the countryside where land is cheaper? In many cases the choices are obvious, and the factors that make them obvious are related to the characteristics of a particular place. For example, the availability of labor or energy resources, or the proximity to a market or specialized input suppliers may determine the choices of a firm. Geography, which is the study of the characteristics of places, is an important consideration for firms, and in turn has significant effects on trade.

Trade and geography are linked in two fundamental ways. First, a place may pull in economic activity because it is close to a market. Cities, for example, become centers of economic growth because they offer firms a market and the lowest cost opportunity for expansion. Second, a place may offer firms the opportunity to find critical inputs, including skilled labor, and to stay abreast of current developments. For both of these reasons, on the output side and the input side the characteristics of places are an important part of firm decision making. And as a result, geography plays a key role in some trade.

Geography, Transportation Costs, and Internal Economics of Scale

For most manufactured goods it is not practical to produce next to each market because there are some economies of scale. For example, it would not make sense to locate car assembly firms next to every car dealership. Production would be at too small a scale and costs would be extremely high. Instead, car production tends to be concentrated in a few areas and the final product is shipped to the markets where it is sold. As a result, there are significant transportation costs, both in bringing in the parts that are assembled into the final car and in shipping the car to its final market. Accordingly, car companies think carefully about the location of their activities, and try to mitigate their high transportation costs by locating near their markets.

Not all types of manufacturing have the same level of transportation costs, and services have few or none, but to one degree or another, the cost of bringing parts to the assembler and then shipping the final product to market are important considerations for many firms. If there were no internal economies of scale, then it would be possible to locate production next to the market where the good will be sold, but the presence of scale economies makes that impractical for most production. Milk and eggs tend to be produced locally because there are more limited scale economies and higher transportation costs, while aircraft are highly concentrated in their production because there are large scale economies and relatively smaller transportation costs.

Transportation costs and scale economies are characteristics of manufacturing that help explain several patterns observed in the global economy. For example, it was noted in Chapter 4 that most foreign investment in the world today is directed toward high-income countries, not toward developing countries. Largely this is because high-income countries have larger markets and firms find it convenient to locate next to the market. All else equal, the lower transportation costs often outweigh other costs that might be higher. It also explains the southward shift of U.S. car manufacturing in the 1990s, as firms in Michigan and Ohio moved to Texas in order to be closer to the new final assemblers that were springing up in Mexico. The cost of transporting the large number of parts that are assembled into a car or truck requires that assemblers and parts suppliers are in close proximity to one another.

CASE STUDY

The Shifting Geography of Mexico's Manufacturing

Approximately two-thirds of the trade between the United States and Mexico is intrafirm. Most of this occurs within the context of Mexico's special export processing sector, called the **maquiladora** industry. Orignially limited to its border with the United States but later expanded to the whole country, the maquiladora industry began in 1965. The original purpose of the government was to generate employment along Mexico's northern border. In the long run, the maquiladora industry became a major source of manufacturing activity, a major employer, and one of the country's main sources of exports.

The maquiladora industry is an example of an **export processing zone (EPZ)**. In EPZs, both domestic and foreign firms produce goods for export without paying tariffs on the parts and materials they import. This allows domestic and foreign firms such as General Motors and Sony to set up in Mexico and pay no tariffs on the inputs they bring into the country from abroad, as long as they export the output.

The number of firms in the export processing industry grew slowly but steadily and by 1980, fifteen years after the initial legislation, there were 620 plants with 120,000 workers. Nevertheless, the export processing industry was an exception to the dominant trend in Mexican manufacturing that remained firmly focused on production for the domestic market. Until the middle of the 1980s, Mexico's development strategy was inward looking and most firms found that it was less profitable to export than to produce for the home market since goods sold domestically were protected from competition and goods sold abroad were not.

In 1982, a financial crisis struck Mexico and policymakers began to rethink the country's development model. Up until then, the focus on production for the domestic market caused most firms to locate near Mexico City or one or two other major urban areas such as Monterrey or Guadalajara. The choice of locations reduced their transportation costs by locating production near their final market, and allowed them to take advantage of their internal economies of scale since they operated out of only one or a small number of plants. In an unforeseen way, Mexico's development model during the 1950s, '60s, and '70s caused Mexico City to grow into one of the world's largest cities and resulted in a very high proportion of the population becoming concentrated in the country's largest urban centers.

In the middle of the 1980s, Mexican policymakers shifted toward a more neutral policy with respect to production for domestic or foreign markets. They did this by removing many of the tariffs and other protections that had kept domestic firms free from foreign competition. High import tariffs raise the profitability of producing for the domestic market because they limit foreign competiton, but one of the costs of this type of policy is that is becomes relatively less profitable to produce exports, which do face competitive pressures. By reducing and in some cases eliminating tariffs and other measures that limited imports, policymakers created a more level playing field for exports producers. In effect, this made it relatively more profitable to produce goods for sale in foreign markets since it took away the advantages of producing for the domestic market.

Partly as a consequence of these policy changes, the export processing industry along Mexico's northern border took off. By the middle of 2000, the maquiladora industry employed more than 1.3 million workers in more than 3,700 firms and was responsible for more than half of Mexico's total exports. The industry began running large trade surpluses and by 2006, the last year of available data, it was generating more than $24 billion in trade surpluses.

The maquiladora industry grew rapidly because the new incentives caused both Mexican and non-Mexican firms to locate near the border with the United States, rather than in Mexico City. Under the new rules, the largest profitable market is the United States rather than Mexico City. Given internal economies of scale and transportation costs, location as close as possible to the U.S. market made a great deal of sense, and cities on Mexico's northern border, such as Tijuana, Ciudad Juarez, and others, began to grow rapidly almost a decade before the free-trade agreement between the United States, Mexico, and Canada.

External Economies of Scale

External economies of scale occur when firms become more productive as the number of firms in the industry increases, but individual firms may or may not have an economic incentive to increase in size. This may occur for several reasons. First, if the firms in a region produce similar products, then there are likely to be knowledge spillovers that help keep all firms abreast of the latest technology and newest developments. Close physical proximity enhances knowledge spillovers because it creates more opportunities for information exchange through formal and informal networks of people. Regional industry associations can be important, but so can soccer teams, churches, Girl Scouts, and other civic organizations that bring together people that work in different firms. Knowledge spillovers are particularly important in frontier industries undergoing rapid technological change, and they seem to be very sensitive to the face-to-face contact that is impaired by geographical distance.

A second form of external economies of scale occurs when the presence of a large number of producers in one area helps to create a deep labor market for specialized skills. If an industry is large enough to attract a steady stream of potential employees with specialized skills, it reduces the search costs of firms and also offers them the best available skills. This advantage is particularly important in industries that demand highly technical or scarce skills.

A third potential advantage to a large geographical concentration is that it can lead to a dense network of input suppliers. Manufacturers of intermediate inputs prefer to locate near the market for their products since it holds down transportation costs and may keep them better informed. In high-tech sectors, a large number of nearby supplier firms will lower the cost of finding a producer of a specialized input and will also create a wider and deeper selection of input goods and services. All of these effects hold down producer costs. The linkage from producers back to their suppliers can also occur in the other direction. If the concentrated industry manufactures intermediate goods or services, it may attract firms that use its products to make a final good or service. This gives firms more information about their market and may also lead to closer collaboration between suppliers and purchasers of intermediate inputs.

Trade and External Economies

One of the essential features of geographical concentration is that it is self reinforcing. For example, as firms attract skilled workers or specialized input suppliers, the increase in the availability of high-quality inputs creates feedback leading to more firms in the same industry locating in the area. In turn, this leads to a stronger pull for workers and input suppliers. In effect, each of the elements acts on each other to propel the system forward.

One implication of these features is that small differences in initial conditions may lead to large differences in outcome. That is, a region with a small head start or other small initial advantage in attracting firms may develop significant scale economies before other regions. Once the scale advantages become significant, the gap between the lead region and its competitors can widen, and may turn into a permanent competitive advantage. The source of the initial advantage can be anything, including historical accidents. For example, during World War II, as jet engines were being developed in Great Britain, the Allies decided to locate production in the United States on the West Coast where it minimized the probability that the Axis powers could destroy the factories with air raids. Ultimately, this led to a supplier industry around the major jet aircraft manufacturers (Boeing, Lockheed, and McDonnell-Douglas), and helped in the development of specialized labor skills such as aerospace engineering. As a result of a historical accident and the Allies' decisions during the war, the United States dominated the commercial jet aircraft industry for several decades, until a consortium of European governments used large subsidies and other interventions to foster a European competitor, Airbus.

Once the U.S. lead was established, then other countries with essentially the same technological ability as the United States could never catch up, even though in theory they had the capacity to achieve the same level of efficiency. The development of U.S. regional agglomerations (for example, the concentration of specialized aerospace manufacturing firms in the Seattle and Southern California regions) gave the United States a head start and a competitive advantage that could not be easily overcome. U.S. planes were always available at lower prices than a newer, less developed, industry could offer. In this instance, trade stifles the development of an industry that may be as competitive as existing producers.

In theory, it is possible that trade may stifle the development of a new industry that is more efficient than the existing one. Suppose, for example, that Europeans are potentially more efficient at making commercial aircraft than Americans. Their potential can only be realized, however, after a period of experimentation and development. The initial problem they face is that the efficiency advantage goes to the United States because of its better developed linkages between suppliers and producers. In this case, trade and the initial availability of U.S. planes at a lower cost remove the incentive for Europeans to invest in their industry and prevent the development of what would be a more efficient industry. As long as U.S. planes are available at a lower price than European planes, there is no economic reason why anyone would buy European, and the lack of an initial market for their planes guarantees the Europeans a period of financial losses, thereby discouraging investment. In effect, the historical accident of locating jet aircraft production in the United States in order to avoid Hitler's bombers is locked in by trade.

The aircraft example is instructive because it illustrates a case in which trade may not be beneficial. In every other case we've examined so far, trade is beneficial. However, under the circumstances outlined above, it is potentially harmful since, in this hypothetical case, it reduces global efficiency by concentrating world production in the less efficient producer. The aircraft example also illustrates how small initial differences can cascade into large differences in outcome and how with external economies, trade patterns can be a result of completely unpredictable accidents of history.

Industrial Policy

Faced with a more competitive U.S. aircraft industry, what can Europeans do to get their own industry off the ground? This was the question asked several decades ago by the governments of Britain, France, Germany, and Spain. Their answer was to pool the resources of their domestic aircraft and aerospace firms to provide generous subsidies from the four governments to help the consortium absorb the initial losses and to develop their own industry. The result was Airbus, the large European challenger to the U.S.-based Boeing company.

The creation of Airbus is a prime example of governments using **industrial policies** to direct economic activity explicitly. As the name and example imply, industrial policies are government policies designed to create new industries or to support existing ones. Industrial policies are widely pursued around the globe by developed and developing countries and they can have profound impacts on trade and trade patterns. Airbus, for example, now exports commercial aircraft around the world and is a serious competitive force.

It should not be a surprise that industrial policies are controversial, so much so, that recent international agreements limit the scope of action that countries can take to support their industries. In addition, it is clear that in some cases they are politically motivated and end up wasting huge amounts of money. Brazil and Indonesia, for example, have also used industrial policies to develop regional commercial jet aircraft industries, targeted at the 20- to 100-passenger plane market. While Brazil has had commercial success, the Indonesian industry wasted billions of tax dollars and used a large number of engineers and other skilled workers whose talents could have been put to work developing the Indonesian economy. In the European case, however, it is clear that there are small differences between the United States and Europe. Both regions have a comparative advantage in aircraft, while Indonesia does not.

There is no doubt that comparative advantage can change, and someday Indonesia may have a comparative advantage in aircraft production as educational attainment rises, as the infrastructure of roads and ports improve, and as capital becomes more abundant. Comparative advantage is not immutable but it is a leap of reason to argue that a country can successfully pick the specific industry it wants to develop. Aircraft are beyond the reach of Indonesia at this time, and large-scale commercial jetliners may be beyond the reach of Brazil, but how should a country decide which industries it can successfully develop? And, even more basic, why should countries target any particular industry at all? Why not provide the basic components of a well functioning economy, such as education, stable institutions, the rule of law, and so on, and let the market decide whether to produce aircraft, high-speed trains, or some other product?

Industrial Policies and Market Failure

When the private market economy fails to deliver an optimal quantity of goods and services, it is called a **market failure**. Market failure is one of the main theoretical justifications for industrial policies. An optimal quantity is one where the full value of the goods to private consumers and society is equal to its full cost of production. It follows that too little or too much of a good is a market failure. There are many different ways to approach this concept, but one of the clearest is to view market failures as a divergence between **private returns** and **social returns**. A frequent cause of a divergence between private and social returns is that some of the costs or benefits of an activity are externalized, or outside the area of concern of the economic agents engaged in the activity. For obvious reasons, economists refer to the market failure that results from the externalization of costs or benefits as an **externality**. The idea behind the concept of externalities is that not all of the costs or benefits of an action go to the people or companies engaged in the economic activity. That is, they externalize the costs or benefits. For example, a steel mill that pollutes a river imposes a cost on inhabitants downstream, and parents who vaccinate their child create a benefit for their neighbor's children. In an accounting sense, the private returns are the cost and benefits to the steel mill or the parents with the vaccinated child, while the social returns include the private costs and benefits, but also take into account the costs and benefits to the rest of society—the downstream inhabitants or the neighbor's children. Note that externalized costs or benefits do not mean that they disappear and are of no consequence. From an economic viewpoint, they are as important as any other costs or benefits even though they do not fall on the individuals or firms that created them.

There are two simple rules for analyzing cases of market failure. First, when social returns are greater than private returns, a free-market economy produces less than the optimal amount. This follows from the fact that not all the benefits are captured by individuals or firms that produce the benefits, so naturally they do not consider the entire set of benefits when they decide how much to produce. The second rule is that when social returns are less than private returns, a free-market economy produces more than the optimal amount. In this case, economic agents do not take into account the costs that spill over onto others and that reduce the value to society of the good or service.

The divergence between private and social returns is shown in Figure 5.1. Supply and demand are plotted for a competitively produced good that generates external benefits when it is produced. The supply curve S_{priv} is a normal market supply curve, embodying all of the private costs encountered by firms that engage in production. It is labeled with the subscript "priv" to indicate that only the private costs, the costs paid by the firms producing the good, are taken into account. Since production entails some external benefits to members of the society (who are not specified in this model), we can offset some of the costs of production with the external benefits. These are subtracted from the supply curve to derive the social supply curve, S_{soc}, which embodies the private costs minus the external benefits. The supply curve S_{soc} is more comprehensive than S_{priv} since it takes into consideration all of the costs and benefits to society, not simply the private ones.

As can be seen in Figure 5.1, private markets lead to output Q_1 at price P_1. From the standpoint of the social optimum, however, the price is too high and the quantity is too low. The social optimum, at P_2 and Q_2, takes into account the costs and benefits that are external to the producing firms and their internal costs and benefits. In effect, private agents earn less than the social return, which includes the external benefit that firms cannot capture. As a result, there is less than the socially optimal amount of investment in the activity generating the returns. For advocates of industrial policies, the solution is activist government intervention to increase the level of the desirable activity. The tools and problems associated with this type of intervention are discussed next.

There are many reasons why social returns and private returns may differ. Knowledge spillovers are a common example and are often cited as a reason for industrial policies. Social and business interactions among workers in different firms can spread knowledge about new products and new processes. In this case, the social return to the new knowledge is greater than the private return because

FIGURE 5.1   **Market Failure: Externalities**

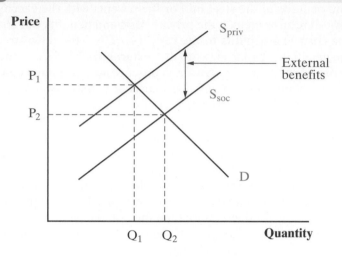

When social returns exceed private returns, markets produce less than the optimum and sell it at too high a price.

some of the value of the knowledge spills over from the firm that created it into other firms. An important case of knowledge spillovers comes from the first entrant into a particular industry. The first firm in an industry provides valuable information about the feasibility of the industry. The first firm may also leak marketing and technological information to other firms, and again, under any of these circumstances, the social returns are higher than the private ones.

A related knowledge spillover occurs in the area of research and development (R&D). Firms that develop new technologies may create breakthroughs that pay handsome profits. Often, before too much time goes by, the new product will be taken apart and improved upon by a competitor. In essence, the competitor bene-fits from the original research and development by being able to copy and improve upon it. Although the original innovator is unable to capture the full monetary benefit of its R&D, the benefits are not lost since other elements in society capture them. A variation of the effect of R&D is the problem of obtaining existing infor-mation. Often, existing technology may provide a solution to a common problem, but information about the technology may lie buried, for example, in a govern-ment research lab or in a Japanese technical journal. Firms could pay to search these sources for technical information, but once they find the answer to their problem, there is a high probability that all of their competitors will be able to copy it because it is difficult to keep information secret within a single firm.

Another source of divergence between private and social returns is capital mar-ket imperfections. According to this argument, new firms may have difficulty attracting sufficient start-up capital. The same applies to existing firms that need to borrow to develop new products or processes. If banks and other lenders in the financial system lack the information they need to make loans, many solid prospects may not receive funding. Imperfect capital markets may also lead to market failure when economies of scale are involved. Proponents of industrial policies cite the fact that many large-scale projects require a set of interdependent investments to be made all at once. For example, a potentially competitive steel industry may require simultaneous investment in port and rail linkages. By itself, each piece may be unprofitable, but taken together the result would be a large, competitive sector.

Strategic Trade

In addition to addressing market failures, a second justification for industrial policies is **strategic trade policy**. The two essential ingredients for strategic trade policy are that an industry has economies of scale and firms in the industry have market power that enables them to earn higher than normal profits. Strategic trade policy is the selective use of trade barriers and industry subsidies in order to capture some of the profits of foreign firms. Setting aside for a minute the practical difficulties of enacting strategic trade policy, in theory it is possible to convince foreign firms to leave the industry by starting a well-publicized and credible system of subsidies to new domestic firms. The size of the subsidy should be sufficient to enable the home country firms to earn profits. As long as home country firms gain a market share, their presence reduces the output of their competitors and, due to economies of scale, drives up the costs of production for foreign firms.

The following example illustrates these ideas. We return to the case of aircraft production. Regional commercial jet aircraft are smaller than the behemoths produced by Boeing and Airbus, and are used for shorter trips, with 20- to 100-seat planes often flying between destinations inside a country. Approximately 90 percent of the world's production is evenly split between Canada's Bombardier and Brazil's Embraer. Given that these firms can satisfy 90 percent of world demand, it can be assumed that there are significant economies of scale in production. The Brazilian firm, Embraer, is the younger of the two. It started in 1969 as a government-owned firm producing aircraft for the Brazilian military, and has moved into the commercial jet business, where it has several current planes and several more under development. In 1994, the company was privatized, but the Brazilian government retains stock shares and veto power over certain business decisions.

This example imagines a time before the entry of Embraer, when Bombardier was a dominant firm. The problem faced by the Brazilian firm was that the capital investment required to enter the market was enormous, in the tens of billions of dollars, and it was too much to risk in a speculative venture that would certainly run into stiff competition from an already established and profitable Canadian firm.

Table 5.3 presents a set of hypothetical payoffs to Embraer and Bombardier as the younger firm contemplates entering the market. As the Brazilian firm surveys its options, it notes that it has a choice of entering the market and losing −10, or staying out and losing 0. Obviously, staying out of the market is the better choice, given that the Canadian firm is already in the market and is not likely to leave. The dominant strategy under these circumstances is that Bombardier stays in the market and Embraer stays out. Suppose, however, that the Brazilian government

TABLE 5.3	A Hypothetical Payoff Matrix	
	Brazil's Embraer (BE)	
Canada's Bombardier (CB)	Enter Market	Stay Out of Market
Stay in Market	BE (–10)	BE (0)
	CB (–10)	CB (25)
Leave Market	BE (25)	BE (0)
	CB (0)	CB (0)

The dominant strategy is for Embraer to stay out of the market and for Bombardier to stay in. The outcome is the payoff in the upper-right corner.

decides to offer a subsidy. The subsidy should be enough to keep its company profitable regardless of whether the Canadian company leaves the market or stays in it. Let's say that the government offers a subsidy of 15 if Embraer enters the market. Under these conditions, the payoffs will be those detailed in Table 5.4.

With the subsidy (Table 5.4), the dominant strategy is for Brazil's Embraer to enter the market. If it stays out, it earns 0, but if it enters, it earns either 5 or 40, depending on the reaction of Canada's Bombardier. The latter, however, knows for certain that Embraer will enter the market and that, consequently, its own choice is between –10 if it stays in the market, or 0 if it leaves. The rational decision for Bombardier is to leave, ensuring that the Brazilian firm captures the above normal profits that were accruing to the Canadian firm.

Is this scenario feasible? Something like this has already happened in the aircraft industry, both in the large-scale, transcontinental commercial aircraft market and in the smaller, regional aircraft market. The WTO's rules for international competition make it difficult to offer direct subsidies, but in both market segments of this industry, every firm has tried to establish that its competitor is subsidized. For example, Canada and Brazil each have brought the other into the dispute settlement process at the WTO, and tensions have run high over allegations of unfair competition.

While these examples illustrate how subsidies may permit a country to capture, for itself or its firms, the profits of a foreign company, there are at least two practical problems that have been ignored so far. These are in addition to the fact that subsidies violate the WTO's rules for fair competition, and that using them can lead to a trade war. First, we assumed that governments have far more detailed information about costs and profits than is likely. Second, we assumed that there are no counter subsidies offered by the government of the company that loses out.

Industrial Policy Tools

Although there are a variety of techniques used to carry out industrial policies, they all share the same objective of channeling resources to the targeted industry. This can be accomplished in various ways, but the most obvious is to offer direct subsidies to firms in the targeted industry. As noted, this runs into the

TABLE 5.4	The Payoff Matrix after a Subsidy of 15	
	Brazil's Embraer (BE)	
Canada's Bombardier (CB)	**Enter Market**	**Stay Out of Market**
Stay in Market	BE (5)	BE (0)
	CB (−10)	CB (25)
Leave Market	BE (40)	BE (0)
	CB (0)	CB (0)

The dominant strategy is for Embraer to enter the market and for Bombardier to leave it. The outcome is the payoff in the lower-left corner.

practical difficulty that Uruguay Round rules of the WTO prohibit subsidies for competitive products. Nevertheless, the rules do allow governments to subsidize "precompetitive" activities such as research, and the distinction between the two can be blurry at times. It is not necessary, however, to provide direct subsidies to targeted industries in order to support them. Governments have a wide range of options, ranging from providing information about conditions in foreign markets (many countries do this through their embassies and consulates), helping negotiate contracts, lobbying foreign governments to adopt home country technical standards, or tying foreign aid to purchases from home country firms.

One common practice used by governments in some newly industrializing countries is to sell foreign exchange to targeted firms at below-market prices, thereby enabling them to buy capital goods from abroad at below-market prices. A second common technique is to provide government loans to private firms at below-market interest rates or, alternatively, to provide government guarantees on loans obtained from the private sector, thereby enabling borrowers to obtain favorable interest rates. Similarly, governments may provide special tax treatment to targeted industries. Governments also use their own purchases as a way to develop an industry. This can affect a wide range of activities, including medical equipment for state-owned hospitals, power generating equipment for state-owned utilities, telecommunications equipment for state-owned phone and broadcast media, military hardware, and so on. In some cases—for example suppliers of military hardware in the United States—firms are guaranteed a profit on the development of new products, which essentially removes all risk to the firm and shifts it to taxpayers.

Governments often support industries by encouraging firms to work together, either through the direct funding of the research done by consortia and/or through the relaxation of antitrust laws. This decreases the probability that competing firms will spend resources duplicating each other's research and development, but it increases their market power. Finally, governments may directly own firms, although this is less common after several recent waves of privatization in capitalist countries and the collapse of communism. In countries where government ownership is not unusual (France for example), the firms are run more or less like private firms.

Proponents of industrial policies stress that no matter which technique is used to target an industry, it is critical for governments to refrain from coercion. Firms should be allowed to refuse assistance (with the inevitable strings attached), and governments should recognize that any action they take to penalize noncooperation is likely to weaken the industry and lower the probability of a successful program.

Problems with Industrial Policies

While every economist recognizes that markets do not always produce the optimal outcome, many are skeptical about the practicality of using industrial policies to solve problems of market failure. One basic problem is that it is difficult to obtain the information necessary to measure the extent of market failure. For example, an efficient industrial policy requires governments to provide precisely the right amount of additional resources to the targeted industry. This implies that governments should keep adding resources as long as the external benefits are greater than the cost of the resources, but in most cases no one is capable of precisely measuring the benefits, particularly if they are spread throughout the economy and if they are only realized over a long period of time. Without the advantage of hard numbers, it is easy to imagine a situation where a government program spends $100 million to capture $50 million of external benefits. Similarly, the implementation of a successful strategic trade policy requires governments to know the costs of production for foreign firms and to be able to anticipate their reaction correctly when they face subsidized competition. While it is conceivable that the production costs may be known, it is impossible to know their reactions.

Even if these objections could somehow be met, there remains the problem of determining which industry to target. If everyone acknowledges that a particular industry has a bright future, then entrepreneurs and investors will jump on it and government support is unnecessary. On the other hand, we know that external benefits lead markets to underinvest. Consequently, one possibility for choosing industries to target is to pick the ones that have the largest external benefits. The problem with this strategy is that the positive externalities that develop out of new technologies and inventions are usually a surprise to everyone involved and it is impossible to know beforehand that they will occur. In 1990, for example, almost no one foresaw the advent of the Internet.

Another strategy that has been advocated for selecting the industries to target is to target high-value-added industries, where **value added** is the difference between the cost of materials and the value of the output. Value added is partly determined by the contribution of labor to production, and high-value-added industries are usually ones where wages are high. Value added is also determined by the contribution of capital, and therefore it may be high because an industry uses a lot of capital or a lot of highly skilled labor, or both. High-value-added industries are often selected as desirable ones to target because they tend to pay high wages or use new technologies that are viewed as important for future prosperity. The problem with this strategy for selecting an industry to target is that it often makes no sense in practice. For example, two of the highest-value-added industries in the United States are petroleum refining and tobacco products. No one, to my knowledge, has argued that these industries should be targeted for future development. In any case, it is not clear why high-value-added industries will not develop more efficiently through market processes. That is, there is nothing inherent in their nature that creates more external benefits than in other industries.

Another problem with industrial policies is that they encourage **rent seeking**, which is any activity by firms, individuals, or special interests that is designed to alter the distribution of income in their favor without adding to the amount of total income in the economy. When lobbyists persuade Congress to impose a tax on steel imports, for example, it raises the income of the U.S. steel industry, but lowers the income of steel users. (More steel will be produced, but as a consequence, fewer other things are.) If firms know that governments are willing to use industrial policies, they will spend resources to obtain some of the subsidies. This may require the hiring of lobbyists, economists, or engineers whose jobs are to persuade the legislature or some other rule makers. The downside is that it uses resources but does not add to total output.

The extent to which industrial policies encourage resources to be wasted in lobbying and other non-economically productive activities partly depends on the administrative process through which targeted industries are chosen, and the political culture of the country enacting the industrial policy. Countries that have a greater degree of corruption in their political system are likely to have a much harder time choosing between industries on the basis of scientific, technological, or economic criteria. Even in relatively corruption-free environments, however, the problem of industrial policies encouraging rent seeking is real.

Another problem with industrial policies is that it is impossible to contain the external benefits of R&D spending within national boundaries. New technologies soon spread to every nation that has the technological sophistication to take advantage of them. One set of estimates puts the benefits to foreigners of R&D spending by the home country at around one-fourth of the total benefits. The fact that many U.S. firms have separate joint ventures in research and production with European and Japanese firms increases the chances that a new breakthrough will spread to firms in other countries.

Despite these obstacles, industrial policies remain an intensely debated topic, particularly in the arena of economic development. Japan and South Korea used them extensively and are frequently cited as models for developing countries. Opponents of industrial policies continue to argue that sound macroeconomic policies, high rates of saving and investment, and high levels of schooling were the keys to success in those two countries, and that industrial policies were a distraction at best. Proponents view this line of reasoning as an ideological opposition to state-directed economic policy. Given the difficulties of determining cause and effect in economic development, an active debate between opponents and proponents will probably continue for some time. We will examine the East Asian case in greater detail in Chapter 16.

U.S. Industrial Policies

Throughout U.S. history and until World War II, a policy of high tariffs was a regular component of U.S. support for specific industries, but the use of direct subsidies was infrequent. Not counting the extensive involvement of state and federal governments in the development of transportation infrastructure (roads, canals, railroads, seaports, highways, and airports), the two main examples of direct subsidies were agriculture and defense industries.

Agriculture experiences externalities from the ability of neighboring farms to copy each other's innovations. Since a farmer who innovates cannot capture all the rewards of his or her innovation, we know that the private market economy will underproduce agricultural research. This principle was intuitively understood by U.S. farmers and legislators and in 1862 the U.S. Congress passed the Morrill Act, giving federally owned lands to states for the purpose of establishing agricultural research colleges. The Morrill Act was followed in 1887 by the Hatch Act setting up agricultural research stations, and in 1914 by the Smith-Lever Act establishing a system of cooperative education for farmers.

It is difficult to disentangle the effects of these policies from several other factors that worked to create a strong agricultural sector in the United States. The climate, the availability of land, soil fertility, the high level of farmer literacy, the ability to overcome labor shortages with innovations in farm machinery, and the development of a transportation infrastructure all worked to create a comparative advantage in agriculture. In all likelihood, the United States would have emerged as a world supplier of grains and other commodities with or without the support of the universities, research stations, and extension service. These institutions undoubtedly made agriculture more productive, but it seems unlikely that they created a comparative advantage in agriculture that would not have been there otherwise.

The theoretical justification for industrial policies in the defense industry is fairly clear. Defense is a public good (if one person gets it, everyone does, whether they pay for it or not) and public goods often create market failures since the economic incentive is for everyone to free ride and let others pay. For this reason, most economists agree that it is impossible for markets to provide defense and that it must be done by governments. This does not mean, however, that governments necessarily have to be directly involved in the production of war goods. In the post–World War II era, the weapons and tools of the U.S. defense forces have been produced by private firms, although the U.S. government has provided substantial resources to keep these firms in business, under the assumption that it would be detrimental to U.S. defense capability if the nation had to rely on foreign producers for major weapon systems.

Few people would disagree in general with this view, although there are disagreements about the optimal level of defense spending and the types of military equipment that are necessary. The main issue about defense spending in the context of industrial policies is that some economists argue that the United States has used the rhetoric of building a strong defense to hide a wide variety of industrial policies that are targeted at commercial developments. The research consortium Sematech is a case in point. Sematech was founded in 1987 by the Department of Defense in response to the growing use of Japanese semiconductors in U.S. jet aircraft. It is an R&D consortium open to any U.S.-based firm and is funded by its members and the federal government. Its initial goal was to regain technological superiority in the manufacture of semiconductors, and it seems to have largely succeeded. Many people, however, view Sematech as simply a subsidy to IBM, Motorola, Texas Instruments, and other U.S. corporations—one given to help restore their international competitiveness, although it was justified on the basis of a military need.

At two specific points in American history the debate over commercial, non-military, industrial policies has heated up. In both periods, the country felt threatened by outside economic forces. The first period was in the 1790s when the United States feared domination by Great Britain and the second period was in the 1970s and 1980s when fears of Japanese technological and manufacturing superiority began to surface. The first episode gave rise to the classic *Report on Manufactures* by Secretary of the Treasury Alexander Hamilton. Hamilton's report called for a national effort to develop greater manufacturing competitiveness and to lessen U.S. dependence on Britain for manufactured items. The second period of debate began in the late 1970s when U.S. steel production, then consumer electronics, autos, and semiconductors seemed either to vanish or to be on the verge of collapse as waves of Japanese imports captured increasing market shares.

From the vantage point of the twenty-first century, we can see two trends that prompted the questions about using industrial policy. The first occurred in the 1980s when world trade and foreign investment began to reach levels of competitive intensity that were new to the United States. Since the end of World War II, U.S. cars and other products had been relatively insulated from foreign competition, but by the 1980s, American businesses could no longer be complacent about foreign competition. Suddenly, it seemed, a number of highly competitive foreign products were taking away domestic sales from U.S. producers. A second trend was the painful loss of comparative advantage in a number of traditional, labor-intensive industries. This did not happen overnight, but with the rise of foreign competition, industries such as steel, consumer electronics, and a number of others were shown to be less competitive.

CASE STUDY

Subsidizing Commercial Aircraft

The manufacture of commercial aircraft is closely tied to the defense industry, both in its origins and in its current corporate relations. Given the importance of airpower in modern warfare, that fact alone makes the commercial aircraft industry an important strategic asset. But commercial aircraft also combine leading technologies in materials science, power systems, electronics, communication technology, and other key areas at the frontier of industrial performance. Hence, once most countries reach a certain level of industrial development, they try to develop aircraft manufacturing, repair, parts supply, or other related activities that tie them into the world's production system.

The market for multi-passenger commercial aircraft is dominated by the four companies previously mentioned: Airbus (France, Germany, Spain, and the United Kingdom), Boeing (United States), Bombardier (Canada), and Embraer (Brazil). Other countries, such as India, China, Italy, Taiwan, and Japan, have their own aircraft industries, but they are confined strictly to military planes and/or they work as suppliers to the big four or to smaller companies making light aircraft. Airbus, for example, has fifteen hundred suppliers in thirty countries. There are significant barriers to entering the markets dominated by the big four because it takes many billions of dollars to develop a new generation of airplanes. Once in, however, there are large but intangible benefits in the form of the strategic military advantages, national prestige, and experience working with cutting edge technologies.

Whether it makes more sense for a nation to buy its planes or produce them is a complicated question with no clear answer. What is clear, however, is that all four of the dominant companies have received substantial direct and indirect subsidies from their national governments and other public entities. This has raised a number of complaints within the world trading system. Brazil has challenged Canada and vice versa, while the United States has challenged the governments in Europe that support Airbus and those governments have challenged the U.S. support for Boeing.

In general, subsidies are considered an unfair advantage, although in some cases (agriculture for example) there are few international rules, and in other cases, the subsidy does not damage the economic interests of another country. Subsidies are a common source of friction, however, and therefore it is useful to have agreements as to when they can and cannot be used. In 1979, the Tokyo Round of the GATT prohibited all export subsidies on manufactured items, but left production subsidies alone. (Export subsidies are payments that go to a producer if and only if they export the product, while production subsidies support production regardless of whether the good is sold domestically or exported.) This was amended and extended by the Uruguay Round agreement, which defined prohibited subsidies (including export subsidies) and "actionable" subsidies, which are not prohibited outright but can be challenged under the dispute resolution mechanism in the WTO if they cause "adverse effects" to a third party.

According to the WTO, a subsidy is a financial contribution by a government or public agency that confers a benefit. Specific examples include grants, loans, loan guarantees, provision of goods or services, and fiscal incentives. The WTO left the door open for subsidies that do not hurt third parties, and for financial contributions that go to support basic research and development or what it calls pre-competitive technologies.

Since 1994, there have been two complaints leveled by Canada against Brazil based on a Brazilian program that helped foreign companies finance the purchase of Embraer planes. Similarly, there have been two complaints filed by Brazil against Canada for the support it gave Bombardier, which Brazil claimed was equivalent to export subsidies. Both Canada and Brazil won partial judgments against the other and were required to dismantle some of their financial support. Needless to say, their support continues but in somewhat subtler forms. Meanwhile, the United States filed a complaint against the European Union, alleging that its support for Airbus constituted export subsidies, and simultaneously, the European Union filed against the United States, alleging the same concerns. The U.S.-EU dispute is complicated and promises to be a lengthy one, with billions of dollars hanging in the balance. In the interim, Airbus and Boeing continue to integrate their design and production systems into the world economy, and both look less and less like nationally based companies.

Summary

- Comparative advantage cannot account for a significant part of world trade. In many countries, well over 50 percent of their merchandise trade is intraindustry, and for the United States and a number of other large economies, it is over two-thirds.

- Intraindustry trade is not based on comparative advantage since it consists of the export and import of similar products and occurs mostly between countries that have similar productivity, technology, and factor endowments. Intraindustry trade is based on economies of scale and product differentiation.

- Economies of scale occur whenever average costs decrease as production increases. Economies of scale are an important determinant of trade patterns because they form a separate basis for trade that is in addition to comparative advantage-based trade.

- Economies of scale can be either internal, external, or both. With internal economies of scale, the gains from trade include a wider selection of consumer choices and lower prices. With external economies of scale, the gains from trade are less certain since, in theory, they can lock in production in a less efficient country and prevent the development of production in a more efficient country.

- External economies of scale lead to regional agglomerations of firms. Firms are attracted by several positive factors derived from operating in close geographical proximity to each other. The three main factors are large pools of skilled labor, specialized suppliers of inputs, and knowledge spillovers.

- Industrial policies are premised on the idea that markets may fail to develop an industry that is essential for future prosperity, or that there will be less development than is optimal if many of the benefits of an industry are external to the firms in the industry.

- Historically, governments have used a number of tools to foster the development of industries that they thought were essential to future prosperity. These tools included a number of different types of direct and indirect subsidies. The Uruguay Round of the GATT agreement has made it illegal to subsidize a commercial product.

- Problems with industrial policies include the absence of a reliable method for selecting the industry to target, rent seeking, international spillovers, and the difficulty of correctly estimating the optimal amount of support to provide.

Vocabulary

export processing zone (EPZ)

external economies of scale

externality

Grubel-Lloyd (GL) index

industrial policy

interindustry trade

internal economies of scale

intraindustry trade

maquiladora

market failure

monopolistic competition

oligopoly

private returns

product differentiation

rent seeking

social returns

strategic trade policy

value added

Study Questions

1. What is intraindustry trade, how is it measured, and how does it differ from interindustry trade? Are the gains from trade similar?

2. Comparing U.S. trade with Germany and Brazil, is trade with Germany more likely to be based on comparative advantage or economies of scale? Why?

3. What are the differences between external and internal economies of scale with respect to the size of firms, market structure, and gains from trade?

4. What are three key incentives for firms in a particular industry to cluster together in a geographical region?

5. How might trade hurt a country if it imports goods that are produced under conditions of external economies of scale?

6. When the United States signed a free-trade agreement with Canada (1989), no one thought twice about it. When the agreement with Mexico was signed (1994), there was significant opposition. Use the concepts of interindustry and intraindustry trade to explain the differences in opposition to the two trade agreements.

7. What are the theoretical justifications for targeting the development of specific industries?

8. What are some common problems in implementing industrial policies?

9. Figure 5.1 illustrates the case of an industry that generates external social benefits with its production. Draw a supply and demand graph for an industry that creates external costs with its production. Compare and contrast the market determined price and output level with the socially optimal price and output levels.

APPENDIX

A Graphical Illustration of Prices and Costs with Monopolistic Competition

Figure 5.2 illustrates the relationship among the number of firms in the industry, average costs, and output prices. The horizontal axis measures the number of firms in the industry, while the vertical axis measures average costs and prices. Line segment P shows the relationship between the number of firms and prices. It slopes downward to the right because as more firms enter the market, it puts downward pressure on prices. Line segment AC shows the relationship between the average cost for each individual firm and the total number of firms in the market.

FIGURE 5.2

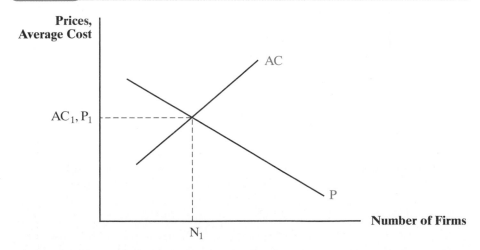

In monopolistic competition, an increase in the number of firms drives down prices and drives up each firm's average costs. Equilibrium occurs when price equals average cost.

It slopes upward because as more firms enter the market, the quantity each existing firm sells is reduced and the average cost of production increases. At prices above P1, new firms have an incentive to enter the market since price exceeds average costs. At prices below P1, just the opposite occurs and some firms will leave the market because their costs are greater than the market price.

Figure 5.2 also makes obvious the reason why firms want to export. Any firm that exports will be at a competitive advantage since it will have the greater sales it needs to drive down its costs. This idea is illustrated in Figure 5.3, where the alternative cost curve, AC*, is identical to AC except that it belongs to a larger market. For any given number of firms, AC* shows that average costs are lower in a larger market. This follows from the economies of scale that each firm experiences and the fact that if the number of firms is held constant, each firm sells more when the size of the market expands.

Export markets enable firms to expand production and to realize their scale economies. Scale economies, together with competition among firms, lead directly to the gains from trade. Increased production causes average costs to fall, while competition forces firms to pass the cost savings on to consumers in the form of lower prices.

FIGURE 5.3

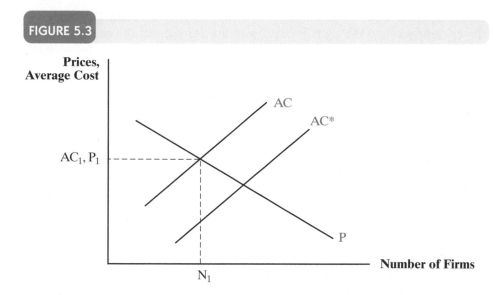

For any given number of firms, an increase in the size of the market through the creation of foreign sales allows economies of scale to be realized and pushes down average costs.

The Theory of Tariffs and Quotas

Introduction: Tariffs and Quotas

Chapters 6 and 7 are an introduction to the theory and policy of tariffs and quotas. In the economics literature, this analysis is called *commercial policy*. Chapter 6 is an introduction to tariff theory and Chapter 7 focuses on an empirical estimate of the direct costs of protectionism and the arguments used by proponents of restricted trade. The inefficiency and expense of tariffs and quotas as a means to protect industries and jobs will be apparent after measuring their direct costs.

Analysis of a Tariff

Barriers to trade come in all shapes and sizes. Some are obvious or **transparent**, whereas others are hidden or **nontransparent**. Quotas directly limit the quantity of imports, while tariffs indirectly limit imports by taxing them. Tariffs and quotas cause consumers to switch to relatively cheaper domestic goods or to drop out of the market altogether. They also encourage domestic producers to increase their output because demand switches from foreign to domestic goods.

   In the analysis that follows we will look only at the effects of tariffs and quotas on the industry in which they are imposed. For example, the economy-wide effect of a tariff in, say, the steel industry will not be analyzed. In the language of economics, the analysis in Chapter 6 is known as *partial equilibrium analysis* because it considers the effects of tariffs and quotas on only a part of the economy—the market in which the trade barrier is erected. Before we turn to tariff analysis, however, we must introduce two important concepts: consumer and producer surplus.

Consumer and Producer Surplus

What is the maximum price you would be willing to pay for a gallon of milk? The answer is likely to be different for each consumer, depending on income, how much he or she likes milk, whether he or she has kids who need it, whether he or she can tolerate lactose or not, and a number of other factors, many of which are subjective. The subjective value that consumers place on milk is contained in the market demand curve for milk, which describes the total quantity of a good that consumers are willing and able to buy at each and every price. As the market price falls, a greater quantity is purchased because more consumers will feel that the lower price is equal to or below the value they place on the milk.

Suppose, for example, that you are willing to pay $3.50 for a gallon of milk, but the price is only $3.20. In essence, each gallon of milk provides $0.30 of value that is "free" in the sense that it is over and above what you must pay. This excess value, called **consumer surplus**, is the value received by consumers that is in excess of the price they pay. It occurs because everyone values each good differently, yet for most goods there is only one price. Consumer surplus can be measured if the demand curve is known. Since the demand curve is a summary of the value that each consumer places on a particular good, the area between the demand curve and the price line is a measurement of consumer surplus.

Figure 6.1 shows hypothetical market demand and supply curves for milk. At the market equilibrium price of $3.20 per gallon, 10,000 gallons will be supplied and demanded. Many people value milk at a higher price, however, and the value they receive in consuming milk is greater than $3.20. In Figure 6.1, consumer surplus is the area below the demand curve and above the price line of $3.20. The size or value of consumer surplus is the area of the triangle given by the formula ($\frac{1}{2}$) × (height) × (width), or ($\frac{1}{2}$) × ($1.30) × (10,000), which is equal to $6,500. This equals the difference between the subjective value of the milk consumed and the total amount consumers spent for it.

Consumer surplus is a real savings to consumers. If firms had a way to determine the maximum price that each consumer was willing to pay, then theoretically they could charge every individual a different price and thus reduce consumer surplus to zero. Luckily for those of us not in the milk business, firms usually cannot get this

FIGURE 6.1   **Consumer and Producer Surplus**

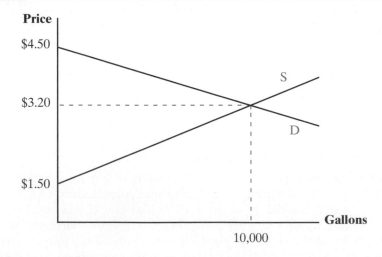

Consumer surplus is the area below the demand curve and above the price line. Producer surplus is the area above the supply curve and below the price line.

information without going through a long and costly interview procedure. As a result, it is usually impractical (and in some cases, illegal) for firms to charge different customers different prices. Nevertheless, some firms such as car dealers manage to charge different prices for the same goods. The easiest strategy for most firms is simply to charge everyone the same price, so consumer surplus is a real savings for most consumers in most markets.

On the production side, the analogous concept is called **producer surplus**. In our hypothetical milk example, if you owned a dairy farm and were willing and able to produce milk at $3.00 per gallon, you would receive producer surplus of $0.20 per gallon if you sold milk at $3.20. Recall that the supply curve for a market is the sum of supply curves for the firms in the market and that it reflects the minimum price firms will accept to produce a given amount. In Figure 6.1, some firms are willing to produce at $2.00 per gallon, and at every price above $1.50 at least some firms will have output to sell. Every firm that is willing to sell for less than the equilibrium price of $3.20 earns revenue that is above the minimum it needs. This excess or surplus revenue is a firm's producer surplus.

As in the case of consumer surplus, we can measure producer surplus. Measurement in this case depends on knowing the parameters of the supply curve (where it crosses the price axis and its slope) because producer surplus is the area above the supply curve and below the price line. In our example, it is equal in value to the triangle given by the formula $(\frac{1}{2}) \times (\$1.70) \times (10,000)$, which equals $8,500. This is the revenue received by producers that is in excess of the minimum amount of revenue that would be required to get them to produce 10,000 gallons of milk.

Prices, Output, and Consumption

We will use the concepts of producer and consumer surplus when we discuss the income distribution effects of tariffs and quotas. Before we analyze those effects, however, we must begin with a description of the effects of tariffs on prices, domestic output, and domestic consumption.

Figure 6.2 shows the domestic or national supply and demand for an imported good. We are assuming that there is one price for the good, which we will call the world price, or P_w, and that foreign producers are willing to supply us with all of the units of the good that we want at that price. This is equivalent to assuming that foreign supply is perfectly elastic, or that the United States does not consume a large enough quantity to affect the price. We will drop this assumption when we discuss the case of a large country. Note that the world price is below the domestic equilibrium price. This means that domestic producers are not able to satisfy all domestic demand at the market price of P_w and that consumers depend on foreign producers for some of their consumption. Specifically, at price P_w, consumers demand Q_2, but domestic producers supply only Q_1. The difference, $Q_2 - Q_1$, or line segment Q_1Q_2, is made up by imports.

Now suppose that the government imposes a tariff of amount "t." Importers will still be able to buy the good from foreign producers for amount P_w, but they will have to pay the import tax of "t," which they tack onto the price to domestic

| FIGURE 6.2 | Domestic Supply and Demand for an Imported Good |

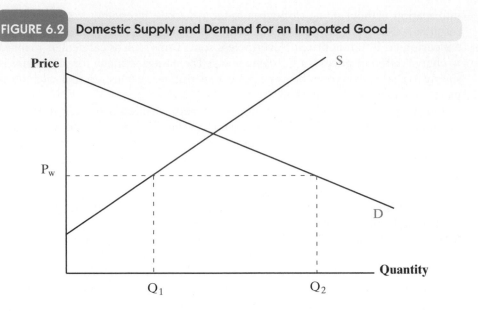

The difference between domestic demand and domestic supply, $Q_2 - Q_1$, is the quantity of imports at price P_w.

consumers. In other words, the price to consumers rises to $P_w + t = P_t$, as shown in Figure 6.3. The price increase in the domestic market has effects on domestic consumption, domestic production, and imports. First, the price increase squeezes some people out of the market, and domestic consumption falls from Q_2 to Q_2^*. Next, on the production side, the higher price encourages domestic production to increase from Q_1 to Q_1^*. The increase in domestic production occurs because domestic firms are able to charge a slightly higher price $(P_w + t)$ in order to cover their increasing costs while remaining competitive with foreign firms. Finally, imports decrease from Q_1Q_2 to $Q_1^*Q_2^*$. To summarize, tariffs cause the domestic price to rise by the amount of the tariff, domestic consumption falls, domestic production rises, and imports fall.

Resource Allocation and Income Distribution

Tariffs have more subtle effects than just a rise in prices and a fall in imports. The increase in domestic production requires additional resources of land, labor, and capital to be reallocated from their prior uses into the industry receiving protection under the tariff. Also, when the price changes, consumer and producer surplus do too.

First, let's consider the effect on consumer surplus. Figure 6.3 shows both the pre- and post-tariff price and output levels. Remember that consumer surplus is the entire area above the price line and below the demand curve. When consumers pay price P_w, it is areas a + b + c + d + e + f. After the tariff is imposed and

FIGURE 6.3 | **The Effects of a Tariff**

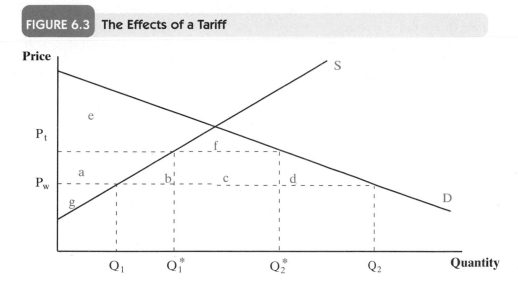

Tariffs cause an increase in domestic prices and domestic production, and a fall in domestic consumption. They increase producer surplus and government revenue, but decrease consumer surplus.

the price rises to P_t, consumer surplus shrinks to $e + f$. The difference, area $a + b + c + d$, represents a loss to consumers.

Unlike consumer surplus, producer surplus grows. Pre-tariff producer surplus is area g, and post-tariff is $g + a$. The difference, area a, is the additional revenue that is above the minimum necessary to encourage domestic firms to increase their output from Q_1 to Q_1^*. On net, producers are better off, and consumers are worse off, but what about the nation as a whole?

If we consider the whole loss to consumers, areas $a + b + c + d$, we see that it can be subdivided into several different areas. Part of the loss, area a, is a transfer from consumer surplus to producer surplus. Although the loss makes consumers worse off, it makes producers better off by the same amount. Therefore, the nation as a whole is neither better nor worse off unless it can be established that giving the resources to producers somehow benefits or harms national welfare. This part of the lost consumer surplus is an income distribution effect of the tariff, since it rearranges national income by transferring resources from one group (consumers) to another group (producers).

Another income distribution effect of the tariff is represented by area c. Note that the height of this area is equal to the tariff, and the width is the amount of imports after the tariff is imposed. Therefore, this part of lost consumer surplus is equal to (tariff) × (imports), which is the amount of revenue collected by the government when it enacts the tariff. In this case, the income distribution effect is a transfer from consumers to the government. Again, it is assumed that there is no net effect on national welfare since the loss by consumers is exactly matched by the gain of government. As long as this transfer does not change national welfare, there is no net effect.

The two remaining areas of lost consumer surplus are b and d. Both represent net national losses, and both involve a misallocation of resources. Consider area d first. Along the demand curve between Q_2^* and Q_2, there are consumers that value the good above the cost of purchasing it at the world price. As a result of the tariff, however, they have been squeezed out of the market and are not willing or able to pay price P_t. The fact that consumers value the good above the cost of obtaining it in the world market but cannot purchase it is a net loss to the nation. Economists refer to the destruction of value that is not compensated by a gain somewhere else as a **deadweight loss**. Area d is this type of loss.

The final area to consider is b. Along the domestic supply curve between Q_1 and Q_1^*, output is increased at existing plants. Given that the supply curve slopes upward, firms can only increase their output if the price is allowed to rise. In other words, in order to obtain the additional output, domestic producers must be able to charge a higher price that will cover their rising costs for each additional unit. At the pre-tariff price of P_w, the total cost of imports $Q_1 Q_1^*$ would have been the price times the quantity, or $(P_w) \times (Q_1 Q_1^*)$. The cost of producing the same goods at home is equal to the cost of the imports plus area b. In other words, the triangle b is the additional cost to the nation when it tries to make the extra output $Q_1 Q_1^*$ at home instead of buying it in the world market at price P_w. Area b is a resource misallocation and a net loss to the nation because the same goods $(Q_1 Q_1^*)$ could have been acquired without giving up this amount. Area b is another deadweight loss, sometimes referred to as an **efficiency loss** because it occurs on the production side.

We can summarize the net effect of the tariff on the nation's welfare by subtracting the gains of producers and government from the losses of consumers: $(a + b + c + d - a - c) = b + d$. The two triangular areas are losses for which there are no compensating gains; therefore, they represent real losses to the nation as a whole. Table 6.1 on page 126 summarizes the effects of tariffs that we have noted.

CASE STUDY

A Comparison of Tariff Rates

The Doha Development Agenda of the World Trade Organization (WTO) is focused on the trade problems of developing countries. One impetus for the start of the Doha negotiations, and a factor behind the emphasis on economic development issues, is the complaint by many developing countries that they did not derive sufficient benefits from the Uruguay Round of trade negotiations that concluded in 1993. At issue for many developing countries are the levels of tariffs and other industrial country barriers that block access to agriculture, clothing, and textile markets. These product lines tend to be areas where developing countries have comparative advantage, particularly in cases where climate is a factor or where production uses abundant labor but requires little capital.

For their part, many industrial countries, the World Bank, and the WTO have argued that a major part of the problem faced by developing countries is the relatively high level of protection among developing countries themselves. High tariffs limit their ability to sell into each other's markets—and consequently their ability to follow their comparative advantage.

Figure 6.4 shows trends and levels of tariff rates in three groups of countries that are arranged according to their income levels. In 2007 U.S. dollars, low-income countries have per capita income levels below $936, middle income ranges from $936 to $11,455, and high income is anything above the middle group.

Because it is difficult to gather information on tariff rates for a large number of countries, we must interpret the data in Figure 6.4 with caution. The year-to-year data in each group of countries varies in the number of countries included in the group average. Furthermore, tariffs are only one form of protection, as we will see later in this chapter.

Despite the data limitations, two notable patterns are visible in Figure 6.4 and are widely accepted as qualitatively accurate. First, the higher a country's income, the lower its tariffs are likely to be. There are exceptions, of course, and one can point to low- and middle-income countries with low tariffs (for example, Botswana, Chile, and Turkey) and high-income countries with relatively high tariffs (Bermuda and Korea), but in general, low income implies relatively higher

FIGURE 6.4 **Average Tariff Rates, 1986–2007**

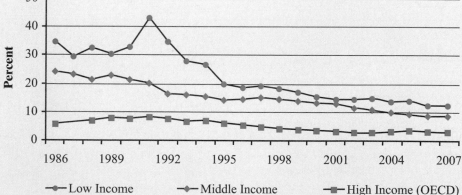

Tariff rates in high-income countries tend to be lower, and since the mid-1980s, tariff rates in nearly all countries have fallen.

Source: World Bank, Data on Trade and Import Barriers, "Trends in average applied tariff rates in developing and industrial countries." http://go.worldbank.org/LGOXFTV550

tariffs and high income implies the opposite. Second, tariffs have come down over time. In each of the three groups mentioned, the average tariff fell by about 50 percent between 1986 and 2003.

Why then, if trade is beneficial for growth, do low-income countries tend to have higher tariff rates? Although the complete answer varies by country circumstances, one of the most important reasons is that tariffs are a relatively easy tax to administer and often form an important part of government revenue. Taxes on income, sales, and property require more complex accounting systems and formal markets through which a large share of economic activity passes. In countries with large informal markets, where sales of goods and services are not recorded, it is difficult to apply many kinds of taxes. In addition, taxes on income and property run into powerful interest groups that have the power to prevent the creation or payment of taxes. Consequently, tariff revenue is an important source of operating revenue for governments in many developing countries.

Other Potential Costs

These effects of tariffs are the ones that are most predictable and quantifiable. In Chapter 7 there are some actual estimates of the production and income distribution effects of tariffs and quotas for a number of industries in the United States and Japan. These are not the only effects of tariffs, however—three others should be noted: the effects if trading partners retaliate, the impact of protection on domestic innovation and productivity, and the incentive for firms to engage in

TABLE 6.1	Economic Effects of the Tariff in Figure 6.3	
Variable	Free Trade	Post-tariff
Price to consumers	P_w	P_t
Domestic consumption	Q_2	Q_2^*
Domestic production	Q_1	Q_1^*
Imports	$Q_1 Q_2$	$Q_1^* Q_2^*$
Consumer surplus	$a + b + c + d + e + f$	$e + f$
Producer surplus	g	$g + a$
Government revenue	0	c
Deadweight consumption loss	0	d
Deadweight production (efficiency) loss	0	b

Tariffs reallocate income from consumers to producers and government. They also create deadweight losses, one on the consumption side and one on the production side.

rent-seeking behavior. Each of these effects broadens our focus to a consideration of more than the directly affected industry.

Retaliation   Retaliation can add to the net loss of a tariff by hurting the export markets of other industries. For example, in 1995 the United States imposed a tariff on European (mainly Italian) pasta because of some trade practices that the United States felt discriminated against its pasta manufacturers. In return, the European Community retaliated by imposing tariffs on U.S. manufacturers of vegetable oils — corn, soybean, safflower, and other cooking oils. The cost of the U.S.-imposed tariff not only affected U.S. consumers of Italian pasta who were forced to pay higher prices, but also affected workers and owners of capital in the U.S. vegetable oil industry. In essence, in addition to the deadweight losses brought on by the tariff, the vegetable oil industry lost export markets. A further problem is that retaliation can quickly escalate. For example, in the 1930s, many depressed nations reduced imports through tariffs. The result was that they gained jobs in industries that competed with imports but lost jobs in industries that produced exports. In the end, no jobs were gained, trade declined, and everyone had a lower standard of living.

Innovation   A costly effect of tariffs is that they isolate domestic firms from foreign competition and reduce the incentive to introduce new products or upgrade the quality and features of existing ones. It is difficult to measure this effect, but as Chapter 1 described, there are several types of evidence showing that open economies grow faster than closed ones.

Rent Seeking   Hypothetically, tariffs could stimulate product improvement if domestic producers know that the tariffs are temporary and if they believe they will be removed. The problem is that firms with tariff protection can hire lobbyists and work to keep the protection in place. Economists use the term rent seeking to describe this type of behavior. Rent seeking is any activity that uses resources to try to capture more income without actually producing a good or service. If it is easier to lobby a government for protection than it is to become more competitive, then firms will use rent seeking tactics. If, on the contrary, lobbying is not likely to succeed in gaining protection, then firms are less likely to engage in that particular form of rent seeking. For this reason, political systems that do not easily provide protective tariffs are much more likely to avoid one source of wasted resources.

The Large Country Case

Economists distinguish between large and small countries when it comes to tariff analysis. As a practical matter there may not be much difference between the two, but in theory it is possible for large countries to actually improve their national welfare with a tariff as long as their trading partners do not retaliate. In economic terms, a large country is one that imports enough of a particular product so that if it imposes a tariff, the exporting country will reduce its price in order to keep some of the market it might otherwise lose.

An example of the **large country case** tariff is shown in Figure 6.5. Suppose that the United States, a large country, imposes a tariff of size t on its imports of

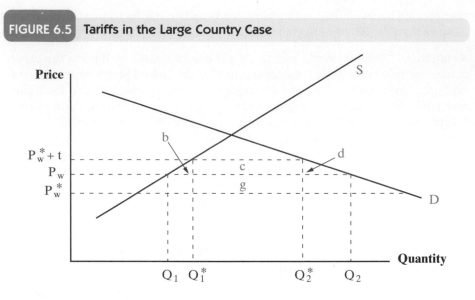

FIGURE 6.5   **Tariffs in the Large Country Case**

A tariff in a large country reduces demand so much that foreign producers cut their prices.

oil. The fall in U.S. demand brought on by the tariff causes P_w, the world price, to fall to P_w^*, offsetting some or all of the deadweight loss from the tariff.

Looking more closely at Figure 6.5, we can compare the large and small country cases. The situation before the tariff is the same as the one shown in Figure 6.3. The main difference between the two cases stems from the fact that foreign suppliers cut the price to P_w^* after the tariff is levied. Consequently, less additional domestic production occurs, and fewer consumers are squeezed out of the market. In other words, areas b and d in Figure 6.5 are smaller than they would be in the small country case where there is no price drop. A smaller deadweight loss is not the only effect, however. In Figure 6.5, area g represents tariff revenue, which together with area c is the total tariff revenue collected. However, compared to the pre-tariff situation, area g is a net gain to the importing nation. Pre-tariff, area g was part of the money paid for imports. After the tariff, and due to the price decline, it is part of the revenue collected by the government and, hence, stays within the nation.

As long as $g > b + d$, a large country can improve its welfare by imposing a tariff. This outcome, however, assumes that there is no retaliation, rent seeking, or harmful effects on innovation.

Effective versus Nominal Rates of Protection

One of the ironies of tariff protection is that often it is not what it seems. In fact, the amount of protection given to any one product depends not only on the tariff rate but also on whether there are tariffs on the inputs used to produce it. Suppose, for example, that the United States decided to impose a tariff on imports of laptop computers. If American-made laptops have foreign parts in them, then the amount of protection they receive from a U.S. tariff depends also on whether there are tariffs on their imported inputs. It is conceivable, in other words, that the protection given by a tariff on laptops could be completely undone by forcing laptop manufacturers to pay tariffs on their imported inputs.

Economists distinguish between the **effective rate of protection** and the **nominal rate of protection**. The nominal rate is what we have discussed so far in this chapter—the rate that is levied on a given product. The effective rate of protection takes into account the nominal rate and any tariffs on intermediate inputs. Consequently, it gives a clearer picture of the overall amount of protection that any given product receives. The effective rate of protection is related to the concept of value added. Value added is the price of a good minus the costs of the intermediate goods used to produce it. **Value added** measures the contributions of capital and labor at a given stage of production. The effective rate of protection is defined as follows:

$$(VA^* - VA)/VA$$

where VA is the amount of domestic value added under free trade, and VA* is the amount of domestic value added after taking into account all tariffs, both on final goods and intermediate inputs.

Consider the example shown in Table 6.2. Suppose that laptop computers sell for $1,000, and foreign producers are willing to sell to the United States all it wants at that price. In order to make a laptop, American manufacturers must import $600 worth of parts, so that a domestic laptop actually has $400 of value added in the United States ($1,000 − $600 = $400). If the United States imposes a 20 percent tariff, then the price rises to $1,200. Value added in the United States is now $600 ($1,200 − $600), and the effective rate of protection is 50 percent (($600 − $400) / $400). That is, a 20 percent tariff provides 50 percent protection! This happens because a large share of the value of the final product is produced elsewhere, so all of the domestic protection falls on the share produced in the United States.

Now consider what happens if the United States decides also to protect domestic component manufacturers and levies a large tariff on intermediate inputs. If the tariff on foreign parts is 50 percent, then the cost of intermediate inputs rises from $600 to $900. With a 20 percent tariff on the value of the final product, the price of imports stays at $1,200, which is the price American laptop makers must meet. Value added with the tariff on intermediate inputs is $300 ($1,200−$900), and the effective rate of protection is now −25 percent (($300 − $400) / $400). That is, even with a 20 percent tariff on foreign laptops, American laptop makers receive *negative* protection. The tariff on the final product is more than offset by the tariffs on the intermediate products, so that the overall situation leaves producers more exposed to foreign competition than if there were no tariffs levied at all.

Negative rates of effective protection are not uncommon. Part of the reason stems from the fact that tariffs are enacted in a piecemeal fashion over long periods

TABLE 6.2	Nominal and Effective Rates of Protection		
Variable	No Tariff	A 20% Tariff on the Final Product	A 20% Tariff Plus a 50% Tariff on Imported Inputs
Price of a laptop computer	$1,000	$1,200	$1,200
Value of foreign inputs	$600	$600	$900
Domestic value added	$400	$600	$300
Effective rate of protection	0	50%	−25%

Effective rates of protection are higher than nominal rates if intermediate inputs are imported tariff free. If intermediate inputs are subject to tariffs, it reduces the effective rate of protection and can even turn it negative.

and are not constructed in a planned and coherent way. Pressures from domestic lobbyists, considerations of strategic interests, and numerous other forces go into the shaping of national tariff systems. Consequently, it is not surprising to find contradictory tariff policies where newer tariffs undo the effects of older ones.

This discussion should add a note of caution to attempts to determine exactly which industries are protected. Clearly, the notion of effective rates of protection is more relevant than nominal rates. With tariff rates, what you see may not always be what you get.

CASE STUDY

The Uruguay and Doha Rounds

The Uruguay Round negotiations concluded in 1993 after seven years of negotiations. They took three years longer than planned, and included one complete breakdown in the talks. The agreement was signed in 1993, ratified by most of its 123 participating countries in 1994, and implemented in 1995.

Table 6.3 summarizes the four main categories of negotiations. Trade barriers were reduced through several mechanisms, including tariff reductions, clarification of the rules on subsidies, a number of new areas of agreement, and institutional reforms within the framework of the existing General Agreement on Tariffs and Trade (GATT). Most notably, the Uruguay Round created the WTO as a body to oversee the implementation and further refinement of the various agreements.

One of the biggest potential changes in world trade patterns coming out of the Uruguay Round was the negotiation of a separate Agreement on Textiles and Clothing (ATC). Until 1994, textiles and clothing had a separate international agreement, called the Multi-Fiber Arrangement, which was a system of quotas and tariffs. Under the ATC, textiles and clothing were integrated into the WTO

TABLE 6.3	The Uruguay Round
Category	**Results**
Tariffs	■ Most industrial product tariffs cut by 40 percent ■ Conversion of some agricultural quotas to tariffs
Subsidies	■ Subsidies defined ■ Classifies prohibited and actionable subsidies
New agreements	■ Agreement on Textiles and Clothing ■ Trade Related Aspects of Intellectual Property Rights ■ Trade Related Investment Measures ■ General Agreement on Services
Institutional	■ Creates the World Trade Organization reorganization ■ Refines the dispute settlement process ■ Implements periodic trade policy reviews

The Uruguay Round included far more than tariff cuts.

system, with a complete phase-out of all quotas by 2005, and with allowance for the application of temporary rates of protection in the event of a sudden surge in imports. Subsequently, however, the European Union (EU) and the United States have both negotiated side agreements with China to limit the volume of Chinese textile and clothing exports.

Other notable accomplishments of the Uruguay Round were separate agreements on trade in services—General Agreement on Trade in Services (GATS), an agreement on intellectual property enforcement—Trade Related Aspects of Intellectual Property Rights (TRIPS), and an agreement on investment—Trade Related Investment Measures (TRIMS). The Uruguay Round also reorganized the GATT into an organization called the WTO. The WTO takes the lead in multilateral trade negotiations, administers all of the agreements (ATC, GATS, TRIPS, TRIMS, GATT), and provides a more efficient dispute settlement process. In addition, the WTO conducts periodic reviews of individual country trade policies, which it makes available (with much more information) on its Web site at http://www.wto.org.

The Doha Round was launched in 2001 in Doha, Qatar. The goal was to reach an agreement by the end of 2005, but that proved impossible, and in July 2006, the talks were suspended. Not surprisingly, the areas where talks broke down were trade barriers and subsidies in agriculture and textiles and apparel.

The initial Doha Declaration included twenty-one subjects for negotiation, several of which were dropped along the way. Doha is called the Doha Development Round because the needs of developing countries were given greater visibility. For example, a key issue is the problem of many developing countries in implementing Uruguay Round commitments. In addition, access to life-saving medicines under the terms of the TRIPS agreement has been a problem, and the important developing country sectors of agriculture and textiles and apparel continue to face significant barriers to entering developed country markets.

Agriculture and agriculture support policies have been the most significant obstacle to progress in the Doha Round talks. High-income countries and regions such as the EU, the United States, and Japan find it difficult to agree to a reduction in agricultural support policies, or to open their markets to foreign producers. Consequently, issues of agricultural subsidies and market access have become stumbling blocks to a new agreement. At the same time, the United States and the EU are pushing developing countries to further reduce their trade barriers for manufactured items. At this point in time it is impossible to predict the outcome of the talks, or even if the Doha Round will be completed.

Analysis of Quotas

The economic analysis of quotas is nearly identical to that of tariffs. Quotas are quantitative restrictions that specify a limit on the quantity of imports rather than a tax. The net result is much the same: tariffs and quotas lead to a reduction in imports, a fall in total domestic consumption, and an increase in domestic production. The main difference between quotas and tariffs is that quotas that are not followed up with additional policy actions do not generate tariff revenue for the government. The lost tariff revenue can end up in the hands of foreign producers as they raise their prices to match demand to supply. Hence, the net loss from quotas can exceed that from tariffs.

In terms of Figure 6.3, consumers still lose area a + b + c + d, but the government does not collect area c as a tax. (We will examine what happens to area c, but try to reason it out for yourself first.)

Types of Quotas

The most transparent type of quota is an outright limitation on the quantity of imports. Limitations are sometimes specified in terms of the quantity of a product coming from a particular country, and at other times there is an overall limit set without regard to which country supplies the product. For example, in the apparel sector, until 2005 the United States set quotas for imports of each type of garment (men's suits, boys' shirts, socks, and so on). The quota for each good was further divided by country, so, for example, Hong Kong and Haiti had different limits on each type of apparel that they could export to the United States.

Another type of quota is an import licensing requirement. The United States uses this form infrequently, but a number of other nations have relied on these quotas for the bulk of their protection. For example, until 1989 they were the main form of protection in Mexico. As the name implies, import licensing requirements force importers to obtain government licenses for their imports. By regulating the number of licenses granted and the quantity permitted under each license, import licenses are essentially the same as quotas. They are less transparent than a quota because governments usually do not publish information on the total allowable quantity of imports, and foreign firms are left in the dark about the specific limits to their exports.

A third form of quota, and the one that has been common in U.S. commercial policy, is the **voluntary export restraint (VER)**, also known as the *voluntary restraint agreement* (VRA). Under a VER, the exporting country "voluntarily" agrees to limit its exports for some period. The agreement usually occurs after a series of negotiations in which the exporter may be threatened with much more severe restrictions if they do not agree to limit exports in a specific market. Given that there is usually more than a hint of coercion, it may be a misnomer to call these restrictions "voluntary."

VERs were popular forms of protection in the 1970s and 1980s, but new limits on their use were implemented under the Uruguay Round agreement. In 2005, however, both the United States and the EU negotiated export restraints in textiles and apparel with China.

The Effect on the Profits of Foreign Producers

The main difference between tariffs and quotas is that there is no government revenue from quotas. In place of tariff revenue, there are greater profits for foreign producers, called **quota rents**.

In Figure 6.6, the world price is set at P_w, domestic production is Q_1, and imports are Q_1Q_2. Suppose that the government decides to set a quota on imports of quantity $Q_1Q_2^*$. At price P_w, demand exceeds supply, which is equal to

FIGURE 6.6 **Analysis of a Quota: 1**

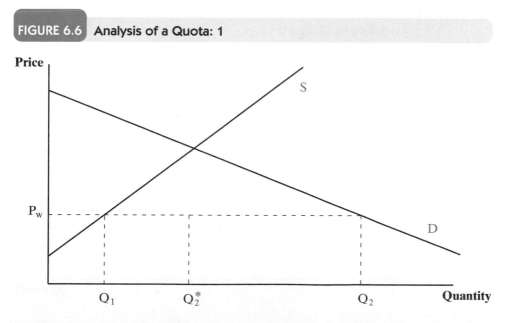

A quota restricts imports to line segment $Q_1Q_2^*$ and creates excess demand equal to Q^*Q_2.

Q_1 domestic plus $Q_1Q_2^*$ imports. Consequently, the price rises until supply equals demand when the gap between the domestic supply curve and the domestic demand curve is equal to $Q_1Q_2^*$. This is illustrated in Figure 6.7, where domestic supply is shown as having grown to Q_1^*, and the domestic price is P_q, which is above P_w. $Q_1^*Q_2^*$ is equal to $Q_1Q_2^*$ in Figure 6.6.

Figure 6.7 looks the same as Figure 6.3, which shows a tariff in a small country case, because they have nearly identical effects on production, consumption, and prices paid by consumers. Indeed, for any given quota there is some tariff that will accomplish the identical import restriction. One difference stands out, however. In the tariff case, the government earned revenue from imports—area c in Figures 6.3 and 6.7. In the quota case, no revenue is earned unless the government auctions the quota. Instead, area c represents the extra profits of foreign producers due to the higher prices.

A second important difference between tariffs and quotas relates to their effect on producer surplus over time, as demand for the good increases. If a quota remains fixed, an increase in consumer demand also increases the price paid by consumers and the quantity of producer surplus garnered by domestic firms. In contrast, an increase in consumer demand for an item that has an import tariff increases the quantity of imports and leaves the price intact. This assumes that the country is relatively small and the increase in its demand does not alter the world (pre-tariff) price. Given this difference, it is not surprising that domestic firms prefer quotas over tariffs as a form of protection for their industry.

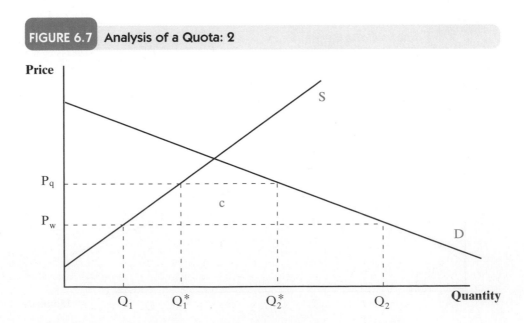

FIGURE 6.7 **Analysis of a Quota: 2**

The quota generates extra revenue for foreign producers in area c.

Two circumstances can mitigate or limit the ability of foreign suppliers to earn extra profits. First, if there is a large number of foreign suppliers, then competitive conditions may prevent them from raising their prices. And second, a clever government can extract the extra profits from foreign producers and domestic importers through the implementation of an auction for import licenses.

Suppose that the country imposing the quota decides to auction off the right to import. How much would a domestic importer be willing to pay? In Figures 6.6 and 6.7, foreign suppliers are willing to sell the amount of the quota ($Q_1Q_2^*$ in Figure 6.6, or $Q_1^*Q_2^*$ in Figure 6.7) at price P_w. A domestic importer, recognizing that he or she can sell the good at price P_q, should be willing to pay an amount equal to something slightly less than the difference P_q minus P_w. In other words, he or she pays P_w for the good that sells for P_q. If he or she pays anything less than $P_q - P_w$ for the right to sell in the market with the quota, he or she makes a profit. In equilibrium, an auction market should lead to bids for the right to sell that are more or less equal to the projected price increase. With an auction market, then, the government can potentially collect the same revenue with a quota that it would with a tariff. Of course, administrative costs of a quota may be higher, since the government must implement its auction market.

Hidden Forms of Protection

While outright quantitative restrictions, import licensing requirements, and VERs are all forms of quotas, there are numerous other forms of protection that function the same as quotas. Any kind of trade barrier that reduces imports without imposing a tax functions more or less like a quota. Therefore, economists divide the different forms of protection into two main categories: tariffs and **nontariff barriers (NTBs)**. Nontariff barriers can be subdivided into quotas and **nontariff measures**. Nontariff measures are often nontransparent, or hidden, in that they are not presented as trade barriers or forms of protection even though they serve that purpose.

Nontariff measures cover a wide variety of formats and economic activities. In many cases, it is difficult to decide if they are directly intended as trade-related measures, or if they exist for some other purpose, but have impacts on trade flows. They include excessively complicated customs procedures, environmental and consumer health and safety precautions, technical standards, government procurement rules, limits imposed by state trading companies, and others. In general, nontariff measures include any regulatory or policy rule other than tariffs and quotas that limits imports. Often, it is difficult for nonspecialists to determine whether a nontariff measure is imposed in order to protect an industry, or out of some other concern. For example, the United States and the EU have a long-running disagreement over the EU's prohibition on imports of beef and pork from livestock that is fed growth hormones. The EU claims that this is to protect the health of its consumers, while the United States argues that there is no scientific evidence to support the ban. The WTO agrees with the United States, but the EU insists that the meat has long-run health effects. Does the EU continue to ban imports in order to protect its beef and pork producers, or is it simply exercising a reasonable level of caution?

While there is no consensus about the dollar value of economic losses due to nontariff measures, there is a consensus among economists that the world economy would be better off if they were reduced. Research indicates that benefits would accrue through the lowering of prices for many goods, increases in export and import volumes, increases in production levels, and overall economic welfare. In this respect, they are not much different from tariffs or quotas. They are generally much more difficult to eliminate, however, as they are embedded more deeply in national economic policies.

CASE STUDY

Intellectual Property Rights and Trade

Intellectual property is usually divided into copyrights and related rights for literary and artistic work, and industrial property rights for trademarks, patents, industrial designs, geographical indications, and the layout of integrated circuits. The rules for respecting **intellectual property rights** as they relate to trade were negotiated during the Uruguay Round (1986–1994), and culminated in the **Trade Related Aspects Intellectual Property Rights (TRIPS)** agreement.

The growth of world trade over the last half of the twentieth century led to a greater awareness of the importance of intellectual property. More and more, traded goods and services incorporated specialized knowledge and unique ideas. Pharmaceuticals, computer hardware, telecommunications equipment, and other high technology products are valuable because of the innovation and research they incorporate, while software, movies, music, and other artistic expressions are valued for their creativity. The protection given to creators and innovators varied greatly until standardization began with the signing of the TRIPS agreement.

The lack of intellectual property protection is viewed as a nontariff measure since the failure or inability to protect intellectual property restricts trade flows. Exporters are reluctant to sell products into a market if they know that their ideas or brands will be stolen and copied by local producers. Hence, there were strong pressures by developed countries to reach an agreement on enforcement of protections for intellectual property. Since the implementation of the Uruguay Round in 1995, there have been twenty-four intellectual property complaints settled by the WTO, most having to do with patents, and a large share of those related to pharmaceuticals.

It is probably impossible to prevent copyright infringements that happen through informal networks of families and friends. For example, friends copying each other's music on their iPods or sharing their copy of Microsoft Office cannot easily be stopped when it is done outside a formal market. On the other hand, many countries have very large and very visible markets where fake goods with counterfeit trademarks and illegal copies of DVDs and software are sold. Beijing's famous Silk Market is an example that attracted a lot of attention. In

2005, as part of its commitment to fulfill its WTO obligations, Chinese courts imposed fines on the landlord of the market and began the process of eliminating fake goods, many of which had counterfeit labels from European luxury brands. Furthermore, intellectual property violations in the industrial arena (for example, through copying patented technologies) involves billions of dollars in losses.

The fundamental economic rationale for the TRIPS agreement is that by protecting innovation it gives a financial incentive to firms and individuals to do research and to continue to innovate. Nevertheless, the TRIPS agreement is not uniformly seen as a positive step for world prosperity. Among others, Nobel Laureate Joseph Stiglitz has criticized it for the costs it has imposed on China, Mexico, and other developing countries that must devote scarce resources to its implementation. Mexico, he argues, has spent over $50 million in its implementation. Also, it is not empirically well established that the benefits of innovation outweigh the costs of access, particularly for developing countries. This is particularly true for developing countries that find their access to new technologies curtailed when they must pay royalties and other fees.

Pharmaceuticals are a case in point. With the AIDS crisis in full force in a number of countries, access to anti-AIDS drugs is critical. If patent enforcement under the TRIPS agreement prevents the production of inexpensive copies, then it is harmful to world prosperity. Although a number of exceptions were written into the agreement in order to allow access to life-saving medicines and other critical technologies, it is difficult for many developing countries to take advantage of the exceptions because they lack the technical know-how to make generic varieties of expensive and sophisticated drugs.

In the end, many countries simply lack the resources to fully implement the TRIPS agreement. Nevertheless, it remains an area of active interest, particularly by rich developed country markets with large numbers of patents, copyrights, and trademarks to protect.

Summary

- Tariffs increase domestic production and employment at the cost of greater inefficiency and higher prices. Production and distribution effects are measured by estimating the changes in producer surplus and consumer surplus.

- In addition to short-run welfare and efficiency effects, tariffs have long-run costs of increased rent seeking, slower innovation, and the loss of export markets through the retaliation of trading partners.

- In theory, a large country can improve its welfare with tariffs. In general, welfare-improving tariffs tend to be small, and they only improve welfare if there is no retaliation by supplying nations and no external costs such as increased rent seeking.

- Economists distinguish between nominal and effective rates of protection. The effective rate is the difference in domestic value added with and without tariffs, expressed in percentage terms.

- Quotas have similar effects as tariffs, although the overall national losses are greater due to the transfer of quota rents to foreign producers. Auction markets, in which governments auction the right to import an item under a quota, can reduce the amount of quota rents and, in the limit, provide the same revenue as an equivalent tariff.

- Administratively, quotas take many forms. They can be well-specified quantitative restrictions on imports, negotiated limits on a trading partner's exports, or requirements to obtain a license to import.

- Nontariff measures include a wide variety of regulations and policies that effectively reduce the volume of international trade. They often act as hidden forms of protection, and are commonly embedded deeply in a country's rules and institutions. Together with quotas, they make up nontariff barriers to trade.

Vocabulary

consumer surplus

deadweight loss

effective rate of protection

efficiency loss

intellectual property rights

large country case

nominal rate of protection

nontariff barrier (NTB)

nontariff measure

nontransparent

producer surplus

quota rents

Trade Related Aspects Intellectual Property Rights (TRIPS)

transparent

value added

voluntary export restraint (VER)

Study Questions

1. Graph the supply and demand of a good that is produced domestically and imported. Assume that the country is not large enough to affect the world price. Illustrate the effects that a tariff on imports has. Discuss the following:

    a. Income distribution effects

    b. Resource allocation effects

    c. Domestic production and consumption effects

    d. Government revenue effects

    e. Price of the good effects

2. Suppose the world price for a good is 40 and the domestic demand-and-supply curves are given by the following equations:

Demand: $P = 80 - 2Q$

Supply: $P = 5 + 3Q$

    a. How much is consumed?

    b. How much is produced at home?

    c. What are the values of consumer and producer surplus?

    d. If a tariff of 10 percent is imposed, by how much do consumption and domestic production change?

    e. What is the change in consumer and producer surplus?

    f. How much revenue does the government earn from the tariff?

    g. What is the net national cost of the tariff?

3. Under what conditions may a tariff actually make a country better off?

4. In addition to the production and consumption side deadweight losses, what are some of the other potential costs of tariffs?

5. The Uruguay Round of the GATT began a process of phasing out the use of voluntary export restraints. Why did they come into widespread use in the 1980s? For example, given that VERs are a form of quotas, and that they create quota rents and a larger reduction in national welfare than a tariff, why did nations use them instead of tariffs?

6. The GATT strongly favors tariffs as a protective measure over quotas or other nontariff measures. It encourages new members to convert quotas to their tariff equivalents. One of the main reasons that tariffs are preferred is because they are more transparent, particularly by comparison to nontariff measures. Explain the idea of transparency, and how nontariff measures may be nontransparent.

7. Suppose that in the United States bikes are built from a combination of domestic and foreign parts.

    a. If a bike sells for $500 but requires $300 of imported parts, what is the domestic value added?

    b. If a 20 percent tariff is levied on bikes of the same quality and with the same features, how do the price and the domestic value added change? (Assume that the United States cannot cause the world price to change.)

    c. What is the effective rate of protection?

    d. If, in addition to the 20 percent tariff on the final good, a 20 percent tariff on imported parts is levied, what is the effective rate of protection for U.S. bike manufacturers?

Commercial Policy

Introduction: Commercial Policy and Jobs

An argument was made in Chapter 6 that tariffs and quotas lower national welfare by creating deadweight losses. In this chapter, we examine the dollar value of the effects of tariffs and quotas in the European Union (EU), Japan, and the United States. The overall level of tariffs and quotas in these three economic regions is about average for industrial economies. They are also fairly low, implying that the total deadweight loss imposed on each region is relatively minor. The purpose of this exercise, however, is to compare the costs and benefits of trade barriers. As we will see, even low trade barriers have a high ratio of costs to benefits, and should make us question the strategy of trying to gain jobs in this way.

After a look at the dollar costs of protection in three sectors of the EU, Japan, and the United States, we examine the most common reasons given for protecting specific industries. Again, the purpose is not to question the goals that nations set for themselves, but to look at the efficiency of tariffs and quotas in reaching them. Finally, the chapter ends with a discussion of the mechanisms used to provide protection.

Protection in the European Union, Japan, and the United States

Between the end of World War II and the early 1990s, tariffs around the world fell substantially. With the signing of the General Agreement on Tariffs and Trade (GATT) Uruguay Round agreement in 1994, the 123 founding members of the World Trade Organization (WTO) agreed to cut their rates by another 40 percent, and by 2002, average nominal rates were 3.9 percent in the United States, 3.3 percent in Japan, and 3.9 percent in the EU. A few industries have seen much smaller decreases in protection, however, and in nearly all of the leading industrial countries and regions, agriculture, clothing, and textiles remain heavily protected. As we saw in the last chapter, developing countries tend to have higher rates in general, and all countries have high levels of protection in particular industries that they deem "sensitive."

In addition to tariffs and quotas, many countries provide generous subsidies to some of their agricultural producers. Among high-income countries, this benefit is particularly prevalent in the EU, Japan, and the United States. Although these subsidies are not explicitly trade barriers, in effect they have the same import reducing effect as tariffs and quotas.

Direct Costs and Jobs Saved in Agriculture, Clothing, and Textiles

Very few countries apply tariffs uniformly across all industries. For example, prior to the complete adoption of the Uruguay Round's 40 percent reduction in tariffs, twenty-two protected sectors in the EU accounted for about one-half of the total costs of EU tariffs and quotas to consumers. Similarly, twenty-one sectors in the United States accounted for one-half of the lost consumer surplus, and in Japan, forty-seven sectors accounted for nearly all of the loss of consumer surplus.

Since the phase-in of the Uruguay Round tariff reductions, average tariffs have fallen 40 percent, but few sectors are average. In particular, three sectors have had much smaller changes in tariffs and quotas: agriculture, clothing, and textiles. In the United States, for example, World Bank data shows that while average tariffs fell by 40 percent, tariffs on agricultural goods fell by 12 percent and clothing and textiles by 14 percent each. In addition, all three sectors in the EU, Japan, and the United States have significant nontariff barriers applied to them, and agriculture is given large subsidies by all of the national governments.

Table 7.1 itemizes the impact of EU, Japanese, and U.S. tariffs and quotas in the three areas discussed. These are not the only products with trade barriers, but all three geographical areas have stiff protection for these sectors. Furthermore, Table 7.1 is based on the largest tariffs and quotas and does not include the cumulative effects of many smaller tariffs and nontariff barriers. Because a significant part of EU, Japanese, and U.S. production in these sectors exists only because of protective measures, trade in these goods has become the focus of an intense debate between developing countries and high-income countries. These tend to be lines of production where developing countries have significant comparative advantages but encounter high-trade barriers when they attempt to enter industrial country markets.

Column A of Table 7.1 shows the producer surplus gained at the expense of consumers, column B is tariff revenue, column C shows the quota rents that occur due to the increase in prices charged by foreign suppliers, and column D is the consumption and production side deadweight loss. Because many product lines in these three sectors have tariffs and quotas, all of the items show both tariff revenue generated (B) and quota rents (C) that mostly accrue to foreign producers. The final column, C + D, measures the net reduction in national welfare from the direct effects of the tariffs and quotas.

Table 7.1 also shows that in the EU and Japan, the largest national losses occur in agriculture, while in the United States, national losses in agriculture are relatively smaller, but in clothing they are much higher. European losses in agriculture are mostly efficiency losses that result from keeping relatively less efficient producers in operation, whereas in Japan they are efficiency losses plus

TABLE 7.1	EU, Japanese, and U.S. Protection in Three Sectors (Mid-1990s, Millions of US$)				
	Producer Surplus Gained	Tariff Revenue	Quota Rents	Deadweight Losses	National Welfare Loss
European Union	**A**	**B**	**C**	**D**	**C+D**
Agriculture	4,717	3,001	341	4,879	5,219
Clothing	1,464	1,450	2,239	1,461	3,161
Textiles	2,290	1,490	1,716	571	2,288
Japan					
Agriculture	43,192	1,085	6,906	7,186	14,093
Clothing	1,605	386	2,673	1,701	4,375
Textiles	772	275	142	14	156
United States					
Agriculture	1,775	176	646	350	996
Clothing	9,901	3,545	5,411	2,301	7,712
Textiles	1,749	632	713	181	894

Three sectors account for a large share of protectionism in the three countries and regions. These sectors support the proposition that older sectors tend to be the most protected, particularly in cases where a country has lost a substantial part of its comparative advantage.

Sources: Messerlin (2001) *Measuring the Costs of Protection in Europe*; Sazanami, Urata, and Kawai (1995) *Measuring the Costs of Protection in Japan*; Hufbauer and Elliott (1994) *Measuring the Costs of Protection in the United States*. Published in Washington, DC by Institute for International Economics.

large quota rents paid to foreign suppliers. That is, despite its protection for its farm sector, Japan is still one of the world's largest food importers. Similarly, the United States imports large quantities of clothing, and its commercial policy creates large net national losses from quotas.

Table 7.2 carries the analysis one step further. The first column of Table 7.2 is the total cost to consumers in the form of lost consumer surplus. It is equal to the sum of columns A, B, C, and D in Table 7.1. The second column shows estimates of the direct number of jobs saved by the tariffs and quotas, and the third column is the cost to consumers per job saved (column 1 divided by column 2). In each of the sectors and in all three countries, the cost per job saved exceeds $100,000 per year, often by a large amount. The least expensive jobs to save are in European agriculture, but given that average wages were around $17,000 per year in the mid-1990s, even those jobs look expensive to preserve by this means. In Japan and the United States agriculture is the most expensive, while in the EU jobs in textiles are most costly.

The purpose of this exercise is to illuminate the hidden costs of using tariffs and quotas to achieve employment objectives. It does not analyze whether societies are better off if they preserve employment in these sectors. That is, this

TABLE 7.2	Jobs Saved through Tariffs and Quotas		
	Cost to Consumers (Millions of US$)	Jobs Saved	Cost per Job Saved (US$)
European Union			
Agriculture	15,130	121,192	106,751
Clothing	7,735	39,383	167,928
Textiles	7,096	33,160	182,968
Japan			
Agriculture	58,058	76,600	762,000
Clothing	879	13,800	461,313
Textiles	166	2,700	445,864
United States			
Agriculture	2,947	6,053	486,866
Clothing	21,158	152,583	138,666
Textiles	3,275	16,203	202,123

Saving jobs with tariffs and quotas is grossly inefficient and has costs per job saved that are far greater than the average annual income of workers in the protected industry.

Sources: Messerlin (2001) *Measuring the Costs of Protection in Europe*; Sazanami, Urata, and Kawai (1995) *Measuring the Costs of Protection in Japan*; Hufbauer and Elliott (1994) *Measuring the Costs of Protection in the United States*. Published in Washington, DC by Institute for International Economics.

analysis is not useful for understanding the role of agriculture in national culture, or the desirability of preserving garment manufacturing. Rather, it only tells us about the costs of preserving employment when it is accomplished with tariffs and quotas. From this perspective, it shows how grossly inefficient commercial policy is at achieving the objective of job preservation. The analysis also points to the issues of concern in the Doha negotiations. Namely, it raises the question of whether trade barriers to protect these industries in high-income countries have the unintended consequence of increasing poverty in low-income countries.

Agriculture, clothing, and textiles were singled out because they tend to be the most highly protected sectors of industrial countries and because the problem of access to those markets has harmful effects on developing countries. The results shown in Table 7.1 and Table 7.2 are not unique in terms of the cost per job saved, however, and other sectors in all three regions have similar or worse performance when evaluated in those terms. For example, voluntary export restraints imposed by the United States on Japanese automobiles in the 1980s cost U.S. consumers well over $100,000 per job saved, and in the EU, the cost per job of its trade barriers was estimated at over €550,000 in the 1990s. Even when tariffs are relatively low, the cost per job saved tends to be high.

The Logic of Collective Action

Given that the costs to consumers are so high for each job saved, why do people tolerate tariffs and quotas? Ignorance is certainly the case for some goods, but for some tariffs and quotas, the costs have been relatively well publicized. For example, many people are aware that quotas on sugar imports cost each man, woman, and child in the United States between $5 and $10 per year. The costs are in the form of higher prices on candy bars, soft drinks, and other products containing sugar. Few of us work in the sugar industry, so the argument that our jobs depend on it is weak at best.

In a surprising way, however, we probably permit our tariffs and quotas because of a version of the jobs argument. The economist Mancur Olson studied this problem and similar ones and noticed two important points about tariffs and quotas. First, the costs of the policy are spread over a great many people. Second, the benefits are concentrated. For example, we all pay a little more for candy bars and soft drinks, but a few sugar producers reap large benefits from our restrictions on sugar imports. Olson found that in cases such as this, there is an asymmetry in the incentives to support and to oppose the policy. With trade protection, the benefits are concentrated in a single industry and, consequently, it pays for the industry to commit resources to obtaining or maintaining its protection. The industry will hire lobbyists and perhaps participate directly in the political process through running candidates or supporting friendly candidates. If people in the industry think their entire livelihood depends on their ability to limit foreign competition, they have a very large incentive to become involved in setting policy.

The costs of protection are nowhere near as concentrated as the benefits because they are spread over all consumers of a product. The $5 to $10 per year that sugar quotas cost each of us is hardly worth hiring a lobbyist or protesting in Washington. Thus, one side pushes hard to obtain or keep protection, and the other side is silent on the matter. Given this imbalance, an interesting question asks why there are not more trade barriers.

CASE STUDY

Agricultural Subsidies

Agricultural issues have long sparked conflict among the members of the WTO. Some cases have pitted high-income countries against each other, among them disputes between the United States and Japan over apples and EU-U.S. disputes over bananas. More recently, the WTO's Doha Development Agenda has tried to address agricultural issues that are central to relations between developing and industrial countries. In particular, three issues are on the table: tariffs and quotas (market access), export subsidies given by countries to encourage farm exports, and production subsidies granted directly to farmers.

Direct subsidies are viewed as harmful because they lead to overproduction, squeeze out imports, and in some cases result in the dumping of the surplus product

TABLE 7.3	Agricultural Subsidies, 2007	
	Agricultural Subsidies (Millions of US$)	As a Percent of Farm Receipts
Australia	1,827	6
Canada	7,001	18
European Union	134,318	26
Japan	35,230	45
United States	32,663	10

The EU provides the largest subsidies, both in absolute terms and as a share of GDP but Japanese farmers are more dependent on agricultural subsidies.

Source: OECD, Producer Support Estimate by Country. http://www.oecd.org/tad/support/psecse.

in foreign markets. The original GATT agreement included language on agriculture, but there were so many loopholes that it had little impact. Not until the Uruguay Round was finalized in 1993, nearly 50 years after the signing of the original GATT agreement, were significant changes made in the rules for agricultural trade. Many quotas were converted to tariffs, and industrial countries agreed to reduce their direct support for the farm sector by 20 percent. Indirect supports such as research and development and infrastructure construction were recognized as necessary, desirable, and permissible.

While direct-support payments were curtailed, the Uruguay Round left intact direct payments to farmers that theoretically do not increase production, are part of a country's environmental or regional development plan, or are intended to limit production. If you think these are a lot of loopholes, you are right. Consequently, the current round of trade negotiations, the Doha Development Agenda, has taken up the issue of agriculture again, and developing countries in particular are pushing to limit government practices that block their access to markets in high-income countries or that subsidize production by industrial countries.

Table 7.3 shows the range of direct-support payments to agricultural producers in many industrial nations. The twenty-seven members of the EU are grouped together because their trade and agricultural policies are formulated at the EU level, not at the national level. In terms of both absolute support and the percentage of its GDP that it transfers to farmers, the EU is the biggest subsidizer. Japan is close in percentage terms but is at about one-half the level in absolute dollar amounts. The United States is also a large subsidizer, and Canada is similar. Not all countries subsidize agriculture, however. Australia's supports are less than one-half the level of the United States as a share of GDP, and despite the lower support levels, it uses its comparative advantages to be among the top fifteen agricultural exporting countries in the world.

Why Nations Protect Their Industries

Countries use tariffs for a variety of reasons, not the least of which is the revenue they generate. In a developing country's economy, a large percentage of economic activity is unrecorded. Subsistence farmers sell their surplus in the town market, and repairmen and craftsmen take on jobs without leaving a paper trail of work orders or receipts. In this environment, income taxes and sales taxes are difficult if not impossible to impose. Tariffs, on the other hand, can be relatively easily collected by inspectors at the ports and border crossings. They simply have to value the goods coming in and levy a fee (the tariff) on the person transporting the goods. The United States is a case in point, as tariff revenues were the single greatest source of income for the U.S. government until well into the twentieth century.

In addition to the need for revenue, there are four broad categories of reasons that nations give for imposing trade barriers.

The Labor Argument

The labor argument is a perennial justification for trade barriers. It was used throughout the nineteenth century, and most recently, has been resurrected by many opponents of expanded trade agreements. The argument states that nations must protect their markets against imports from countries where wages are much lower because otherwise the advantage of lower wages will either wreck the domestic industry or force it to match the lower wages. For example, in the debate leading up to the ratification of NAFTA, opponents argued that Mexico would have an unfair advantage in trade with the United States because Mexican firms pay their workers a fraction (on average, about one-eighth) of the wages paid to American workers.

The labor argument fails to consider productivity differences. Mexican workers, for example, earn about one-eighth of the salary of U.S. workers because their productivity, on average, is about one-eighth of the level of U.S. workers. Mexico has lower productivity because the education and skill levels of its workforce are less than in the United States, Mexican workers have less capital at work than U.S. workers, and the infrastructure of the Mexican economy is not as developed as the infrastructure of the United States. As Mexican workers gain more skills and education, and as the capital available on the job and in the surrounding economy increases, their productivity will rise, and so will their wages.

The labor argument also fails to consider the issues raised at the beginning of this chapter, where we saw that tariffs and quotas are an expensive way to protect jobs. If the goal is an adequate number of jobs to reach full employment, then appropriate macroeconomic and labor market policies are better instruments. Monetary and fiscal policies (see Chapter 11) that maintain economic growth, and labor market policies that provide adjustment assistance to dislocated workers and incentives for employers to hire them are far less expensive than trade policy for this purpose. If the goal is to keep a particular sector alive, then direct subsidies to the producers are preferable because they do not have the distortions that result from forcing consumers out of the market.

The Infant Industry Argument

A much more sophisticated argument for protection is the **infant industry** argument. The argument is mainly associated with the tariff policies of developing nations that protect their "infant" industries against the competition of more mature firms in industrial countries. Nevertheless, industrial countries use this argument on occasion to justify protection in some high-technology cases (for example, Japanese skis). Two beliefs lie at the root of the infant industry argument. The first is that market forces will not support the development of a particular industry, usually because foreign competition is too well established, but also possibly because the industry is too risky. The second belief is that the industry in question has some spillover benefits, or positive externalities, that make the industry more valuable to the national economy than simply the wages and profits it might generate. Whenever there are spillover benefits, the market may not support the development of an industry to the optimum level. With positive externalities, many of the benefits of production are captured by other firms or individuals outside of the producing firm. Since the producers do not get the full benefit of their own production, they produce less than the amount that is most beneficial for society.

Positive externalities are usually argued to be in the form of linkages to other industries or of a technological nature. As an example of the linkage case, many nations have attempted to start their own steel industries because they assumed it would create a cheaper source of steel for other industries, such as cars. The problem with this argument is that it does not demonstrate that there is some inherent advantage in making something as opposed to buying it, or in other words, that the car industry will have a special advantage if it can buy steel from local producers. If the car industry is forced to buy locally at prices above world levels, protection on the domestic steel industry may actually harm the car industry. This is what happened to firms in Brazil when the government tried to start a domestic computer industry by keeping out foreign producers. The policy actually had negative linkage effects on Brazilian businesses because they had to pay higher prices for computers and got lower-quality machines in the bargain. Brazil would have been better off importing its computers, as it does now.

Technological externalities can happen when workers change jobs and take the skills they have learned to their new employment, or whenever an industry creates information or technology that is useful somewhere else in the economy. As a practical matter, however, it is difficult to know in advance when there will be technological spillovers, and, accordingly, it is difficult to judge which industries should be protected.

Even if technological externalities are present, it is not enough to establish the validity of the infant industry argument. Two more conditions must hold. First, the protection that is offered must be limited in time, and second, the protected industry must experience falling costs. The time limits on protection ensure that the industry does not become a permanent recipient of transfers from consumers, while the presence of falling costs ensures that the policy will eventually pay for itself and that the industry will become competitive.

The National Security Argument

Every nation protects some industries as a way to guard its national security. In trade terms, national security can be interpreted in the narrow sense of military capability or in a broader sense of cultural identity. The most obvious examples of national security in a narrow sense include weapons industries, and somewhat more broadly, strategic technologies. Some nations also include strategic minerals such as the exotic ores used in jet aircraft, but protection for the sake of making available specific resources is not an optimal policy. A better policy is to build stockpiles of the mineral by buying large quantities in peacetime when it is cheap.

A broader definition of national security includes the cultural industries—movies, television programming, music, print media, and theater. Some nations worry that if they allow completely free trade in the cultural industries, then the most commercially viable firms will dominate, and the cultural values of the home country will be obscured and forgotten. Since the United States has the strongest presence in much of the entertainment industry, the goal of protecting national cultural values is usually an argument in favor of protecting a nation's filmmaking, television programming, and music production against complete domination by its U.S. counterparts. For example, the precursor to the North American Free Trade Agreement, called the Canadian-United States Free Trade Agreement (signed in 1988), established the right of Canada to require its TV and radio stations to broadcast a certain proportion of Canadian produced programs. There are similar requirements in music, theater, and the print media. U.S. television and movie producers naturally opposed this limitation on free trade and demanded the right to sell an unlimited amount of U.S.-produced entertainment. They lost this argument, however, and they lost again when the Uruguay Round of the GATT was signed. It allows all nations to place similar restrictions on their film, television, and other cultural industries.

The issue of free trade in military and cultural industries inevitably involves noneconomic values and issues. How, for example, can we begin to assess the effects on Canadian culture and society of limitations on U.S. television programming? Given that many industries argue that their products are absolutely essential to maintaining military capability, how can we assess the strategic value of particular products or technologies? Economists tend to defer to the judgment of scientific and engineering experts on questions of strategic importance, pointing out that a less costly option is stockpiling the needed materials when possible. In the case of protection for cultural industries, economists can point out some of the trade-offs, but they cannot estimate the cultural benefits of, say, a nationally based film industry.

The Retaliation Argument

A final category of reasons given by nations to justify trade barriers is retaliation for unfair trade practices. When a country decides that another country's trade practices unfairly discriminate against it, a common response is to impose a trade barrier. Retaliatory tariffs and quotas can provide an incentive for negotiations, but they can also lead to escalating trade wars.

Economic analysis is of limited utility in understanding this situation, since the outcome depends on political processes that determine how nations respond to pressure, their willingness to negotiate, and the outcome of negotiations. There are three camps of economists on this issue. One camp argues that free trade is beneficial regardless of the actions of a country's trading partners. If other countries choose to protect their markets, this argument goes, then it lowers their standard of living, and we would be foolish to do the same by imposing trade barriers in retaliation. Another camp argues that since free trade is beneficial, it is in everyone's interest to see it followed as widely as possible. Therefore, if a tariff today will cause other nations to open their markets tomorrow, the world economy will benefit in the long run.

A third group argues that countries that have a closed market or that restrict market access by imposing barriers to trade have an unfair advantage, particularly in high-technology products. They have a domestic market all to themselves, and they can compete freely in other markets that are more open than their own. In cases where the size of the market is important, the ability to sell to a market larger (home plus foreign) than their competitor's may give the firms in the protected market a competitive advantage. If firms in the open market are forced out of business, then the technology, skills, and expertise that go with them will exist only in the firms from the country that adopted the strategy of protecting its market. To ensure that this scenario does not play out, and so that we do not lose critical technologies, some would argue that we should use the threat of retaliation to force open markets that are presently closed.

CASE STUDY

Traditional Knowledge and Intellectual Property

Traditional knowledge forms part of the cultural heritage of traditional societies and indigenous communities. It is often embedded in cultural practices and everyday activities as a part of a world view and cultural life, but it can also embody intellectual knowledge of plants, animals, and the natural world, which has been gathered over generations. Those who practice Chinese traditional medicine, traditional healers in indigenous cultures, small-scale farmers, and hunters and gatherers have knowledge of plants and animals that has commercial potential. When that knowledge is expropriated and used by outsiders without recognition of its origin, it is not only unfair to the originators of the knowledge but also has the potential to harm them.

For example, researchers in the United States asked for a patent on turmeric, which they showed to be effective in healing skin cuts and lesions. Turmeric is the bright yellow spice used in curries and other dishes, and has been used for over four thousand years in Indian traditional medicine. Nevertheless, Patent No. 5,401,504 was granted by the U.S. Patent Office to the University of Mississippi for its use as a healing agent. As a practical matter, the patent would probably have been unenforceable, but it might have imposed a legal requirement on traditional users to pay royalties. The Indian government protested, arguing that it was a part of their traditional knowledge base and that it had long been used as a healing agent in India. After they produced ancient Sanskrit texts describing its use, the patent was overturned.

Brazil and India are foremost among a group of tropical countries that are working to provide protection for their traditional knowledge and their biodiversity. One fear is that "bio-prospectors" will collect plant samples shown to them by traditional healers in indigenous communities, isolate the key compounds in their laboratories, patent a new pharmaceutical, and ignore the interests of the traditional community or the nation where they live.

Traditional healers in Samoa use the bark of the mamala tree for a variety of medicinal purposes, including combating hepatitis. Guided by traditional knowledge, researchers discovered that it was an effective agent for making prostratin, an anti-AIDS compound. This story appears to end well since revenue from the development of the drug is expected to be shared with the village and the families that assisted in its discovery, and for further AIDS research, but without aggressive enforcement and vigilance it is feared that traditional knowledge will not be recognized and respected.

In another example, new plant varieties are adapted from traditional ones and patented by a seed company. In the African nation of Mali, the Bela community uses a wild rice that is more resistant to blight and other crop-destroying diseases. Researchers from the University of California, Davis, were able to clone the gene responsible and use it to strengthen traditional varieties of rice. They patented this gene, which raises the question of the connection between the new, genetically modified rice with the blight-resistant gene, and the interests of the Bela people. In the end, a Genetic Resource Recognition Fund was created to pay for fellowships for agricultural students from Mali and other countries where the wild rice grows.

Given the potential stakes, both monetary and cultural, a number of international organizations take an active interest in these issues. Among the most visible are the World Intellectual Property Organization (WIPO), the International Union for the Protection of New Plant Varieties (UPOV), the Food and Agriculture Organization (FAO), the WTO, the United Nations Development Program (UNDP), the World Health Organization (WHO), and the United Nations Environmental Program (UNEP). There are many international agreements, but the issues are relatively new and it is an area of international law that will continue to evolve over time.

Source: World Intellectual Property Organization, *Intellectual Property and Traditional Knowledge*. No date. http://www.wipo.int/freepublications/en/tk/920/wipo_pub_920.pdf

The Politics of Protection in the United States

Although U.S. trade with the rest of the world has grown, political pressures to protect domestic industries have frequently been intense. Part of the reason stems from the fact that Congressional reforms removed some of the insulation from industry lobbyists that Congress enjoyed in the 1950s and 1960s. Another reason stems from the end of the Cold War and the lessening of U.S. willingness to sacrifice trade issues for the sake of maintaining close geopolitical alliances. A third reason is the rise of the export-oriented East Asian newly industrializing countries (NICs), including China, and the pressure they have put on a number of domestic U.S. industries. Finally, the growth of the U.S. trade deficit and the widespread fear in the 1980s that the United States had lost its competitive edge also contributed to a greater reluctance to open U.S. markets without reciprocity by other countries. More recently, the rapid increase of the U.S. trade deficit and the loss of manufacturing jobs since 2000 are conditions that are likely to bring back the competition fears of the 1980s. For each of these reasons, trade conflicts have intensified.

Protection in the United States is usually obtained through direct action by the president (for example, the Voluntary Export Restraints [VERs] on Japanese autos in the 1980s) or through one of the following different legal procedures:

- Countervailing duties
- Antidumping duties
- Escape clause relief
- Section 301 retaliation

In each case, a firm, an industry trade association, or a government agency may petition the federal government to initiate an investigation into foreign country or foreign firm practices.

Countervailing Duties

A **countervailing duty (CVD)** is a tariff that is granted to an industry that has been hurt by foreign country **subsidies** of its national firms. Since subsidies permit a firm to sell its goods at a lower price and still make a profit, an effect of subsidies is to make firms more competitive. The goal of a countervailing duty is to raise the price of the foreign good to a level high enough to countervail the effect of the subsidy. The idea is to level the playing field between domestic firms that receive no subsidies and foreign ones that do.

Countervailing duties are used less often than other forms of protection, such as antidumping duties. In the United States, there has been an average of four to five cases per year since 1985. Countervailing duties require a clear definition of a subsidy since they are intended to counteract the effects of subsidies. One of the benefits of the Uruguay Round is that it standardized the definition as a financial contribution by a government (national or local) or public agency that confers a benefit. Subsidies take on a variety of forms, including grants, low interest loans, preferential tax treatments, provision of goods or services for free or below cost, or any of a number of other financial benefits.

Antidumping Duties

An **antidumping duty (ADD)** is a tariff levied on an import that is selling at a price below the product's **fair value**. The determination of fair value introduces an element of subjectivity into the process of justifying an antidumping duty, as does the fact that the legal analysis and the economic analysis of dumping are not in agreement. Consequently, antidumping duties have become a source of significant trade tension between countries; it is not surprising that a number of countries would like to strengthen the WTO's rules regarding antidumping duties by making them harder to apply.

According to the rules of the WTO, **dumping** occurs when an exporter sells a product at a price below what it charges in its home market. It is not always possible to compare the home market and foreign market prices, however, and wholesalers, transportation costs, and other add-ons to the price may limit the usefulness of the comparison. Therefore, two other methods may be used to determine if a good is being dumped. Comparisons can be made with the price charged in third country markets, or to an estimate of the cost of production. Comparison to prices in another country is similar to the comparison between prices in the exporter's home market and the complaining country's market, and may be uninformative for the same reasons. Therefore, the WTO allows the third method whereby a country estimates the foreign firm's production costs and uses that measure to determine if dumping is occurring. In this case, an exporter does not need to sell below the cost of production to be found guilty of dumping. Dumping charges are supported if the foreign firm is not selling at a price that provides a normal rate of return on invested capital.

One final criterion must be met before antidumping duties are allowed. The country claiming dumping must also be able to show that the dumping has caused material injury to its firms. If dumping occurs, but there are no harmful effects on domestic firms, then antidumping duties are not allowed. This would happen if the dumping margin is too small to matter.

At their most basic level, antidumping duties are a tool of commercial policy that protects against predatory pricing by foreign firms. Selling below cost as a strategy to drive the competition out of business is widely perceived as unfair, and allowing it to happen can harm the economic interest of a country. This is particularly likely if it results in higher prices after the domestic producers have been driven out of the market. Since 1985, the United States has imposed an average of twenty-one new antidumping duties per year.

Problems arise, however, because the economic theory and the legal definition are not completely in agreement. First, in order for a firm to sell in a foreign market at a price that is below its cost of production, it must have market power at home that allows it to earn higher than normal profits so it can subsidize its foreign sales. If a firm is not earning above average profits somewhere, it cannot maintain a price somewhere else that is below its cost. Yet, when countries investigate a dumping complaint, market structure is rarely considered. This problem is compounded by the use of estimated production costs to determine dumping, since estimated values require some guesswork about technology and other inputs, and this creates a significant margin of error.

Second, within the scope of normal commercial operations, firms often sell below cost. The most obvious case is that of goods that are likely to spoil. A fresh fish exporter with a load sitting on a dock somewhere is likely to lower his or her price progressively as time passes. In this case, the cost of producing the shipment of fish represents sunk costs that have already been incurred, and the only option is to sell the goods for whatever is possible. Firms also sell selected items below cost as a technique for penetrating markets. This is similar to the behavior of large retail chains that offer some goods at an extremely low price in order to create a reputation as a value-oriented retailer. And finally, firms will go for extended periods selling at prices that do not cover the cost of their capital and other fixed costs as long as the costs of their variable inputs such as labor and materials are covered. Since capital costs such as interest on their loans have to be paid no matter what is produced, in the short run, the chief consideration is whether the price is high enough to cover labor costs and material input costs. In the long run, a firm that cannot sell at a high enough price to meet its capital costs will have to shut down, but in the short run, it continues to produce.

The increasing use of antidumping duties has generated a great deal of interest in defining their usage more carefully. As things now stand, there is a wide variation among countries in their application and their willingness to negotiate their usage. Some countries rarely apply them, and some trade agreements, such as the one between Canada and Chile, ban their usage except under exceptional circumstances. Other countries use them frequently—often it seems, as a politically expedient way to satisfy an important industry lobbying group.

In the United States, the procedure for firms to obtain protection requires that a petition be filed with the International Trade Administration (ITA) in the Department of Commerce. The ITA investigates whether dumping (or subsidization in the case of a petition for countervailing duties) has occurred. If its finding is positive (dumping has occurred), the case is turned over to the United States International Trade Commission (USITC), an independent regulatory commission. The USITC conducts an additional investigation to determine if substantial harm has been done to the domestic industry and if an antidumping or countervailing duty is warranted. The relative success of U.S. firms in proving that foreign companies are dumping has encouraged a growing number of antidumping petitions in recent years.

Escape Clause Relief

Escape clause relief is so named because it refers to a clause in the U.S. and GATT trade rules that permits an industry to escape the pressure of imports by temporarily imposing a tariff. Escape clause relief is a temporary tariff on imports in order to provide a period of adjustment to a domestic industry. It is initiated when an industry or firm petitions the USITC directly for relief from a sudden surge of imports. The burden of escape clause relief is on the firm; it must establish that it is been harmed by imports and not by some other factor, such as bad management decisions. In practice, it has become so difficult to obtain relief from import competition under this procedure that few cases are filed.

Section 301 and Special 301

Section 301 of the U.S. Trade Act of 1974 requires the president's chief trade negotiator, the United States Trade Representative (USTR), to take action against any nation that persistently engages in unfair trade practices. The action usually begins with a request for negotiations with the targeted country. The goal of the negotiations is to change the policies of countries that restrict U.S. commerce unreasonably or unjustifiably. Note that it is left to the United States to define unreasonable and unjustifiable restrictions on U.S. commerce.

The types of trade practices that the USTR is required to investigate are quite broad. Recent cases have included an investigation of China's management of its exchange rate, Ukraine's actions to enforce intellectual property rights, and the EU's lack of compliance with a WTO ruling against its blockage of imports of hormone-fed beef.

A similar program to Section 301 is known as **Special 301**. This part of U.S. trade law requires the USTR to monitor property rights enforcement around the globe. In 2005, the USTR surveyed ninety countries and identified fifty-two as lacking adequate enforcement or as denying market access to U.S. artists and industries that rely on intellectual property enforcement. Inclusion on this list means that the USTR has some concerns and will continue to monitor the situation.

CASE STUDY

Economic Sanctions

Economic sanctions are a form of trade restriction. Unlike tariffs and quotas, which affect imports alone, often sanctions are on exports as well as imports and may include financial components as well. Access to international credit through privately owned banks or international lending agencies may be limited or blocked, as may investment by domestic firms in the country singled out for sanctions. Examples of export prohibitions included the U.S. rule during the Cold War prohibiting computer sales by domestic firms to the Soviet Union, and current prohibitions on selling goods or services to Cuba and North Korea. The world community's boycott of investment in South Africa before the ending of apartheid is an example of an investment and trade sanction.

Economic sanctions go beyond simple trade or investment measures. In most cases they are used as one of several tactics aimed at achieving a broader policy objective—the ending of Soviet expansion or Iranian terrorism or South African apartheid. Another feature of sanctions is that they are often accompanied by additional measures, ranging from diplomatic pressure to military invasion.

The logical question to ask about sanctions is "Do they work?" In an important two-volume study of this question, three economists analyzed 120 episodes of economic sanctions throughout the world since World War I. Table 7.4 summarizes their findings. The economists found it useful to categorize the goals of sanctions into five separate groups: those designed to create a relatively modest policy change (for example, to free a political prisoner or to limit nuclear proliferation); those intended to destabilize a government; those aimed at disrupting a military adventure of another nation (for example, stopping Iraq's invasion of Kuwait); those designed to impair another nation's military potential; and a fifth category of other goals, such as stopping apartheid, or the Arab League's boycott of oil sales to the United States in retaliation for support for Israel.

In order to be classified as a success, the policy outcome must have been the one desired by the country imposing the sanctions, and the sanctions must have been a contributor to the policy outcome. Hufbauer, Schott, and Elliott find 41 successes in the 120 cases they examined, but they report a drop in the number of successes after about 1973. They determined that sanctions are more effective when the target country is small, economically weak, and politically unstable; the target country is an ally; sanctions are imposed quickly and decisively; the costs to the sending country are small; and the goal is a relatively small change.

The more difficult the goal, the more likely is the need for military force to back up the sanctions. The U.S. invasion of Iraq in 2003 is a case in point. United Nations sanctions against Iraq undoubtedly helped to cripple its economy, even though the sanctions were never successfully enforced completely. In that sense, they contributed to the success of U.S. policy in replacing Iraq's government. Still, without a military invasion, it seems unlikely that the sanctions alone would have led to a change of government.

TABLE 7.4	Economic Sanctions since World War I	
Goal	Number of Cases	Successes
Modest policy change	51	17
Destabilize a government	21	11
Disrupt a military adventure	18	6
Impair military potential	10	2
Other	20	5

Sanctions imposed between World War I and 1990 had about a 38 percent success rate.

Source: Gary Clyde Hufbauer, Jeffrey J. Schott, and Kimberly Ann Elliott. *Economic Sanctions Reconsidered.* Washington, DC: Institute for International Economics. 1990; "Executive Summary," 1998.

Summary

- Regardless of their cost or their ability to achieve a desired objective, every nation uses trade barriers. In most industrial nations, they are not used to develop comparative advantage in new industries, but rather to protect old industries that can no longer compete or to temporarily protect industries that are under pressure from new competitors. Agriculture, clothing, and textiles are the most protected sectors in many industrial countries.

- Tariffs and quotas are inefficient mechanisms for creating (or keeping) jobs. Because the costs are hidden in the prices consumers pay for foreign and domestic goods, few people realize how inefficient they are.

- The primary beneficiaries of trade barriers are producers who receive protection and governments that receive tariff revenue. The losers are consumers. Because the gains are concentrated among a relatively few people, and the losses are dispersed across many, there is usually a small economic incentive to oppose trade barriers but a large incentive to seek them.

- The valid arguments in favor of protection involve economic returns to society that are undervalued or not counted by markets. That is, it must be the case that the market does not take into consideration the gains that spill over from production. The total value of producing a good, including any spillovers, is extremely difficult to measure, however, and it is often impossible to know the future value of the skills or technology an industry will create.

- In addition to presidential action, there are several forms of protection in the United States: countervailing duties to counter a foreign subsidy, antidumping duties to counter dumping of foreign goods, escape clause relief to counter an import surge, and Section 301 actions to retaliate against foreign trade practices that have been labeled as unfair. Except for escape clause relief, each type of tariff requires a demonstration that foreign products are competing unfairly in the U.S. market and that they have harmed domestic producers. The most common form of tariff imposition is an antidumping duty.

Vocabulary

antidumping duty (ADD)

countervailing duty (CVD)

dumping

escape clause relief

fair value

infant industry

Section 301

Special 301

subsidies

Study Questions

1. Which industries are more heavily protected in the United States and Japan? Are high-income or low-income nations more affected by American and Japanese trade barriers? Explain.

2. What new areas of trade and investment received coverage under the agreement signed after the Uruguay Round of the General Agreement on Tariffs and Trade?

3. Given that tariffs and quotas cost consumers and that they are grossly inefficient means for creating or preserving jobs, why do citizens allow these policies to exist?

4. What four main groups of arguments do nations use to justify protection for particular industries? Which are economic, and which are noneconomic?

5. Evaluate the labor and infant industry arguments for protection.

6. Are tariffs justified as a retaliatory measure against other nations? Justify your answer.

7. What are the four legal procedures that American firms have at their disposal for seeking protection? What are the conditions that would generate a request for each kind of protection?

International Trade and Labor and Environmental Standards

Introduction: Income and Standards

Since the end of World War II, many of the formal barriers to international trade have been removed. This was accomplished through the sustained efforts of the world's trading nations, often working through the negotiating frameworks provided by the General Agreement on Tariffs and Trade (GATT), the World Trade Organization (WTO), and more recently, the regional trade agreements around the globe.

As trade barriers are removed, however, new obstacles to increased international economic integration begin to appear. These obstacles are driven by two distinct but equally important forces. First, it sometimes happens that national laws and regulations that were adopted for strictly domestic reasons unintentionally limit international commerce in a more integrated economic environment. For example, a law designed to capture economies of scale by giving one company a monopoly in telephone services makes it impossible for foreign telephone companies to enter the market.

A second obstacle to increased international economic integration is the conflict over standards. These extend from disputes over technical product standards, to health and safety standards, to labor and environmental standards. Issues arise in these areas for a variety of reasons. For example, the adoption of a common set of product standards gives a significant commercial advantage to firms that are already producing to the standard, and hence, each country would like to see the wider application of its own standards. Another reason behind many of the conflicts over standards is the wide variation in world income levels. Trade between developed and developing countries is usually based on comparative advantage and it moves countries along their production possibility curves, causing greater specialization in production. Although each nation's gains from trade may be large, greater specialization creates winners and losers inside each country, and raises questions of fairness.

Economic conditions and living standards inside developing countries are vastly different from conditions inside high-income economies such as the United States. In particular, lower wages, longer hours, less safe working conditions, dirtier industries, and less regard for environmental degradation are relatively more common in low-income than in high-income countries. When trade occurs between countries with different living standards, people begin to wonder about the inexpensive goods they import from low-income countries. Does their production exploit children, are working conditions safe and healthy, do workers have political and civil rights, and are the methods employed environmentally friendly? And if not, can trade barriers such as tariffs, quotas, or complete prohibition of imports effectively pressure the exporting country into changing its practices?

Setting Standards: Harmonization, Mutual Recognition, or Separate?

Two or more economies can be deeply integrated even if they have different rules, regulations, and standards governing their individual economies. The United States is an obvious example, since individual states impose different standards on vehicle emissions, minimum wages, teacher training, food safety, construction codes, and product availability, to name just a few. Lesser forms of integration between sovereign nations, such as partial trade agreements, free-trade areas, customs unions, and common markets are likely to vary even more with respect to rules, regulations, and standards.

Harmonization of product and process standards is one option for countries seeking to expand their commercial ties. **Harmonization of standards** refers to the case where two or more countries share a common set of standards in an area of concern, such as product safety, labor, environment, fair competition, and so on. Another option is **mutual recognition of standards**, in which countries keep their own product and process standards, but accept the standards of others as equally valid and sufficient. For example, a medical doctor trained in a foreign country may not receive the same training as medical doctors in the home country, but under a system of mutual recognition he or she is qualified to practice in either country. A third option is **separate standards**. In this case, countries keep their own standards and refuse to recognize those of anyone else. For example, if the home country has a more stringent rule for pesticide residue left on vegetables after harvest, then with separate standards it prohibits imports that are considered unsafe. Most regional trade agreements and the WTO agreements practice a combination of harmonization, mutual recognition, and separate standards.

There are no general rules to determine which approach is most efficient or fairest in all cases. Often it is the case that the harmonization of technical standards having to do with product design or performance is useful, since it leads to a larger, more unified market and creates greater efficiency. Simple examples such as the number of threads per centimeter on screws, or the size of electrical plugs on home appliances are illustrations of cases where harmonization unifies a market and creates efficiency gains across the economy. In other cases, harmonization of standards may pose the potential problem of freezing into place a set of inferior standards. New technologies are a case in point, since the evolution of new products and processes is impossible to forecast, and freezing technical standards into legal requirements may have a harmful effect on future developments. In addition, there are many cases such as labor or environmental legislation where it is unclear which country has the "best" rules. Mutual recognition is a superior option under these conditions, as it allows competition between different standards, which may help clarify the costs and benefits of each one.

Harmonization of standards sometimes poses an additional problem in its failure to take into account the differences between countries. Generally speaking, the lower a country's average income, the less administrative, scientific, and technical capacity it has to design and enforce standards. In addition, national priorities change as income levels change, and there is no reason why the priorities of one group of countries should dominate. Differences in income levels are not always an obstacle to the harmonization of standards, however, because many product standards are technical considerations where the adoption of a common set of rules makes a great deal of sense if it widens the market and lowers prices.

When standards across countries vary by the level of development, it is generally better to mutually recognize each other's standards, or if that is not possible for safety or other reasons, to maintain separate standards. While trade theory is clear on this point, many people living in high-income countries find it hard to accept, particularly with respect to labor and environmental standards. Many fear that in the absence of a common set of labor and environmental standards, low standards abroad create competitive pressures for domestic firms to lower their standards, or to move to a foreign location in order to reduce their costs. This possibility has been labeled a **race to the bottom**, where the bottom is the lowest possible level of standards. In the following sections, we examine this issue and others, in the context of labor and environmental standards.

CASE STUDY

Income, Environment, and Society

The World Bank uses four categories to classify the countries of the world according to their income levels. **High-income** countries have per capita incomes (2007, U.S. dollars) of $11,456 or more, **upper-middle-income** countries range between $3,706 and $11,455 per person, **lower-middle-income** countries range between $936 and $3,705 per person, and **low-income** countries have per capita incomes of $935 or less.

Most of the world's population and a majority of countries are either low-income or middle-income (see Table 8.1). In dollar terms, a majority of the world lives on less than $3,706 (2007) per person per year. By contrast, the average per capita income for the world's high income countries was $37,571 in 2007. Income differences that are this large lead inevitably to differences in social and environmental indicators, as shown in Table 8.2.

Table 8.2 displays four indicators that are important to the economy, society, and the environment. The first variable, infant mortality, is a key measurement of health conditions. It shows a strong and consistent tendency to decline as income

TABLE 8.1	Income and Population by World Bank Categories, 2007		
Income Category	Number of Countries	Population (Millions)	Average Income per Person (US$)
Low	49	1,295.8	574
Lower middle	54	3,434.5	1,905
Upper middle	41	823.7	7,106
High	65	1,056.3	37,571

Most of the world's population lives in countries classified as low- or lower-middle-income.

Source: World Bank, *World Development Indicators.*

grows due to the benefits of improved sanitation and nutrition along with wider access to health care and health care of improved quality. The second variable, access to safe drinking water, is one of the most significant public health problems in the world and can also be considered an environmental problem with direct health effects. As incomes rise, the percentage of the population with access increases significantly until virtually all citizens in high-income countries have access to safe drinking water. This should not be interpreted to mean that high-income countries do not have water problems; it simply means that their citizens have access to safe drinking water.

The other two indicators show a mixed pattern. In the one case, carbon dioxide emissions, conditions deteriorate with income growth. Carbon dioxide, or

TABLE 8.2	Income Levels, Society, and the Environment			
Income Category	Under 5 Mortality, per 1000, 2007	Percent of Population with Access to Safe Drinking Water	CO_2 Emissions, Metric Tons per Person, 2005	Percent Change in Forest Reserves, 1990–2005
Low	126.4	68	0.6	−10.5
Lower middle	49.9	88	2.8	−2.5
Upper middle	24.2	95	5.5	−3.3
High	7.1	100	12.6	+1.1

Some conditions improve with income growth, some worsen, and some vary widely.

Source: World Bank, *World Development Indicators.*

CO_2, is a major contributor to global warming and is produced when we burn fossil fuels. High-income economies burn more energy than low-income ones, hence they generate more than twenty times as much carbon dioxide per person. Middle-income countries are intermediate but show the same pattern of increased fuel consumption and increased CO_2 emissions as income rises. Some environmental indicators, water quality for example, tend to improve with income, at least after a threshold level. Others have no clear pattern, although there is a long-run tendency for improvement. In Table 8.2, forest reserves are an example. Low-income countries are removing forests at the highest rate, middle-income countries are intermediate but variable, and high-income countries are increasing their forest reserves, albeit relatively slowly.

In sum, when thinking about labor and environmental standards, it is useful to keep in mind the general patterns across countries of highly different income levels.

Labor Standards

Recently, the United States and other countries have demanded that labor and environmental standards be included in all future trade negotiations. This is a politically charged issue that is likely to come and go over time, depending in part on the political party in power, but it also reflects rising worldwide interests in issues related to human rights and the environment. To date, the United States' trade agreements with Canada and Mexico (the North American Free Trade Agreement), Jordan, and Chile contain language on labor and environmental standards, either in the treaty itself, or as a side agreement. In each case, the language specifies that each country must enforce its own standards or face monetary fines. Many labor and environmental activists view this as inadequate and are pushing to include trade sanctions as part of the enforcement mechanism, both in existing agreements and in future agreements, including those reached by the WTO.

The complaints against trade by labor and environmental interests are relatively similar. In both cases, it is alleged that trade with countries that have lower standards creates a race to the bottom in standards, and that countries with high standards are forced to lower their standards or experience a loss of jobs and industry. Furthermore, it is alleged that this type of trade is unfair, since the failure to enact or to enforce standards gives firms in the countries with lower standards a commercial advantage. Before addressing these issues, it is useful to clarify what is meant by standards, particularly in the case of labor standards.

Defining Labor Standards

The concept of labor standards is multifaceted, since it covers a wide variety of potential rights, stretching from basic rights such as the right to be free from forced labor, to civic rights such as the right to representation in a union. At present, there is no core set of work-related rights that everyone views as universal human rights.

As a starting point we take the following five labor standards proposed as basic rights by the **International Labor Organization (ILO)** (see the ILO Case Study in this chapter) and revised by the Organization for Economic Cooperation and Development (OECD):

- Prohibition of forced labor
- Freedom of association
- The right to organize and bargain collectively
- An end to the exploitation of child labor
- Nondiscrimination in employment

Most people would probably agree to these rights, although there is a fair amount of ambiguity attached to each of them. For example, conditions that are considered exploitative in a high-income country might seem acceptable in a poor one. Or cultural or religious values regarding employment opportunities for men and women may be at odds with the idea of nondiscrimination.

Other potential standards are significantly more contentious. For example, universal standards for minimum wages, limits on the number of hours someone can work in a day, and health and safety issues in the workplace are difficult to define given the wide variation in incomes and living conditions around the world. High-income countries, where unskilled labor is relatively scarce, face an entirely different set of economic constraints compared to those faced by low-income countries where unskilled labor is relatively abundant. For example, if low-income countries are forced to pay a minimum wage high enough to satisfy critics in high-income countries, many people fear that the result would be the closing down of production and a rise in unemployment rather than an increase in living standards. In other words, too high a minimum wage may be well intentioned, but it may reduce living standards in low-income countries. Even this is ambiguous, however, since it is no easy matter to determine how high is too high.

CASE STUDY

Child Labor

The most common definition of a child is a person under 18 years of age. This is the definition set forth by the United Nations and the International Labor Organization (ILO, see next case study), and accepted by most countries. Many children are economically active without falling into the negative category of child labor because their work is light, their hours are not long, and they work to supplement their studies or to learn a skill.

It is easy to be opposed to the evils of child labor, particularly when it is hazardous to the physical and psychological well being of children. Opposition becomes more

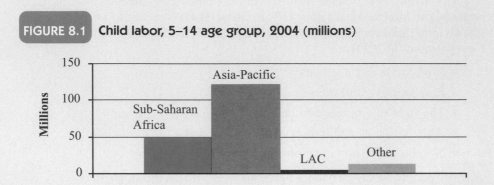

FIGURE 8.1 Child labor, 5–14 age group, 2004 (millions)

Asia has the most child labor, followed by sub-Saharan Africa. LAC is Latin America and the Caribbean.

Source: F. Hageman, Y. Diallo, A. Etienne, and F. Mehpa (2006). *Global Child Labor Trends, 2000–2004*. Geneva: ILO.

complicated, however, when schools do not exist and impoverished families depend on the few cents their children can bring home. In these cases, children and their work contribute to family survival and a humane policy requires more than a simple prohibition of work by children.

Child labor appears to be in decline worldwide, but it is still common in some parts of the world. The ILO estimated that the number of economically active children, ages 5–14, was 190.7 million in 2004. Of those, 165.8 million were estimated to be engaged in child labor, of which 74.4 million were engaged in work that was hazardous to their physical or psychological well-being. Geographically, they are most numerous in the Asia-Pacific region, followed by sub-Saharan Africa (Figure 8.1).

FIGURE 8.2 Percent of children working, 5–14 age group

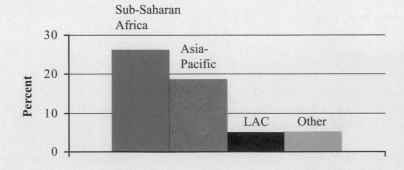

Sub-Saharan Africa has the highest proportion of children working, followed by the Asia-Pacific region.

Source: F. Hageman, Y. Diallo, A. Etienne, and F. Mehpa (2006). *Global Child Labor Trends, 2000–2004*. Geneva: ILO.

Sub-Saharan Africa has fewer child laborers than the Asia-Pacific region, but a larger percentage of its children are pressed into labor. In 2004, more than one in four children in the 5–14 age group were working (Figure 8.2). Poverty, a lack of educational opportunities, and agriculture are the main causes. Agriculture is the primary user of children's labor, and 69 percent of all child labor is located in that sector, with services employing 22 percent and industry (manufacturing, construction, mining, and utilities) employing only 9 percent of the total. Very few children work in sectors that are export oriented and, in general, the incidence of child labor declines as GDP increases. It also decreases as opportunities for schooling become available. The ILO and others argue that child labor is most effectively combated by supporting the expansion of schooling.

Labor Standards and Trade

The major source of disagreements between trade economists and labor activists is over the use of trade barriers to enforce labor standards. That is, should one country use trade barriers to pressure another country into altering its labor standards? Trade economists tend to be more skeptical about the use of trade barriers, partly for the reasons outlined in Chapter 7 where it was shown that they are expensive and grossly inefficient policies for reaching most of the goals for which they are used. In addition to the deadweight losses in consumption and production at home, the use of trade barriers to enforce standards abroad raises several other concerns for economists. These include their effectiveness in creating change in an exporting country, the hazy borderline between protectionism and concern over standards, the lack of agreement over the specific content of standards, and their potential to erupt into a wider trade war. We will examine each of these points next.

Effectiveness   In addition to the deadweight losses and income redistribution effects of trade barriers, it is clear that only large countries can hope to use barriers successfully, since a small country cannot have a large enough impact on demand. That is, if a small country such as the Netherlands decides that garment producers in Haiti are exploiting children, then any trade barrier that the Netherlands erects against imports from Haiti are not likely to reduce demand enough to stop the offending Haitian practice. Only countries that constitute a significant share of the Haitian market could erect barriers that would impose costs on Haitian producers, and even then only if there are no alternative markets for Haitian goods. Nor would this necessarily lead to changes, since there are numerous examples (Cuba, Myanmar, and others) where countries have suffered large costs from trade sanctions but have not altered their policies in response. In effect, the general rule is that the effectiveness of the trade barrier increases as more countries join to impose them. For example, the strong unity of the world's industrial economies against South Africa was at least partly responsible for ending the policy of apartheid.

In addition to the problem of creating a coalition of countries, an additional obstacle to the effectiveness of trade barriers is that in some cases they will make conditions worse rather than better. This outcome occurs when sanctions cause producers inside a country to move their facilities into the informal, unregulated economy where it is out of sight of domestic inspectors and regulators. Some share of production in every economy takes place in the **informal economy**. The informal economy does not necessarily produce illegal goods such as drugs, but it is untaxed, unregulated, and uninspected. In developing countries this tends to be a relatively larger share of overall economic activity than in industrial economies, and it is typically composed of small firms operating with little capital. Employees in these enterprises usually earn less and suffer harsher working conditions. If sanctions against a country create incentives for its employers to avoid the scrutiny of labor inspectors, then a larger share of the working population could find themselves laboring under worse conditions.

Hazy Borderline between Protectionism and Concern   When does the concern over foreign labor practices become a justification for protectionism? There is no definitive way to answer this question, although it is certain that special interests sometimes use the issue of labor standards as a means to justify their real goal, which is to obtain protection against foreign competition. Indeed, this is the fear of many developing countries, and explains why their governments resist negotiating labor standards. Developing countries tend to have abundant supplies of unskilled labor and they depend on low-wage, low-productivity jobs for a large share of their employment. In these countries, proposals to set labor standards and to use trade barriers as an enforcement mechanism are widely viewed as a new form of protectionism on the part of high-income countries. Given that most high-income countries continue to protect their markets in key areas of developing country production—agriculture, clothing, and textiles—there is a strong suspicion that calls for labor standards are a way to undermine the comparative advantage of low-income countries and to close the markets of high-income countries in selected areas.

The Specific Content of Labor Standards   The problem of reaching agreement on the specific content of standards has yet to be resolved. We have seen how child labor varies by income, and that even the definition of a child varies across countries. For example, disputes over the minimum age at which someone may legally enter the labor force have so far blocked international agreement on child labor, other than vague condemnations of the practice. Other standards are equally contentious, although it is always conceivable that an international consensus may develop in the long run. At the present time, however, the lack of international agreement on the specific content of labor standards, other than the relatively vague proposals from the OECD and ILO, means that trade sanctions are unilateral measures with a large potential for creating conflict and undermining international economic relations.

The Potential to Set Off a Trade War   One of the primary obligations of countries in the WTO is to treat other members the same. That is, discrimination by one WTO member against another is not allowed. There are exceptions, as in the case of national security, or in the case of the special benefits given to members of a free-trade area, but in general, discriminatory trade practices are not allowed. Consequently, the use of trade sanctions to enforce labor standards places a country out of compliance with its WTO obligations and opens it to the risk of retaliation by the targeted country. Where this ends is indeterminate.

Evidence on Low Standards as a Predatory Practice

One of the concerns expressed by the proponents of trade sanctions is that low standards may reflect a deliberate policy to capture markets and foreign investment. That is, a country may use its coercive power to hold down or repress labor standards, and thereby reduce the costs of producing goods. While theoretically possible, this too has a number of issues that must be examined empirically.

In practice, there is little or no support for the view that countries use low labor standards to attract foreign investment. While there is evidence that a country can reduce production costs by outlawing unions, or by some other repressive practice, there is no evidence that this type of policy has succeeded in giving any country a comparative advantage in lines of production that it did not already have. In other words, low standards can reduce production costs, but they do not change a country's comparative advantage.

This result does not affect the case of competition between countries with the same or similar comparative advantages. Within a particular line of production, such as the clothing industry, countries may compete by lowering labor standards, but then the harmful competitive effects of low standards are on other countries with low standards, not on countries with high standards and with an entirely different comparative advantage.

While low labor standards may help a country compete against another low labor standards country, there is clear evidence that low labor standards are not a successful strategy for attracting foreign investment. The reason is simple. Low labor standards are highly correlated with a labor force that is abundant in illiterate, unskilled labor. Furthermore, it is a sign that the nation's infrastructure of roads, ports, power supply, telecommunications, schools, and sanitation are also undeveloped. Hence, the labor cost savings of low labor standards is more than likely to be offset by higher costs everywhere else in production. Consequently, empirical studies show that countries with low labor standards are less successful at attracting foreign investment.

Finally, there is the case of intolerable practices, such as apartheid in the old South Africa, the gulags of the former Soviet Union, and slavery in Sudan and elsewhere. These types of practices raise a number of moral issues, which make it unreasonable to rely solely on economic analysis. Clearly, however, the more united the world is against a particular inhumane labor practice, the more likely sanctions are to succeed. For example, the United States is isolated in imposing sanctions on

Cuba, and although it has imposed significant costs on Cuba's economy, the lack of international support for U.S. policies has prevented the sanctions from successfully changing Cuban policies.

CASE STUDY

The International Labor Organization (ILO)

The International Labor Organization (ILO) "seeks the promotion of social justice and internationally recognized human and labour rights." The ILO began in 1919 and is the only surviving element of the League of Nations, which was founded after World War I and was the precursor of the United Nations (UN). In 1946, the ILO was incorporated into the United Nations and since then, most of the world's countries have become members.

The ILO uses several tools to attain its goals. Most prominently, it develops labor standards that are embodied in specific Conventions and Recommendations. Individual countries are encouraged but not required to ratify the ILO Conventions. Currently, there are 183 conventions, about 26 of which have been shelved and are no longer proposed, leaving 157 in force.

On June 18, 1998, the ILO adopted the "Declaration on Fundamental Principles and Rights at Work and its Follow-up." This document specifies the eight **core labor standards** it believes all countries should respect, regardless of which conventions they ratified. The ILO groups the eight core standards into four areas:

- Freedom of association and recognition of the right to collective bargaining
- Elimination of all forms of forced labor
- Effective abolition of child labor
- Elimination of discrimination in employment and occupations

The most serious type of complaint handled by the ILO concerns cases where worker's organizations, firms, or governments file a formal complaint that a member government is not enforcing core labor rights. The process for handling such complaints begins with a consultation with the alleged offender, followed by an official investigation if the consultation does not resolve the issue. The investigating committee may make recommendations, which the target country may appeal to the International Court of Justice. If there is an appeal, afterwards the ILO can propose actions against the offending country. Economic actions such as trade sanctions are within the legal framework of options available to the ILO. It should be noted, however, that throughout its lengthy history, the ILO has recommended actions against one country only, and it has never proposed trade sanctions.

The ILO's reluctance to use the full extent of its power, along with the failure of some of its members to support it, results in a fairly weak organization. Throughout its lengthy history, the ILO has proposed trade sanctions against only one country, Myanmar. The Southeast Asian nation uses forced labor throughout the country, particularly to fill the ranks of its military. Myanmar came under ILO scrutiny in 1998 and in 2000 the international organization recommended trade sanctions. The sanctions recommendation was withdrawn in 2001 after Myanmar gave assurances that it was addressing the problem. Five years later, in mid-2006, little has changed—Myanmar continues to use forced labor while giving assurances that it is ending the practice, and trade sanctions have not been imposed.

In addition to handling complaints and proposing conventions, the ILO also provides technical assistance in all aspects of labor policy, including labor law, worker benefit programs, vocational training, development and administration of cooperatives, and many other areas.

Sources: International Labor Organization, http://www.ilo.org. Elliott, Kimberly Ann, "The ILO and Enforcement of Core Labor Standards." Washington, DC: Institute for International Economics. July 2000. http://www.iie.com/NEWSLTR/news00–6.htm. Accessed 10-9-00. "Gathering Mild Rebuke: Myanmar," *The Economist.* September 2, 2006.

Trade and the Environment

Over the last forty years, the realization has grown that our activities profoundly affect the natural environment. Unfortunately, our production and consumption choices do not always reflect the environmental costs of our decisions, and in the short run, our economies too often perform as if environmental costs and limits are irrelevant. When economic agents are allowed to ignore the environmental costs of their actions, then conflict between financial and environmental interests are inevitable. Most high-income countries have a significant amount of such conflict, and trade, along with other economic activities, has received its share of environmental criticism.

Transboundary and Non-Transboundary Effects

There is a considerable overlap between environmental standards and labor standards. For example, many proponents of putting environmental standards into trade agreements believe that trade sanctions—tariffs, quotas, prohibitions on imports—should be used as enforcement mechanisms, while the critics of trade sanctions have the same concerns raised earlier: They are relatively ineffective, there is a hazy borderline between protectionism and concern for the environment, there is a lack of international agreement, and there is a potential to start trade wars.

There are some differences between labor and environmental standards, however, beginning with the fact that some but not all environmental impacts are transboundary. In other words, low standards in one country can degrade the environment in another country or countries. When it comes to trade policy, the distinction between **transboundary and non-transboundary environmental impacts** is an important one. We will look at non-transboundary, or exclusively national impacts, first.

Trade and Environmental Impacts That Do Not Cross Borders   Proponents of trade barriers to enforce environmental standards base their analysis on two types of claims. First, they argue that environmental standards reduce industrial competitiveness. This induces an environmental race to the bottom where countries are forced to rescind standards in order to stay competitive. Second, they argue that standards in rich countries cause them to "export pollution" to developing countries by relocating their dirty industries there. Both effects are harmful to the environment, as they lead to downward pressures on environmental standards and the concentration of dirty industries in a few developing countries.

The first claim, that environmental standards reduce industrial competitiveness, is theoretically valid since standards must raise the costs of production. Essentially, environmental standards prohibit the shifting of environmental costs to the public at large and thereby force firms to take a more complete measure of all their costs of production. If the standards are correctly implemented, they raise national well-being and lead to an economically optimal level of production. This implies that the argument against standards by firms that are subject to them is an argument between their interests and the nation's interests. Clearly, the nation is better off if the production of dirty industries is curtailed somewhat, even though the workers and firms in the shrinking industry may be worse off in the short-to-medium runs. The idea that the sectional interests are so politically strong that they can force environmental deregulation (race to the bottom) or prevent the introduction of new standards altogether may have some merit, but in general, environmental standards in most countries have gotten tougher over time, not more lax.

Countries that compete by offering foreign firms a reduced set of environmental compliance requirements are known as **pollution havens**. Note the essential similarity between the pollution haven concept and the claim that countries compete for foreign investment by lowering their labor standards. Empirically, there is evidence that some dirty industries from high-income industrial economies moved to developing countries in the 1970s when the industrial economies first began cracking down on environmental polluters. Steel and chemical industries fall into this pattern, although it is possible that the developing countries were gaining a comparative advantage in these areas as high-income countries were losing theirs. Regardless, there is strong evidence showing that the idea of pollution havens is invalid. That is, it is impossible to identify any country that successfully competes for new investment on the basis of low environmental standards. The fact that there are no pollution havens is good news, but it does not mean that individual firms cannot move to escape the environmental regulations of a high-standards country. Undoubtedly, there are cases of this, although numbers and overall importance are uncertain.

From a trade perspective, the issue is complicated by the fact that differences in income and preferences make the optimal set of environmental standards variable by country. An optimal set of standards in Europe, for example, might be entirely different from the optimal set in North Africa or central Asia. The fact that budgets and regulatory abilities are limited implies that countries cannot do everything, and that they must prioritize their efforts. Biodiversity and habitat preservation may receive top priority in one place, while clean water and soil conservation are first in another. When the optimality of standards varies across countries, the introduction of trade barriers as a means of enforcing one country's standards in another country's production system would actually lower global welfare rather than raise it.

Trade and Transboundary Environmental Problems   Transboundary environmental impacts happen when one country's pollution spills over into a second country, for example, when a shared watershed is polluted by the upstream user, or industrial production in one country creates acid rain in another country. It can also happen in a mutual way, for example, when heavy truck traffic between two countries creates air pollution in both. And finally, transboundary environmental impacts can occur as the result of similar activities in many countries, leading to global impacts such as global warming and ozone depletion. There are a variety of potential actions that countries may contemplate, from tariffs on the output of the polluting industries, to embargoes, to multi-country or global negotiations.

The analysis of labor standards applies here, as unilateral actions by one country are unlikely to have any effect whatsoever except in the large country case. Even then, the more isolated the sanctions-imposing country is, the lower the probability that its actions will successfully alter the policies of the offending countries.

CASE STUDY

Trade Barriers and Endangered Species

The connection between trade and endangered species protection is an area where the environmental movement has been critical of the WTO. The original precedent-setting case began with the U.S. ban on imports of tuna that were caught with nets that were particularly harmful to dolphins. Under the terms of the Endangered Species Act of 1973, the United States imposed a ban on tuna imports that were not certified as "dolphin-safe." Mexico lodged a complaint, and the outcome of the investigation was a GATT ruling that countries cannot prohibit imports based on the method of production, as long as the goods are legal. Because the United States allowed tuna to be sold in its market, it could not keep out tuna harvested in a way that hurt dolphins.

The U.S. prohibitions on certain shrimp imports was the next important case to draw attention to the conflict between trade and the protection of endangered species. The United States sought to protect endangered sea turtles that are harmed by shrimp trawlers that do not use turtle excluder devices (TEDs) on their nets. In 1987, it issued guidelines requiring shrimp trawlers to use TEDs and in 1989 it announced that beginning in May of 1991 it would ban shrimp from countries that were not certified. The guidelines applied only to the Caribbean and the western Atlantic, and countries were given three years to come into compliance. In 1996, a number of additional conditions were placed on shrimp imports, the guidelines were extended worldwide, and countries were given four months to come into compliance.

India, Malaysia, Pakistan, and Thailand immediately protested to the WTO. The primary basis of the protest was that they were given four months to comply with the U.S. rules, while countries in the Caribbean were given three years and technical assistance. In addition, they cited the dolphin-tuna case, and argued that the GATT rules forbid discrimination against imports based on the process of production. After the United States and the Asian nations failed to resolve their dispute through informal consultations, the Asian nations asked the WTO's Dispute Settlement Body to establish a panel to resolve the issue. The issue wound its way through the dispute resolution process of rulings and appeals and finally culminated in a decision acknowledging the right of countries to impose import barriers in order to protect endangered species. However, the final decision also stated that the United States' failure to negotiate or confer with the affected countries put it in violation of WTO rules. Furthermore, by treating the Asian nations differently, the United States acted in a discriminatory manner. In response, the United States began a series of negotiations with the countries that filed the complaint. In the end, it revised its timetable and procedures for certification, and agreed to provide technical assistance in the use of TEDs.

This case is important because, in the words of the WTO, "We have not decided that the sovereign nations that are Members of the WTO cannot adopt effective measures to protect endangered species, such as sea turtles. Clearly, they can and should." In effect, the WTO forced a multilateral solution by arranging for the United States—which places a relatively high value on sea turtles—to assist a number of developing countries—which place a relatively higher value on their commercial fishing industries—in acquiring the technology they need. This enables the United States to extend its protection of an endangered species worldwide, while the fishing fleets of South Asia remain commercially viable.

The WTO also clarified the controversial issue of products versus processes that first began with the dolphin-tuna dispute. In its ruling, the WTO states that trade measures are permitted to protect endangered species. At the same time, the ruling stressed the need to negotiate a solution and disallowed unilateral action.

Source: World Trade Organization, "United States-Import Prohibition of Certain Shrimp and Shrimp Products," AB–1998–4. http://www.wto.org/english/tratop_e/dispu_e/58abr.doc

Alternatives to Trade Measures

Currently, it is impossible to predict how, or even if, trade rules might eventually change in order to accommodate labor and environmental standards. These are new issues for the world trading system, and it is possible that they will become a permanent source of tension in international economic relations. As long as there are large income gaps between rich and poor countries, it seems unlikely that differences in standards will disappear. If trade tensions over standards are likely to continue in one form or another, then it is important to look for ways to preserve the benefits created by world trade while simultaneously resolving the conflicts over standards.

In the search for alternatives to trade measures, it is useful to recognize the general economic principle that efficient policies go directly to the root of the problem they are designed to correct. This was illustrated in Chapter 7, where it was demonstrated that trade barriers are an expensive way to solve the problem of job shortages in a particular industry. In the cases of environmental degradation and the exploitation of labor, the root of the problem lies in the production and/or consumption of particular goods, not in their trade. If a steel mill pollutes a river or exploits children, the direct cause of the environmental and human harm is the set of production standards employed by the mill, not the fact that the steel is exported. In some cases of negative environmental effects (for example, air pollution caused by gas-burning cars) the root of the problem is consumption, not production. Given that environmental degradation and labor exploitation are by-products of production and consumption decisions, the optimal policies for addressing them is at the level of production and consumption, not at the level of trade measures, since the latter create production and consumption inefficiencies in the country that imposes them. In some cases, such as countries that still allow slavery, trade measures may be the only available option short of military intervention, but in most international conflicts over labor and environmental standards, there are more efficient policies than trade measures.

Labels for Exports

The idea of labeling is widespread and has been implemented with mixed success. This idea is a certification process producing a label that is attached to the good when it is exported. The label is designed to tell consumers that the good was produced under conditions that are humane or environmentally sustainable. This method is already in place in a few instances, although not always successfully. For example, in 1999 the United States and Cambodia agreed that the United States would increase its quota of Cambodian textiles and garments if the country allowed foreign observers to visit its factories. Cambodia agreed to the intrusion of labor inspectors because it is desperate for the export business. The initial result was a heightening of conflict between Cambodian unions and employers, and a threat by producers to move elsewhere. Coffee is a somewhat more successful example, where retailers have used independent inspection agencies that offer services to firms that import coffee and other tropical products. This allows retailers to advertise that they sell one or more types of coffee that are certified as beneficial to small farmers. Similarly, some cosmetic brands and retailers certify that their products are not tested on animals.

Labeling probably has an important role to play in resolving conflicts, but not in its present form. First, many countries will resist what they consider an infringement of their sovereignty when foreign inspectors are allowed to probe into the details of labor and environmental conditions. A second problem is that consumers will have to be convinced that the label provides reliable information. If a sweater made in Cambodia has a label saying it was made under humane conditions, what degree of confidence should you put on that information? As the procedure of labeling becomes more widespread, it is possible that the true information value of labels will decrease. These problems are not insurmountable, but they have to be addressed before labeling is adopted on a larger scale.

Requiring Home Country Standards

A second alternative to trade measures is to require home country firms to follow home country standards whenever they open foreign operations. An example is the Sullivan Principles, which asked multinationals operating in South Africa during the apartheid era to practice nondiscrimination. In the case of labor standards, a domestic firm in a high-standards country that wants to open a plant in a developing country would be required by law to adhere to the same labor standards as the ones it must follow at home. This does not mean that wages and benefits must be the same, since the cost of labor varies, but minimum wages might be included, along with some benefits, workplace health and safety standards, child labor standards, hours of work standards, and so on. In the environmental sphere, it is not uncommon for firms to adopt the same standards abroad as they use at home, since environmental control is often built into the technology and a least-cost strategy usually involves the adoption of one set of standards rather than multiple standards.

The advantage of this approach is that it addresses the issue of a race to the bottom by making it impossible for a home-based company to exploit low labor or environmental standards abroad, while, at the same time, preserving access to the low-wage labor of labor-abundant countries. Furthermore, this technique shifts the costs of improved standards to firms and consumers in high-income countries—which is where most of the concern originates. It might seem strange to regulate companies operating outside the nation, but it is well within the legal right of nations to impose standards on domestic firms that operate abroad, as long as the standards do not conflict with the laws of the host country. Given that the required standards are meant to be more stringent than those in the host country, this should not be a problem.

One weakness of this approach, however, is that it only addresses the problem of firms in high-standards countries that go abroad, but does not address the problem of foreign-owned and foreign-operated firms that export into the domestic market. In other words, firms based in countries with low standards are untouched by this type of rule. More problematically, a clothing manufacturer based in a high-standards country might outsource its production through contracts with firms based in low-standards countries. This puts part of the production at arm's length and makes it more difficult to ensure that working conditions are satisfactory. Since the firms doing the actual cutting and sewing are foreign-owned, they may lie completely outside the reach of the regulations governing the clothing manufacturer located in the high-standards country.

Nevertheless, regulations placed on domestic firms operating abroad address a significant share of the fears of a race to the bottom. In particular, they remove the threat by domestic firms to relocate abroad if standards are not reduced at home, and ensure that the attraction of foreign-based production is the foreign comparative advantage, not the ability to lower labor standards or ignore the environment. In addition, they help avoid the problems created when high-income countries appear to be dictating labor and environmental standards for low- and middle-income countries. Each country sets its own standards, but when firms cross national boundaries, they must conform to whichever standards are higher, either those in the sending country or the receiving country.

Increasing International Negotiations

A third alternative to trade measures is to increase the level of international negotiations, using either existing international organizations such as the ILO for labor, or creating new agreements and organizations for the environment. In the labor standards arena, proponents of increased negotiations would like to see the ILO publicize examples where countries are out of compliance with core labor rights. It could do this with the information it already gathers on the labor practices of its member countries. An expanded role for the ILO is supported by the growing recognition that it has the technical capability to assess labor policies, whereas the WTO does not.

In the environmental arena, the WTO reports that there are about two hundred multilateral environmental agreements (for example, the Montreal Protocol regulating the use of chlorofluorocarbons, the Basel Convention regulating the transportation of hazardous waste, and the Convention on International Trade in Endangered Species) and that about twenty of them have the potential to affect trade. In cases where two or more countries have signed an agreement and the agreement allows trade sanctions as part of its enforcement mechanism, the WTO's position is that disputes should be resolved within the environmental agreement and not within the WTO. In cases where there are no environmental agreements, however, as with the United States' shrimp import ban, then WTO rules of nondiscrimination apply.

It is significant that the WTO has staked out a position on the issue of multilateral environmental agreements. The WTO recognizes explicitly that it is not an environmental organization and that it has no expertise in this area. However, it has left room for environmental agreements to develop their own enforcement mechanisms. This does not change the fact that trade sanctions are unlikely to be the optimal (lowest cost) technique for resolving environmental disputes, but it does leave it up to the nations involved to decide on their own methods of enforcement.

Summary

- The increase in world trade over the last fifty years has reduced tariffs and eliminated quotas, but as a result, many domestic policies have become unintentional barriers to trade. Examples include competition policies, product standards, health and safety standards, and labor and environmental standards.

- Countries do not need to harmonize standards in order to trade. In many cases, harmonization would remove some of the differences between countries and eliminate the gains from trade. Alternative treatment of standards include mutual recognition and maintaining completely separate standards.

- Differing labor and environmental standards have become a point of significant conflict between high-income and low-income countries. Standards differ primarily because of differences in income and factor endowments.

- Core labor standards defined by the OECD and the ILO include prohibitions against forced labor, freedom of association and collective bargaining, the elimination of child labor, and nondiscrimination in employment.

- Child labor is most common in Africa and Asia. Asia has the most children working, but a larger proportion of African children under age fourteen are at work. Child labor is most common in agriculture and in small-scale, family-operated businesses.

- Proponents of using trade barriers to enforce labor and environmental standards abroad argue that differences in standards are an unfair competitive advantage for the low-standards countries. They also fear that trade and foreign investment cause a race to the bottom in standards and that low environmental standards make some countries "pollution havens."

- Evidence is scarce that countries use low standards to attract industry. In practice, low standards are associated with low levels of foreign investment. In addition, there is no evidence of pollution havens.

- Most economists oppose the use of trade measures to enforce standards because they are relatively ineffective, do not go to the root of the problem, are not based on an agreement regarding the content of standards, encourage protectionism in the guise of support for standards, and can lead to wider trade conflict.

- Environmental problems can be transboundary or non-transboundary. International conflicts over both types of problems are similar to conflicts over labor standards. Transboundary problems, in particular, require international negotiations.

- Alternatives to trade measures include labeling, enforcement of home country standards on home country firms operating abroad, and increased international negotiations. Greater support for the ILO and increasing support for international environmental agreements are also more efficient alternatives to trade measures.

Vocabulary

core labor standards

harmonization of standards

high-income, upper-middle, lower-middle, and low

informal economy

International Labor Organization (ILO)

mutual recognition of standards

pollution havens

race to the bottom

separate standards

transboundary and non-transboundary environmental impacts

Study Questions

1. What are the three ways for countries to handle different standards abroad? Do standards have to be the same for countries to be integrated?

2. What are the advantages and disadvantages for countries that adopt the same standards?

3. When high-definition television (HDTV) was first considered a possibility in the United States, the U.S. government held a competition to select the technical standards that would be used nationwide. Why would the government see an advantage to setting one standard, and what are the pros and cons for the private businesses that were interested in producing for the U.S. market?

4. Why do standards vary across countries? Illustrate your answer with examples in the area of labor standards.

5. What are labor standards, and why are arguments about labor standards confined primarily to arguments between high-income countries on the one hand, and low- and middle-income countries on the other?

6. Discuss the reasons why using trade barriers to enforce labor or environmental standards may be less efficient than other measures.

7. What are the arguments in favor of using trade barriers to enforce labor and environmental standards? Assess each argument.

8. One common critique of the WTO is that it overturns national environmental protections and forces countries to lower their standards. For example, when the United States tried to protect endangered sea turtles, the WTO prevented it. Assess this claim.

9. What are the alternatives to trade measures for raising labor and environmental standards? What are the strengths and weaknesses of each one?

International Finance

Trade and the Balance of Payments

Introduction: The Current Account

The international transactions of a nation are divided into three separate accounts: the *current account*, the *capital account*, and the *financial account*. For most countries, the capital account is relatively minor, and the two most important accounts are the current and financial accounts. The **current account** tracks the flow of goods and services into and out of the country, while the **financial account** is the record of the flow of financial capital. The **capital account** is the record of some specialized types of relatively small capital flows. This chapter examines the accounting system used to keep track of a country's international transactions. One of its primary goals is to understand the accounting relationships among domestic investment, domestic savings, and international flows of goods, services, and financial assets. In addition, we will use the international accounts to examine the meaning of international indebtedness and to discuss its consequences.

The Trade Balance

In 2008, the United States purchased $2,522 billion in goods and services from foreign suppliers. The composition of the purchases included a wide array of tangibles and intangibles, from Japanese Nintendos to Venezuelan oil and from luxury Mexican vacations to tickets on the European rail system. In the same year, U.S. firms exported $1,827 billion worth of aircraft, software, grains, trips to Disneyworld, and other goods and services. The difference between exports and imports of goods and services is called the **trade balance**. For the United States, the 2008 trade balance was $1,827 billion minus $2,522 billion, or –$695 billion. Because the number is negative, the United States had a trade deficit.

Exports and imports include both goods and services, so the trade balance can be decomposed into the balance on goods and the balance on services. In the case of the United States, the goods balance was in deficit by $840 billion, while the services balance was in surplus by $144 billion. In 2008, services were 30 percent of total exports, and for many years they have been a growing part of U.S. and world trade. The main items in services trade include travel and passenger fares; transportation services; royalties and license fees; and education, financial, business, and technical services.

Although the U.S. trade balance for services is in surplus, total trade in services is still too small a share of overall trade to counteract the very large deficit in the merchandise goods trade balance.

The Current Account Balance

The merchandise goods trade balance is the most commonly cited measurement of a nation's transactions with the rest of the world. The widespread dissemination of the monthly merchandise trade balance statistics through press releases and news articles makes it the most familiar concept in international economics as well as the basis of most people's understanding of U.S. international economic relations.

A more comprehensive statistic is the **current account balance**, which measures all current, nonfinancial transactions between a nation and the rest of the world. It has three main items: (1) the value of goods and services exported, minus the value of imports; (2) income received from investments abroad, minus income paid to foreigners on their U.S. investments; and (3) any foreign aid or other transfers received from foreigners, minus that given to foreigners. Each of the items—**goods and services**, **investment income**, and **unilateral transfers**—has credit (positive) and debit (negative) components. The simplest framework for conceptualizing these three components is in terms of credits and debits, as portrayed in Table 9.1.

The investment income items in Table 9.1 are not movements of investment capital but the income received or income paid on previous flows of financial capital. For example, financial capital sent to Germany to buy a bond would not be included, but the interest received on the bond would be. (The funds that leave the United States are counted in the financial accounts of the United States and Germany.) It is useful to think of investment income flows as payments for the use of another nation's financial capital. If U.S. mutual funds invest in the Mexican stock market, for example, the initial investment will not show up directly in the current account but will be included in the financial account. The subsequent flow of dividends back to the mutual fund in the United States will be counted in the United States as income received and in Mexico as income

---

TABLE 9.1	Components of the Current Account	
	Credit	Debit
1. Goods and services	Exports	Imports
2. Investment income	Income received on foreign investments	Income paid to foreigners on their U.S. investments
3. Unilateral transfers	Transfers received from abroad	Transfers made to foreigners

There are three main components to the current account. Each component is divided into debit and credit elements.

paid. Conceptually, it is as if U.S. investors are receiving payment for the rental of U.S. capital to Mexican firms, which makes it similar to payments for a service.

The third item in the current account balance includes payments made that are not in exchange for a good or service, such as foreign aid, or the remittances (sending home of the wages) of immigrants temporarily residing in another country. In the U.S. case, these payments are usually relatively small, but they can figure very importantly in the current account balances of developing countries receiving either substantial foreign aid or large remittances from their citizens working abroad.

Table 9.2 gives a picture of the U.S. current account in 2008. The $706,068 million deficit is part of the growing trend in U.S. current account deficits, as shown in Figure 9.1. Large deficits in the current account began around 1982, and have been more or less a constant feature of the U.S. economy since then. Although the deficit turned into a small surplus of $6.6 billion in 1991 (partly due to large unilateral transfers received by the United States as payment for Operation Desert Storm), since then it has deteriorated significantly.

We will explore the causes and consequences of large current account deficits later, but here it should be noted that it is not simply a sign of weakness. On the contrary, through much of the 1990s, rapid economic growth in the United States raised incomes and created a voracious appetite for imports. Meanwhile, economic

TABLE 9.2	The U.S. Current Account Balance, 2008
	Millions of Dollars
1. Goods and services	
Exports of goods	1,276,994
Exports of services	549,602
Imports of goods	–2,117,245
Imports of services	–405,287
2. Investment income	
Investment income received	764,637
Investment income paid	–646,406
3. Net unilateral transfers	–128,363
Memoranda	
Goods and services balance	–695,936
Current Account Balance	–706,068

The U.S. current account deficit in 2008 was $706,068 million. The deficit is largely the result of merchandise goods imports exceeding exports. The United States has surpluses in services and investment income.

Source: U.S. Department of Commerce, Bureau of Economic Analysis, http://www.bea.doc.gov/.

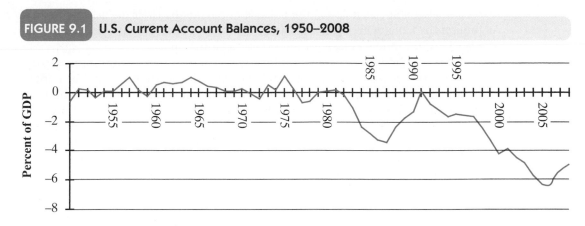

FIGURE 9.1   U.S. Current Account Balances, 1950–2008

There are two periods of large current account deficits in the United States. The first lasted through most of the 1980s, while the second began in the early 1990s and continues today.

Source: U.S. Department of Commerce, Bureau of Economic Analysis, http://www.bea.gov.

growth among the United States' main trading partners ranged between negative and sluggish so that foreign incomes did not rise as rapidly. Consequently, foreign demand for U.S. exports grew less rapidly than the U.S. demand for imports. Therefore, it can be argued that the current account deficit is a sign of relative U.S. economic strength. It would be a mistake to carry this argument too far, however, since everyone agrees that the deficit is not sustainable in the long run and that there is a potential for it to create serious future problems. We will look at this issue later in the chapter after we introduce a few more concepts.

Introduction to the Financial and Capital Accounts

The financial and capital accounts are the primary record of the international flow of financial capital and other assets. In most countries, the capital account is of lesser importance and the financial account is the primary statement of international financial flows. The capital account includes transfers of specific types of capital, such as debt forgiveness, the personal assets that migrants take with them when they cross international boundaries, and the transfer of real estate and other fixed assets, such as transfer of ownership of a military base or an embassy. The annual total of these flows is relatively small for most countries.

The financial account is divided into three categories: (1) net changes in U.S.-owned assets abroad, (2) net changes in foreign owned assets in the United States, and (3) net change in financial derivatives. Assets include bank accounts; stocks and bonds; and real property such as factories, businesses, and real estate. The value of financial derivatives is determined from the value of a variable such as interest rates, exchange rates, or commodity prices, which underlie them. They are complex financial contracts that are traded in a variety of forms, and until recently were not included in the balance of payments. Their inclusion in 2006 is thought to have eliminated a growing source of measurement error, as derivatives have become increasingly important in global finance.

Table 9.3 shows the capital and financial accounts in relation to the current account. Two points about the capital and financial accounts should be kept in mind. First, both accounts present the flow of assets during the year and not the stock of assets that have accumulated over time. Second, all flows are "net" changes rather than "gross" changes. Net changes are the differences between assets sold and assets bought, as when U.S. residents purchase shares in the Mexican stock market while simultaneously selling Mexican bonds. The net change in U.S.-owned assets is the difference between the value of the

TABLE 9.3 The U.S. Balance of Payments, 2008	
	Millions of Dollars
Current Account	
1. Goods and services	
Exports	1,826,956
Imports	–2,522,532
2. Investment income	
Investment income received	764,637
Investment income paid	–646,406
3. Net unilateral transfers	–128,363
Capital Account	
4. Capital account transactions, net	953
Financial Account	
5. Net change in U.S. assets abroad (increase/outflow (–))	–106
6. Net change in foreign assets in the United States (increase/inflow(+))	534,071
7. Net change in financial derivatives	–28,905
Statistical Discrepancy	200,055
Memoranda	
Balance on current account (1 + 2 + 3)	–706,068
Balance on capital and financial accounts (4 + 5 + 6 + 7)	506,013

The financial and capital accounts measure capital inflows and outflows and are equal to the current account, with sign reversed. The statistical discrepancy measures the amount by which we mismeasure.

Source: U.S. Department of Commerce, Bureau of Economic Analysis, http://www.bea.doc.gov/.

shares purchased and the bonds sold. If the stocks and bonds are equal in value, then the net change is zero. Net changes are informative because they measure the monetary value of the change in a country's financial stake in foreign economies.

Under the accounting procedure used to tabulate credits and debits in the financial account, outflows of financial assets are a debit item while inflows are a credit item. This point is most easily understood by considering home country financial outflows as payments for the purchase of foreign-owned assets, and financial inflows as receipts from the sale of home country assets to foreigners. In this manner, the negative and positive signs of asset flows are conceptually similar to imports and exports. In other words, the purchase of foreign assets requires capital outflows and are counted as debit (negative) entries in the financial account. Conversely, when foreigners purchase home country assets, there is a capital inflow and a credit (positive) entry in the financial account.

The current, capital, and financial accounts are interdependent. While the current account measures the flow of goods and services between a country and the rest of the world, the capital and financial accounts measure the flow of financing that is used to acquire the goods and services. More specifically, the sum of the capital and financial accounts is equal in absolute value to the current account, but with the opposite sign. For example, if a country has a $20 billion current account deficit, then it has a $20 billion surplus (inflow of financing) in its combined capital and financial accounts. The inflow of financial capital can take many forms, including foreign deposits in domestic banks, foreign purchases of domestic stocks and bonds, or foreign purchases of real estate and businesses, to name a few.

A large share of a nation's financial account transactions, however, is not in response to the current account flows of goods and services. For example, a London-based investment company may buy stock in a Chilean firm, lend money to the government of Thailand, and engage in any number of financial transactions that have nothing to do with the movements of goods and services on the current account. In an accounting sense, these purely financial transactions must have a net value of zero. The reason they add to zero is that the purchase of an asset is simultaneously the sale of an asset of equal value. For example, if you buy a share of stock, you obtain the asset of partial ownership while the person selling the share obtains your cash. It is the same internationally. If a Canadian citizen buys shares in the Mexican stock market (capital outflow), he or she must sell Canadian dollars or some other asset (capital inflow). (If he or she pays for the shares by writing a check drawn on a Mexican bank, then it does not enter the financial account since it is a change of one foreign asset for another.) As a result, the financial account is a complete picture of net flows of financial assets during the year.

At the very bottom of Table 9.3, the last item entered is in the row labeled "Statistical discrepancy." Previously, it was stated that the sum of the current account, capital account, and financial account must total zero. In an accounting sense they are zero, but not everything can be measured precisely, and the **statistical discrepancy** is the amount of mismeasurement. It is calculated as the sum of the current, capital, and financial accounts, with the sign reversed. In 2008 it was calculated as follows:

$$(-1) \times (-706,068 + 506,013) = 200,055$$

The statistical discrepancy exists because our record of all of the transactions in the balance of payments is incomplete. Although the errors could be in any of the three accounts, it is believed that most of the errors are in the financial account since it is the hardest one to measure accurately. Financial flows are intangible, and in certain cases such as money laundering associated with the illegal drug trade, the sending or receiving agents have incentives to hide them.

Types of Financial Flows

One of the primary concerns of most governments is the form of financial flows entering and leaving their country. Some financial flows are very mobile and represent short-run tendencies. These flows are often vehicles for transmitting a financial crisis from one country to another, or for generating sudden responses to changes in investor expectations about the short-run prospects of an economy. The degree of mobility of financial flows and the potential of some flows to introduce a large element of volatility into an economy have turned the consideration of the type of flows a country receives into a major issue.

As a first approach to a more detailed representation of the financial account, it is useful to subdivide the financial flows in Table 9.3 into categories that reference their origin in the public (governmental) or private sector. In most countries, the bulk of financial flows are private, although in times of crisis this can change. Table 9.4 shows the 2008 financial account for the United States, divided into five subcategories representing the main components of inflows and outflows in terms of public and private assets.

Official reserve assets are mainly the currencies of the largest and most stable economies in the world, such as U.S. dollars, EU euros, British pounds, and Japanese yen. Reserve assets also include gold and special drawing rights (SDR), the artificial currency of the International Monetary Fund (IMF). Reserve assets are used to settle international debts and, consequently, central banks and treasury ministries use them as a store of value. For example, when an importer in a small country such as Chile purchases a shipload of goods from Europe, payment may be in dollars or euros or pounds, but it is unlikely that the supplier would accept Chilean pesos from the purchaser. The importer must convert some pesos into a reserve currency, such as U.S. dollars, and use them to pay for its imports. If the Chilean central bank is unable to provide dollars or another reserve currency to Chilean banks and importers, then the import business grinds to a halt unless the importer is able to secure some form of credit from the seller.

Since all forms of international debts are settled with reserve assets, especially key currencies, they play a very prominent role in international finance. When they become scarce in a country, it signals that potentially serious problems are arising. For example, as discussed in Chapter 12, when Mexico's economy collapsed in late 1994 and early 1995, it was because Mexicans owed dollars to various international investors, but the sudden outflow of dollars from Mexico during 1994 had severely reduced the supply of dollars and, in the short run, made it impossible for firms and the government to pay their dollar denominated debts. Relief came when Mexico was able to arrange several loans from the IMF, the United States, and Canada, which replenished its supply of official reserve assets.

The fallout from the Mexican crisis of 1994–1995 was a disastrous recession and changes in the government's data reporting system so that everyone could track the inflows and outflows of reserve assets in a more timely manner. Note, however, that since the financial account reports on financial flows, it does not indicate the stock, or total supply, of assets available. From Table 9.4, we see that the United States had a debit of −$4,848 million in its change in official reserve assets. This represents payment for the purchase of official reserve assets, but there is no indication given in this accounting procedure for the total amount of reserve assets available to the United States.

Row 1.B in Table 9.4 includes other assets acquired by the federal government. These mainly represent loans to foreign governments, the rescheduling of past loans made to foreign governments, payments received on outstanding loans, and changes in nonreserve currency holdings, such as Mexican pesos or Israeli shekels. Line 2.A of Table 9.4 is symmetrical with 1.A. When the federal government needs to borrow money in order to cover its deficit or to refinance its debt, foreign governments usually purchase a share of the Treasury bills or bonds sold, and it shows up in line 2.A. U.S. Treasury securities are equivalent to reserve assets for foreign governments because they are easily sold for dollars and the dollar is universally accepted as payment for international debt. Private foreign interests may also purchase U.S. Treasury or other securities, however, and these purchases show up in line 2.B, along with other private investments in the U.S. economy.

TABLE 9.4   Components of the U.S. Financial Account, 2008

	Millions of Dollars
1. Net change in U.S. assets abroad (increase/outflow (–))	−106
A. U.S. official reserve assets	−4,848
B. U.S. government assets, other than official reserve assets	−529,615
C. U.S. private assets	534,357
2. Net change in foreign assets in the United States (increase/inflow (+))	534,071
A. Foreign official assets in the United States	487,021
B. Other foreign assets in the United States	47,050
3. Net change in financial derivatives	−28,905

There are six main categories of financial flows. Each of these categories can be further subdivided.

Source: U.S. Department of Commerce, Bureau of Economic Analysis, http://www.bea.doc.gov/.

The largest value in Table 9.4 is in row 1.C. Since financial outflows are a debit item, a positive value for net outflows tells us that on average, domestic firms disinvested abroad and brought their assets home to the United States. As a result, there was a net inflow (positive item) of private investment abroad. The movement of private assets shown in Rows 1.C and 2.B in Table 9.4 are broken into their subcomponents in Table 9.5.

In addition to the net change in financial derivatives, Table 9.5 shows three main subcomponents for net private outflows and inflows. The first subcomponent is **foreign direct investment (FDI)**. FDI was discussed in Chapter 4 where Dunning's OLI theory was presented. FDI in the financial account includes tangible items such as real estate, factories, warehouses, transportation facilities, and other physical (real) assets. The second and third subcomponents can be considered portfolio investment since they represent paper assets such as stocks, bonds, and loans. The similarity between FDI and **foreign portfolio investment** is that they both give their holders a claim on the future output of the foreign economy. They are very different, however, in their time horizons and this can have dramatic effects on the host country, where assets are located. Direct investments usually involve a longer time horizon because they are difficult to liquidate quickly and therefore represent a long-term position in the

TABLE 9.5 — Private Flows in the U.S. Financial Account, 2008	Millions of Dollars
1. U.S. private assets abroad, net (increase/outflow(–))	534,357
Subcomponents:	
A. Direct investment	–332,012
B. Foreign securities	60,761
C. Loans to foreign firms, including banks	805,608
2. Foreign-owned assets in the Unites States, other than official assets, net (increase/inflow(+))	47,050
Subcomponents:	
A. Direct investment	319,737
B. U.S. securities and currency	99,069
C. Loans to U.S. firms, including banks	–371,756
3. Net change in financial derivatives	–28,905

Private assets flows are the largest part of the financial account. Both private outflows and inflows are usefully divided into three symmetrical subcomponents. The net change in the value of financial derivatives comprises the other major category of private flows.

Source: U.S. Department of Commerce, Bureau of Economic Analysis, http://www.bea.doc.gov/.

host country. Portfolio investments in stocks and bonds tend to be more short term. While many investors may decide to hold their foreign securities through all the ups and downs, by their nature, stocks and bonds are much more liquid than real estate or factories. It is common, therefore, for portfolio investors to have a shorter time horizon, and to move quickly if they expect a downturn.

Shifts in expectations can lead to a sudden cessation of inflows followed by large and destabilizing outflows of financial capital. Economist Guillermo Calvo has labeled this a **sudden stop**. Sudden stops have been involved in most of the financial crises of the last thirty years. In terms of Table 9.5, they would appear as a sudden change from one year to the next in categories 2.B and 2.C, which would shift from positive to negative and possibly cause the entire financial account balance to become negative. Recall that a negative financial account means that there are no net inflows for financing a current account deficit and that the current account must move from a negative balance to a positive one, usually by reducing imports and increasing exports. In many cases, such a drastic shift in a country's trade relations leads to a deep depression.

The problems caused by a sudden stop can be compounded by the pattern of internal lending in the borrowing country. Frequently in international markets, banks and other financial institutions borrow funds that are denominated in a foreign currency, such as the dollar or the euro. The financial inflow of borrowed money is then used to increase lending at home after converting the funds to a local currency. If a sudden stop occurs, banks and other institutions are at risk since they have debts that are denominated in a foreign currency but revenues that are in the local currency. Access to the dollars or euros that they need in order to service their debts may be limited. Furthermore, if the sudden stop is accompanied by a fall in the value of the local currency, then institutions that have relied on borrowed financial inflows are also saddled with an increase in the size of their debts when measured in the domestic currency terms.

Limits on Financial Flows

Until a few years ago, most nations limited the movement of financial flows across their national borders. A typical pattern was to allow financial flows that were related to transactions on the current account, but to limit and regulate financial account transactions. If an importer needed a foreign loan to purchase goods abroad, or if an exporter needed foreign financing in order to buy materials needed to make export goods, then these financial flows were regulated but generally allowed. Conversely, if a bank wanted to borrow abroad in order to make loans at home then the inflow of financial capital to the bank was prohibited or subjected to such onerous terms and conditions that it was undesirable. These types of restrictions on financial flows were a normal part of the international economic landscape, even in industrial economies, until the 1980s and 1990s. For example, the members of the European Union did not completely liberalize financial flows between member countries until 1993.

In the movement toward more open markets over the last several decades, there has been a significant lifting of controls on financial flows across international boundaries. This change in international economic policy was seen as desirable because restrictions on financial flows limit the availability of financial capital. Developing countries, in particular, were thought to benefit from liberalization since they have the greatest scarcity of financial capital and their ability to raise incomes and living standards depends greatly on access to adequate financial capital.

In addition, it is difficult to disentangle financial flows related to financing current account transactions from flows that are purely financial account transactions. This makes it difficult to regulate or control international financial flows, and many economists argue that the attempt to do so creates unnecessary red tape and bureaucratic delay and arbitrariness, and reduces economic efficiency. For over a decade, through much of the 1980s and 1990s, the consensus among economists was that it is better to allow financial capital to move freely across international borders.

More recently, the extreme volatility in some financial markets and the severe damage it has caused to a number of countries has revived interest in some form of controls or regulations to limit the damage caused by unexpectedly large financial outflows. It is easy to understand the tensions involved, however. On the one hand, foreign capital inflows are beneficial because they enable countries to increase their investments in factories and ports and other physical assets that help raise living standards and incomes. On the other hand, the sudden outward flight of foreign financial capital can generate a debt crisis and throw a country into deep depression. The key is to capture the benefits of increased investment while minimizing the risks of capital flight. At this point there is not much consensus among economists about the best policies. We will look at this issue in more detail in Chapter 12 after we introduce several more concepts.

CASE STUDY

The Crisis of 2007–09 and the Balance of Payments

The global financial crisis that began in 2007 had both medium-run and short-run impacts on the balance of payments. It is too early to tell what the long-run impacts might be, but in its earliest stages the crisis was confined to financial markets and institutions and did not have an immediate impact on GDP or employment. In the United States and elsewhere, the first stages of the crisis began in the late summer of 2007 with severe strains in financial markets. These strains continued into 2008 and then intensified with the bankruptcy of a number of large financial services firms that had significant international business. Throughout late 2007 and into 2008, banks and other financial services firms such as insurance companies and securities dealers reassessed their portfolios and tried to reduce their risk exposure by selling their foreign assets in large quantities. The goal was to build reserves of short-term, highly liquid and secure assets such as cash and U.S. Treasury securities.

Banks and financial firms knew that some of the assets they held were "toxic" and unlikely to maintain their value or any value at all in some cases. As the crisis progressed, problems grew more intractable as it became increasingly difficult to determine a market value for assets that stopped trading and had no reference prices available. If banks could not build their reserves against their potential losses, the consequences would be disastrous, since they would lack the means to pay their own debts. The shifts in financial markets that began in late summer and early fall of 2007 were sudden, and continued throughout 2008. The sudden and large reversal in the normal pattern of global finance is illustrated in Table 9.6, which shows the main components of the financial account of the United States for 2007 and 2008.

Table 9.6 shows that both foreign and U.S. domestic interests shifted toward a defensive stance from 2007 to 2008 as they stopped accumulating each other's assets altogether, or greatly reduced their purchases. In 2007, U.S. private interests purchased 1.449 trillion (millions of millions) dollars of foreign assets (line 1.B), but in 2008 they sold over one-half trillion dollars (534 billion) of foreign assets. The primary source of the change was in the form of loans to foreigners (line 1.B.iii), and the secondary source was in the purchase of foreign securities (1.B.ii). Foreign

TABLE 9.6	The U.S. Financial Accounts, 2007–2008 (Millions of Dollars)	
	2007	**2008**
1. U.S.-owned assets abroad, excluding financial derivatives (increase/financial outflow (-))	**–1,472,126**	**–106**
A. U.S. government assets	–22,395	–534,463
B. U.S. private assets	–1,449,731	534,357
i. Direct investment	–398,597	–332,012
ii. Foreign securities	–366524	60,761
iii. Loans, including banks and non-banks	–684,610	805,608
2. Foreign-owned assets in the United States, excluding financial derivatives (increase/financial inflow (+))	**2,129,460**	**534,071**
A. Foreign official assets in the United States	480,949	487,021
B. Other foreign assets in the United States	1,648,511	47,050
i. Direct investment	275,758	319,737
ii. U.S. securities and currency	661,784	99,069
iii. Loans, including banks and non-banks	710,969	–371,756

Source: U.S. Department of Commerce, Bureau of Economic Analysis, http://www.bea.doc.gov/

direct investment by U.S. firms declined slightly but did not change very much.

U.S. government outflows partially offset the decline of private outflows (line 1.A.). These were primarily due to new agreements between the Federal Reserve Bank and the European Central Bank and the Bank of Japan, which provided dollars to Europe and Japan by buying and holding foreign currencies. The primary increase in U.S. government assets was European currencies other than the euro.

Line 2 shows that foreigners accumulated far fewer U.S. assets in 2008 than they did in 2007. The biggest change occurred in the area of loans to U.S. banks and non-financial firms, which moved from a net inflow to the United States of nearly $711 billion to a net outflow of $372 billion (line 2.B.iii). At the same time, foreign purchases of securities fell by over $550 billion.

In general, Table 9.6 illustrates how firms in both the United States and abroad sought to protect themselves against the spreading crisis by reducing new investments outside their home country and by bringing liquid assets home.

The Current Account and the Macroeconomy

There are two important practical reasons for learning about the balance of payments. One is to understand the broader implications of current account imbalances and to analyze the policies that might be used to tame a current account deficit. This is particularly important for small countries that are easily buffeted about by changes in the global economy, but it is also of interest to a big economy such as the United States, where very large current account deficits have been the norm for several years. A second practical reason for studying the balance of payments is to try to understand how countries might avoid a crisis brought on by volatile financial flows, and what policies will minimize the harmful affects of a crisis if it occurs. Economic analysis is still in its infancy when it comes to the problem of volatile financial flows, and there is some distance to travel before there is likely to be a consensus agreement on issues such as free versus restricted capital mobility, or the links from financial flows to economic growth. Nevertheless, there are some basic points of agreement among economists, and we will discuss them in Chapters 10 and 12. Before then, we must examine the relationship of the current account to the macroeconomy, which requires a brief review of basic concepts from the principles of macroeconomics.

The National Income and Product Accounts

The internal, domestic accounting systems used by countries to keep track of total production and total income are called the **national income and product accounts (NIPA)**. These accounts are very detailed presentations of income, output, and other measures of a nation's macroeconomy. We will use the most fundamental concepts from this accounting system, beginning with the concept of **gross domestic product (GDP)**. Recall from the principles of economics that a nation's gross domestic product is the market value of all final goods and services produced inside its borders during some time period, usually a year. GDP is the most common measure of the size of an economy, although it is widely recognized that it ignores some important considerations, such as the value of leisure time and environmental degradation that takes place during the process of producing the nation's output. In addition, GDP only includes goods that pass through organized markets, so household production (cooking, sewing, landscaping, childcare, and so on) and other non-market-oriented production are left out. For these and other reasons, economists caution against using GDP as a sole determinant of the well-being of a society. In spite of these limitations, however, it provides a starting point for understanding different economies.

In order to avoid the problem of double counting, GDP only includes the value of *final* goods and services. This is actually a strength of the measure, since if we added the value of steel sold to a car maker and the value of the cars, we would be counting the steel twice: once as steel and a second time as part of the value of the car. The final part of the definition states that GDP must be measured over some time period, usually a year. Most countries measure GDP every three months, but for most purposes, including ours, the most useful time period to consider is the span of one year.

An alternative concept for measuring a nation's output is **gross national product (GNP)**. For most countries, the difference between the two concepts is very small, because GNP is the value of all final goods and services produced by the labor, capital, and other resources of a country, regardless of where production occurred. In an accounting sense, GNP is equal to GDP plus investment income and unilateral transfers received from foreigners minus investment income and unilateral transfers paid to foreigners:

$$\text{GDP} + \text{foreign investment income received}$$

$$- \text{ investment income paid to foreigners}$$

$$+ \text{ net unilateral transfers} = \text{GNP}$$

Note that the difference between GNP and GDP is precisely equal to lines 2 and 3 in Tables 9.1, 9.2, and 9.3: the investment income and unilateral transfers components of the current account balance. This fact is useful because GDP includes exports minus imports and it enables us to bring the entire current account concept into the picture.

The usefulness of adding net foreign investment income (investment income received minus investment income paid) plus net unilateral transfers is apparent when we look at the definition of GDP based on its four main components. Table 9.7 defines the necessary variables. GDP is equal to the sum of consumer expenditures plus investment expenditures plus government expenditures on goods and services plus exports of goods and services minus imports of goods and services:

$$\text{GDP} = C + I + G + X - M \qquad (9.1)$$

TABLE 9.7	Variable Definitions
Variable	Definition
GDP	Gross domestic product
GNP	Gross national product
C	Consumption expenditures
I	Investment expenditures
G	Government expenditures on goods and services
X	Exports of goods and services
M	Imports of goods and services
CA	Current account balance
S	Private savings (savings of households and firms)
T	Net taxes, or taxes paid minus transfer payments received

Given that GNP is equal to GDP plus net foreign investment income and net unilateral transfers:

$$GNP = GDP + (\text{Net foreign investment income} + \text{net transfers}) \quad (9.2)$$

or

$$GNP = (C + I + G) + (X - M + \text{Net foreign investment income} \quad (9.3)$$
$$+ \text{net transfers})$$

we can write the definition of GNP in terms of the current account balance. Rewriting Equation (9.3) in a simpler form gives us the following:

$$GNP = C + I + G + CA \quad (9.4)$$

Equation (9.4) explicitly shows the relationship between the current account and the main macroeconomic variables such as consumer spending, investment, and government purchases.

As the total value of goods and services produced by the labor, capital, and other resources of a country, GNP is also the value of income received. This follows from the fact that the production of final goods and services generates incomes that are equal in value to output and is embodied in the basic macroeconomic accounting identity stating that every economy's income must equal its output. From the point of view of the income recipients, there are three choices or obligations: They may consume their income (C), save it (S), or use it to pay taxes (T). In reality, all of us do a combination of the three. This permits us to rewrite the definition of GNP in terms of income and its uses as follows:

$$GNP = C + S + T \quad (9.5)$$

Since Equations (9.4) and (9.5) are equivalent definitions of GNP—one in terms of the components of output, the other in terms of the uses of income—we can set them equal to each other as follows:

$$C + I + G + CA = C + S + T \qquad (9.6)$$

Subtracting consumption from both sides and rearranging terms gives us the following:

$$I + G + CA = S + T \qquad (9.7)$$

or

$$S + (T - G) = I + CA \qquad (9.8)$$

Equation (9.8) is an accounting identity, or something that is true by definition. It is worth memorizing because it summarizes the important relationship between the current account balance, investment, and public and private savings in the economy. Equation (9.8) does not reveal any of the causal mechanisms through which changes in savings or investment are connected to the current account balance, but it does provide insight into the economy. For example, if total savings remains unchanged while investment increases, then the current account balance must move toward, or deeper into, deficit.

In order to see this, it is necessary to be certain that you understand the term on the left side, $(T - G)$. This is the combined (federal, state, and local) budget balances of all levels of government, or, to say it another way, government savings. It is savings because (T) is government revenue (or income) and (G) is government expenditure. A positive $(T - G)$ states that the combined government budgets are in surplus, which in the governmental sector is equivalent to savings. Conversely, a negative $(T - G)$ is a deficit, or dissavings. By placing governmental budget balances on the left-hand side, we are emphasizing that there are two sources of savings in an economy: the private sector (S) and the public or governmental sector $(T - G)$. If governments dissave (run deficits), then they must borrow from the private sector, which reduces total national savings on the left-hand side.

From Equation (9.8) we see that a nation's savings (private plus public) is divided into two uses. First, it is a source of funds for domestic investment (I). This role is crucial because new investments in machinery and equipment are a source of economic growth. Investment is essential as the means to upgrade the skills of the labor force, to provide more capital on the job, and to improve the quality of capital by introducing new technology. According to Equation (9.8), if government budgets are in deficit, the total supply of national savings is reduced, and, all else equal, investment will be less than it might otherwise have been. Conversely, a surplus in government budgets will augment private savings and increase the funds available for investment, all else equal.

The second use for national savings is as a source of funds for foreign investment. If the current account is in surplus, national savings finances the purchase of domestic goods by foreign users of those goods. In return, or as payment, the domestic economy acquires foreign financial assets. Recall from the discussion of the relationship between the current and financial accounts that the financial account is more or less a mirror image of the current account. In other words, a positive current account is associated with a negative financial account, which is an outflow of financial capital. Equivalence between the outflow's magnitude and the current account surplus ensures that foreigners obtain the financial resources they need to buy more goods and services than they sell in world markets. In a sense, the surplus country provides its savings to the rest of the world, thereby enabling it (the surplus country) to sell more goods abroad than it buys. For a surplus country, a financial capital outflow is an investment because it involves the acquisition of assets that are expected to pay a future return. It is not the same as domestic investment, however, because the assets are outside the country. Hence, another name for the current account balance is *net foreign investment*. A positive balance implies positive foreign investment, while a negative balance implies negative investment (disinvestment), or a reduction in net foreign assets.

With the exception of 1991, when it received large income payments in compensation for the Gulf War, the United States has had a current account deficit every year since 1981 (see Figure 9.1). In 2008, the deficit was 5.0 percent of GNP. Figure 9.2 shows the current account balance since 1990 and the three related macroeconomic variables from Equation (9.8). Since 1990, the general trend in private savings (S) is down while the trend in investment (I) is up. Both of these factors are related to a decline in the current account balance, holding public savings (T – G) constant. (T – G) was not constant, however, and the increase in public savings during the second half of the 1990s could have provided increased funds for domestic and foreign investment, except for the fact that private savings deteriorated as public savings increased. Since 2000, the decline in the government accounts has consumed the slight increase in private savings and the current account has continued to decline.

The four macroeconomic variables in Figure 9.2 demonstrate that there is not a fixed relationship between current account balances and government budget balances, or between savings and investment. Each of the four variables are determined by the other three and a change in any one of them influences all of them. For example, during an economic recession, many countries have budget deficits. In 2009, Spain's budget deficit was approximately 9.6 percent of its GDP, and Singapore, which normally runs a budget surplus, had budget deficits equal to 4 percent of its GDP. But while Spain's current account deficit was similar to its budget deficit (7.5 percent of GDP), Singapore's current account was in surplus by an amount equal to nearly 15 percent of its GDP.

The availability of global financial flows has made it easier for current account deficit countries to obtain the outside financing they need when their domestic savings is inadequate. Global capital flows have not completely broken the link between domestic savings and domestic investment, as most countries have savings and investment levels that are roughly similar, but this is not true for every country and in recent years it has been less and less true overall. For example, developing countries with relatively low savings such as Honduras, Ethiopia, and Kenya have managed to invest much larger shares of their GDP than they could if they relied on their domestic savings alone. This is possible because capital inflows are available to finance their current account deficit and to provide an additional source of funding for investment.

Are Current Account Deficits Harmful?

The relationship between the current account balance, investment, and total national savings is an identity. Consequently, it does not tell us why an economy runs a current account deficit or surplus. In Equation (9.8)

$$S + (T - G) = I + CA$$

the left and right sides are equal by definition. Consequently, we cannot say that the current account is in deficit because saving is too low any more than we can say it is because investment is too high.

FIGURE 9.2   **U.S. Savings and Investment, 1990–2007**

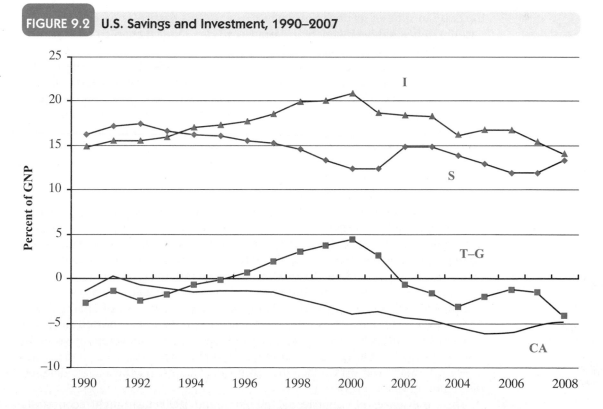

During the 1990s, private saving (S) fell while investment (I) rose. The gap between saving and investment was filled by increased public saving (positive T − G) and capital inflows (negative CA).

Source: U.S. Department of Commerce, Bureau of Economic Analysis, http://www.bea.gov.

There is a general tendency in the media and the public to interpret a current account deficit as a sign of weakness and as harmful to the nation's welfare. Another interpretation is that the deficit enables more investment than would be possible otherwise, and since higher investment is correlated with higher living standards, the current account deficit might be interpreted as beneficial. In addition, the capital inflows that are associated with current account deficits are an implicit vote of confidence by foreigners. For example, between 1980 and 1991, Japan invested more than $25 billion of its trade surplus in U.S. manufacturing. By the start of the 1990s, the Japanese owned 66 steel works, 20 rubber and tire factories, 8 major car assembly plants, and 270 auto parts suppliers, employing more than 100,000 workers. Furthermore, the investment came at a time when the three major U.S.-based auto manufacturers (Chrysler, Ford, and GM) were laying off workers and relocating production abroad. Some of the Japanese firms were acquisitions (which may have closed if they had not been bought) and many were new plants built from scratch with Japanese savings. During the deficits of the 1990s, foreign investors continued to pour in capital, enabling the United States to raise its level of investment and increase its productivity in spite of its declining savings rate. In this particular case, the current account deficit has been beneficial because, all else equal, it enabled more investment than was possible otherwise, given the savings rate.

Current account deficits can also generate problems, however. The capital inflows that occur with a current account deficit increase the stock of foreign-owned assets inside the home country, raising the possibility that a change in investor expectations about the economy's future can lead to a sudden surge in capital outflows. In the worst case scenario, capital flight is followed by a depletion of international reserves and a financial crisis. This is an experience shared by a number of developing countries since the 1980s, but it should not lead you to believe that the optimal policy for a country is to avoid current account deficits. As we have just seen, such deficits allow countries to invest more than they could otherwise, and this is particularly important for developing countries where investment capital is especially scarce. Furthermore, current account surpluses are no guarantee that a country will be able to avoid a crisis if one develops among its trading partners. International financial crises, like some biological diseases, tend to be contagious. When Mexico slipped into the peso crisis in late 1994 and early 1995, for example, economists and journalists began to write about the "Tequila effect" on Latin America. Similarly, when the currency of Thailand (the baht) lost a large share of its value in July of 1997, the media reported stories of "baht-ulism" spreading across East Asia and the rest of the developing world. In both cases, the size of a country's current account balances was not a good predictor of whether it was drawn into the crisis. (See Chapter 12 for a more detailed discussion of financial crises.)

The experiences of countries in the 1980s and 1990s has taught economists that financial crises are determined by more than the size of the current account deficit, and that there are no absolute thresholds between safe and dangerous levels of a deficit. While deficits of 3 to 4 percent of GDP begin to raise red flags, and deficits of 7 to 9 percent are considered extremely risky, there are too many other factors that must be taken into consideration before the probability of a crisis can be determined.

CASE STUDY

Current Account Deficits in the United States

Figures 9.1 and 9.2 illustrate the growing problem of the U.S. current account deficit. In 2008, the deficit was over $700 billion and nearly 5 percent of GDP. For most developed countries, current account deficits in the range of 4 to 5 percent of GDP usually trigger adjustments that force a reduction in their size. It seems only natural to ask whether the the crisis that began in 2007 is related to the size of the U.S. current account deficit.

In Figure 9.1, there are two periods of widening current account deficits. In the 1980s, the deficit widened, then closed. The second episode began in the early 1990s with a deficit that continued to expand until very recently. While the current account deficits look similar in these two episodes, the movement of the other variables in Equation (9.8) were significantly different.

Beginning around 1981, the budget of the federal government turned the overall (federal-state-local) government balance, (T − G), into a large negative number. Given the lack of private savings to finance both domestic investment (I) and public sector dissaving, foreign finance filled the gap and the current account turned negative. The 1990s story is different in several ways, but perhaps most importantly, in that over the course of the decade, the federal budget moved from a large negative to a positive. If everything had remained the same, this would have reduced the need for foreign savings and pushed the current account in the direction of surplus, but (S) and (I) were not constant. The decade saw sharp increases in investment spending as corporations bought new computer technology and the telecommunications equipment they needed to stay competitive. In addition, a stock market boom followed by a housing market boom made consumers much wealthier, with the result that households rapidly increased their consumption and decreased their personal savings. Therefore, the changes in the government budget were overwhelmed by the increases in investment and by the decline in savings, resulting in a large and growing current account deficit. In 2002, large federal budget deficits returned and put additional pressure on the United States to seek foreign financing for its domestic and foreign investment.

Before the crisis that began in 2007, a central concern of some observers was whether or not the U.S. current account deficit posed a danger to the U.S. economy. After the crisis began, a separate set of questions surfaced about the role of the deficit in creating the crisis itself. While no one argued that the current account deficits caused the crisis, there is perhaps a significant relationship between the two having to do with the long-run consequences of global imbalances.

In order for the United States to run a significant current account deficit over many years, it had to be financed by countries with surpluses that collectively matched it. In terms of the balance of payments, U.S. current account deficits were financed by capital inflows in its financial account. These net capital inflows represented the trade surpluses of countries such as Germany, Japan, and China, which were invested in the United States. In other words, the counterpart to U.S. deficits was a series of surpluses elsewhere in the global economy.

In effect, the willingness of governments and firms outside the United States to invest their earnings inside the United States enabled it to run large current account deficits over a long period while maintaining a low level of public and private savings. This had a number of consequences, including the housing boom of the 2000s and the consumption spree (low savings rates) of many Americans. Housing finance became awash in funds to lend, consumer credit was extremely easy to get, and many Americans had lifestyles that were supported by their indirect access to the savings of households, firms, and governments abroad. In Germany, Japan, China, and other surplus countries, savings rates were high, consumption ran well below incomes, and trade surpluses grew larger and larger, particularly after 2000.

If these global imbalances were short run, or if they were used to make a series of investments that raised productivity (which they did, in part), then the problems they caused would not be severe. However, some economists argue that the global imbalances were at the root of the crisis that began in 2007 because they persisted for a long time and encouraged the gradual accumulation of problems that eventually became extremely severe. To begin, financial market regulators were not prepared for large inflows of foreign capital, and lacked sufficient experience to understand the hidden dangers if the inflows persisted over a long period. Banks and securities firms that received deposits felt pressure to make loans so they would have earnings to cover the interest on their deposits. Over a period of many years, the steady availability of funds from surplus countries helped hold interest rates down and encouraged borrowing, especially for big-ticket items such as houses and cars. Easy money for home loans raised the demand for housing and pushed up home prices. Rising home prices made them seem like a safe investment, which only encouraged more borrowing and further building. Given the nature of many of the loans that were made for the purchase of housing, when home prices began to fall, the entire system unraveled, causing enormous losses for the banks and others that were tied up in the home loan market.

International Debt

Current account deficits must be financed through inflows of financial capital. Recall from Table 9.5 and the previous discussion that capital inflows take different forms, from direct investment to purchases of stocks, bonds, and currency, to loans. Loans from abroad add to a country's stock of **external debt** and generate **debt service** obligations requiring interest payments and repayment of the principal. Debt is defined as money owed to nonresidents that must be paid in a foreign currency. It includes the debts on borrowings by both governments and the private sector, and long and short term debt, where short term is anything under a year. Theoretically, foreign loans are no more harmful than any other type of debt. That is, as long as the borrowed funds are used to increase skills and production levels, the borrower will be able to service the debt without difficulty. In practice, however, it is not uncommon for borrowed funds to be used in a manner that does not contribute to the expansion of the country's productive capacity, and often debt service becomes an unsustainable burden that holds back economic development.

All countries, rich and poor, have external debt. In the case of high-income countries, debt service is rarely an issue, because the amount of debt is usually relatively small compared to the size of the economy. Low- and middle-income countries are another matter. In a number of cases, the size of the external debt burden is unsustainable, given the economy's ability to make interest payments and to repay the principal.

Unsustainable debt occurs for a number of reasons. In some cases, countries are dependent on exports of one or two basic commodities such as copper and coffee. The shock of a sudden drop in world commodity prices reduces the value of exports and sometimes generates unexpectedly large current account deficits. In other cases, countries experience natural disasters such as hurricanes and earthquakes that create a need for relief and foreign assistance, or civil conflicts that fuel a demand for arms purchases. Corruption too can play a role, as described later in the case of the Democratic Republic of the Congo. Even electoral politics may be a factor, as when officials try to gain support through unsustainable expenditures targeted at important constituents. Finally, the behavior of foreign lenders also plays a role, as described next.

Debt is a serious problem. In 2007, the world's low- and middle-income countries had total debt obligations of nearly 3.5 trillion dollars, which required more than 500 billion dollars a year in interest and principal repayment. Debt burdens worsen the budget position of central governments by adding payments that must be made to outsiders, and they reduce the availability of funds for important domestic needs such as infrastructure projects, schools, and health care. Excessive debt burdens may also intensify and spread an economic crisis, such as occurred with the East Asian Crisis of 1997–1998.

Table 9.8 shows the five largest low- and middle-income country debtors as of 2007. The table shows total debt as well as two measures of the burden of debt; debt service (interest plus principal repayment) to exports and debt service to GNP. Debt service payments as a percentage of exports gives a good idea of the share of a country's foreign exchange earnings that it must use to make debt payments, while debt service to GNP gives an idea of the share of total production that must be devoted to debt payments. The largest debtor, China, appears to have sustainable debt levels given that its total debt service requires slightly more than 2 percent of its export earnings, and its debt levels are equal to only

TABLE 9.8	The Five Largest Developing Country Debtors, 2007		
Country	Debt, Billion US$	Debt Service as a Percent of GNP	Debt Service as a Percent of Exports
China	373.6	1.0	2.2
Turkey	251.5	7.5	32.1
Brazil	237.5	4.4	27.8
India	221.0	3.5	7.7
Mexico	178.1	4.0	12.5

Larger economies can handle more debt, but even some large economies find that a large share of their exports must go to debt service.

Source: World Bank, World Development Indicators.

1 percent of its gross product. Turkey, on the other hand, is also a large country but its debt levels are relatively more burdensome and require nearly one-third of its export earnings. This limits the use of Turkey's foreign exchange earnings and poses a significant burden on its economy, which must devote 7.5 percent of its total production to servicing its debt.

Debt problems of developing countries have received considerable attention in recent years from multilateral organizations such as the World Bank, from high-income-country governments, and from private organizations that have argued for debt relief. One notable movement is the Highly Indebted Poor Country (HIPC) program, which is a join venture of the World Bank, the IMF, and high-income-country governments. The goal of the HIPC program is to provide debt forgiveness for a select group of countries that must qualify based on high levels of poverty and debt and a track record of economic reform. There are currently forty countries in the HIPC program, thirty-three of which are in sub-Saharan Africa, and to date they have had 80 percent of their debt erased.

CASE STUDY

Odious Debt

Thirty-three of the forty HIPC countries are in sub-Saharan Africa. The average income per capita of the forty countries is $468 and life expectancy at birth is fifty-three years. Given the countries' conditions of extreme poverty, it is hard to argue against debt relief, yet some people question its value. Their primary argument is that it would be wasted money since the conditions that created debt are likely to persist, leading to a new round of borrowing and a return to previous levels of debt. Others worry that debt relief might cause some countries to borrow excessively in the belief that their debt burden will be forgiven later.

Economists do not have a single point of view on this issue, although many favor some sort of debt relief despite the arguments just made. The cost of debt forgiveness for the most severely indebted poor countries is inconsequential compared to the economies of the high-income countries, which are the ones that would be called upon to forgive the debts. In addition, some share of the debt is classified as odious debt and in those cases the arguments in favor of debt relief are impossible to ignore. **Odious debt** is legally defined as debt incurred without the consent of the people and that is not used for their benefit. It is associated with corrupt governments and countries where freedom is severely limited or does not exist.

Many cases of odious debt can be found among the forty countries that qualify for the HIPC initiative. For example, in sub-Saharan Africa, the Democratic Republic of the Congo (formerly Zaire), Kenya, and Uganda almost certainly fall into this category, while at least part of the debt of many other countries would as well. Between 1972 and 1999, about 60 percent of the loans to HIPC countries went to regimes considered "not free" by Freedom House, an international organization that ranks countries as free, partly free, or not free. And between 1985 and 1995, about 67 percent of the loans made to HIPC countries went to places that were considered corrupt by the *International Country Risk Guide*, a risk analysis service.

The Democratic Republic of the Congo (DRC) is a clear-cut case. From 1965 to 1997, the DRC was ruled by the dictator Joseph Desire Mobutu. During Mobutu's reign, real GDP, measured in the equivalent of U.S. dollars at 2000 prices, fell from $317 per person to $110 per person while the regime amassed billions of dollars in foreign aid and loans. Mobutu's personal fortune was estimated to have reached $4 to $6 billion, most of which was deposited in Swiss bank accounts. In 2004, per capita income was at $88 and international debts were around $12 billion. The latter was equivalent to about 225 percent of GDP and 1,280 percent of a year's exports.

Given the continued decline in incomes and the large number of unfinished projects that were financed by various governments and multilateral agencies, there is little evidence that the borrowed money was successfully used for development purposes. Furthermore, lenders knew the situation when they made their loans, but they went ahead anyway since they wanted to secure access to the DRC's mineral deposits of cobalt and other strategic metals. Cases like the DRC make it difficult to argue that its citizens should be forced to pay off the debt. In 2003, the DRC was admitted to the HIPC program and qualified for up to 80 percent debt forgiveness, depending on its macroeconomic performance.

Sources: Birdsall and Williamson, *Delivering on Debt Relief*, 2002, Center for Global Development and Institute for International Economics, Washington, DC; World Bank, *Global Development Finance*, 2003, World Bank, Washington, DC.

The International Investment Position

Each year that a nation runs a current account deficit, it borrows from abroad and adds to its indebtedness to foreigners. Each year that it runs a current account surplus, it lends to foreigners and reduces its overall indebtedness. If the total of all domestic assets owned by foreigners is subtracted from the total of all foreign assets owned by residents of the home country, the result is the **international investment position**. If the international investment position is positive, then the home country could sell all its foreign assets and have more than enough revenue to purchase all the domestic assets owned by foreigners. If it is negative, then selling all foreign assets would not provide enough revenue to buy all the domestic assets owned by foreigners.

As an example of the international investment position, consider the United States at the end of 2008. The market value of all assets outside the United States and owned by governments, businesses, and residents of the United States was $19,888 billion. Among other things, these assets included factories, shares of stock, bonds, foreign currency, and bank loans. At the same time, the market value of assets located in the United States and owned by governments, businesses, and residents abroad was $23,357 billion. As a result, the international investment position of the United States at the end of 2008 was –$3,469 billion. To summarize:

International investment position

= domestically owned foreign assets − foreign owned domestic assets

= $19,888 billion − $23,357 billion

= −3,469 billion

The large current account deficits of the 1980s, 1990s, and 2000s have eroded the United States' investment position from a positive $288.6 billion in 1983 to zero in 1989, and negative since then. Each year a country experiences a current account deficit, foreigners acquire more assets inside its boundaries than its residents acquire abroad, and the international investment position shrinks further.

We have considered many of the costs and benefits of capital inflows. They enable countries to invest more than would otherwise be the case, but they also make it possible for governments and consumers to spend more (save less). One of the benefits not discussed so far is the possibility of **technology transfer**. When capital inflows take the form of direct investment, they may bring new technologies, new management techniques, and new ideas to the host country. This transfer is particularly important for developing countries that lack access or information about newer technologies, but it is also important for high-income countries. Technology transfer is by no means an inevitable outcome of foreign direct investment, and much of the current research on this type of capital flow seeks to understand the conditions that encourage or discourage it.

One of the costs of capital inflows that has not been discussed is their potential to provide access to political power. Much depends on the political culture of the host country receiving the capital inflows, but large direct investment flows, as well as portfolio investment flows, are likely to provide access to politically significant people. This is the case in large and small countries, but it is particularly important in low- and middle-income countries, where wealth encounters fewer countervailing powers or contending interests.

Summary

- Every nation's transactions with the rest of the world are summarized in its balance of payments. The balance of payments has three components: the current account, the capital account, and the financial account. The two most important components are the current and financial accounts.

- The current account is a record of a nation's trade, investment income, and transfers between it and the rest of the world.

- The financial account is a record of financial capital flows between a country and the rest of the world. The financial account is equal to the current account plus the capital account, with the sign reversed. This follows from the accounting principle that every purchase or sale of a good or service must generate a payment or a receipt.

- Capital flows in the financial account are grouped together as governmental and private. Private flows are the bulk of international capital flows. They are grouped into categories of direct investment and portfolio investment. In general, direct investment is longer-term and, therefore, less volatile.

- Large, sudden outflows of financial capital have created economic instability in many countries, particularly during the 1990s. This has created an active debate over the merits of restricting foreign capital flows. Economists are divided on this point, with some favoring restrictions and some favoring free capital mobility.

- There is a fundamental economic identity that total private and public saving in an economy must be equal to domestic investment plus net foreign investment. The current account balance is equal to net foreign investment, and a negative balance is equivalent to disinvestment abroad.

- Current account deficits enable a country to invest more than it could otherwise, which has a beneficial effect on national income. If deficits are too large, however, they increase the vulnerability of a country to sudden outflows of financial capital.

- Forty low-income countries are classified as highly indebted poor countries (HIPC). Thirty-three of the countries are in sub-Saharan Africa. All forty have unsustainable debt levels, some of which may be considered odious debt because it is debt incurred without the consent of the country's citizens and is not used for their benefit.

- The international investment position is the difference between foreign-based assets owned by residents in the home country and home-based assets owned by residents of foreign countries.

■ Foreign investment has costs and benefits for the host country. While it may lead to technology transfer and higher investment levels, it can also become a mechanism for spreading a crisis and give foreigners a voice in the nation's internal political affairs.

Vocabulary

capital account

current account

current account balance

debt service

external debt

financial account

foreign direct investment (FDI)

foreign portfolio investment

goods and services

gross domestic product (GDP)

gross national product (GNP)

international investment position

investment income

national income and product accounts (NIPA)

odious debt

official reserve assets

statistical discrepancy

sudden stop

technology transfer

trade balance

unilateral transfers

Study Questions

1. Use the following information to answer the questions below. Assume that the capital account is equal to 0.

Net unilateral transfers	250
Exports of goods and services	500
Net increase in U.S. government's nonreserve foreign assets	30
Net increase in foreign ownership of U.S.-based nonreserve assets	400
Net increase in U.S. private assets abroad	250
Invest income received in the United States	200
Net increase in U.S. ownership of official reserve assets	20
Imports of goods and services	600
Net increase in foreign ownership of U.S.-based reserve assets	100
Investment income paid abroad by the United States	300

   a. What is the current account balance?
   b. Does the financial account equal the current account?
   c. What is the statistical discrepancy?

2. Look at each of the cases below from the point of view of the balance of payments for the United States. Determine the subcategory of the current account or financial account that each transaction would be classified in, and state whether it would enter as a credit or debit.

    a. The U.S. government sells gold for dollars.

    b. A migrant worker in California sends $500 home to his village in Mexico.

    c. An American mutual fund manager uses the deposits of his fund investors to buy Brazilian telecommunication stocks.

    d. A Japanese firm in Tennessee buys car parts from a subsidiary in Malaysia.

    e. An American church donates five tons of rice to the Sudan to help with famine relief.

    f. An American retired couple flies from Seattle to Tokyo on Japan Airlines.

    g. The Mexican government sells pesos to the United States Treasury and buys dollars.

3. Weigh the pros and cons of a large trade deficit.

4. Is the budget deficit of a country linked to its current account balance? How so? Explain how it is possible for the United States' current account deficit to grow while the budget deficit has disappeared.

5. Compare and contrast portfolio capital flows with direct investment capital flows.

6. Why is a current account surplus equivalent to foreign investment?

Measuring the International Investment Position

It may seem like a straightforward job to add up the value of assets, but nothing could be further from the truth. Consider the following problem: The United States ran trade surpluses in the 1950s and 1960s and accumulated large holdings of foreign assets. In the 1980s and 1990s, the United States ran trade deficits and foreigners accumulated large holdings inside the United States. By 2008, a sizable proportion of U.S.-owned assets had been purchased decades ago when prices were much lower, and foreign-owned assets were purchased recently, after the worldwide inflation of the 1970s and the early 1980s. If asset values are tallied using their historical costs (the price at the time of purchase), then foreign-owned assets appear more valuable, not necessarily because they are but because they were acquired more recently when world prices were higher.

It seems logical to expect that the reporting of asset values would be done on a current cost basis, rather than a historical cost basis, where current cost is the cost of purchasing the asset in the current period. Unfortunately, it does not happen this way. In the United States, firms use historical cost as the basis for valuation of assets in company records, and they use this when they report their foreign holdings to the agency that collects the data, the Bureau of Economic Analysis. The difference between current cost and historical cost does not affect the measurement of portfolio investment, which is relatively short term, but it has significant effects on the measurement of direct investment since it is held for longer time periods.

Until 1991, the United States only calculated the historical cost of U.S.-owned foreign assets. As a result, the U.S. international investment position appeared to become negative very rapidly as large trade deficits in the mid-1980s led to a rapid accumulation of new assets in the United States by foreign interests. More recently, in the 1990s, the United States began to report all assets on a current value basis. The primary deficiency in this data as it now stands is that it cannot be broken down into country-specific or industry-specific data. Therefore, we know the overall international investment position for the United States, but we cannot accurately examine the U.S.-Japan bilateral investment position, since we have U.S. assets in Japan only on a historical cost basis.

APPENDIX B
Balance of Payments Data

Current account and international investment data are readily available for most nations of the world.

Bureau of Economic Analysis

The Bureau of Economic Analysis is the official source of national income and product and international accounts data for the United States. It has an easy-to-use Web site with a complete set of data for both the current and historical periods. It is located at http://www.bea.gov.

International Financial Statistics (IFS)

This is a regular publication of the International Monetary Fund. It appears monthly, with an annual *Yearbook* at the year's end. As the name implies, the IFS focuses on financial data, but it also contains information on current accounts and international capital flows. Coverage is of most of the world's nations, and the most recent *Yearbook* usually contains a decade of data for each country. The IMF publications are one of the sources used by many international agencies and private enterprises. Nearly all university libraries and many city libraries will have the IFS.

Balance of Payments Statistics (BOPS)

This is a sister publication of the IMF that complements the data in the *IFS*. The *BOPS* has the most up-to-date and detailed current account statistics of any international data source. In addition, it contains detailed breakdowns of capital flows.

Exchange Rates and Exchange Rate Systems

Introduction: Fixed, Flexible, or In-Between?

The topics of exchange rates and exchange rate systems are less settled than most issues examined so far. The lack of consensus is partly because countries must decide on the type of exchange rate system that best suits their conditions, and there is a fairly extensive menu of choices for selection. Some of the choices are relatively recent innovations, such as crawling pegs or target rate zones, and their performance characteristics under a wide array of economic conditions have yet to be fully analyzed. In general, the choice of an exchange rate system varies along a continuum from completely flexible rates that are determined by the market forces of supply and demand, to completely fixed rates that are set and maintained by a country's central bank. Between these two poles there are many intermediate forms combining various degrees of fixity and flexibility in the determination of the exchange rate.

A further complication is that each type of exchange rate requires a different set of policies by government officials and each responds differently to pressures from the world economy. All three of these factors—exchange rate system, government policy, and the world economy—interact in ways that are at times impossible to predict and, as a result, have given rise to an active set of debates over the selection and management of a country's exchange rate system.

Exchange Rates and Currency Trading

The **exchange rate** is the price of one currency stated in terms of a second currency. An exchange rate can be given in one of two ways, either as units of domestic currency per unit of foreign currency or vice versa. For example, we might give the U.S.-Mexico exchange rate as dollars per peso (0.10 dollars) or pesos per dollar (10 pesos). The custom varies with the currency. For example, the U.S. dollar–British pound exchange rate is usually quoted in terms of dollars per pound, but the U.S. dollar–Mexican peso exchange rate is usually pesos per dollar. In this chapter and the rest of the book, the exchange rate is always given as the number of units of domestic currency per unit of foreign currency. For the United States, this means it is dollars per peso and dollars per pound.

Exchange rates are reported in every newspaper with a business section and on numerous Web sites. Figure 10.1 shows several years of average U.S. dollar values for three of the most frequently traded currencies: the European Union's euro, the Japanese yen, and the British pound. The rates are taken from the U.S. Federal Reserve Bank's Web site, and are the interbank rate that one bank charges another when buying large amounts of currency. Tourists and individuals purchasing relatively small amounts would have paid more.

All three are flexible exchange rates, meaning that they are not fixed over time. Consequently, you can see that the euro began to appreciate against the dollar sometime in 2001 and gradually rose in value from just under 90 cents to nearly $1.50 per euro in 2008. The trajectory of the British pound over the same time was similar, but the Japanese yen was much more variable and did not move in just one direction.

Note also that one euro is less valuable than one pound and that one yen is worth a fraction of a pound or a euro. It is a common mistake to interpret this to mean that the yen is weaker than both of the other currencies and the euro is weaker than the pound. Currencies are scales like centigrade and Fahrenheit, or miles and kilometers. It does not matter how many of one (kilometers, yen, degrees Fahrenheit) it takes to equal another (miles, euros, degrees centrigrade); we cannot use the words *weak* and *strong* to describe them in this sense. A currency is considered weak, or weakening, if it is depreciating against another. The euro appreciated against the dollar from approximately 2001 until 2008. The dollar was weak against the euro during that period because it had a persistent tendency to lose value when measured in euro terms. During the entire period shown in Figure 10.1, the dollar was neither consistently weak nor strong against the yen, but it was generally weak against the pound.

FIGURE 10.1   **Dollar Exchange Rates for Commonly Traded Currencies, 1999–2008**

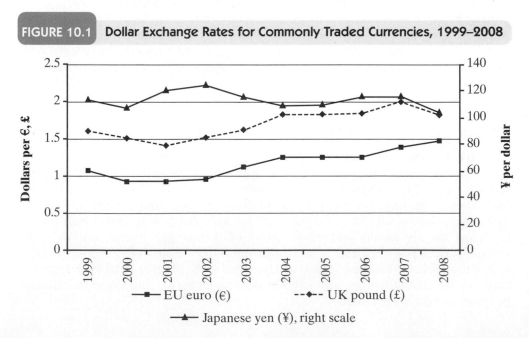

Reasons for Holding Foreign Currencies

Economists identify three reasons for holding foreign currency. The first is for trade and investment purposes. Traders (importers and exporters) and investors routinely transact in foreign currencies, either receiving or making payments in another country's money. Tourists are included in this category because they hold foreign exchange in order to buy foreign goods and services.

The second reason for holding foreign exchange is to take advantage of interest rate differentials, or **interest rate arbitrage**. Arbitrage conveys the idea of buying something where it is relatively cheap and selling it where it is relatively expensive. Interest rate arbitrage is similar in that arbitrageurs borrow money where interest rates are relatively low and lend it where rates are relatively high. By moving financial capital in this way, interest rate arbitrage keeps interest rates from diverging too far, and also constitutes one of the primary linkages between national economies. Capital inflows to the high interest rate countries put downward pressure on interest rates, while the outflow from the low interest rate countries dries up the supply and puts upward pressure on rates. This drawing together of interest rates in different countries is one way in which economic conditions are transmitted across national borders. Various other factors intervene in this relationship, such as perceptions of risk, but in general, interest rate arbitrage is a powerful force in the world economy and tends to be one of the main reasons for holding foreign currency.

The third reason for holding foreign exchange is to speculate. Speculators are businesses who buy or sell a currency because they expect its price to rise or fall. They have no need for foreign exchange to buy goods or services or financial assets; rather, they hope to realize profits or avoid losses through correctly anticipating changes in a currency's market value. Speculators are often reviled in the popular press, but in fact they help to bring currencies into equilibrium after they have become over- or undervalued. If speculators view a currency as overvalued, they will sell it and, in the process, drive down its value and thereby realize the result they anticipated. If they guess wrong, however, they tend to lose a lot of money since they place their bets on a result that does not materialize. For this reason, some economists have argued that speculation either serves the useful function of bringing currency values into proper alignment, or its practitioners lose money and go out of business. Not everyone agrees with this view, however, and some economists feel that speculation against a currency can be destabilizing in the sense that it does not always push an exchange rate to its equilibrium value, but instead will sometimes lead to a grossly over- or undervalued currency, which is a major problem for the country involved. Needless to say, the role of speculation in the market for foreign exchange is an issue that has not reached a consensus.

Institutions

There are four main participants in foreign currency markets: retail customers, commercial banks, foreign exchange brokers, and central banks. Of these four, commercial banks are the most important. Retail customers include firms and individuals that hold foreign exchange for any of the three reasons given in the previous section—to engage in purchases, to adjust their portfolios, or to profit from expected future currency movements. In most cases, they buy and sell through a commercial bank. Commercial banks in many parts of the world hold inventories of foreign currencies as part of the services offered to customers. Not all banks provide this service, but those that do usually have a relationship with several foreign banks where they hold their balances of foreign currencies. When a surplus accumulates, or a shortage develops, the banks trade with each other to adjust their holdings.

In the United States, foreign exchange brokers also play an important role. It is not very common for U.S. banks to trade currency with foreign banks. Instead, U.S. banks tend to go through foreign exchange brokers, who act as middlemen between buyers and sellers since they do not usually hold foreign exchange. Brokers can also serve as agents for central banks. The market, then, works as follows. An individual or firm that needs foreign exchange calls its bank. The bank quotes a price at which it will sell the currency. The price is based on one of two possible sources of supply: The bank may have an account with another bank in the country where the currency is used, or it may call a foreign exchange broker. The broker keeps track of buyers and sellers of currencies and acts as a deal maker by bringing together a seller and a bank that is buying for its customer.

In most cases, currency trades take the form of credits and debits to a firm's bank accounts. For example, a local U.S. importer that must make payment in yen can call and tell its bank to transfer yen to the Japanese bank of the firm that supplies the importer with goods. The importer will have a debit to its local bank account that is equivalent to the cost of the yen. If the U.S. bank has a branch or correspondence bank in Japan, it can electronically notify the branch to debit the yen from the account of the U.S. bank and credit it to the Japanese bank of the supplier. If the U.S. bank goes through a currency trader instead of dealing directly with a Japanese bank, then it first buys yen that are in an account with a Japanese bank. Next, it requests that some or all of its yen assets be transferred to the bank of the Japanese supplier of the U.S. importer.

Exchange Rate Risk

Firms that do business in more than one country are subject to **exchange rate risks**. These risks stem from the fact that currencies are constantly changing in value and, as a result, expected future payments that will be made or received in a foreign currency will be a different domestic currency amount from when the contract was signed.

Suppose, for example, that a U.S. semiconductor manufacturer signs a contract to send a British computer manufacturer a shipment of microprocessors in six months. If the U.S. manufacturer agrees on a price in British pounds, it must know the value of the pound six months from now in order to know the dollar equivalent of its future revenue. If the U.S. manufacturer specifies that the microprocessors be paid for in dollars, then it shifts the exchange rate risk to the British firm. The U.S. company knows the exact dollar amount it will receive in six months, but the British firm is uncertain of the price of the dollar, and therefore the pound price of microprocessors.

Financial markets recognized this problem long ago and, in the nineteenth century, they created mechanisms for dealing with it. The mechanisms are the forward exchange rate and the forward market. The **forward exchange rate** is the price of a currency that will be delivered in the future; the **forward market** refers to the market in which the buying and selling of currencies for future delivery takes place. Forward markets for currencies are an everyday tool for international traders, investors, and speculators because they are a way to eliminate the exchange rate risk associated with future payments and receipts. Forward foreign exchange markets allow an exporter or importer to sign a currency contract on the day they sign an agreement to ship or receive goods. The currency contract guarantees a set price for the foreign currency, usually 30, 90, or 180 days into the future. By contrast, the market for buying and selling in the present is called a **spot market**. The prices of foreign currencies quoted in Figure 10.1 are "spot prices."

Suppose the U.S. semiconductor manufacturer signs a contract to deliver the microprocessors to the British firm in six months. Suppose also that the price is stated in British pounds. The manufacturer knows precisely how many pounds it will earn six months from now, but it does not know whether the pound will rise or fall in value, so it does not know what it will earn in dollar terms. The solution is to sign a forward contract to sell British pounds six months from now in exchange for U.S. dollars at a price agreed upon today. Using the forward market, the U.S. manufacturer avoids the risk that comes from exchange rate fluctuations.

Forward markets are important to financial investors and speculators as well as exporters and importers. For example, bondholders and other interest rate arbitrageurs often use forward markets to protect themselves against the foreign exchange risk incurred while holding foreign bonds and other financial assets. This is called **hedging** and it is accomplished by buying a forward contract to sell foreign currency at the same time that the bond or other interest-earning asset matures. When interest rate arbitrageurs use the forward market to insure against exchange rate risk, it is called **covered interest arbitrage**.

The Supply and Demand for Foreign Exchange

The value of one nation's money, like most things, can be analyzed by looking at its supply and demand. Under a system of flexible, or floating, exchange rates, an increase in the demand for the dollar will raise its price (cause an **appreciation** in its value), while an increase in its supply will lower its price (cause a **depreciation**). Under a fixed exchange rate system, the value of the dollar is held constant through the actions of the central bank that counteract the market forces of supply and demand. Consequently, supply and demand analysis is a useful tool for understanding the pressures on a currency regardless of the type of exchange rate system adopted. For this reason, we begin with the assumption that exchange rates are completely flexible. After examining the usefulness of supply and demand analysis, we will turn to alternative systems, including gold standards and other variations on fixed exchange rates.

Supply and Demand with Flexible Exchange Rates

Figure 10.2 shows the demand for British pounds in the United States. The curve is a normal downward-sloping demand curve, indicating that as the pound depreciates relative to the dollar, the quantity of pounds demanded by Americans increases. Note also that we are measuring the price of the pound—the exchange rate—on the vertical axis. Since it is dollars per pound ($/£), it is the price of a pound in terms of dollars and an increase in the exchange rate (R) is a decline in the value of the dollar. In other words, movements up the vertical axis represent an increase in the price of the pound, which is equivalent to a fall in the price of the dollar. Similarly, movements down the vertical axis represent a decrease in the price of the pound.

For Americans, British goods are less expensive when the pound is cheaper and the dollar is stronger. Hence, at depreciated values for the pound, Americans will switch from U.S. or third-party suppliers of goods and services to British suppliers. However, before they can purchase goods made in Britain, first they must exchange dollars for British pounds. Consequently, the increased demand for British goods is simultaneously an increase in the quantity of British pounds demanded.

Figure 10.3 shows the supply side of the picture. The supply curve slopes up because British firms and consumers are willing to buy a greater quantity of American goods as the dollar becomes cheaper. That is, they receive more dollars per pound. However, before British customers can buy American goods, first

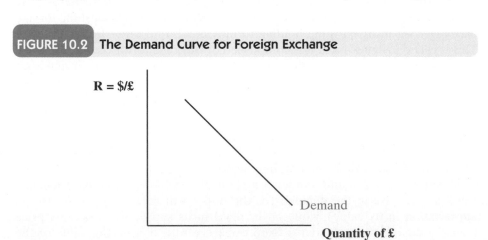

FIGURE 10.2 **The Demand Curve for Foreign Exchange**

R = $/£

Demand

Quantity of £

As the exchange rate falls, the dollar appreciates and the dollar price of British goods falls. The quantity of pounds demanded by the U.S. market increases as U.S. consumers and firms purchase more goods and services in Britain.

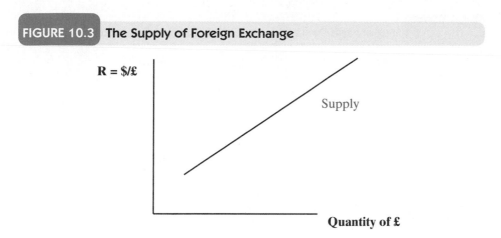

FIGURE 10.3 The Supply of Foreign Exchange

As the exchange rate rises, the dollar depreciates and the pound price of U.S. goods falls. The quantity of pounds supplied to the U.S. market increases as British consumers and firms purchase more goods in the United States.

they must convert pounds into dollars, so the increase in the quantity of American goods demanded is simultaneously an increase in the quantity of foreign currency supplied to the United States.

Figure 10.4 combines the supply and demand curves. The intersection determines the market exchange rate and the quantity of pounds supplied to the United States. At exchange rate R_1, the demand and supply of British pounds to the United States is Q_1.

Exchange Rates in the Long Run

We have determined that the supply curve slopes up to the right and the demand curve slopes down. The next step in supply and demand analysis is to consider the factors that determine the intersection of supply and demand and the actual exchange rate. We will continue to assume that the exchange rate is completely flexible. Later in the chapter we look at exchange rates that are fixed, and at intermediate rates between fixed and flexible.

In Figure 10.5, an increase in the U.S. demand for the pound (rightward shift of the demand curve) causes a rise in the exchange rate, an appreciation in the pound, and a depreciation in the dollar. Conversely, a fall in demand would shift the demand curve left and lead to a falling pound and a rising dollar. On the supply side, an increase in the supply of pounds to the U.S. market (supply curve shifts right) is illustrated in Figure 10.6, where a new intersection for supply and demand occurs at a lower exchange rate and an appreciated dollar. A decrease in the supply of pounds shifts the curve leftward, causing the exchange rate to rise and the dollar to depreciate.

The causal factors behind the shifts in the supply and demand are easier to conceptualize if we divide the determinants of exchange rates into three

FIGURE 10.4   Supply and Demand in the Foreign Exchange Market

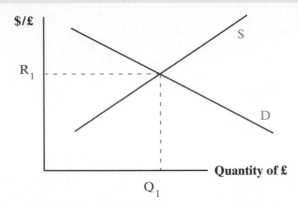

The intersection of the supply of British pounds to the U.S. market and the U.S. demand for British pounds determines the quantity of pounds available in the United States (Q_1) and their dollar price (exchange rate R_1).

periods: long run, medium run, and short run. This seems to be accurate empirically, as not all the factors that determine an exchange rate show up instantaneously. In fact, some causal factors take a very long time—a decade or more—to exert their full influence, and in the meantime, a number of short-run or medium-run factors may push in a completely opposite direction.

Looking at the long run first, **purchasing power parity** states that the equilibrium value of an exchange rate is at the level that allows a given amount of money

FIGURE 10.5   An Increase in Demand for British Pounds

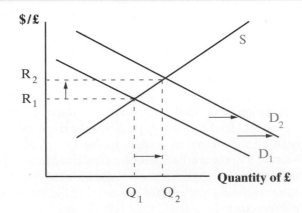

An increase in the U.S. demand for British pounds (rightward shift of the curve) causes the dollar to depreciate.

FIGURE 10.6   An Increase in the Supply of British Pounds

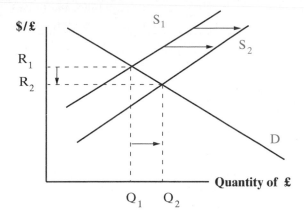

An increase in the supply of British pounds to the U.S. market (rightward shift of the curve) causes the dollar to appreciate.

to buy the same quantity of goods abroad that it will buy at home. By this criteria, the equilibrium exchange rate is the point where the dollar buys pounds at a rate that keeps its purchasing power over goods and services constant. That is, $100 buys the right amount of pounds to enable the purchase of the same basket of goods and services in Britain that $100 buys in the United States. Table 10.1 illustrates this idea.

In Table 10.1, a basket of goods costs $1,000 or £500, depending on the country where it is purchased. Accordingly, the long-run tendency is for the exchange rate to move to $2 per £. If it is above that, the pound is overvalued and the dollar is undervalued. An overvalued pound buys more in the United States than in Britain since it would be possible to convert £500 to more than $1,000 and buy a larger basket of goods than can be bought in Britain. Exchange rates less than $2 would imply the opposite—the pound is undervalued and the dollar overvalued.

It should be stressed that this is an underlying tendency and not a description of actual exchange rates at any point in time. Over the long run, purchasing power parity exerts influence over exchange rates, but in the short to medium run, there are significant deviations from this pattern. If you have traveled outside your home country, you are probably aware of cases where your domestic currency buys you so much foreign currency that your standard of living is higher when you travel. You might be able to stay in a better class of hotel, eat in better restaurants, and shop for items that you cannot afford at home. Or you may be familiar with the opposite, where your standard of living declines because you get so little foreign currency in exchange for your domestic currency that everything seems inordinately expensive.

Purchasing power parity influences currency values indirectly. When a currency is overvalued or undervalued, it creates profit-making opportunities for merchants that can move goods across international borders. Suppose, for example,

TABLE 10.1	A Hypothetical Example of the Exchange Rate in the Long Run	
	Cost of the Same Basket of Goods in Each Country	
Price in dollars	$1,000	
Price in pounds	£500	
Long-run equilibrium exchange rate	($1,000/£500) = $2/£	

Purchasing power parity states that dollars will tend to exchange for pounds at a rate that maintains a constant purchasing power of a given quantity of currency.

that the dollar is overvalued and that instead of $2 per pound, the exchange rate is $1.75 per pound. Prices are assumed to be the same as those shown in Table 10.1. In this case, $1,000 buys £571.43 (1,000/1.75). If merchants take the £571.43 and buy British goods and then ship the goods to the United States, they can earn more than $1,000. (They earn $1,142.86 since goods prices are 2 to 1.) In the long run, the demand for British pounds increases and, as shown in Figure 10.5, the exchange rate rises. The process will continue until the exchange rate hits $2 per £, and there are no more profit-making opportunities from shipping goods from Britain to the United States.

The process just described is reinforced by the flow of goods from Britain to the United States. The supply of goods shrinks in Britain, leading to rising prices there. In the United States, supply rises and, under normal competitive conditions, prices will fall. These effects will take a while to exert themselves, but they are another factor reinforcing purchasing power parity. In this case, however, prices are moving in the direction that equalizes the purchasing power of the two currencies instead of equalization through exchange rate movement as in the previous example. In theory, it does not matter which changes—prices or exchange rates—but given that prices in many countries tend not to fall easily, while exchange rates are relatively easily moved, most of the equalization probably occurs through exchange rate movements.

The story of goods arbitrage—buying where the goods are cheaper and selling where they are more expensive—which stands behind purchasing power parity, obviously has a few unrealistic assumptions. In particular, it requires that goods flow costlessly across international borders and that all goods and services can be traded. In reality, there are transportation costs involved with moving goods. This means that our merchant who buys £571.43 of goods in Britain and sells them for $1,142.86 in the United States loses some of his or her $142.86 profit to shipping, insurance, and other transaction costs. In addition, he or she pays a fee to a bank or a currency broker when buying the needed pounds.

Nor is this the only obstacle standing in the way of profits. Few nations have eliminated all their barriers to the entry of foreign goods and services. The merchant may face a tariff, import license fees, inspection fees, or some other barrier at the border that adds to his or her cost. In the limit, imports of the goods in question may be prohibited and goods arbitrage may be impossible at any price differential. In addition, some goods and many services are not traded. For example, restaurant meals, haircuts, landscape maintenance, and a host of other services that must be consumed on the spot are rarely, if ever, traded.

Once the assumptions of purchasing power parity are examined, it is not surprising that it exerts its influence over exchange rates only in the long run. If there are significant profit-making opportunities through goods arbitrage, then in spite of today's obstacles, entrepreneurs will work to create the conditions that will allow them to take advantage of the price differentials across markets. They will look for ways to lower transport costs, to minimize the costs of compliance with import rules and regulations, and to change the rules where it is feasible. All of these steps take time, but in spite of the real obstacles to its operation, purchasing power parity remains a significant long-run force in the determination of exchange rates.

Exchange Rates in the Medium Run and Short Run

While purchasing power parity is working slowly in the background, other forces have more immediate impacts on the position of the supply and demand curves for foreign exchange. We turn first to the forces that are correlated with the business cycle, the natural but irregular rhythms of expansion and recession that every country undergoes. Given that the time period from the peak of one expansion to the next is usually several years in duration, the forces that are tied to the business cycle can be considered medium run. That is, they are pressures on an exchange rate that may last for several years, but almost always less than a decade and usually less than five to seven years.

The most important medium-run force is the strength of a country's economic growth. Rapid growth implies rising incomes and increased consumption. When consumers feel secure in their jobs and at the same time experience a rapid growth in their incomes, they spend more, some of which will be on imports and travel abroad. As a result, rapid economic growth at home is translated into increased imports and an outward shift in the demand for foreign currency, as shown in Figure 10.5. Holding constant a host of short-run forces that may be in play at the same time, the effect of rapid economic growth at home is a depreciating currency.

The effect of growth is symmetrical, both with respect to slower growth at home, and with respect to the rate of economic growth abroad. Slower growth, such as a recession during which output declines (negative economic growth), raises consumer uncertainty about jobs and reduces many people's incomes. For the economy as a whole, as consumption expenditures fall, expenditures on imports decline as well, and the demand for foreign exchange falls. A leftward shift of the demand curve reduces the exchange rate and appreciates the currency. In other words, just as more rapid economic growth can cause a depreciation in a country's currency, slower growth sets forces in motion that lead to an appreciation.

Growth abroad does not have a direct effect on the home country's demand for foreign exchange (although it may have an indirect effect through its stimulation of the home economy), but it will directly affect the supply curve. More rapid foreign growth leads to more exports from the home country, and slower foreign growth results in fewer exports. More exports to foreigners increase the supply of foreign currency and shift the supply curve rightward, as shown in Figure 10.6. Fewer exports have the opposite effect. You should practice drawing the effects of changes in the rates of home and foreign economic growth on the supply and demand curves for foreign exchange.

Turning from the medium run of the business cycle to short-run periods of a year or less, a number of forces are constantly at work shaping currency values. The foremost short-run force is the flow of financial capital. The effects of financial flows range from minor and subtle to dramatic and, at times, catastrophic. They are as capable of creating slight day-to-day variations in the value of a currency as they are of creating complete financial chaos and bringing down governments. The degree of volatility in financial flows varies greatly and is highly responsive to governmental policies and conditions in the world economy. The impact on exchange rates of large-scale, short-run movements in financial capital has become one of the most serious issues in international economics.

Two variables in particular are responsible for a large share of short-run capital flows: interest rates and expectations about future exchange rates. These two forces often influence each other and are capable of creating unpredictable interactions, as when a change in interest rates reshapes investor confidence or catalyzes speculative actions in currency markets.

The role of interest rates in the short-run determination of exchange rates is crucial. The interest rate–exchange rate relationship is summed up in the **interest parity** condition, which states that the difference between any pair of countries' interest rates is approximately equal to the expected change in the exchange rate. The appendix at the end of this chapter develops the algebra of this relationship, but the intuition is not difficult to grasp. Suppose an investor has a choice between investing at home and earning interest i, or investing abroad and earning interest rate i*. If foreign interest rates are higher than domestic ones, it may seem advantageous to invest abroad, but this is not necessarily the case. The best choice is also determined by exchange rate movements during the investment period. If investors want to convert their future earnings back into their home currency, then exchange rate movements must be taken into account during the investment period. In order to protect against unanticipated losses due to currency fluctuations, cross border investors can sign a forward contract to sell the foreign exchange from their future earnings. This is known as covered interest arbitrage and is a common way to take advantage of interest differentials while guarding against the risk of exchange rate losses.

A simple example will help clarify. Suppose a U.S.-based investor has a choice between a one-year certificate of deposit (CD) issued by a U.S. bank or a German bank. For the sake of simplicity, assume that they are similar with respect to risk, transaction costs, and other characteristics. The U.S. investment is denominated in dollars and pays 3 percent (i) while the German investment is in euros and pays 2 percent (i*). In one year, $1,000 invested in the United States will pay $(1 + 0.03)$ thousand, or $1,030, while the return on the German CD depends on the fixed interest rate and the exchange rate a year from now. If the dollar-euro spot rate is 1.2 today, then the investor can use the $1,000 to buy $(1,000/1.2)$, or €833.33, which can be invested at 2 percent in Germany. In one year, the investor will have $833.33 \times (1 + 0.02)$, or €850. If the exchange rate is 1.3 a year from now, then $1,000 converted to euros today and invested in Germany will pay 850×1.3, or $1,105. That is, the investor earns $(1.3/R) \times (1 + 0.02)$ in one year, where R is today's spot rate of exchange.

The problem for the investor is that he or she cannot know what the exchange rate will be one year from now. Our example fudged this point by assuming that the rate was 1.3 dollars per euro in one year's time, but in fact we cannot know what the spot exchange rate will be in a year. Given this uncertainty, investors turn to the forward market where they can sign a contract guaranteeing them a fixed amount of dollars for the euros they will have in one year when the CD matures.

Let F stand for the forward exchange rate and R for the spot rate. The difference between the two is the expected appreciation or depreciation. If $F > R$, then the dollar is expected to depreciate, and is said to be selling at a discount. If $F < R$, then the dollar is expected to appreciate and is selling at a premium. Given information about F and R, our investor is prepared to select between the dollar and euro CDs.

In our previous example, R is 1.2 and F is 1.3, implying that the dollar is at a discount in the forward market and people expect it to depreciate over the next year. The choices are as follows. An investor with $1,000 can earn $1,000 \times (1.03)$, or $1,030 in the United States. Or he or she can earn $(1.3/1.2) \times (1.02) \times \$1,000$, which is $1,105 if he or she invests in Germany. Clearly the German investment is better and will attract capital. Money flowing into German CDs will push down German interest rates (i* falls) and increase the spot price of the euro (R rises). Both changes reduce earnings on the German CD until, in the end, we reach the interest parity condition

$$i - i^* \approx (F - R)/R$$

which says that interest rate differences are approximately equal to the expected change in the exchange rate.

The utility of the interest parity condition is that it brings together capital flows, domestic interest rate policy, and exchange rate expectations. Suppose, for example, that domestic interest rates are above foreign rates, so that $i > i^*$. In that case, investors expect a discount in the forward market, so that $F > R$. If the expected depreciation in the domestic currency is not sufficient to compensate for higher interest rates at home, then capital flows into the country, increases demand for domestic currency, and pushes down domestic interest rates until the difference between i and i* is approximately equal to the percentage difference between the forward and spot exchange rates.

Consider another example. Suppose that home interest rates are less than foreign rates $(i < i^*)$ and that forward rates are less than spot rates $(F < R)$ by an appropriate amount so that the interest parity condition holds. Beginning at this point, home policymakers decide for some reason to raise their interest rates to the same level as foreign rates: $i = i^*$. Now, investors in both home and foreign markets will invest more at home because they earn the same rate of interest, and they expect domestic currency to appreciate in value (since $F < R$). Figure 10.7 illustrates these shifts. Note that both the demand curve for foreign currency and the supply curve of foreign currency shift, with demand moving in and supply moving out. Taken together, both shifts reinforce a downward movement in the spot rate. As R falls, domestic currency appreciates and the gap between F and R closes. If $i = i^*$, the process ends when $F = R$.

In addition to their impact on the forward-spot rate differential, expectations play a crucial role in the determination of exchange rates in another way. A sudden change in the expected future value of an exchange rate can have a dramatic and often self-fulfilling impact on a country's currency. For example, if investors suddenly come to believe that a currency must depreciate more than they had anticipated, it lowers the expected value of assets denominated in that currency. This can create a sudden exodus of financial capital and put enormous pressure on the country's supply of foreign exchange reserves. To a significant extent, episodes of capital flight can be self-fulfilling in their expectations about an exchange rate. If investors expect depreciation, they try to convert their assets to another currency. This raises the demand for foreign exchange and depresses the supply, fulfilling the expectation of a depreciation.

There are numerous potential causes of this type of volatility in financial capital flows and exchange rate shifts. It also seems likely that technological changes in telecommunications have altered the sensitivity of markets toward changes in expectations, although this is yet to be established definitively. Nevertheless, it is certain that a frequent cause of sudden shifts in expectations is the realization that a particular government is practicing economic policies that are internally inconsistent and unsustainable. We will examine this in more detail in Chapters 11 and 12,

FIGURE 10.7   **The Effects of an Increase in Home's Interest Rate**

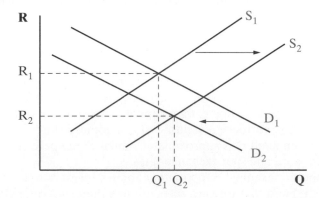

An increase in domestic interest rates causes a decrease in demand and an increase in supply of the foreign currency. Both effects cause an appreciation in the exchange rate from R_1 to R_2.

but it is relatively easy to get a sense of the meaning of inconsistent policies. An example is policies that are designed to stimulate the economy strongly (more growth → more imports → more demand for foreign exchange) when the supply of foreign exchange is severely limited (not enough exports, very low interest rates).

CASE STUDY

The Largest Market in the World

In 2007, the world's foreign exchange markets traded an estimated $3,210 billion worth of currency per day. Another way to look at this is that every 4.3 days, currency trades equaled the value of U.S. annual GDP. These estimates come from a survey of fifty-four central banks that is conducted every three years by the Bank for International Settlements (BIS), a "central bank for central banks." The BIS survey is the *Triennial Central Bank Survey of Foreign Exchange and Derivatives Market Activity in April 2007*, and is available from the BIS at *http://www.bis.org*.

Between 1992 and 2007, the volume of exchange rate transactions grew from $880 billion per day to $3,210 billion. This is an annual growth rate of over 9 percent per year and far higher than the growth of the world economy. In 2007, 86.3 percent of every currency trade involved the U.S. dollar, and 33.0 percent involved the EU's euro (see Table 10.2). Not surprisingly, the U.S. dollar/euro exchange was the most common, with 27 percent of all transactions, followed by the U.S. dollar/yen (13 percent) and the U.S. dollar/UK pound (12 percent).

TABLE 10.2   **Composition of Currency Trades, April 2007**

Currency	Percent of Total Trades
U.S. dollar	86.3
EU euro	37.0
Japanese yen	16.5
UK pound	15.0
Swiss franc	6.1
Australian dollar	6.8
Canadian dollar	6.7
Emerging markets	4.2
Other	27.5

Source: Bank for International Settlements, http://www.bis.org.

TABLE 10.3	Currency Trading Centers
Location	**Percent of World Currency Trading**
United Kingdom	34.1
United States	16.6
Japan	6.0
Singapore	5.8
France	3.0
Hong Kong	4.4
Australia	4.2
Switzerland	6.1
Other	19.8

Source: Bank for International Settlements, http://www.bis.org.

Note that the total in Table 10.2 is 200 percent rather than 100 percent because every sale is simultaneously a purchase. The dollar is so often traded because it is used as an international medium of exchange and because of the cross-trading that occurs between pairs of currencies. That is, a Chilean importer may pay his or her Mexican supplier in U.S. dollars, or he or she may use Chilean pesos to buy dollars and use the dollars to buy Mexican pesos. It is unlikely that the Mexican exporter would accept Chilean pesos, so one way or another the importer has to come up with dollars.

Currency trading is concentrated in four main centers: London, New York, Tokyo, and Singapore. London is by far the largest center of foreign exchange trading, as is illustrated by the BIS survey's finding that more U.S. dollars are traded in London than in New York (see Table 10.3). Given the preponderance of the U.S. dollar in currency trades and the importance of London as a trading center, it follows that most of the trades in London do not involve the British pound.

The mechanisms from inconsistent policy to exchange rate crisis and collapse are fairly well understood, but this begs the question about the cause of a sudden shift in expectations. Many recent episodes of sudden exchange rate shifts have occurred when investors lost confidence in a particular currency. Yet why the sudden change in investor confidence? Government policies had been in place for years in some cases, yet suddenly they were deemed unsustainable and likely to lead to a severe depreciation. In order to understand this, economists will have to develop a far deeper understanding of the subtle relationships between actual economic conditions and psychological expectations. Reaching this goal is far off at this point.

TABLE 10.4	Major Determinants of an Appreciation or Depreciation	
	R Falls: An Appreciation in the Domestic Currency	R Rises: A Depreciation in the Domestic Currency
Long run: Purchasing Power Parity	Home goods are less expensive than foreign goods	Home goods are more expensive than foreign goods
Medium run: The Business Cycle	Domestic economy grows more slowly than foreign	Domestic economy grows faster than foreign
Short run (1): Interest Parity	Home interest rates rise, or foreign rates fall	Home interest rates fall, or foreign rates rise
Short run (2): Speculation	Expectations of a future appreciation	Expectations of a future depreciation

Table 10.4 summarizes the long-, medium-, and short-run factors that have been discussed. The list is not exhaustive, but the main elements are included.

The Real Exchange Rate

The concept of the exchange rate that has been used so far and that is exemplified by the values shown in Table 10.2 does not really tell us what a foreign currency is worth. Exchange rates tell us how many units of domestic currency we give up for one unit of foreign currency, but unless we know what foreign prices are, we still do not know the purchasing power of our domestic money when it is converted to a foreign currency. As an illustration of this problem, suppose that the U.S. dollar–Malaysian ringgit exchange rate is $0.25 and that it stays constant over the year. However, suppose also that Malaysian inflation is 4 percent while U.S. inflation is 1 percent. After one year, the four ringgits that cost one dollar will buy 3 percent less in Malaysia than the dollar buys in the United States. The relatively higher inflation in Malaysia erodes the value of a dollar's worth of ringgits more rapidly than the dollar loses value at home. Consequently, when converted to ringgits, the real purchasing power of the dollar has declined even though the exchange rate is still $0.25 per ringgit.

From the point of view of tourists and business people who use foreign exchange, the key item of interest is the purchasing power they get when they convert their dollars, not the number of units of a foreign currency. An American importer trying to decide between Malaysian and Chinese textiles does not really care if he or she gets four ringgits per dollar or eight Chinese yuan per dollar. The biggest concern is the volume of textiles that can be purchased in Malaysia with four ringgits and in China with eight yuan.

The **real exchange rate** is the market exchange rate (or **nominal exchange rate**) adjusted for price differences. The two are closely connected. By way of illustration, let's consider the case of a wine merchant who is trying to decide whether to stock his or her shop with American or French wine. Let's say that French wine of a given quality cost €200 and American wine of the same quality costs $180. What the merchant needs to know is the real exchange rate between French and American wine. Suppose that the nominal rate is $1.20 per euro so that $180 is equivalent to €150 in the currency market. In this case, French wine costs one-third more than American wine, and the real exchange rate is 1⅓ cases of American wine per case of French wine. The algebra is straightforward:

Real exchange rate

= [(Nominal exchange rate) × (Foreign price)] / (Domestic price)

= [($1.20 per euro) × (€200 per case)] / ($180 per case)

= ($240 per case of French wine) / ($180 per case of American wine)

= 1⅓ cases of American wine per one case of French wine

Since the real purchasing power of the dollar is much less in France than in the United States, the choice facing the wine merchant is obvious.

In this example, the main lesson is clear. What matters most to exporters and importers is not the nominal exchange rate, but the real exchange rate—in other words, how much purchasing power they have in the countries under comparison. Let R_r symbolize the real exchange rate, R_n the nominal rate. Since we are interested in the whole economy rather than just one market such as the market for wine, we will use a price index to measure overall prices in the two countries. Price indexes are equivalent to the average price of a basket of goods and services in each economy. Let P stand for the home country price index, and P* represent foreign prices. Then, following the algebra of the wine merchant's calculation:

Real exchange rate

= [(Nominal exchange rate) × (Foreign prices)] / (Domestic prices),

or, more compactly,

$$R_r = R_n (P* / P)$$

Suppose, for example, that the U.S. dollar–EU euro nominal exchange rate is $1.20 per euro and that both price levels are initially set at 100. In this case, the cost of a basket of goods and services is the same in real terms in both countries and

$$R_r = R_n (P* / P) = R_n (100 / 100) = R_n$$

The real rate equals the nominal rate when the purchasing power is the same in both countries. Note that purchasing power parity indicates that this is the long-run equilibrium. Over time, however, if inflation is higher at home than in the foreign country, P rises more than P*, and R_r falls, meaning the domestic currency appreciates in real terms.

By way of illustration, suppose that the United States has 10 percent inflation while the EU has 0 percent. Then, the real U.S.-EU exchange rate (in terms of dollars per euro) would be as follows:

$$R_r = (\$1.20 \text{ per euro}) \times (100 / 110) = \$1.0909 \text{ per euro}$$

Tourists, investors, and businesspeople can still trade dollars and euros at the nominal rate of $1.20 per euro (plus whatever commissions they pay to the seller), but the real purchasing power of the U.S. dollar has risen in the EU compared to what it buys at home. The real exchange rate of $1.0909 per euro tells us that EU goods are now 9 percent cheaper than the U.S. goods that have risen in price. As a result, unless the nominal rate changes, the dollar goes further in the EU than at home. In real terms, the euro has depreciated and the dollar has appreciated.

Changes in the value of real exchange rates play an important role in international macroeconomic relations. When countries control the value of their nominal exchange rate, for example, they must be certain that their prices do not change in relation to the prices of their trading partners. If inflation runs higher at home, then the real value of their currency appreciates. Over a period of time, if uncorrected, this can lead to a build-up in the current account deficit as imports increase and exports decrease. In a number of cases, the end result has been currency crises and the collapse of nominal exchange rates. (For example, Mexico in December 1994 and Thailand in July 1997.)

Alternatives to Flexible Exchange Rates

Exchange rate systems are all modifications of two fundamental categories: fixed and floating (flexible) exchange rate systems. The differences are basic. In a **fixed exchange rate system**, the value of a nation's money is defined in terms of a fixed amount of a commodity, such as gold or in terms of a fixed amount of another currency, such as the U.S. dollar. In a **flexible (floating) exchange rate system**, the value of a nation's money is allowed to "float" up and down in response to the market forces described earlier in the chapter. Through the first seventy years of the twentieth century, fixed exchange rates were the norm, often within a framework that defined the value of a country's currency in terms of a fixed amount of gold. After World War II, many nations shifted away from gold and pegged the value of their currencies to the U.S. dollar or to the currency of another country with which they had strong historical ties. For example, a number of former French colonies in sub-Saharan Africa fixed their currencies to the franc. Beginning in the 1970s, the use of fixed exchange rate systems began a swift decline, first in the high-income industrial economies, and then in many developing countries during the 1980s and 1990s. By the end of the twentieth century, flexible exchange rate systems were the norm in every region of the world.

Although the weight of current economic opinion probably favors floating exchange rates, there is widespread recognition that individual country conditions are unique and that there is no single type of exchange rate system appropriate for every country. The analysis of the pros and cons of different systems in the context of individual country conditions is a very active area of research, and no one can say whether the trend toward flexible rates during the last few decades is irreversible, or if world economic conditions might not change in ways that encourage countries to return to some form of fixed exchange rate.

Fixed Exchange Rate Systems

Gold standards are a form of fixed exchange rates. Under a pure gold standard, nations keep gold as their international reserve. Gold is used to settle most international obligations and nations must be prepared to trade it for their own currency whenever foreigners attempt to "redeem" the home currency they have earned by selling goods and services. In this sense, the nation's money is backed by gold.

There are essentially three rules that countries must follow in order to maintain a gold exchange standard. First, they must fix the value of their currency unit (the dollar, the pound, the yen, and so on) in terms of gold. This fixes the exchange rate. For example, under the modified gold standard of the **Bretton Woods exchange rate system** that was developed at the end of World War II (1947–1971), the U.S. dollar was fixed at $35 per ounce and the British pound was set at £12.5 per ounce. Since both were fixed in terms of gold, they were implicitly set in terms of each other: $35 = one ounce of gold = £12.5, or 2.80 dollars per pound (2.80 = 35 / 12.5).

The second rule of the gold standard is that nations keep the supply of their domestic money fixed in some constant proportion to their supply of gold. This requirement is an informal one, but is necessary in order to ensure that the domestic money supply does not grow beyond the capacity of the gold supply to support it. The third rule of a gold standard is that nations must stand ready and willing to provide gold in exchange for their home country currency.

Consider what would happen if a country decided to print large quantities of money for which there is no gold backing. In the short run, purchases of domestically produced goods would rise, causing domestic prices to rise as well. As domestic prices rise, foreign goods become more attractive, since a fixed exchange rate means that they have not increased in price. As imports in the home country increase, foreigners accumulate an unwanted supply of the home country's currency. This is the point at which the gold standard would begin to become unhinged. If gold supplies are low in relation to the supply of domestic currency, at some point the gold reserves will begin to run out as the country pays out gold in exchange for its currency. This spells crisis and a possible end to the gold standard.

Under a fixed exchange rate system, the national supply and demand for foreign currencies may vary but the nominal exchange rate does not. It is the responsibility of the monetary authorities (the central bank or treasury department) to keep the exchange rate fixed. Figure 10.8 illustrates the task before a national government when it wishes to keep its currency fixed. Suppose that the United States and United Kingdom are both on the gold standard and the U.S. demand for British pounds increases.

FIGURE 10.8 | **Fixed Exchange Rates and Changes in Demand**

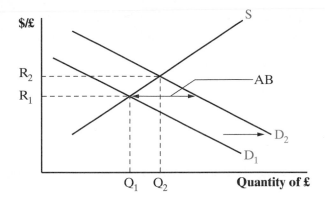

An increase in the demand for British pounds puts pressure on the exchange rate and will cause the dollar to depreciate to R_2 unless the increase in demand is countered by an increase in supply equal to line segment AB.

In the short run or medium run, a rise in demand for pounds from D_1 to D_2 is caused by one of the factors listed in Table 10.4: increased U.S. demand for UK goods, higher UK or lower U.S. interest rates, or speculation that the value of the dollar might not remain fixed for much longer. If R_1 is the fixed U.S.-UK exchange rate, then the United States must counter the weakening dollar and prevent the rate from depreciating to R_2. One option is to sell the United States' gold reserves in exchange for dollars. This puts gold in the hands of merchants, investors, or speculators who are trying to obtain British pounds. The quantity of gold that must be sold is equivalent to the value of the pounds represented by line segment AB. In effect, the United States meets the increased demand for British pounds by supplying international money—gold—to the market through a sale of some of its gold stock. Since gold and pounds are interchangeable, an increase in the supply of gold is equivalent to an increase in the supply of pounds, as shown in Figure 10.9, and the exchange rate stays at R_1.

Under a pure gold standard, countries hold gold as a reserve instead of foreign currencies and sell their gold reserves in exchange for their own currency. This action increases the supply of gold—which is international money—and offsets the pressure on the home currency to depreciate. Actually, there are two possibilities for the home country as it sells its gold reserves. Either the demand for gold is satisfied and the pressure on its currency eases, or it begins to run out of gold. If the latter happens, the home country may be forced into a devaluation that is accomplished by changing the gold price of its currency. As an illustration, if the dollar is fixed at $35 per ounce of gold, a devaluation would shift the price of gold to something more than $35, say $50, and each ounce of gold sold by the United States buys back a greater quantity of dollars.

FIGURE 10.9 Selling Reserves of Pounds to Counter a Weakening Dollar

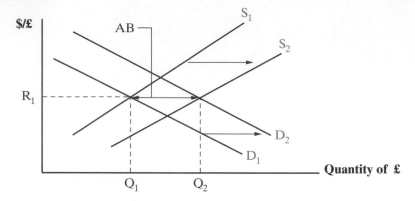

By selling gold equal in value to AB pounds, the United States prevents a depreciation in the dollar-pound exchange rate.

Pure gold standards have been rare since the 1930s. More commonly, countries have adopted modified gold standards, such as the Bretton Woods system (1947–1971) (see the Case Study), or fixed exchange rate systems called **pegged exchange rates**. Pegged exchange rate systems operate similarly to a gold standard except that instead of gold, another currency is used to "anchor" the value of the home currency.

One potential source of problems with a pegged currency is that the home currency's value is synchronized with its peg, so changes between the peg and a third-party currency are identical for the home currency and the third party. An example will clarify. Suppose that Thailand decides to peg its currency to the U.S. dollar at the rate of 25 Thai baht per U.S. dollar. The goal of Thailand's central bank must be to supply dollars whenever it is asked to redeem its own baht. If the dollar appreciates against the Japanese yen, then so does the Thai baht, and at the same rate. Appreciation against the Japanese yen may or may not be a problem for Thailand's producers, depending on the importance of the Japan-Thailand trade relationship. In 1997, it turned out to be very important, and declining Thai competitiveness from its appreciating currency played a prominent role in triggering the Asian financial crisis of 1997–1998.

The simplest way to avoid this type of problem is to peg the currency not to one single currency, but to a group of currencies. This is, in fact, closer to Thailand's actual policy in 1997. While this is slightly more complex arithmetically, it reduces the importance of any single country's currency in the determination of the home country's currency value. Typically, countries that adopt this strategy select the currencies of their most important trading partners as elements of the basket.

Pegged exchange rates can work very well under many circumstances, but another factor that can cause them to unravel is a significant difference in inflation rates between the home country and its peg. We saw previously that real exchange rates play a greater role in determining trade patterns than nominal rates. Using the United States–Thailand example, and looking at the equation that describes the relationship between real and nominal exchange rates from Thailand's point of view (as the home country), we have the following:

$$R_r = (25 \text{ baht per dollar}) \times [(\text{U.S. price level}) / (\text{Thai price level})]$$
$$= R_n (P^* / P)$$

Relatively high inflation in Thailand appears as a faster rate of change in P, and leads to a real appreciation in the baht. Under these circumstances, Thai producers are less competitive and U.S. producers are more so (in Thailand). If the situation persists, speculators will likely step in and begin to sell bahts in the expectation that the pegged nominal rate of 25 baht per dollar will be devalued to offset the appreciation in the real rate. Moving the nominal peg from 25 to 30 or 40 baht per dollar may be necessary to restore balance.

The most common technique for dealing with this problem is through the adoption of a **crawling peg**. Crawling pegs are fixed—that is, pegged—exchange rates that are periodically adjusted. The idea is to offset any differences in inflation (changes in P) through regular adjustments in R_n. If correctly handled, the real exchange rate remains constant and the impact of inflation differences never shows up as a change in competitiveness.

There are several other variations on the theme of managed exchange rates. One of the key points to keep in mind is that purely fixed or purely flexible exchange rate arrangements are rare. When a currency is fixed in value, it is still subject to market pressures of supply and demand which, at times, can force governments to alter its value. Similarly, when countries adopt a flexible exchange rate system, there is usually some degree of government intervention in currency markets to try to shape its value. Consequently, many countries that claim to have a flexible exchange rate actually have adopted a **managed float** in which they occasionally sell or buy their currency as they try to nudge the exchange rate up or down.

CASE STUDY

The End of the Bretton Woods System

The Bretton Woods system of exchange rates was enacted at the end of World War II. It included most nations outside the former Soviet Union and its allies. The exchange rate system was a major component of the institutions that were designed to manage international economic conflict and to support international economic cooperation. In addition to the exchange rate system, the other institutions that were created at the same time included the International Monetary Fund (IMF), the International Bank for Reconstruction and Development (IBRD) or World Bank, and the General Agreement on Tariffs and Trade (GATT). (See Chapter 2.)

Each institution had its own role in the management of world economic affairs. The roles of the exchange rate were to provide stability by eliminating excess currency fluctuations, to prevent nations from using exchange rate devaluations as a tactic for gaining markets for their goods, and to ensure that there was an adequate supply of internationally accepted reserves so that nations could meet their international obligations.

In the Bretton Woods exchange rate system, the dollar was fixed to gold at the rate of $1 equalling ⅟₃₅ of an ounce of gold, or $35 per ounce. Every other currency within the system was fixed to the dollar and, therefore, indirectly to gold. Unlike a pure gold standard, however, countries could use U.S. dollars as their international reserve and did not have to accumulate gold or tie their money supply to their gold reserves.

The Bretton Woods exchange rate system had one fatal flaw—the dollar. The United States was in a privileged position since its currency was treated the same as gold. This meant that the United States could simply increase its money supply (the supply of dollars) and gain increased purchasing power over European, Japanese, and other countries' goods. Other nations preferred the United States to maintain a relatively robust supply of dollars, since this ensured that there was an adequate supply of international reserves for the world economy.

Problems with this arrangement began when the U.S. economy expanded at a different rate than the economies of its trading partners. In the mid-to-late 1960s, the United States deepened its involvement in the Vietnam War while it simultaneously created the "War on Poverty" at home. Both policies generated large fiscal expenditures that stimulated the economy. While U.S. expansion raced ahead of expansion elsewhere, Europeans found themselves accumulating dollars more rapidly than they desired. The dollars were a by-product of U.S. economic expansion and partially reflected the price increases that were accompanying the expansion.

Under a different type of exchange rate system, it would have been appropriate for the United States to devalue its currency. U.S. prices had risen relative to foreign prices, the real exchange rate had appreciated as a consequence, and trade deficits were beginning to become a permanent feature of the U.S. economy.

One policy would have been to devalue the nominal dollar exchange rate, but this was not an option. Since every currency was tied to the dollar, there was no way for the United States to devalue against a group of other currencies selectively. An alternative was for the United States to devalue against all currencies by changing the gold value of the dollar. By the late 1960s, it was becoming apparent that this would be necessary.

Persistent U.S. deficits had led to an accumulation of dollars outside the United States, which greatly exceeded the United States' supply of gold. In other words, the United States lacked the gold reserves to back all of the dollars that were in circulation. Official recognition of this fact led to the **Smithsonian Agreement** of December 1971, in which the major industrialized countries agreed to devalue the gold content of the dollar by around 8 percent, from $35 per ounce to $38.02. In addition, Japan, Germany, and other trade surplus countries increased the value of their currencies.

Although the Smithsonian Agreement was hailed by President Nixon as a fundamental reorganization of international monetary affairs, it quickly proved to be too little and of only temporary benefit. The gold value of the dollar was realigned again in early 1973, from $38.02 to $42.22. In addition, further devaluation occurred against other European currencies. The end of the system came in March of 1973 when the major currencies began to float against each other. A few currencies, such as the British pound, had begun to float earlier.

In each case, the strategy of allowing the exchange rate to float in response to supply and demand conditions was adopted as a means of coping with speculation. When speculators had perceived that the dollar was overvalued at $38 per ounce or $42 per ounce, they sold dollars in anticipation of a future devaluation. Nor was the dollar the only currency speculated against. Other weak currencies such as the pound and the Italian lira had also been correctly perceived as overvalued and had been sold off by speculators. In the end, the central banks of the weak-currency countries found it impossible to support an unrealistically high value of their currency. The costs of buying up the excess supply of their currencies at overvalued prices proved to be too great. The simplest solution was to let the currencies float.

Choosing the Right Exchange Rate System

Given the menu of choices for exchange rate systems, an active area of economic research has focused on the performance characteristics of systems under different economic conditions and institutional arrangements. For many years, economists debated the pros and cons of fixed and flexible rates, but as the variety of exchange rate options has grown, as capital mobility has increased, and as international trade and investment relations have deepened, researchers have become more concerned with understanding how varying degrees of flexibility or fixity might best serve the interests of individual countries. In particular, economists have tried to learn how different exchange rate systems might influence the core elements of a country's macroeconomy such as the rate of economic growth, the rate of inflation, and the frequency of currency crises.

Traditional views held that countries with fixed exchange rate systems were better at controlling inflation, but that they paid a price in the form of slower economic growth. The reasoning behind this view was that in order to maintain a fixed rate, governments have to be very careful about issuing new money. Since most of the episodes of hyperinflation during the second half of the twentieth century resulted from overexpanding the money supply, it seems reasonable that an exchange rate policy that limits the supply of money would also help avoid inflation. However, in the view of some economists, the limits placed on the ability of a country to manipulate its money supply also remove an important tool that governments use to help manage the rate of economic growth. Therefore, the tradeoff was lower growth for lower inflation.

More recent research, particularly with data from the 1990s, has failed to demonstrate a strong relationship between the type of exchange rate system and either inflation or economic growth. Prior to the 1990s, countries with fixed or pegged exchange rates tended to have lower rates of inflation, but during the 1990s their advantages on the inflation front diminished substantially. Similarly, there is evidence that countries with more flexible rates tend to have higher average rates of economic growth, but this result depends on the classification of the fastest growing Asian economies. Technically, many of these countries have flexible exchange rates, but at the same time they manage them very closely. When they are omitted from the analysis, there is no significant difference in the rate of growth between countries with relatively fixed and relatively flexible rates. And finally, neither fixed nor flexible rates seem to offer superior protection against a currency crisis. As a result, no particular system seems to rank above any other in its ability to provide superior macroeconomic performance.

Insofar as economists have been able to devise a set of rules for selecting an exchange rate system, they are very general and very basic. If the goal is to find the system that helps minimize negative shocks to an economy, then the source of the shock determines whether a more flexible or more fixed system should be adopted. When the shocks originate in the monetary sector—for example, a central bank that goes overboard in printing new money—a fixed rate is better (Argentina is a good example). On the other hand, if the shocks to an economy originate in the external environment—for example, a sudden change in the price of imported oil—then relatively more flexibility in the exchange rate enables the country to adapt to the changes more easily. The general argument here is that individual country characteristics matter a great deal. The problem with these rules, however, is that the source of the shocks to an economy are likely to vary from episode to episode and, as a consequence, the basic rules outlined above provide less practical guidance than desired.

One interpretation of these two rules is that smaller economies that are open to the world economy will do better with more flexible exchange rates. Flexibility will help to minimize the potentially negative effects of shocks that originate in the world economy by allowing changes in the exchange rate to absorb some of the shock and to act as a buffer between the domestic economy and the rest of the world. Given that the actual trend for many small, open, developing economies has been toward greater use of flexible exchange rate systems, theory and practice seem to confirm each other.

On the other hand, exchange rate pegs are still popular, particularly with many developing countries. There are a couple of reasons for this. First, all economists agree that one of the most important elements of an exchange rate system is its credibility. That is, no matter what type of exchange rate is adopted, a successful system must generate confidence and the widespread belief that it is sustainable. Exchange rate systems that lack credibility are guaranteed to fail in their basic job of providing a smooth and reliable conversion between domestic and foreign money. Under some conditions, exchange rate pegs may offer greater credibility. One of the conditions, and the second reason why some countries continue to peg their currencies, is a relatively high degree of trade dependence on a single, major economy. Consider the case of Mexico, with about 80 percent of its trade with the United States. Given its trade dependence on the United States, Mexico pegged its peso to the U.S. dollar for many years. Because Mexican inflation ran higher than the U.S. rate, a crawling peg was favored as the means of keeping the real exchange rate relatively constant. The purpose of the dollar peg was to provide benefits to Mexican businesses and consumers by eliminating some of the price variation in Mexican imports and exports. The rule seems to be that when a country is closely tied to the economy of a large, industrial country such as the United States, pegging to its currency may provide additional stability and help businesses to plan their futures with greater confidence.

This view is shared by many, but at the same time it is widely accepted that, in Mexico's case at least, the use of a flexible exchange rate has served it better than the pegged rates it used before 1994. The reason for the discrepancy between what might work in theory and what has worked in practice highlights the complexity of choosing an exchange rate system when every country has unique economic factors and its own set of institutions shaping its economic outcomes. In Mexico's case, due to a set of agreements between the business sector, organized labor, and government, it was unable to make the periodic adjustments to its nominal exchange rate that are required with a crawling peg. In effect, Mexico's institutional inability to adjust its nominal exchange rate undermined the credibility of the exchange rate system. The lack of credibility led to periodic bouts of speculation against the peso whenever it was perceived to be overvalued and vulnerable. Several of these speculative bouts were followed by a peso collapse and economic recession. The lesson, in the end, seems to be that the first criterion for choosing an exchange rate system is that it must have credibility in currency and financial markets.

CASE STUDY

Monetary Unions

Some countries prefer not to have their own currency. Sixteen of the twenty-seven countries of the EU use a common currency, the euro, and more are expected to join. Panama adopted the dollar as a legal tender alongside its own currency, called the cordoba, in the early twentieth century, and in 2000 Ecuador and El Salvador eliminated their currencies altogether and adopted the dollar.

Dollarization, or the adoption of another country's currency, differs from a monetary union such as the EU that make up the European Monetary Union (EMU). In a monetary union there is a common central bank that issues the currency and carries out monetary policy. By contrast, the central banks of El Salvador and Ecuador have no ability to issue money and they have no control over their monetary policy since they cannot expand or contract their money supply. There is no barrier in international law to using another country's money, but in doing so a country becomes powerless to influence its exchange rate or the quantity of money in circulation.

There are currently four monetary unions in the world. These are the EMU, the Eastern Caribbean Currency Union (ECCU), the West African Economic and Monetary Union (WAEMU), and the Central African Economic and Monetary Community, which is known by its French acronym, CEMAC. Another monetary union, the West African Monetary Zone (WAMZ) is close to starting and will tie together five English-speaking countries in West Africa, including Nigeria, the largest African nation.

The EU case is discussed in detail in Chapter 14. The two African unions, WAEMU and CEMAC, are the oldest of the monetary unions. Both were formed out of former French colonies in Western Africa and both use the CFA franc as their currency. (CFA stands for Communauté Française Africaine, or French African Community.) Both the WAEMU and the CEMAC have central banks that issue their currencies and both fix it to the euro at approximately 655 CFA francs per euro. While both are convertible into euros or other currencies, they are not directly convertible into each other's CFA francs. The French Treasury Department backs both currencies and stands ready to provide currency reserves if either of the two central banks of the monetary unions run short.

According to most observers, the advantages of CFA francs over independent currencies is that they have lowered inflation in the participating countries and reduced macroeconomic instability. Since the central banks are responsible for more than one economy, it has probably reduced the political influence of individual governments and led to a steadier, less volatile monetary policy. The

TABLE 10.5   Monetary Unions

Monetary union	Members	Exchange rate system	Exchange rate, July 2009
European Monetary Union (EMU)	Sixteen of twenty-seven European Union countries	Flexible	1 euro = 1.39 US$
West African Economic and Monetary Union (WAEMU)	Eight countries in sub-Saharan west Africa	Fixed to euro	461.657 CFA francs = 1 US$
Central African Economic and Monetary Community (CEMAC)	Six countries in west-central Africa	Fixed to euro	Same as above
Eastern Caribbean Currency Union (ECCU)	Six island countries and two British territories	Pegged to dollar	2.62 EC dollars = 1 US$

disadvantages are the same as those for a fixed exchange rate: Changes in the value of the currency cannot be used to protect the domestic economy against shocks that begin outside the country. For example, as the euro gained value against the dollar after 2000 (see Figure 10.1), the CFA franc also appreciated against the dollar and goods produced in the CFA franc zone became more expensive when priced in dollars. This particularly affected the WAEMU, which mainly exports cotton and other agricultural products.

Each of the monetary unions are also economic unions (EU), common markets (ECCU is the basis for the Caribbean Common Market), or customs unions (WAEMU and CEMAC). Monetary union implies a high level of integration and coordination and is only worthwhile if other elements of the economy are also integrated. There is not a great deal of agreement as to the value or necessity of monetary unions, but without additional economic integration they make little sense.

Single Currency Areas

On January 1, 1999, eleven of the (then) fifteen members of the EU adopted the euro as their currency. Shortly thereafter, a twelfth member joined the euro group. Initially, the use of the euro was limited to government bonds and other financial instruments, and it served mainly as an accounting unit. By 2002, euro coins and paper money circulated, and shortly thereafter, the francs, marks, and pesetas of the twelve members were withdrawn from circulation. As of 2009, sixteen of twenty-seven EU members use the euro. The adoption of a single currency has been under serious consideration since the 1970s (at least), and the official agreements between the member states have been in place since the early 1990s. Given that one of the strongest symbols of national independence is a nation's money, the thirty years it has taken to arrive at the point where the citizens and policymakers of the EU are willing to give up their centuries-old forms of money may not seem so long.

The EU's experience with the euro is examined in more detail in Chapter 14, but any discussion of single currency areas has to recognize that it has excited the imagination of people all over the world. Researchers have begun to analyze other regions to see if they are suitable areas for the use of a single currency, and within the EU itself there has been a huge amount of discussion of the single currency. The starting point for the economic analysis of the pros and cons of adopting a single currency is the work by the Nobel Prize–winning economist Robert Mundell, whose work on the theory of **optimal currency areas** developed the criteria used to determine whether two or more countries would be economically better off sharing a currency rather than maintaining their own national money.

There are at least four potential reasons why a group of countries might want to share a common money. First, a single currency eliminates the need to convert each other's money and thereby reduces transaction costs in a number of ways. It eliminates the fees paid to banks or to the currency brokers that arrange the conversion, it simplifies accounting and bookkeeping, and it enables consumers and investors to compare prices across international boundaries more accurately. Each of these advantages provide some gain in efficiency and a reduction in business costs. Second, a single currency eliminates price fluctuations that are caused by changes in the exchange rate. When speculators move their money into or out of a country, or when temporary interest rate changes in one country alter the supply and demand for foreign exchange, one country may become (temporarily) cheaper or more expensive for business. As a result, business decisions may reflect temporary shifts in currency values rather than underlying issues of economic efficiency. The elimination of misleading price signals that result from exchange rate fluctuations is also a potential gain in efficiency.

Third, the elimination of exchange rates through the adoption of a single currency can help increase political trust between countries seeking to increase their integration. A single currency removes some of the friction between integrating nations by eliminating the problems that are caused by exchange rate misalignments. An example may help clarify this point. On the EU's way to a single currency, it experienced a speculative episode that was directed against the British pound and the French franc, among other currencies. After some initial attempts to fend off the speculation against the pound, Britain let it depreciate. France, on the other hand, raised its interest rates in order to increase the demand for the franc. As a result, the pound was suddenly, significantly depreciated against the franc. European businesses in France and elsewhere noted this development and moved several factories from the continent to England and Scotland. As you can imagine, this did not sit well with politicians in France and Holland (which also lost jobs to Britain). This episode illustrates the benefits of eliminating exchange rate misalignments, or sudden dramatic changes in exchange rates. For most pairs of countries, this is not an important issue, but for members of a regional trade alliance, particularly one that is seeking deeper levels of integration than simply free trade, it can be a very important political benefit from a single currency.

Fourth, and finally, for some developing countries the adoption of a common currency may give their exchange rate system greater credibility. This is particularly applicable if the common currency is the dollar or the euro or some other widely traded currency. Use of such a currency can reduce exchange rate fluctuations and create greater confidence in the financial system of the adopting country, possibly leading to lower interest rates and an increased availability of credit, although this depends on the overall soundness of the financial system.

Nations that give up their national money do not do so without cost. In addition to its political symbolism, the adoption of a common currency also means that the country no longer has its own money supply as a tool for managing its economic growth. The topic of monetary policy is taken up in more detail in Chapter 11, but the basic point is easy to grasp. Countries with their own currency can influence the rate of growth of the economy in the short run (but not in the long run) through a change in the supply of money. While these policies are somewhat controversial, most countries use changes in the money supply to counteract an economic slowdown. When a country adopts a common currency with one or more other countries, it gives up this tool. After the introduction of the common currency, there is only one money supply and, consequently, one rate of growth of the money supply. New York, for example, shares a common currency with California and, as a consequence, both states experience the same changes in the money supply. If New York is growing fast and California is growing slowly, it would be impossible for the Federal Reserve to alter the money supply in a way that would speed up growth in California and slow it down in New York. With a single currency, there is a "one-size-fits-all" monetary policy.

Conditions for Adopting a Single Currency

Economic analysis offers four conditions for determining if the gains from a single currency will outweigh the costs of giving up a national money. None of these conditions is absolute, and if one is not met, it may be compensated for in one of the other three. Ultimately, the desirability of a single currency is not subject to hard and fast rules and it is a judgment call for the economists, politicians, and citizens of the affected nations.

The first criterion relates to the cost just noted. If countries have relatively similar economic experiences, then they tend to enter expansions and recessions at more or less similar points in time and a one-size-fits-all policy for expanding or contracting the money supply will be appropriate for all members of the currency area. In this case, there is little or no cost associated with the loss of the national money as a tool to expand or contract the national economy. In fact, however, few countries are that well synchronized in their business cycles. Even the states of the United States enter and leave recessions at different points in time, and the national figures on growth only reflect an average across all 50 states.

The second condition is a high degree of labor and capital mobility between the member countries. This allows workers and capital to leave countries or regions where work is scarce and to join the supply of labor and capital in booming regions. In effect, free migration of the factors of production smooths out some of the differences in the business cycle by taking unemployed inputs and moving them to where they are needed. This is how the fifty states of the United States compensate for a lack of complete synchronization in the business cycles of individual states. When conditions are bad in one region, workers and investors move their labor and capital to another region, freeing inputs from areas where they are not needed and providing them to areas where they are.

While capital tends to be relatively mobile, labor is less so, even within countries. Therefore, a third condition is that there are regional policies capable of addressing the imbalances that may develop. Depressed areas may remain depressed if people cannot move or choose not to because the psychological or other costs are too high. Insofar as the economics of regional policies are concerned, they may be determined at any level, from the currency area (multicountry) to individual nation-states, to subnational units (provinces or cities). The key point is not the agency responsible, but that there are effective policies for assisting regions that may not be synchronized with the majority of the currency area's economy.

Finally, the first three conditions point to the fourth: The nations involved must be seeking a level of integration that goes beyond simple free trade. Free trade requires that nations remove their tariffs, quotas, and other border barriers that inhibit the flow of goods. If this is the goal, a common currency is unnecessary. If something much deeper is sought, however, such as a greater harmonization of national economies and much closer economic and political ties, then a single currency can be helpful, provided the other three conditions are observed. This condition is admittedly ambiguous and is part of the reason why policymakers do not always agree in their analysis. It is somewhat circular reasoning, but true nevertheless, that the desirability of a single currency partly depends on the goals of the countries involved.

CASE STUDY

Is the NAFTA Region an Optimal Currency Area?

The EU is one model for the creation of a single currency. In the EU model, an entirely new currency is created and each joining country gives up its national money. The discussion of a single currency in the NAFTA countries has favored a different model. So far, discussion has centered on the adoption of the U.S. dollar by all three countries instead of the creation of an entirely new currency. Either model leads to the same outcome: a single currency area. Is the discussion realistic? That is, are the proponents of a single currency dreaming or is there something to be gained in such a move?

It is clear that whatever the long-run advantages or disadvantages of a single currency might be, there is a long way to go before the NAFTA countries meet the four conditions necessary for a single currency area to be an optimal policy. First, the business cycles of the three countries have not been synchronized, at least historically. While the macroeconomies of Canada and the United States have often moved together, Mexico has historically had a very different pattern of business cycles. This may be changing, however, since the Mexican cycle appears to be much closer to that of the United States since 1994. Second, given the legal restrictions on labor movement and the political obstacles to opening a North American labor market, labor flows cannot be counted on to help synchronize national business cycles. Third, there are no regional policies within the NAFTA framework as there are within the EU. In the EU, national governments tax themselves to create a regional fund that is used to provide assistance to areas that lag in economic growth. This is useful for overcoming regional imbalances and removes some of the sting that a region might feel if the EU's other policies are not supportive. And finally, NAFTA was originally conceived as a means to reduce border barriers. While its ultimate goal will surely evolve over time, at present there does not appear to be a consensus that it should be something more than a free-trade area.

As it is presently constituted, the NAFTA region is clearly not an optimal currency area. Nevertheless, it is a safe bet that dollarization will continue to be explored, particularly in Mexico. In part, this is because there are counterarguments to each of the above objections: A single currency will help synchronize the three economies; it is possible to formulate an agreement that allows a guest worker program such as the United States and Mexico had in the 1940s, 1950s, and 1960s; regional policies are simply a matter of political will and financial means, but they would not require huge expenditures; and closer integration of the NAFTA partners is inevitable.

Summary

- People hold foreign currency in order to buy goods and services, to take advantage of interest rate differentials, and to speculate. The primary institutions in the exchange-rate market are commercial banks and foreign exchange brokers.

- Exchange rates can be analyzed with supply and demand analysis, as if they are just another commodity in the economy. Increases (decreases) in the supply of foreign exchange cause the domestic currency to appreciate (depreciate). Increases (decreases) in the demand for foreign exchange cause the domestic currency to depreciate (appreciate).

- Exchange rates are unpredictable because they are simultaneously influenced by long-run, medium-run, and short-run factors. In the long run, purchasing power parity is important. In the medium run, the business cycle is important, and in the short run, interest-rate differentials and speculation are important.

- The interest parity condition says that the interest rate differential between two countries is approximately equal to the percentage difference between the forward and spot exchange rates.

- Firms use forward exchange rate markets to protect against exchange rate risk.

- Real exchange rates are equal to nominal or market exchange rates adjusted for inflation. They give a better picture of the purchasing power of a nation's currency.

- Fixed exchange rate systems were thought to help limit the growth of inflation, but there is little evidence of this over the last two decades. Fixed exchange rates eliminate the ability of governments to use monetary policies to regulate the macroeconomy.

- Flexible exchange rate systems were thought to help increase growth, but there is little evidence of this over the last two decades. Flexible exchange rates free a nation's macroeconomic policies from the need to maintain a fixed exchange rate.

- All exchange rate systems are on a continuum between fixed and flexible rates. Pegged exchange rates, crawling pegs, and a managed float are examples of intermediary-type systems. The most important rule for countries is that their exchange rate system is credible.

- Optimal currency areas are geographical regions within which it is optimal for countries to adopt the same currency. The criteria for an optimal currency area are a synchronized business cycle, complete factor mobility, regional programs for lagging areas, and a desire to achieve a higher level of economic and political integration.

Vocabulary

appreciation

Bretton Woods exchange rate system

covered interest arbitrage

crawling peg

depreciation

dollarization

exchange rate

exchange rate risk

fixed exchange rate system

flexible (floating) exchange rate system

forward exchange rate

forward market

gold standard

hedging

interest parity

interest rate arbitrage

managed float

nominal exchange rate

optimal currency area

pegged exchange rate

purchasing power parity

real exchange rate

Smithsonian Agreement

spot market

Study Questions

1. Draw a graph of the supply of and demand for the Canadian dollar by the U.S. market. Diagram the effect of each of the following on the exchange rate; state in words whether the effect is long, medium, or short run; and explain your reasoning.

   a. More rapid growth in Canada than in the United States

   b. A rise in U.S. interest rates

   c. Goods are more expensive in Canada than in the United States

   d. A recession in the United States

   e. Expectations of a future depreciation in the Canadian dollar

2. Suppose the U.S. dollar–euro exchange rate is 1.20 dollars per euro, and the U.S. dollar–Mexican peso rate is 0.10 dollars per peso. What is the euro-peso rate?

3. Suppose the U.S. dollar–yen exchange rate is 0.01 dollars per yen. Since the base year, inflation has been 2 percent in Japan and 10 percent in the United

States. What is the real exchange rate? In real terms, has the dollar appreciated or depreciated against the yen?

4. Which of the three motives for holding foreign exchange are applicable to each of the following?

    a. A tourist

    b. A bond trader

    c. A portfolio manager

    d. A manufacturer

5. If U.S. visitors to Mexico can buy more goods in Mexico than they can in the United States when they convert their dollars to pesos, is the dollar undervalued or overvalued? Explain.

6. In a fixed exchange rate system, how do countries address the problem of currency market pressures that threaten to lower or raise the value of their currency?

7. In the debate on fixed versus floating exchange rates, the strongest argument for a floating rate is that it frees macroeconomic policy from taking care of the exchange rate. This is also the weakest argument. Explain.

8. Brazil, Argentina, Paraguay, and Uruguay are members of MERCOSUR, a regional trade area that is trying to become a common market. What issues should they consider before they accept or reject a common currency?

9. Suppose that U.S. interest rates are 4 percent more than rates in the EU.

    a. Would you expect the dollar to appreciate or depreciate against the euro, and by how much?

    b. If, contrary to your expectations, the forward and spot rates are the same, in which direction would you expect financial capital to flow? Why?

10. Why do some economists claim that the most important feature of any exchange rate system is its credibility?

APPENDIX

The Interest Rate Parity Condition

The following variables are defined as in the chapter:

   i = home country interest rate
   i^* = foreign interest rate
   R = the nominal exchange rate in units of home country currency per unit of foreign currency
   F = the forward exchange rate

The forward rate and the interest rates have the same term to maturity.

An investor has a choice between i and i*. Letting the dollar be the home currency, \$1 invested today will return \$1(1 + i) next period if invested at home. To make the comparison with a foreign investment, the dollar first has to be converted into the foreign currency, then invested, and the earnings must be converted back into dollars. The equivalent of \$1 in foreign currency is 1 / R. If 1 / R is invested abroad, at the end of the next period it returns (1 / R)(1 + i*), which is in units of foreign currency. The reconversion to dollars can be done in the forward market where the exchange rate for a forward contract is F. Therefore, in dollars, \$1 invested abroad will return (1 / R)(1 + i*)F in the next period.

The interest parity condition states that investors will be indifferent between home and foreign investments (of similar risk), implying that they will move their funds around and cause interest rates and exchange rates to change until the returns are the same in the two cases:

$$1 + i = (1 / R)(1 + i^*) \, F = (1 + i^*)(F / R)$$

Divide by (1 + i*):

$$(1 + i) / (1 + i^*) = F / R$$

Subtract 1 from both sides:

$$[(1 + i) / (1 + i^*)] - [(1 + i^*) / (1 + i^*)] = F / R - R / R$$

$$[(1 + i) - (1 + i^*)] / [(1 + i^*)] = (F - R) / R$$

$$(i - i^*) / (1 + i^*) = (F - R) / R$$

The left-hand side denominator is close to 1 for small values of i* (this is why we state the interest parity condition as an approximation). The right-hand side is the percentage difference between the forward and spot rates. If it is negative, markets expect an appreciation in the home currency. Rewriting the last equation,

$$i - i^* \approx (F - R) / R,$$

which says that the difference between home country and foreign interest rates is approximately equal to the expected depreciation in the home country currency.

An Introduction to Open Economy Macroeconomics

Introduction: The Macroeconomy in a Global Setting

Chapters 9 and 10 introduced the concepts of the balance of payments and the exchange rate. In this chapter we look more closely at their relationship to each other and to the overall national economy. After a brief review of a few key macroeconomic concepts, the chapter focuses on the interactions among the current account, exchange rates, and key components of the macroeconomy—consumption, investment, and government spending. National governments are important to this chapter since they rarely take a passive role in the economy. Indeed, since the worldwide Great Depression of the 1930s, and especially since the end of World War II, national governments have shouldered a significant share of the responsibility for keeping the growth of the economy on track, the unemployment rate low, and prices stable. This role is particularly evident in the crisis that began in 2007 and the recession that followed in 2008. Therefore, a major focus of this chapter is the impact of macroeconomic policies on the exchange rate and current account.

The impacts of activist macroeconomic policies are one focus of this chapter, but it is also important to recognize that these are not the only links between a nation's macroeconomy and the rest of the world. Usually governments control a significant share of the national product and as a consequence, their normal, day-to-day operating decisions affect exchange rates and the current account. The same is true for consumers and businesses. In most economies, expenditures on consumption goods and services comprise the largest single component of the macroeconomy, and as we have already seen, an increase in economic growth causes consumers to draw in a greater quantity of imports, increasing the demand for foreign exchange and pushing the current account toward the deficit side.

Aggregate Demand and Aggregate Supply

Table 11.1 shows the four main economic agents in the macroeconomy: households, businesses, government, and foreigners. In our simplified model of the macroeconomy, households supply all the factors of production (land, labor, and capital) that businesses need to produce the nation's output. In return, the revenue that businesses

TABLE 11.1	The Main Economic Agents in the Macroeconomy
Agent	Function
Households	■ Supply factors (land, labor, capital) to business ■ Purchase consumer goods and services (C) ■ Save ■ Pay taxes
Businesses	■ Use the factors supplied by households to produce the nation's output ■ Purchase investment goods (I)
Government	■ Purchase government goods and services (G) ■ Collect taxes (T)
Foreigners	■ Purchase exports (EX) ■ Supply imports (IM)

There are four main agents in the macroeconomy. Each one is a different source of demand for goods and services.

earn when they sell their goods is used to pay for the factors supplied by households. Accordingly, all of the income generated in the economy accrues to households since they supply all of the factor inputs. This is a fundamental identity in the macroeconomy: The income for the economy as a whole equals the value of its output.

When we track income and output, it is important to understand the position of **intermediate inputs**—goods purchased by one business from another to use in production. For example, a car manufacturer hires not only labor, land, and capital (for which it pays wages and salaries, rents, interest, and dividends) but it also purchases glass, tires, steel, and so on. The payment for auto glass is not directly income to households because it is paid to another business, but if we trace it back, it ultimately becomes income. For example, the glass manufacturer receives payment from the car company and it uses the payment to pay wages, rent, interest, and dividends, as well as its suppliers. We can keep following the flow of payments, through the suppliers to the glass firms, or more simply, we can recognize that all of the payments are incorporated into the value of the car. That is, the purchase price of the car ultimately generates an equivalent amount of income. As a result, the fundamental identity holds between income and output.

The identity between total expenditures on final goods and services and the value of total output in an economy can be looked at in another way. Figure 11.1 is similar to a graph of supply and demand in a single market, except that the demand curve is total demand for all final goods and services and the supply curve is total output. In other words, the curve with a negative slope is **aggregate demand (AD)**, and the curve with a positive slope is **aggregate supply (AS)**. In a simple supply and demand graph, the horizontal axis measures quantity and the vertical axis measures price, but in the AD/AS graph shown in Figure 11.1, all final goods (GDP) are included on the horizontal axis and the price level, (P) is shown on the vertical axis. The price level is equivalent to the consumer price index or another measure of economywide prices. Points along the AD curve show the equilibrium levels of output and prices that are consistent on the demand side of the economy, while the AS curve shows the points that are consistent from a supply-side point of view. Together, they show the levels of equilibrium output (Q_1) and prices (P_1) at a given point in time.

The shape of the aggregate supply curve is designed to call attention to three regions of GDP. On the horizontal part of the AS curve, the economy is operating below full employment. Theoretically, the availability of unemployed workers and other idle resources allows an increase in output to occur without putting upward pressure on prices. Workers and the owners of other factors cannot demand higher wages or other payments in return for more inputs of labor and capital because there are plenty of idle workers and other resources willing and able to contribute at the going rate. Hence, an increase in production can be relatively easily achieved without causing shortages of inputs or increases in prices. The middle, upward-sloping part of the AS curve symbolizes the range of GDP where inputs begin to become scarce. Some wage increases or other factor price increases are necessary in order to obtain more inputs and to produce more output. In the vertical region of the AS curve, the economy is at full employment

FIGURE 11.1   **Aggregate Demand (AD) and Aggregate Supply (AS)**

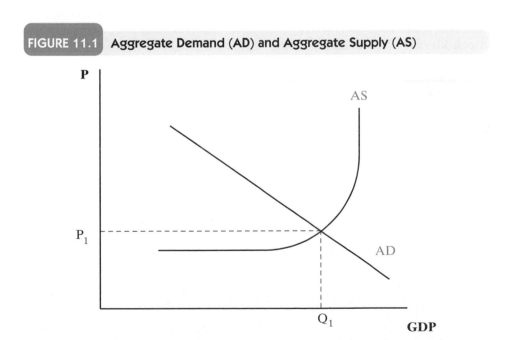

The aggregate demand (AD) curve shows the levels of output (GDP) and price (P) where expenditure decisions and production decisions match; aggregate supply (AS) shows the levels of output and prices where decisions to supply inputs and production decisions match. Together they show the levels of equilibrium output (Q_1) and prices (P_1).

and no more output is possible until new workers enter the labor force or new factories and machines are built. Figure 11.1 portrays this region as an absolute limit to production. In fact, it is possible to exceed this level for short periods of time, for example, during wars or other extraordinary events that cause people to work longer hours or at a faster pace than they are willing to maintain over the long-run. Given that output levels beyond the vertical region can be sustained only for a short period, it is useful to think of the vertical portion of the AS curve as signifying the full-employment level of GDP.

In the short-run and medium-run, the focus is on changes in aggregate demand that are initiated by one or more of the economic agents listed in Table 11.1. Significant changes in expenditures are not at all uncommon over the course of a year or more. For example, as an economy goes into recession, consumers and businesses may quickly alter their expectations and their spending (C and I) as they reassess their economic circumstances. Similarly, recessions, wars, natural disasters, and other factors can cause large shifts in government tax (T) and expenditure (G) policies, as well as changes in other policies that directly affect consumer and business spending. And finally, economic booms or depressions abroad sometimes cause a rapid change in foreign purchases of products exported (EX) from the home country.

Figure 11.2 illustrates the case of an increase in aggregate demand. The source of the change could be an increase in expenditures by any one of the economic agents listed in Table 11.1. That is, it could be due to an increase in consumption expenditures (C), business investment (I), government purchases of final goods

---

FIGURE 11.2   A Shift in the AD Curve

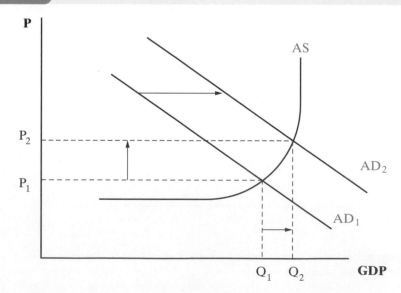

An increase in aggregate demand will cause an increase in GDP and a rise in the price level.

and services (G), government tax cuts that stimulate consumer or business spending, or exports (EX) purchased by foreigners. The net result of any of the changes is qualitatively the same. Prices rise slightly from P_1 to P_2 as factor inputs become scarcer, and GDP rises from Q_1 to Q_2. If the economy initially happened to be on the horizontal part of the AS curve, then prices would not have risen, but output would still have gone up. If the changes commenced from a position of full employment on the vertical part of the AS curve, then all of the change would have been in the price level, and no increase in output would occur. If AD falls instead of rising, the effects are symmetrical and in the opposite direction of the changes caused by an increase in AD.

Although the simple relationships between AD, AS, P, and GDP portrayed in Figures 11.1 and 11.2 are a useful way to conceptualize the interactions of a number of key macroeconomic variables, the graphs and the description hide a great deal of complexity. For example, the graphs illustrate only one point in time, and they do not show what happens as the economy grows over time. If an economy grows, it must have more labor or more physical capital or natural resources and be capable of producing more output. Hence, economic growth could be added by shifting the whole AS curve rightward. Consequently, the changes in Figure 11.2 must be viewed as short-run or medium-run changes that take effect separately from economic growth.

Another factor that is hiding behind Figure 11.2 is the actual mechanism that moves the economy from one level of GDP (Q_1) to a higher level (Q_2). Suppose, for example, that AD begins to shift rightward due to rising business optimism that prompts many firms to increase their investment spending. Firms order new machines or start new construction projects, and total spending in the economy goes up. This is not the end of the story, however, as the firms that supply the machines or do the construction will have to increase their output levels, and that will put additional income in the hands of their owners and workers. Those suppliers and their workers are likely to spend at least part of their additional income. Statistical analysis over long periods of time has shown that there is a very close quantitative relationship between income received by households and household consumption patterns. That is, as income rises, so do expenditures. Consequently, the workers and business owners who supply goods and services to the investing firms increase their own expenditures as well. They buy houses, furniture, cars, college education, medical care, and all the other things that households spend money on, thus creating another round of income increases and expenditures.

In effect, the original increase in investment spending causes an increase in production. Because output equals income in the macroeconomy, incomes go up by an amount that is equal to the value of the increased production. In turn, higher incomes lead to another set of expenditures and production increases and another round of income increases. And so on. When a new equilibrium is eventually reached and the effect of the original change in spending has completely worked its way through the economy, the total increase in GDP is greater than the original increase in spending. This is the **multiplier effect** of an increase in aggregate demand. For any given increase in spending that is not directly caused by an increase in income, the impact on equilibrium GDP is greater than the initial spending increase. There is no consensus among economists about the size of the multiplier effect, although most empirical estimates have put it between 1.0 and 2.0, with a majority in the middle of that range. If the multiplier is 1.5, it would mean that a sudden increase in spending of, say, $100 million would raise equilibrium GDP by $150 million. The multiplier undoubtedly varies in different countries and even in the same country at different times, and the source of the initial increase in aggregate demand is important so that an increase in consumption spending may not have the same ultimate impact as an increase in government spending.

The multiplier process of spending-production-income-spending and so on might seem as if it could go on forever, but in fact the impact of the original expenditure gets smaller and smaller, rather like the waves that radiate out from a rock thrown into a pond. There are several forces that dampen the impact over time and that bring GDP to a new equilibrium level. Three of the dampening forces are taxes, saving, and imports. In most countries, each successive increase in income will lead to additional taxes and saving, as well as additional spending. On average, when incomes rise people spend part of the increase, pay taxes with part of the increase, and save part of the increase. Taxes vary by country, and as we saw in Chapter 9, the amount saved varies as well. The larger the part that is taken by government or that is saved by households, the faster the impact of the original expenditure dissipates.

Each successive increase in income in the spending-production-income-spending cycle will also trigger an increase in imports. We can be certain of this effect because part of what households buy is imported, so that if they increase their purchases, they will also be buying more imported goods. All three of the variables—taxes, savings, and imports—cause the next round of spending on goods that are domestically produced to be less than the first round; therefore, they ensure that the income and spending effects moving through the economy are becoming smaller and smaller in each successive round. In addition, the three variables also show why the multiplier varies from country to country. The greater imports are as a share of spending, savings, taxes, the more each successive round of spending is reduced from the previous. That is, countries with larger propensities to import, higher saving rates, or higher tax rates will have smaller multipliers.

Fiscal and Monetary Policies

The discussion of aggregate demand, aggregate supply, and the multiplier is background for the analysis of the effects of fiscal and monetary policies on GDP and prices. **Fiscal policy** includes government taxation and expenditures, while **monetary policy** covers the money supply and interest rates. The institutions that enact fiscal and monetary policy vary across countries, but generally the legislative and executive branches are responsible for tax policy and for determining spending priorities, and the central bank and the finance ministry set monetary policy, sometimes with direct input from the executive branch of government. Recently, there is a trend toward granting central banks complete independence in setting monetary policy, as has historically been the case in a number of countries, including the United States.

Fiscal Policy

Government's fiscal policies of expenditure and taxation are an important element of every country's macroeconomy, because they are a major determinant of the total demand for goods and services. All else equal, when a government increases its spending the increase ripples through the economy as a series of production-income-spending increases that lead to higher levels of equilibrium GDP. Similarly, when governments cut their expenditures the same effect occurs, but in the opposite direction as production, income, and spending all decrease.

Changes in tax levels are similar in their analysis. A decrease in taxes will raise household income—what is available to save or spend—because fewer taxes are withdrawn from paychecks. The increase in after-tax income will in turn lead to increases in spending, production, and income again. Figure 11.2 can be interpreted as either an increase in government spending or a cut in taxes. In both cases, the AD curve shifts rightward, and both GDP and the price level rise.

For obvious reasons, cuts in taxes and increases in government spending are referred to as **expansionary fiscal policy**. The opposite, **contractionary fiscal policy**, is a tax increase or a cut in government spending, both of which reduce the level of equilibrium GDP by shifting the AD curve to the left. Contractionary policy is symmetrical with expansionary policy, so that tax increases and government spending cuts have a negative multiplier effect on total output, while tax cuts and government spending increases have a positive multiplier effect. It is important to note that we are assuming that nothing else changes other than the single change in fiscal policy. For example, there is no assumption that government budgets are balanced, and an increase in government spending does not imply a simultaneous increase in taxes. Similarly, cuts in taxes are not countered by cuts in spending, nor are tax increases balanced by government spending increases.

For many macroeconomists of the 1940s and 1950s, the discovery of the multiplier effect of fiscal policy was like finding the holy grail of macroeconomics. It seemed to offer a technique for managing the economy and, most importantly, for avoiding disasters such as the Great Depression of the 1930s. Needless to say, most economists today are much more cautious about the use of fiscal policy. The reasons are not hard to understand. First, expansionary policies tend to cause inflation, which offsets some of the increased consumer spending by absorbing it into higher prices instead of higher output. Second, there is a substantial margin of error in the estimation of the size of the multiplier. Does a $50 billion tax cut lead to a $50 billion, $75 billion, or $100 billion increase in income? Third, the use of fiscal policy is complicated by its variation in effects stemming from the different possibilities for financing an expansionary policy. If governments accommodate the expansionary fiscal policy with an expansion of the money supply, the multiplier is larger than if there is no accommodation. Taken together, the three technical problems of inflation, the margin for error in measuring the multiplier, and variation in the multiplier's size depending on the means of paying for the expansion make it difficult to use fiscal policy precisely.

But this is not all. The politics of turning government spending off and on, or turning taxes off and on, is a long, drawn-out, and complicated process. By the time the legislation is passed, the purpose for which it was originally intended may have disappeared entirely. In other words, fiscal policy as a tool for managing the economy to avoid recessions and curtail inflation is politically cumbersome. Taken together, the political problem plus the technical problem of measuring its precise effects make fiscal policy a less used tool for managing the economy. Nevertheless, it is still important to study, since government spending and taxation policies have significant impacts on the macroeconomy and the current account, regardless of whether they are implemented to achieve a particular macroeconomic objective.

Monetary Policy

Monetary policy is the other main category of policies that national governments use to influence the macroeconomy. As noted, in the United States, the European Union, and a growing number of other nations, monetary policy is determined by an independent central bank. Therefore, it reflects the views of the central bank and its responses to economic conditions rather than the views of a particular political party or the executive branch of government.

Monetary policy works through a combination of changes to the supply of money and changes to interest rates. When the central bank changes the supply of money, it does so by changing the quantity of funds in financial institutions that are available for lending. The most frequently used technique for accomplishing this is called **open market operations**. Open market operations are simply the buying and selling of bonds in the open market. When a central bank sells bonds, banks and other financial institutions give up some of their cash. Consequently, cash reserves shrink throughout the financial system. Buying bonds has the opposite effect on the financial system's reserves of cash and is the primary technique for expanding the money supply.

As cash reserves in the financial system increase, there is likely to be more investment. That is, financial institutions such as banks need to generate revenue by making loans. Money sitting in the vaults earns the bank no revenue, so an increase in bank reserves leads banks to make more loans. In order to encourage businesses to borrow additional funds, however, interest rates must fall.

Figure 11.3 illustrates the process of a fall in interest rates with a simple supply and demand diagram showing an increase in the supply of money. The horizontal axis measures the quantity of money in the system, where money is defined to be cash, checking accounts, and other easily spendable assets such as money market accounts that allow check writing. The easier it is to spend an asset, the more *liquid* it is considered to be. Cash is the most liquid asset, while checking accounts are slightly less so, but still highly liquid compared to, say, stocks or bonds.

The supply curve is represented with a vertical line instead of the more common upward sloping supply curve because we are assuming that the central bank fixes the quantity of money at a given level, and that the quantity does not vary with the level of interest rates, measured on the vertical axis. The interest rate can be considered similar to the price of money. There are two reasons for this: It is the price you pay to borrow money and it is the opportunity cost of holding your assets in the form of money instead of some other, interest-earning, form. This is admittedly a simplification, since borrowing costs and the return on savings are always different, and since some types of money earn interest (for example, money market accounts). Still, it is a simplification that is useful and one that captures the essential relationship between interest rates and the quantity of money in the economy.

The fall in interest rates shown in Figure 11.3 is the key to the increase in investment that comes about as a result of an expansionary monetary policy. Once investment increases, the expenditure multiplier takes over and the production-income-spending cycle is set in motion. Hence, an increase in the money supply will expand the economy and increase incomes. Not surprisingly, monetary policy is also symmetrical with respect to its contractionary and expansionary impacts, so a decrease in the money supply will result in a decline in production and incomes.

Expansionary monetary policy involves an increase in the money supply and a fall in interest rates, leading to a positive expansion in income. **Contractionary monetary policy** is exactly the reverse, and involves a decrease in the money supply and a rise in interest rates, leading to a contraction in income. As with fiscal policies, both expansionary and contractionary monetary policies work through the multiplier process to raise or lower income, depending on whether the policy is expansionary or contractionary.

FIGURE 11.3 **Money Supply and Demand**

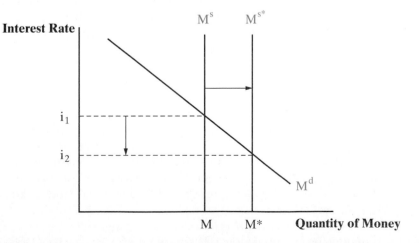

An increase in the supply of money reduces the rate of interest.

CASE STUDY

Fiscal and Monetary Policy during the Great Depression

The Great Depression is the name Americans give to the worst economic period in modern American history. It was a worldwide phenomenon, however, and most countries felt hard times. The onset of the crisis varied from country to country, but in the United States, it started in July 1929, with an unnoticed modest decline in economic activity. Stock prices continued to rise through the summer of 1929, in spite of the overall decline in output and income. September and October were bad months for the market, culminating in the panic of Black Thursday on October 24, when the market fell by more than one-third. Most people thought that the worst was over and many argued that the stock market collapse was good for the economy since it squeezed out excess speculation.

The small recession that began during the summer of 1929 grew into one of the worst decades in American history. By 1933, over 25 percent of the labor force was unemployed and real GDP had fallen by nearly 26 percent. Out of the cauldron of the Great Depression came Social Security, the Fair Labor Standards Act to regulate working conditions and wages, the Securities and Exchange Commission to oversee stock trading, the Federal Deposit Insurance Corporation to protect bank deposits, the Tennessee Valley Authority, and a host of other programs that inserted the federal government much deeper into American economic life.

Most Americans probably think of the 1930s and the Great Depression as synonymous, but there were two separate recessions in the United States during the decade. The first and most severe, is the one that began in 1929 and lasted until 1933. The second began in 1937 and lasted into 1938. Between these two downturns in economic activity, there was a strong recovery, and by 1936, real GDP was above where it had been in 1929, the last year of overall positive growth until 1934. Figure 11.4 illustrates the annual rate of growth, 1930–1941.

In hindsight, it is easy to see the policy mistakes that prolonged the recession and made it far more severe than it needed to be. Based on what we know today about expansionary fiscal and monetary policy, the federal government should have done one or more of the following: raise government spending for goods and services, cut taxes, or increase the money supply to lower interest rates. The problem in the 1930s was that no one was aware of the relations discussed in this chapter. In a very real sense, if you read the first part of this chapter, then you know more about fiscal policy than presidents Roosevelt and Hoover and all of their advisers knew.

Instead of using increases in government spending and cuts in taxes to stimulate the economy, presidents Hoover (1929–1933) and Roosevelt (1933–1945) worried about the federal budget deficits that emerged during the 1930s. Both

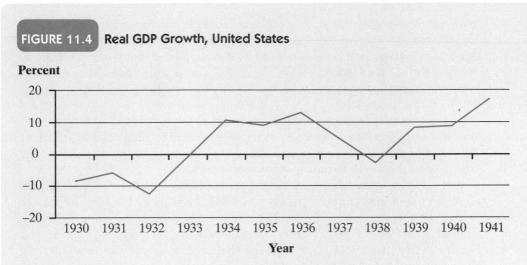

FIGURE 11.4   **Real GDP Growth, United States**

Source: Bureau of Economic Analysis.

Roosevelt and Hoover thought that budget deficits undermined business confidence and were a major reason for the recession. Consequently, the budget deficit became a major issue of the 1932 presidential election, in which Roosevelt successfully campaigned on the platform of a balanced federal budget. As it turned out, however, the federal budget was in deficit during every year of Roosevelt's presidency.

Hoover and Roosevelt tried to balance the budget. Both presidents unsuccessfully opposed legislation to offer war veterans early payment of the retirement money they were owed, and both presidents supported tax increases when deficits began to appear after 1929. Hoover introduced a dramatic tax increase in 1932, while Roosevelt increased taxes at several points in time, most dramatically with the beginning of social security taxes in 1937. Given the contractionary impact of tax increases, it is not surprising that 1932 was the worst year of the depression, nor that the economy slipped back into recession in 1938 after the implementation of the new social security tax.

If fiscal policy was not helpful during the 1930s, monetary policy was a disaster. Between 1929 and 1933, the money supply (currency, checking accounts, and savings deposits) fell by nearly 31 percent. Credit became scarce and investment disappeared. In other words, if fiscal policy could be considered more or less neutral during most years of the Great Depression (neither expansionary nor contractionary), then monetary policy was contractionary.

In retrospect, it is easy to understand the failure to use expansionary fiscal policy. No one in the 1930s understood the macroeconomy well enough to discern how to use fiscal policy to fight the recession. It is more difficult to justify the misuse of monetary policy, however, because more was known about the relationships between the money supply, bank reserves, and investment. For many years, prominent economists such as Nobel Prize winner Milton Friedman argued that the Federal Reserve was simply incompetent. This view cannot be ruled out, but more recent scholarship has shed new light on this historic episode. Rather than incompetence, the Fed's actions reflected a different set of priorities. In particular, it may have been acting responsibly if its first priority was to protect the gold standard.

Under the rules of the gold standard, central banks are required to use interest rates and monetary policy to attract gold whenever gold reserves run low. This usually means an interest rate hike in order to increase the demand for the domestic currency and to reduce the demand for foreign currencies.

In 1928, U.S. monetary policy turned contractionary as the Fed was worried about speculation in the stock market and wanted to make it more difficult for brokers to borrow from banks. The Fed raised interest rates and, unintentionally, created an inflow of gold to the United States. U.S. policy put pressure on European countries, which began to lose their gold reserves. Consequently, the contractionary policy in the United States spread across the Atlantic as countries began to raise their interest rates and slow their rate of money growth in order to stop the outflow of gold. The irony is that each country was acting responsibly according to the dictates of the gold standard, but they were following polices that resulted in a worldwide economic catastrophe.

At several points during the years that followed, U.S. and foreign policies turned even more contractionary. In 1931, it was widely expected that the United Kingdom would leave the gold standard altogether, and speculation turned against the pound. In September 1931, Britain left the gold standard and speculators immediately shifted their attention to the dollar. Expecting a similar decline in the value of the dollar, they began to sell dollars and dollar-denominated assets, all of which resulted in gold outflows. Once again, the Fed responded by raising interest rates in September and October 1931, and the U.S. economy continued its downward spiral.

It is no coincidence that the first countries to leave the gold standard (the United Kingdom and the countries that followed it out of the gold standard in September 1931) were the first to experience recovery. Once their policies were freed from the constraint of supporting a fixed rate of exchange, they could turn them toward economic expansion. In the United States, Roosevelt's first act after taking office in March 1933 was to suspend the gold standard. It seems unlikely that he completely understood the relationship of gold to the depression, but it was a good move, as the economy began its recovery from the worst economic crisis of the twentieth century.

Current Account Balances Revisited

Chapter 9 described the identity between private savings, government budget balances, investment, and the current account as follows:

$$S + (T - G) = I + CA$$

Now we are ready to look more closely at this identity and to incorporate the links between monetary and fiscal policy, income, and the current account. The goal is to analyze how a change in income caused by a change in monetary or fiscal policy influences the country's current account. We will do this in two steps. In the first step we will explore the links between changes in monetary and fiscal policies, interest rates, and exchange rates. The link from monetary policy to interest rates has already been described, but as we will see, fiscal policies have interest rate effects as well. In the second step we will put together policy changes, interest rates, exchange rates, and the current account balance. Once we have done this we will have a much clearer understanding of the policies a country must follow if it needs to eliminate a trade imbalance in its current account.

It is important to emphasize that we are looking at changes in income and other macroeconomic variables that are likely to take place over the span of a few years or less, while ignoring long-run impacts that may take many years, perhaps even a decade or longer, to materialize. We will return to this point later in the chapter when we try to distinguish long-run, permanent changes from short-run changes.

Fiscal and Monetary Policies, Interest Rates, and Exchange Rates

From Chapter 10 and the interest parity condition, we know that interest rate increases lead to an appreciation of the domestic currency (the exchange rate, (R), falls) and interest rate decreases lead to a depreciation (the exchange rate rises). Recall that this occurs through changes in the demand and supply of foreign currency. As interest rates rise, they increase the supply of foreign currency since interest arbitrageurs are constantly searching for the highest possible rate of interest. Similarly, a decline in interest rates reduces the inflow of foreign financial capital, decreasing the supply of foreign currency. Demand side effects are present in both cases as well, since home country interest arbitrageurs have the same motivation to move their capital in and out of the country.

The exchange rate effects of monetary policy are easily identified. We have already seen how an expansion of the money supply increases bank reserves and pushes down interest rates. Consequently, in addition to increasing income, expansionary monetary policy must also cause a depreciation of the exchange rate. Given the symmetry between expansionary and contractionary policies, monetary contraction reduces bank reserves and drives up interest rates, leading to an appreciation of the exchange rate.

Since a rapidly depreciating currency is a feature of most international financial crises, contractionary monetary policy is a very commonly adopted technique to stop a depreciation. This technique is discussed more fully in Chapter 12, but it should be noted that the downside of using monetary policy this way is a contraction in income and possibly even the cause of a recession. This illustrates once again that it is not unusual for a trade-off to exist between a country's exchange rate goal and its goals for income growth and employment. The Fed's action to raise interest rates to protect the dollar in 1931 is a classic example of a conflict between the needs of the domestic economy and the desire to protect the exchange rate.

The interest rate effects of fiscal policy are less easily identified, but they are present nonetheless. The key to understanding these links lies in the behavior of households and the changes they make when their incomes rise or fall. Looking first at the case of a rise in household income, we know that consumption expenditures will also rise. Furthermore—and this is key—rising incomes cause households to reevaluate the division of their assets between liquid forms such as money, and relatively less liquid forms such as stocks and bonds. When income rises, the average household will hold more money. In economic terms, the demand for money increases, as shown in Figure 11.5.

Why do households increase their demand for money when their incomes increase? The reasons are straightforward. First, at higher levels of income, they consume more. That is, they need a higher level of money holdings to pay for their purchases. Second, the opportunity cost of the interest they lose on holding money instead of an interest-paying asset becomes less burdensome. In other words, when households have more income, they can "afford" to hold more money.

Lest this seem too abstract and immaterial to your personal situation, think about what you might do if your income doubled. Most likely, you would increase the amount of money in your wallet and checking account. You would also probably put aside some of your increased income into long-term savings. The point is that if you are more or less average in your spending behavior, an increase in income would cause you to spend more and you would facilitate your

FIGURE 11.5   An Increase in the Demand for Money

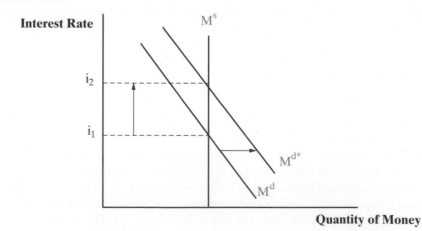

An increase in income causes households to increase their money holdings. As a consequence, interest rates rise.

increased spending by carrying around more cash and larger balances in your checking account.

Now we have all of the pieces to analyze the exchange rate effects of fiscal policy. Expansionary fiscal policy will raise incomes and consumption. One outcome of these effects is an increase in the demand for money which, as shown in Figure 11.5, leads to higher interest rates. Given the relationship between interest rates and exchange rates, we know that higher interest rates, all else equal, lead to an inflow of foreign capital and a fall in the exchange rate (an appreciation). As usual, the effects of contractionary policy are symmetrical. A cut in government spending or an increase in taxes will cause income and money demand to fall, followed by a drop in interest rates and a rise in the exchange rate (depreciation).

Fiscal and Monetary Policy and the Current Account

Once the exchange rate effects of monetary and fiscal policy have been identified, it is relatively easy to describe their effects on the current account. As we will see, the effect of fiscal policy on the current account is definite, while the effect of monetary policy is ambiguous. We turn now to the analysis of these impacts.

Taking the case of expansionary monetary policy first, we have seen that an increase in the money supply reduces interest rates and causes a depreciation in the domestic currency. Exchange rate depreciation switches some consumer spending from foreign goods (imports) to domestic goods, because foreign goods become relatively expensive. The effect of **expenditure switching** is to partially or completely offset the increase in imports caused by rising incomes. As a result, there is a more robust expansion of the domestic economy because less of the expansion of demand leaks out of the economy as an increase in imports. In other words, expansionary monetary policy is reinforced by the changes in the exchange rate.

Contractionary monetary policy has an opposite effect. Interest rates rise, causing an appreciation of the domestic currency, which makes imports relatively cheaper. As a consequence, consumers switch some of their expenditures away from domestic goods toward foreign ones. The reduction in demand for domestic goods reinforces the impact of contractionary monetary policy on income, consumption, and investment, and leads to a more vigorous decline in economic activity than would occur in a closed economy.

To summarize, the impact of monetary policy on income is magnified by its exchange rate effects. We cannot definitely say, however, what the effects are on the current account balance since the income effect of monetary policy on the current account is the opposite of the exchange rate effect. The current account balance could rise or fall with either expansionary or contractionary policy. However, a key idea in the chain of causation is the notion of expenditure switching. This refers to switching back and forth between domestic and foreign goods which, in this case, is in response to a change in the exchange rate. Expenditure switching magnifies the effects of monetary policy. Note, however, that this result depends on exchange rate flexibility. In an economy with a fixed exchange rate, changes in the money supply will not cause expenditure switching.

The effect of fiscal policy on the current account is more certain. As shown, expansionary fiscal policy increases interest rates, causing an exchange rate appreciation. Appreciation switches expenditures toward foreign goods since it makes them relatively cheaper, thereby increasing imports and reducing the current account balance. The expansionary fiscal policy leads to more imports, both from the rise in income and from exchange rate appreciation, which creates a feedback effect on domestic income. The shift in expenditures toward foreign goods offsets some of the increase in the demand for domestic goods and diminishes the impact of expansionary fiscal policy. Similarly, the exchange rate effect of contractionary fiscal policy switches expenditures away from foreign goods and toward domestic goods, diluting some of the contractionary effects of the policy.

The major short-run to medium-run effects of fiscal and monetary policy are summarized in Table 11.2. The differences between the two begin with their interest rate effects and carry over to exchange rates and current accounts. In the case of monetary policy, changes in the exchange rate and income have offsetting effects on the current account, but with fiscal policy changes in the exchange rate and income have reinforcing effects on the current account. As a result, the impact of monetary policy on the current account is indeterminate, while the impact of fiscal policy is definite.

The Long Run

How permanent are the effects? Economists more or less agree that in the long run the level of output in an economy tends to fluctuate around a level that is consistent with full employment. Note that full employment does not mean that everyone has a job. No matter how strong the economy is, there is always some unemployment from the entry of new workers into the labor force, or the return of workers after an absence from work. While searching for their jobs, both

TABLE 11.2	The Main Effects of Fiscal and Monetary Policies			
	Monetary Policy		Fiscal Policy	
	Contractionary	Expansionary	Contractionary	Expansionary
Y and C	$\Downarrow$	$\Uparrow$	$\Downarrow$	$\Uparrow$
i	$\Uparrow$	$\Downarrow$	$\Downarrow$	$\Uparrow$
R*	$\Downarrow$	$\Uparrow$	$\Uparrow$	$\Downarrow$
CA	$\Uparrow$ or $\Downarrow$	$\Uparrow$ or $\Downarrow$	$\Uparrow$	$\Downarrow$

Monetary and fiscal policies have different impacts on interest rates, exchange rates, and the current account. Monetary policy's impact on exchange rates and income partially offset each other's impact on the current account.

*A fall in R is an appreciation, while a rise is a depreciation.

groups are considered unemployed. In addition, there are always a number of people who have voluntarily quit their jobs to look for better ones, and people who lack the job skills they need to find a job.

In a strong economy, unemployment may temporarily fall to a very low level, but this tends to resolve itself. Initially, employers may grab whoever is available to fill their job vacancies, but as the pool of the unemployed dries up, they raise wages and look for ways to get by with fewer workers. Ultimately, this returns the unemployment rate to its normal level. Conversely, in a weak economy unemployed workers put downward pressure on wages, which ultimately resolves the problem of unemployment, since employers hire more workers when wages fall. The most controversial issue is how long these changes might take. Some observers believe they happen fast, while others are skeptical, particularly about the speed at which wages fall. In one sense, the debate over the amount of time it takes an economy to reach its long-run equilibrium at full employment is a debate over the meaning of the long run. Is it two years, five years, or ten?

In Chapter 10, we saw that in the long run, purchasing power parity determines exchange rates. Fiscal and monetary policy may cause deviations from purchasing power parity, but in the long run, a combination of exchange rate changes and changes in domestic prices will restore balance to the purchasing power of national currencies.

The current account must also tend toward balance in the long run. No nation can run deficits forever, nor can it run surpluses forever. Since deficits are equivalent to foreign borrowing and surpluses equivalent to foreign lending, there are limits in each direction. The limits are not well defined, however, and countries such as the United States have been able to run enormous deficits for long periods, while countries such as Japan have run surpluses.

CASE STUDY

The Limits to Macroeconomic Policy

In 1900, Argentina was among the richest countries in the world. Its good fortune was not to last, however, and by mid-century its per capita income had fallen behind. Although it still had the highest per capita income in Latin America, the gap with western Europe and North America was substantial, and it was not getting smaller when it was hit by the Latin American debt crisis and the Lost Decade of the 1980s (see Chapter 15). The debt crisis was vicious and hard to shake off. In 1989, seven years after it began, Argentina was still caught in it, and its GDP fell 7 percent while inflation hit 3,080 percent. Politicians tried a variety of experiments to get out of the recession and hyperinflation, but none of them led to sustained growth or brought down the inflation rate. In 1991, a radical experiment was tried. The country fixed its currency to the dollar at a 1:1 rate and dramatically restricted the creation of new money. For every new Argentine peso put into circulation, the central bank was required to have a dollar to back it up, and a newly created **currency board** was there to oversee the exchange rate system and enforce the rules.

The currency board worked extremely well through most of the 1990s. Argentina was back on a strong growth path with low inflation and was widely viewed as a successful model for other countries. Problems began to develop in 1998, however, when the global fallout from a crisis in East Asia spread to Latin America. Argentina's main trading partner, Brazil, devalued its currency in early 1999, giving Brazilian firms an advantage and putting Argentine firms at a disadvantage since goods valued in pesos were now more expensive. Argentina's current account balance developed a relatively large deficit of 4–5 percent of its GDP, and the loss of exports led to a recession in 1999.

At this point, conventional economic theory prescribed a demand-side stimulus for Argentina. Total expenditures in the economy were down, in part because it was more difficult to export, so the country should have cut taxes, raised government spending, increased the money supply, or some combination of those policies. There were a few obstacles, though. First, anything that might upset the 1:1 exchange rate was viewed as a potential problem. All else equal, exapnsionary macroeconomic policies cause prices to rise, and it was feared that deliberately increased government deficits might undermine confidence in the anti-inflation committment of the government. Argentina was already running a budget deficit that was hard to control, and increased spending and tax cuts were not an option. Monetary expansion was also out since that would undermine the peg to the dollar by increasing the circulation of pesos beyond the level of dollars available to back them up.

Secondly, a currency devaluation, whether intentional or not, would be a problem. During the growth years of the 1990s, Argentine firms and Argentina's government had borrowed dollars in international capital markets. There was nothing particularly unusual about Argentina's borrowing, except that its ability to raise revenue to service its debts was constrained by domestic political factors. Taking on debt denominated in dollars is common, but it imposes a high price when there is a currency devaluation, since the dollar value of the debt does not change, but the domestic currency value rises. Given that the government and most firms earned revenues in pesos, but that their international debts were in dollars, anything that caused the value of the peso to decline would increase the burden of debt.

The debate over policy was intense: Should Argentina devalue and increase the debt burden or maintain the exchange rate and continue to watch the current account deficit grow and the economy shrink? Cut government spending to create confidence in the fiscal soundness of the government; or, use expansionary fiscal policy to address the recession while undermining confidence in the government's committment to the 1:1 exchange rate? In effect, there were two choices. On the one hand, the government could use expansionary macroeconomic policies to try to combat the recession, but at the cost of a probable devaluation of the peso since no one would believe that it was still committed to anti-inflation policy and fiscal prudence. On the other hand, it could maintain the peso's link to the dollar at the 1:1 ratio, but at the cost of ignoring the recession.

Argentina's recession began in 1999. Two year later, in 2001, the country was still in recession and prospects seemed to be getting worse. As people lost confidence in the government's ability to maintain the 1:1 exchange rate, they decided that a devaluation was coming and began to take their money out of banks. After enormous losses in the banking sector, the government closed all banks in early December 2001. When they reopened in January 2002, the peso's link to the dollar had been cut. The peso began a steady decline, dropping from 1 peso per dollar to 0.7 pesos on January 7, to 0.545 pesos on Juanuary 22, and on down in value. Eventually, around June 2002, it stabilized around 0.27 pesos per dollar. In the end, it lost about three-fourths of its value.

Some observers argue that Argentina should have sought more flexibility in its policies by severing the one-to-one relationship between the peso and the dollar much earlier—in 1997 or 1998. Others argue that it should have made deeper cuts in its budgets, because that was the only way to maintain confidence in its currency. At first, the government tried the latter approach, but political and institutional obstacles prevented the budget cuts from being large enough.

The Argentine case still poses questions for economists. Recessions caused by a decline in demand are most effectively fought by increasing demand, either through government spending, tax policy, or monetary policy. However, if a country needs to demonstrate to the world that it is fiscally prudent because doing so will prevent speculation against its own currency and maintain the inflow of foreign currency, then expansionary macroeconomic policies may be impossible. Does this mean that developing countries cannot use expansionary macroeconomic policies?

Macro Policies for Current Account Imbalances

Fiscal, monetary, and exchange rate policies are essential tools for eliminating a current account imbalance. While any persistent imbalance can be portrayed as a problem, in practice the most dangerous imbalances are large current account deficits. Persistently large surpluses may bother a country's trading partners, but they rarely threaten a national economy the way that large deficits sometimes do. The macro policies for addressing a current account deficit are a combination of fiscal, monetary, and exchange rate policies, often collectively called **expenditure switching policies** and **expenditure reducing policies**. Both are essential.

We have already seen one type of expenditure switching policy when we talked about the exchange rate effects of fiscal and monetary policy. In general, an appropriate expenditure switching policy for eliminating a current account deficit is one that turns domestic expenditures away from foreign-produced goods and toward domestic goods. As discussed, an exchange rate depreciation is one way to do this. Recall that a depreciation raises the domestic price of foreign goods. An alternative type of expenditure switching policy is a trade barrier such as a temporary tariff to make foreign goods more expensive.

Expenditure reducing policies are simply contractionary fiscal or monetary policies that cut the overall level of demand in the economy. In most cases, they are necessary along with expenditure switching policies because without overall expenditure reductions, inflation ensues as home country domestic expenditures switch away from foreign producers and toward domestic producers. For this reason, expenditure switching policies must be accompanied by reductions in overall expenditures.

While expenditure shifts without expenditure reductions are inflationary, expenditure reductions without shifts toward domestic producers are recessionary. This makes the expenditure shifts necessary, since a shift in spending toward domestic producers offsets the decline in demand and leaves the economy with the same level of output but without a current account deficit. Given the need to use both types of policies simultaneously, expenditure reductions and expenditure shifts are not viewed as alternatives to each other but rather as two equally essential components of a macroeconomic policy designed to address a current account deficit.

The Adjustment Process

The term **adjustment process** is used to describe changes in the trade deficit that are caused by a change in the exchange rate. We have already seen that a depreciation raises the real price of foreign goods, making domestic substitutes relatively

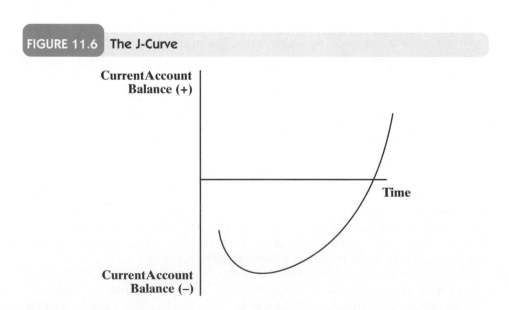

FIGURE 11.6   The J-Curve

Initially, depreciations often cause the current account balance to deteriorate further. With time, substitutions of domestic goods for foreign goods leads to an improvement in the balance.

more attractive. While this is an accurate description of the general pattern, depreciations often have delayed effects. In the United States, for example, there is a median average lag of about nine and a half months between a change in the exchange rate and an impact on U.S. exports. The median average lag for import responses is slightly less, but still more than seven months. Consequently, it is a mistake to think that exchange rate changes will affect trade flows overnight.

In addition to the lag effects, the first impact of a depreciation on the current account may be a further deterioration rather than an improvement. This deterioration is known as the **J-curve**, and is shown in Figure 11.6.

After a depreciation, there is usually a short period of no noticeable impact on the flow of goods and services. When imports and exports begin to respond, the immediate change is an increase in the value of imports, pushing the current account balance deeper into deficit. The size of the deterioration and the length of time before there is an actual improvement varies from country to country. In the United States, a depreciation results in an improvement in the trade balance only after a year or more. The reasons are straightforward. A depreciation makes foreign goods immediately more expensive, but it takes time for households and businesses to find substitutes. In the short-run they lack information, and it takes time to find new suppliers in the domestic economy, to check the quality of their products, and to negotiate contracts. Meanwhile, until the alternative suppliers are found, foreign goods continue to be used even though they cost more.

CASE STUDY

The Adjustment Process in the United States

From the third quarter of 1980 to mid-1987, the U.S. trade deficit widened from 0.48 percent of GDP to over 3.5 percent of GDP. In 1985, the Plaza Accord among the G5 (France, Germany, Japan, the United States, and the United Kingdom) created a cooperative effort to bring down the value of the dollar. The dollar began to fall in early 1985 with the introduction of a new team of officials at the Treasury Department; from January 1985 to January 1987, it fell from an index of 152.83 to 101.13, or nearly 34 percent.

While the dollar was falling, the trade deficit continued to widen. This was unsettling to a number of politicians, economists, and others, who had predicted a significant decline in the U.S. trade deficit as a result of the depreciation. Some journalists and politicians began to argue that the trade deficit would never respond to a change in the value of the dollar, that foreign trade barriers would make it impossible for the United States to substantially expand exports, and that our own open market would ensure a growing volume of imports regardless of the dollar's value.

Nevertheless, after a little more than two years, the trade balance began to respond to the fall in the dollar. Figure 11.7 shows the change in the value of the dollar and the trade balance from 1980 to 1988. Note that the time scale for the trade deficit is offset two years to reflect the long lag in the adjustment process. This offset pairs the exchange rate with the value of the trade balance two years later. It is apparent that there is a striking similarity in their movement, once adjustment is made for the two-year lag.

The question economists have debated since this episode is why it took so long for trade balances to respond to the decline in the value of the dollar. There are several possible explanations. One is that the prior increase in the dollar's value had padded the profit margins of foreign producers. From 1980 to 1985, their exports to the United States rose in terms of their domestic prices even though they sold in the United States for the same dollar prices. Consequently, when the dollar began to fall, foreign producers were initially able to keep dollar prices constant and absorb the decline in its value by realizing lower profits in terms of their domestic currency.

Another possible reason for the long lag is that there were still impacts from earlier appreciations working through the system. A third reason for the long lag is that exports began to increase from a much lower base than imports, and needed to increase much more rapidly in percentage terms in order for the trade deficit to begin to close.

FIGURE 11.7   **The U.S. Trade Balance and the Exchange Rate, 1980–1988**

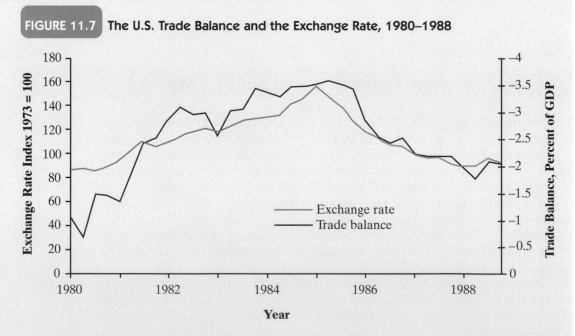

In the 1980s, changes in the U.S. trade balance mirrored changes in the exchange rate with a lag of two years.

Source: Business Cycles Indicators, BCI DataManager, Gary F. Langer; *Economic Report of the President.*

Macroeconomic Policy Coordination in Developed Countries

Coordination of macroeconomic policies is a frequent issue for the leading industrial economies. The annual meetings of the old G8 (Canada, France, Germany, Italy, Japan, Russia, the United Kingdom, and the United States) and the new G20 are often an extended discussion of shared macroeconomic issues, international economic relations, and relations with developing countries. When global economic imbalances arise, for example large U.S. current account deficits and growing Chinese surpluses, macroeconomic coordination becomes a topic of discussion. Actual coordination of macroeconomic policies is fairly rare, but not impossible. For example, the previous case study describes the agreement between five leading industrial economies to arrange a coordinated depreciation of the dollar, known as the Plaza Accord.

There are a variety of objectives sought with macroeconomic policy coordination, from achieving a desirable level of world economic growth to avoiding a global economic crisis. The purpose of coordination is to avoid imposing a disproportionate burden on one of the major world economies. Unequal burdens result when one country pays a large share of the costs of economic adjustment. As an illustration, suppose that the world economy is in a period of relatively slow growth. Not every economy will experience this, but it may be the case that enough economies are in recession or growing slowly so that the average rate of growth throughout the world is too slow to raise living standards or to pull people out of poverty. If a group of industrial economies decide jointly to expand their economies with fiscal and monetary policies, then growth in their incomes raises incomes around the world as their demand for imports stimulates production in other countries. If all economies expand simultaneously, then no one country is burdened by a sudden excess of imports over exports—their exports grow along with their imports and with the growth in demand in their trading partner's economies. For a variety of reasons, such as existing large budget deficits, or fear of the inflationary effects of expansionary policy, some countries may choose not to expand their economies. In this case, the effectiveness of the expanding economies as engines of growth across the globe is reduced. Furthermore, the country or countries using expansionary policy will probably experience a deterioration in their current accounts since their trading partners are not growing at the same rate. If expansionary fiscal policies cause interest rates to rise, then a further deterioration in the current account is likely due to the appreciation of the currency as a result of the inflow of foreign capital.

The way out of this dilemma is for a coordinated effort at macroeconomic expansion. There are both political and economic problems with coordination, however. The political problem is that there is no international organization capable of arranging a multilateral agreement among nations, nor is one possible without a significant sacrifice of national sovereignty. The economic problem is that there is rarely a period in which nations find it in their own interest to pursue the same policies as their trading partners. Countries enter and leave slow growth periods and recessions at different points in time and it is rare that one policy is suitable for everyone. Coordination remains a topic of discussion among the world's leading economies, however, since it is always in one or more countries' interest.

Summary

- Households supply all the factors of production (land, labor, and capital) that businesses need to produce the nation's output. In return, they receive all the income, or factor payments, which are payments for the use of their land (rents), labor (wages and salaries), and capital (dividends, profits, and interest). The income received by households is equivalent to the value of the output produced by businesses.

- Businesses use financial institutions to borrow household savings. They use the savings to invest. Businesses also produce the nation's output. Governments spend on goods and services, using tax revenues from the income flow going to households. The foreign sector supplies imports and demands exports.

- Fiscal policies are government tax and expenditure policies. Monetary policies are for interest rates and the money supply. Expansionary policies raise GDP and national income, while contractionary policies do the opposite.

- Fiscal and monetary policies work by changing total demand. Fiscal policies either change government spending on goods and services, which is a direct change in demand, or they change household income through a change in taxes. This is an indirect change in total demand. Monetary policies work through a change in interest rates, which changes investment.

- The multiplier explains how an initial change in spending (demand) is multiplied through the economy into a larger change in spending.

- Fiscal policy is considered more difficult to implement than monetary policy because it requires Congress to pass legislation that must be signed by the president. Monetary policy is easier because it is conducted by the Federal Reserve.

- Both fiscal and monetary policy influence exchange rates and the current account balance. In each case, the effect is through a change in interest rates brought on by the fiscal or monetary policy. Neither policy is likely to have long-run effects on income.

- In order to reduce or eliminate a current account deficit, countries must practice expenditure switching and expenditure reducing policies. Expenditure switching policies turn demand away from the foreign sector and toward domestic production. Expenditure reducing policies cut back on the overall level of demand.

- The J-curve describes how a policy designed to eliminate a current account deficit may initially make it larger before reducing it. The lag between a depreciation and a reduction in the size of a current account deficit is one to two years in the United States.

Vocabulary

adjustment process	expenditure switching
aggregate demand (AD)	expenditure switching policy
aggregate supply (AS)	fiscal policy
contractionary fiscal policy	intermediate inputs
contractionary monetary policy	J-curve
currency board	monetary policy
expansionary fiscal policy	multiplier effect
expansionary monetary policy	open market operations
expenditure reducing policy	

Study Questions

1. Using aggregate demand and aggregate supply, graph the effects on the price level and GDP of each of the following:
   a. A cut in income taxes
   b. An increase in military spending
   c. A drop in export demand by foreign purchasers
   d. An increase in imports
   e. A decline in business investment spending

2. Explain the concepts of fiscal and monetary policy. Who conducts them and how do they work their way through the economy?

3. What are some of the problems in trying to use fiscal and monetary policies? Why can't economists and politicians make precise predictions about the effects of a policy change on income and output?

4. Describe the mechanism that leads from a change in fiscal policy to changes in interest rates, the exchange rate, and the current account balance. Do the same for monetary policy.

5. Some countries have fixed exchange rate systems instead of flexible systems. How does the exchange rate system limit their ability to use monetary policy?

6. The United States is currently running a large current account deficit. If Congress and the White House decide to enact policies to reduce or eliminate the deficit, what actions should they take? Describe the set of policy options available to them.

7. Describe the larger economic effects of the policies in the previous question. That is, what would be the effects on income, consumption, employment, interest rates, and real exchange rates of policies designed to reduce or eliminate a current account deficit?

8. During the second half of the 1980s, the United States depreciated the dollar in hopes that it would reduce the current account deficit. After a year, the deficit was actually larger and newspaper editorialists were writing columns claiming that there is no link between the exchange rate and the current account. Explain why they got this wrong.

9. Suppose the United States, Japan, and many other places around the world go into recession, but growth remains strong in Europe. Why would macroeconomic policy coordination help, who should coordinate, and what are some of the obstacles to coordination?

International Financial Crises

Introduction: The Challenge to Financial Integration

Increasing international economic integration has created opportunities for growth and development, but it has also made it easier for crises to spread from one country to another. The worldwide recession that began in 2008 was triggered by a financial crisis that started in 2007, and while it is perhaps the most severe example of a crisis since the 1930s, there are several other recent examples. In 1992, currency speculation against the British pound and a few other European currencies nearly caused the collapse of monetary arrangements in Europe, and inflicted high costs on a number of countries in the European Union. In late 1994, speculation against the Mexican peso led to its collapse, and spread a "Tequila effect" through South America. In 1997, several East Asian economies were thrown into steep recession by a wave of sudden capital outflows, and in 1998, Russia's default on its international debt sent shockwaves as far as Latin America.

Financial crises are not new, but the way they develop and spread continues to evolve with the world's financial and economic integration. In some instances, they are an almost predictable result of inconsistent or unrealistic macroeconomic policies, but in other cases, countries with fundamentally sound macroeconomic policies have been pulled into a currency or **financial crisis** for no obvious reason. This makes financial crises difficult to predict, but it also increases the value of a set of early warning indicators. The **contagion effects** of a crisis do not conform to a single pattern and they reinforce the idea that there are different types of crises with their own rules of behavior.

Financial crises have brought down governments, ruined economies, and destroyed individual lives. Their enormous costs have created an intense amount of research into causes, prevention, and treatment. This chapter reviews some of the basic themes of this literature. It begins by describing two types of crises that have been observed during the last twenty years. Then it turns to a discussion of several key issues, including the steps that a country might take to avoid or minimize a crisis, and the policy choices it faces once one begins.

Much of the research in this area is designed to formulate sound principles for international financial reforms. The many reform proposals that have appeared in recent years are usually referred to as proposals for reform of the **international financial architecture**.

Often their contents revolve around a set of proposed changes to the International Monetary Fund (IMF) and other multilateral institutions with a role in international financial relations. The final section of this chapter looks at two of the main questions in that discussion: Does the world economy need a **lender of last resort**, and what type of conditions should a lender impose on the recipients of its assistance?

Definition of a Financial Crisis

Financial crises have a variety of potential characteristics, but the term usually refers to an exchange rate crisis, a banking crisis, or some combination of the two. Exchange rates and banking systems are not the only components, but in recent crises they have been points of vulnerability, partly because they are often the variables through which the contagion effects of a crisis are spread from one country to another, and between the financial system and the rest of the economy.

A **banking crisis** occurs when the banking system becomes unable to perform its normal lending functions, and some or all of a nation's banks are threatened with insolvency. A bank, like any other business, is considered insolvent or bankrupt if its assets are less than its liabilities, or, to put it another way, if its net worth is negative. The recession that began in 2008 is part of the fallout from a banking crisis that started in 2007. A variety of financial institutions, including banks, were involved.

The primary role of banks is **intermediation** between savers and borrowers. Simply put, banks and other financial institutions pool the savings of households and make them available to businesses that want to invest. If the businesses that borrow from a bank go under, then the bank cannot repay its depositors, and the bank may go out of business as well. **Disintermediation** occurs when banks are unable to act as intermediaries between savers and investors—it is a serious problem with negative economic consequences.

When a bank, insurance company, or securities firm fails, the investors that purchased its financial products lose some or all of their savings. Bank depositors in many countries are covered by deposit insurance, but holders of insurance annuities or securities purchased through a brokerage house rarely are. The loss of savings causes households to cut back on consumption and spreads the recessionary effect wider and wider through the economy. This is one way a crisis gets transmitted within an economy. Unaffected banks may stop making new loans as they take a cautious approach, new investment slows or stops altogether, layoffs occur, and the economy falls deeper into the vicious circle of a downward spiraling recession.

An **exchange rate crisis** is caused by a sudden and unexpected collapse in the value of a nation's currency. This can happen under a fixed, flexible, or intermediate type of exchange rate. If the exchange rate system is some form of a fixed exchange rate, the crisis entails a loss of international reserves, followed by a sudden devaluation once it appears that the reserves will run out. Devaluation is intended to accumulate reserves or to conserve existing reserves by making the rate of exchange less favorable to people trying to convert their domestic currency to dollars or another international reserve currency. If a country uses some form of flexible exchange rate, an exchange rate crisis involves a rapid and uncontrolled depreciation of the currency. While no type of exchange rate system guarantees safety, current research favors the idea that countries that adopt a pegged exchange rate may be more vulnerable to an exchange rate crisis.

Similar to the effects of a banking crisis, an exchange rate crisis often results in a steep recession. There are several channels through which recessionary effects may be transmitted, but one of the most common channels is the banking system. For example, prior to the Asian crisis of 1997 and 1998, banks borrowed dollars in international capital markets. When their home country currencies collapsed, the dollar value of their debt increased enormously. Consequently, many banks failed, disintermediation took place, new investment stopped, and the economies slid into a deep recession.

Two Sources of International Financial Crises

It is safe to say that every international financial crisis is unique in its origins and in the way it causes domestic economies to unravel. Nevertheless, it is helpful to consider two separate origins of crises. The first type is a result of definite and identifiable macroeconomic imbalances. For this type, the moment of crisis onset is difficult to predict, but unless the underlying conditions are corrected, it is almost certain to occur eventually. The second type is brought on by volatile flows of financial capital that move into and out of a country quickly. A sudden change in investor expectations may be a triggering factor, and underlying fragility in the banking and financial sector may be present. Still, this type of crisis can be puzzling because in several recent cases it has affected countries with particularly strong international positions and stable macroeconomic policies.

Crises Caused by Macroeconomic Imbalances

Over the last few decades, a number of crises have been triggered by severe macroeconomic imbalances, often accompanied by an exchange rate system that intensifies the country's vulnerability. The crisis that began in 2007 can partially be described that way. Exchange rate vulnerability did not play a role, but the large global imbalances of current account deficits and surpluses set the stage for the crisis (see the case study later in the chapter). There were many unusual features about the crisis that began in 2007, but one of the most surprising was that it originated in an advanced economy, the United States. In hindsight, it may be completely understandable that the global crisis began in the United States, but before it started, no one could have predicted it. The U.S. dollar did not play a significant role, in part because the dollar's status as the primary international reserve currency makes it highly demanded, even more so when there is a crisis.

Macroeconomic imbalances in government budgets, trade balances, and currency values have set off several crises in developing countries over the last decades. Frequently, these are the result of over-expansionary fiscal policies that cause the budget and current account balances to deteriorate and an appreciation in the exchange rate. When tax systems are inefficient or unreliable, it can compound the problems. Governments are then forced to borrow to finance their expenditure programs. In many low-income and middle-income countries the capital markets are less developed and few businesses or individuals are willing and able to buy bonds, particularly if they have an alternative place to put their savings. Consequently, governments have frequently obligated the central bank to buy its bonds and the money supply increases by the amount borrowed, leading to inflation and undermining confidence in the exchange rate.

With a fixed exchange rate system or a crawling peg system, higher rates of inflation lead to real appreciation of the exchange rate if the nominal rate does not adjust or if it adjusts more slowly than the inflation differential. Recall from Chapter 10 that the real rate is dependent on the nominal rate and prices at home and abroad. If prices at home rise, then the nominal rate has to depreciate by a similar percentage in order to keep the real rate steady. With fixed or pegged exchange rate systems, keeping the real rate constant becomes impossible when inflation is higher at home because it requires constant adjustment of the nominal rate and destroys confidence in the idea of a fixed or pegged exchange rate. Crawling pegs can do better in theory, since they involve an automatic adjustment, sometimes daily, but in practice they too tend to lead to overvalued exchange rates when inflation is higher at home.

Once people suspect that the exchange rate is overvalued, then capital flight out of the country begins. The incentive is to sell domestic assets, convert them to foreign exchange before the currency is devalued or depreciated, and invest outside the country, if possible. The goal is to preserve the value of the assets. After the domestic currency falls and once it is stabilized, then capital can return.

The scenario just described—unsustainable macroeconomic policies followed by deficits in the budget and trade accounts, an expected currency devaluation, and capital flight—is a basic description of the origins of many financial crises that occurred over the last several decades. They usually began in developing countries and they have the same treatment of **austerity** that was prescribed in Chapter 11 when discussing expenditure switching and expenditure reduction policies for curing a current account deficit. Recall that expenditure reducing policies address the budget deficits through tax increases and expenditure cuts, while expenditure switching policies address the current account deficit and the run on international reserves through devaluation of the currency and temporary measures against imports. These policies are relatively straightforward to describe but very painful to implement. In most cases they result in recession, if one has not already developed by the time they are put into place.

The precise causes of the crisis that began in 2007 will be debated for some time, but in a completely different way from the pattern just described, macroeconomic imbalances may have played a key role. Between approximately 2000 and 2007, large global imbalances developed between high-saving countries such as China, Japan, and Germany on the one hand, and high-consumption countries such as the United States, the United Kingdom, and Spain on the other. The flow of capital from high savers, which also included many oil exporters, to high spenders was reflected in large and persistent current account imbalances, and was partly responsible for the boom in house prices that occurred in the United States and many parts of western Europe. Capital flows kept interest rates low and made it easy to get loans for buying homes. The role of these imbalances is examined in greater detail, along with other factors, in the case studies later in the chapter.

Crises Caused by Volatile Capital Flows

Not all crises are the result of macroeconomic imbalances or unsustainable expansions in fiscal and monetary policies. National economies are increasingly vulnerable to the effects of technology that instantaneously shift vast sums of financial capital from one market to another. Together with the high degree of financial openness achieved in the last few decades, the contagion effects of crisis can spill across oceans and national borders. The best example of this kind of crisis is the one that hit some of the economies of East Asia in 1997 and 1998. While several economies had underlying weaknesses in their financial sectors, others such as Singapore, Hong Kong, and Taiwan were adversely affected even without the same weaknesses.

The fundamental cause of this type of crisis is that financial capital is highly volatile and technological advances have reinforced this volatility. The discovery of large emerging markets and the drive by financial investors in high-income countries to diversify their portfolios caused hundreds of billions of dollars to be invested throughout the world. Most savings in a nation never leaves, but an increasingly large volume of savings has entered international capital markets, where it moves relatively freely in response to interest rates, exchange rate expectations, and economic activity. This creates opportunities as well as problems. For example, one of the main problems in financial markets is that portfolio managers look at the actions of each other for information about the direction of the market. This creates a kind of herd behavior that takes over at critical moments and intensifies a small problem, turning it into a major crisis as large numbers of investors simultaneously lose confidence in a country. What begins as a trickle of funds out of a country can be interpreted as bad news about underlying conditions and lead to an avalanche of capital flight. When that happens, international reserves disappear, exchange rates tumble, and the financial sector can suddenly look very weak.

A weak financial sector can also intensify the problems. A case in point is a banking sector that borrows internationally and lends locally. If the funds obtained in the international market are short-term and are used to fund long-term loans such as real estate, problems arise when the international loans must be repaid. As long as international lenders are willing to roll over the debt and extend new loans, everything moves along smoothly. As soon as the lenders believe that there is a problem with a borrowing bank, they refuse to roll over the debt, creating a liquidity problem if the bank's assets are tied up in real estate loans. In the short-run, real estate is relatively illiquid and cannot be used to make a payment. When a number of banks are confronted with similar problems, their attempt to unload real estate depresses prices even further and undermines the solvency of the banking system since every bank with real estate investments is suddenly holding a portfolio of declining value.

This type of scenario is particularly troubling because it can go either way. That is, it may resolve itself without a crisis if international lenders are willing to extend additional credit while banks sell their long-term assets. Alternatively, if international investors expect a crisis and as a result are unwilling to give domestic banks the time they need to convert illiquid assets into liquid ones, then the crisis becomes a self-fulfilling prophecy. The belief in a crisis causes lenders to refuse to roll over the banking debts, and the banks, which are illiquid, become insolvent.

Several parts of this scenario are unsettling to economists and policymakers. First, there are multiple possible outcomes, or in economic terms, there are *multiple equilibria*, depending on the responses of international lenders. Second, one of the possible outcomes is a crisis, but the crisis is self-fulfilling. It is not predetermined, nor is it necessary. Third, the crisis affects banks that are fundamentally sound, but that have mismatches between the maturities of their debts and their assets. In other words, they are illiquid, but not insolvent.

These factors seem to imply that it should be possible to avoid this type of crisis. In part, it requires that banks pay closer attention to the maturity match between their debts and assets. In some cases, this requires a higher degree of supervision and regulation on the part of the banking authorities. For their part, international lenders must be more informed about the activities of their borrowers. This requires greater information flows, the use of standard accounting practices, and overall greater transparency in domestic and international financial systems. And, as a final point, once a crisis occurs, international agencies such as the IMF that are called in to make emergency loans need to be able to distinguish between insolvency and illiquidity. The distinction is more complex than it seems, but it is crucial, since the appropriate response will vary depending on the short- to medium-run prospects of the borrowing country.

CASE STUDY

The Mexican Peso Crisis of 1994 and 1995

The collapse of the Mexican peso and the ensuing crisis that began at the end of 1994 has elements of a crisis caused by macroeconomic imbalances and one caused by volatile capital flows and financial sector weakness. On the one hand, there were definite signs of macroeconomic imbalances, including an overvalued real exchange rate and a large current account deficit. On the other hand, the Mexican government operated a relatively austere fiscal policy, and not counting foreign interest payments on its debt, the government budget was in surplus, not deficit. Similarly, inflation came down during the early 1990s and reached 7 percent overall in 1994, down from 22.7 percent in 1991. Between

1990 and 1993, Mexico experienced capital inflows of $91 billion, or an average of about $23 billion per year, the most of any developing country. The capital inflow was in the form of private portfolio investments ($61 billion), direct investments ($16.6 billion), and bank loans ($13.4 billion).

The administration of President Salinas (1988–1994) actively encouraged large inflows of foreign capital as a way to maintain investment rates far above the level that domestic Mexican savings could support. Recall from Chapter 9 the macroeconomic identity that private savings plus the government budget balance must equal domestic investment plus the current account balance:

$$S_p + (T - G) = I + CA$$

In 1994, Mexican savings of around 14 percent of GDP could not support investment of more than 20 percent of GDP unless there was an inflow of savings from the rest of the world. Mexico ran large current account deficits equal to 5 percent of GDP in 1991 and 6.5 percent in 1992 and 1993. The enormous inflow of foreign goods and services permitted more investment by providing capital goods that Mexico could not make itself, and by satisfying consumption through foreign goods and thereby allowing domestic factories to produce investment goods. This was the strategy of the Salinas government, and it seemed to be working. The North American Free Trade Agreement (NAFTA) between Canada, the United States, and Mexico took effect on January 1, 1994, and throughout the year U.S.-Mexican trade expanded by almost one-fourth (23.7 percent). NAFTA inspired confidence in Mexico's institutional stability and guaranteed access to the wealthy U.S. market for any goods made in Mexico.

During 1994, the world capital market began to shift toward a more conservative, risk-averse stance. In February 1994, interest rate movements in the United States and exchange rate movements around the world led to large losses for a number of banks and other investors. Portfolio managers began to reassess their investments and look for ways to reduce their exposure to risk. Political events also prompted investors to reassess their financial positions in Mexico. First, on January 1, 1994, at the moment NAFTA began implementation, subsistence farmers in the poorest Mexican state of Chiapas revolted against the federal government. Second, in March the leading presidential candidate was assassinated while campaigning for office. While the lead-up to the signing and implementation of NAFTA had encouraged the view that Mexico was a safe, stable, and modernizing country, these events shocked investors into taking a closer look. Financial prudence seemed to call for reducing the level of exposure to Mexico, and many investors inside and outside the country sold their peso-denominated assets.

Less than three weeks after taking office in early December 1994, President Ernesto Zedillo finally agreed that the peso was overvalued and announced a 15 percent devaluation. Ordinarily this measure might have been interpreted as a cautious and responsible move to address the problem of an overvalued currency. Unfortunately, currency traders and economists had expected a 20 to 30 percent devaluation, and President Zedillo's actions made it appear as if his administration did not understand the severity of the crisis. Consequently, rather than the calming effect he had hoped for, Zedillo's announcement of a 15 percent devaluation sent currency and financial markets into even greater turmoil. More capital fled the country, dollar reserves shrank, and the credibility of Mexico's exchange rate policies came under severe questioning.

Two days after announcing the devaluation, the government of Mexico announced that it would move to a floating exchange rate system. Although this was the right move, the damage had been done, and both foreign and domestic capital continued to leave the country. By March 1995, the peso had fallen to more than seven per dollar, a loss of more than 50 percent of its value compared to early December 1994 (see Figure 12.1).

Zedillo addressed the short-run problems of the crisis by seeking financial support from the NAFTA partners and the IMF. Relief came in late January 1995, in the form of a line of credit and loans. Within weeks, currency markets were calmed down and the rate of capital flight slowed as the holders of peso-denominated assets began to relax in the knowledge that the government would be able to convert any amount of pesos to dollars. The peso regained some of its lost value, and by the end of April 1995, it was trading at six per dollar.

The medium- and long-run problems were addressed with a package of austerity measures that cut government spending, increased taxes (T up, G down), and reduced consumption. The large current account deficit at the end of 1994 increased the vulnerability of Mexico's financial system to capital flight and had been partly responsible for the draining of dollar reserves. Expenditure reduction policies were therefore an appropriate step taken to address the crisis, because tax increases and government expenditure cuts would help reduce the current account deficit. Electricity prices and gasoline prices were raised (both were supplied through government-owned enterprises), and credit was restricted

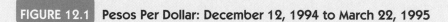

FIGURE 12.1   **Pesos Per Dollar: December 12, 1994 to March 22, 1995**

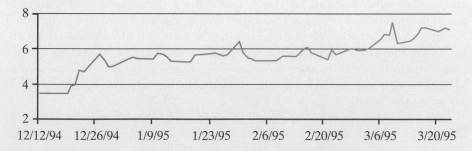

The peso lost over half its value between December 20, 1994, and March 9, 1995.

Source: Federal Reserve Board, http://www.federalreserve.gov/releases/H10/hist/.

through steep increases in interest rates and new limits on bank lending. These measures reduced consumption and boosted saving, provided a greater pool of domestic funds for investment purposes, and decreased the country's dependence on foreign capital inflows. However, the fall in consumption and government expenditures brought a recession; Mexico's GDP fell by 6.2 percent in 1995, and more than 500,000 people lost their jobs.

Analysts are still digesting the lessons of the peso collapse, but a few things stand out. For Mexico, the policy of relying on large foreign inflows of world savings through a large financial account surplus (current account deficit) proved to be unstable. Too much of the foreign capital was invested in short-term portfolios rather than longer-term direct investment. This distribution is not inherently unsafe, but once the peso became overvalued, both foreign and domestic investors feared that a surprise devaluation would destroy the value of their assets, and they began to convert large numbers of pesos into dollars. In addition, the peso crisis demonstrated how hard it is to arrange an orderly devaluation in a crawling peg system. Mexico's 15 percent devaluation was a cautions step in the right direction, but instead of calming market fears, it undermined credibility in the exchange rate system. Since then, many economists have argued in favor of completely fixed exchange rates with no discretionary monetary policy, or a floating exchange rate such as Mexico has followed since the crisis.

Domestic Issues in Crisis Avoidance

Not all crises are avoidable. Nevertheless, there are steps that countries can take to try to minimize the likelihood of crises and the damage they cause when they happen. In addition to the need to maintain credible and sustainable fiscal and monetary policies, governments must engage in active supervision and regulation of the financial system and provide timely information about key economic variables such as the central bank's holding of international reserves.

In these areas, the design of effective policies is relatively straightforward, but in other areas there is a wide array of expert opinion, and consensus remains elusive. Should countries bail out their banks if they fail, and what type of penalties should they impose if they do? Should they try to limit foreign capital inflows and outflows? Which type of exchange rate system is most stable? It is possible that in some areas there is no single optimal policy for avoiding a crisis and countries have a variety of equally viable options? In those cases, it is also possible that there are choices that are better for some countries, but not others, depending on the conditions inside the country?

Moral Hazard and Financial Sector Regulation

When a country's financial sector becomes dysfunctional, problems spread to the rest of the economy. Credit dries up, investment disappears, households worry about their lost savings, consumption falls, and the economy falls into recession.

Hence, there is a big incentive to keep the financial sector operational, even if it means that governments have to spend revenues in order to keep the sector in working order.

This creates a dilemma for policymakers, since the knowledge that you will be bailed out if you fail usually leads people, including bankers, to take greater risks than are prudent. That is, if the costs of failure are removed, the incentive for the decision makers inside financial institutions to take normal precautions and to behave responsibly are also removed.

In economic terms, this is the problem of **moral hazard**. Moral hazards occur when there is an incentive to withold essential information or to act in a manner that creates personal benefits at the expense of the common goal. For example, when selling a used car, the seller has a financial incentive not to divulge negative information about the car, and people seeking life insurance have an incentive not to divulge negative information about their health. Similarly, in the financial sector, banks and other institutions have an incentive to make riskier investments that pay a higher return if they know that they will be bailed out.

Moral hazard problems are particularly acute when the government of a country uses the credit system to make loans for specific economic development goals, or even worse, for satisfying important political constituencies. For example, a government may determine that the development of a particular steel plant is in the interests of the country, or that the economic enterprises of politically well-connected elites should be supported with easy credit. Many governments use state-owned banks to make such loans, or they provide financial incentives or threats to private banks to get them to make the loans. The result in either case is that the loans may not meet market criteria for lending, and there are either implicit or explicit guarantees to the banking sector that they will be bailed out if something bad happens. In the Asian crisis of 1997 and 1998, these types of loans gave rise to the term **crony capitalism**. The definition of crony capitalism is ambiguous, however. Many Asian politicians and observers pointed out that in the West, politicians and business people often rely on tight networks of acquaintances and associates, which are little different from the charges of insider-dealing that are implied by the term *crony capitalism*.

The problem of moral hazard is inescapable if there is a general policy of protecting the financial system from collapse. In effect, no matter how it is administered, the policy of protecting the sector is a form of insurance, and all insurance systems have moral hazard elements. There is no way to eliminate the problem of moral hazard completely, but it can be minimized through various actions.

To this end, bank regulators from the industrial countries met in Basel, Switzerland, under the auspices of the Bank for International Settlements (BIS) to agree on a set of operational standards, including supervision and regulation, for internationally active banks (see Chapter 10 for a brief description of the BIS). This led to the 1989 **Basel Capital Accord**, which was eventually adopted by more than 100 countries. In 2001, a New Basel Capital Accord, Basel II, was issued, updating the previous standards.

Basel II is a set of recommended best practices that emphasizes the three areas of capital requirements, supervisory review, and information disclosure. **Capital requirements** help to reduce moral hazard elements in the banking sector by requiring the owners of banking institutions to invest a percentage of their own capital in their bank so that bank losses are personal losses to shareholders and other bank owners, as well as losses to the bank's depositors. Bank **supervisory review** and regulations are designed to act as oversight to assist with risk management and to provide standards for daily business practices. Inadequate bank supervision and the inexperience of local bank managers actively involved in international financial markets were key weaknesses in the economies of East Asia and were partly responsible for the onset of the crisis in 1997. Hence, supervision and oversight of financial markets, including banks, has become a central component of recommendations for avoiding crises. The final area, **information disclosure**, is designed to encourage market discipline by requiring banks to disclose all the relevant information that lenders, investors, and depositors need to understand the full scope of a particular bank's operations.

The three pillars of Basel II are key to a healthy global financial system, but they were not sufficient to prevent the global crisis that began in 2007. Most international financial services firms adhered to Basel II requirements, but new forms of finance and financial instruments were not part of the regulatory framework. One of the key weaknesses is thought to be the standards for capital adequacy. Consequently, there has been a great deal of recent discussion about capital adequacy in the case of new financial instruments, and a series of revisions and enhancements to the Basel II framework. These enhancements are targeted at many of the new types of financial instruments and at accounting procedures that allows firms to exclude some assets and liabilities from their accounts.

Exchange Rate Policy

Through the 1970s and 1980s, many countries adopted a crawling peg exchange rate system, often as part of an anti-inflation strategy. Recall from Chapter 10 that the "pegged" part of a crawling peg involves fixing the exchange rate to a major world currency such as the dollar or the euro, or to a basket of currencies that include the home country's major trading partners. The "crawling" part of the exchange rate involves regular—often daily—devaluations of a fixed amount. Theoretically, a crawling peg allows a country to increase or decrease the value of its currency periodically, but since pegs are usually intended to stabilize the real exchange rate in a country with higher inflation than its trading partners, most crawling pegs are set to a constant rate of devaluation rather than revaluation. That is, if domestic inflation is higher than foreign inflation, nominal devaluation keeps the real exchange rate constant. Given the definition of the real rate as

$$R_r = R_n (P^*/P),$$

then if the change in P (domestic prices) is greater than the change in P* (foreign prices), the nominal rate, R_n, must rise (devalue) in order to keep the real rate constant. Maintaining the peg requires the monetary authority to exercise discipline in the creation of new money, and is anti-inflationary in that sense. In addition, many countries tried to reinforce the anti-inflation tendency of the crawling peg by intentionally devaluing at a slower pace than the difference between home and foreign inflation. This created real appreciation in the exchange rate, and was intended to act as a brake on domestic inflation. Foreign goods steadily became cheaper in real terms, limiting the price increases that domestic producers were able to impose. The use of the exchange rate in this manner had mixed success in helping to control inflation, but in a number of cases it led to severe overvaluation of the real exchange rate and increased the country's vulnerability to a crisis.

Another way in which a crawling peg exchange rate system increases a country's vulnerability to crisis is that it is politically difficult to find a way to exit from the system if it becomes overvalued. When a government announces a change in the system, it runs the risk of losing its credibility. Both domestic and foreign economic agents accommodate the existing system, and a sudden large devaluation leads to economic losses and a loss of confidence in the country's policymakers. Consequently, it is common for countries to delay addressing the problem of overvaluation, and when the correction comes, it has to be larger. The end of Mexico's crawling peg in 1994 is a good example.

Currently, many economists believe that countries should adopt either a "hard peg," which is akin to a fixed exchange rate, or they should use a floating exchange rate, which is managed by the central bank. Hard pegs include fixed rates, dollarization, and the use of currency boards. In any of its possible forms, the monetary authority must exercise discipline in the creation of new money. Credibility of the peg is of the utmost importance to its survival, and it is only assured if there is a tight control on the money supply. Floating exchange rates allow more flexibility in the conduct of monetary policy, but they raise the specter of a lack of monetary discipline and a return to deficit financing through the printing of money. They also lead to greater volatility as the domestic currency swings up and down. For these reasons, many countries are reluctant to adopt flexible exchange rates.

Capital Controls

Many economists hold that the free movement of capital is a desirable objective because it allows investors to send their financial capital wherever the return is highest, which raises world welfare by putting financial capital to its most valuable use. At the same time, capital mobility allows countries to invest more than is possible with their domestic savings alone, which again raises world welfare when there are valuable investment projects and insufficient savings to realize them. Others, however, claim that the benefits of complete capital mobility are based on theory, but are never fully demonstrated empirically. In addition, capital mobility generates very high costs in the form of macroeconomic crises, and these costs must be offset against any economic gain.

This issue is unsettled, and although economists agree that trade in goods and services raises a country's welfare, there is less agreement about the benefits of free capital movements. The sources of the disagreement cover not only the potential benefits of capital inflows versus the potential costs of sudden capital outflows, but also include debates over the actual ability of **capital controls** to prevent capital movements, whether controls on the movement of capital can stop a crisis once it begins, and whether it is better to limit inflows, outflows, or both.

Through much of the twentieth century, countries guarded against the problems of capital mobility by restricting its movement. This seems to imply that countries are able to prevent capital from crossing their borders, but what may have been true in 1970 is much more doubtful today. The growth of emerging stock markets and the implementation of technology to facilitate capital transfers have created both the incentive and the means for investors to send their capital abroad.

Ordinarily, capital flow restrictions are imposed by limiting transactions that are part of the financial account of the balance of payments. (See Chapter 9 for a discussion of the components of the balance of payments.) Capital movements to support transactions on the current account are usually permitted since they are necessary for trade. Consequently, one of the primary ways in which firms can get around capital account restrictions is to overinvoice imports. This allows them to make payments abroad that are larger than necessary for the purchase of imports. Alternatively, they can underinvoice exports so that the reported payments received are smaller than the actual payments, and the difference can be invested outside the country without reporting to authorities. While these techniques are common, and perhaps fraudulent, outright corruption in the form of bribes is also a possibility for getting money out of the country.

Whether these types of practices make controls on capital outflows completely ineffective is open to debate, but they clearly reduce the effectiveness of capital controls. For this reason, as a general rule, restrictions on inflows are seen as more workable than restrictions on outflows. Inflow restrictions can take a variety of forms, but they share the common goal of trying to reduce the inflow of volatile, short-run capital, which may add to the stock of liquid assets ready to flee the country.

Restrictions on capital inflows cannot stop a crisis once it begins, however. Consequently, there is an ongoing debate over the utility of imposing restrictions on capital outflows once a crisis starts. Since many crises include a speculative attack against the home country currency, some argue that a temporary limitation on capital outflows could help to stop a crisis by artificially reducing the demand for foreign exchange. In theory, this would prop up the value of the domestic currency and eliminate expectations of a large decline in its value.

In the midst of the Asian crisis, Malaysia followed this policy in spite of a number of warnings that it would undermine investor confidence in Malaysian policies, cut them off from international capital markets, and do long-term damage to the economy. None of the dire predictions materialized and Malaysia recovered from the crisis at about the same speed as Korea, which went the other way and eliminated some of its controls on capital flows. The fact that two different policies led to more or less similar outcomes is a measure of how much we do not know.

CASE STUDY

The Asian Crisis of 1997 and 1998

The Asian financial crisis began in Thailand in July 1997. From there, it spread to a number of other countries, including Malaysia, the Philippines, Indonesia, and South Korea. The outward symptoms of the crisis were fairly similar across countries: currency speculation and steep depreciations, capital flight, and financial and industrial sector bankruptcies. It is tempting to interpret these symptoms as signs of the region's weaknesses, but ironically, the causes are at least in part due to the region's great strengths.

Current Account Deficits and Financial Account Surpluses

The most severely affected countries all had large trade deficits. Table 12.1 shows current account deficits in 1996, the year before the crisis. For the five countries in the top panel, deficits averaged 5.2 percent of GDP in 1996. In Thailand, where the crisis began, the current account deficit was nearly 8 percent of GDP. The three countries in the bottom panel of Table 12.1 all felt reverberations from the crisis in spite of their small deficits (Hong Kong) or large surpluses (Singapore and Taiwan).

Large current account deficits necessarily imply large financial account surpluses, and the countries listed in the top half of Table 12.1 all experienced large capital inflows. Foreign investors were more than willing to send their capital to East Asia as the region had averaged about 5 percent growth per year in real GDP for the last thirty years, and there was no reason to believe that would change anytime soon. Furthermore, slow growth in Japan and Europe during much of the 1990s caused many international investors to scour the globe looking for higher returns, and the stable and dynamic economies of Southeast Asia stood out prominently. Low inflation, small budget deficits or consistent government surpluses, and the high rates of economic growth made them highly desirable places to invest and to loan funds.

Exchange Rate Policies

Exchange rate policies in the region usually involved pegging to the dollar, so that as the dollar appreciated in the mid-1990s, it caused many exchange rates to appreciate along with it, resulting in a number of significant currency misalignments. The pegged exchange rates became harder and harder to sustain, partly because they made it more difficult for the pegged countries to export. According to some observers, this problem was exacerbated by China's devaluation of its fixed exchange rate in 1994 and the significant depreciation of the Japanese yen throughout the period of dollar appreciation. The movements in these two currencies made the exports of Thailand and several others less competitive.

TABLE 12.1 **Current Account Balances and Currency Depreciations**

	Current Account Balance, 1996, Percent of GDP	Currency Depreciation in Dollars, 7/1/97 to 12/31/97
Countries with large deficits		
Indonesia	−3.4	−44.4
Malaysia	−4.9	−35.0
Philippines	−4.7	−33.9
South Korea	−4.9	−47.7
Thailand	−7.9	−48.7
Countries with small deficits or surpluses		
Hong Kong	−1.3	0.0
Singapore	+15.7	−15.0
Taiwan	+4.0	−14.8

Large current account deficits led to large depreciations. Nevertheless, some countries were hit with depreciations even when they had large surpluses.

Source: Goldstein, Morris, *The Asian Financial Crisis: Causes, Cures, and Systemic Implications*, Washington, DC: Institute for International Economics, June 1998.

Financial Sector Problems

The downturn in export revenues exposed several other weaknesses, including those in regulatory systems, corporate structures, and financial systems. Many countries in East Asia rely on corporate structures built around family ties and personal networks. This can have significant advantages for small and medium-size enterprises, but as firms grow, the lack of disclosure and transparency make it difficult for outside lenders to assess the microeconomic risks of lending. In addition, the lack of hard data and information make it difficult to implement the kinds of regulatory controls that all economies need for stability, especially in the financial sector. For example, many banks experienced the kind of mismatches between the maturities of their assets and liabilities that is described as a serious vulnerability earlier in the chapter. These firms took out short-term loans in international capital markets and used the money to finance real estate developments with long and risky payoffs.

Crisis and Contagion

The event that triggers a crisis is often relatively unimportant. For example, some analysts blame the decline in Thailand's export earnings that stemmed from the downturn in prices for computer chips. In any case, the huge trade imbalance and the disappointment on export revenues undermined investor confidence in Thailand's ability to keep its exchange rate pegged to the dollar. People began to expect a devaluation and did not want to be holding the Thai baht when it came. Furthermore, many of the loans to the Thai financial sector were short-term loans obtained in international capital markets, and required repayment in dollars. This raised the cost of a devaluation because Thai financial institutions earned revenue in baht, but owed a fixed amount of dollars. Any change in investor confidence could undermine the entire economy.

How the Thai crisis spread internationally is one of the less certain components of the overall crisis. One hypothesis is that Thailand served as a "wake up call" for investors to examine more closely their holdings in other countries. Another hypothesis is that the Thai devaluation made exports from several neighboring countries less competitive and forced them to engage in competitive devaluations. Regardless, there was a contagion element in the Thai crisis and it soon spread to countries as far away as Brazil and Russia.

Some of the consequences of the Asian crisis are easily visible in Table 12.2, which shows the growth rate of real GDP in 1998 and 1999. With the exceptions of Singapore and Taiwan, every country affected by the crisis experienced a recession in 1998. Given their large trade surpluses and their ample international reserves, Singapore and Taiwan were able to focus on their domestic economies rather than trying to defend their currencies, thereby avoiding recessions. By the second quarter of 1999, every country had returned to positive growth.

The rapid recoveries shown in Table 12.2 caught most analysts by surprise, yet the flexibility and fundamental soundness of macroeconomic policies throughout East Asia facilitated swift recovery. Still, Table 12.2 does not tell the whole story since poverty rose significantly throughout the region and will take many years to return to its pre-crisis level. In addition, without fundamental financial sector reform, the chances of a repeat episode remain fairly high.

Crisis Management

Three issues in crisis management remain unresolved after this episode. First, did the IMF make a mistake in advising the borrowing countries to defend their currencies with interest rate hikes? Second, were there moral hazard elements present, perhaps as a result of the Mexican bailout in 1995? Third, are capital controls helpful as a temporary measure to stem a crisis?

The first issue is a specific instance of the dilemma referred to earlier. Should countries try to protect their domestic economies or must they defend their currencies? For countries with large trade surpluses and ample international reserves, defense of the domestic economy through lower interest rates seems feasible. The real question applies to the five countries with large current account deficits. Some critics of the IMF blame it for turning a financial panic in those countries into full blown depressions by counseling them to raise their interest rates. The critics charge that the IMF treated the crisis as if it

TABLE 12.2	Real GDP Growth	
	1998	1999
Real GDP growth in countries with large current account deficits		
Indonesia	–13.2	+0.2
Malaysia	–7.5	+5.4
Philippines	–0.6	+3.3
South Korea	–6.7	+10.7
Thailand	–10.2	+4.2
Real GDP growth in countries with small current account deficits, or surpluses		
Hong Kong	–5.1	+3.0
Singapore	+0.4	+5.4
Taiwan	+4.6	+5.7

Many countries experienced deep depressions in 1998, but by the second quarter of 1999, virtually every crisis country had returned to positive growth.

Source: Asian Development Bank, "Economic and Statistics, Regional Data," available at http://www.adb.org/Statistics/regdata.asp [February 24, 2001].

were the same as the Latin American debt crisis of the 1980s, in which governments had large budget deficits and high rates of inflation. In East Asia, governments were running surpluses or small deficits, so there was no need to temporarily contract the economy with interest rate increases. Defenders of the IMF argue that interest rate hikes were necessary as a means to stop the slide in currency values.

A second issue relates to the moral hazard of bailing out a bank or corporation. If banks know they will be bailed out if they make bad lending decisions, then they have less reason to exercise prudence and caution, and more reason to take greater risks that offer higher returns. Some critics allege that the IMF loans to Mexico set a precedent that taught lenders that their mistakes would be covered by loans from the IMF, and consequently the Asian crisis became more likely. The counterargument is that "bailouts" are not really bailouts in the full sense of the word because they do not protect investors from losses. Most investors in East Asia saw sizable reductions in the values of their portfolios, so they have plenty of reason to exercise caution when lending.

A final unresolved issue is the problem of capital flight. Can it be stopped, at least in the short term, with controls on capital outflows? Malaysia thought so, and implemented capital controls that appeared to have some success in removing pressures on the Malaysian ringgit to depreciate. Malaysia acted in spite of a number of warnings that it would lose its access to international capital markets, yet its recovery from the crisis was as rapid as in any of the other affected countries. On the other hand, Korea went the other way and removed some of the controls it had on capital flows, and it also recovered quickly. Did capital controls make a difference? As with the previous two issues, an answer awaits further research.

Domestic Policies for Crisis Management

It is relatively easy to prescribe a cure for financial crises that result from inconsistent macroeconomic policies. For example, if a crisis is triggered by a collapsing currency, which, in turn is the result of large government budget deficits financed by money expansion with a fixed or crawling peg exchange rate, then the prescription is relatively straightforward in economic terms: Cut the deficit, raise interest rates to help defend the currency, and, perhaps, let the currency float. In other words, the solution to a fiscal crisis brought on by macroeconomic imbalances is to correct the imbalances.

The problem is that the economic austerity of budget cuts and higher interest rates may not be politically feasible. In addition, several economic problems are often present. Tax systems in many countries are unenforceable, meaning that tax increases may not generate more revenue. The adoption of a floating exchange rate system may undermine the credibility of the government's commitment to fighting inflation, since financial sector interests often fear that it will remove the last bit of restraint over money creation and lead to hyperinflation. Governments may not be able to cut expenditures easily, since government employees may be unionized with multiyear contracts, may provide essential domestic services, or other elements of the budget may support powerful domestic interests.

The case of a crisis brought on by sudden capital flight in the context of relatively stable and credible macroeconomic policies is even more difficult to resolve. Given that this type of crisis may have multiple equilibria outcomes, depending on the direction taken by expectations, there is a powerful argument for addressing the problem of a collapsing currency through interest rate hikes, sales of reserves, and other actions that might help convince investors that the currency is strong. On the other hand, high interest rates and other actions to defend the currency are likely to intensify bankruptcies and other contractionary forces that develop during a crisis. Hence, defending a currency may push a small downturn into a full-blown depression.

In crises caused by either macroeconomic imbalances or sudden capital flows, there is a strong desire to avoid a recession. In the first type, however, both fiscal and monetary policies are usually overextended and the crisis is partly a result of policies that are unsustainable and overly expansionary. In effect, this forecloses fiscal and monetary policies as tools to avoid the recessionary aspects of the crisis and the only way out is usually through some sort of recession.

In the second case, however, fiscal and monetary imbalances may not be part of the initial problem, so the use of fiscal and monetary policies is not entirely ruled out. However, the dilemma faced by governments in this position is that expansionary policies include a reduction in interest rates, which can cause a further depreciation in the domestic currency. If domestic firms have debts that are denominated in dollars or another foreign currency, a depreciation implies a sudden increase in the size of their debts and spreads additional bankruptcies through the economy.

In effect, this implies that fiscal and monetary policies are limited if there is an international component to the crisis. It also creates a stark set of choices for handling the crisis. Either defend the currency with high interest rates and spread the recessionary effects of the crisis, or defend the domestic economy against the recessionary effects of a crisis and intensify the problems of a collapsing currency. Much of the debate over the policies recommended by the IMF during the Asian Crisis of 1997 and 1998 (raise interest rates to try to stabilize the collapsing currencies) turned on precisely this point. Clearly, if there was an easy, nonrecessionary, way to end a crisis, policymakers would use it.

Reform of the International Financial Architecture

The frequency of international financial crises coupled with their high costs has generated a great deal of interest in finding the right policies for avoiding a crisis and for handling one if it begins. Taken as a whole, the discussion of new international policies for crisis avoidance and management is referred to as reforming the international financial architecture. In particular, a lot of attention is focused on the role of the IMF and the conditions it imposes as part of its loan packages.

A number of ideas for reforming the international financial architecture have been advanced in recent years. Private think tanks such as the Council on Foreign Relations, the Overseas Development Council, and the Centre for Economic Policy and Research in London have each published proposals, as have multilateral agencies such as the United Nations Conference on Trade and Development (UNCTAD) and government appointed bodies such as the International Financial Institutions Advisory Commission of the U.S. Congress. In the aftermath of the crisis of 2007–2008, reform is also a major topic of discussion at international meetings of finance ministers and country leaders.

The proposals for international financial reform express a variety of conflicting viewpoints, but they agree that two issues are at the center of the discussion. The first is the role of an international lender of last resort, and the rules governing its lending practices. A second issue is the type of conditions such a lender might impose on its borrowers. In effect, both of these issues are questions about the role of the IMF and its current practices.

A Lender of Last Resort

Recall from Chapter 2 that a lender of last resort is a source of loanable funds after all commercial sources of lending have disappeared. In a national economy, this role is usually filled by the central bank. In the international economy, it is filled by the IMF, often with the support of high-income, industrial economies such as Canada, France, Germany, Japan, and others. As a lender of last resort, the IMF is often asked to intervene when countries reach a crisis point in their finances and cannot make payment on their international loans, or cannot convert their domestic currency into dollars or another foreign currency due to an insufficiency of international reserves.

Not everyone agrees that there should be a lender of last resort, and some observers worry about the moral hazard problems of such lending. This is particularly problematic as a crisis begins to develop and some firms are on the verge of collapse. The moral hazard problem can intensify since managers of failing firms have a large incentive to gamble on high-stakes, high-risk ventures that, if they pay off, will cover all their losses. In response, those who favor maintaining the IMF in its current role as an international lender of last resort stress the importance of financial sector regulation, including the elements outlined in the Basel Capital Accord. If the owners of financial firms risk a substantial loss in the event of financial meltdown, they are less likely to take on excessive risk.

Three other issues that are central to the discussion of the IMF's role as a lender of last resort are the question of how high an interest rate it should charge when it makes loans, the length of the payback period, and the size of its loans. Taking the interest rate issue first, the traditional prescription for a lender of last resort is that it lends at a relatively high, or penalty level, interest rate. Most IMF loans are at a rate of interest that is equivalent to a weighted average of short-term government borrowing rates in leading industrial economies, plus a slight surcharge. In practice, these tend to be fairly low-interest loans and definitely not a penalty rate.

Some fear that this encourages countries to borrow, while others argue that the interest rate does not affect the incentive to borrow in a crisis. It may affect the length of time that countries take to pay back the loan, however, and in this sense, a higher rate may encourage countries to get out from under their IMF debt. Some proponents of higher interest rates on IMF loans also believe it is necessary to shorten the loan period, while others point out that higher interest rates will encourage countries to pay off their loans faster. The length of IMF loans varies by type of loan, with some as short as one year, and others as long as ten years, depending on whether the loan is for immediate relief or long-term structural adjustment.

The final issue about the rules for IMF loans is the size of the loan. Countries pay a subscription, called a *quota*, to join the IMF. The size of the quota mainly depends on the size of the economy and its strength. The quota determines how much a country can borrow in a "normal" crisis, as well as how many votes the country has in setting IMF policy. Generally, countries can borrow up to 300 percent of their quota, but in extraordinary circumstances such as the Mexican peso crisis, the Asian crisis, or other crises with the potential to spread, the limits on country borrowing are determined more or less by the needs at the time, as well as the amounts available directly from other governments.

Although some countries have borrowed enormous sums that are well above 300 percent of their quota, the limits on borrowing have not kept up with the growth in the size of national economies. Some argue that borrowing limits should be greatly expanded, while others propose differentiating between crises that have a high probability of spreading and those that are contained within a single country. In many cases, it may not be possible to determine the difference, but systemwide crises definitely have the potential to impose greater costs. Hence, there is a clear rationale for intervening with larger sums if it will stop a crisis faster. This seems to be a point on which most countries agree. At the 2009 meeting of the twenty largest economies, called the G-20, there was agreement to treble the resources available to the IMF from US $250 billion to US $750 billion, for a total increase of US $500 billion.

Conditionality

The second set of issues surrounding the role of a lender of last resort such as the IMF is the issue of conditionality. IMF **conditionality** refers to the changes in economic policy that borrowing nations are required to make in order to receive IMF loans. Conditionality typically covers monetary and fiscal policies, exchange rate policies, and structural policies affecting the financial sector, international trade, and public enterprises. The IMF makes its loans in **tranches**, or installments on the total loan, with each additional tranche of the loan dependent on the completion of a set of reform targets. For example, a loan recipient may have to promise to develop a plan for privatization in order to receive the first tranche, have a workable plan in order to receive the second tranche, begin implementation for the third tranche, and so on.

Often these types of reforms generate significant opposition since they seem to override national sovereignty and generally impose contractionary macroeconomic policies. Some economists argue that conditionality requirements intensify the recessionary tendencies of a crisis, although there is a debate over whether countries recover faster with IMF assistance than without it. Until the early 1990s, the IMF focused its efforts on economic policy reforms in a way that more or less ignored their social consequences. Public outcry against the effects of conditionality on the vulnerable members of societies forced a closer look at the social impacts of policies, and the IMF has tried to make adjustments. Even so, there are still widespread complaints that IMF conditionality is too punitive and too contractionary, and a few countries in crisis have refused IMF assistance. The most notable example is Malaysia during the Asian crisis of 1997 and 1998. Apparently, refusing to work with the IMF did not hurt, since Malaysia recovered from the crisis as fast as any other country.

Prior to the 1970s, IMF conditionality focused primarily on correcting the immediate source of the problem that led to a crisis, and avoided involvement with underlying economic issues, such as trade policy and privatization. This was criticized as too short-sighted, and it was agreed that the Fund should involve itself beyond short-run economic policy. New loan programs were developed to provide money and technical assistance to countries that needed help in restructuring their economies. This shift involved the IMF in far more than crisis resolution, as it took on an active role in assisting in privatization, the design of social policies, trade policy reform, agricultural policies, environmental policies, and a number of other areas.

By the late 1990s, there was growing recognition that "mission creep" had become a problem and that the Fund had taken on responsibilities that were better left to the World Bank, regional development banks, or some other agency designed to address the long-run issues of economic development. Several of the proposals for reforming the international financial architecture envision a reduced role for the IMF in this area.

In addition to dealing with the problem of mission creep, several of the reform proposals argue in favor of a set of requirements that countries must pass before they will be allowed to borrow. These proposals favor a prequalifying examination of country policies as a means to avoid crises in the first place. Proponents argue that in order to receive assistance, countries should first demonstrate that they meet a number of requirements such as open financial markets, adequate bank capital, transparent reporting of financial sector data, and others. Those who propose this type of prequalification for IMF assistance argue that it will force countries to adopt fundamentally sound financial sector policies that will minimize the probability of a crisis.

Critics of the prequalification idea point out that prequalification will not avoid crises since it does not deter speculative attacks on a country's currency. It may even promote instability if it induces complacency about a country that prequalifies. In addition, it would be impossible for the IMF to ignore the needs of member countries that fail to prequalify, and this would lead to other, less open ways to handle a crisis. Finally, the IMF has already implemented a prequalification procedure for one type of loan, but to date no country has tried to prequalify since it might be interpreted as a signal to the rest of the world that problems are developing.

Two additional issues are worth mentioning as part of the reforms of the international financial architecture. First is the issue of a set of standards for transparency and data reporting in the financial sector. The purpose of greater transparency is to make a country's financial standing clearer to potential lenders. The issue of transparency and data reporting is moving forward with the Basel Capital Accord and the IMF's own development of standards for data reporting, called the **data dissemination standards**.

The second issue is the need to find ways to coordinate private sector involvement in times of crisis. Less progress has been made on this issue than on the data dissemination issue, and it continues to be a serious concern. When a country reaches a crisis, the insistence by numerous private creditors that they be paid first can make it more difficult to resolve a crisis. Hence, proposals have been put forward for **standstills**, in which the IMF officially recognizes the need for a country in crisis to stop interest and principal repayments on its debt temporarily. This would also impose a burden on the country's creditors, and reduce the moral hazard element in their lending practices.

Conflict between private creditors over who deserves first repayment has often been an obstacle to resolving a crisis. Consequently, many analysts see the need for **collective action clauses** in all international bond loans. A collective action clause would require each lender to agree to a collective mediation between all lenders and the debtor in the event of a crisis. This avoids the problem that an uncooperative creditor may be able to block a solution that is agreed to by a majority of the lenders. It would also promote a quicker resolution to a crisis caused by a borrowing country's insolvency.

Reform Urgency

In the aftermath of the Asian crisis, a wide number of reform proposals were circulated among academics, government officials, and the staff of multilateral organizations. The crisis drove home the points that international financial flows had grown dramatically over the previous decades, that many developing countries are now active participants in world finance, and that contagion effects can instantaneously spread a crisis from one country or region to another. Reform, beginning with a reconsideration of the role of the IMF, was at the top of everyone's agenda.

A decade after the Asian crisis began, the world was enveloped in a much broader and potentially deeper crisis. Yet, as the Asian crisis faded in memory, the urgency for reform diminished and not much had happened by the time the crisis in the U.S. housing market exploded in 2007. Reform is difficult and without the urgency of a crisis it proved to be impossible. A relatively stable world economy after 1998, and the rise of issues such as terrorism, energy prices, climate change, and security, crowded out the issue of international financial reform. With the onset of a global financial crisis in 2007, and its conversion into a deep recession across most of the globe, the topic is once again timely and in the news.

CASE STUDY

The Global Crisis of 2007

The most recent financial crisis began in the United States in the fall of 2007. The first visible stage was called the subprime crisis in reference to housing loans made in the United States that were given to borrowers with less than prime credit ratings. Many of these borrowers proved unable to manage the housing payments they had taken on, and many of the loans turned out to have clauses that made it financially impossible for homeowners who could not refinance their loans within a year or two. When home prices started falling, refinancing became difficult or impossible for homeowners who now owed more than their houses were worth.

Problems in the housing sector quickly spread through the banking sector and into other parts of the financial services industry such as insurance companies and investment banks that had bought mortgage-backed assets. This would have posed serious problems for the United States under any circumstances, but it is at this stage that the problem became global. Three critical factors or preconditions turned a national, U.S. problem into a global one. First, the world's financial markets had undergone a relatively steady transformation over several decades with the development of new and innovative financial products. The financial services industry of 2007 did not look at all like the industry it was in the 1960s or 1970s. Second, financial markets had become much more integrated. Open capital markets and flexible exchange rates created new global flows of financial capital that were not possible in earlier decades. These larger and more integrated capital flows were augmented by high rates of savings in a number of emerging markets, such as China, that had played virtually no role in global finance before the 1980s or 1990s. Third, a spirit of deregulation had captured the thinking of many economists, politicians, and regulators. This permitted new forms of very risky finance to develop without close supervision, and without consideration for the fact that some of the new forms of finance posed risks not only for the individual financial institutions using them, but to the entire economic system as well.

By early 2008, the subprime crisis had spread beyond the United States. One of the causes of its rapid contagion was the high level of innovation that occurred over the previous several decades. In the 1970s and 1980s, banks accepted deposits, which they lent to borrowers who wanted to buy homes. Beginning in the 1980s and increasingly through the 1990s into the twenty-first century, banks and other "non-bank financial entities" such as car financing firms, consumer credit firms, insurance companies, and others began to enter the market. Their strategy was not to profit from the interest they earned on the home loans, but to group a large number of loans together and sell shares in the entire package. This is known as **securitization**. It applies not only to home loans, but can also be done with car loans, consumer credit loans, and a wide variety of other types of debt. If you buy a share in the securitized package, you receive a return that is based on the interest that the ultimate borrowers—home owners, car owners, credit card owners, etc.—pay to their lenders. The company that creates the securitized package of loans can, in turn, sell shares to another bank, a foreign-based insurance company, a foreign government, or virtually anyone willing and able to buy. Needless to say, if homeowners in the United States cannot pay what they owe, then the owners of shares in the securitized package lose money.

The growing integration of global finance meant that these new products could be sold just about anywhere and finance crossed international boundaries with increasing ease. Pension funds in Wisconsin bought products that originated in Iceland, city governments in Germany bought securities based on Southern California real estate, and Hungarian home owners took out loans in Swiss francs from Swiss banks. Housing markets in developed countries experienced a boom—finance was easy to obtain, prices were going up, and demand for new homes, either to live in or as investments, continued to increase. In the United States, home prices rose nearly 90 percent between 2000 and 2006, and the United Kingdom, Spain, and a number of other markets experienced increases as large or larger. These increases fed on themselves as they pulled more finance into the housing market. The growing international integration of financial services meant that capital for home loans could be moved from one country to another, and that the United States, Spain, Ireland and other locations where there were rapid increases in home prices could continue to borrow to purchase even more homes.

New innovations in financial products and the growing integration of capital markets challenged regulators to keep up. With the growth of computer modeling and the application of advanced mathematics, many new financial products are complicated beyond nearly everyone's ability to understand, including the regulators and the corporate heads and risk managers of the companies that created them. Few, if any, regulators in the United States or elsewhere expressed concern, however. As explained by Alan Greenspan, the ex-chairman of the U.S. Federal Reserve Bank, most regulators were persuaded that financial firms would self-regulate since it is not in their interest to lend to someone that will default on his or her loan. His perspective reflected a much more general view that close regulation of financial markets was not in the national interest since regulators were likely to impose limits that reduced efficiency while favoring the objectives of the regulators over the interests of market participants. The thought that the global financial system was at risk was inconceivable to all but a few analysts. Almost no one believed that the most advanced countries of the world could stumble into a crisis that would lead to the near collapse of their economies.

Financial innovation, global financial integration, and financial deregulation can explain a lot of what happened. They do not, however, tell us why the crisis began in 2007 rather than earlier or later. As with many other crises, it is impossible to pinpoint an event that triggered the onset, but there is one more factor that played a very significant role and without which it is unlikely that there would have been the housing boom or the crisis. This factor is the large global savings imbalances that built up in the world financial system over the course of the first decade of the twenty-first century. In order to explain this, we need to briefly return to the Asian crisis of 1997–1998.

The Asian crisis caused a reaction among many developing countries, both in Asia and elsewhere. The countries that suffered the greatest crisis were those that lacked sufficient dollars, euro, yen, and other international reserves to defend their national currencies. Their solution was to accumulate a large supply of international reserves by increasing their savings and running large current account surpluses that they could use to purchase dollars, U.S. Treasury securities, and other secure, highly liquid, financial assets. Large and important countries such as China began to increase their holdings of dollars, mostly in the form of short-term bonds, both government and private. Due to the sheer size of these accumulations, they began to play an important role in international finance. The savings held by governments are called **sovereign wealth funds**, but private entities also increased their savings.

Globally, current account balances must total to zero. If China and other countries run large current account surpluses in order to accumulate international reserves, their counterparts are large deficit countries. The country with the largest current account deficit, both over time and in all recent years, is the United States. Table 12.3 shows the five largest surplus countries and the five largest deficit countries between 2000 and 2007. The first column of numbers is the surplus or deficit for 2007 while the second is the cumulative surplus or deficit from 2000 through 2007. The table shows that there are mainly, but not only, two kinds of surplus countries: Asian exporters and oil producers. Germany is an outlier, but is also one of the world's largest exporters. While five countries is not a lot to generalize from, the pattern holds with some exceptions if we look at all countries of the world together.

The importance of large imbalances is that they were a supply of savings that became available globally to countries such as the United States, where households and businesses wanted to borrow in order to maintain higher levels of current consumption and investment. Without the savings of China, Japan, Germany, and the others borrowing in the United States, the United Kingdom, Spain and the others would have been much more expensive and the bubble in housing markets would have been less likely. As a result, we probably would not

TABLE 12.3   **Current Account Deficits, 2000–2007 (Billions of US$)**

Country	Current Account Balances	
	2007	Cumulative, 2000–2007
Surplus countries		
China	371.8	973.8
Germany	252.9	768.9
Japan	244.0	1,175.0
Saudi Arabia	95.1	399.7
Russia	76.2	460.0
Deficit countries		
United States	−731.2	−4,660.1
Spain	−145.4	−494.1
United Kingdom	−78.8	−393.8
Australia	−57.7	−245.7
Italy	−51.0	−180.4

Source: World Bank, World Development Indicators, 2009.

have seen the boom in house prices, low interest rates, and the easy lending that took place in the high-deficit countries. Global imbalances should be added to the other three elements that made the crisis possible. They all were important, but if we can consider innovation, integration, and regulation to be micro-economic factors, then global savings and investment imbalances were the primary macroeconomic factor.

The policy implications of the crisis will be analyzed and debated for years. Each of the elements described in this case study has generated a set of questions with multiple answers and no consensus. For example, financial innovation has brought many benefits to economies by providing more sources of capital for investment and consumption and new mechanisms for insuring against risk. Yet, some new instruments may increase systemic risk if they are not carefully used. Is all financial innovation a good thing? Financial market regulation could, in theory, provide oversight, but what kind of regulation and by whom? Global financial integration has increased efficiency, but are all forms of integration equally desirable? These and other questions await a clear set of answers.

Summary

- International financial crises are generally characterized by financial disintermediation in the crisis country, a collapsing currency value, and a steep recession.

- One type of crisis is caused by severe macroeconomic imbalances, such as large budget deficits, hyperinflation, overvalued real exchange rates, and large current account deficits.

- Another type of crisis is the result of a speculative attack on a currency that prompts large outflows of financial capital and a run on the country's international reserves. This type of crisis can be self-fulfilling because economic agents that believe an attack on the currency is imminent will abandon the currency, which is equivalent to an attack on the currency.

- The Mexican peso crisis of 1994–1995 had elements of both types of crises, as did the Asian crisis of 1997–1998. However, several countries in East Asia were subjected to speculative attacks on their currencies even though their underlying macroeconomic fundamentals were very strong.

- Responding to a crisis is complicated by the problem of moral hazard. If the government or the IMF bails out the banks and other firms hit by crisis, it may encourage future risky behavior. The problem of moral hazard is particularly acute if the government has directed credit to specific enterprises for political or developmental purposes because directed credit either explicitly or implicitly includes a government guarantee.

■ The Basel Capital Accord and Basel II are a set of recommendations for internationally active banks and financial enterprises. They cover the supervision and regulation of enterprises, minimum capital requirements, and standards for information disclosure.

■ Many economists believe that crawling peg exchange rates makes countries more vulnerable to a crisis because they become overvalued more easily and there is no smooth way to abandon them when a crisis begins to brew.

■ Capital controls on capital outflows are generally viewed as ineffective in the long run, although there is some debate about their temporary efficacy in times of crisis. Capital controls on the inflow of short-term financial capital have more supporters, but there is no consensus on their efficacy in avoiding crisis. Some research shows that they can help a country avoid a small crisis, but are less effective at avoiding a large crisis.

■ The optimal response to a crisis depends on its causes. If it is caused by macroeconomic imbalances, then changes in macroeconomic policies are essential. If it is caused by sudden, unexplained capital flight, then the optimal response is less certain. Some economists, particularly those at the IMF, argue that stabilizing the currency with high interest rates will lead to a quicker recovery, even though this intensifies the contractionary elements of the crisis in the short run. Others favor expansionary fiscal and monetary policies to minimize the short-run effects of a recession.

■ Reform of the international financial architecture includes a revaluation of the role of the IMF and other international agencies. A few favor abolishing the IMF as a lender of last resort, while most favor keeping it but reconsidering some of its policies. In particular, questions have been raised about the interest rates it charges on its loans, the length of the loan period, and the limits on the size of loans.

■ The most contentious element of IMF lending policies is conditionality. In particular, there is widespread agreement that the IMF tries to support too many different types of reform and that it should refocus on its core competencies, which include financial sector reform, balance of payments assistance, and exchange rate policies. There is some discussion about whether it should require countries to prequalify before they are eligible for its lending programs.

■ Other issues in the international financial reform discussion include standards for data dissemination and policies to create greater involvement of private creditors in working out the solutions to international financial crises when they occur.

■ The crisis that began in 2007 had three microeconomic components and one macroeconomic one. Financial innovation, global financial integration, and a regulatory philosophy of "hands-off" or *laissez faire* each played a role. The primary macroeconomic cause was the presence of large global imbalances between high-savings and high-spending nations.

Vocabulary

austerity	financial crisis
banking crisis	information disclosure
Basel Capital Accord	intermediation
capital controls	international financial architecture
capital requirements	lender of last resort
collective action clauses	moral hazard
conditionality	securitization
contagion effects	sovereign wealth funds
crony capitalism	standstills
data dissemination standards	supervisory review
disintermediation	tranches
exchange rate crisis	

Study Questions

1. What is an international financial crisis, and what are the two main causes?

2. In the text, the point is made that the expectation of a crisis from volatile capital flows is sometimes a self-fulfilling crisis. How can a crisis develop as the self-fulfillment of the expectation of a crisis?

3. What are three things countries can do to minimize the probability of being hit by a severe international financial crisis?

4. Why are crises associated with severe recessions? Specifically, what happens during an international financial crisis to create a recession in the affected country or countries?

5. What type of exchange rate is associated with a higher probability of experiencing a crisis? Why?

6. In a crisis not caused by macroeconomic imbalances, economists are uncertain whether a country should try to guard against recession or try to defend its currency. Why are these mutually exclusive, and what are the pros and cons of each alternative?

7. Explain the moral hazard problems inherent in responding to a crisis.

8. Some people argue that U.S. loans to Mexico in 1995 led to the Asian crisis. Explain the logic of this argument.

9. Some countries impose capital controls as a means of preventing a crisis. Evaluate the pros and cons of this policy.

10. How has the role of the IMF come under scrutiny in the recent discussion of reforms in the international financial architecture?

Regional Issues in the Global Economy

13 Economic Integration in North America

Introduction: Expanding Economic Relations

After several years of negotiations, the North American Free Trade Agreement (NAFTA) came into effect on January 1, 1994. In Mexico NAFTA was greeted by a group of armed rebels that seized several towns in the southern state of Chiapas. In the United States NAFTA was ratified by Congress after a close and bitter debate in which both the proponents and opponents had exaggerated—and misread—the likely impacts. The debate in Canada was not nearly as dramatic, however. Canadians had just gone through a similarly divisive struggle over the **Canadian-U.S. Trade Agreement (CUSTA)** that began in 1989, and Canadian commerce with Mexico is relatively small.

For many U.S. economists, it seemed odd that a relatively dry and straightforward agreement would turn into one of the most contentious economic issues of the 1990s. After all, U.S. barriers to Mexican imports were already low; if Mexico decided to lower its barriers to U.S. and Canadian products, what could be so controversial? Plenty, as it turns out.

Economic and Demographic Characteristics of North America

Before we turn to the history and controversy over NAFTA, it is useful to have an idea of the size of the combined North American market. Table 13.1 shows population and GNP comparisons measured in two different ways. By any measure, the combined market is enormous. With more than 439 million residents in 2007, the NAFTA region continues to be one of the largest trade agreement areas in the world today.

International income comparisons are more complicated than population comparisons. The fourth column in the table is a typical way to make comparisons. Mexican and Canadian incomes are converted to U.S. dollars using the average exchange rate over the entire year. This method shows that the average Canadian income is about 88 percent of the United States' average income, and the average Mexican income is around 21 percent. The first problem with this comparison is that regardless of changes in either nation's output, fluctuations in the exchange rate can lead to dramatically different values for Mexican or Canadian GDP when measured in U.S. dollars. A second problem is that real prices vary across countries. Haircuts, restaurant meals, and maid services, for instance, cost far less in real terms in Mexico than in the United States. These goods and services are not traded, and Mexico's relative abundance of labor makes production of labor-intensive goods cheaper. As a consequence, the average annual income in Mexico of $9,715 buys more goods and services than a similar income in the United States.

The last column shows income comparisons in **purchasing power parity** terms. Purchasing power parity comparisons use an artificial exchange rate to make adjustments for differences in prices. It can be interpreted as the U.S. dollar value of the real quantity of goods and services that a typical Mexican income buys. In other words, GDP per person in Mexico is enough income to buy goods and services that would cost $14,104 in the United States. However, if a Mexican citizen took that amount of pesos, converted them to dollars, and brought them to the United States, he or she would only get $9,715 worth of goods and services.

Measurements of GDP per capita at market exchange rates and at purchasing power parity both convey important information. Market exchange rates tell what a nation can buy externally (outside the nation), while purchasing power parity tells what it can buy internally (inside the nation). As an exporter, one would be more interested in the former, but as someone interested in knowing how Mexico's living standards compare to those of the United States, one would want to know the latter.

Two more points about Table 13.1 are worth considering. First, even though Mexico is a developing country, the NAFTA market is very rich. Few countries have a higher GDP per capita than the weighted average of Canada, Mexico, and the United States, and total GDP at market exchange rates is over $16 *trillion*.

Second, NAFTA combines nations that are at very different levels of economic development. Even though Mexico is one of the wealthiest nations in

TABLE 13.1	Population and GDP for NAFTA Countries, 2007			
Country	Population (Millions)	GDP (US$ Billions)	GDP per Capita (US$)	GDP per Capita (US$, PPP)
Canada	33.0	1,330	40,329	32,812
Mexico	105.3	1,023	9,715	14,104
United States	301.6	13,751	45,592	45,592
Total	439.9	16,104	36,609	37,321

The NAFTA market includes more than 430 million people with a combined gross domestic product of more than $16 trillion.

Source: The World Bank, *World Development Indicators.*

North American Free Trade Agreement Members

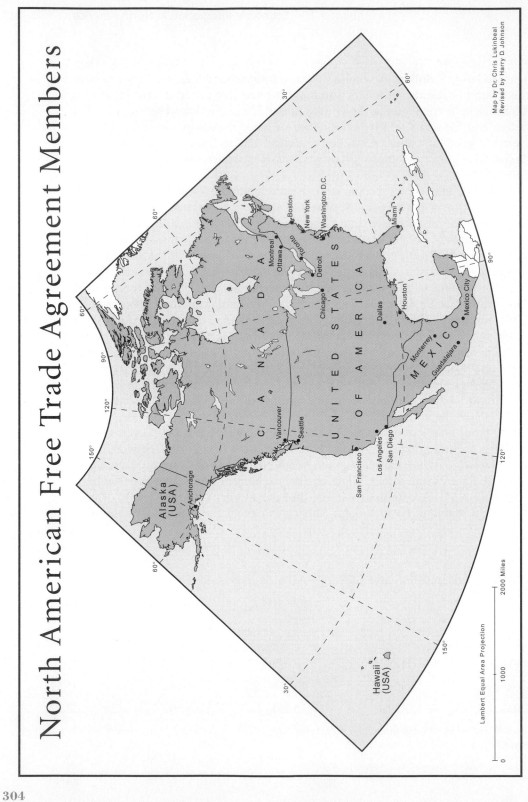

Map by Dr. Chris Lukinbeal
Revised by Harry D. Johnson

Lambert Equal Area Projection

0   1000   2000 Miles

TABLE 13.2	Merchandise Trade within the NAFTA Region, 2007 (Millions of US$)			
	Exports by:			
Imports by:	Canada	Mexico	United States	World
Canada	—	6,491	248,437	370,450
Mexico	4,627	—	136,541	225,850
United States	332,065	223,426	—	1,895,690
World	420,853	271,874	1,163,000	—

A large share of total trade by NAFTA countries is with each other, particularly for Canada and Mexico.

Sources: International Monetary Fund, *Direction of Trade Statistics*.

Latin America, the gap between its per capita income and that of the United States adds a layer of political and social tension to NAFTA. Issues such as immigration and environmental and labor standards are more contentious than in other trade blocs.

Table 13.2 shows the importance of trade between each pair of countries. Note that the trade between each pair of countries is an important share of each nation's overall trade, with the exception of Canada-Mexico. Both Canada's and Mexico's trade with the United States is far greater than their trade with any other country. In 2007 Canada was the United States' number one trading partner, and Mexico was number three, behind China.

Mexico and Canada depend on trade more than the United States does. Recall that one way to measure how much a country depends on trade is to calculate its openness ratio ((Exports + Imports) / GDP). Using this measure, 2007 trade was equal to nearly 71.2 percent of Canada's GDP, 64.5 percent of Mexico's GDP, and 27.3 percent of the United States' GDP. These numbers reflect the general proposition that the smaller a nation, the more it must trade in order to achieve a given level of prosperity.

The Canada-U.S. Trade Relationship

The United States and Canada trade more than any pair of countries in the world. In 2007 total trade between the two was valued at $676 billion. Figure 13.1 illustrates the nearly constant upward trend in bilateral trade. On average, from 1985 to 2008 Canada-U.S. trade grew at 7 percent per year and doubles approximately every decade.

Given the history of close ties and the importance of trade, it is not surprising that the United States and Canada would join together to form a free-trade area and that they would do so before NAFTA was created. The Canadian-U.S. Trade Agreement, or CUSTA, was signed in 1988 and implemented on January 1, 1989, exactly five years before NAFTA. CUSTA, however, was not the first important

FIGURE 13.1   Canada-United States Total Trade, 1985–2008

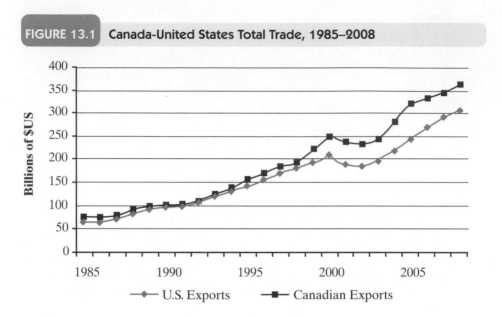

Canadian-U.S. trade in goods and services has grown almost 7 percent per year since 1985. At that rate, it doubles every ten years.

Source: U.S. Bureau of Economic Analysis.

trade agreement between Canada and the United States. In 1965, twenty-four years before the implementation of CUSTA, Canada and the United States signed an agreement on trade and investment in automotive products, the single largest component of U.S.-Canadian trade.

The Auto Pact of 1965

Although the **Auto Pact** agreement was limited to trade in automotive products, it is a very successful example of gains from trade. By removing barriers to trade, the pact permitted the big three Detroit automakers (General Motors, Ford, and Chrysler) to produce for a single, combined market. Prior to the agreement, Canadian content laws required that cars sold in Canada had to be mostly produced there as well. The relatively small market size caused factories in Canada to lose some of the economies of scale of their American counterparts, and not surprisingly, Canada's productivity in automotive products was around 30 percent below the U.S. level.

With the coming of free trade in cars and car parts, Detroit automakers (who were also Canadian automakers) were able to reorganize production in Canada and the United States, and both locations began to produce for both markets. The impact on trade was stunning. Between 1963 and 1969, when firms began to anticipate an opening of Canada-U.S. auto trade, Canadian exports to the United States grew 169 percent, while U.S. exports to Canada grew 114 percent. Most of the trade growth was in automotive products, and even today they remain the single largest component of trade between the United States and Canada.

The Canadian-U.S. Trade Agreement (CUSTA) of 1989

From the Canadian viewpoint, the 1980s brought to the foreground two trends that had to be addressed. First, the United States began to be a less reliable trade partner. The problem was the United States' expanded use of countervailing and antidumping duties, and "voluntary" export restrictions (VERs). In addition, U.S. rhetoric indicated a greater willingness to use these measures as a means of gaining political support from declining U.S. industries. Although VERs and antidumping and countervailing duties did not directly affect an important share of U.S.-Canadian trade, the specter of the United States turning increasingly protectionist was a problem for Canada. Its dependence on international trade meant that protectionism in the United States was a direct threat to its standard of living.

The second problem facing Canada in the 1980s was the need to restructure many of its firms and industries in order to keep them competitive in a more global environment. Many observers inside Canada felt that Asian manufacturing was beginning to exert strong competitive pressures on Canadian firms and without significant modernization and rebuilding, Canadian firms were likely to lose markets at home and abroad.

Creating a free-trade agreement with the United States was one solution to the problem of growing U.S. protectionism and increasing Asian competitiveness in manufacturing industries. This solution locked the United States into an international agreement requiring it to keep its market open and, at the same time, put pressure on Canadian manufacturers to make the necessary changes.

The impacts of CUSTA were more or less as expected. Between 1989 and 1994, Canadian exports to the United States grew 55 percent ($47 billion increase), while U.S. exports to Canada grew 46.6 percent ($36.5 billion increase). In percentage terms this growth is not quite as rapid as the period before and after the implementation of the Auto Pact, but given that trade was already at a high level in 1987, a 50 percent increase represents an enormous volume of trade.

The debate over U.S.-Canadian free trade was low key and dispassionate in the United States. In Canada, however, a heated public discussion erupted when it was announced that the United States and Canada were negotiating an agreement. The opponents of the trade agreement feared that (1) Canada might not be able to compete with U.S. firms, which had the advantages of economies of scale; (2) expanded trade might force Canada to jettison many of its social programs; and (3) Canadian culture might come to be dominated by the U.S. news, information, arts, and entertainment industries.

The issue of Canadian competitiveness was largely one about the need to gain economies of scale and to increase productivity through organizational or technological changes within firms. For the most part, the real issue for a high-income, industrialized country such as Canada is the length of time over which the changes can be expected to occur, and not whether firms are capable of competing.

The Canadian opponents of CUSTA also argued that it would erode Canada's social programs. For many citizens, Canada's more extensive social programs, such as universal health care and income maintenance, are part of a national identity that make Canada unlike the United States. The opponents of CUSTA argued that the intensification of competition with the United States would undermine these social programs. They reasoned that social programs would be cut in order to reduce business taxes and make Canadian firms more competitive. Given that taxes are but one component of business costs, and that in some cases there are offsetting reductions in cost elsewhere, it was not at all certain what the final impact of free trade would be on Canadian social programs. In the case of health care, for example, it makes more sense to argue that the United States' system is a competitive disadvantage, since it raises the cost of hiring workers when they must be provided with health care benefits by their employer. In Canada, by contrast, health care coverage is universal and is paid for out of general government revenues and individual taxes.

The final and most contentious issue from the Canadian point of view was the possibility of U.S. cultural domination. A very wide spectrum of opinion, including both opponents and proponents of expanded free trade, argue that the combination of Canada's smaller population and its proximity to the United States will destroy its national identity if it allows completely free trade in the cultural industries. These industries include music in all of its venues, as well as radio, television, newspapers, book publishing, magazines, drama, cinema, and painting. Under the rules of CUSTA, Canada is allowed to protect its national identity by imposing quantitative restrictions on imports of "cultural products." In most cases the rules allow Canada to impose domestic content requirements on television, radio, and theater. The content requirements make it illegal for a radio or TV station to program content originating in the United States 24 hours a day. Cable TV companies give preferences to Canadian-based TV networks, and there are national rules that favor Canadian theater companies, artists, and writers.

Recent Mexican Economic History

Canada's interests in CUSTA were relatively straightforward, but Mexico's interests in signing NAFTA were more complex. Like Canada, Mexico wanted to guarantee its access to the U.S. market; unlike Canada, however, Mexico needed to alter its economic strategy fundamentally. The decision to seek closer economic ties to the United States was one of many major policy changes that Mexico made between the late 1980s and early 1990s. By the time the agreement was ratified in 1993, Mexico had completely abandoned the economic policies it had followed since the end of World War II.

The Slowdown in Economic Growth

Mexico's shift from a closed and inward economic orientation to an open and outward set of policies began in the mid-1980s after a long period of crisis caused by international trends and a series of domestic policy mistakes. The most important

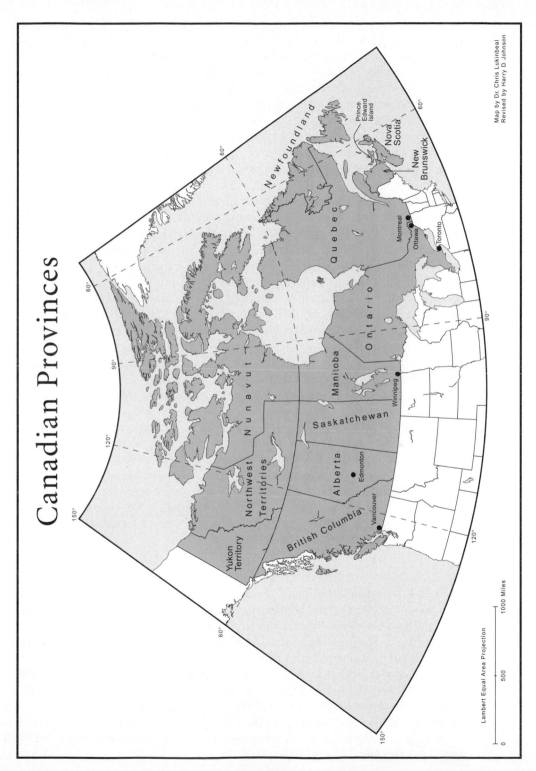

Canadian Provinces

Newfoundland

Prince
Edward
Island

Nova
Scotia

New
Brunswick

Quebec

Montreal

Ottawa

Toronto

Ontario

Manitoba

Winnipeg

Saskatchewan

Nunavut

Alberta

Edmonton

Northwest
Territories

British Columbia

Vancouver

Yukon
Territory

150°

120°

90°

60°

60°

60°

90°

120°

150°

60°

Map by Dr. Chris Lukinbeal
Revised by Harry D. Johnson

Lambert Equal Area Projection

0   500   1000 Miles

international trend was the slowdown in world economic growth that began in the early 1970s, more than a decade before the shift in policies. Economists disagree about the causes of the growth slowdown, but it affected all of Latin America, Africa, Europe, North America, and the Soviet Union. A few areas in Asia escaped the trend, but most countries around the world found that it was impossible to maintain the same rates of growth they had achieved in the 1950s and 1960s.

In the 1970s national governments across Latin America, including Mexico, began to borrow heavily in order to obtain the financial resources needed to keep their economies expanding. Capital markets were relatively open to international lending, and banks in New York, London, and other financial centers were driven to make large loans by the huge deposits they had received from oil producing countries. Mexico and a number of other countries moved away from the cautious fiscal and monetary policies they had followed in the 1950s and 1960s, and accepted large budget deficits and expansionary monetary policies as the price of economic growth in a slowing world economy.

Budget deficits and expansionary monetary policies seemed to work at first, but they came at a high cost. Recall from earlier chapters that monetary expansion can lead to higher and accelerating rates of inflation that, in turn, cause a real appreciation of a currency. The demand stimulus from deficit spending plus the real appreciation of the Mexican peso resulted in growing current account deficits. This pattern was not confined to Mexico, nor to Latin America, but was repeated in many parts of the world.

The first crisis hit Mexico in 1976, and was followed by an IMF bailout and cuts in government spending. The restraints were temporary, however; in 1978, Mexico's large oil reserves began to reach the world market. According to international lenders, this made the country a good credit risk as Mexico's reserves were large and it was widely believed that the price of oil would continue to rise. Unfortunately for the lenders and for Mexico, oil prices began to fall in 1981. By 1982 the country was no longer able to pay interest or repay principal on its foreign loans. In relatively rapid succession, a number of countries were also exposed as lacking sufficient international reserves to service their debt. This began the **debt crisis** of the 1980s.

The Lost Decade of the 1980s

Once it was revealed that many developing country borrowers were no longer able to service their debts, international lending stopped. In Mexico the crisis brought on a series of devaluations in the peso that fueled inflation by making imported goods more expensive. The devaluations resulted in some expenditure switching, as consumers shifted from imported goods to domestic goods; however, it was not sufficient to counteract the large expenditure reduction caused by the cuts to government spending. Furthermore, many private firms had become dependent on international borrowing, and the sudden cessation in foreign loans led to a steep decline in private spending by businesses. The culmination of these forces was a deep economic depression many refer to as the "**Lost Decade.**"

Ordinarily, the solution for a country in this situation would be to export its way out. Ideally, by exporting goods and services that other countries want to buy, it could accumulate dollars that could be used to pay debts and to revive the economy. This is essentially how the East Asian economies escaped from their financial crises of 1997–98. In Mexico's case, however, the ability to export was undermined by four decades of **import substitution industrialization (ISI)** policies.

ISI policies target the development of manufacturing through various kinds of support for the production of goods that substitute for imports. ISI was the dominant development strategy in Latin America and most of the developing world from approximately the end of World War II until the middle of the 1980s. This will be discussed in more detail in Chapter 15. ISI theorists believed that industrial development could be accomplished through a series of stages beginning with a focus on simple consumer goods (foodstuffs, beverages, furniture, apparel). In the second stage, ISI policies prescribed support for more complex consumer goods and intermediate industrial goods (appliances, autos, pumps, generators), and finally, in the last stage, support for the development of complex industrial goods production (chemicals, electronics, machine tools). By the time a country reached the last stage, it would be among the industrial economies of the world.

Various tools were used to support ISI policies, including subsidies and high levels of protection against competition from imports. By raising the private benefits of investment in the production of goods intended for the domestic market, Mexico and other ISI countries pulled land, labor, and capital into those favored industries, but unintentionally made exports relatively less profitable, since they were not as favored with subsidies, tax breaks, and protection from imports. Several decades of protection from foreign competition meant that Mexico's manufacturing sector was not very competitive in the early 1980s, precisely the time it needed exports in order to earn dollars. Ironically, ISI policies that had tried to strengthen industrial development and increase self-sufficiency caused the opposite to occur.

Economic Policy Reforms in the Mexican Economy

The debt crisis of the 1980s led to a steep fall in real incomes and wages. Between 1983 and 1988, real wages fell by 40 to 50 percent, and real per capita GDP fell by 15 percent between 1982 and 1986. As a result, health care, education, and income support programs were all hit hard.

There were three main lessons that Mexico's policymakers learned from the crisis. First, management of the macroeconomy had to improve. Lack of concern for budget and trade deficits led to severe crises in 1976 and 1982, and in the future, economic policymakers could not ignore macroeconomic imbalances. In effect this meant that government could no longer use public expenditures as the main support for economic growth. Second, it was seen that markets needed to play a larger role in resource allocation decisions, in part to increase the competitiveness of Mexican firms and to attract the capital Mexico needed for investment and growth. Third, ISI policies were no longer viewed as the best policy for industrial development, and more traditional ideas of comparative advantage began to take center stage. This point was driven home by other trends in the world economy, including a number of multicountry academic studies that were critical of ISI, and the tremendous success of several export-oriented Asian economies that abandoned ISI in the late 1960s and early 1970s. (See the Case Study of the Republic of Korea in Chapter 3.)

President Salinas entered office in December 1988. He faced an economy that was weakened by several years of negative or subpar growth, a private sector that was unwilling to risk new investments, and large foreign debts that took all or nearly all of the country's export earnings. Salinas's primary goal was to raise capital for investment, but in order to do that he needed to change the expectations of potential investors, both domestic and international. This required a stronger market orientation so that investors would know that their success was dependent on market forces and not government rules that seemed to change arbitrarily.

Salinas continued many of the reforms that began under his predecessor, de la Madrid (1982–1988), including progress on bringing the federal budget under control. He also increased the rate of privatization of businesses that began under de la Madrid, and Mexico saw a decline in state-owned firms from 1,155 in 1982 to 217 by 1992. In May 1990 Salinas announced that Mexico would reprivatize its banking sector, and early in his presidency he began to tackle the debt crisis.

In 1989 when the United States announced the start of the **Brady Plan** for international debt relief, Salinas quickly put Mexico first in line to qualify for the partial debt forgiveness proposed under the terms of the plan. Named after U.S. Secretary of Treasury Nicholas Brady, the plan offered modest amounts of debt relief in return for domestic policy reforms, most of which Mexico had accomplished by 1989 (see Chapter 15 for a more detailed discussion of the Brady Plan). More important than the small amount of debt relief, the plan significantly altered international perceptions about Mexico and its economic stability and future.

On the trade front, Salinas continued to reduce tariffs and eliminate import licensing requirements. These reforms, along with privatization, curbs on inflation, and a fiscally prudent budget, were not necessarily permanent. Until the electoral reforms of the 1990s, Mexican presidents concentrated a great deal of power in their office, and all of the reforms could be overturned by a future president. In order to confront this problem, in 1989 Salinas took the very bold and unexpected step of proposing a free-trade agreement with the United States. He had two central goals he wanted to achieve. First, Salinas wanted to tie up the reforms in an international treaty, making a return to inward-oriented and protectionist policies all but impossible. Second, he wanted to add to the low level of domestic savings by attracting foreign capital for development of the Mexican economy.

Closer economic ties with the United States seemed to offer Mexico the guarantees that international investors wanted. Not only would it make future policy reversals more difficult, it offered full access to the wealthy American market for anyone that produced their goods in Mexico. The proposal seemed to accomplish its goals; capital began to pour into Mexico from both foreign investors and from Mexican nationals who had sent their savings out of the country during the turmoil of the 1980s. Between 1990 and 1993, Mexico attracted over $90 billion in outside capital, or about one in every five dollars that went to developing countries from private sources.

CASE STUDY

Ejidos, Agriculture, and NAFTA in Mexico

The majority of Mexico's farmers work on a type of collective farm called *ejidos*. Ejido members can farm their individual pieces of land as independent farmers, planting whatever crops they choose, and their children can inherit the land. However, they cannot sell the land and they cannot rent it out to someone else. In theory, they either farm it or lose it. The first ejidos were created about a decade after the Mexican Revolution (1910–1917) and continued to be formed until the constitutional reforms of 1992. Mexico's constitution put limits on the amount of land one person could own and gave landless agricultural laborers the right to petition the government for the excess land. The 1992 reforms stopped the creation of new ejidos and created a process for breaking up existing ones by turning them into private landholdings. The reforms do not require change, and most ejidos continue to operate the same as they did before the reforms, although some have been privatized and the land has been sold. At the same time that the government opened an avenue for buying and selling ejido lands, it cut many of the subsidies it had given to small farmers. In the long run, changes in the level of subsidies for small farmers have been more important than the new markets for ejido lands—and not always for the best.

According to the Mexican Census of Agriculture, in 2007 there were 31,518 ejidos, with 4,210,899 members (including people living on the communal lands of indigenous communities). This is approximately 72–73 percent of the labor force in agriculture in Mexico. On average, ejido farmers tend to own less valuable lands, have smaller individual plots of land than more commercially oriented farms, and produce a disproportionately small share of the nation's agricultural output. This is not to say that all ejido farmers are poor, but many of them lack access to markets, to capital, and to technical knowledge that would allow the members to earn a decent living.

In 1992, Mexico rewrote the section of its constitution that allowed for the creation of ejidos. The administration of Mexico's president, Carlos Salinas, argued that ejidos created disincentives for investment in agriculture, which kept productivity low and contributed to rural poverty. Some economists shared this view but others were not so certain. The argument of the reformers was that the lack of complete ownership rights and the small plot sizes on ejidos inhibited the use of machinery and other productivity enhancing investments. Regardless of the analytical correctness or incorrectness of the causes of low productivity on ejidos, the vast majority of Mexico's poor people lived in rural areas and worked in agriculture, often as members of an ejido. In 1992, about 25 percent of the labor force was in agriculture, but it produced only 9 percent of GDP. One explicit purpose of the change in subsidies for small farmers and in ownership rights of ejido members was to reduce the size of the agricultural labor force by creating incentives to combine land holdings and to apply modern production technologies. In 1992, the undersecretary of agriculture stated that the goal was to reduce the share of labor in agriculture from 25 percent of the labor force to 15 percent.

Seventeen years later, in 2009, 12.7 percent of the labor force is in agriculture (compared to less than 2 percent in the United States and Canada) and the figure is shrinking. The worst forms of poverty and its highest levels continue to be concentrated in rural areas, and the agricultural sector is generally described as in crisis. NAFTA opponents frequently blame the trade agreement, but Mexican agricultural policy plays a far larger role. Corn shows why. Corn is a dietary staple for many Mexicans and the main crop on many small farms. Under NAFTA, Mexico's import duties on corn were scheduled to be phased out over a fifteen-year period but Mexico unilaterally cut tariffs ahead of schedule and increased imports from the United States, in part to lower the price of corn for animal feed, increase the size of the country's livestock herds, and expand the amount of animal protein in the diet of the average Mexican citizen. Mexico's larger and more commercial farmers expanded their corn production along with the growth in imports, and the total amount produced nationally increased. Nevertheless, small-scale, isolated, and impoverished farmers were badly hurt by this strategy since it lowered corn prices at the same point in time that the government cut subsidies to small farmers.

NAFTA allows each country to subsidize its farms as little or as much as it chooses. Mexico provided approximately US $6 billion in farm supports (subsidies) in 2007, but much of this went to farmers who were relatively better off. This level of subsidies is equal to 14 percent of the gross receipts of farmers. In the United States, farm subsidies are 10 percent of farm receipts (see Table 7.3), according to the *Agricultural Outlook* of the Organisation for Economic Co-operation and Development (OECD). Farm support policies in Mexico were not designed to keep poor farmers on their land; rather the government's original policy was to offer them very little or no farm-related assistance in order to encourage them to leave farming altogether. In that sense, the policy worked. However, the decision to downsize the agricultural sector was independent of the decision to sign a trade agreement with the United States and Canada and did not take into account the plight of farmers who have few options other than a small plot of corn.

The North American Free Trade Agreement (NAFTA)

Trade flows between the United States and its NAFTA partners increased significantly in the 1990s. Given that trade flows were growing before the implementation of NAFTA, and that they have continued to grow afterward, it is impossible to say how much of the increase in trade is directly due to the trade agreement. Some of the increase before NAFTA's implementation may have been in anticipation of freer trade, while much of the growth since then may have occurred without the agreement. Given that tariffs on about half of the goods traded between the United States and Mexico were eliminated immediately in 1994, it makes sense to think that NAFTA caused at least some of the growth in trade. U.S.-Canadian trade also expanded, even though there was little change in trade barriers. In part, the growth in trade among NAFTA partners was a reflection of the overall growth of the three economies. NAFTA, however, facilitated the trade growth.

The first important feature of NAFTA is that most forms of trade barriers came down. Since the United States and Canada were relatively open economies with few trade barriers before NAFTA, most of the change came on the Mexican side. For example, between 1993 and 1996, average U.S. tariffs on Mexican goods fell from 2.07 to 0.65 percent. By contrast, Mexican tariffs on U.S. goods fell from 10 to 2.9 percent. These reductions in tariffs under NAFTA were a continuation of the reduction in trade barriers that began in the mid-1980s. Between 1982 and 1992, the percentage of Mexico's imports that required import licenses from the government declined from 100 to 11 percent and tariffs fell from an average level of 27 to 13.1 percent. By 1994, Mexico's economy was substantially open to the world.

The phase-out period for the remaining tariffs and investment restrictions varied from sector to sector. In cases where there was expected to be significant new competition, industries were given a longer grace period to prepare themselves. Although each country wants the gains from trade, it also wants to avoid a sudden disruption of its economy.

A second feature of NAFTA is that it specifies North American content requirements for goods that are subject to free trade. That is, in order to qualify for free trade or the reduced tariff provisions of the agreement, a specified percentage (usually 50 percent) of the value of the good must be made in North America. The purpose of local content requirements is to prevent non-NAFTA countries from using low tariffs in one NAFTA country to gain access to all three. Most trade economists dislike these provisions because they increase the likelihood of trade diversion. Production of inputs in lower-cost, nonmember countries could be reduced if firms move their operations to NAFTA countries in order to meet the content requirements. Trade diversion occurred in the apparel industry, for example. Firms moved from the Caribbean to Mexico even though Mexico was not the lowest-cost producer. Mexico's exports to the United States paid zero tariffs, so goods produced there could sell for less than goods produced in lower-cost countries facing high tariffs when entering the United States. Nevertheless, content requirements were politically necessary in order to pass the agreement in Canada and the United States.

A third feature of the agreement is that it establishes a system of dispute resolution. When a disagreement arises, any country may request an investigation. This will set in motion a bi-national panel that investigates the issue and makes a report.

Both countries are bound by the results of their analysis. It is hoped that this will lead to greater consultation and cooperation between countries and prevent trade disputes from escalating.

The NAFTA Debate in the United States

The proposal for a trade agreement with Mexico reignited the debate over free trade in the United States. In particular, organized labor and environmental groups opposed the agreement, along with a handful of specific industrial and agricultural interests that feared stiffer competition with Mexico. Non-economic opposition to NAFTA came from a number of politicians and citizens who expressed doubts about signing a trade agreement with a country that lacked strong democratic institutions.

Labor Issues

Blue-collar industrial labor unions were the most vocal opponents of NAFTA. Their reasons parallel the discussion of trade, jobs, and labor standards in Chapters 7 and 8. Recall that the labor argument rejects free trade because of the fear that competition with low-wage countries will drive down wages at home, cause jobs to migrate overseas, and create a race to the bottom in labor standards. The relevant ideas have been discussed in the earlier chapters, but it is worth repeating that the core mistake of this view is the failure to take into account the productivity differences between U.S. and foreign workers. Labor in Mexico, for example, earns less for three reasons: (1) average Mexican education and skill levels are lower than in the United States; (2) the average Mexican worker has less capital at work; and (3) the public infrastructure of roads, ports, water systems, communication systems, and power and waste disposal systems is less reliable and less developed than in the United States. The net outcome of these three fundamental differences in human and physical capital is that productivity levels are lower in Mexico, and, as a consequence, wages are lower.

Recall, however, that the Stolper-Samuelson theorem predicts that U.S. workers with skills that are in abundance in Mexico may be hurt by the agreement. Given that Mexico is relatively well endowed with low-skilled labor and that the United States is relatively well endowed with skilled labor, trade between the United States and Mexico is likely to exert downward pressure on the wages of low-skilled U.S. labor. Garment workers, low-skilled and semiskilled autoworkers, and low-skilled assembly line workers may find their wages held down or their jobs moved out of the country. As always, the key question is how big an effect there will be, particularly in comparison to the macroeconomic policies of the Federal Reserve, which, in the short run, exert far more influence over wages and jobs than trade. In addition, since Mexico's GDP is only about 5 percent as large as that of the United States, its ability to absorb capital investment is limited.

During the NAFTA debate, labor unions formed the core of a pressure group that pushed the Clinton administration to seek a separate agreement on labor issues. The agreement came to be known as the side agreement on labor, or, more formally, the **North American Agreement on Labor Cooperation**. It was one of two such agreements, the other dealing with environmental issues. The labor side agreement requires both the United States and Mexico to enforce their own labor laws, especially laws pertaining to child labor, minimum wages, and workplace safety. Countries are required to permit investigators to examine alleged infringements of these protections, and fines may be levied. The agreement does not permit investigations into the rights of workers to organize, nor does it cover this aspect of labor law. Because it does not force the release of information, investigators often have a hard time obtaining evidence. Some critics of trade agreement point to this as evidence that the labor side agreement is not meant to investigate conditions but is mainly for show. Proponents of the side agreement counter that it is often instrumental in shining a light on harmful practices and that it has facilitated reforms.

Environmental Issues

The second major side agreement is called the **North American Agreement on Environmental Cooperation**. This agreement was motivated by two main concerns. One was the desire to prevent U.S. and Canadian firms from relocating to Mexico where they might take advantage of less stringent environmental enforcement. The second concern was the growth of environmental pollution along the U.S.-Mexico border. Mexico's environmental laws are quite good in general, but enforcement has often been lacking, due to a lack of resources, a lack of administrative capacity, or corruption. The high visibility of this issue in North America required Mexico to get tougher in its enforcement, and in this way NAFTA has helped generate some desirable environmental outcomes.

Recall from the discussion in Chapter 8 about trade and the environment the distinction between transboundary and non-transboundary environmental problems. In the context of NAFTA, transboundary pollution along the U.S.-Mexico border is an issue of considerable importance to both countries. Since the 1980s, rapid population growth on both sides of the border has created a number of environmental challenges that are compounded by the rapid growth of manufacturing in northern Mexico. A significant share of the *maquiladora* manufacturing is located in cities on the border, as close as possible to the U.S. market and the U.S. transportation network. In many cases, U.S. and Mexican cities share watersheds, air basins, and ecological habitats, making whatever happens on one side of the border of concern to the other side.

The rapid influx of people to the border region, coming from elsewhere in the United States to take advantage of the warm climate and sunny weather, and coming from the interior of Mexico to find jobs and a decent income, has put a heavy burden on roads, sewers, water systems, and other public infrastructure. Unfortunately, a large increase in population and manufacturing growth on the Mexican side of the border occurred in the 1980s, during the debt crisis in Mexico when there were few resources for urban development. Consequently, sewage and water capacity have been strained beyond capacity and there is a backlog of projects needing attention and resources.

As noted in Chapter 8, it is unrealistic to expect environmental standards, clean-up preferences, or resource commitments to be identical in countries with different income levels. Nevertheless, NAFTA provides an excellent opportunity to address the issue of transboundary environmental problems. Specifically, the side agreement on the environment creates a mechanism for investigating environmental disputes, such as cases where it is alleged that Mexico (or the United States or Canada) is gaining competitive advantages by not enforcing environmental laws. Investigation of these cases is followed by a resolution of the dispute through binding arbitration if both sides cannot agree.

The side agreement also established the **North American Development Bank (NADBank)** to help finance border cleanup costs. NADBank has several hundred million dollars of initial funds provided by the United States and Mexico. Estimates of border cleanup costs vary widely, from $2 billion to $8 billion. In addition to the NADBank, the environmental side agreement created the Border Environmental Cooperation Commission (BECC) to analyze and certify the technical and scientific components of border cleanup proposals for NADBank funding. The NADBank, the BECC, and other bi-national, cooperative, border environmental programs (Border XXI, for example), are targeted at issues such as increasing the availability of clean drinking water, wastewater treatment, air quality monitoring and improvement, solid and hazardous waste disposal, and other issues of mutual concern.

Like the labor side agreement, the environmental side agreement has a mixed record. This fact, coupled with the fact that the NADBank has been slow in distributing funds for projects, has led many to complain that the positive institutional features of the side agreements are little more than window dressing and that they do not confront the real problems of trade between industrial United States and developing Mexico.

Immigration

Immigration is the most contentious issue in U.S.-Mexico relations. No one knows precisely how many Mexican citizens reside in the United States, but the U.S. Census Bureau's 2005–2007 American Community Survey counted over 37 million foreign-born residents of the United States, of which 30.7 percent (11,430,000) were born in Mexico. The Census Bureau does not attempt to determine citizenship status, so its count does not distinguish between legal and undocumented immigrants. The Pew Hispanic Center is a private research institute that uses government data sources to estimate the number of undocumented. Their estimates for 2008 are that there were approximately 11.9 million undocumented immigrants in the United States, and 59 percent (about 7 million) were of Mexican origin. Most are concentrated in the border states of California, Texas, Arizona, and New Mexico, but they are increasingly dispersed across the country.

Chapter 4 discussed the basic economic factors behind migration, including **demand-pull**, **supply-push**, and **social networks**. All of these factors are relevant to U.S.-Mexico migration. For example, once in the United States, migrants are easily able to find jobs in agriculture, construction, restaurants and hotels, building and landscape maintenance, meat packing, and other sectors, while penalties for hiring undocumented workers are infrequently enforced. These jobs are very attractive to ambitious Mexicans who often face economic uncertainties in their home communities. For example, the average manufacturing wage in the U.S. border state Arizona was $48,000 per year in 2001; across the border in the Mexican border state of Sonora, manufacturing production workers earned the annual equivalent of $5,220 at market exchange rates, about one-ninth the U.S. level.

The United States is conflicted by the issue of illegal immigration from Mexico. On the one hand, migrants who enter without authorization are breaking the law and that bothers many Americans. On the other hand, they often settle in the United States, raise families, and contribute to community life. Majority opinion does not support the idea of mass deportations and it is rare that the federal government attempts to enforce laws against hiring undocumented immigrants; when they do, there is an outcry from the businesses and communities that have come to depend on immigrant labor. Under these circumstances, the politically expedient policy is to try to close the border, except at legal points of entry and exit. In effect this is what the United States has done by increasing the level of vigilance along the border and by building fences and other barriers. Most research shows that this strategy is not effective, however, and that the annual number of unauthorized immigrants has increased since the implementation of stricter border enforcement policies.

There are three reasons why increased border enforcement has not worked. First, the border is 2,000 miles long, spans two major North American deserts and several mountain ranges, and is impossible to patrol effectively. Second, the economic incentive to enter the United States is high. Wages are higher, jobs are plentiful in normal years, and the probability of being caught and deported is low once a migrant finds work in the United States. Third, nearly one-half of all illegal immigrants in the United States enter legally, but overstay the duration of their visas. These individuals come through legal ports of entry and are not hindered by fences.

For political reasons, many proponents of NAFTA chose to emphasize the claim that it would reduce immigration. President Salinas, for example, picked up this theme. When addressing U.S. audiences, he often rallied support by stating, "Mexico wants to export goods, not people." His point was that NAFTA would give Mexico greater access to the U.S. market and would create faster growth in Mexico. As a result, the nation would experience a greater capacity to absorb labor into the national economy. Most simulations of the effects of NAFTA found a similar effect. The faster the Mexican economy grows, the weaker the supply-push factors will be. Nevertheless, in the short- and medium-run, the immigration-increasing supply-push factors are probably stronger than the long-run immigration-reducing supply-push factors. That is, in the short-run, agricultural reorganization and market opening probably have a bigger impact in the determination of the number of Mexican migrants than does overall economic growth and the spread of jobs and opportunities across Mexico. The net effect is that NAFTA probably causes less migration from Mexico to the United States than if there was no agreement; however, changes in the Mexican economy cause migration to increase.

Migration remains a topic of serious debate both inside the United States and between the United States and Mexico. Before September 11, 2001, it appeared that the two countries might reach an accord that would permit Mexican nationals to work in the United States for a limited period each year as "guest workers," but the terrorist attack on the United States halted the political momentum toward agreement. Pressures for an agreement, however, will not go away completely for two essential reasons. First, economic changes in Mexico generally guarantee that a large share of its labor force will continue to be mobile. Older industries are disappearing and new ones are developing, but during the lifespan of an average worker, there are a limited number of opportunities for significant economic advancement. Most Mexican workers can increase their real wages by at least five or six times if they migrate to the United States. This is a powerful driver, particularly when future economic conditions in Mexico are uncertain. Second, while some Americans are bothered by the social and cultural changes that occur with increased migration, many powerful economic interests in the United States want access to Mexican labor. Consequently, Mexico continues to push for an agreement to open the border for at least a proportion of its labor force, and many U.S. interests continue to propose guest-worker and temporary visa programs.

CASE STUDY

Manufacturing in the United States

In what year did the United States produce its highest output of manufactured goods? When asked to a large group, the guesses range from the 1960s to the 1990s. The correct answer is usually "last year." Figure 13.2 illustrates this by plotting on the right scale the real value added in manufacturing, 1960–2008. Given that a recession began in 2008, there was a slight downturn since manufacturing is sensitive to the business cycle. As the graph shows, however, there is a long-run upward trend in manufacturing output that is interrupted briefly by the occasional recession.

The left scale shows manufacturing employment. Employment peaked in 1979 at 19,426,000, and began a long-run decline after that. In 1980 the United States entered a mild recession, and then a more severe one in 1981–1982. Manufacturing employment recovered some of its losses in 1984, but continued its trend downward.

Within the story of the growth of manufacturing output, there are a couple of other stories not directly shown in the graph. First, there is the story of manufacturing relocation within the United States. Traditional industrial states in the north central part of the United States, such as Ohio and Michigan, have seen many jobs leave for other parts of the country. Some jobs have gone overseas, but quite a few have also gone to southern states such as South Carolina, Tennessee, and Texas. When coupled with the overall

FIGURE 13.2   **Real Value Added and Employment in Manufacturing, 1960–2008**

Since the late-1970s, manufacturing employment has declined, while manufacturing output has constantly risen except during recessions.

Source: U.S. Bureau of Economic Analysis; U.S. Bureau of Labor Statistics.

decline in the total number of jobs, the plight of older manufacturing states has been grim. This has also contributed to the mistaken perception that the United States no longer has a vibrant manufacturing sector, but the story of Figure 13.2 is that the United States continues to produce a large and growing quantity of manufactured goods.

The second story is the rapid increase in productivity in the manufacturing sector. Fewer workers but more output means each worker is producing more, and output per hour worked in manufacturing has increased at a very rapid rate. This has occurred in part through the application of new technologies and new processes, and while productivity growth speeds up and slows down, it is usually much more rapid in manufacturing than in services or agriculture. Hence, even if we consume the same quantity of manufactured goods, we would expect a smaller share of the labor force to produce them for us.

Jobs, Politics, and the Future

The most common issue in the internal U.S. debate over NAFTA was its effects on U.S. jobs. Many trade economists were discouraged by this because the key effect of any trade agreement is the increased productive efficiency that comes with a reallocation of resources, not job gains or losses. Placing the focus of the debate on workers who might be dislocated was politically inevitable, but it ignored the real economic advantages of expanded trade.

Most people also lost sight of the fact that the Mexican economy is not very large when compared to the United States. In 2007, total GDP, measured in dollars at market exchange rates, was equal to about 8 percent of U.S. GDP, which made it slightly smaller than the state of New York and quite a bit smaller than Texas or California. In 1994, when NAFTA was implemented, Mexico was less than 5 percent of the size of the United States in economic terms. Consequently, the direct effects on the United States of expanded trade cannot be dramatic. This point is well illustrated by an examination of the predicted effects of NAFTA on the U.S. economy. Before its implementation, a number of forecasts were made by academic economists and various interest groups. In each category (employment effects, wage effects, impact on overall U.S. current account balance), a majority of forecasts predicted either no effect on the national economy or effects too small to be measured. Note that this does not imply that there are no local effects, particularly along the border or in states that have a relatively large share of their overall trade with Mexico—for example, Texas.

As shown in Figure 13.3, U.S.-Mexico trade has grown significantly for more than a decade. U.S. exports have grown from $31 billion in 1989 to $175 billion in 2008, while Mexican exports expanded from $33 billion to $236 over the same period.

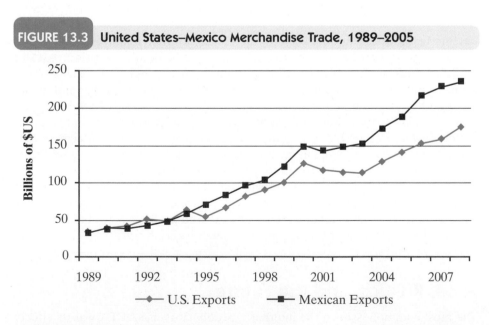

FIGURE 13.3 United States–Mexico Merchandise Trade, 1989–2005

U.S.-Mexican goods and services trade has grown 9 percent a year since the opening of NAFTA negotiations in 1989. At that rate, trade doubles every eight years.

Source: U.S. Bureau of Economic Analysis.

Some aspects of Mexico's recent economic history are a clear illustration of trade and growth driven by economies of scale (see Chapter 5). The inward orientation of Mexican economic policy up until the mid-1980s meant that production for the internal market was favored over exports. Consequently, firms with high fixed costs and high transport costs tried to locate near the internal Mexican market, leading to the rapid growth of Mexico City and its environs. In the 1980s, as policy changes made it more profitable to export, firms began to locate as close as possible to foreign markets, in this case, the United States. The result is the extremely rapid growth of population and manufacturing production in northern Mexican states along the U.S.-Mexico border. In the medium to long run, this rapid northern growth is perhaps the most dramatic effect of the opening of the Mexican market through trade liberalization and NAFTA. The rapidly industrializing northern states of Mexico now have per capita regional incomes (regional GDP) that are three to five times greater than some of the poorest states in Mexico, most of which are located in the south. Such regional disparity within the country is a source of great concern, as the parts of the country that are not well connected to the world economy are falling further behind the more prosperous areas.

Estimating the number of jobs created or destroyed by NAFTA is difficult. It is possible to estimate the number of workers needed in order to produce exports, and the number of jobs that would be created if imports were produced at home, but these values are not the same as job creation and destruction due to a trade agreement. For example, imports may supply a firm with capital or intermediate goods that make it more competitive and enable it to survive and perhaps to export. And exports may supply a firm that moved abroad but previously produced the entire value of its goods at home. Hence, some imports create jobs, while some exports only exist because jobs at home have been destroyed. Given the conceptual difficulties, actual estimates of the number of jobs gained or lost are usually politically motivated. Groups that are pro-NAFTA show job gains, while anti-NAFTA organizations show job losses. In either case, however, neither side of the debate can show large job gains or losses in the United States. Given that the United States creates more than two million net new jobs in an average year, most estimates of job losses or gains due to the trade agreement are well below 5 percent of the measured total change.

The politics of trade make discussion of job impacts necessary even though the ability of an economy to generate jobs is determined by labor market policies and fiscal and monetary policies, not by trade policies. Furthermore, there is widespread agreement among economists that the real test of success or failure for a trade agreement is whether it leads to a more efficient allocation of resources. By this criterion, the growth in trade between all three NAFTA partners is a positive indicator of increasing specialization, economies of scale, and efficiency. It is interesting that this tendency predates NAFTA and has simply continued since its implementation.

It is tempting to downplay the importance of NAFTA, especially in the United States and Canada. From the Canadian perspective, trade with Mexico is growing, but it is still a relatively small share of Canadian trade. Additionally, the 1989 CUSTA locked in most of the gains from trade with the United States. From the United States' perspective, Mexico's relatively small economy, about 8 percent of the U.S. economy, means that it is unlikely that trade can have a major impact on the national economy, even if there are pockets of the United States that feel the effects, both positive and negative. In Mexico, however, NAFTA has solidified the openness of the Mexican economy and acted as an impetus for a broad set of economic reforms in trade, agriculture, industrial policy, and increasingly, the legal system. From a purely economic perspective, the conclusion seems to be that NAFTA is important to Mexico, and relatively unimportant to the United States and Canada. It is a mistake, however, to limit our view in this way.

Mexico is the most populous Spanish-speaking country in the world, and as the country with the second largest GDP in Latin America, it is viewed as a leader throughout the hemisphere. It is at the forefront of economic and political change in Latin America, and has a young population that migrates in large numbers; however, it has also become a destination for increasing numbers of U.S. and Canadian retirees. Along the Mexican border with the United States, an urban population is rapidly growing around clusters of manufacturing industries in electronics, autos, medical devices, and others. Cultural and linguistic integration in the border regions is very advanced, and family and social networks knit together many communities spanning the international boundary. NAFTA has facilitated the creation of new bi-national and tri-national organizations for managing specific issues, such as labor and environmental concerns. It has also indirectly supported the development of numerous civic and business organizations, and helped to widen the channels of communication between the member countries. NAFTA has played a key role in moving all three nations toward greater awareness and understanding of each other's interests and concerns. In the long run, the direction of historical change in key indicators such as population movements, language, investment patterns, civic engagement, and regional planning all point toward deeper and more permanent forms of integration.

The Expansion of NAFTA

In July 2005 the United States ratified the Dominican Republic–Central American Free Trade Agreement (DR-CAFTA), with the Dominican Republic and five Central American countries: Guatemala, Honduras, El Salvador, Nicaragua, and Costa Rica. Canada and Mexico were not part of the agreement, however, Mexico has individual free-trade agreements with each of the countries except the Dominican Republic, and Canada has a free-trade agreement with Costa Rica, but not with the others.

The extension southward is a natural development, particularly since the United States provided expanded access to its markets for Caribbean and Central American countries beginning in the 1980s with various unilateral cuts in trade barriers. As shown in Table 13.3, the nations in DR-CAFTA add over forty-five million people to the North American market, although problems of poverty and inequality are enormous. Other than Costa Rica and the Dominican Republic, most of the countries are relatively poor, and the six nations combined have a regional GDP less than many metropolitan areas in the United States. For example, the Los Angeles metropolitan area (Los Angeles and Long Beach) has a regional personal income that is more than four times the GDP of the six countries listed in Table 13.3.

The countries shown in Table 13.3 are small and not likely to register a strong impact in the United States. Nevertheless, they have been able to capture some of Mexico's apparel trade with the United States and pose a challenge to some producers in Mexico, particularly those that use large amounts of unskilled and semiskilled labor. Given that labor costs are generally higher in Mexico than in Central America, the biggest impact in the NAFTA region will be on Mexico. More importantly, however, the agreement is likely to be felt strongly in Central America, particularly as U.S. agricultural products gain greater access and challenge traditional and small-scale producers of corn (maize) and other basic grains. Other major effects are likely to be felt as U.S. service companies gain greater access to insurance, banking, and telecommunications markets.

The Future of NAFTA: A North American Community?

By comparison to the European Union (see Chapter 14), Canada, Mexico, and the United States are in an early stage of economic integration. A free-trade agreement is in place and capital flows freely as it would in a common market. But restrictions on the movement of labor are very strong and there are no permanent NAFTA organizations comparable to the governing bodies of the European Union. Additionally, almost all policies are made independently by each of the

TABLE 13.3	Population and GDP for the DR-CAFTA Countries, 2007			
Country	Population (Millions)	GDP (US$, Billions)	GDP per Capita (US$)	GDP per Capita (PPP, US$)
Costa Rica	4.5	26.3	5,887	10,842
Dominican Republic	9.7	36.7	3,772	6,706
El Salvador	6.9	20.4	2,973	5,804
Guatemala	13.3	33.9	2,536	4,562
Honduras	7.1	12.2	1,722	3,796
Nicaragua	5.6	5.7	1,022	2,570
Total	47.1	135.1	2,869	5,428

Population in the DR-CAFTA countries is a little more than one-tenth of the NAFTA nations, but aggregate GDP is less than 1 percent of NAFTA.

Source: World Bank, *World Development Indicators*.

three members, including market access rules for nonmembers, environmental standards, telecommunications, transportation, and most business laws.

The timing and speed of further integration is dependent on politics; however, there are a number of next steps that follow systematically from what has already been accomplished. One option is to do nothing, or even to begin the dismantling of the agreement, although it is hard to imagine either case over the long run. Slowly, market forces are knitting together the three national economies, and already the costs of trying to undo the agreement would be very high. Three issues top the agenda of those who would like to see NAFTA evolve into a North American Community:

- A customs union
- Improved trilateral organizations for managing a more integrated community
- A focus on development and closing the economic gap between Mexico and the other members

One of the inefficiencies of free-trade areas is that they require **rules of origin**. Rules of origin define which goods qualify for free trade, and which are imports from outside the region. The problem is that many goods are a combination of North American and non–North American inputs, so it is far from straightforward to determine which goods qualify for free movement within the NAFTA countries. For example, a car may be assembled in Mexico out of parts that are made in Mexico and ten or fifteen other countries, including the United States and Canada. For the assembled car to be classified as Mexican or North American in origin, there has to be a rule about the percent of the value that is created in North America. Given that autos are assembled from tens of thousands of parts, this is a complicated accounting process that ties up significant resources without actually contributing to the production of a single car. Verification of the origin of shipments slows the flow of trade at the borders, and adds significantly to transaction costs.

In a customs union, member countries have the same tariffs toward nonmembers. Consequently, any goods entering the NAFTA region would pay the tariff owed and then move freely within the NAFTA region. This reduces transaction costs, speeds up trade flows, and simplifies accounting. The cost to each country is partly political in that it must give up its ability to set its own tariffs independently of the other members of the customs union. In addition, there may be a revenue loss to a member government if it is required to reduce its tariffs in order to comply with the customs union. In the case of the NAFTA countries, Mexico has the overall highest tariffs toward nonmembers and would likely lose some of its revenue if the three countries formed a customs union.

A second item on the agenda of a North American Community is the creation of additional permanent organizations for managing economic relations. Some fear that this would duplicate the many large bureaucracies of the European Union, while others argue that the lack of organizational structure in NAFTA creates chaos and disorganization. NAFTA began the development of trilateral organizations, but these are limited in scope and do not address many of the issues that have emerged since the agreement was signed. For example, there are potential benefits from organizations that can manage a North American security perimeter, that develop new infrastructure for a more efficient North American transportation system, that address regional disparities, and that begin to propose solutions to the development gap.

Third, a North American Community must develop mechanisms for managing migration in an amicable and less contentious way. Some argue that the migration debate in the United States must be broadened to a discussion of development in Mexico since, in the long run, migration will end when the high level of economic uncertainty facing Mexican families and communities is reduced. This will not happen suddenly, and as long as a Mexican worker can increase his or her income by a factor of five or six simply by crossing the border, migration will continue. However, it is possible to think about migration in terms of development, and to manage the entire process in a more humane way.

CASE STUDY

Doing Business in Canada, Mexico, and the United States

In 1989 Peruvian economist Hernando de Soto published *The Other Path*, a brilliant work that argued against cumbersome, complex, and unnecessary business regulations in developing countries. De Soto made his case with a simple yet powerful experiment: He hired a small team of researchers in Lima, Peru, to work full time at obtaining a business license for a small textile firm. The researchers spent 289 days, or nearly 10 months and paid an amount equal to thirty-two times a monthly minimum wage to obtain the signatures and permits required to register their business officially. Then they duplicated this experiment in a number of other developing countries to show that Peru is not atypical. Ultimately, these barriers constrain the economic growth of national economies by limiting the growth of small business.

De Soto's work found its way onto a larger stage at the World Bank where his ideas were built into an ongoing research project and an online database comparing the ease of doing business in 181 countries. Using a standardized methodology, the Doing Business Web site (http://www.doingbusiness.org) issues an annual report on the degree of regulation, regulatory outcomes, legal protections for investors, and employment flexibility. Table 13.4 shows comparisons for Mexico, Canada, and the United States for 2009.

Looking at the categories in Table 13.4, Mexico's biggest obstacles for business are the complexity of the tax system and tax compliance, along with problems in hiring workers. The United States and Canada rank high overall but Canadians have a relatively lower ranking in the areas of contract enforcement and trade rules, while the U.S. tax system is relatively burdensome.

TABLE 13.4 **Doing Business in the NAFTA Countries, 2007**

Process	Rank among 181 Countries		
	Mexico	Canada	United States
Overall: Doing Business	56	8	3
Degree of regulation			
Starting a business	115	2	6
Dealing with licenses	33	29	26
Registering property	88	32	12
Closing a business	23	4	15
Regulatory outcomes			
Enforcing contracts	79	58	6
Trading across borders	87	44	15
Ease of employing workers	141	18	1
Legal protections			
Paying taxes	149	28	46
Protecting investors	38	5	5
Getting credit	59	28	5

Mexico ranks 56 out of 181 countries for the overall ease of doing business; Canada is eighth and the United States is third.

Source: World Bank, http://www.doingbusiness.org.

Summary

- Canada is the United States' closest ally. In addition, it is mostly English-speaking, has a similar standard of living, and a long democratic tradition. Mexico, on the other hand, is a vastly different society with historical reasons for wariness toward the United States. Furthermore, economic integration with Mexico is much more contentious than with Canada. Labor and environmental standards, worker displacement, poorly developed infrastructure, corruption in the political and judicial systems, immigration, and the drug trade are all areas of existing or potential conflict.

- The United States and Canada have had a free-trade agreement since 1989 (CUSTA). It was preceded by an agreement in 1965 (the Auto Pact) to allow free trade in autos and automobile parts between the two countries.

- Mexico's long process of opening its economy began in the mid-1980s and was a result of the collapse of its traditional economic policy of import substitution industrialization (ISI). ISI stresses self-sufficiency and independence from world markets. The collapse of the Mexican economy in 1982 was due to its inability to repay its international loans; that episode began the Third-World debt crisis. The recessions that followed came to be known throughout Latin America as the "Lost Decade."

- The most contentious issues in the United States related to the signing of the NAFTA agreement were issues of labor policy, environmental policy and enforcement, and migration.

- To date, the main impact of NAFTA has been to continue an ongoing trend toward increased trade. It is impossible to accurately measure the effects of NAFTA on jobs and wages, but most economists estimate a small, positive effect on job creation.

- U.S. benefits from NAFTA are political as well as economic. It offers the opportunity to develop institutions that provide formal mechanisms for discussion, consultation, and resolution of issues.

Vocabulary

Auto Pact

Brady Plan

Canadian-U.S. Trade Agreement (CUSTA)

debt crisis

demand-pull

import substitution industrialization (ISI)

"Lost Decade"

North American Agreement on Environmental Cooperation

North American Agreement on Labor Cooperation

North American Development Bank (NADBank)

purchasing power parity

rules of origin

social networks

supply-push

Study Questions

1. How does Mexico's GDP per person compare to that of the United States? Discuss the different approaches economists can use to make this calculation.

2. Why is the openness indicator for Canada greater than that for the United States?

3. Explain how an increase in U.S. and Canadian intraindustry trade altered the level of productivity in the affected Canadian sector.

4. What were Canada's motives for proposing and signing the Canadian-U.S. Free Trade Agreement?

5. What were the forces at work in the Mexican economy that led to the market reforms and market opening of the mid-1980s?

6. What were Mexico's motives for proposing and signing the North American Free Trade Agreement?

7. In what areas are there NAFTA side agreements? Discuss the pros and cons of these agreements.

8. What are the three main categories of factors that determine the number of immigrants to the United States from Mexico? Give specific examples of each.

9. Explain why claims about job creation and job destruction due to NAFTA are likely to be misleading and inaccurate.

The European Union: Many Markets into One

Introduction: The European Union

The **European Union EU** is an economic union of twenty-seven nations with over 494 million citizens and more than $16,843 billion in output. It is the largest, oldest, and most integrated of regional agreements. It helped put an end to over a century of wars on the European continent, and its incorporation of new members from central Europe has reintegrated several countries that had been cut off from their historical and cultural ties to western Europe. There are a number of lessons to be learned from the struggle of the EU to expand and deepen the economic ties of its member nations.

Since 2004 twelve new members have joined, including three newly independent nations that were part of the former Soviet Union and seven ex-socialist countries in central Europe. The rapid accession of many new members is not the first expansion of the EU. Since its inception in 1957 it has undergone several periods of growth in its numbers and its responsibilities. In 1979 the nine members of what was then called the **European Community (EC)** linked their exchange rates in a system designed to eliminate wide fluctuations among currencies. By 1986 the EC had grown from six to twelve members, and in 1987, they signed the **Single European Act (SEA)**, with the intention of creating a single European identity that would form an umbrella over the various national cultures, economies, and political systems. The Single European Act turned the EC into a common market by allowing for the free movement of labor and capital as complements to the already free movement of goods and services. In 1992 the members signed the **Treaty on European Union**, which led directly to the creation of the common currency, the euro, in 1999.

None of these changes has been easy, or carried out according to a preconceived master plan. Instead, the member states have been forced to act pragmatically as world events called for changes. The shift from fixed to floating exchange rates in the 1970s and 1980s, the fall of the Berlin Wall in 1989, the collapse of communism, the integration of world capital markets and increasing international capital flows, and the rise of environmental awareness, have shaped the EU's development. As changes in the world economy have led to new arrangements and new responsibilities for EU institutions, the goal of peaceful political, social, and economic integration has stayed on track. In this regard, the EU is a truly remarkable achievement,

European Union

Lambert Equal Area Projection

0   500   1000 Miles

Map by Dr. Chris Lukinbeal
Revised by Harry D. Johnson

particularly when one considers the bloody history of twentieth-century Europe and the low expectations of most observers when the original documents were signed in 1957.

The EU is the most ambitious integration agreement in the world today. It has its own revenue and budget, a set of institutions for making laws and regulating areas of common interest, a common currency, and freedom of movement for people, money, goods, and services. Despite this profound integration, it has managed to protect the sovereignty of its member states and to avoid homogenization of cultures and linguistic regions. Indeed, integration in the larger sphere of nation-states has enabled a number of historical national identities to re-emerge and to claim greater autonomy in their political systems. Examples include the Catalans of Spain and the Welsh and Scots of the United Kingdom.

Before proceeding, it is useful to clarify the various names given over time to the European Union (EU). In 1958, when it was formed, the EU was a free-trade area only and was called the **European Economic Community (EEC)**. As it took on more social and political responsibilities, and as the economic community became more integrated, the name changed to the European Community (EC). In 1993, with the implementation of treaty agreements to form an economic union, the EC became the European Union.

The Size of the European Market

Before discussing the history or economics of economic integration in western Europe, let us define the nations and groups that are important to get an idea of the size of the market. In terms of population, the EU is the largest integrated market in the world. By implication, the EU is likely to have a major role in determining future international political arrangements, trade patterns and rules, and international economic relations in general. Few countries will be able to grow and prosper without selling their goods in the European market, which is a powerful incentive to accept European leadership on international issues.

Table 14.1 lists the members of the EU and their population and incomes in 2007. As shown in Table 14.1, income is measured in absolute and per capita terms, and at market exchange rates and purchasing power parity rates. Comparisons at market exchange rates are a less accurate indicator of living standards than comparisons at purchasing power parity rates, but they are a more accurate indicator of the size of each market in terms of its ability to buy goods and services that are imported. Several features of Table 14.1 are worth highlighting. First, not all west European nations are members. Norway, which voted against joining in 1970 and in 1995, and Switzerland are noticeably absent. In addition, a number of the smaller nations, including Iceland, Liechtenstein, San Marino, and Monaco are not members, although Iceland has applied. Second, the majority of nations in the EU are relatively small. The unification of Germany in the early 1990s created the largest country in the EU, but only six of the twenty-seven nations (France, Germany, Italy, Spain, Poland, and the United Kingdom) can be considered large, and none are as populous as the United States or Mexico. Third, the combined EU market is very similar to the size of the NAFTA market, in terms of population and GDP. In 2007 the EU counted 494 million people while the NAFTA nations counted 439 million; GDP comparisons were $16,843 billion in the EU and $16,104 billion in NAFTA.

TABLE 14.1 Population and Income in the European Union, 2007

Country	Population (Millions)	GDP (US$, Billions)	GDP per Capita (US$)	GDP per Capita (US$ PPP)
Original Members				
Belgium	10.6	453	42,609	34,935
France	61.7	2,590	41,970	33,674
Germany	82.3	3,317	40,324	34,401
Italy	59.4	2,102	35,396	30,353
Luxembourg	0.5	49	103,042	79,485
Netherlands	16.4	766	46,750	38,694
Entered 1973–1995				
Austria	8.3	373	44,879	37,370
Denmark	5.5	312	57,051	36,130
Finland	5.3	245	46,261	34,526
Greece	11.2	313	27,995	28,517
Ireland	4.4	259	59,324	44,613
Portugal	10.6	223	20,998	22,765
Spain	44.9	1,437	32,017	31,560
Sweden	9.1	454	49,662	36,712
United Kingdom	61.0	2,772	45,442	35,130
Entered 2004–2007				
Bulgaria	7.7	40	5,163	11,222
Cyprus	0.9	21	24,895	24,789
Czech Republic	10.3	175	16,934	24,144
Estonia	1.3	21	15,578	20,361
Hungary	10.1	138	13,766	18,755
Latvia	2.3	27	11,930	16,377
Lithuania	3.4	38	11,356	17,575
Malta	0.4	7	18,203	23,080
Poland	38.1	422	11,072	15,987
Romania	21.5	166	7,703	12,369
Slovak Republic	5.4	75	13,891	20,076
Slovenia	2.0	47	23,379	26,753
Total, EU-27	494.5	16,843	34,061	29,954

The twenty-seven members of the European Union have income and population totals that are comparable to those for the NAFTA region.

Source: World Bank, *World Development Indicators*.

Before the European Union

The EEC was born on March 25, 1957, with the signing of the **Treaty of Rome** by the original six members. The treaty went into effect about nine months later, on January 1, 1958. The treaty remains the fundamental agreement while more recent agreements, such as the Single European Act and the Maastricht Agreement were passed as amendments to the original treaty. The six founding members include the Benelux countries (Belgium, Netherlands, and Luxembourg), France, West Germany, and Italy.

The Treaty of Rome

The EEC grew out of the reconstruction of Europe at the end of World War II. The goals of the founders of the EEC were to rebuild their destroyed economies and to prevent the destruction from happening again. The original vision of the founders of the EEC was for a political union that they hoped to create through economic integration. In 1950 the first step was a proposal by Robert Schuman, the foreign minister of France, to pool the European coal and steel industries. Coal and steel were chosen because they were large industrial activities that served as the backbone of military strength. Schuman's plan was to pool the industries of Germany and France, the two largest west European antagonists, but Luxembourg, Belgium, the Netherlands, and Italy signed on as well. The **European Coal and Steel Community (ECSC)** Treaty was signed in 1951 and included provisions for the establishment of the ECSC High Authority, an international agency with regulatory powers. Coal and steel trade between the six members grew by 129 percent in the first five years of the treaty.

The success of the ECSC led to early attempts at integration in political and military areas (the European Defense Community and the European Political Community), but these efforts failed when they were rejected by the French Parliament in 1954. At that point, European leaders decided to focus their efforts on economic integration. In 1955 the six foreign ministers of the ECSC countries launched a round of talks in Messina, Italy, to discuss the creation of the European Economic Community and **European Atomic Energy Community (EAEC** or **Euratom)**. The goal of the former was to create a single, integrated market for goods, services, labor, and capital. The latter sought jointly to develop nuclear energy for peaceful purposes. Two separate treaties were signed in 1957 in Rome, creating the EEC and Euratom.

Institutional Structure of the EEC

The founders of the EEC debated the terms of their political affiliation. The key issue was and remains the degree of authority and power to grant the European institutions, and how much to reserve for national states. Officially, the EU is not a federation of states or provinces such as the United States or Canada, but a unique union of independent states that collaborate on transnational issues but maintain sovereign authority on others.

In EU jargon, **subsidiarity** describes the relationship between national and EU areas of authority, and between national and EU institutions. Subsidiarity is defined as the principle that the union will only have authority to tackle issues that are more effectively handled through international action than by individual nations acting alone. In some cases, these issues are easily defined, but in others they are not. Currently, the EU is responsible for trade policy, competition policy, environmental policy, regional development, research and technology development, and economic and monetary union.

Areas that are fuzzier and that contain an element of controversy include social policy, such as the social safety net and health care, and labor market policy, such as rules regarding working hours, safety, vacations, and wage rates. The conflict between policies that reflect national values and the desire to obtain greater gains from trade through economic integration is a pervasive problem in every instance of economic integration. Given that nations rarely speak with a single voice, but are themselves composed of factions and special interests, the struggle over the transfer of sovereignty is all the more contentious.

There are three main governing bodies in the EU and several additional key institutions. The three governing bodies are the **European Commission**, the **Council of the European Union**, and the **European Parliament**. These three institutions represent the citizens of the EU and form the backbone of EU governance. Table 14.2 shows the number of votes in each, as well as the range of votes granted the various countries, depending on their size.

The European Commission   The executive body of the EU is the European Commission. Each country has one vote in the commission. Future members will also be given one vote. Commissioners serve five-year terms that are renewable, and they are appointed by national governments with the mutual approval of the member states. The commission elects one of its own members to serve as its president. Work is divided in a way that gives each commissioner responsibility for one or more policy areas, but all decisions are a collective responsibility.

The commission's primary responsibility is to act as the guardian of the treaties, ensuring that they are faithfully and legally enforced. This role includes responsibility for creating the rules for implementing treaty articles and for EU budget appropriations. As the executive branch, the commission has the sole right to initiate EU laws and the same right as the national governments to submit proposals.

TABLE 14.2   Votes in the Main EU Institutions

		Votes per Country	
	Total Votes	Minimum	Maximum
European Commission	27	1	1
Council of the European Union	345	3	29
European Parliament	785	5	99

The Council of the European Union   The council is the primary legislative branch of the EU, a responsibility it shares with the European Parliament. Each country has between three (Malta) and twenty-nine (France, Germany, Italy, United Kingdom) votes. The council is the primary body for enacting laws proposed by the commission and has more control over the budget than the parliament or the commission. Its membership consists of ministers from each nation, with participation varying according to the topic under discussion. For example, labor ministers convene to discuss labor issues, and environmental ministers to discuss environmental legislation. Most legislative decisions require either unanimity among all countries or a **qualified majority**, which is a majority of countries and 255 of 345 votes (73.9 percent).

The council's presidency rotates among the member states in six-month terms. The chance to serve as president of the council for six months is an important mechanism for individual member states to bring up their own legislative agendas and has been instrumental in the adoption of key EU regulations.

The European Parliament   The European Parliament has 785 members, directly elected by the people for five-year terms and apportioned among the member states according to population. Members associate by political affiliation rather than national origin. The parliament has three main responsibilities as follows:

- Passing laws
- Supervising other institutions within the EU
- Passing the final EU budget

EU laws are usually a co-decision of the council and parliament, although the council alone may make laws in certain areas. The parliament also provides oversight of the work of the other main bodies, such as the commission. And finally, passage of the annual budget of the EU requires approval of the parliament. Over time, the role of the parliament has probably changed more than any other institution. In its early years it was primarily an advisory body with little real authority, but as the EU has grown it has taken on more authority, in part because it provides democratic legitimacy as the only institution directly elected by the citizens of the EU.

Other Institutions   There are six additional institutions that play important roles in EU governance and administration. These include the EU's supreme court (Court of Justice), the monitor of EU finance and regulations (Court of Auditors), institutions that focus on regions (Committee on Regions), broad economic and social issues (Economic and Social Committee), and investment (European Investment Bank). Finally, the **European Central Bank** conducts monetary policy and has played a crucial role in the fight against the recession that began after the crisis of 2007.

The Treaty of Lisbon   The **Treaty of Lisbon** was signed on December 13, 2007, by all twenty-seven members of the EU, but must be ratified by each nation, according to its own rules, before it becomes EU law. The treaty is an attempt to streamline governance and decision making, while at the same time giving the EU a greater voice in world affairs by consolidating defense, security, and foreign policies. It includes a Charter of Fundamental Rights, which is a statement of political and civil liberties granted to each citizen. It was originally intended to take force in January 2009, but controversy arose over the issue of national sovereignty, and not all countries have ratified the agreement. If it eventually becomes law, EU decision making will be less cumbersome and there is a chance that it may overcome traditional obstacles to speaking with a common voice on defense and foreign policy. If the EU were to provide a single foreign policy position on key issues, its weight in international affairs would increase, but most likely at the expense of some of its individual members.

Financing the European Union   The total budget of the EU for 2008 was €129.1 billion ($190 billion). This amounts to slightly more than 1 percent of the gross national income of the member states, and is a relatively small amount of revenue by comparison to that of national governments, which often have total revenue equivalent to 30 to 50 percent or more of the nation's gross national income. The budget is financed through three main sources:

- Tariffs on goods entering the EU
- An EU share of national value added taxes
- A payment from each member country based on the size of its economy

The latter category is by far the largest, accounting for about 67 percent of the total revenue collected by the EU.

The two largest expenditure categories of the EU are for agricultural support, both direct payments in the form of subsidies and indirect payments in the form of rural development, and **cohesion funds**. Agricultural support programs take nearly 42 percent of the budget directly, with another uncertain amount, which is counted as rural development or cohesion expenditures. Cohesion funds take almost 30 percent of the budget and are used to support the less developed regions within the EU, particularly the new members from central Europe that have incomes below the EU average. This is accomplished through infrastructure development, particularly environmental projects such as water treatment and transportation projects.

Deepening and Widening the Community in the 1970s and 1980s

When Europeans speak of increasing the level of cooperation between member countries, they use the term *deepening*. Deepening refers to economic and noneconomic activities that cause increased levels of integration of the national economies. For example, the movement from a free market to a customs union, the harmonization of technical standards in industry, or agreements to develop a common security and defense policy are deepening activities that increase interactions between the member states. On the other hand, when Europeans speak about extending the boundaries of the EU to include new members, they use the term *widening*. Between 1957, when the agreement was signed to create the EEC, and 1995, nine new members were added, bringing the total from six original members to fifteen. In 2004 ten more members were added and in 2007 Bulgaria and Romania joined. In the next section of this chapter we will look at the various stages of deepening.

Before the Euro

In 1979 the members of the EEC began to link their currencies in an effort to prevent radical fluctuation in currency values. The EC wanted to prevent competitive devaluations, in which one country devalues in order to capture the export markets of another country. **Competitive devaluations** inevitably generate conflict and lead to a breakdown in cooperation, since the devaluing country is viewed as gaining exports and jobs at the expense of others. Nations sometimes find it difficult to resist devaluation, especially during recessions. This tactic is viewed as unfair, however, and in the medium to long term, it is usually ineffective since the nondevaluing countries are obliged to follow suit and retaliate with their own devaluations.

In addition to looking for a mechanism that might discourage competitive devaluations, the EC sought to remove some of the uncertainty and risk from trading and investing across national boundaries. While forward markets can be used to protect against exchange rate risk, they only work about six months into the future.

The goal was to create an environment in which trade and investment throughout the EC was determined by considerations of comparative advantage and efficient resource allocation, rather than by changes in exchange rates. The result was the **European Monetary System (EMS)** and the **exchange rate mechanism (ERM)**. The formation of the EMS in 1979 was a significant deepening of the EC and served to prepare the way for the eventual introduction of a single currency. It was designed to prevent extreme currency fluctuations by tying each currency's value to the weighted average of the others. The group average, the **European currency unit (ECU)**, was used as a unit of account, but not as a means of payment.

The ERM system was an example of an exchange rate band. Each currency in the band was fixed to the ECU, but was allowed to fluctuate several percentage points up or down. If a currency began to move out of the bandwidth of several percentage points around the fixed rate, the central bank of the country was obligated to intervene by either buying its currency in order to prop it up, or by selling currency in order to push it down in value. In September 1992, for example, the United Kingdom spent an estimated $30 billion in just a few days, in an attempt to protect the British pound from market speculators who had become convinced that it was going to fall in value. In the end, the speculators were right, and the Bank of England lost a lot of money trying to move against the market.

Given the ineffectiveness of market intervention in the face of a strong and determined market movement, most analysts predicted that the ERM would fail as a mechanism for maintaining stable European currency values. An ERM-type arrangement was attempted in 1973, but it soon collapsed as a result of the first oil shortage and its effects on national inflation rates. When the EC proposed a similar arrangement in 1979, many were skeptical that it would survive for very long or that it would effectively stabilize currencies. To most economists' surprise, the ERM effectively linked EC exchange rates for two decades.

The ERM experienced several adjustments, but none of them threatened the functioning of the system until 1992. Oddly enough, it was the reunification of Germany that caused the system to nearly collapse and led to a much weaker linkage between exchange rates. Because German reunification had a profound effect on the ERM, and because it is an interesting lesson in the costs of tying currencies together, it is useful to look at this episode in more detail.

Problems began in 1990 with Germany's decision to speed up its reunification with the German Democratic Republic (East Germany) after the fall of the Berlin Wall in November 1989. Economic conditions in East Germany were worse than expected, and it was soon apparent that the costs of building a productive economy would be enormous. The infrastructure (roads, bridges, ports, utilities, schools, hospitals) was in worse shape than most people realized, and environmental pollution was significant. In order to build a prosperous economy in its eastern region, Germany had to raise the productivity levels of the people living there, which required huge investments in infrastructure and the environment. The unexpectedly large expenditures to raise the productivity of East Germany resulted in a very large fiscal stimulus to the German economy. Such large expenditures by both the government and private sector were also expected to have an inflationary impact, and the Bundesbank (Germany's central bank) acted to counteract the increased probability of future inflation by raising interest rates. An increase in interest rates is expected to slow the economy by increasing the costs of using borrowed capital. Germany, therefore, had an expansionary fiscal policy that was partially offset by a contractionary monetary policy.

High interest rates in Germany made German financial instruments more attractive and caused capital to flow into Germany from the other EC countries. This resulted in the selling of British pounds, French francs, and other currencies in order to buy German marks (and then German bonds) and caused the pound, the franc, and other currencies to fall in value. At first, the movement was within the 2.25 percent bandwidth, and most of the EC hoped that they would somehow muddle through without making any drastic changes in the ERM or the EMS.

One solution would have been for the countries with falling currencies to raise their interest rates to match Germany's. This would have stemmed the outflow of financial capital looking for better rates of return in Germany. Some of the countries—the United Kingdom, for example—were entering recessions in 1990 and 1991 and did not want to raise interest rates just as a recession was taking hold. The likely effect would have been to hasten and deepen the recession, something no policymaker wants to be accused of doing. Other countries, France for example, were not yet entering the recessionary phase of their business cycle, but they had very high unemployment rates, and contractionary monetary policy was not desirable.

The dilemma faced by the EC countries is a good example of a recurring theme in the history of exchange rate systems. By tying their exchange rates to each other, the EC countries gave up a large measure of independence in their monetary policies. Because Germany was the largest country and the one with the most influential central bank, its monetary policy set the tone for the rest of the EC, and, at a time when many of the members wanted expansionary monetary policy, they were forced to adopt contractionary policies. The 1992 episode illustrates the recurrent tension that occurs between the appropriate external policies (exchange rate management) and the appropriate internal policies (full employment, reasonable growth, low inflation) when nations tie their exchange rates. Since the "right" policy choice for meeting the exchange rate problem was diametrically opposite to meeting the needs of the internal economy, EC members were left with a tough decision. They would have to honor their commitments to the ERM and make their unemployment and growth rates worse, or do the right thing for internal growth and watch the ERM fall apart. In the French case, an interest rate increase threw the country into recession, but France remained within the ERM. In Italy and the United Kingdom, the ERM was abandoned, and their currencies were allowed to freely float against other EC currencies. A third option was chosen by Spain, where the parity, or center of the band, was shifted. In order to lessen the probability of future repeats of this problem, the bandwidth was widened in 1993 from ±2.25 percent to ±15 percent.

The Second Wave of Deepening: The Single European Act

Other than the creation of the EMS in 1979, the changes in the EC were minor through the 1970s and the first half of the 1980s. In the early 1980s most west European countries suffered through a recession that left their unemployment rates high, even as their economic growth recovered in 1984 and 1985. The European economies seemed stale and incapable of new dynamism and many in the United States began to refer to the European situation as "Eurosclerosis," signifying a permanent hardening of the arteries of commerce and industry.

By the late 1980s, people in North America and Europe had stopped using "Eurosclerosis" and begun to speak of "Europhoria." While both terms were exaggerations, dramatic events had reshaped the EC in the intervening years. What was previously dismissed in the early 1980s as a hopeless case of bureaucratic inefficiency was now regarded as a dynamic, forward-looking, integrated regional economy. Europe seemed to be "on the move."

The Delors Report

Reshaping the EC got under way with the selection of the former French finance minister, Jacques Delors, to serve a five-year term as president. Delors was a compromise candidate, and no one expected unusual or dramatic changes in the

CASE STUDY

The Schengen Agreement

The Schengen Agreement was signed by five countries (Belgium, France, Germany, Luxembourg, and the Netherlands) in the town of Schengen, Luxembourg, in 1985. The purpose of the agreement was to eliminate all passport and customs controls at the common borders of the five nations. Given that they enjoyed free trade, and given the flow of people between the countries, the purpose of examining passports or checking customs paperwork seemed inefficient and unnecessary. Over the next few years, more members of the EU joined the agreement. When the Single European Act was completely implemented, the idea of a common market allowing free movement of people gave it added logic. By 1995, the agreement was extended to more countries and more areas of activity, including cooperation among police forces, drug enforcement agencies, and the sharing of criminal justice information. Originally, the Schengen Agreement and its subsequent extension were outside the legal framework of the EU, but in 1999 it was incorporated into EU law. Eventually non-EU countries, among them Iceland and Norway, were allowed to participate.

The dismantling of border-control stations, including passport and customs inspections, undoubtedly has had a positive effect on EU efficiency, because it reduces travel time for both goods and people. It also demonstrates a high degree of social trust among the member nations and contributes to goodwill and better relations. In effect, it shifts customs and passport controls to the perimeter of the EU, where non-EU citizens and goods first enter the region. While this is beneficial, two main problems have arisen from the shifting of control to the perimeter.

First, Ireland and the United Kingdom have not accepted the dismantling of passport controls at the border because they fear the freedom of movement this will give terrorists. However, as members of the EU, they must extend the rights of all other EU citizens to travel freely and reside inside their borders, even as they maintain passport checks at the border. Second, the eventual extension of the Schengen Agreement to the twelve new members since 2004 depends on those members' ability to demonstrate control over their own borders to the east, and on the development of a new EU data system for sharing information about individuals and lost or stolen objects. The timetable for extending Schengen beyond its current membership (thirteen EU members, plus Norway and Iceland) is flexible.

EC under his stewardship. Delors's vision of the EC, however, was of a fully integrated union, and as president of the EC's executive branch he had a platform from which he could initiate significant change. His vision was shaped in part by the belief that the institutions of the EC could help return individual national economies to economic prosperity and by the desire to complete the task of building an economic and political union.

Delors' first step, and perhaps his most significant one, was to issue a report called "Completing the Internal Market," which detailed 300 specific changes necessary for the EC to move from a quasi-customs union to an economic union. It laid out a timetable for completing the changes and removed the need for unanimous voting in the Council of Ministers. Delors proposed that most measures be allowed to pass with a "qualified majority" and that unanimity be reserved for only the most momentous issues, such as taxes. Although the qualified majority still allowed a minority of countries to block a measure, it prevented any single country from blocking a proposed change.

After some relatively minor changes in the **Delors Report**, it was adopted in its entirety in 1987, as the Single European Act (SEA). Of the 300 steps, or "directives," 279 were included in the SEA. Many of the 21 not included were considered too difficult to accomplish in the time period the EC gave itself, but were taken up as goals of the next round of deepening. For example, monetary union under a single currency was moved forward to the next round of deepening.

The date for implementation of the SEA was January 1, 1993. By the end of 1992, it was expected that the "four freedoms" (freedom of movement for goods, services, capital, and labor) spelled out in the SEA would be instituted and, as a result, the EC would be at the common market level of economic integration. In order to accomplish these goals it was necessary to determine the method of implementation of each of the 279 directives and for each of the 12 member nations to make the necessary changes in their internal laws, standards, and customs practices. While some areas remain incomplete, the vast majority of the directives were put into practice by the end of 1992, and the EC achieved common market status.

The steps taken to implement the SEA can be broadly divided into three areas: (1) the elimination of physical barriers, such as passport and customs controls at the borders between member countries; (2) the elimination of technical barriers, such as differences in product and safety standards; and (3) the elimination of fiscal barriers, such as differences in taxes, subsidies, and public procurement. Each of these poses its own benefits and challenges and will be discussed in more detail. First, we will consider the gains that the EC hoped to reap from the elimination of these barriers.

Forecasts of the Gains from the Single European Act

One of the central reasons for supporting the SEA was to achieve gains in economic efficiency. One set of gains was anticipated to come from the freeing of the movement of goods and services. While the SEA did not mandate the elimination of border inspections, it did grant freedom of movement to people and goods. In many cases, border controls were dismantled, also with support from the Schengen Agreement, but in some cases "tax inspections" replaced customs inspections due to the EU's inability to establish a common system of value-added taxation. Nevertheless, substantial progress has been made in eliminating long border waits and in speeding up the distribution of goods throughout the EC.

Integration also created economic benefits from greater economies of scale and increased competitiveness. Economies of scale are possible because EC firms are able to produce at one site, or in a fewer number of sites for the entire European market and will not have to duplicate production facilities across national boundaries. This enables some companies to consolidate their operations and to avoid duplication in their production and support services, such as accounting. The increase in competitiveness comes from several sources. For example, the increased pressure of competition will force some firms to make productive investments that they would not otherwise have made. In addition, the openness of the competitive environment will generate a larger, more mobile pool of labor that carries skills from one firm to another. Finally, the free flow of goods and services will generate a greater flow of information and ideas so that firms have easier access to the best new ideas.

Problems in the Implementation of the SEA

One of the most interesting lessons of the Single European Act is that it is still difficult to reduce barriers to trade and investment even when the citizens, businesses, and governments of the involved countries are united in their desire to do so. According to all the polls, the SEA enjoyed very broad support throughout the EC. Still, from the time when it was first proposed in 1985 until its final implementation in 1993, there were very difficult negotiations among the member countries.

The Effects of Restructuring   As we saw in Chapter 3, when a national economy goes from a relatively closed position to a relatively open one, economic restructuring takes place. The less efficient firms are squeezed out, and the more efficient ones grow; overall economic welfare expands as countries concentrate on what they do best, which inevitably means abandoning some industries and expanding others. In the case of the EC, it was forecast that almost all manufacturing industries would see shrinkage in the number of firms. The most extreme case was the footwear industry, which was predicted to lose 207 of its 739 firms. In some cases, the majority of the disappearing firms were concentrated in one or two countries, such as the UK carpet industry, where it was predicted that 31 of 52 manufacturers would go out of business.

The firms that go out of business are part of the economy-wide shift to a more efficient use of labor and capital resources, but it is obvious that there are immediate human costs. In the long-run, it is easy to show that the gains in efficiency and the improvement in living standards outweigh the costs of restructuring, but in the short-run individuals and communities can feel acute pain. Due to the inevitable costs from restructuring, many people predicted that adversely affected firms and labor unions, along with the communities and regions that depend on the firms, would fight to prevent the full implementation of the SEA.

The auto industry is the best example of an economic interest that fought to prevent the full realization of the goals of the SEA. Car prices vary throughout the EU due to a lack of harmonization of national technical standards, documentation requirements, and rates of taxation. Ordinarily, such large price differences would present an opportunity for consumers and distributors to move cars from the low-price countries to the high-price ones and, in the process, bring about a reduction in price differences. The auto industry is covered by a separate set of tax laws, however, that require buyers to pay the tax rate of the country where they register the car, not where they buy the car. This effectively discourages buyers from crossing national borders in order to search out the best deal on car prices and helps maintain the status quo in automobile production.

One significant reason why there have not been more exceptions to the dropping of trade barriers is that the EU has a broad array of programs to address the problems of structural change. Some of these programs are funded out of the EU budget, and others are national in origin. Programs include the EU's Regional Development Funds, which can be used to address problems of structural unemployment, and the member nations' income maintenance, education, and retraining funds. The latter vary across the member countries, but in general they reduce the costs to individuals and communities of unemployment and structural change by providing a generous social safety net for laid-off workers. The programs can also have positive effects in reducing political opposition to economic change.

Harmonization of Technical Standards   A second major obstacle to the creation of the four freedoms was the problem of harmonizing standards. These include everything from building codes, industrial equipment, consumer safety, and health standards, to university degrees and worker qualifications. The EU estimated that there were more than 100,000 technical standards that required harmonization in order to realize the benefits of a completely integrated market. Many of the technical standards involved rules that directly touch upon cultural identities. Nowhere was this more true than in the case of food processing. For example, there were discussions around the allowable level of bacteria in French cheese, the type of wheat required to make Italian pasta, the ingredients of German beer, and the oatmeal content of English bangers (breakfast sausages). In the end, the EU recognized that complete harmonization of standards would generate significant hostility and that the work required to agree on a set of common standards was beyond its capacity. Consequently, a combination of harmonization and mutual recognition of standards was adopted. In particularly sensitive cases, mutual recognition is the rule, but individual nations are allowed to keep their own national production requirements. For example, German beer must be certified as having been made according to the German standards, but Germany must allow all brands of beers to be sold within its borders.

As the discussion in Chapter 8 noted, standards do not have to be the same in order to create a single market, but the gains in economic efficiency that come from sharing the same standard can be significant. Shared standards permit manufacturers to produce to one standard, rather than many, and to capture important economies of scale in the process. These economies also pass outside the EU, since U.S. or Japanese manufacturers share the benefits of being able to produce to one set of standards as well.

Value-Added Taxes   A third difficulty standing in the way of completely realizing the four freedoms is the issue of value-added taxes (VAT). These taxes function essentially like sales taxes and are levied by each of the EU members but at a wide variety of rates and coverage. When the SEA was first proposed in 1987, there were significant differences in the dependence of the member governments of the EU on value-added taxes, ranging from 19 to 35 percent of total government revenue. The European Commission studied the United States to determine the effects of different rates of sales taxation on states sharing common borders and found that once the difference in sales taxes exceeded 5 percent, the higher-tax state lost revenues, sales, and jobs to the neighboring lower-tax state. In other words, a 5 percent difference was enough to cause consumers to cross state boundaries to make purchases. The standard VAT rate in the EU before the SEA varied from 12 percent at the low end (Luxembourg and Spain) to 20 percent in the Netherlands, 22 percent in Denmark, and 25 percent in Ireland. In addition, there were special rates for sensitive goods, which varied a great deal more than the standard rates.

VAT rates proved impossible to completely harmonize because they go to the heart of national political philosophy. High-tax countries expect the state to play a relatively greater role in national economic life, while low-tax countries are closer to the laissez-faire end of the political economy spectrum. The level of value-added taxes, and the degree to which the national government depends on them, are in large part determined by the political philosophy of the nation. In turn, these philosophical attitudes are shaped by economics, as well as complex historical, cultural, and social factors..

The attempt to harmonize value-added taxes created an inability to agree on a single rate. What was accomplished, however, was the creation of minimum and maximum rates that were set at 15 and 25 percent. Since the difference still exceeds the 5 percent differential that is the threshold at which high-tax countries lose revenue and sales, a number of controls were established to prevent revenue loss, even though these controls prevent the complete realization of the four freedoms.

Public Procurement   Public procurement is the purchase of goods and services by governments or government-owned enterprises, such as state-run television companies, utilities, or hospitals. Most nations of the world tend to use procurement processes that discriminate in favor of nationally owned suppliers, although there are limits on their ability to do so if they belong to the World Trade Organization (WTO).

Since 1970, the EU has attempted to eliminate discrimination in public procurement, but this has proved difficult. It is a problem particularly in the areas of telecommunications, pharmaceuticals, railway equipment, and electrical equipment. These are often the areas of economic activity where governments have state-owned enterprises or national firms that were considered critical to national prosperity, and therefore received significant support, including government's purchase of output.

CASE STUDY

The Erasmus Program and Higher Education

It is easy to forget that during the first part of the twentieth century, the European continent was engulfed in one of the most brutal and violent periods in human history. Wars, depression, and genocide marked the history of every country until the end of World War II. How then did the countries that comprise the EU manage to deepen their ties and to form an economic union? The answer is multidimensional, contentious, and would take volumes, but one thing we know is that the EU built political, social, professional, and commercial networks across national borders. The processes of building networks is ongoing, and student mobility is a fundamental component.

The most prominent effort is the **Erasmus program**. Erasmus began in 1987 and since then more than 1.9 million students have gone abroad within the EU and over 90 percent of all EU-based universities have joined the exchange program. Erasmus students receive a mobility grant that does not cover all expenses, but does cover the difference in living expenses caused by studying in another country. Students do not pay fees to the host institution, and course credits and study periods are recognized and accepted by the institution of origin. The language of instruction is often the language of the host institution, although not always. Erasmus also provides support for faculty who teach abroad.

With an annual budget of around €400 million ($540 million), Erasmus has served as a base for higher education innovation and reform. It was key to the development of the Bologna Process, which is an agreement among the twenty-seven EU countries, joined by nineteen non-EU members (forty-six in total, with more countries holding observer status), to form a Higher Education Area by 2010. Bologna has created common structures for higher education around three degrees: bachelor's, master's, and doctorate. It has also created a common set of unit requirements for degrees, and harmonized the recognition of credits. Bologna's intent is to reduce the variability in higher education degrees by creating a common set of standards that will ensure quality. The Erasmus Program also helped start Erasmus Mundus, a worldwide program of exchanges targeted at the master's degree level and involving both students and faculty.

The objectives of these programs are to increase student mobility, foster language acquisition, and increase the sophistication and international understanding of graduates. In the long run, the goal is to develop international networks among business people, intellectuals, government workers, and other educated labor.

The Third Wave of Deepening: The Maastricht Treaty

By 1989, planning for the implementation of the SEA in January 1993 was well under way. Europe had seen several years of economic expansion, and the excitement of the SEA seemed to signal that the time was right to consider some of the directives proposed in the Delors Report that had been set aside because they were seen as too complex to accomplish by 1993. In 1990 the European Commission convened an Intergovernmental Conference on Economic and Monetary Union. The purpose of the conference was to bring together the leaders of the twelve nations to discuss the steps necessary to create a monetary union under a single currency. There were other issues on the agenda, but this was the one that attracted the most interest inside and outside the EU.

The Intergovernmental Conference continued through most of 1991. The final draft of the proposed agreement was completed in December in the Dutch town of Maastricht and, ever since, has been known as the **Maastricht Treaty**. Many of the provisions in the agreement were technical and covered such arcane issues as the tax treatment of holiday homes in Denmark, or the status of the pope in trade disputes with the Vatican. Other issues dealing with basic EU social policy were much more fundamental. For example, the Maastricht Treaty called for the creation of a "Social Charter" defining a uniform set of labor laws and worker rights. It defined the right of all residents in a community to vote and stand for election in local contests, regardless of the resident's nationality; it put more control over health, education, cultural, and consumer safety issues in the hands of the European Commission; it called for a common defense and security policy along with a common military force; and it defined the steps for achieving a common currency under the control of a European Central Bank by 1999.

It is the last goal that attracted the most attention. Achieving a single currency required each country to give up its ability to set its own monetary policy and instead accept whatever contractionary or expansionary policy the European Central Bank chooses. This is the most controversial feature of the Maastricht Treaty, inside and outside of the EU. The controversy stems from the fact that there are economic risks associated with voluntarily giving up one of the few tools that governments have to counteract recessions. If, for example, Germany is booming, but Spain is in an economic slump, there is no common monetary policy that will be suitable to both countries. Germany would need a contractionary policy to cool off the economy and to prevent the ignition of inflation, while Spain would need an expansionary policy to create employment and growth. These controversies led to a very different public reception for the Maastricht Treaty than that received by the SEA. Whereas citizens, businesses, and governments were solidly behind the SEA, support for the Maastricht Treaty was much more tentative.

Monetary Union and the Euro

The timetable for monetary union under a single currency was scheduled to occur in three separate stages. Stage one began in 1990 with the lifting of controls on the movement of financial capital within the EU. Stage two began in 1994 with the creation of the European Monetary Institute, based in Frankfurt, Germany. The institute was charged with the responsibility for coordinating the move to monetary union and gradually took on elements of a supranational central bank. The third stage began in 1999 with the phased-in introduction of the **euro** and the European Central Bank.

During stages one and two, nations were expected to bring their monetary and fiscal policies into harmony so that the introduction of the euro would not happen under wildly different sets of monetary and fiscal policies. In order to judge when individual national policies were in agreement, the EU developed a set of **convergence criteria**. These were objective measures that signaled whether the national policies were in conflict or in agreement, and whether individual nations were ready for monetary union. Table 14.3 lists the specific monetary and fiscal variables that are required to be coordinated and the target ranges for each.

Initially, nations were expected to meet all five goals for monetary union. The experience of the first half of the 1990s, however, indicated that no nation, except perhaps Luxembourg, could consistently maintain each of these targets and that some countries would never meet them. For example, Italian and Belgian central government debts were well over 100 percent of their annual GDP, and there was no way to change this in the span of a few years. Some economists questioned why these particular criteria were chosen in the first place, since a country that can maintain its interest rates, debts, deficits, inflation, and exchange rates in the target range is already doing what the EU hopes to achieve with monetary union. In other words, meeting the convergence criteria was an indicator that the nation can do what monetary union does but without actually giving up its currency. Why, then, should countries surrender control over monetary policy, and why should they give up their national currency, particularly since there are hidden costs?

TABLE 14.3	Convergence Criteria for Monetary Union
Goals	**Targets**
1. Stabilize exchange rates	Maintain currency within the ERM band
2. Control inflation	Reduce it to less than 1.5 percent above the average of the three lowest rates
3. Harmonize long-term interest rates	Bring to within 2 percent of the average of the three lowest rates
4. Government deficits	Reduce to less than 3 percent of national GDP
5. Government debt	Reduce to less than 60 percent of national GDP

These five goals were designed to harmonize fiscal and monetary policies in preparation for the single currency.

Costs and Benefits of Monetary Union

There is no doubt that there are benefits to having one currency in a market as large as the EU's. For example, the average cost of currency conversion for travelers is 2.5 percent of the amount converted. A trip from Portugal to Sweden, with stops along the way, can quickly eat up a sizable portion of one's vacation money. Businesses fare much better, however, and if they buy in quantities greater than the equivalent of US $5 million, then the costs are a much smaller 0.05 percent, or $5,000 to convert $10 million. One estimate combining tourists and businesses puts the total costs of currency conversion at 0.4 percent of the EU's GDP. This is not a trivial sum, but it is not huge, either. The 0.4 percent figure could be higher, however, given the costs of maintaining separate accounting systems and separate money management processes for the different currencies.

A second reason for desiring monetary union is to reduce the effects of exchange-rate uncertainty on trade and investment. Since orders for goods are often placed long before delivery occurs, traders face a good deal of uncertainty about their earnings (if they export) and their payments (if they import). A single currency eliminates this uncertainty in the same way, for example, that California manufacturers can always be certain of the value of payments they will receive when they ship goods to New York. Recall from Chapter 10 that traders and investors can protect themselves from currency fluctuations with forward markets. Therefore, it should not be surprising that there is not much evidence that the elimination of currency fluctuations through a monetary union will increase cross-border trade and investment. On the other hand, tests of this idea are difficult because there are few examples of monetary unions. Recently, however, some evidence has emerged that shows large positive effects on trade and investment flows from the creation of a single currency. Ultimately, the EU's experience will prove to be a valuable case study.

Given these considerations, the benefits of a single currency appear to be uncertain. The same cannot be said for the potential costs. A single currency does not allow individual nations to pursue an independent monetary policy, in the same way that the state of New York cannot have a monetary policy that differs from California's or the rest of the United States'. In a single-currency area, there is a "one size fits all" monetary policy. It is optimal to have a single currency and to eliminate the costs of currency conversion and other transaction costs, as long as the regions in the single currency area have synchronized business cycles and mobile labor forces. Synchronization of business cycles means that there is a single monetary policy—expansionary, neutral, or contractionary—that is appropriate for everybody. A mobile labor force guarantees that if some regions are not well synchronized, labor will move from the shrinking region to the expanding one, making the business cycles move together. If, however, the business cycles are not synchronized and labor is relatively immobile, then the single monetary policy will be right for some areas but wrong for others.

Business cycles in Europe have never been synchronized, although the convergence criteria were partly designed with this goal in mind. In addition, the

SEA's guarantee of freedom for labor mobility does not seem to have created significantly more continent-wide labor mobility, and Europeans are far less mobile than Americans. Given that most conventional measures show that the EU fails both criteria for being an optimal currency area, it seems natural to ask why it took this momentous step.

The Political Economy of a Single Currency

Most policies that offer uncertain benefits and potentially large costs should be rejected. Why, then, did monetary union push ahead? This is the question that many economists have asked, and the answers are less than clear. The easiest answers are that the leaders of the EU believed that monetary union would create substantial trade and investment flows, or that the leaders of the EU were simply swept up in a euphoric rush to greater political and economic unity. The latter explanation suffers from the defect that the EU has been unable to forge a consensus around a common defense and security policy, as evidenced by the divisions over the conflict in the former Yugoslavia.

The best explanation for the push to monetary union seems to be that it was politically necessary in the wake of the capital market liberalization required under the SEA. Prior to 1990, many countries had controls on the movement of foreign exchange into their country. Regulatory measures were common, such as taxes on foreign currency holdings, or on assets denominated in foreign currencies, and limitations on the uses of foreign currencies were widespread. The removal of these controls made it easier to speculate in foreign currency markets. One outcome of the removal of capital controls was the turmoil of 1992, when speculators became convinced that a number of currencies in the ERM would ultimately have to be devalued, prompting them to sell off large quantities of the currencies. During the sell-off, Portugal, Ireland, and Spain all devalued; Italy temporarily suspended participation in the ERM; and the United Kingdom dropped out permanently. Ultimately, the British pound fell by 25 percent from its peak before the speculative attacks. Soon after it left the ERM, there were several cases of firms that announced their intentions to close plants inside EU countries and move to the United Kingdom. Philips Electronics, the giant Dutch firm, for example, closed plants in Holland, and SC Johnson and the Hoover Company closed French plants, all in order to open new plants in the United Kingdom where French and Dutch currencies bought more land, labor, buildings, and machinery.

Political friction increases and cooperation decreases when one country loses jobs to another as a result of currency depreciations. The desire to reduce these types of frictions is the reason why the EMS, with its ERM, was created in 1979. Consequently, it is the reason why a flexible exchange rate system was not an option. Although floating exchange rates have the advantage of permitting the greatest amount of flexibility in a nation's monetary policies, the EU's economic integration plans have closed the door on the use of flexible exchange rate systems.

Given that flexible rates are ruled out, it seems logical to ask why the EU did not choose to institute a system of fixed exchange rates. In fact, the ERM acted somewhat like a fixed exchange rate system because it tied each country's currency to a weighted average of the other currencies. Exchange rates were not completely fixed, however, and there were bands that the currencies tried to stay within. The EU's problem with a fixed exchange rate system is that it lacked the ability to keep the currencies within their bands, let alone to completely fix them. International currency markets know that there are definite limits to the resolve and the resources of member countries trying to defend their currencies. The EU partially solved this by changing the bandwidths from ±2.25 percent to ±15 percent, which removed the minor short-term speculative pressures against particular currencies by letting them float down more before intervention became required. This, however, did nothing about the serious pressure against a currency that the United Kingdom and Italy experienced in 1992. In other words, the EU is not willing to defend its fixed rates if the costs grow too high, which means that fixed rates are not really "fixed."

Implementation of the Single Currency

The inability of the EU to maintain a set of fixed rates, coupled with the political undesirability of floating rates, made the single-currency option an attractive choice. Membership in the monetary union, however, is a subset of the EU. The United Kingdom left the ERM and, along with Denmark and Sweden, did not join the move to a single currency. Few, if any, of the countries met the convergence criteria for compliance by the 1998 deadline. Nevertheless, in May of 1998, it was announced that eleven countries (the fifteen members of the EU, minus the United Kingdom, Sweden, Denmark, and Greece) would adopt the single currency on January 1, 1999. Greece adopted the euro one year later.

In the first stage of the implementation process, countries kept their national currencies, but fixed their exchange rates to each other. Until euro coins and notes began to circulate in 2002, each of the euro area countries continued to use its own national money, which was fixed in value to the euro and, therefore, to the money of the other member countries. During the transition period before the introduction of euro coins and notes, national currencies were managed as separate, national manifestations of the euro. The German mark, for example, was worth about one-half a euro, just as two quarters are worth one-half a U.S. dollar. Consequently, speculation against any one currency was equivalent to speculating against all of them. The euro itself is on a flexible exchange rate system, so it is free to move up or down against the dollar, the yen, and other currencies. The euro is managed by the European Central Bank (ECB), which also conducts monetary policy in the euro region.

Since its introduction in 1999 at US $1.18, the euro value has varied significantly (see Figure 14.1). Or, one might say that the dollar's value has fluctuated significantly; either way, the same meaning is implied. The euro lost about one-fourth of its value within the first eighteen months and since then has rapidly gained it all back. The decline and the subsequent rise were larger than expected. The decline in 1999 and 2000 was attributed to high—and rising—U.S. interest rates, the high rate of growth in the United States, and the soaring U.S.

FIGURE 14.1   **The U.S. Dollar-EU Euro Exchange Rate, 2000–July, 2009**

The euro has gained value against the dollar since 2001.

Source: The Federal Reserve Bank, *Foreign Exchange Rates.*

stock market. The rise in the euro that began in 2002 is perhaps related to the ballooning U.S. trade deficit and the expectation of future declines in the dollar that will be necessary to restore balance, along with the historically low level of U.S. interest rates.

Widening the European Union

After the achievement of monetary union, one of the most pressing problems facing the EU was the timetable and conditions under which new members would be added.

Central and Eastern Europe

Ten countries joined the EU in 2004 and two more joined in 2007. Ten of the twelve new members are from central Europe and have undergone profound economic and political transformations as they abandoned relatively closed socialist economies in favor of democratic and capitalist systems.

There are three criteria for membership. First, each of the countries must be stable, functioning democracies. Second, they must have market-based economies, and third, they must formally adopt the EU-wide rules, called the ***acquis communautaire***. These include technical standards, environmental and technical inspections, banking supervision, public accounts, statistical reporting requirements, and other elements of EU law. The *acquis* is sovereign over national laws and must be completely adopted by each new member before it is granted full membership.

In the years leading up to membership, the EU consults and provides technical assistance to candidate nations. To qualify for admission, prospective members must develop the administrative capacity for implementing and enforcing EU rules. Building this capacity requires training legions of professional and technical workers, including judges, lawyers, environmental health and safety inspectors, financial institution supervisors, accountants, and a number of other skilled occupations. The professionals in these areas must become versed in EU law, technical standards, and administrative processes. Failure to demonstrate an ability to enforce the rules can lead to a denial of admission into the EU.

There are four major problems with the planned expansion. The first is agriculture and agricultural policies. Several of the new members in central Europe have large agricultural sectors. Poland, for example, is a large country, with a population of thirty-eight million and about 18 percent of its labor force in agriculture. Agriculture is important to several other new members as well, because it generates exports and earns much needed foreign exchange. Large agricultural sectors are a problem for the EU, however, because of the EU's agricultural policies, known collectively as the **Common Agricultural Policy (CAP)**. The CAP is the world's most extensive set of farm price supports and farm income maintenance programs. One indicator of the importance of the CAP is that it continues to be the largest item in the EU budget at 42 percent in spite of a number of ongoing reforms to the agricultural support system. In addition, a significant share of expenditures on regional development is agricultural supports that have been reclassified for administrative reasons and to avoid complaints filed through the WTO system.

The CAP sets farm prices, guarantees a market for farm products, and provides direct income payments to farmers. Under a set of reforms passed in 2005, direct payments to farmers will be phased out gradually and decoupled from production. While desirable on their own account, the reforms are necessary in part due to the accession of the new members with large agricultural sectors and low incomes. Agricultural support payments on the same scale as those given to the EU-15 are impossible, given the budget of the EU. The twelve new members will receive some payments that are phased in gradually over a ten-year period.

The second major issue of expansion is migration. The SEA created the right for all EU citizens to move freely and reside wherever they choose. Furthermore, it attempts to create a single labor market that allows workers to search for employment in any member country. Nevertheless, in 2004, when ten countries joined, only the United Kingdom offered an open labor market, and no countries have shown signs of opening their doors to Romanian and Bulgarian workers, whose countries joined in 2007. Under the rules of accession, countries that were members before 2004 have up to seven years before they must open their labor markets to the new members. New members must also wait for the dismantling of passport controls on their movement (see the Case Study on the Schengen Agreement).

A third issue with expansion is governance. As the original six members of the EEC grew into the fifteen members of the EU, and then added twelve more members, the institutions and governing bodies of the EU became too complex and cumbersome. The proposed solution, the Constitution for Europe, was intended to simplify decision-making processes, among other things, but the proposed document has not been well received by the citizens of the EU and it is unlikely that it will pass.

Fourth, income difference between the new and existing members is much larger than any previous differences. This creates a variety of tensions, from potential migration pressures to differences in institutional capacity and demands on the EU budget for agricultural support payments, cohesion funds, and regional development funds. In the short-to-medium term, the EU has addressed the migration issue by allowing countries to delay the opening of their labor markets for seven years. It has addressed the institutional gap with a lengthy accession period in which it provided technical assistance and financial support to the new members in order to assist the development of their legal, administrative, and regulatory institutions and to ensure that the new members were capable of enforcing the EU's body of rules and regulations, or the *aquis communitaire*.

The most serious potential problems associated with the accession of relatively poor members from central Europe can be ameliorated, if not eliminated completely, by a closing of the income differences between the new and old members. In this regard, the recent experiences of Ireland, Spain, Portugal, and Greece are instructive. Their accession in the 1970s and 1980s led to a similar gap between the richest and poorest members, although not quite as large as the current gap. Recognizing the tensions created by large disparities, the EU created the Cohesion Fund and expanded its Regional Development Fund. These and other sources of financing are now being used to build infrastructure and to connect the new regions to western Europe and the global economies.

Turkey

Turkey officially submitted its application for membership in 1987, and in 2004 the European Commission recommended to start negotiations in 2005. Turkey's population of 73.9 million in 2007 would make it the second largest member, although its GDP per capita was only $12,955 at purchasing power parity rates of exchange and $8,877 at market exchange rates. The market rate is less than 20 percent of the EU average, but more than some of the current members, such as Romania and Bulgaria.

The political challenges posed by Turkey's accession are significant. In order to begin negotiations, potential members must demonstrate that they are a stable democracy with respect for human rights, including protections for ethnic minorities, have a functioning market economy, and can implement and enforce the rules and laws of the EU. Turkey fulfilled these criteria as a precondition for opening negotiations over accession, but it must continue its reforms. In particular, EU officials have warned that the country continues to stifle freedom of speech, that it has not curbed the use of torture in its prisons, and that it has not established civilian control over its military. In addition, Turkey's accession is hampered by the problem of Cyprus, a member of the EU that is geographically divided into two ethnic regions, a northern half that is Turkish and a southern territory that is ethnically mixed, but largely Greek. Turkey's reluctance to open its ports to Cypriot ships is another barrier to its accession, in part due to the fact that Cyprus can block Turkey's accession under EU rules that grant member countries veto rights over the accession of new members.

It is not certain that Turkey will join the EU eventually. If it does, the situation will be reminiscent of the situation of Mexico in the NAFTA region. Both are large developing countries with similar per capita income levels. EU pre-accession support programs in financial and technical assistance and post-accession supports with Cohesion Funds and Regional Development Funds will be critical.

CASE STUDY

Spain's Switch from Emigration to Immigration

Spain's period of highest emigration was from 1881 to 1930, when approximately 4.3 million people left. In 1910 its population was just under 20 million, so a loss of 4.3 million people was significant. The decade with the highest out-migration was 1910 to 1920, when 1.3 million people, or well over 5 percent of the population, left.

Emigration was slowed by the world depression of the 1930s and World War II, but began again in earnest after 1950. Unlike the earlier migrations, when the majority of migrants went to the Americas, increasing numbers headed for other countries in central and western Europe. In particular, France, Germany, and Switzerland were major recipients of Spanish citizens.

By the time Spain joined the EU in 1986, changes were occurring in the Spanish economy that were reducing the supply-push forces that cause emigration. In 1950 Spain's work force was nearly 50 percent agricultural, but by 1970 agriculture's share of the labor force had fallen to less than 25 percent. With more industry came higher productivity and a shrinking wage gap with France, Germany, and even Switzerland. By the early 1990s, Spain's economic success was turning it into a net attractor of migrants, rather than a net sender. As a result, in the second half of the 1990s, immigration to Spain was accelerating, particularly from North Africa, South America, and western Europe. Well-off

Europeans discovered Spain's Mediterranean coast, while Colombians, Ecuadorians, Moroccans, and Mauritanians came for jobs and wages that were significantly higher than what they could earn at home. In 2004 42 percent of the foreign population residing in Spain was from the Americas; they were predominantly Colombians who wished to escape the ongoing violence at home and Ecuadorians looking for work and higher wages. Another 33 percent were Europeans, mostly from western Europe and relatively wealthy, and 19 percent were Africans, predominantly from Morocco.

Immigration creates a reaction in most countries where the numbers of immigrants are large. The U.S.-Mexican case is famous but there are numerous others. Mexico itself resists immigration from Guatemalans on its southern border, while Costa Ricans appreciate the hard work of Nicaraguans who come to pick the coffee crop, but they complain about their behavior and use of social services. Germans have a long love-hate relationship with Turks, the French with Algerian immigrants, and so on around the globe. Spain's policy has been relatively accommodating toward immigrants, including six amnesties for undocumented workers since 1990. Its last amnesty occurred in 2005 and offered legal status to more than 700,000 foreigners. At the same time, Spain increased its program of border enforcement, which is primarily aimed at deterring Africans. It also built walls around Ceuta and Melilla, two Spanish territories located inside Morocco, and stepped-up its coastal patrols.

Migration policies are fraught with uncertain side effects, but one of the most frequent consequences of increased enforcement at the border is a displacement of immigrants to alternative points of entry. In the Spanish case, the walls around Ceuta and Melilla, together with increased vigilance along the coast, resulted in migrants moving their point of departure from Morocco to Western Sahara, a disputed territory on Morocco's southern border. From there, migrants could reach the Canary Islands, which is Spanish territory. When Spain increased its patrols off the coast of Western Sahara, migrants moved their departure points south to Mauritania, and then farther south to Senegal when Spain began to target Mauritania.

It is difficult to name a country that has not gone through a period of high rates of out-migration at some point in its development. Europeans went to the Americas, U.S. citizens went west into what was Mexico and the frontier, Koreans spread around the globe, and the Japanese went to North and South America. Spain's period of high emigration is over, and it is now one of the desirable target countries where emigrants prefer to settle.

The Demographic Challenge of the Future

As the EU looks toward the future, a number of challenges are visible. In the short-to-medium run, it must continue to create convergence in income and living standards between its poorest and its most well-off members. Over the medium run, it must also prepare for further widening, in particular for the possible accession of Turkey, a large nation with per capita income levels about one-fifth of the EU average. And finally, in the long run, it must adapt its economies and social support systems to prepare for a much older population.

One of the primary determinants of social spending in virtually all countries is the age structure of the population. As populations age, they need more health care, more pensions, and more long-term care. Each of these entails increases in public spending, and given that older citizens regularly vote, democracies usually respond to their demands. A small part of increased spending on services for the elderly will be offset by decreases in educational spending and unemployment benefits, as a smaller share of the total population will need schooling or experience involuntary unemployment. However, these savings will not begin to offset the increases in social spending associated with an aging population. According to estimates carried out by the European Commission, if current policies are left in place, the average EU government will have to increase the public sector by 10 percent simply to maintain its existing programs at their current levels.

Table 14.4 shows a projection of EU population (twenty-seven countries) through 2040. By 2040 the percent of the population 65 and over is expected to reach nearly 28 percent of the total, up from below an estimated 18 percent in 2010. The ability of governments to manage a much larger population of retired people will be constrained by the fact that after 2011, the working age population is forecast to begin declining, and after 2018, the total number of people working is projected to start declining as well. Corresponding to the increase in the population over 65 is a nearly equal drop in the working age population, as shown in Table 14.4. Fewer workers means that the rate of economic growth will fall, and that new resources for supporting an aging population will be harder to acquire. At the same time, the number of available workers to support the production of

TABLE 14.4	Population Forecast, 2010–2040: Twenty-Seven Members of the European Union			
	Population, 2010 (Millions)	Percent, 2010	Population, 2040 (Millions)	Percent, 2040
Total	489.0	100.0	468.6	100.0
By age category				
Ages 0–15	74.6	15.3	63.2	13.5
Ages 15–64	328.7	67.2	274.5	58.6
Ages 65+	85.7	17.5	130.9	27.9

Population in the European Union will stop growing and begin to age rapidly after 2010.

Source: U.S. Census Bureau.

social services needed by the aging population will be both relatively and absolutely smaller.

Migration can play a role at the margin to ameliorate the changes, but it is unlikely that migration alone will have a major impact. Simply to return the estimated 2040 working age population (15–64) to its 2010 estimates would require the immigration of more than 54 million people, or 11 percent of the predicted 2040 population. And this still would not compensate for the absolute increase in the number of people 65 and over. Nevertheless, given the potential for EU expansion beyond its current members along with the migration pressures emanating from North Africa and elsewhere, any assumption about the capacity of the EU to absorb migrants may turn out to be false.

The Commission of the European Union has begun to analyze trends and to recommend changes to pension and health care systems. Several countries have begun to experiment, for example linking pensions to changes in life expectancy, and to encourage workers to postpone retirement. Demographic changes are clearly visible and well understood; whether or not the EU and the national governments respond will depend on the flexibility and adaptability of their electorates.

Summary

- The twenty-seven-member European Union was created in several stages. The earliest stage involved agreements over open trade for coal and steel (ECSC), followed by cooperation over the peaceful development of nuclear energy (Euratom) and a free-trade agreement.

- The main institutions of the European Union are the European Commission, the Council, the Court of Justice, the Court of Auditors, and the European Parliament. The roles of these institutions have evolved.

- The Treaty of Rome was signed in 1957 and was put into effect in 1958, creating a six-country, free-trade area that was phased in gradually over the next ten years.

- The next wave of deepening was the creation of the European Monetary System in 1979, linking exchange rates.

- Following the EMS, the Single European Act was passed, creating a common market by 1993. While preparations were taking place for the implementation of the SEA, the Maastricht Treaty, or Treaty on European Union, was signed in 1991 and approved by the national governments in late 1993.

- The Maastricht Treaty created a common currency. In preparation, a set of convergence criteria was developed with targets for interest rates, inflation, government spending, and government debt.

- While the European Union was undergoing its several rounds of deepening integration, it was also widening membership to nearly all of western

Europe. Between 1958 and 1995, it expanded from the original six members to fifteen. In 2004 ten more countries joined, followed by two more in 2007.

- Eastward expansion of the European Union created problems in the areas of agricultural policy, governance, income differences, and migration.

Vocabulary

acquis communautaire

cohesion funds

Common Agricultural Policy (CAP)

competitive devaluation

convergence criteria

Council of the European Union

Delors Report

Erasmus Program

euro

European Atomic Energy Community (EAEC or Euratom)

European Central Bank

European Coal and Steel Community (ECSC)

European Commission

European Community (EC)

European Currency Unit (ECU)

European Economic Community (EEC)

European Monetary System (EMS)

European Parliament

European Union (EU)

exchange rate mechanism (ERM)

Maastricht Treaty

qualified majority

Single European Act (SEA)

subsidiarity

Treaty of Rome

Treaty of Lisbon

Treaty on European Union

Study Questions

1. What were the three main stages of deepening that occurred in the European Community after the Treaty of Rome was passed?

2. What are the five main institutions of the European Union, and what are their responsibilities?

3. The Single European Act is a case in which it was difficult to create an agreement, despite the fact that there was near unanimity in support of an agreement. If everyone wanted the agreement, why was it hard to negotiate?

4. How did the European Union expect to create gains from trade with the implementation of the Single European Act?

5. A sudden sharp increase in the demand for the German mark almost destroyed the Exchange Rate Mechanism in 1992. Explain how a rise in the demand for a currency can jeopardize a target zone or exchange rate band.

6. Discuss the pros and cons of the single currency.

7. What are the pressures on the European Union to admit new members?

8. What problems arose from the admission of twelve new members between 2004 and 2007?

9. How does the European Union compare and contrast to the NAFTA region in size, institutional structure, and depth of integration?

CHAPTER 15

Trade and Policy Reform in Latin America

Introduction: Defining a "Latin American" Economy

Latin America stretches from Tijuana on the U.S.-Mexico border to Cape Horn at the southern tip of South America. Within this vast geographic area lies such a diversity of languages and cultures that any definition of Latin America must have exceptions and contradictions. For example, *Merriam-Webster's Collegiate Dictionary* defines the region as Spanish America and Brazil, a standard view that must leave out a few small countries in Central and South America (Belize, Suriname, Guyana, and French Guiana) and the island nations of the Caribbean that were outside the region of Spanish and Portuguese settlement. *Webster's* second definition, "All of the Americas south of the United States," is more inclusive, but it is perhaps less important to give a precise definition than it is to recognize the variety of physical geography, cultures, and income levels that coexist within any definition. In fact, the variety is so great that it is worth asking whether these nations can truly constitute a single world region. In other words, what is the "Latin American" experience, and how does it allow us to group together nations as different as Argentina, with its European culture and relative prosperity, and Guatemala, with its indigenous culture and great poverty?

The diversity within Latin America should make us careful not to overgeneralize. Nevertheless, there are several common themes shared by all, or nearly all, the nations in the region. First, there are common historical threads, beginning with the fact that a great many nations share a heritage of Spanish and Portuguese colonization, and a common linguistic base. In some countries, however, the languages of indigenous people are important as well. A second part of their shared histories is that many Latin American countries gained their national independence from Spain and Portugal during the nationalist revolutions of the early and middle nineteenth century. This differentiates them from the colonial experiences of Africa and Asia, and implies that the national identities of Latin Americans are perhaps deeper than in many parts of the developing world.

During the twentieth century, Latin American nations had much in common. The Great Depression of the 1930s, for example, caused most nations to shift their policies away from an outward, export orientation toward an inward, targeted industrial strategy. The new strategy eventually developed its own theoreticians and came to be known as "import substitution industrialization." More recently, most nations were borrowers in the 1970s, and severely indebted in the 1980s. Finally, beginning in the

1980s and continuing through to the twenty-first century, the region began a wide-ranging set of economic policy reforms, similar in scope to the transformation of central and eastern Europe after the collapse of communism.

In this chapter, we examine the origins and extent of the economic crisis that hit Latin America in the 1980s and analyze the responses. Before we examine the crisis of the 1980s and the economic reforms of the late 1980s and 1990s, first we must step back and look at the long-run performance of the economies of Latin America. When seen in the light of history, we understand why the miserable economic growth record of the 1980s gave rise to a dramatic shift in policies.

Population, Income, and Economic Growth

Table 15.1 is a snapshot of the current levels of income and population. The nations of Latin America are home to more than 550 million, or 120 million more people than the three nations of NAFTA, and 62 million more than the twenty-seven nations of the European Union.

Table 15.1 shows the extent to which four countries account for the bulk of the population and production in Latin America. These are, in order by size of population: Brazil, Mexico, Colombia, and Argentina. Together they add up to about 67 percent of the population of Latin America and over 77 percent of the GDP.

For long stretches of the twentieth century, Latin America was one of the fastest-growing regions of the world. In particular, from 1900 to 1960 the region's real GDP per capita grew as fast or faster than that of Europe, the United States, or Asia. Individual experiences varied, but most countries saw adequate to excellent growth along with rising living standards. After World War II, most countries in Latin America experienced good rates of growth, as did most regions in the world, and the two largest countries, Brazil and Mexico, had remarkable increases in their per capita income levels. Circumstances began to change as world economic growth slowed after 1973 and Latin American experiences became more varied. Some countries grew faster in the 1970s and some grew slower, but nearly all relied more heavily on government expenditures to stimulate growth. The undoing of this period was the onset of the Latin American Debt Crisis, which began in 1982 and is described later in the chapter. The Debt Crisis turned the 1980s into a **Lost Decade**, as growth was negative, inflation skyrocketed, and poverty increased across most of the region—all at a time when several developing countries in East Asia were growing at unprecedented rates. In Latin America, the Debt Crisis brought an end to nearly fifty years of economic policy, as one country after another tried bold new experiments in search for a way to restore economic growth.

Import Substitution Industrialization

Economic policy reform in Latin America brought the demise of the economic development strategy known as **import substitution industrialization (ISI)**. Every Latin American country—and many developing countries outside the region—

TABLE 15.1	Population and GDP for Latin America and the Caribbean, 2007			
	Population (Millions)	GDP (US$, Bil.)	GDP per Capita (US$)	GDP per Capita (US$, PPP)
Andean Community				
Bolivia	9.5	13.1	1,379	4,206
Colombia	44.0	207.8	4,724	8,587
Ecuador	13.3	44.5	3,335	7,449
Peru	27.9	107.3	3,846	7,836
Central American Common Market				
Costa Rica	4.5	26.3	5,887	10,842
El Salvador	6.9	20.4	2,973	5,804
Guatemala	13.3	33.9	2,536	4,562
Honduras	7.1	12.2	1,722	3,796
Nicaragua	5.6	5.7	1,022	2,570
MERCOSUR				
Argentina	39.5	262.5	6,644	13,238
Brazil	191.6	1,313.4	6,855	9,567
Paraguay	6.1	12.2	1,997	4,433
Uruguay	3.3	23.1	6,960	11,216
Other Countries				
Chile	16.6	163.9	9,878	13,880
Dominican Republic	9.7	36.7	3,772	6,706
Haiti	9.6	6.7	699	1,155
Mexico	105.3	1,022.8	9,715	14,104
Panama	3.3	19.5	5,833	11,391
Venezuela, RB	27.5	228.1	8,299	12,156
Latin America and Caribbean	560.6	3,615.9	6,450	9,970

Source: World Bank, *World Development Indicators.*

had used the ISI strategy since at least the 1950s, when it became the consensus theory of economic development. In Latin America, ISI policies were brought to an end by their inability to resolve the crisis of the 1980s, together with the growing perception that they were creating long-term economic inefficiencies. Because these policies were so central, and because they illustrate an attempt to foster economic development through an inward orientation, they are worth learning about in greater detail.

Origins and Goals of ISI

From the second half of the nineteenth century until the middle of the twentieth century, most of Latin America relied on exports of agricultural commodities (tropical fruits, coffee, cotton, and grains) and minerals (petroleum, copper, and tin) to earn foreign revenue. These export sectors were often developed or controlled by foreign capital and had few economic linkages to the domestic economy, functioning instead as foreign enclaves within the nation. In cases where the export sector was domestically owned, it usually brought wealth to a relatively small number of people and added greatly to the inequality of power and money that is pervasive in Latin American society.

World War I and the Great Depression of the 1930s disrupted the flow of Latin American exports and severely reduced export earnings. World War II partially reversed this trend, as many countries turned to Latin America for the minerals and foodstuffs they could no longer make at home due to the war, but at war's end there was another drop in demand for Latin America's commodities. In the late 1940s, a young Argentine economist, Raul Prebisch, and a German exile, Hans Singer, developed a theory to explain the loss of foreign exchange earnings. In their view, the fall in demand for Latin American commodities was not solely due to the end of the war, but was also a long-run tendency for the prices of primary commodities to fall. Singer and Prebisch argued that coffee, tin, copper, bananas, and other primary commodity exports would inevitably experience price declines relative to the prices paid for manufactured goods.

In trade analysis, the ratio of average export prices to average import prices is called the **terms of trade (TOT)**:

$$\text{TOT} = (\text{Index of export prices})/(\text{Index of import prices})$$

Latin America exported raw materials and imported finished goods, so the Prebisch-Singer prediction was that the terms of trade for the region would decline. For obvious reasons, this view was given the label **export pessimism**.

The reasoning behind export pessimism included both statistical studies and economic theory. Statistical analysis showed raw material prices falling over periods as long as several decades. More recent analysis shows that while prices may fall for extended periods of time, there is no long-run trend up or down. Economic theory holds that as incomes rise, people spend a smaller share of their overall income on foodstuffs and other raw-material-based goods such as textiles and apparel, and they spend more on manufactured items. Consequently, the demand for raw materials declines in relation to the demand for manufactured goods. Note, however, that this effect does not necessarily lead to a decline in the terms of trade for raw material producers. In particular, productivity increases in manufacturing can overwhelm increases in demand and push down the real prices of manufactured goods.

Latin America

Export pessimism formed the basis of orthodox economic policy from roughly the 1950s through the 1970s. As the head of the United Nations' **Economic Commission on Latin America** (**ECLA** in English; **CEPAL** in Spanish), Prebisch guided economic policies throughout Latin America and reinforced a shift that had begun with the destruction of trade in the 1930s. The loss of markets during the Great Depression temporarily forced Latin America away from dependence on raw material exports and toward industrial development through the replacement of imported manufactured goods with domestically produced ones—hence the name "import substitution industrialization." Ironically, domestic production of manufactured import substitutes required the importation of large quantities of capital goods (machinery and parts), and in order to earn the revenues needed to buy these imports, most nations continued to depend on raw material exports in the decades after World War II. Primary commodities still make up a significant share of today's exports from Latin America.

ISI is a form of industrial policy that focuses on those industries that produce substitutes for imported goods. According to Prebisch and Singer, the inevitable decline in the terms of trade for primary commodities means that the biggest constraint on industrial development is the shortage of foreign exchange. Lower export prices mean that countries find it harder and harder to earn the foreign exchange they need in order to buy the machinery and other capital goods they cannot produce themselves. One of the most important roles of import substitution is to reduce the need for foreign exchange that is used to buy goods that could be made at home.

ISI theorists argued that a country should begin by producing inexpensive and relatively simple consumer items, such as toys, clothing, food products (e.g., beverages and canned goods), and furniture. Gradually, the focus of industrial targeting should move on to more complex consumer goods (e.g., appliances and autos) and intermediate industrial goods (e.g., pumps, generators, basic metals). In the third stage, complex industrial goods would be produced (e.g., chemicals, electronic equipment, machine tools).

Criticisms of ISI

The economic tools for implementing ISI are the same as those for industrial policies discussed in Chapter 5. These include a variety of different types of government support, from subsidies of all kinds to trade protection and monopoly power in the domestic market. In retrospect, import substitution industrialization generated a number of unintended consequences that caused inefficiencies and wasted resources. Among the many criticisms that have been leveled at ISI are the following: (1) governments misallocated resources when they became too involved in production decisions; (2) exchange rates were often overvalued; (3) policy was overly biased in favor of urban areas; (4) income inequality worsened; and (5) ISI fostered widespread rent seeking.

Foremost among the problems of ISI are those related to an overconfident and naive belief in the ability of the state to direct resources efficiently into their best uses. In the 1950s and 1960s, it was often assumed that **market failures** were far more common in developing nations than in industrial ones, and that one of the main goals of any state should be to correct these through selective and careful state intervention in the economy. In this context, ISI can be interpreted as a set of policies in which government uses its economic and political power to improve on the market. Recall from Chapter 5 how difficult it is to measure market failures and to know the required corrective action.

This model is not totally wrong, but it overestimates the technical ability of government officials to identify market failures and their solutions. It also assumes that government bureaucrats are selfless individuals who ignore political considerations and focus only on economic efficiency and what is best for the nation as a whole. This naive model of political reality caused an underemphasis on problems related to the implementation of economic policies, such as corruption and the lobbying power of economic elites. It also failed to take into account the slow accumulation of special provisions, favors, and economic inefficiencies that built up over time when policies were heavily influenced by politics. Naturally, this problem was magnified by the inequality in wealth and income throughout Latin America. Powerful interest groups were able to use ISI policies to their own benefit, rather than in the national interest.

A second problem of ISI was the development and persistence of overvalued exchange rates. Overvaluation was a deliberate policy in some countries, while in others it was a chronic problem stemming from the maintenance of a fixed exchange rate under conditions of higher inflation than among the countries' trading partners. As a deliberate policy, overvaluation of the exchange rate accomplished several goals. In particular, it made it easier for the targeted industries to obtain the imported capital goods they needed. It also helped to maintain political alliances between the urban working classes and the political parties in power. It did this by providing access to relatively less expensive foreign goods, which kept living standards higher than they would have been otherwise. As evidence of this point, when governments were forced to depreciate in the 1980s and 1990s, they often lost the political support of the urban classes.

Although overvalued exchange rates had some benefits, they also had costs. Most importantly, they made it difficult to export because they raised the foreign price of domestic goods. This hurt the agricultural and traditional export sectors because it made exports less profitable. In turn, capital was directed away from agriculture, causing productivity and income in rural areas to remain low and stagnant.

Overvalued exchange rates also stung the parts of industry that did not produce substitutes for imports because it was less profitable to export. In addition, the overvalued exchange rate made foreign machinery less expensive and caused industrial investment to be too capital intensive and insufficiently labor intensive. Consequently, industry did not create enough new jobs to absorb the growing labor force and the labor that left agriculture for the cities. Furthermore, since most industry is located in urban areas, government investment in infrastructure improvements—such as transportation, communication, and water—were heavily targeted toward cities and their environs. As a result, subsistence farmers and their families did not benefit from, or contribute to, national economic development, and Latin America continued to have the highest levels of inequality of any region in the world.

In addition to a persistent tendency toward overvalued exchange rates, ISI trade and competition policies were heavily protectionist and often favored the creation of domestic monopolies. The lack of foreign and domestic competition meant that manufacturing remained inefficient, uncompetitive, and inwardly focused. With profits from a protected domestic market, many producers saw no reason to invest in modern equipment, further reinforcing the uncompetitiveness of their products. It is ironic that as a consequence of ISI many countries became more vulnerable to economic shocks that originated outside of Latin America, which was precisely the opposite effect from the one that motivated ISI in the first place.

A final problem of ISI is the development of widespread rent-seeking behavior. When governments intervene in the planning and directing of industrial development, they give government officials and bureaucrats a wide range of valuable commodities to distribute. These include the many subsidies and licenses that are a part of ISI policies. For example, in order to protect the domestic market and to ensure access to needed imports, governments often required import licenses and at the same time provided foreign exchange at subsidized prices to the importer. When government policy creates something of value, such as the license to import or a subsidy to buy foreign exchange, the private sector will spend resources to obtain it. In the absence of strong institutions to ensure the independence of the bureaucracy—and, often, even when they are present—bribes and corruption become a part of the decision making. Ultimately, some decisions are made for the wrong reasons, and economic waste is the result.

CASE STUDY

ISI in Mexico

The Mexican constitution of 1917 established the power and the responsibility of the federal government to intervene in the economy in order to act as the leading agent of economic growth and as the referee of social conflict. This role was not institutionalized inside the Mexican government until the Mexican revolution was consolidated in the 1930s under the presidency of Lázaro Cárdenas, whose son was a leading opponent of the dismantling of ISI during the reforms of the 1980s and 1990s.

In order to lead and direct economic growth, government could legitimately claim the need to be powerful—otherwise, powerful social classes could resist the government's directives and initiatives, particularly those with distributional goals or consequences. Therefore, economic policy served not only to meet the needs of the country for economic growth and a fairer distribution, but also to increase the political power of government. Mexico nationalized its oil industries in 1938, and throughout the twentieth century a number of sectors were nationalized and turned into state-run monopolies (telephones, airlines, banks, railroads, and mineral development companies). The use of the government budget in this manner guaranteed access to investment funds, while monopoly markets ensured that the favored firms would succeed, at least within the nation.

The government also offered loans and loan guarantees to many firms in targeted industries. Loans and loan guarantees helped firms obtain capital at interest rates that were below what they would have normally paid. Similarly, the government sold foreign exchange at artificially low prices to targeted firms who needed to buy imports. Mexican exporters were required to convert their foreign exchange earnings into pesos at an overvalued peso rate—too few pesos per dollar—which made exporting relatively less profitable; the government then sold the cheaply acquired foreign exchange to targeted industries. In effect, exporters were subsidizing the development of the targeted industries.

Unlike many ISI nations, Mexico limited foreign investment. Like most ISI nations, however, when investment was permitted (e.g., autos), performance requirements were placed on the foreign firms. A common requirement was that the foreign firm balance its foreign exchange requirements so that each peso of imports was matched by a peso of export earnings. Further interventions occurred in the area of commercial policy where import licenses limited many types of imports. Recall that import licenses are essentially quotas. By the 1970s about 60 percent of all imports were subject to licensing.

From 1950 to 1973, Mexico's real GDP per capita grew at the rate of 3.1 percent per year. By comparison, the United States grew 2.2 percent per year, the fourteen largest Organisation for Economic Co-Operation and Development (OECD) nations grew 3.5 percent per year, and growth in the six largest Latin American economies was 2.5 percent. At the same time that the economy was undergoing relatively rapid economic growth, industrialization was changing the structure of the economy. Mexico's manufacturing sector expanded from 21.5 percent of GDP to 29.4 percent. Growth began to slow in the 1970s, as it did in many parts of the world.

One widely shared view is that Mexico's growth began to stall because the country was running out of easy targets for industrial development. Light manufacturing and simple consumer goods industries are relatively easy to start up, and the conversion of a part of the nation's economy from subsistence agriculture to simple manufacturing makes growth rates look good. The next stages require more sophisticated manufacturing, however, and are relatively harder to start up. According to this view, Mexico had run out of simple industries to start and was inevitably having a harder time producing more sophisticated goods that were further from its comparative advantage.

In spite of rapid economic growth during the 1950s and 1960s, poverty and income inequality continued. Large numbers of Mexicans, many of them indigenous people living in rural areas, did not participate in the growth of the economy. This is evidenced by the fact that in the 1980s much of the agricultural industry was still at a subsistence level, using 26 percent of the nation's labor force to produce just 9 percent of the nation's GDP. The urban bias in Mexico's development strategy turned Mexico City into one of the largest metropolises in the world, with more than fifteen million people in the greater metropolitan area by the late 1980s. The sensational growth and crowding of people and industry into the basin that holds Mexico City resulted in serious pollution problems.

There is no consensus among economists as to the role played by ISI in Mexico's debt crisis of the 1980s. Certainly, ISI policies expanded the role of the federal government in economic activity and increased government expenditures and borrowing during the 1970s. Nevertheless, overall economic growth remained fairly robust until the mid-1970s. One widespread view is that the easy gains of ISI were gone by the 1970s, and in order to keep growth on track, Mexican presidents used their power over public finances to increase expenditures dramatically. At first the government argued that it could easily afford to borrow in foreign capital markets because the nation had recently, in 1978, become a major oil exporter. Ultimately, the government's fiscal policies generated enormous public sector deficits, fears of devaluation, and capital flight. By 1982, a year after the price of oil fell, the nation had run out of international reserves and could no longer service its international debt. If the government had not resorted to unsustainable macroeconomic policies, would it have fallen into the debt crisis and rejected ISI policies in the mid-1980s?

Macroeconomic Instability and Economic Populism

Many economists are convinced that while ISI policies are suboptimal, they had less of a direct effect in creating the economic crisis of the 1980s than did misguided macroeconomic policies. The reasons are relatively straightforward. ISI policies involve trade barriers and government support for selected industries. Collectively, these policies may lower a nation's income by a few percentage points, but they rarely lead to a full-blown economic crisis. Faulty macroeconomic policies, on the other hand, often lead to hyperinflation, depression, and balance of payments crises. In addition, while most of Latin America used ISI policies from the 1950s through the 1980s, economic growth remained at fairly high levels for most countries until the early 1980s when growth turned negative in nearly all countries. While it is possible that the 1980s crisis was the culmination of several decades of ISI policies, it is certain that the crisis was directly linked to the faulty macroeconomic policies of the late 1970s and early 1980s.

Populism in Latin America

Many Latin America specialists blame the faulty macroeconomic policies of the region on populist or economic populist political movements that use economic tools to reach specific goals, such as obtaining support from labor and domestically oriented business, or isolating rural elites and foreign interests. Examples of populist leaders abound: in Argentina, Juan Perón (1946–1955 and 1973–1976) and Raúl Alfonsín (early 1980s); in Brazil, Getúlio Vargas (1951–1954), João Goulart (1961–1964), and José Sarney (1985–1990); in Chile, Carlos Ibáñez (1952–1958) and Salvador Allende (1970–1973); in Peru, Fernando Belaúnde Terry (1963–1968), Juan Velasco Alvarado (1968–1975), and Alan García (1985–1990); in Mexico, Luis Echeverría (1970–1976) and José Lopez Portillo (1976–1982); in Venezuela, Hugo Chavez (1998–). Populist movements in Latin America share nationalistic ideologies and a focus on economic growth and income redistribution. The central economic problem generated by these movements is the use of expansionary fiscal and monetary policies without regard for the importance of inflation risks, budget deficits, and foreign exchange constraints.

Economic populism is usually triggered by three initial conditions. First, there is a deep dissatisfaction with the status quo, usually as a result of slow growth or recession. Second, policymakers reject the traditional constraints on macro policy. Budget deficits financed through printing money are justified by the existence of high unemployment and idle factories, which offer room for expansion without inflation. Third, policymakers promise to raise wages while freezing prices and to restructure the economy by expanding the domestic production of imported goods, thereby lessening the need for foreign exchange. In the words of one analyst, the policies call for "reactivating, redistributing, and restructuring" the economy.

Early in the populist regime, there is a vindication of the policies. The economic stimulus of government expenditures and newly created money leads to rising growth rates and rising wages. Soon, however, bottlenecks begin to set in. For example, construction firms run out of particular inputs, such as cement or specialized steel products, and manufacturing firms cannot find the parts they need to repair their machinery. Prices begin to rise, and the budget deficit grows. In the next stage, inflation begins an extreme acceleration, and shortages become pervasive throughout the economy. The budget falls into serious deficit as policies become unsustainable, and wage increases cease keeping up with inflation. In the final stage, countries experience massive capital flight as fears of a devaluation develop. The flight of capital out of the country depresses investment and further depresses real wages.

In the end, real wages are often lower than before the cycle began, and there is an international intervention under the sponsorship of the IMF, which is designed to stop the high inflation and end a balance of payments crisis. Typically, the IMF oversees the implementation of stabilization and structural reform policies that call for serious budget cuts, a slowdown in the growth of the money supply, a reduction in trade barriers, and in general, greater reliance on market mechanisms and less government intervention. While these stages of the populist cycle are an idealization, they capture the essence of the populist experience as it has occurred in many Latin nations.

The Debt Crisis of the 1980s

In August of 1982 Mexico announced that it lacked the international reserves it needed to pay the interest and principal due on its foreign debt. Mexico was not the first country to declare its inability to service its debt, but it was the biggest up to that point. Its announcement soon led to the realization that a number of other countries, including most of Latin America, were in similar circumstances. Thus began the Lost Decade.

Proximate Causes of the Debt Crisis

In Mexico's case, the collapse of oil prices in 1981 undermined its ability to earn the revenue it needed to service its debt. The problem was compounded by the fact that a significant portion of its debt was owed in dollars at variable interest rates and that efforts to combat inflation in the United States and elsewhere had resulted in a higher level of world interest rates. Consequently, interest payments on Mexico's debt rose at the same time that the nation's ability to earn dollars shrank.

The collapse of oil prices in 1981 and the rise in world interest rates were not the only external shocks to the economies of Latin America. In 1981–1982, the world's industrial economies entered a deep recession that reduced world demand and prices for many of the raw materials produced in Latin America and elsewhere. In Mexico's case, oil was the critical commodity, but a number of other primary commodity exports experienced a similar decline in their world price.

The price decline for Latin America's exports and the rise in interest rates were significant parts of the mix of events that led up to the debt crisis. These external economic shocks probably would not have caused a generalized debt crisis without some additional factors, however. Historically, debt crises not only require a set of external shocks to the indebted countries but also an acceleration of international lending, which occurred between 1974–1982. Added to these two factors was the complicating problem of mismanagement of national macroeconomic policies in the late 1970s and early 1980s.

During the 1970s, financial institutions throughout the developed world were awash in money that they were anxious to lend. The rise in oil prices in 1973 and 1974, and again in 1979, led to an enormous expansion of bank deposits by the oil-rich nations of the world. Banks in New York, London, Paris, and Frankfurt were anxious to lend these deposits and aggressively sought new borrowers beginning in 1974. For Latin America and the Caribbean, long-term, publicly guaranteed debt rose from slightly over $37 billion in 1973 to more than $261 billion in 1983. The sudden acceleration in commercial bank lending and the rise in the amount of debt made the economies vulnerable to a sudden and unforeseen economic shock.

Table 15.2 shows the size of the debt for some of the most heavily indebted countries after the first year of the crisis. The second column of numbers expresses the debt in net terms (gross debt minus debt owed by foreigners) as a percentage of GDP. The third column shows the net interest payments owed as a percentage of exports of goods and services. This is a useful indicator because nations ultimately have to pay the interest on their international debts out of the

TABLE 15.2	Debt Indicators at the Onset of the Debt Crisis, 1983		
Country	Gross External Debt (Millions of US$)	Net External Debt as a Percentage of GDP	Net Interest Payments as a Percentage of Exports
Argentina	43,634	75.3	62.8
Bolivia	3,328	141.9	38.5
Brazil	92,961	48.3	38.7
Chile	17,315	87.6	32.9
Colombia	10,306	25.1	18.8
Costa Rica	3,646	137.8	45.4
Mexico	86,081	63.8	32.1
Peru	10,712	52.4	20.1
Venezuela	32,158	38.8	9.6

A large percentage of the exports of indebted countries went to pay interest on their debts.

Source: Cline, William, *International Debt Reexamined,* 1995; World Bank, *World Debt Tables,* 1987.

revenues they earn from their exports. What we see is that between 10 and 63 percent of the revenue earned by exports went to pay interest and, consequently, was unavailable for purchasing imports or for investing domestically.

Responses to the Debt Crisis

Initially, most analysts in the United States and in the international financial institutions such as the IMF perceived the debt crisis to be a temporary, short-run liquidity problem. Under this assumption, the reasonable response is to increase capital flows to Latin America and other indebted regions so that they would have the financial resources to service their debts. If additional capital flows can stimulate higher rates of economic growth, then it is a reasonable policy because an adequate growth rate would allow the countries to outgrow their debt.

From the standpoint of U.S. policy, the key to growth was viewed as increased investment, which was only possible if capital flows into the region were restored. The first policy proposal along these lines was that of U.S. Treasury Secretary James Baker in 1985. The **Baker Plan** tried to organize a renewed lending program by commercial banks. The problem was that most banks that had Latin American loans in their portfolios were trying to reduce their exposure to the region, not increase it. Consequently, few resources were forthcoming under this plan.

Without capital flows from developed country banks, the choices were not attractive. Outright default and disavowal of the debt would cut off most of a nation's trade and investment linkages. The consequences for investment and growth would be risky and potentially disastrous, depending on the reaction of the United States and other governments. On the other hand, if they continued to make interest payments, and potentially principal repayment, it would require huge trade surpluses in order to earn the revenue they needed to pay for imports plus interest on the debt.

Interest payment on the debt owed to foreigners enters the current account as a debit in the category of income paid abroad, as discussed in Chapter 9. Consequently, interest payments severely increased the current account deficits of many countries. Recall the fundamental accounting balance of an open economy,

$$S_p + T - G = I + CA,$$

where S_p is private savings, $T - G$ is government (public) savings, I is investment, and CA is the current account balance. Without financial capital inflows to finance their current account deficits, countries must eliminate the deficit through a combination of increased exports and reduced imports. The policies that accomplish this are expenditure-switching and expenditure-reducing policies. Recall from Chapter 11 that expenditure-switching policies such as devaluations of the currency turn the demand for foreign goods into a demand for domestic goods and raise CA directly. Expenditure-reducing policies, such as tax increases and cuts in government spending, raise $T - G$ and, indirectly, reduce consumption, investment, and imports. The net effect of expenditure-reducing policies is often a recession in which the demand for domestic and imported goods falls due to a fall in domestic income.

In other words, in order to accumulate the resources they needed for their interest payments, governments were forced to follow contractionary policies that caused deep recessions throughout the region. Between 1982 and 1986, the average rate of growth of real per capita GDP was –1.8 percent per year in Latin America and the Caribbean.

By 1987 it was apparent to analysts throughout the world that restoring capital flows was not enough. There was a need for deep reform in the economies of Latin America. First, it was observed that the faulty macroeconomic policies of the region consistently left aggregate national expenditure above national income and that the likelihood of a return to growth was small as long as the gap between the two remained. Second, in their attempt to keep government expenditures higher than warranted, many countries had resorted to printing money, which resulted in high and increasing rates of inflation. Third, the burden of the debt itself was becoming apparent to everyone inside and outside Latin America. After the interest and principal payments were made, insufficient export earnings remained for domestic investment and consumption, and growth was stunted. By 1988–1989, both creditors and the multilateral lending agencies such as the IMF were in agreement that debt relief was in everyone's interest.

The growing consensus on the need for debt relief led to the **Brady Plan** in 1989, named after the secretary of the treasury during the Bush administration, Nicholas Brady. Essentially, the Brady Plan gave something to everyone. Creditors were expected to restructure some of the old debt into longer-term debt with a lower interest rate and to make some additional new loans. The multilateral lending agencies, such as the IMF, were expected to provide additional loans on concessional terms, that is, below market interest rates, and borrowers were required to provide evidence of their willingness to begin serious economic reform before any new loans would be forthcoming. The Brady Plan did not end the debt crisis, but it was a significant step toward greater stability in the region. Countries that renegotiated their debt with the Brady Plan package were perceived to have greater credibility and sounder finances by the international financial community. Consequently, after 1989 capital flows began to return to Latin America but this time not in the form of bank loans. Rather, savers and investors in the United States, Europe, and Asia began to increase their direct investment in Latin America, as well as their holdings of various financial assets, such as stocks and bonds issued by private companies doing business there. While large inflows of capital can present problems, particularly if they reverse and flow out, they are the additional savings and investment that are needed if the region is to return to its historical levels of growth. To a large degree, the new capital that has been flowing into the region since 1989 is a vote of confidence by investors around the world.

From the vantage point of the first decade of the twenty-first century, the most lasting effects of the debt crisis—other than the forgone output due to the recessions of the 1980s—are the deep economic reforms that have taken place in country after country. These reforms are key to explaining the return of capital flows to Latin America. Reforms vary by country, both in kind and degree, but they mark a historical shift away from the protectionist and interventionist policies of ISI and economic populism and toward more open and market-oriented policies.

Economic Policy Reform and the "Washington Consensus"

By the late 1980s most countries in Latin America had started a series of economic policy reforms that began to alter the fundamental relationships between business and government and between their national economy and the world. After 1989 the reforms intensified and became more general. In most cases, the reforms consisted of three separate but interrelated features. First, and with varying degrees of success, governments implemented stabilization plans to stop inflation and to control their budget deficits. Second, most countries began privatizing the government-owned parts of their economies, such as manufacturing enterprises, financial and other services, mining operations, tourism, and utility companies. Third, trade policies became more open and less discriminatory against exports.

Throughout Latin America, this package of reforms has come to be known as the **"neoliberal model"** or neoliberalism, because it represents a partial return to classic nineteenth-century European liberalism that favored free markets and minimal government intervention in the economy. By 1992 growth had returned to most countries.

In spite of the benefits of policy reform, however, many problems persist. Poverty and inequality continued to increase in many countries, since growth did not filter down into all sectors. The problem of poverty was compounded by the lack of adequate infrastructure, which made it harder for all segments of society to benefit from economic growth. The absence of schools, health clinics, roads, clean water, and other infrastructure elements, particularly in rural areas where poverty is greatest, limits the reach of restored economic growth.

Stabilization Policies to Control Inflation

Many countries sought to avoid the recessionary consequences of the onset of the debt crisis by increasing government spending. The only way to finance government spending, however, was through the printing of more money, because tax systems were inadequate and government borrowing abilities were limited by the debt crisis. The reckless printing of money to finance government spending drove a number of nations into periods of hyperinflation, as detailed in Table 15.3.

The solution to the hyperinflation experienced by Argentina, Bolivia, Brazil, and Peru is simple to prescribe: Cut government spending and stop printing money. The implementation of this prescription was difficult, however. In the short run, if price increases outstrip wage increases, as is often the case in a period of disinflation, then the burden of bringing down the rate of inflation falls mainly on wage earners who experience a fall in their real wages. Consequently, anti-inflation policies create economic hardship and alienate the political support of many wage earners, making governments unpopular with a large share of the population.

TABLE 15.3   Inflation Rates, 1982–1992

Country	Inflation (in Percents)		
	Average 1982–1987	Average 1987–1992	Highest 1982–1992
Argentina	316	447	4924 (1989)
Bolivia	776	16	8170 (1985)
Brazil	158	851	1862 (1989)
Chile	21	19	27 (1990)
Colombia	21	27	32 (1990)
Mexico	73	48	159 (1987)
Peru	103	733	7650 (1990)
Venezuela	10	40	81 (1989)

High rates of inflation were a common problem of the 1980s.

Source: Edwards, Sebastian, *Crisis and Reform in Latin America*, 1995.

A further complication was the lack of agreement over the causes of inflation. Some argued that it was caused by inertia since everyone expected future inflation to be high. This caused producers to raise prices in anticipation of higher future input costs. The problem of inflation developing a momentum of its own, and a lack of empirical information about the depth of this problem, led to two different policy prescriptions for controlling inflation: the orthodox model and the heterodox model.

The **orthodox model** minimizes government involvement in the economy. Consequently, its anti-inflation prescription is straightforward—cut government spending, reform the tax system to increase compliance and revenues, and limit the creation of new money. The heterodox model calls for the same actions plus the freezing of wages and prices. In the **heterodox model**, inflationary expectations are so embedded in economic decision making that price increases will continue even if government spending and new money creation cease. In practice, heterodox plans often ignored the budget deficits that were part of the problem.

Between 1986 and 1992, Brazil implemented five separate heterodox stabilization plans to end inflation, and not one of them worked. Similarly, heterodox plans in Argentina and Peru in 1985 succeeded for approximately a year but then failed as inflation returned with a vengeance. Nevertheless, Brazil and Mexico each ultimately controlled inflation using heterodox methods.

An issue that continued to plague many nations was the problem of inconsistency between inflation stabilization and exchange rate policy. Mexico's experience is a good example of the problem and stems from the fact that the exchange rate is a powerful weapon in the fight against inflation. Mexico fixed its peso to the dollar in the mid-1980s as part of its anti-inflation strategy. Argentina and Brazil did the same under their stabilization plans of 1991 and 1994, respectively. Domestic producers that compete with U.S. goods were forced to avoid price increases so they would remain competitive. Furthermore, prices did not increase on imports of U.S.-made capital goods, which were essential to Mexican industry, thereby helping to hold down Mexican prices for finished manufactured goods. Since Mexico's inflation was still slightly higher than U.S. inflation, the peso became overvalued over a period of time. Ultimately, this contributed to a serious trade imbalance and the collapse of the peso in December 1994, followed by a deep recession in 1995. Since 1994, Mexico has let the peso float against the dollar and has stopped trying to use the exchange rate as an anchor against the current of inflation. Argentina's struggle to control inflation and its use of the exchange rate is discussed in the Case Study in Chapter 11.

Structural Reform and Open Trade

Stabilization policies to control inflation and curtail large budget deficits are usually one part of a package that also includes **structural reform policies**. One way to keep the two types of policies separate is to recognize that stabilization generally focuses on macroeconomic policies, for example, inflation and government budgets, while structural reform tends to be more microeconomic, dealing with issues of resource allocation. Structural reform policies include the privatization of government-owned enterprises, deregulation and redesign of the regulatory environment of overregulated industries such as financial services, and the reform of trade policy.

The many initiatives to privatize and reform the regulatory environments of the economies of Latin America are quite remarkable, but this section will focus on the most impressive area of structural reform to date: the economic integration of the region with the world economy. Prior to the onset of the debt crisis, the economies of Latin America had the most restricted trade systems of all the nations in the noncommunist world. In many countries, the debt crisis reinforced the belief that isolation from the world economy was the only way to protect a nation from shocks that originated in the external environment.

In the 1970s, Chile broke with this tradition and began to reform its trade policies. Mexico and Bolivia followed in 1985 and 1986, and by 1987–1988, it was apparent throughout Latin America that trade had to be more open if economic growth was to be restored. In the late 1980s and early 1990s, nearly all the countries of Latin America began reducing both the level of tariffs and nontariff barriers (NTBs) and the variability of tariff rates across industries and goods. Table 15.4 shows the changes in tariffs that occurred between the mid-1980s, when the reforms began, and the early 1990s. As large as the tariff reductions were, the effect of the elimination of nontariff barriers such as quotas and import licensing requirements was even more dramatic, as many countries eliminated all or nearly all these barriers. By the early 1990s, most of the tariff and nontariff changes had been implemented, and countries began to turn to alternative forms of market opening.

The three main goals of trade reform were to reduce the anti-export bias of trade policies that favored production for domestic markets over production for foreign markets, to raise the growth rate of productivity, and to make consumers better off by lowering the real cost of traded goods. In response to the changes in

TABLE 15.4	**Average Tariff Rates, in Percents, Selected Countries**	
	1985	2007
Argentina	28	12
Brazil	80	12
Chile	36	6
Colombia	83	12
Mexico	34	13
Peru	64	10
Venezuela	30	13

Latin American countries have dramatically reduced their trade barriers, including tariff rates. Most of the opening occurred between 1985 and 1995.

Source: Inter-American Development Bank; World Trade Organization.

TABLE 15.5	Openness Indexes, 1985 and 2007		
	1985	2005–07	% Change
Argentina	18	45	148.9
Brazil	19	26	35.8
Chile	54	76	41.1
Colombia	26	42	60.4
Mexico	26	65	148.1
Peru	39	48	22.1
Venezuela	42	56	34.3

Openness indexes increased significantly with the change in policies.

Source: World Bank, *World Development Indicators;* World Trade Organization.

trade policy, the growth rate of exports picked up in most countries, while nontraditional exports increased dramatically. Furthermore, productivity rose in a majority of countries for which there is data. The productivity increase is at least partly the result of trade opening due to the impact of technology transfers, the improved investment climate, and the pressures on local firms to remain competitive.

Table 15.5 shows the openness indexes for seven countries. Since 1985, the average percentage change in openness was 70 percent for the countries listed. The pattern of openness conforms to the usual one, in which trade has a greater weight in the GDP of smaller countries than it does in larger ones, but the pattern of increase across nearly all countries, both big and small, is remarkable. Table 15.5 does not distinguish between intraregional trade that occurs within the framework of a regional trade agreement and interregional trade with nonmembers. Regardless, there were significant increases in the relative importance of trade to Latin American economies.

CASE STUDY

Regional Trade Blocs in Latin America

Latin America has more regional trade agreements than any other world region, and it has some of the oldest agreements as well. The first wave of agreements were signed in the 1960s as Prebisch and others began to recognize that ISI strategies eliminated the possibility for economies of scale and productivity increases that come with it. As long as production was limited to the home market, firms in many sectors would not be large enough to invest in research and development and to compete internationally. The solution was to encourage

Latin America: Trade Blocs

Map by Dr. Chris Lukinbeal
Revised by Harry D. Johnson

Robinson Projection

regional trade agreements such as the Central American Common Market (1961), the Caribbean Free Trade Association (1966, now called the Caribbean Community and Common Market) and the Andean Pact (1969, now called the Andean Community). The goals of these agreements are shown in Table 15.6. While the agreements conferred commercial advantages on firms located in member countries, they did not significantly alter trade patterns nor did they increase the flow of trade within the regions. Countries resisted pressures to lower their tariffs and momentum toward freer trade within trade blocs quickly dissipated. By the 1980s, the agreements were on paper only and were having scant effects on member countries.

With the onset of trade reforms in the mid-to-late 1980s, regional trade agreements once again became popular. Mexico took the lead with its announcement in 1989 that it was pursuing a free-trade agreement with the United States. In addition to economies of scale, trade agreements seemed to hold the promise of attracting foreign investment as well as increasing market access and possibly diversifying trade partners. Two years after the North American Free Trade Agreement (NAFTA) negotiations began, Brazil, Argentina, Paraguay, and Uruguay signed the Treaty of Asunción, establishing the Common Market of the South, or MERCOSUR. While MERCOSUR was in its infancy, Mexico, Canada, and the United States signed NAFTA (1994) and the Andean Pact was reborn as the Andean Community (1996).

The NAFTA agreement between Canada, Mexico, and the United States was implemented on January 1, 1994, and in December of the same year, leaders from thirty-four countries in the Western Hemisphere committed to a **Free Trade Area of the Americas (FTAA)** no later than 2005. By 2002, the FTAA idea was nearly dead, but Latin American countries have continued to sign bilateral and plurilateral agreements. In addition to the four customs unions listed in Table 15.6, the Organization of American States (OAS) reports that Latin American countries have signed forty-two free-trade agreements and thirty-four partial trade agreements, both inside and outside Latin America. A complete list is available through the OAS's Foreign Trade Information System, http://www.sice.org.

TABLE 15.6	Regional Trade Blocs		
	Year	Members	Goals
Andean Community	1969	Bolivia, Colombia, Ecuador, Peru	Customs union
Caribbean Community (CARICOM)	1973	Antigua and Barbuda, the Bahamas, Barbados, Belize, Dominica, Grenada, Guyana, Haiti, Jamaica, Montserrat, St. Kitts and Nevis, Saint Lucia, St. Vincent and the Grenadines, Suriname, Trinidad and Tobago	Customs union
Central American Common Market	1961	Costa Rica, El Salvador, Guatemala, Honduras, Nicaragua	Customs union
Dominican Republic-Central America Free Trade Agreement (DR-CAFTA)	2005	Costa Rica, Dominican Republic, El Salvador, Guatemala, Honduras, Nicaragua, United States	Free-trade area
MERCOSUR	1991	Argentina, Brazil, Paraguay, Uruguay, Venezuela	Customs union
NAFTA	1994	Canada, Mexico, United States	Free-trade area

The Washington Consensus

The term **Washington Consensus** was coined by the economist John Williamson as shorthand for a set of economic policies that constitute a broad consensus among conservative and liberal economists. Williamson developed the list while thinking about Latin America, and its elements provide a clear picture of the first generation of reforms that were implemented beginning in the mid-1980s. The "Washington" part of the name refers not only to the central site of the U.S. government, but also the site of the leading institutions in the international financial community (IMF and World Bank) and the unofficial community of think tanks that is centered there. The "Consensus" part of the name refers to the fact that these were thought to be uncontroversial elements that a majority of economists in the U.S. government, IMF, World Bank, and Washington think tanks believe to be good economic policy.

The Washington Consensus, as proposed by Williamson, has ten elements and can be divided into five macroeconomic components and five microeconomic ones.

Macroeconomic reforms:

1. Avoid large budget deficits.
2. Spend public money on health, education, and basic services rather than special interests or huge projects.

3. Cut taxes, but tax a wider range of activities and make the collection system effective.
4. Make certain that real interest rates are positive, limiting the use of preferential rates.
5. Make the exchange rate competitive and credible.

Microeconomic reforms:

6. Use tariffs instead of quotas, and gradually reduce them.
7. Encourage foreign direct investment.
8. Privatize state enterprises in activities where the market works.
9. Remove the barriers to firm entry and eliminate restrictions on competition.
10. Guarantee the security of property rights.

Williamson suggested these ten points for policymakers as a lowest common denominator of ideas that he believed were shared by analysts on both the political right and the political left. He did not think that he had designed a blueprint for development and he willingly acknowledged that the consensus did not address a significant number of important issues for which there is no consensus. Among the most important omissions were the appropriate government response to market failures, the priority to be given environmental concerns, how best to address problems of inequality and poverty, and the need to make economies better able to withstand international financial crises.

The subsequent history of the Washington Consensus is a lesson in how ideas take on a life of their own. It was quickly interpreted on the political right as further support for free-market policies and as a complete list of the all things governments should do in order to return to growth and prosperity. On the political left, observers agreed with the meaning of the consensus, but were in complete disagreement over its validity. While Williamson tried to argue with both sides in favor of a more sophisticated view of the consensus as a starting point and not as an ending point for policymakers, common usage of the term usually means something closer to the conservative, free-market interpretation, rather than Williamson's own idea.

The Next Generation of Reforms

The Washington Consensus overlaps with stabilization policies and structural reforms, and they are commonly mixed together under the label neoliberalism. Neoliberalism is a negative term throughout most of Latin America, primarily because the reforms of the last two decades have created uncertainty and change, but they have not begun to fulfill expectations of growth and prosperity. That is, the narrowly defined Washington Consensus may have helped some countries to end hyperinflation or runaway budget deficits, but it has not solved some of the region's most pressing and fundamental long-term problems. Inadequate growth rates, dramatic inequality, and vulnerability to macroeconomic crises and volatility continue to plague most of the countries of the region. After the reforms of the 1980s and 1990s, economic growth rates increased, but were still too low to offer much encouragement, and rates of poverty and levels of inequality hardly changed. Analysts in the mid-1990s began to talk about "reforming the reforms" and a "second generation of reforms," while popular frustration over the lack of material improvement in many countries led to widespread disillusionment with the reforms. Several countries (Brazil, Venezuela, Bolivia, Ecuador, Nicaragua) elected leaders who promised an end to the reforms or to at least moderate them, and while the new set of policies have varied, there is generally a much stronger element of nationalism and a reduction in market-friendly policies. Some leaders, for example Hugo Chavez in Venezuela, have called for the creation of a socialist bloc in Latin America and a complete repudiation of the last two decades of reforms.

More moderate reformers have begun to develop a second generation of reforms that take into account the region's institutions, and that address the problems of social and economic inequality. The reformers' goals are to develop a more inclusionary economic system by creating opportunities for excluded groups, to make countries less prone to macroeconomic crises, and to create greater flexibility by addressing some of the legal and institutional rigidities. For example, many small firms and individual-owned businesses or homes are located on property for which owners do not have a formal title. This situation makes it impossible for them to use their assets as collateral for loans, or to participate in the formal financial system. In effect, it limits growth by disallowing the full economic participation of a large share of small-scale entrepreneurs. To address this problem, bureaucratic processes must be redesigned and simplified, while legal and judicial structures must be reorganized to meet the needs of small businesses and individuals, rather than large companies and powerful political interests. Similarly, bankruptcy laws that encourage risk-taking, competition policies that break up monopolies, and financial sector supervision that limits unnecessary or unwanted risk are all areas that need work.

Mechanisms for addressing Latin America's highly unequal distribution of income are also on the agenda. In many countries, a long history of exclusion has blocked economic opportunity for particular groups, including indigenous people, African Americans, and isolated subsistence farmers. Although conditions vary greatly, most countries share an income distribution that is among the least equal of any region of the world. The mechanisms for addressing inequality are politically difficult because inevitably they involve an increase in tax collections and the redirecting of expenditures toward groups and regions that tend to be among the least powerful and the least influential. Nevertheless, an increase in expenditures for rural infrastructure to connect isolated groups to the national economy, along with education, health care, and microcredit lending programs, will all play a role in solving the long-standing problem of inequality.

Over the last twenty years, a few countries, including Mexico and Chile, have become among the most open and outward-oriented countries anywhere. In a relatively short period, Latin America has undergone a historical shift from a closed, inwardly oriented region of the world to one of the most open and outwardly oriented. This shift has required fundamental changes in economic policy and in the thinking of politicians and citizens. In many respects, the region had no choice because the previous strategy of ISI was floundering and unable to ease the debt crisis of the 1980s. So far, the results of these reforms are disappointing, but they highlight the need for reformers to consider more than economics alone as they struggle to find the sources of economic development in a more integrated world environment.

CASE STUDY

The Chilean Model

Chile suffered through a brutal dictatorship in the 1970s and 1980s. General Augusto Pinochet came to power in 1973 after a military coup that overthrew the democratically elected Salvador Allende. Pinochet tortured and jailed an unknown number of Chilean citizens, and tortured and killed an estimated two thousand to three thousand more. He was an extreme nationalist who knew little about economics and preferred advisors that had no affiliation with previous governments. After the failure of his first economic advisor, he selected an ambitious group of Chilean academics who were outside the country's political establishment and who had received training at the University of Chicago. The University of Chicago was known for its free-market ideology and Pinochet's economic advisors came to be known as the Chicago Boys.

The Chicago Boys quickly ended Chile's import substitution policies. They rapidly privatized banks, copper companies, and other firms that had been nationalized. They cut tariffs steeply, ended most import licensing requirements, and opened the Chilean economy to the world. Agricultural subsidies were cut and government supports were dismantled. The economy, which had been in crisis, began to grow two years after Pinochet gained power and after a disastrous recession in 1975. But the growth was illusory, and when a worldwide recession started in the early 1980s, Chile's economy collapsed. Banks were renationalized, and many of the trade reforms were turned back.

After two more years of crisis, the economy began to recover in 1984. This time, the Chicago Boys practiced a more pragmatic style of policymaking and growth remained strong through the remainder of the 1980s. By 1990, Pinochet was gone and democracy had been restored. A coalition of center and left parties, called Concertación, came to power, and has been in office since. The presidency has alternated between centrist Christian Democrats and leftist Socialists, but economic policy has remained relatively constant. Ricardo Lagos, the Socialist Concertación president from 2000 to 2006, explained,

I do believe ... that to have sound economic policies is not something of the right-wing or the left-wing parties. It's simply sound economic policies—now (that) took some time to learn.

Under the Chicago Boys and the brutal dictator Pinochet, and under Socialist and center-right (Christian Democrat) members of Concertación, Chile implemented a broad spectrum of market reforms. These governments introduced school vouchers that subsidize students, not schools. They established a system of individual retirement accounts that workers manage like a mutual fund account. They built infrastructure such as roads, but if the government's budget was stretched too thin, they made them toll roads and got the private sector to construct them. They implemented a uniform tariff that is the same on all goods so it does not divert investment away from one sector and toward another, and they slowly reduced the tariff over time.

The governments that came after the Pinochet dictatorship kept many of the same market-oriented policies, even when the Socialists controlled the presidency. They added a series of new initiatives, however, in order to provide greater social justice. Health care was expanded, along with retirement funds for people who were too poor to have built up an individual account, and infrastructure spending was increased to connect the country and to increase mobility of goods, services, and people. Poverty rates fell, incomes rose, and Chile became a model for many other countries. Lagos explained the government's perspective in the following way:

It's one thing to say, "Look, we have a market economy." It's a different story to say, "I don't want to have a market society." I think it is really the big issue today in the world. It's true we are living in a global world where the market is allocating resources, but where to allocate resources in the area of public goods and services is something that remains in the domain of the citizen.

Summary

- Latin America has been one of the fastest-growing regions of the world throughout most of the twentieth century. Growth came crashing to a halt in the 1980s, however, and only began to return in the late 1980s and early 1990s.

- Until the recent reforms, Latin American economic growth has focused on inward development rather than outward orientation. Productivity in subsistence agriculture has lagged behind overall growth, leading to much higher rates of poverty in rural areas than in urban ones.

- The primary development strategy of Latin America was adopted in the 1930s, 1940s, and 1950s. It came to be called import substitution industrialization and focused on the inwardly oriented development of industries that could produce goods that would substitute for imports. This model of development was favored because it was thought that Latin America would suffer ever-declining terms of trade for its primary commodity exports, and that ISI would reduce the need for foreign exchange and imports, thereby making the region less vulnerable to economic shocks from outside.

■ Economic growth under ISI was adequate, but ultimately it led to an inefficient manufacturing sector, excessive rent seeking, a persistent tendency toward overvalued exchange rates, and too great a concentration of resources on the urban sector.

■ ISI policies were often made worse by the tendencies of many countries to elect or support economic populists. Populists favored economic growth and redistribution while, in the extreme, they ignored economic constraints such as government budgets and foreign exchange shortages.

■ Populist policies generated macroeconomic instability, which often led to hyperinflation and falling real wages.

■ The debt crisis that began in 1982 affected every country of the region, even those without high levels of debt or debt problems. As a result of the crisis, it became extremely difficult to borrow internationally.

■ The main causes of the debt crisis were the increases in lending during the 1970s and the external shocks of interest rate hikes and primary commodity price decreases, especially oil. The faulty macroeconomic policies of many Latin American governments during the late 1970s and early 1980s made them more vulnerable to the shocks.

■ The debt crisis resulted in negative growth throughout the region for most of the period from 1982 through 1987. By 1987–1988, the need for significant reforms in economic policy was apparent to almost all governments.

■ From the mid-1980s through the present, the governments of Latin America have engaged in serious reforms of economic policy. The reforms have first tried to create macroeconomic stability through controlling inflation and reducing budget deficits. Stabilization policies have been followed by structural reforms that have opened trade, privatized, and reduced and redesigned the regulatory environment.

■ Growth has returned to most of Latin America, but dissatisfaction with the economic reforms is widespread. Job creation is less than desired, inequality persists, and economic growth is below the rate necessary to significantly reduce poverty.

Vocabulary

Baker Plan

Brady Plan

Economic Commission on Latin America (ECLA, or CEPAL in Spanish)

economic populism

export pessimism

Free Trade Agreement of the Americas (FTAA)

heterodox model

import substitution
industrialization (ISI)

Lost Decade

market failure

"neoliberal model" or neoliberalism

orthodox model

structural reform policies

terms of trade (TOT)

Washington Consensus

Study Questions

1. What were the main characteristics of economic growth in Latin America from the end of World War II until the debt crisis of the 1980s?

2. What is import substitution industrialization? Explain its goals and methods.

3. What are the main criticisms of import substitution industrialization? Did ISI fail?

4. Describe a typical cycle of economic populism. Why does it often leave its supporters worse off than before the cycle begins?

5. Explain how economic populist policies usually lead to overvalued exchange rates and large trade deficits.

6. What were the proximate causes of the debt crisis? How did the United States and other industrial countries respond?

7. Why did the Latin American debt crisis of the 1980s cause recessions in each country?

8. What is the difference between stabilization policies and structural adjustment policies? Give examples of each.

9. What is neoliberalism? Why do some people consider it a negative term?

10. What was the content of Latin American trade reforms of the late 1980s and 1990s? How do the actions taken relate to the desired goals?

Export-Oriented Growth in East Asia

Introduction: The High-Performance Asian Economies

One of the most interesting and important economic stories of the last fifty years is the success of several Asian economies. In Chapter 17 we will look more closely at China and India, but in this chapter the focus is on the group of countries that the World Bank designated **high-performance Asian economies**, or **HPAE**. The eight countries that comprise the HPAE are Hong Kong (now a part of China, but a British protectorate until July 1, 1997), Indonesia, Japan, Malaysia, Singapore, South Korea, Taiwan, and Thailand. These countries vary in living standards but they share an outward orientation that many observers see as fundamental to their high growth rates and declining poverty. Their experiences and relative successes have influenced economic policy around the world.

The severe economic and financial crisis that hit the HPAE in 1997 was a major setback for the region, yet it also demonstrated the long-run resilience of their economies, as most countries quickly returned to positive growth rates in the range of 5 to 10 percent per year. However, they have not been immune to the global recession that began in 2008, and in the long run, it may pose a greater challenge to their export-driven economic strategies since it is not certain that the rest of the world can continue to absorb their export surpluses. Nevertheless, their experiences are well worth examining, particularly since they were developing countries that used international trade and the international economy to achieve high rates of economic growth.

Before proceeding, it is useful to explain some of the terms used to describe this part of the world. A common name for one group of countries that began a rapid economic growth period shortly after Japan took off in the 1950s is the **Four Tigers**. This group includes the two city-states of Hong Kong and Singapore, and South Korea and Taiwan. They are also sometimes referred to as the *Four Dragons*, or the *Little Dragons*, and all four are classified by the World Bank as high income. Another group, which is broader and not confined to East Asia, is the **newly industrializing economies**, or **NIE**. There are a number of these economies in Latin America (Argentina, Brazil, Chile, and Mexico), as well as East Asia. NIE in the HPAE are Indonesia, Malaysia, and Thailand. China may also be considered one of the NIE, but it is usually placed in its own category due to its size and the legacy of communism. All of the NIE began their high rates of economic growth after the economies of the Four Tigers took off.

High-Performance Asian Economies (HPAE)

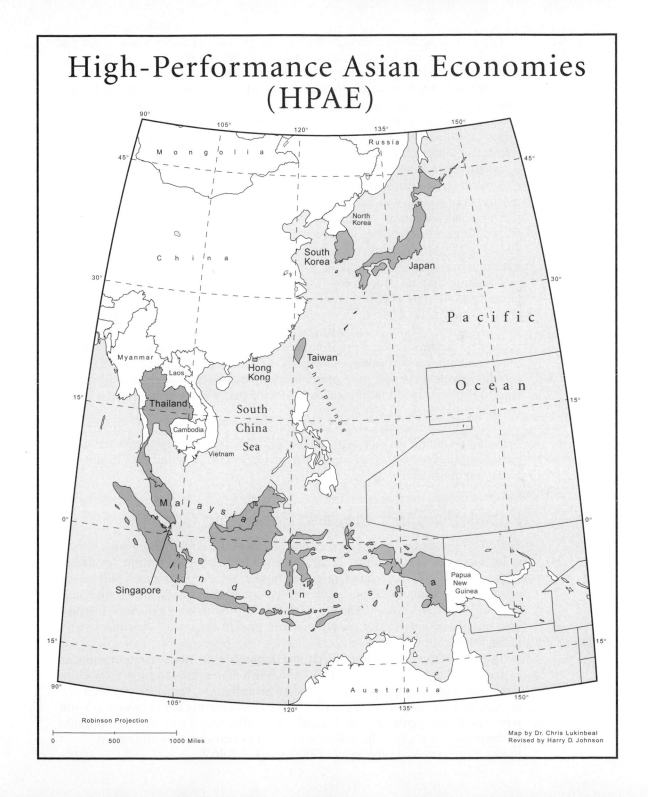

Robinson Projection

0   500   1000 Miles

Map by Dr. Chris Lukinbeal
Revised by Harry D. Johnson

Economists agree on several facts about the HPAE and their economic success. First, they were careful to maintain stable macroeconomies. Second, they had strong and credible commitments to sharing the benefits of economic growth, in part through expanded access to health care, education, and housing. These policies and others enabled them to develop a skilled workforce with high rates of literacy that was very attractive to multinational firms. Third, they promoted their exports, but they remained more open to imports than most other developing countries. Exports provided foreign exchange earnings and forced firms to make competitive products, while imports brought new technologies and new products.

Several questions about the HPAE experience remain unanswered. For example, the importance of industrial policies, or industrial targeting is unclear. Were these policies incidental, or were they instrumental in creating growth? Another series of questions revolves around the use of interventionist government policies and the avoidance of rent seeking. Specifically, in the various government interventions in economic activity, how did HPAE nations avoid the problem of rent seeking that has been so costly to Latin America? On the other hand, some have argued that they did not avoid it, and that it is one of the reasons for the collapse of the financial sector in several countries during the summer and fall of 1997. Does the "East Asian Miracle" represent a new model for economic growth or are the HPAE doing fundamentally the same thing that the United States and other industrialized nations did to achieve high incomes? And finally, can their model of export promotion be adopted elsewhere, or does it inevitably lead to the type of global imbalances that are partly responsible for the world recession that began in 2008?

This chapter examines these and several other questions as it explains the issues surrounding the successes of the East Asian high-growth economies. In particular, the contrast with Latin America is emphasized, along with East Asian trade and international economic relations.

Population, Income, and Economic Growth

Table 16.1 illustrates the size and income levels of the HPAE along with several other large Asian economies. In contrast to Latin America, income levels are high in the HPAE. Measured in either market exchange rates or purchasing power parity terms, GNP per person is high in Singapore, Japan, Hong Kong, Taiwan, and South Korea. The three remaining countries, Thailand, Malaysia, and Indonesia, began their period of rapid growth later and are considerably behind the other five.

Table 16.2 shows that the HPAE and a number of other Asian economies experienced high growth in the 1980s and much higher growth rates than Latin American economies. It is one of the most important contrasts between the regions and it is also a primary reason why East Asia attracted attention in Latin America. China's growth record might also qualify it as a member of the "high-performance" club, but the differences in its policies and institutions make it unlike any other Asian economy in Tables 16.1 and 16.2.

TABLE 16.1	Population and GDP for the HPAE, 2007			
	Population (Millions)	GDP (US$, Billions)	GDP per Capita (US$)	GDP per Capita (US$, PPP)
HPAE				
Hong Kong, China	6.9	207	29,912	42,306
Japan	127.8	4,384	34,313	33,632
Indonesia	225.6	433	1,918	3,712
Korea, Republic	48.5	970	20,014	24,801
Malaysia	26.5	187	7,033	13,518
Singapore	4.6	161	35,163	49,704
Taiwan, Republic of China	23.0	383	16,661	
Thailand	63.8	245	3,844	8,135
Other				
China	1,318.3	3,206	2,432	5,383
Philippines	87.9	144	1,639	3,406
Vietnam	85.2	69	806	2,600

HPAE countries, except Indonesia, have attained a high level of economic success, and several have joined the ranks of high-income countries.

Source: World Bank, *World Development Indicators;* Taiwan, Republic of China, *National Statistics*.

A Note on Hong Kong On July 1, 1997, Great Britain officially returned the colony of Hong Kong to China after more than 150 years of British rule. China has pledged itself to follow the policy of "one country, two systems" in its relations with Hong Kong. In practical terms, this means that China will allow Hong Kong to keep its own currency, will limit migration between Hong Kong and the mainland, and will generally try to preserve Hong Kong's current system. Statistics for Hong Kong and China are treated separately.

According to the "Rule of 72," if a variable (income, for example) grows at the rate X, then it doubles in approximately $72/X$ years. In other words, Korea's 8.2 percent annual rate of growth between 1980 and 1990 implies that its per capita real GDP doubled in 8.8 years (72/8.2), and over the decade, its income more than doubled. While the majority of developing countries have not begun to close the gap with high-income countries, income differences between the HPAE and the world's richest countries have been shrinking for several decades. Table 16.2 also shows the rate of growth of GDP per person for the high-income

TABLE 16.2	Average Annual Growth in Real GDP per Capita, 1980–2007	
	1980–1990	1990–2007
HPAE		
Hong Kong, China	5.7	3.1
Japan	4.3	3.1
Indonesia	3.4	1.2
Korea, Republic	8.2	4.8
Malaysia	2.5	3.9
Singapore	5.0	4.1
Taiwan, Republic of China	6.7	5.4
Thailand	5.9	3.7
Other		
China	8.5	9.4
Philippines	-1.6	1.7
Vietnam*	0.9	6.1
Low-income countries[+]	2.0	2.9
Middle-income countries[+]	1.1	3.0
High-income countries[+]	1.7	2.4

*Vietnam is 1984–1990; [+]Low-, Middle- and High-Income Countries are 1990–2005.

Real GDP per capita has grown faster in the HPAE over several decades than in most of the rest of the world.

Source: World Bank, *World Development Indicators;* Heston, Summers, and Aten, *Penn World Table Version 6.2;* Taiwan, Republic of China, *National Statistics;* author's calculations.

countries. As shown in the table, growth rates for each of the HPAE exceed the high-income average, except in the case of Indonesia, which was hit particularly hard by the Asian Crisis of 1997–1998.

General Characteristics of Growth in the HPAE

Recall from Chapter 15 that from the end of World War II until the mid- to late 1980s, economic growth in Latin America was characterized by high levels of inequality, periods of macroeconomic instability, and an inward orientation. The contrast with the HPAE could not be more striking, since their growth was built around falling inequality, generally sound macroeconomic fundamentals, and the promotion of exports. It is worth looking at each of the elements in more detail.

Shared Growth

One of the most remarkable features of growth in the HPAE is that it was accompanied by rising economic equality. This feature is even more remarkable when it is realized that inequality in income and wealth was already relatively low at the start of the period of high growth. Since the 1950s pioneering work of the economist Simon Kuznets, it was thought that growth in developing countries would first result in falling economic equality, followed later by rising equality. While Kuznets's work was based on measurements from a large number of countries, the East Asian experience has called into question the idea that economic growth in developing countries follows a "Kuznets's curve," in which equality first declines and then rises.

Table 16.3 compares income distribution in the HPAE with the largest countries in Latin America. The columns show the percent of the nation's income received by the bottom 20 percent of households, the top 20 percent, and the ratio of the two. The poorest households in the main Latin American economies receive between approximately 2 and 5 percent of total income, while the poorest in the HPAE receive between 5 and 10. On the high end, the richest 20 percent in Latin America receive between approximately 54 and 62 percent, while in the HPAE the range is from 36 to 51 percent. Consequently, the HPAE have a much more equal structure of income than Latin America.

The conditions that led to greater income equality were rooted in the unique historical experiences of each country. Nevertheless, each of the HPAE had a similar set of highly visible wealth-sharing mechanisms. Specifically, these included land reform, free public education, free basic health care, and significant investments in rural infrastructure, such as clean water systems, transportation, and communication systems. These policies did not equalize incomes, but they provided people with the tools they needed to raise their individual incomes and gave hope for the future. This had several positive effects. For example, when purchasing power is spread more widely through a society, it increases the opportunities for small- and medium-scale entrepreneurs that produce for the local market. The experiences gained in meeting local demand helps small firms develop into larger enterprises and may carry over into numerous other activities. In addition, rising incomes across a broad spectrum of socioeconomic groups raise hopes in general for future improvements and encourage cooperation among the different classes of society while conferring legitimacy on the ruling governments. Both factors contribute to political stability as well as the willingness by the business elites to commit to long-term investments.

Rapid Accumulation of Physical and Human Capital

Rising levels of equality were closely tied to very rapid rates of accumulation of physical and human capital. Rapid accumulation of physical capital is synonymous with high levels of investment. Investment, in turn, depended on high savings rates. The level of savings in the HPAE is considerably higher than in many other parts of the world. The explanations for high savings are varied. In part, it is a result of the rapid **demographic transition** experienced by those nations after World War II.

TABLE 16.3	Measures of Income Distribution, East Asia and Latin America			
	Year	Income Share of Bottom 20%	Income Share of Top 20%	Ratio
HPAE				
Hong Kong, China	1996	5.3	50.7	9.6
Indonesia	2005	7.2	47.3	6.6
Japan	1993	10.6	35.7	3.4
Korea, Republic	1998	7.9	37.4	4.7
Malaysia	2004	6.4	44.4	7.0
Singapore	1998	5.0	49.0	9.7
Thailand	2004	6.1	49.0	8.1
Latin America				
Argentina	2005	3.4	53.9	15.9
Brazil	2007	3.0	58.7	19.4
Colombia	2006	2.3	61.6	26.6
Mexico	2006	4.6	53.3	11.5
Peru	2006	3.9	54.0	13.9
Venezuela	2006	4.8	54.0	11.1

Income in the HPAE is more equally distributed than in Latin America. Note that income comparisons must rely on data from different years.

Source: World Bank, *World Development Indicators*.

The demographic transition is the shift from high birth rates and high death rates to low birth and death rates that accompanies modernization. Countries that have completed a demographic transition have fewer children below working age and a larger percentage of the population engaged in economically productive work. Hence, they tend to have higher savings rates.

Savings rates were also boosted by the stable macroeconomic environment of low inflation, but it is likely that the most important underlying factor in the creation of high savings was the rapid rate of income growth. That is, savings and income growth are interdependent, and the HPAE seemed to have created a "virtuous cycle" in which rapid income growth caused high savings. Savings led to high rates of investment, which fed back into a second round of income growth and high savings.

Investment in people was as important as the accumulation of physical capital. One of the key features of the HPAE's educational policy is that public investment in education was focused on the primary and secondary levels. Educational dollars go further at this level, and the social impact is much greater per dollar spent than at the university level. These investments raised literacy rates dramatically and laid the foundation for a highly skilled workforce that was capable of tackling increasingly sophisticated forms of production. In effect, the continuous rise in human capital endowments of the HPAE constituted an ongoing shift in the comparative advantages of those nations so that new investments could continually push into new product lines.

Rapid Growth of Manufactured Exports

Each of the eight HPAE actively and successfully promoted exports, although each began its development pushes with import substitution policies. Import substitution industrialization (ISI) policies, however, were quickly replaced with an emphasis on export promotion. The timing of the switch from ISI to export promotion varied by country. Japan began promoting exports in the late 1950s and early 1960s, the Four Tigers (Hong Kong, Korea, Singapore, Taiwan) started in the late 1960s, and the newly industrializing economies, NIE (Indonesia, Malaysia, and Thailand) began in the early 1980s.

Table 16.4 shows the results of the export push. Between 1965 and 2000 the HPAE more than doubled their share of total world exports and total world manufactured exports. In part, the success of the export promotion drives was the result of education policies that favored primary and secondary schooling. These policies created widespread literacy and an adaptable and easily trained labor force. In addition, each of the HPAE pursued various export promotion policies. For example, Japan and the Four Tigers made export financing credit readily available, they required export targets for firms that wished to receive favorable credit terms or tax benefits, and they provided tariff-free access to imports of capital equipment used to manufacture exports. Policies in the NIE were somewhat less interventionist and relied to a greater extent on attracting direct foreign investment in export activities.

The connection between export promotion and high rates of growth is an area of some controversy in economics. There are several possible connections that are explored in greater detail later in the chapter. A second controversy is the possibility of other nations using similar export promotion strategies. In many cases, these policies generate trade conflicts and may be at odds with the rules for fair trade agreed to by the members of the WTO.

Stable Macroeconomic Environments

A fourth and final characteristic of the HPAE is the maintenance of stable macroeconomic environments. Chapter 15 argued that one of the persistent problems of Latin America has been the frequent reoccurrence of macroeconomic crises. Even before the crisis of 1997, the high-performance economies of East Asia were not completely free of macroeconomic crises, but when they occurred, policy responses were usually quick and appropriate. Responses to the 1997 crisis were no different in this regard. Macroeconomic stability can have

TABLE 16.4	The Share of HPAE in World Exports, 1965–2000		
	HPAE Share of World Exports		
	1965	1980	2000
Total Exports	7.9	13.1	19.9
Exports of Manufactures	9.4	17.3	21.3

HPAE exports have significantly increased their share of world exports.

Source: World Bank, *The East Asian Miracle*; and World Bank, *World Development Indicators, 2003*.

several components, and the factors that are usually emphasized in this context are a commitment to keeping inflation under control, good management of both internal government debt and externally owed foreign debt, and the quick resolution of crises when they occurred. In general, macroeconomic policy has been characterized as "pragmatic and flexible."

On average, budget deficits and foreign debt were not dramatically smaller than in other regions of the world although there was a significant amount of variation across countries. The difference in the HPAE, however, is that with the exception of the recent crisis, deficits and debts remained manageable. High growth rates helped ease the constraints imposed by a given level of debt, partly because the high levels of exports earned the foreign assets necessary for debt servicing. The crisis of 1997 is the exception that proves this rule, since one of the key triggers of the crisis was a significant reduction of export earnings in a couple of countries and the growth of large current account deficits. To many foreign investors, these deficits began to seem larger than was warranted, and this triggered significant capital flight.

The commitment to low inflation helped keep real interest rates stable and enabled firms to take a longer-run view of their investments. In addition, low inflation helped avoid severe real appreciations in the exchange rate. Low inflation also meant that variations in the real exchange rate, the real interest rate, and the inflation rate were relatively low. In turn, this helped to foster a greater security in the minds of investors.

The Institutional Environment

Economic success stems from an ability to mobilize and allocate resources. In the HPAE, large flows of savings were generated, they were channeled into the financial system, and they were lent to business enterprises that used them productively. Simultaneously, governments emphasized education and universal literacy. Ultimately, an efficient mobilization and allocation of resources is based on the decisions of individuals and businesses that own resources. In order to ensure that individuals and businesses use their resources in the most productive manner, governments must create rules that foster efficient outcomes. In this regard, the institutional environments of the HPAE are essential to their success.

Several components of the institutional environment are critical insofar as they help to make government policy credible. In particular, property rights are relatively secure and free from the threat of nationalization. Bureaucracies are generally competent, individuals and businesses are free to make contracts that will be enforced, access to information is widespread, and regulations tend to be clear and well publicized. Of course, there are exceptions to each of these features, depending on the time and place, but in general they characterize the institutional environments of the HPAE.

These characteristics should not be confused with the characteristics of open, democratic societies. The fact that several of the HPAE do not support political and civil liberties raises a question about the relationship between authoritarian rule and economic growth. Specifically, do the lack of political and civil liberties and the concentration of power in the executive branch of government confer advantages for economic development?

The answer to this question is complex and beyond the scope of this book. Nevertheless, it should be noted that many dictatorships have failed in their bid to mobilize and allocate resources. Dictatorships or authoritarian regimes may be as likely to prey upon society as they are to foster its economic development. However authoritarian they are, the HPAE fostered growth rather than the enrichment of a small elite at the expense of the majority.

A second issue that arises from the general lack of traditionally defined democratic rights is the relevancy of the HPAE experience to other regions of the world, such as Latin America. Some social scientists argue that the context of authoritarian rule makes the HPAE experience irrelevant to nations such as Bolivia and Argentina, where policy reform is taking place within an institutional setting that allows far more dissent.

The relationship between authoritarian rule and economic growth and the applicability of the HPAE experience to the rest of the developing world are contentious and lack consensus. Generally speaking, there does not seem to be a correlation between the type of government (democratic or authoritarian) and the ability to put good policies into place.

Fiscal Discipline

Democratic or not, governments must create a stable macroeconomic environment in order for economic growth to succeed. The characteristic of macroeconomic stability has already been discussed, but it is worth revisiting because of its central importance and its contrast with the experiences of other regions such as Latin America.

The maintenance of a stable macroeconomic environment requires fiscal discipline and an acceptance of the resource constraints that limit government actions. Budget deficits and foreign debt must be kept manageable, and the real exchange rate must be relatively stable. The benefits of accepting these limitations are that it increases the credibility of government policy and builds the private sector's confidence. The result is more investment and less capital flight.

Business-Government Relations

Stable macroeconomic policies are necessary for growth, but they are no guarantee. For example, macroeconomic stability does not address the very significant problem in all developing countries of the coordination of interdependent investment projects. The coordination problem results from the fact that many private sector investments are interdependent. That is, their profitability depends on the simultaneous or prior creation of a complementary investment. The same often holds true for private sector/public sector investments. For example, profitable investment in warehousing facilities at a seaport depends on the prior investment in sufficient port infrastructure to provide an adequate flow of goods through the warehouses. Yet the port and related transportation linkages may not be worthwhile unless there is a simultaneous investment or a guarantee of future investment in the warehouses.

CASE STUDY

Deliberation Councils in the Ministry of International Trade and Industry (MITI)

Japan's use of deliberation councils has been more extensive than any other country's. In Japan, the councils are attached to a particular ministry, or bureaucracy, such as the Ministry of International Trade and Industry (MITI). Since MITI is one of the largest bureaucracies in Japan, and because it has more control over Japanese economic policy than any other bureaucracy—with the exception of the Ministry of Finance—it has numerous deliberation councils. According to one account, in 1990 there were seventeen major regular deliberative councils attached to MITI.

Councils in MITI are of two basic types. They are industry specific, such as the Textile Industry Council, or they are thematic, such as the Industrial Structure Council. Thematic councils deal with a broad range of issues and, consequently, are composed of numerous committees. For example, the Industrial Structure Council had eighteen committees in 1990, ranging from the Industrial Finance Committee and the Industrial Labor Committee to the Industrial Location Committee.

The method for using deliberation councils involves a feedback process in which the first step is for MITI officials to call a hearing and invite comments from various interested parties. Based on the information they collect, MITI officials issue a draft report that is then forwarded for discussion to a deliberative council. The council may include affected industry representatives, academics, journalists, consumer and labor representatives, former bureaucrats, financial representatives, and politicians. Representation is not proportional in any sense, nor are representatives elected.

Based on the feedback that MITI gets from the council, it makes changes in its draft plan and issues a final document that details the steps that will be taken, such as policy changes or new policy initiatives. The final action taken by MITI is essentially a public relations campaign to sell the plan to the wider public.

Source: Campos and Root, *The Key to the East Asian Miracle*.

The coordination of interdependent investment activities is difficult in a purely free-market framework. The difficulty stems from the fact that the flow of information is not sufficient to let all investors know of the intentions of each other. Six of the eight HPAE surmounted this problem through the creation of **deliberation councils**, a set of quasi-legislative bodies that bring together representatives from the private and the public sectors. In effect, deliberation councils coordinate the information flow between businesses and policymakers.

Individual councils are usually created to deal with a limited set of issues involving one industry or a particular set of policy issues, such as the government budget. By bringing together government officials and affected business groups, the councils reduce the cost of acquiring information about new policies, provide a forum for bargaining over policies, instill greater investor confidence, and raise the level of credibility of the government's policies. More than perhaps any other function, however, deliberation councils serve as a vehicle for the business elites to have a strong voice in the setting of government policy and thereby ensure their cooperation in the overall economic strategy.

Avoiding Rent Seeking

Economic policy in the HPAE has been relatively interventionist. That is, the laissez-faire ideology of letting markets determine outcomes has not been followed. Hong Kong is somewhat of an exception, but even in Hong Kong government has directed and actively participated in the creation of extensive public housing. In the next section, we examine some of the issues related to the effectiveness and extent of government intervention in the economy. Whether extensive or not, however, one of the biggest puzzles surrounding HPAE economic policy was the degree to which most countries were able to avoid the costs and inefficiencies associated with private sector rent seeking.

When governments intervene to help specific industries or to channel resources in a particular direction, they create benefits that are of value to someone. Generally speaking, when private interests perceive the possibility of obtaining something of value from government (for instance, credit subsidies, import protection, and business licenses) they will devote scarce resources to obtaining those benefits. The result, as discussed in several earlier chapters, is wasteful rent seeking.

Government policies in the HPAE created numerous benefits of value to specific industries, yet in spite of this there was relatively little rent seeking by those interests. To be sure, rent seeking still occurs, and there is significant variation by HPAE nations. Nevertheless, there is less overall rent seeking than in many other societies.

It is unlikely that there is a single, simple explanation for this lack of rent-seeking behavior, but the deliberation councils probably played a key role. By providing a policy forum in which various interests can make their views known and have a chance to argue in favor of policies that are particularly beneficial, the need to hire lobbyists is reduced. Furthermore, given that industrial and business interests meet with government officials as a group, rather than single interests by themselves, there is greater transparency and less worry about what competing interests may be doing behind the scenes.

In addition to the role played by deliberation councils, some analysts point to the fact that whenever governments offer something of value, they usually attach performance requirements. For example, firms receiving credit subsidies or import protection are usually required to meet specific targets—often export targets—or else the subsidies are taken away. What is remarkable, and not clearly understood, is how HPAE governments are able to enforce the performance requirements they lay down. Many nations outside East Asia, including many Latin American governments, have used performance requirements as incentive mechanisms, but often they have proven to be unenforceable. That is, when firms have not met their production or export targets, governments outside the HPAE have often been unable to withdraw the special considerations they are providing to the noncompliant firms.

Two key elements that have played a role in enforceability are the presence of a well-educated bureaucracy along with its insulation from the political process. In most of the HPAE, civil service careers are highly respected and well paid. Consequently, bureaucrats are well educated and competent. In addition to ability, their insulation from the political process gives them the room to make decisions based on merit rather than on the basis of special interests.

A final explanation for the relative lack of rent seeking is the commitment to shared growth that we saw at the beginning of the chapter. The fact that business elites are convinced that they will share the benefits of economic growth reduces the pressure for them to seek added benefits through the manipulation of the political process. In effect, greater equality in the HPAE reduces the number of individuals and groups that feel left out of the growth process and eliminates the underlying cause of much rent seeking.

CASE STUDY

Were East Asian Economies Open?

High-growth Asian economies relied on their export sectors for a substantial part of their growth. They actively promoted exports in various ways and to varying degrees, and there is a consensus among economists that manufactured exports played a key role in their economic development. Export promotion is not the same thing as an open economy, however, and there is disagreement about their trade policies and the extent of their openness.

It would seem that it should be easy to settle the debate simply by looking at tariff rates and quotas. Unfortunately, these are inadequate measures of trade policy, particularly if a country has significant non-tariff measures that it uses to block imports. For example, the U.S. auto industry argued for years that red tape and unnecessary safety inspections made their cars uncompetitive in Japanese markets. This may or may not have been the case; U.S. cars were not designed for Japan and the marketing and distribution systems are fundamentally different from those in the United States. Did U.S. cars fare poorly because the playing field was tilted to favor Japanese brands, or was the playing field level and U.S. automakers had products that were less competitive?

It is possible that high-growth Asian economies promoted their exports and severely restricted imports in order to protect domestic markets. In that case, their policies were not market-oriented, but instead reflected a high degree of government intervention with the purpose of determining outcomes selected by planners and bureaucrats. In this view, some East Asian economies followed the policies of mercantilism and viewed exports as the path to wealth creation and imports as destructive to their wealth and prosperity (see Chapter 3). Alternatively, East Asian economies did not set tough constraints on imports, but followed relatively open export promotion policies that contributed to rapid economic growth, more or less in line with market-based incentives.

This is an important debate. The HPAE were the first group of countries since World War II to go from developing to developed, or low and middle income to high income. If mercantilism is the key to their success, it would be an important empirical case against the paradigm of comparative advantage and the gains from trade.

Table 16.5 contrasts imports and exports for high-growth East Asian countries with the main Latin American economies. Imports and exports include goods and services and are measured relative to the size of each country's GDP. Data is provided for two years. In 1980, most of the East Asian economies were practicing export promotion policies, and Latin America had weak export sectors and relatively closed economies. By 2007, Latin American policies had changed toward much greater open policies.

Between 1980 and 2007, every country in Table 16.5 increased its imports relative to its GDP, and every country except Indonesia increased the relative share of exports in its GDP. By 2007, Latin American economies were much more open than they were in 1980 when they were all following import substitution policies, and their imports and exports were much larger shares of their GDP. Nevertheless, trade is still significantly below its importance in East Asia. The partial exception is Japan, which as a large country has a smaller openness index than any of the others in Table 16.5.

East Asian economies apparently did not close their import sectors, but rather imported quite a large amount of goods and services. They still may have used

TABLE 16.5   Imports and Exports as a Share of GDP

	Imports		Exports	
	1980	2007	1980	2007
HPAE				
Hong Kong, China	89.4	199.0	88.9	209.5
Indonesia	20.2	25.4	34.2	28.5
Japan	14.5	17.6	13.6	19.2
Korea, Republic	40.0	45.3	32.1	44.6
Malaysia	54.3	96.7	56.7	113.1
Taiwan, Republic of China	52.6	65.9	24.1	72.2
Thailand	30.4	72.5	51.4	74.1
Latin America				
Argentina	6.5	21.1	5.1	25.1
Brazil	11.3	12.3	9.0	13.9
Colombia	15.6	22.7	16.2	19.5
Mexico	13.0	35.6	10.7	32.4
Peru	19.4	22.6	22.4	28.5
Venezuela	21.8	24.7	28.8	31.0

East Asian economies promoted exports but also absorbed large quantities of imports.

Source: World Bank, *World Development Indicators*; World Trade Organization, *Trade Profiles*.

selective protection for targeted industries, but in general the data do not support the idea that they were relatively closed to imports. This is entirely consistent with theoretical models showing that protectionism often hurts exports by causing the currency to appreciate as a result of a lack of demand for foreign goods, and due to the higher returns protectionism creates for the production of import substitutes. In other words, just as Latin America's depressed imports went hand-in-hand with its depressed exports in 1980, East Asia's high level of exports went hand-in-hand with a relatively high level of imports.

The Role of Industrial Policies

The most influential study to date of the high-performance Asian economies is the World Bank's policy research report entitled *The East Asian Miracle: Economic Growth and Public Policy*. The World Bank's research team concluded that government interventions were common in three areas: (1) targeting of specific industries, that is, industrial policies narrowly defined; (2) directed credit; and (3) export promotion. In this section, we examine the debate over the effectiveness of industrial policies and offer a word of caution about the use of directed credit.

Targeting Specific Industries in the HPAE

Recall from Chapter 5 that industrial policies can be defined in broad or narrow terms. The broad definition is policies that alter a nation's endowment in a way that does not favor particular industries. For example, we have already seen that the East Asian success story involves high rates of primary and secondary schooling that altered the characteristics of the labor force and the high rates of savings and investment that created the infrastructure and capital goods necessary to enter more sophisticated lines of manufacturing.

The narrow definition of industrial policies is the targeted development of specific industries. In effect, targeted industrial policies attempt to change the comparative advantage of a nation through the alteration of its industrial structure. These policies channel resources to favored industries and are often criticized as being "government bureaucrats picking winners and losers."

With the exception of Hong Kong, each of the HPAE has had or still has some form of targeted industrial policy. They were strongest in Japan, Korea, and Taiwan (the "northern tier" of HPAE), but were significant in the other countries as well. In Japan, the focus has been on steel, autos, textiles, shipbuilding, aluminum, electronics, and semiconductors, among others. The height of Korean policies was between 1973–1979 with the Heavy and Chemical Industries (HCI) program, which targeted steel, shipbuilding, petrochemicals, and other heavy industries. While lacking the same clear focus as Japan and Korea, Taiwan's programs have provided research institutes, science parks, and basic infrastructure for a variety of industries and seem to have targeted the development of import substitutes.

Malaysian policies took off in the early 1980s with the Look East policy, which emulated Korea's and Japan's industrial development. Malaysia created the Heavy Industries Corporation of Malaysia (HICOM) to develop steel, nonferrous metals, machinery, paper and paper products, and petrochemicals, but it ran into financial constraints in the late 1980s when a number of the firms under HICOM proved to be unprofitable and required government bailouts. Since then, Malaysia has privatized many firms and reduced the degree of state control in others. Indonesia and Thailand did not make systematic efforts such as Japan and Korea did, but the Thai Board of Investment has promoted industries that it deemed to have the potential for technological learning. Indonesia has attempted to use large state-run enterprises to advance from labor-intensive to high-technology industries. Singapore's policies have focused largely on encouraging technology transfer from firms in industrial nations through the promotion of foreign direct investment.

The tools that nations use to promote specific industries include the instruments of trade policies. Restrictions on imports, through licensing, quotas, or tariffs, and export subsidies were all used. In many cases, protection from foreign competition enabled firms to earn high profits in domestic markets, which compensated for the losses they suffered in foreign markets. In addition to trade policy, the HPAE used numerous other mechanisms to channel resources to targeted industries. Directed credit was one of the most important tools, because even when it was small in size, it signaled the private sector that government policy favored the industry receiving the funds. This official stamp of approval was an important device for encouraging private lending to new and potentially risky industries. Other tools included subsidies, market information—especially with respect to foreign markets, infrastructure construction, and research—and development funds.

There are two essential elements to these policies that make them different from most other national attempts to promote specific industries. First, resources were usually only provided as long as the companies receiving them met specific export targets. If the targets were not met, the resources (protection, credit, and so on) were withdrawn. Export targets are argued to be a better criterion than profits because many firms had monopolies or significant market power in their domestic markets; hence, profitability may be unrelated to efficiency. Second, governments placed macroeconomic stability above industrial policies. If they began to experience fiscal problems that were caused by the industrial promotion programs, they scaled back or abandoned them.

The World Bank view of these programs is that they were insulated from purely political influences so that industrial targeting decisions were based on technical analysis rather than politics. The collapse of the financial sectors in many countries in 1997 and 1998 has called this assumption into question. For example, government use of directed credit programs appears to be one of the main causes of the financial crisis. Government involvement in credit allocation forced financial institutions to make unsound loans. In turn, the failure to apply business criteria led to a mountain of bad debt, which ultimately sank many banks and whole financial sectors. In the future, conventional economic wisdom will undoubtedly be much more cautious about the benefits of directed credit programs to target industrial development.

Did Industrial Policies Work?

The role of industrial policies in the story of HPAE growth is controversial. Ideally, we would like to know the answers to two simple questions. First, did they work? A successful policy would be one that increases the overall rate of GDP growth or the rate of productivity growth. Second, if they worked, were they important? That is, was their contribution to economic growth significant enough to be considered one of the reasons for East Asian success?

With respect to the question of whether they made a positive contribution to growth, opinion ranges from "no effect" to "positive effect." The reason for the lack of consensus on this important issue is that, in general, it is difficult to measure the effects of policy interventions on growth rates. There are conceptual disagreements about the measurements that should be made, and few countries have data of sufficient quality. In the World Bank's view, "reasoned judgments" must be used to settle the issue. Unfortunately, the paucity of data, together with disagreements over measurement techniques, results in the use of qualitative judgments of the sort that inevitably lead researchers to confirm the opinions that they began with.

In spite of these obstacles to assessing industrial policies, the variety of opinions among researchers can be characterized as falling into two camps. One camp is represented by the World Bank's research. In its view, some government interventions fostered economic growth (export promotion and directed credit), but in general industrial policies did not. They assert that industrial policies usually targeted the same industries that market forces were developing and, therefore, were unnecessary. In the cases where the "wrong" industries were targeted, pragmatic and flexible policymakers of the HPAE managed to quickly change policies before any damage was done to the rest of the economy.

The World Bank's analysis rests on two pieces of evidence. First, it compares the growth rates of productivity in the targeted and nontargeted sectors in the three countries with sufficient data (Japan, Korea, and Taiwan). In general, it finds that productivity change in the promoted sectors was high but no higher than in the rest of the economy. Possible exceptions to its general finding are Japan's chemical and metalworking industries and Korea's chemical industry. One problem for the advocates of industrial policies is that the unpromoted textile sector did as well as any of the promoted sectors. Second, it examines the change over time in the industrial structure of the HPAE. If industrial policies worked, they should have led to a different pattern of industrial growth than the pattern that is caused by a change in factor endowments. The World Bank concluded that industrial policies were at most marginally effective, since the sector-by-sector growth pattern is as expected, given the national endowments of labor and the high savings and investment rates.

Critiques of the World Bank's findings usually rest on two points. First, the fact that productivity growth was generally no faster in promoted sectors is irrelevant, according to the critics. The important issue is what the growth rates would have been without promotion. It is conceivable that without industrial policies, growth in the targeted industries would have been much slower than with the policies. Second, the critics point out that the World Bank analysis is overly general. In their view, it is based on industry groupings that are too broad to uncover the details of selective targeting. For example, some components of the textile industry were heavily promoted in both Japan and Korea in the early period of their industrial policies. Therefore, it is not surprising that textiles overall have experienced a rapid increase in productivity and that they remain a larger than expected component of Japanese and Korean industry.

At present, there is no way to resolve this debate. Consequently, there are a variety of opinions about the relevance of industrial policies for developing countries outside the HPAE group. To the extent that there is agreement, most analysts share the view that if industrial policies are to be successful, they should have three key characteristics. Countries must have (1) clear performance criteria such as export targets, (2) institutional mechanisms to monitor compliance and enforce compliance, and (3) low costs so that nontargeted sectors do not suffer.

CASE STUDY

HCI in Korea

Most observers agree that Korean industrial policies have at least partially succeeded. The most enthusiastic observers argue that they have accelerated the rate of overall growth without creating offsetting inefficiencies elsewhere in the economy. Less optimistic observers concede success in generating exports and in changing the industrial structure of the country, but they offset many of those gains with the huge financial costs of the Heavy and Chemical Industries (HCI) promotion in the 1970s.

Korea's industrial promotion drive began a few years after the Korean War in the early 1960s. Early efforts at industrial targeting focused on key industrial materials such as cement, fertilizer, and petroleum refining. The government typically supported large-scale conglomerates, called *chaebol*, which were given monopolies in the domestic market. Trade policy in the form of an aggressive promotion of exports along with high levels of protection was the main tool for targeting industries, but directed credit and tax breaks were important as well.

Industrial targeting evolved into the Heavy and Chemical Industries program, which was at its most active from 1973 to 1979. HCI targeted six specific industrial groups: steel, petrochemicals, nonferrous metals for enhanced self-sufficiency, shipbuilding, electronics, and machinery (especially earth-moving equipment and autos) for export. The tools used to promote these industries were the same as previously described but with a different emphasis. By the mid-1970s, trade policy had become somewhat more liberal, although most industries still received significant protection. Greater emphasis was placed on subsidies, directed credit through loans at below-market interest rates, and special tax exemptions.

The cost of promotion during the HCI period was significant. Direct funds provided to targeted industries were around 5 percent of the overall budget, and tax exemptions amounted to about 3 percent of total tax revenues. In 1977, around 45 percent of the banking system's total provision of domestic credit went to the targeted industries. Gradually, bottlenecks and large debts began to accumulate.

By 1979, when the second oil crisis hit, inflation was high, the exchange rate had appreciated, causing exports to falter, and the targeted industries had significant idle capacity. In addition, the labor-intensive sectors, which had not been targeted, were starved for credits, and bad debts and financial insolvencies were growing in the HCI sector.

Policymakers quickly switched course. HCI promotion was curtailed, the currency was devalued, and financial market and import liberalization were hastened. One of the main efforts of policymakers in the 1980s was to restructure a number of the distressed industries that were overpromoted in the 1970s. The cost to the government budget has been significant, as it has been forced to bail out bankrupt firms and dispose of nonperforming loans.

Was HCI promotion worth it? It is impossible to answer this question definitively because we can never know what would have happened under an alternative set of policies. During the height of the HCI program and its immediate aftermath, Korea's growth rate dipped slightly (from the mid-1970s through the mid-1980s), but the change was slight and growth overall remained extremely high, even by HPAE standards. Korea achieved classification as a high-income nation, a feat that only Japan and the city-states of Singapore and Hong Kong accomplished in the twentieth century.

Source: World Bank, *The East Asian Miracle*; and Westphal, "Industrial Policy in an Export-Propelled Economy: Lessons from South Korea's Experience," in *The Journal of Economic Perspectives*, Summer 1990.

The Role of Manufactured Exports

The promotion of manufactured exports played a significant role in the industrial strategies of each of the HPAE. These policies were largely successful, and the exports of each country grew even faster than its GDP. Given these facts, it is reasonable to assume that there might be a connection between the two. That is, a number of studies of the HPAE and other regions have shown that higher rates of growth of exports are correlated with higher rates of growth of GDP. What is the mechanism that causes this?

The Connections between Growth and Exports

It is true by definition that exports are part of the GDP, so it would seem that growth in exports is simply a part of overall GDP growth. Export growth may not add to GDP growth, however, if it crowds out growth in the output of goods for domestic consumption, such as consumer goods or investment. In effect, the idea that export growth causes faster GDP growth is an assertion that export growth causes the overall capacity of the economy to grow faster than it would have if production was focused on goods for the domestic market.

If production focused on exports results in greater overall growth, then there must be something in the production process or its links to the rest of the economy that is absent from domestically focused production. One possibility is that because exports are produced for the world market, economies of scale come into play in a way that is absent when firms produce for a small domestic market. Larger firms often have lower average costs because they can spread their fixed costs for capital and machinery over a larger volume of output. Another possible reason why exports might foster growth is that as firms produce for a world market, there are added incentives to increase R&D. Economies of scale may make it more worthwhile, and the need to keep up with foreign competition may make it more necessary.

Other connections between export growth and GDP growth are possible as well. Exports may speed up the adoption and mastery of international best practices. Firms that operate in global markets are not protected from competition. In fact, they are going up against the world's best, and the competitive pressures may force firms to stay abreast of the latest developments in their product area and production process. Measurement of this possible effect is complicated by the presence of some form of export promotion in the HPAE. An exporter does not have to be among the world's best if it receives subsidies (for example, direct payment or access to low-interest loans or tax breaks). Firms can be competitive due to subsidies received at home, which may reduce the pressures to compete based on efficiency or quality. Successful export promotion programs, such as those in Korea, are well aware of this problem, and since their goal is to develop firms that are capable of head-to-head international competition without special breaks, they carefully monitor the programs to ensure that the subsidies granted to the exporters do not become the reason for competitive success abroad. In addition, subsidies are gradually reduced. Note, however, that since 1995 the international rules for subsidies have tightened considerably, and it is much harder for countries to provide them within the World Trade Organization (WTO) framework.

Production of exports has several other potential advantages. Exports make possible the purchase of imports. Developing countries are not usually on the technology frontier, and the creation of an efficient manufacturing enterprise is often dependent on imports of machinery and other capital goods. A scarcity of exports impairs a country's ability to purchase imports, with the result that firms are unable to obtain the imported inputs they need in order to raise their efficiency. A related advantage of exports is that the need to meet export targets tied the HPAE to policies that openly encouraged inward foreign direct investment (FDI) and the acquisition of new technology. One way to overcome the backwardness of domestic manufacturing is to encourage foreign firms to invest. Most of the HPAE welcomed FDI; Singapore went so far as to build its industrial policies around it. At the same time that FDI was encouraged, several countries also sought to provide incentives for the foreign firm to license its technology to potential domestic rivals. This was a particularly common strategy in Japan, where the incentive of access to the large Japanese market was sufficient to encourage many firms to sign technology licensing agreements.

The ability to import capital and modern technology is seen by some as the most critical ingredient in policies that successfully close the gap between developing and developed countries. Export promotion can encourage the acquisition of new technologies because in order to succeed, governments must allow access to whatever imports firms need to become efficient. Most of the HPAE selectively protected their domestic markets, but they also adjusted their policies so that exporters were given access to needed imports. In general, they used less protection than other developing areas.

Is Export Promotion a Good Model for Other Regions?

The export promotion model has succeeded so well in East Asia that, inevitably, it is being prescribed for other developing areas. In Latin America, for example, the economic crisis of the 1980s, together with the very visible counterexample of East Asia, has propelled many nations into similar types of policies. A serious question is whether other areas can duplicate the export successes of the HPAE.

If developing countries around the world begin to emphasize export promotion policies, an issue arises as to whether the world's industrial nations can absorb the exports of a series of newly industrializing countries. This is particularly of concern after several years of global imbalances that eventually led to a financial crisis in 2007 and a global recession in 2008. If all of the world's developing countries attempt to export their way to prosperity without purchasing a similar quantity of imports, their export surpluses have to be matched by deficits somewhere else in the system. In the long run, this is not sustainable, and in the short run, after the recent crisis, it is politically difficult-to-impossible.

Perhaps the greatest obstacle for countries that wish to replicate the export promotion policies of the HPAE is the Uruguay Round of the General Agreement on Tariffs and Trade (GATT). Under the rules that went into effect in 1994, developing countries must eliminate any subsidies that are contingent on export performance. Extremely poor countries with per capita GDP less than $1,000 are exempted. Essentially, the new GATT rules eliminate the possibility that developing countries can use the same tools—credit subsidies, tax breaks, direct payments—that the HPAE used. The only exceptions are the poorest countries, which do not export manufactured goods in any quantity. In all countries, subsidies for noncommercial R&D, regional development, and promoting compliance with environmental regulations are allowed.

CASE STUDY

Asian Trade Blocs

The first edition of this text (1994) began this case study as follows: "Asia is the one region of the world without significant trade blocs." Since then, and more particularly since 2000, that has changed dramatically. Table 16.6 shows the progression in Asia of the signing of trade agreements.

Prior to the growth of trade agreements in the 1990s, the **Association of Southeast Asian Nations (ASEAN)** was the most notable example of an Asian cooperation agreement. Founded in 1967 with five members (Indonesia, Malaysia, Philippines, Singapore, and Thailand), it added five more countries (Brunei Darussalam, Vietnam, Lao PDR, Myanmar, and Cambodia) between 1984 and 1999. ASEAN's initial mission was political and security cooperation, but it has expanded into trade and economic arenas. In 1992 it created the ASEAN Free Trade Area (AFTA), which was implemented over a fifteen-year span.

New agreements began to take shape in the 1990s, especially after the Asian Crisis of 1997–1998. Political and business leaders in East Asia decided that their economies and regulatory agencies were not prepared to handle the increase in trade and investment flows, and that they could not rely on the advice of the International Monetary Fund (IMF) or other multilateral agencies. Stronger bilateral and regional relations were accepted as a means for

TABLE 16.6	Free-Trade Areas in Asia and Oceania		
Year	Under Negotiation	Concluded	Proposed
1989	0	3	1
1995	0	22	1
2000	1	39	3
2009	62	109	45

The number of trade blocs in Asia increased dramatically after the Asian Crisis of 1997–1998.

Source: Asian Development Bank, Asia Regional Integration Center. http://aric.adb.org.

building greater regional stability. New agreements were proposed, negotiated, and eventually signed. These agreements take many forms, both with respect to their regional coverage and their scope. Some are bilateral and intra-regional, such as the Japan-Singapore Economic Partnership Agreement, while others are between one country and an existing group, such as the ASEAN-China Comprehensive Economic Cooperation Agreement. Others are bilateral but interregional, such as the Japan-Mexico Free Trade Agreement, or the Korea-Chile Free Trade Agreement.

Nor are trade agreements the only form of regional cooperation that emerged after the crisis of 1997–1998. ASEAN opened negotiations with China, Korea, and Japan to form the **ASEAN+3** group, which serves as a base for several forms of collaboration, including, for example, the **Chiang Mai Initiative (CMI)**, which provides financing to central banks when they are under pressure, and is intended to reduce their reliance on the IMF or other multilateral agency. Through the use of **swap agreements**, or **swaps**, China or another lending country can play a role similar to the IMF, but with greater speed and flexibility, by lending its currency reserves to the central bank of Thailand or some other borrowing country.

ASEAN+3 nations are also a part of a trade region known as the **Asia Pacific Economic Cooperation (APEC)**. APEC has twenty-one members, the thirteen ASEAN+3 countries, Australia, New Zealand, Russia, the United States, Canada, Mexico, Peru, and Chile. The goal of APEC, as set forth in the 1994 Declaration of Common Resolve, is "free and open trade and investment in the region no later than 2010 for the industrialized economies and 2020 for the developing economies." APEC is not a trade bloc in the normal sense since its goal is not only a free-trade area among its members, but also the goal that each member will practice free trade with all other countries and not only other APEC members. It is uncertain if this will be achieved, but meanwhile APEC serves as a forum for regional discussion and coordination.

Sources: Asian Development Bank, http://www.adb.org; Asian Regional Integration Center, http://aric.adb.org; Asia-Pacific Regional Cooperation, http://www.apec.org.

Is There an Asian Model of Economic Growth?

The East Asian "miracle" has given rise to a large number of studies that seek to explain rapid growth in the HPAE and China. While the issue may superficially appear academic, it has become one of the more interesting and heated debates in recent popular economics. Proponents of laissez-faire economics have used the relative openness of the East Asian economies, their use of private markets, and their strong macroeconomic fundamentals to argue for government policies that are less activist. Proponents of a more activist government have pointed to selective interventions, such as export promotion, industrial policies, and deliberation councils, to argue in favor of a larger government role in the economy. Some Asian politicians have pointed to their restrictions on civil and political liberties as laying a foundation for order and the avoidance of chaos.

Is there an Asian model of the economy? That is, have the HPAE managed to achieve their extraordinary growth rates through policies that are fundamentally different from the policy advice dispensed by proponents of the Washington Consensus (see Chapter 15)? At stake are the paths followed by today's developing economies and the future role of government policy in the industrial countries. Naturally, with a question so controversial, there are a variety of answers and opinions. Recent work, however, seems to be pointing toward a robust set of conclusions.

In order to describe some interesting recent studies, we must briefly review the idea of growth accounting. Recall that labor productivity is a measurement that is defined as output per worker. The growth in labor productivity is highly correlated with the growth in income (or output) per member of the population, but they are not the same thing. East Asian growth is remarkable for its growth in per capita income and its growth in labor productivity.

Any given rate of growth of labor productivity can be broken down into the share that is due to more capital and the share that is due to more skills or education. In the economics literature, such an exercise is called *growth accounting*. When growth accounts are constructed for a country or a region, there is always some share of the growth in labor productivity that cannot be explained by the amount of additional capital or education. This share is a measure of the effects of using the available inputs more efficiently. That is, if more growth occurs than can be explained by the growth of capital or education, it must be due to a more productive use of the available inputs. For example, the organization of production may have changed so that people are working more efficiently, or the quality of technology may have changed so that each unit of capital and labor input produces more units of output.

Another name for the share of labor productivity that is not explained by capital or education is **total factor productivity**, or **TFP**. TFP growth reflects changes in output that are unrelated to changes in capital or labor inputs but that are related to new technologies, innovation, and organizational improvements. According to most estimates, over the long run a majority of per capita income growth in high-income countries has resulted from increases in total factor productivity.

Growth accounting may seem a long way from the debate on East Asia, but it is actually very relevant. As it turns out, the vast bulk of Asian growth since 1960 can be accounted for by increases in capital and education, while TFP plays a much smaller role. Table 16.7 provides the details and some comparisons over the same period.

What we observe in Table 16.7 is that in the sample of six HPAE, TFP growth accounts for between 24 and 36 percent of overall growth. In the slower-growing United States, it accounts for 27 percent, and in the other industrial nations the figure is 37 percent. The fact that TFP growth accounts for about the same overall share of growth in the HPAE was surprising to many observers for two reasons. First, the HPAE are not on the frontier of new technologies like the United States and the rest of the industrial world. Consequently, they should be able to more easily borrow techniques that increase their TFP. Second, the proponents of a new Asian model of economic growth have argued that the selective interventions such as industrial policies and export promotion have increased productivity. In fact, what they appear to have done, if anything, is to increase the quantity of capital per worker.

The last point is key to understanding this debate. When growth is decomposed into its various causes, what appears to account for the bulk of HPAE growth is capital accumulation and not increased total factor productivity. These results appear to be fairly strong, since several other researchers have done similar growth accounting exercises and have reached the same conclusions. The growth accounts for East Asia are important because they paint a consistent, if surprising, picture of the East Asian "miracle." They tell us that there may be no miracle at

---

TABLE 16.7   Sources of Growth, 1960–1994 (Percent)

Country/Region		Contribution of		
	Growth of Output per Worker	Capital per Worker	Education per Worker	Total Factor Productivity
Indonesia	3.4	2.1	0.5	0.8
Korea, Republic	5.7	3.3	0.8	1.5
Malaysia	3.8	2.3	0.5	0.9
Singapore	5.4	3.4	0.4	1.5
Thailand	5.0	2.7	0.4	1.8
Taiwan, Republic of China	5.8	3.1	0.6	2.0
Latin America	1.5	0.9	0.4	0.2
United States	1.1	0.4	0.4	0.3
Industrial Nations*	2.9	1.5	0.4	1.1

Economic growth in East Asia is mainly a result of capital accumulation.

*Including Japan, excluding the United States.

Source: Collins and Bosworth, "Economic Growth in East Asia: Accumulation Versus Assimilation," in *Brooking Papers on Economic Activity*, 2: 1996.

all, just the hard work and sacrifice that comes from forgoing today's consumption in order to raise savings and investment rates. For example, between 1966 and 1985, Singapore raised investment from 11 percent of GDP to 40 percent. It is no surprise, then, that capital accumulation accounts for the bulk of its growth.

If these measures are accurate, the argument for a distinct Asian model looks weak. Rather than selective interventions that target specific industries, the keys were high savings and high investment, together with the other factors outlined in this chapter.

Summary

- The major characteristics of economic growth in the high-performance Asian economies are (1) increasing equality, (2) rapid accumulation of savings and high rates of investment, (3) rapid increases in levels of schooling, (4) rapid growth of manufactured exports, and (5) stable macroeconomic environments.

- The institutional environment is instrumental in creating confidence in policymakers. The policymaking bureaucracy tends to be insulated from the push and pull of the political system. This leads some to decry the lack of representation of the population in policy decisions, but it allows decisions to be made on technical merit rather than political expediency. The voice of business and industry, and to a lesser extent other groups such as consumers, is often heard through consultative bodies known as *deliberation councils*. Deliberation councils are a mechanism for the private sector and government policymakers to exchange information and discuss policies.

- One of the key elements of policy is fiscal control over inflation, the budget, foreign debt, and exchange rates. While inflation, budgets, and foreign debt all vary country by country, inflation is kept under control, and budget deficits and foreign debt are kept within the boundaries defined by the government's and the economy's ability to finance them.

- With the exception of Hong Kong, each of the HPAE followed industrial policies that targeted the development of particular industries. These policies were most focused in the "northern tier" of Japan, Korea, and Taiwan. The effects of these policies are difficult to measure, and there is a long and contentious debate about their efficacy.

- Each of the HPAE promoted manufactured exports. These policies largely succeeded, although the mechanisms that link export growth to faster GDP growth are still uncertain.

- Recent empirical work shows that the main contributor to economic growth in the HPAE is the extremely rapid accumulation of physical capital. Consequently, the argument that the HPAE have pioneered a model that leads to more rapid total factor productivity growth appears false, and the keys to growth should be looked for in the policies that raise savings and investment.

Vocabulary

ASEAN+3

Asia Pacific Economic Cooperation (APEC)

Association of Southeast Asian Nations (ASEAN)

Chiang Mai Initiative (CMI)

deliberation councils

demographic transition

Four Tigers

high-performance Asian economies (HPAE)

newly industrializing economies (NIE)

swap agreements, or swaps

total factor productivity (TFP)

Study Questions

1. Contrast the characteristics of economic growth in the HPAE with those characteristics of Latin America.

2. How can passage through a demographic transition lead to high savings and investment rates?

3. What are the characteristics of East Asian institutional environments that contributed to rapid economic growth?

4. Economists are divided over the effectiveness of East Asian industrial policies. Provide a balanced assessment of the issues relevant to understanding the role of industrial policies in fostering growth. Do you think one point of view is better than another? Why?

5. How might manufactured exports contribute to economic growth?

6. Is there a uniquely Asian model of economic growth? What are the issues, and how might we go about answering that question?

China and India in the World Economy

Introduction: The Challenges of Openness

The emergence of China and India from their relative economic isolation is one of the most important contemporary trends in the international economy. Their increased openness and growing interdependence with the outside world have generated positive and negative effects, opportunities, and challenges. Openness and a change in their economic models enabled hundreds of millions of people to escape poverty, caused many manufactured goods and services to become less expensive, and helped hold world interest rates down, due in part to China's enormous pool of savings. The later tendency helped make real estate more affordable, spurred construction in developed countries, and is partly responsible for a boom in housing prices. Simultaneously, producers of manufactured goods in both developed and developing countries experienced intense competitive pressures that forced some of them to downsize, outsource, and change their business practices. For the first time in history, the service sector has begun to move jobs overseas and growing trade imbalances increase the chances of future crises and protectionist reactions.

China and India have a lot in common and a lot that is different. Both are nuclear powers, sites of ancient civilizations, and the two largest populations in the world. Both have transformed their economic systems by moving away from relative isolation and emphasizing markets over state control. Although China's reforms began earlier than India's, both countries succeeded in creating and sustaining high growth rates.

One of the most important differences is that India is the world's largest democracy while China is ruled by the Communist Party. In India decision making is sometimes contentious and must take into account opposing views, while Chinese decision making is highly centralized within a leadership that is never subjected to popular vote. Another difference is that India's manufacturing sector is much smaller than China's, even after adjusting for the overall size of the economy. As a consequence, trade plays a smaller role in India's economy than in China's, and India's impact on world trade is much less. India's command of information technology industries and services has drawn a great deal of attention, while China's ability to export manufactured goods, from apparel to automobiles to sophisticated electronics, has altered trade patterns and challenges the manufacturing sectors of countries around the world.

TABLE 17.1	Population and Income in China and India, 2007			
	Population (Millions)	GDP (US$, Billions)	GDP per Capita (US$)	GDP per Capita (US$, PPP)
China	1,318	3,206	2,432	5,383
India	1,125	1,177	1,046	2,753

India and China are the two most populous countries in the world.

Source: World Bank, *World Development Indicators*.

India and China are potentially great powers and both are beginning to assume positions in the world economy that are consistent with their sizes and histories. When great powers emerge, history tells us that it usually creates a difficult period filled with transitions and tensions. This chapter surveys the major economic issues associated with the emergence in the world economy of China and India.

Demographic and Economic Characteristics

Table 17.1 shows the size of the Chinese and Indian economies. In 2007 their combined population was over three-eighths (38.5 percent) of world population, and over $4 trillion at market exchange rates. At current economic growth rates, China's economy will become the world's largest around the middle of the century. It currently has the world's third largest GDP, behind the United States and Japan, and is about three times larger than India. On a per capita basis, China will lag the world's leaders for many decades even at present growth rates.

The growth of GDP has been remarkable in both countries. Since 1980 real GDP growth has averaged 6.0 percent per year in India and an astonishing 10.0 percent per year in China. Around 1980, 84 percent of China's population and 65 percent of India's lived in extreme poverty. By the first decade of the new century, the figures had fallen to 15 percent for China and 42 percent for India. This represents nearly one billion individuals that were pulled out of extreme poverty by Chinese and Indian economic growth. Incomes that are only slightly better than extreme poverty are still desperately low, but no one can doubt that the economic success of these two countries has created significant benefits for a sizable share of humanity.

While poverty has fallen, a middle class has grown in size. The populations of both countries are so large that even a small middle class represents enormous purchasing power. The size of the middle class in both countries is unknown, but consider the following hypothetical situation. Suppose that 10 percent of both populations is middle class with purchasing power parity incomes of $12,000 or more. That would be a total of 240 million people, or nearly equivalent to the combined populations of France, Germany, Italy, and the United Kingdom. In both countries, but particularly in the case of China, it is this potential future market that has elicited so much international interest and foreign investment. The history of

Western pursuit of the Chinese market is long and mostly unhappy, but many Western firms believe that they cannot afford not to have a presence in China.

Population totals in India and China have more than doubled since 1950, as shown in Figure 17.1. China's limits on family size sharply curtailed its population growth rate, and between 2020 and 2030 India is predicted to pass it in absolute size. China's restrictive population policies mean fewer children and an older population, but a slowing population growth rate. If current trends hold, between 2030 and 2040 it will fall below replacement levels and its population will actually begin to decline. Given China's lack of health care, pension systems, and democracy, an aging population will not exert the same pressures on the government budget as it will in the European Union (see Chapter 14).

Economic Reforms in China and India

Economic reform of China's communist system began in 1978. Under communism, every aspect of China's economy was controlled by the state. Private enterprise did not exist, and the basic decisions that every economy makes about what to produce, how to produce it, and who should receive it were made from the top down by government planners and Communist Party politicians. China had limited contact with outsiders, and the emphasis of its economic policy was self-sufficiency in all goods and services.

India's reforms began in the 1980s, and then gathered momentum in 1991 when the government was forced to respond to a balance of payments crisis. India's economic system was best characterized as socialist, with a mix of state ownership and control, together with private enterprise. Most large industrial enterprises were state-owned, however, and the Indian system of regulation

FIGURE 17.1 **Population and Projections, 1950–2050**

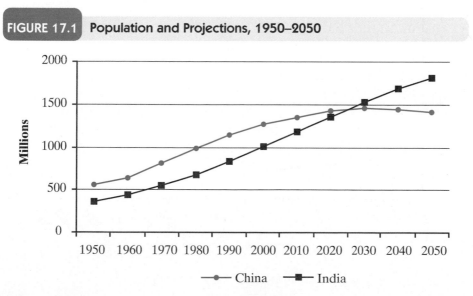

Source: U.S. Census Bureau.

meant that all firms had to obtain permits for even minor changes. If a firm wanted to expand, if it wanted to change its product lines, or even if it wanted to change its board of directors, first it had to obtain a permit from the government.

After their transitions, both countries are much more market oriented and far more outward looking. The remarkable degree of opening is apparent in their openness indexes, 1975–2007, shown in Figure 17.2. The index for both countries increased over the long run. China's jumped immediately with the changes in policy that began in 1978 while India's was relatively unchanged until the early 1990s. The usual negative relationship between country size and openness is weak, as Chinese reforms in particular have emphasized international economic integration through both trade and investment, and have led to an unusually large openness index given its population. China's index is an indication of its dependence on world trade (and by implication, investment) for its continued success.

The Reform Process in China

A country's decision to undertake large scale economic reform can come from many directions. As we saw in Chapter 15, reforms in a number of Latin American countries were a result of the debt crisis of the 1980s together with the failure of traditional policies to resolve the crisis. Other countries, New Zealand for example, began large scale economic reforms without the urgency created by an economic crisis. In China's case there was no immediate crisis, but rather a long period of instability and disappointment with the results achieved under communism. The leader of Chinese

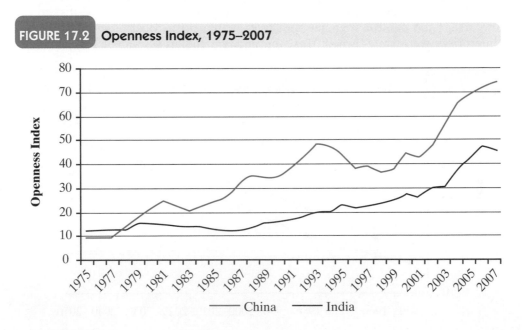

FIGURE 17.2   Openness Index, 1975–2007

Chinese trade began to grow in the late 1970s; India's in the early 1990s.

Source: World Bank, *World Development Indicators*.

economic reforms, **Deng Xiaoping**, put it in terms of a choice between distributing poverty under the old system, and distributing wealth under a new system.

There was no master plan for Chinese reforms, but rather a gradual, steady dismantling of the controls exercised by the state and the Communist Party. Deng Xiaoping is famously reported to have described the reforms as analogous to "feeling the stones to cross the river." You advance one foot, see if it holds, then advance another. The slow and steady pace of reform was dictated in part by a lack of experience and information about how to proceed but also by the fear of a reaction from the hard-line, conservative, anti-reformers.

The first changes were confined to agriculture and involved loosening the constraints on peasant producers by allowing them more control and ownership of individual plots of land. Peasants were allowed to sell their product in markets and were soon increasing the quantity of foodstuff available. Foreign trade under the old system was controlled by twelve **foreign trading corporations (FTC)**, which were attached to the various branches of government. All exports and imports went through the FTC and were strictly regulated with no consideration given to comparative advantage. The reforms gradually opened trade, first through the creation of additional FTC and then through a series of steps that removed price controls and ended export subsidies. In order to limit the initial impact of reforms on the domestic economy and to prevent a political backlash, China created a number of **Special Economic Zones (SEZ)** which were modeled on the concept of export processing zones. SEZ went further by giving provincial and local authorities wide latitude to experiment with radically different economic and trade policies. Incentives were given to form joint ventures with foreign producers who came to the SEZ to set up production facilities. Between 1979 and 1988, China created five SEZ, all of which successfully attracted foreign investment (particularly from Taiwan, Hong Kong, and the overseas Chinese business communities), generated a large flow of exports, and helped raised the rate of economic growth. The SEZ created a demonstration effect for the rest of China and other regions began to push for similar policies.

China also applied to join the General Agreement on Tariffs and Trade (GATT) in 1986. Membership requires a country to describe all trade and economic policies that may affect GATT agreements, and to open bilateral negotiations with individual members over any issues of concern. Negotiations were difficult and lasted until China joined the WTO in 2001. The protracted period of negotiations probably kept the reform process moving forward, and ultimately resulted in a strong Chinese commitment to an open economy, both for trade and investment.

Indian Economic Reforms

Indian reforms began gradually in the 1980s and speeded up considerably after the 1991 crisis. Three forces played significant roles in preparing Indian policymakers for the necessary changes. First, India's primary trade partner, the USSR, suffered a number of setbacks through the 1980s and finally dissolved itself in 1991. India had partially modeled its economic policies on the USSR, and its demise laid bare the failure of its economy to produce prosperity. Second, the success of several East Asian countries was important. In 1960, South Korean and Indian income per capita were about the same, but by 1990, Korea was entering the ranks of the developed world, while India remained stuck at low levels of income. When **Manmohan Singh**, the finance minister who carried out many of the reforms, visited Korea in 1987, he was shocked to see how far behind India had fallen. Third in the list of forces was a financial crisis that developed as a result of heavy borrowing by the government. When the Gulf War drove up oil prices and cut off the flow of remittances back home from Indian workers in the Gulf States, the country was left with inadequate foreign reserves and an inability to finance its debt.

The changes in economic policy that followed touched on a number of areas, including the permitting process. India's regulation of its economy was based on a system of permits that stifled innovation and creativity with their extensive, complicated, and inefficient rules. Permits were intended to be a means for preventing the creation of powerful interests that might undermine democracy and promote inequality. Yet their unintended consequence was that they fostered inefficiency and by protecting Indian businesses from competition, both domestic and foreign, they thereby allowed them to operate without regard for product quality or firm efficiency. Many of the larger firms were state-owned under the belief that the state planners could better select product lines and operating procedures than could markets, and as in the Chinese and Russian cases, the state-owned sector of the economy operated without the imperative of profitability. Firms could lose money for years and still continue in business since they had no hard budget constraints. Losses were covered by the government budget, even as it meant an enormous drain on government revenue and fewer resources for important public projects such as safe drinking water, highways and ports, rural education, and other needs. Denationalization was the second set of reforms begun after the crisis of 1991.

A final critical area that began to receive attention from the reformers was international trade and investment. Indian trade policy was based on the idea of import substitution industrialization (see Chapter 15), as in Latin America and other developing countries after World War II. Domestic firms received high levels of protection, exports were implicitly discouraged, and self sufficiency was the goal. India's famous Ambassador car is an example. Protected from foreign imports, it remained essentially the same for nearly forty years. Why go through the expense of changing the product line if there is a captive market? In addition to dismantling many of the restrictions on trade, India also began to dismantle the restrictions on inward foreign investment.

Remaining Issues

In both the Chinese and Indian cases, profound changes have taken place. The depth and breadth of the reforms represent a break in each country's historical path, and a shift from low-growth, isolationist policies toward high growth and integration with the world economy. The domestic reforms are not over, however, and a number of changes are still in the works.

An indicator of the reform progress in both China and India is the World Bank's Doing Business index discussed in Chapter 13 (http://www.doingbusiness.org). Recall that the index ranks 181 countries on ten dimensions of business regulations.

These range from the ease of starting or closing a business, to employing workers, dealing with licenses, paying taxes, and enforcing contracts, among others. The rankings are based on the number of steps, the amount of time, and the cost to comply with business regulations in each of the ten areas. In 2009 China ranked 83 out of 181, while India was 122. In other words, neither country is a world leader in the ease of doing business.

Given that both China and India are far from being world leaders in the ease of doing business, it is somewhat puzzling how they could have achieved such high rates of growth. Economists do not share a consensus on this issue and it seems that this will be an active area of debate for some time. In the case of China, there are at least two explanations for its growth in spite of its obstacles to doing business. On the one hand, many economists believe that the local enterprises that are found in townships and villages are often owned by local governments and that they provide a counterbalance to the inefficient rules and regulations imposed by the central government. According to the proponents of this explanation, the system is inefficient in its design since it limits market freedoms, but it functions relatively efficiently because the **township and village enterprises (TVE)** are able to respond more quickly to local conditions and because their interests are more aligned with local communities. Not everyone accepts this view. An alternative is that the TVE act in an entrepreneurial way when the central government is not too heavy handed, but a great deal of the growth in China has been fueled by foreign investment, which is subject to a different set of rules and regulations than domestic investment. One of the key points of contention is whether the TVE are publicly or privately owned. Surprisingly, it is difficult to determine the ownership structure, but the proponents of the view that foreign investment has been the key driver of Chinese growth also argue that they are private and that they have been centers of entrepreneurial success in places and at times when the central government has not interfered too much.

CASE STUDY

Why Did the USSR Collapse and China Succeed?

Before the collapse of the Soviet Union, college bookstores and academic presses carried a significant number of works describing the transition from capitalism to socialism, as if it was an inevitable future for some portion of humankind. Almost nothing was published about the reverse process, the transition from socialism to capitalism. Such a book would have seemed strange; no one was writing anything along those lines, and probably few publishers would have given it a second look. When China began its gradual transition in 1978, its meaning was unclear to most observers and it took years to understand that it was abandoning communism. In 1989 when the Berlin Wall fell and central Europeans began to migrate west, no one knew if the USSR or the socialist governments would permit people to leave. And when the USSR announced that it was dissolving into fifteen separate nations, nearly everyone was taken by surprise. It is no wonder then, that the academic and policymaking worlds were unprepared for the transition from socialism to capitalism.

The economies that abandoned socialism or communism in favor of market-based systems came to be known as the **transition economies**. One of the first controversies was over the speed of the transition. "You cannot cross a chasm in two leaps" (go fast) was one view. The other view was that of Deng Xiaoping, the Chinese leader who likened reform to "feeling the stones to cross the river." The International Monetary Fund (IMF) and the U.S. government favored quick transitions, while a number of academics sounded a more cautious note. In many respects, the fortunes of Russia (fast) and China (slow) came to symbolize the two approaches.

Russian reformers quickly moved to create a private economy where none had existed before. This involved an enormous amount of work, not just in the economic realm, but in politics and institution building as well. To begin, the economy had to be stabilized to avoid unsustainable budget deficits and hyperinflation. This was not entirely successful for a variety of reasons, not the least of which was the turmoil caused by the transition and the breakup of the USSR. Throughout the new economy, administrative controls were replaced with market-based mechanisms so that prices could be freed from bureaucratic control. The barriers to firms that prevent them from entering and leaving markets were dismantled, and important new markets were created. New labor markets required unemployment insurance, pension systems, and safety nets, while financial markets needed the regulatory apparatus of banking oversight, security laws, and tax rules. The transfer of property rights was begun, and government officials began the creation of the legal infrastructure for settling disputes and enforcing contracts. One of the most complicated and difficult tasks was the privatization of firms and factories that had been state owned. In Russia, that was nearly the entire productive apparatus of the economy. The end result was an enormous concentration of wealth and a general understanding that the process of privatization favored a small group of insiders. In sum, a wide variety of new institutional structures had to be created.

The outcome was tragic for a large segment of the population. By 1996, Russia's economy was about 64 percent of its size in 1990. Infant mortality increased dramatically, birth rates fell below replacement levels, and wealth became highly concentrated. Russia was not unique in this way, as all but one of the fifteen countries that the USSR split into saw income declines of 25 percent or more. Six countries watched as their incomes fell by more than 50 percent and civil wars broke out in a couple of cases.

By contrast, the Chinese economy did not decline at all during its transition from communism to capitalism. Although its reforms were begun in 1978, until the mid-1980s they mainly affected the agricultural sector. Since China had such a large share of its population in rural areas, the positive effects on food output and rural incomes were significant. Primarily, the agricultural reforms let families and villages take individual responsibility for meeting their production quotas, and allowed them to consume or sell whatever amount they produced above the quota. Villages and communes were allowed to disband the collectivist system of production and individual incentives began to rule the efforts and decision making of producers.

In the mid-1980s, China extended its market-based reforms to a number of Special Economic Zones (SEZ), Economic and Technology Development Zones (ETDZ), High Technology Development Zones (HTDZ), and other special developmental areas, mostly located along the coast. The rules of each type of zone varied, but in general they allowed far more independent, profit oriented, market-based, decision making. The SEZ in particular, were encouraged to experiment with new forms of economic organization, and to develop joint ventures by attracting foreign investment. These areas began to account for the bulk of Chinese growth, exports, and foreign investment.

China's transition strategy is considered a gradualist strategy because it did not attempt to reform the entire economic structure all at once. Rather, it used a **dual track strategy**, which localized reforms to certain areas or sectors (e.g., agriculture) while maintaining traditional, central planning structures in the remainder of the economy. Slowly, subsidized prices were raised to the market level and the mandatory production targets were reduced to a small share of the total output or zero. By the early to mid-1990s, more than 90 percent of retail prices and 80 to 90 percent of agricultural and intermediate goods prices were decontrolled. China has been much slower to privatize its state owned sector.

Many observers argue that the gradual implementation of reforms in a slow but steady sequence removed the pressure to instantaneously develop new institutions and economic relations. By adopting a dual track approach, China allowed the market economy to develop alongside the centrally planned economy, and to gradually take over more and more of its functions. Perhaps even more importantly than avoiding an economic downturn, it gave the Chinese people time to adjust their expectations to fit a market-based system and reduced the shock of change.

The proponents of rapid reform see China as a special case. First, central planning was less extensive in China, with the result that its economy was less distorted and less over-concentrated on heavy industry. Second, and most importantly, China's economy is much more agricultural. In 1978, when China began its reforms, 71 percent of the labor force was in agriculture. The figure for Russia in 1990 at the beginning of its transition was 13 percent. China's heavier concentration in agriculture gives it a large rural labor force with very low productivity. If these workers leave the countryside, the resulting loss of output is small, while the offsetting productivity gains from employment in urban and village industrial enterprises are significant. Hence, China can move labor from agriculture into the new enterprises but Russia had to take labor out of heavy industry to staff the new enterprises.

Janos Kornai, the eminent Hungarian economist and perceptive observer of the transition summarized the debate in the following terms:

Some developments are rapid, others slow. Some call for a one-stroke intervention while many others come about through incremental changes.... The emphasis has to be on consolidation, stability, and sustainability, not on breaking speed records (Finance and Development, September 2000).

China and India in the World Economy

China's accession to the World Trade Organization (WTO) was notable. Accession ended fifteen years of negotiations and established beyond all doubt that China would not turn away from its march toward capitalism. WTO accession also meant that foreign concerns about property rights and market access would be resolved and that investment in China would not be subject to arbitrary rules by the Chinese government or by foreign governments that might try to discriminate against manufacture imports from China.

India was a member of the WTO from the beginning, but its reforms of the 1990s caused exports and imports to take off. With a much smaller manufacturing sector than China, the absolute value of its trade is far less. Nevertheless, its growth rate is high and recent concerns about the outsourcing of services and India's high technology sector are important reasons for a closer look at its trade patterns.

Chinese and Indian Trade Patterns

Figure 17.3 shows the average annual growth of trade, both exports and imports, in constant dollar terms and five-year increments, from 1980 to 2005. In China's case, every five-year period except one (1985–1990) experienced growth in both exports and their rate of growth. India's exports and export growth rate also increased in every period but one (1995–2000), when the growth rate fell slightly but still was above 10 percent. Imports also show strong growth with no periods of absolute decline except 1985–1990 in China.

Figure 17.3 illustrates an important point regarding trade: Exports and imports are tied together. In the case of China this is particularly important to note given the large volume of its exports and the disruption they are causing in trade networks. Chinese exports depend on imported inputs and technology since a large share of its trade consists of commoditized goods that China assembles into a final form and exports. For example, Chapter 4, Table 4.3, lists the top ten Chinese exports to the United States. These are either low technology goods such as footwear, bedding accessories, and briefcases, or high technology goods such as automatic data processing machines. The high technology products, however, are often only assembled in China from parts produced elsewhere. An example is the laptop computer. Taiwan was the leading producer of laptops, but shifted all of its production to China. The processing chips come from Intel, software is supplied by Microsoft, the display panel and memory chips are produced in Korea and Taiwan, and the hard drives are supplied by Japan. China assembles the parts and exports laptop computers (automatic data processing machines).

If China is not presently a high technology producer, it is certainly moving in that direction, in part through its rapid expansion of its science, engineering, research, and development capacity. The number of patents granted by its national patent office was nearly 50,000 in 2005 (versus 164,000 in the United States), and it is spending large amounts on infrastructure that will make the entire society more productive. Nevertheless, at this point it still has limited collaboration with universities and its absorption and diffusion of imported technology is weak. In the present,

FIGURE 17.3   Average Annual Growth of Imports and Exports, 1980–2005

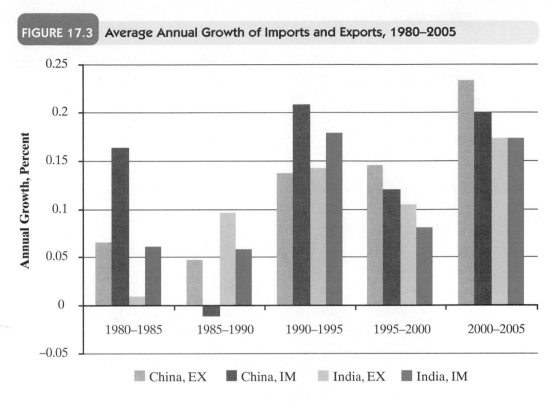

Since 1990, exports and imports have grown much faster than GDP.

Source: World Bank, *World Development Indicators.*

much of its domestic technology sector depends on its ability to copy (often illegally) foreign products, and it continues to depend on foreign direct investment for technology, management, and access to international networks. This is likely to change in the future, however.

Table 17.2 compares Indian and Chinese trade in goods and services. Note first that Chinese exports are about six times larger than India's, and its imports are about four times greater. Even in the area of services, where Indian exports are on the rise and have been much noted, China's total is still about a third larger. Table 17.2 illustrates clearly how much more of an impact China's growth is having on the world economy. Its goods exports account for 8.7 percent of the world's total, and it ranks number two in the world in goods exports and number three in goods imports.

In recent years, Indian trade has captured the world's attention though its ability to participate in the growing area of services trade. Several factors account for this, not the least of which is the fact that English is spoken by educated Indians. In addition, India's leadership has consistently emphasized higher education and technology, and although it has a severe shortage of places in its universities, its leading institutions such as the India Institute of Technology

TABLE 17.2	Chinese and Indian Export and Import Totals, 2007		
	US$, Billions	Share in World Trade	Rank among Countries
India: Exports			
Goods	147	1.0	26
Services	92	2.7	10
India: Imports			
Goods	217	1.5	18
Services	78	2.5	13
China: Exports			
Goods	1,219	8.7	2
Services	122	3.6	7
China: Imports			
Goods	956	6.7	3
Services	129	4.1	6

China's trade sector is much larger than India's, even in services.

Source: World Trade Organization, *Trade Profiles*.

(IIT) are among the world's best. There is possibly no greater example of a sector or a country that has benefited from the advent of the telecommunications revolution than India's high-tech sector.

A closer examination of Chinese and Indian service exports highlights this fact and points to an important difference in the two economies. As shown in Table 17.2, China's service exports are larger than India's, although not by as much as its goods exports. More important is the composition of each country's service exports, which is not shown in Table 17.2. China has a $7 billion deficit in services, which primarily comprise transportation and travel services (shipping costs and business and personal travel). India has a $14 billion surplus in services, which primarily comprise information services and other business services, two high growth areas of services.

Computer and information services and other business services include the call centers that Thomas Friedman (*The World Is Flat*) and others have written about, along with the outsourcing of medical consultations, data entry, legal briefs, and the myriad other activities that are now sometimes performed at a distance and then sent over the Internet to the final user of the information. As described in Chapter 4, the outsourcing of services depends on the telecommunications revolution, with the Internet, video conferencing, satellite communications, and the software to use them. In the past, most services were consumed at the point of production, but as technology allows a separation of production from consumption or use, services have begun to be outsourced in the same way that manufacturing has been for decades.

The Challenges of India and China in the World Economy

There are numerous challenges to existing trade patterns and trade relations posed by the entrance of the world's two most populous countries in the world trading system. We will look at three such challenges: Indian services, Chinese manufacturing, and the demand for resources.

Services

Services such as shipping have been traded for decades as shipping companies hire crews around the world and register their vessels in the most convenient location, selling their services to firms wherever they are in need. Business services and information services, however, are a relatively new to international trade since they can only be traded if technology and infrastructure can pass large amounts of information across long distances at low costs. Since the mid-1990s, this has been possible and trade in information and computer services has taken off. The outsourcing of services from high-income industrial economies to India is a new arena for the application of comparative advantage.

As with all economic changes, some people benefit and some are hurt. It is clear, however, that there are net benefits overall for national economies. Consider the case of the United States. As the hardware for computer and information technology (IT) has become less expensive, IT services and software are taking the majority share of total IT spending by U.S. businesses. Outsourcing reduces the price of IT services and software, makes business-specific applications cheaper to purchase, and allows businesses to achieve higher levels of productivity at a lower cost. Higher productivity, in turn, raises living standards overall, although not necessarily for every individual. It is another case of comparative-advantage-based trade, the same as described in Chapters 3 and 4. In this case, India's comparative advantage allows it to trade with the United States and to contribute to the increase in U.S. productivity while at the same time creating good paying jobs and advancing its own economy.

Those who oppose this form of trade fear that all computer and IT work will end up in developing countries. This seems highly unlikely. For example, the U.S. Bureau of Labor Statistics projects job growth in the United States in IT related occupations to be three times faster than in the rest of the economy until at least 2010. These new workers and many already in the IT services sector will not continue to do the same thing, however, as the comparative advantage of the United States is shifting within the IT field. The danger is not that jobs will disappear, but that the United States will fail to produce enough qualified people, or that the mix of skills and qualifications will not match the demand by businesses, or that new limits on trade in services will put businesses at a competitive disadvantage.

Manufacturing

China's emergence as an export platform and as a high-volume manufacturer of consumer goods challenges existing trade patterns and manufacturing trends. The challenge to emerging markets such as Mexico, Brazil, Malaysia, and Thailand is that they cannot depend on low wages as the primary source of their comparative advantage. The challenge appears in the form of intense competitive pressures from low-cost goods produced in China. Chinese manufacturing wages are estimated to be about one-fourth of the amount paid in Brazil and Mexico, and given China's other advantages, competition on the basis of labor cost alone is increasingly less likely to succeed. For example, Mexico's export processing zone (the *maquiladora* industry, see Chapter 13) lost a large share of its apparel sector when China entered the WTO. Mexico's geographic advantage next to the U.S. market was nullified for products that do not need a rapid turn around between order and delivery. The effect on some of the manufacturing in high-income countries is similar, such as apparel in the United States and Italy. Furthermore, as China begins to expand its exports of more sophisticated products such as cars, the competitive pressure is likely to spread into other sectors of manufacturing.

China has several sources of comparative advantage in manufacturing. Its abundance of low wage, low skilled labor has already been mentioned, and its large domestic market has been alluded to. One way to look at China is as a large free-trade area where firms can take advantage of scale economies when producing for the domestic market. Coupled with overall growth and expansion of its middle class, the demand for manufactured goods is increasing rapidly and will continue to absorb a larger share of Chinese output. A third advantage is China's coastal areas, which have potentially convenient logistics for trading internationally. China continues to invest heavily in its port facilities and coastal infrastructure in an effort to develop its geographic advantages.

There are also a few institutional disadvantages that reduce its competitiveness. One is the overall business climate. While China ranks well ahead of India in the World Bank's Doing Business Index, its position at 83 out of 181 hardly qualifies as world leading. Taxes, the availability of credit, licensing, steps to start a business, or to employ workers and investor protections are all in the bottom half of the world rankings.

A related disadvantage of the business climate is China's inability to enforce intellectual property rights. This was the main point of contention between the United States and China in its accession to the WTO, and continues to be a major issue in China's relations with its trading partners. Some firms routinely resist making investments in China for fear that their products will be copied, and firms that do invest often limit themselves to product lines that do not contain trade secrets. China meets WTO standards but its enforcement is ineffective. Chinese firms frequently reverse engineer products, produce a knock-off at a fraction of the price of the imported good since no royalties are paid, and expand across the domestic market. This has generated a reaction in Europe and the United States, but the problems associated with enforcement of property rights are significant.

Many observers believe that China's enforcement will not become effective until China itself has significant intellectual property to protect.

Resources

China's rapid growth has increased its appetite for natural resources. For resource producers in Latin America and Africa, this has been a boon since China is below the world per capita average in all major natural resources except coal. Copper, oil, iron ore, and other minerals have experienced spikes in their world prices, which are in part related to Chinese demand. Simultaneously, a number of developing countries have been able to sign long-term agreements that will provide them with investment for exploration and supply contracts for the delivery of their resources. China's substantial export earnings are available for purchasing the resources it will need as it continues its development.

The fact that China buys its resources from other developing countries does not guarantee that the countries selling the resources will spend the money well. Furthermore, in some cases these purchases pose a direct challenge to the geo-political strategies of the United States, as China has signed agreements with a number of countries the United States has tried to isolate (e.g., Iran, Sudan, and Venezuela, all of which have signed oil delivery contracts). At this point, Chinese oil purchases have not grown faster than the expansion of known reserves, so it is unlikely that Chinese demand is responsible for much of the increase in world prices.

Unresolved Issues

China's large manufacturing sector and the remarkable growth of its exports has generated a number of concerns. Some concerns are based on misconceptions, others are a projection onto China of problems that originate elsewhere, and some are valid. This part of the chapter looks at three such issues: trade balances, the environment, and the call for political reform in the midst of China's increasing level of unrest.

Unbalanced Trade   Competition created by the rapid growth of China's exports has generated pressures for protectionism in a number of countries. In the United States, for example, a $268 billion merchandise trade deficit with China in 2007 fuels protectionist sentiments and calls for Chinese currency reform. Since the mid-1990s, China has run a significant surplus in both its current account and its trade in goods and services. While large by world standards, neither comes close to being as large as the United States' current account deficit. Figure 17.4 shows the trends in current account balances for China, the euro area, Japan, and the United States. To the extent that world trade is vulnerable from its imbalances, it appears that U.S. deficits and not Chinese surpluses are the source of vulnerability.

A few observers argue that a significant portion of China's manufacturing competitiveness is due to its fixed exchange rate system. Before July 21, 2005, China pegged its currency, the renminbi, to the U.S. dollar. Consequently, when the dollar weakened beginning in 2002, the renminbi weakened with it. In many quarters this was seen as an unfair trade advantage for China. In 2005, China announced that it was adopting a narrow exchange rate band and that it would use a trade weighted index instead of a dollar peg. In other words, the People's Bank of China (PBOC) adopted an exchange rate that is permitted to fluctuate in a narrow band and that is pegged to a weighted average of its major trading partners. Moving the peg off the dollar and setting it on a basket of currencies resulted in an appreciation of China renminbi against the U.S. dollar as the latter lost value in world markets. Since 2005, the dollar has fallen against the renminbi by 20 percent, from 8.19 per dollar to 6.83 (as of mid-August 2009).

A related issue is the effect of China's savings on U.S. government finances. China's trade surplus is related to its relatively high savings rate, as discussed in Chapter 9. The export surplus and the large inflow of FDI have caused it to accumulate the largest foreign reserves holdings of any country in the world, valued at over $2 trillion in mid-2009. The inflow of dollars through trade and FDI leads to an expansion of the Chinese money supply as firms convert their export earnings into renminbi and the PBOC supplies whatever level of domestic currency is needed to mop up the dollars. If it did not do this, the price of the renminbi would

FIGURE 17.4 **Current Account Balances, 1990–2007**

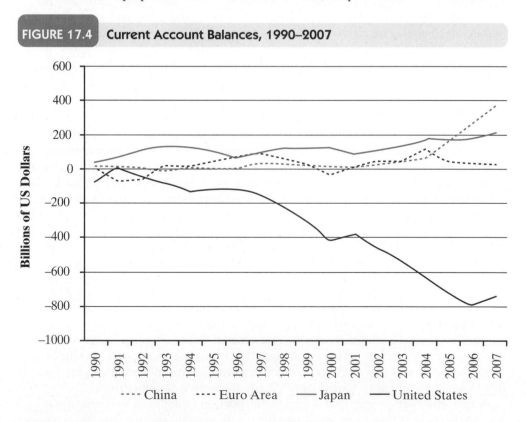

The U.S. current account deficit is much larger and older than China's surplus.

Source: World Bank, *World Development Indicators*.

rise, or in other words, China's currency would appreciate. China then takes a large portion of the newly created renminbi off the market by selling bonds. This is known as **sterilization** because it counteracts the effect on the local currency of the dollar inflow. The local bonds pay low interest rates, and China turns around and buys higher interest foreign assets such as U.S. government bonds with its dollar holdings. In effect, Chinese savings finance U.S. government deficits.

This relationship naturally leads to the fear that if China stopped buying U.S. bonds, it might touch off a crisis in the United States. To the extent this is true, the solution is for the United States to reduce its budget deficits and its trade deficits, which require a large inflow of foreign capital for their financing. According to the U.S. Federal Reserve Bank, China accounts for about 15 percent of the net purchases of U.S. government bonds. This is not a large enough share to have a dramatic direct effect on U.S. interest rates, but it still raises concerns since it would signal a shift in China's willingness to buy U.S. debt and potentially cause other purchasers to change their expectations. Consequently, a change in Chinese purchases of U.S. bonds could tip worldwide investor expectations against the dollar and make it much harder for the United States to finance its deficits. Ironically, this would also hurt China, which currently holds a large supply of U.S. bonds. In a sense, China is stuck with financing U.S. debt, while the United States becomes increasingly vulnerable as its dependence on outside finance grows.

Environmental Pressures   Growth has come at a high environmental cost. Currently China has sixteen of the twenty most polluted cities in the world and 90 percent of its urban groundwater is contaminated. In the last decade, 200 million people have moved from the country to the city, and most live without connection to sewage treatment plants. China's per capita energy consumption is well below the level of the United States, but it is moving up rapidly. Given its large coal deposits (its one abundant natural resource), over the next twenty years it will probably become one of the top contributors to the production of carbon dioxide, a major cause of global warming. If the costs of China's environmental destruction are subtracted from its GDP, its growth rate falls from 9 to 10 percent per year to around 2 percent per year.

China's future economic success is likely to depend significantly on its ability to respond to the negative effects of the environmental destruction created by its growth. Unfortunately, the centralization of control and decision making in the Communist Party works against the creation of flexible and rapid responses to environmental problems. Local areas that are the first to perceive changes in environmental conditions lack a voice in China's highly centralized system and by the time information filters up to the authorities, conditions have deteriorated to the point where far more expensive and disruptive remediation becomes necessary.

Political Reform and Protest   In general, China's leaders recognize their country's environmental problems, but their grip on power and their fear of the consequences if they were to loosen it somewhat prevent them from decentralizing authority and control. Nevertheless, environmental pressures are only one of several forces pressing for greater decentralization of the authority and power of the ruling Communist Party. Some economists have long argued that free markets inevitably lead to political freedoms, but as yet, this has not been the case in China.

In 1993 official Chinese sources reported 8,700 incidents of unrest and/or protest. In 2005 the number was ten times greater, around 87,000. The momentous and rapid changes running through Chinese society are generating increasing levels of unease, discomfort, and anger. China has over 140 million internal migrants who are on the move in search of work and opportunities. Villagers frequently complain about local officials who forcibly take land for the construction of factories, and workers laid off from state-owned factories protest the loss of health care and pension benefits when their unproductive enterprises close without compensation for the workforce. And local citizens complain about provincial authorities that refuse to respond to environmental problems such as toxic spills in local waterways or noxious fumes from manufacturing plants.

China has well over 100 million Internet users, nearly 300,000 nongovernmental organizations (NGOs) and 120,000 newly minted lawyers. The economic changes that it is undergoing are profoundly reshaping society beyond its economy, and while the political system is slow to respond, it is uncertain if the Communist Party will be able to maintain its control.

The Choices Ahead

As China and India succeed, the pressures will mount to limit their participation in world markets. Negotiations for China's accession to the WTO led to a series of bilateral agreements between China and its trading partners that allow voluntary export restraints and other measures to block Chinese exports if they threaten firms in importing countries. The U.S. Congress introduced, and then retracted under political pressure, a measure that would label China's exchange rate management system as an unfair trade advantage. If passed, it would legitimize blocking some Chinese exports from entering the United States. Similar measures have not been proposed for India, although the outsourcing by firms of their IT work has led to calls for the re-examination of policies that may be encouraging firms to go abroad. In the end, however, measures against China and India become difficult to enforce because for every firm hurt by Chinese or Indian imports, others are helped by the low prices and availability of their goods and services. Hence, trade measures to stem trade flows will hurt businesses and consumers that depend on the imports.

If Chinese success in particular is frightening to some politicians, businesses, and workers, Chinese failure should be seen as an even greater threat. For example, the country is unlikely to begin to make serious headway in addressing its environmental problems unless it has political stability and some degree of economic prosperity. It has enormous reserves of coal, which is one of the greatest contributors to global warming when it is burned to generate energy. A switch to cleaner fuels is highly unlikely if the country is struggling against economic failure or political instability. The same holds for its ability to address the problems of water and air pollution, missing urban infrastructure, and other remediation needed in order to counter the effects of rapid economic growth.

A financial crisis in either China or India could radiate in ways that are impossible to predict. As the world's two most populous nations, there are literally hundreds of millions of people who might be affected domestically and the consequences outside of either country could be dramatic. Crises work against stability and peace, and the growth of social protest in China in recent years reduces the likelihood that an economic crisis would be resolved without significant social conflict.

Furthermore, China and India have large parts of their populations that are living in poverty or not far above. While conditions have significantly improved for many, not everyone has benefited from growth and many who have are falling farther and farther behind the new economic elites in both countries. In China this has led to growing dissatisfaction and rising protest. India's democratic system creates more legitimate means for changing leaders who do not deliver, whereas China's growing inequality is seen by many as a potential threat to the current system. A failure of its economic project would undoubtedly worsen economic inequality and lead to greater social unrest.

When governments are undemocratic, social unrest can be a good thing. When they also have nuclear weapons and the world's largest army, too much social unrest can be a threat to the rest of the world. The consequences of a breakdown in order, an economic collapse, or even economic stagnation, are impossible to predict, but any of them would probably pose a serious challenge to prosperity and stability outside China.

Summary

- China and India are the two most populous countries in the world. Taken together, they account for about three-eighths (38.5 percent) of the world's population in 2007.

- Both countries have undertaken extensive economic reforms and both have achieved high rates of economic growth since 1980. China's economy is about three times larger than India's and its growth rate is about 50 percent faster.

- Economic reforms began in 1978 in China and in the 1980s in India. Indian reforms became much more serious and intense after a financial crisis in 1991. China is one of the few formerly communist countries that did not suffer a loss of output during its transition to the market economy. In part this is probably due to the more cautious nature and slower speed of its reforms, but also because of its large agricultural sector. When it began its reforms, about 70 percent of its labor force was in agriculture, much of it very low productivity. A loss of workers to that sector did not result in a decline in output.

- Both China and India score low on the Doing Business Index of the World Bank, indicating that there are a number of institutional changes yet to be made.

- Both countries have seen a very rapid growth of imports and exports. China's manufacturing sector is extremely competitive but relies heavily on technology imports. Its exports are mostly either low technology goods or high technology goods that are assembled in China from imported parts. Exports of Indian business services and computer and information services have taken off since the middle of the 1990s. This type of trade in services represents a new area of trade but is another application of the theory of comparative advantage.

- Trade and growth in China and India pose several challenges for other countries. China's manufacturing sector has a strong comparative advantage in the production of goods that need abundant supplies of low wage labor, while India's production of business services and computer and information services is supported by abundant supplies of English speaking engineers and technicians.

- Large U.S. budget and current account deficits do not depend on China for their financing, but raise the probability of a reaction against China's success in world markets.

- China's inability to enforce intellectual property rights is a constant source of tension between it and its trading partners.

- China's growth has posed an enormous toll on both society and the environment. Its water and air resources are degrading rapidly, and its ability to contain the outbreak and spread of new diseases is under question. The escalation of social protests this has generated has become a major issue for the ruling Communist Party, which seeks to contain the protest.

Vocabulary

Deng Xiaoping

dual track strategy

foreign trading corporation (FTC)

Manmohan Singh

Special Economic Zone (SEZ)

sterilization

township and village enterprises (TVE)

transition economies

Study Questions

1. How are the economies of China and India alike? How are they different?

2. Describe the process of Chinese reforms from their beginning in 1978 up until China's accession to the WTO.

3. What were the factors that led to economic reform in India, and what were the main elements of the reforms?

4. Why did economic reform in Russia and most other transition economies lead to large declines in their GDP but not in China?

5. What are the sources of China's comparative advantage and how does that show up in the goods it trades?

6. What are the factors that make India competitive in business services and computer and information services? Do these factors give it a comparative advantage or do they reflect some other source of competitiveness?

7. What challenges to the world economy do India and China pose?

8. Chinese policies have created a great deal of controversy and discussion. For each of the following topics, describe the issues raised by China's trading partners and evaluate their concerns.

   a. China's trade surplus

   b. China's exchange rate system

   c. Intellectual property

GLOSSARY

Absolute productivity advantage, or **absolute advantage.** A country has an absolute productivity advantage in a good if its labor productivity is higher; that is, it is able to produce more output with an hour of labor than its trading partner can.

Acquis communautaire. The European Union rules governing technical standards, environmental and technical inspections, banking supervision, public accounts, statistical reporting requirements, and other elements of EU law.

Adjustment process. Usually refers to the changes in a country's current account that occur as a result of a fall in the value of its currency.

Aggregate demand (AD). The sum of household consumption, business investment, government spending on final goods and services, and net exports.

Aggregate supply (AS). The total output of an economy.

Antidumping duty (ADD). A tariff levied on imports in retaliation for selling below fair value. *See also* Fair value.

Appreciation. An increase in a currency's value under a floating exchange rate system. *See also* Revaluation.

ASEAN+3. ASEAN+3 refers to bilateral agreements between ASEAN and China, Korea, and Japan.

Asia Pacific Economic Cooperation (APEC). A group of Pacific-region nations founded in 1989 for the purpose of creating free trade among all its members by 2020. APEC includes the United States, Japan, and China, among others. APEC's goal is not a free-trade area; instead, it is to get all members to commit to free trade and open investment flows as a part of their trade policies toward all nations.

Association of Southeast Asian Nations (ASEAN). ASEAN is a community of ten nations with a security component, an economic component, and a socio-cultural component. It was founded in 1967 and has set the date of 2020 for the achievement of a free-trade area.

Austerity. Usually refers to the cuts in government spending and increases in taxes that are implemented to reduce or eliminate a government budget deficit.

Autarky. The complete absence of foreign trade; total self sufficiency of a national economy.

Auto Pact. The 1965 agreement between the United States and Canada that created free trade in the automotive sector.

Baker Plan. The first U.S. plan (1985) to assist indebted nations during the debt crisis of the 1980s.

Banking crisis. A common feature of international financial crises; a banking crisis occurs when banks fail and disintermediation spreads.

Basel Capital Accords. A set of recommended "best practices" designed to help countries avoid banking and financial crises. The accords emphasize capital requirements, supervisory review, and information disclosure.

Brady Plan. A 1989 plan of U.S. Treasury Secretary Nicholas Brady intended to help indebted developing countries. Unlike previous plans, the Brady Plan offered a modest amount of debt relief.

Bretton Woods Conference. A small town in New Hampshire that was, in July 1944, the site of talks establishing the international financial and economic order after World War II. The International Monetary Fund and the World Bank emerged from the Bretton Woods Conference.

Bretton Woods exchange rate system. The exchange rate system that emerged from the Bretton Woods Conference at the end of World War II. *See also* Smithsonian Agreement.

Canadian-U.S. Trade Agreement (CUSTA). A 1989 free trade agreement between the United States and Canada, and a precursor of NAFTA.

Capital account. A record of the transactions in highly specialized financial assets and liabilities between the residents of a nation and the rest of the world.

Capital controls. National controls on the inflow and/or outflow of funds.

Capital requirements. Requirements that owners of financial institutions invest a percentage of their own capital so that all losses are personal losses to shareholders and other bank owners, as well as to depositors.

Chiang Mai Initiative. The Chiang Mai Initiative is an ASEAN+3 agreement to lend currency between central banks.

Cohesion funds. Cohesion funds are a type of EU funding used to support regional development. They are directed toward less developed regions, particularly new members with incomes below the EU average. The funds pay for infrastructure development and environmental projects such as water treatment and transportation projects.

Collective action clauses. A requirement that each international lender agrees to collective mediation between all lenders and the debtor in the event of an international crisis.

Common Agricultural Policy (CAP). The system of support payments and other forms of assistance that is the main agricultural program of the European Union.

Common external tariff. The policy of customs unions in which the members adopt the same tariffs toward nonmembers.

Common market. A regional trade agreement whose member nations allow the free movement of inputs as well as outputs, and who share a common external tariff toward nonmembers.

Comparative productivity advantage, or **comparative advantage.** Achieved in a good when a country has lower opportunity costs of producing the good than those of its trading partners.

Competitive advantage. The ability to sell a good at the lowest price. Competitive advantage may be the result of high productivity and a comparative advantage. Alternatively, it may be the result of government subsidies for inefficient industries.

Competitive devaluation. A devaluation or depreciation in a currency with the intent to gain export markets.

Conditionality. *See* IMF conditionality.

Consumer surplus. The difference between the value of a good to consumers and the price they have to pay. Graphically it is the area under the demand curve and above the price line. *See also* Producer surplus.

Contagion effects. The spread of a crisis from one country to another. This may happen through trade flows, through currency and exchange rate movements, or through a change in the perceptions of foreign investors.

Contractionary fiscal policy. Tax increases and/or cuts in government spending.

Contractionary monetary policy. A cut in the money supply and a rise in interest rates.

Convergence criteria. The five indicators of readiness to begin the single currency in the European Union: stable exchange rates, low inflation, harmonization of long-term interest rates, reduction of government deficits, and reduction of government debt.

Core labor standards. Eight core labor rights developed and advocated by the ILO, and embodied in eight ILO conventions. They cover areas such as freedom from coercion, minimum work age, freedom to bargain collectively, and others.

Council of the European Union. The chief legislative body of the European Union.

Council of Ministers. The legislative body of the EU.

Countervailing duty (CVD). A tariff on imports that is levied in retaliation against foreign subsidies. *See also* Subsidy.

Covered interest arbitrage. Interest rate arbitrage that includes the signing of a forward currency contract to sell the foreign currency when the foreign assets mature. *See also* Interest rate arbitrage.

Crawling peg. A system in which a country fixes its currency to another currency (or a basket of currencies) and makes regular periodic adjustments in the nominal exchange rate in order to offset or control movement in the real exchange rate.

Crony capitalism. A term used to describe conditions in which resources such as bank loans are allocated for political and personal reasons rather than on the basis of market-oriented criteria.

Currency board. A government board that strictly regulates the creation of new money.

Current account. A record of transactions in goods, services, investment income, and unilateral transfers between the residents of a country and the rest of the world.

Current account balance. The broadest measure of a nation's commerce with the rest of the world.

Customs union. An agreement among two or more member countries to engage in free trade with each other and to share a common external tariff toward nonmembers.

Data dissemination standards. The IMF's standards for reporting macroeconomic data.

Deadweight loss. A pure economic loss with no corresponding gains elsewhere in the economy. *See also* Efficiency loss.

Debt crisis. Usually refers to the period between 1982 and 1989 when many indebted developing countries were unable to make interest or principal amortization payments.

Debt service. Principal repayment and interest payments that are made in order to pay off a debt.

Deep integration. Economic integration beyond removal of barriers at each country's border. Deep integration requires changes in domestic laws and regulations that sometimes inadvertently restrict trade.

Deliberation councils. Quasi-legislative bodies that combine representatives from industry with government and that have the purpose of discussing government policy and private sector investment. Japan, Korea, Malaysia, Singapore, and Thailand use deliberation councils.

Delors Report. Named after the president of the European Commission during the 1980s, the report contained three hundred steps that the European Union needed to follow in order to become a common market. The report was adopted in 1987 and led to the creation of a common market under the Single European Act.

Demand-pull. *See* demand-pull factors.

Demand-pull factors. Economic conditions in the receiving country that "pull" in migrants. *See also* Supply push factors.

Demographic transition. The shift from high birth rates and high death rates (characteristic of nearly all pre-industrial societies) to low birth rates and low death rates (characteristic of high-income, industrial societies).

Deng Xiaoping. Chinese leader who began China's reforms in 1978.

Depreciation. A decrease in a currency's value under a floating exchange rate system. *See also* Devaluation.

Derived demand. Demand for a good or service that is derived from the demand for something else. For example, the demand for labor is derived from the demand for goods and services.

Disintermediation. A failure on the part of the banking system that prevents savings from being channeled into investment.

Doha Development Agenda. The name for the trade negotiations that began in 2000 under the auspices of the World Trade Organization.

Doha Round. The current WTO round of trade negotiations. *See* Doha Development Agenda.

Dollarization. The use of the dollar in place of a country's domestic currency. Technically, dollarization can refer to the use of any currency that is not the country's own.

Dual track strategy. China's strategy for transitioning from communism to capitalism is known as a dual track strategy because it localized market reforms to certain geographical areas or economic sectors (e.g., agriculture) while maintaining government planning for the remainder of the economy.

Dumping. Selling in a foreign market at less than fair value. *See also* Fair value.

Economic Commission on Latin America (ECLA, CEPAL). The United Nation's agency that oversees UN activity and information gathering in Latin America.

Economic populism. Economic policies emphasizing growth and redistribution that simultaneously de-emphasize (or deny the importance of) inflation risks, deficit finance, external constraints (i.e., trade and exchange rate issues), and the reactions of economic agents.

Economic restructuring. A movement from one point to another along a country's production possibility curve.

Economic union. The most complete form of economic integration, these unions are common markets that also harmonize many standards while having the same or substantially similar fiscal and monetary policies. Economic unions may include a common currency.

Economies of scale. A decline in average cost while the number of units produced increases.

Effective rates of protection. Effective rates of protection consider levels of protection on intermediate inputs as well as the nominal tariff levied on the protected good. Effective rates are measured as the percentage change in the domestic value added after tariffs on the intermediate and final goods are levied. *See also* Nominal rates of protection.

Efficiency loss. A form of deadweight loss that refers to the loss of income or output that occurs when a nation produces a good at a cost higher than the world price.

Escape clause relief. Temporary tariff protection granted to an industry that experiences a sudden and harmful surge in imports.

Erasmus Program. A EU program for student and faculty mobility at the university level.

Euratom or European Atomic Energy Community (EAEC). An agreement concurrent with the Treaty of Rome that committed the six countries to the peaceful and cooperative development of nuclear energy.

Euro. The new currency of the European Union. Formally introduced as the unit of account in 1999, the euro appeared in January 2002.

European Central Bank. The central bank for the euro area countries.

European Coal and Steel Community (ECSC). A 1951 agreement among the six countries that eventually formed the EEC, creating free trade in the coal and steel industries.

European Commission. The executive branch of the European Union.

European Community (EC). The name for the European Union prior to the signing of the Maastricht Treaty and the creation of the economic union.

European Economic Community (EEC). The original name for the community founded by the Treaty of Rome. The EEC eventually became the EC, and then the EU.

European Monetary System (EMS). An exchange rate system started in 1979 that linked the currencies of each of the members of the EC. The EMS was replaced in 1999 by the euro.

European Parliament. A quasi-advisory body of the European Union. The parliament is the only directly elected government body in the European Union, and it has been moving toward becoming a true legislature.

European Union (EU). Twenty-seven western European nations that are an economic union.

Exchange rate. The price of one currency expressed in terms of a second currency. Exchange rates may be measured in real or nominal terms.

Exchange rate crisis. A collapse of a country's currency.

Exchange rate mechanism (ERM). The system adopted by the EC when it used the EMS. The ERM was a target zone exchange rate that allowed some limited flexibility in an otherwise fixed set of exchange rates.

Exchange rate risk. Risk that occurs when an individual or firm holds assets that are denominated in a foreign currency. The risk is the potential for unexpected losses (or gains) due to unforeseen fluctuations in the value of the foreign currency.

Expansionary fiscal policy. Tax cuts and/or increases in government spending.

Expansionary monetary policy. Increases in the money supply and cuts in interest rates.

Expenditure reducing policies. Policies that reduce the overall level of domestic expenditure. These are appropriate for addressing the problem of a trade deficit, and they include cuts in government expenditures and/or increases in taxes.

Expenditure switching. *See* expenditure switching policies.

Expenditure switching policies. Policies designed to shift the expenditures of domestic residents. If the problem is a trade deficit, they should shift toward domestically produced goods; if the problem is a trade surplus, they should shift toward foreign goods. Examples of these policies are changes in the exchange rate and changes in tariffs and quotas.

Export pessimism. The views of Argentine economist Raul Prebisch and his followers, who believed real prices received by Latin American countries for their exports would fall over time.

Export processing zone (EPZ). A geographical region in which firms are free from tariffs as long as they export the goods that are made from imports. Rules and regulations governing EPZs vary by country, but all of them are aimed at encouraging exports, often through encouragement given to investment.

External debt. Debt that is owed to agents outside a country's national boundaries.

External economies of scale. Scale economies that are external to a firm, but internal to an industry. Consequently, all the firms in an industry experience declining average costs as the size of the industry increases.

Externality. A divergence between social and private returns.

Factor abundance, factor scarcity. These are relative terms because, strictly speaking, all factors are scarce. Relative factor abundance implies that an economy has more of a particular factor in relation to some other factor and by comparison to another economy. Relative factor scarcity implies the opposite.

Fair value. A standard for determining if dumping is occurring. Generally, in the United States fair value is the average price in the exporter's home market or the average price in third country markets. Definitions vary by country, making fair value a source of disagreement.

Financial account. The part of the balance of payments that tracks capital flows between a national economy and the rest of the world.

Financial crisis. Usually involves a banking crisis and may also entail an exchange rate crisis. A financial crisis results in disintermediation and a slowdown in economic activity that may be severe.

Fiscal policy. Policies related to government expenditures and taxation.

Fixed exchange rate system. An exchange rate that is fixed and unchanging, relative to some other currency or group of currencies.

Flexible (floating) exchange rate system. When supply and demand for foreign exchange determine the value of a nation's money.

Foreign affiliate. A foreign-based operation that is owned by a firm in the home country.

Foreign direct investment (FDI). The purchase of physical assets such as real estate or businesses by a foreign company or individual. It can be outward (citizens or businesses in the home country purchase assets in a foreign country) or inward (foreigners purchase assets in the home country). *See also* Foreign portfolio investment.

Foreign exchange reserves. Assets held by the national monetary authority that can be used to settle international payments. Dollars, euros, yen, and monetary gold are examples of reserves.

Foreign portfolio investment. The purchase of financial assets such as stocks, bonds, bank accounts, or related financial instruments. As with FDI, it can be inward or outward.

Foreign trading corporation (FTC). Prior to reform, all foreign trade in China was controlled by twelve enterprises that were attached to various branches of government. These enterprises were called foreign trade corporations.

Forward exchange rate. The exchange rate in a forward market.

Forward markets. Markets in which buyers and sellers agree on a quantity and a price for a foreign exchange or other transaction that takes place in (usually) 30, 90, or 180 days from the time the contract is signed. *See also* Spot markets.

Four Tigers. Hong Kong, Korea, Singapore, and Taiwan. Their economic growth began shortly after Japan's post–World War II development. They are classified by the World Bank as either high-income or upper-middle-income economies. (The Four Tigers are sometimes called the Four Dragons or the Little Dragons.) *See also* High-performance Asian economies and Newly industrializing economies.

Free riding. Occurs when a person lets others pay for a good or service, or lets them do the work when he or she knows that he or she cannot be excluded from consumption of the good or from the benefits of the work.

Free Trade Agreement of the Americas (FTAA). An agreement currently under negotiation to create a free-trade area among thirty-four countries in the Western Hemisphere.

Free-trade area. A preferential trade agreement in which countries permit the free movement of outputs (goods and services) across their borders as long as the outputs originate in one of the member countries.

Gains from trade. The increase in consumption made possible by specialization and trade.

General Agreement on Tariffs and Trade (GATT). The main international agreement covering the rules of trade in most, but not all, goods. The GATT's origins can be traced to negotiations that took place in 1946, after World War II.

General Agreement on Trade in Services (GATS). An attempt to extend the rules and principles of the GATT to trade in services. GATS was one of the outcomes of the Uruguay Round.

Gold standard. A fixed exchange rate system that uses gold as its standard of value.

Gross domestic product (GDP). The market value of all final goods and services produced in a year inside a nation.

Gross national product (GNP). The market value of all final goods and services produced by the residents of a nation, regardless of where the production takes place. GNP equals GDP minus income paid to foreigners plus income received from abroad.

Grubel-Lloyd (GL) index. A measure used to determine the importance of intraindustry trade.

Harmonization of standards. Harmonization of standards occurs when two or more countries negotiate a common standard or policy. Harmonization can occur with respect to safety standards, technical standards, environmental standards, legal standards, certification, or with respect to any requirement set forth by national policies. *See also* Mutual recognition of standards.

Heckscher-Ohlin (HO) trade theory. A trade theory that predicts the goods and services that countries export and import. The theorem states that countries will export goods that require the intensive use of relatively abundant factors to produce, and import goods that require relatively scarce factors to produce.

Hedging. Eliminating risk (e.g., exchange rate risk can be eliminated, or hedged, by signing a forward contract).

Heterodox. A heterodox stabilization policy is designed to cure inflation by the following: cutting government spending, limiting the creation of new money, reforming the tax system, and freezing wages and prices. *See also* Orthodox stabilization policies.

High-income, upper-middle, lower-middle, and Low-income countries. Categories used by the World Bank to classify countries by their level of per capita income. The criteria for categories change over time. Currently, low income is less than $876 per year, lower-middle income is $876 to $3,465 per year, upper-middle income is $3,466 to $10,725 per year, and high income is above $10,725 per year.

High-performance Asian economies (HPAE). The eight high-performance Asian economies of Hong Kong, Japan, Indonesia, Korea, Malaysia, Singapore, Taiwan, and Thailand. *See also* Four Tigers and Newly industrializing economies.

IMF conditionality. The changes in economic policy that borrowing nations are required to make in order to receive International Monetary Fund loans. The changes usually involve policies that reduce or eliminate a severe trade deficit and/or a central government budget deficit. In practical terms, they involve reduced expenditures by the government and by the private sector (to reduce imports) and increased taxes. *See also* International Monetary Fund.

Import substitution industrialization (ISI). An economic development strategy that emphasizes the domestic production of goods that substitute for imports. ISI policies decrease imports and exports.

Index of openness. A measure of the importance of trade to a national economy, consisting of exports plus imports divided by GDP.

Industrial policy. A policy designed to create new industries or to provide support for existing ones.

Infant industry. A young industry. An argument for tariff protection is often made based on the belief that a particular industry is incapable of competing at present but that it will soon grow into a mature and competitive industry that no longer needs protection.

Informal economy. The part of a national or local economy that is unmeasured, untaxed, and unregulated.

Information disclosure. One of the three areas emphasized by the Basel Accord in its list of recommended practices. Information disclosure is intended to encourage market discipline by requiring banks to disclose the relevant information that lenders, investors, and depositors need to understand the full scope of a particular bank's operations.

Institution. A set of rules of behavior. Institutions set limits, or constraints, on social, political, and economic interaction. An institution may be informal (e.g., manners, taboos, or customs) or formal (e.g., constitutions or laws).

Intellectual property rights. Intellectual property is divided into copyrights and related rights for literary and artistic work, and industrial property rights for trademarks, patents, industrial designs, geographical indications, and the layout of integrated circuits.

Interest parity. The notion that the interest rate differential between two countries is approximately equal to the percentage difference between the forward and spot exchange rates.

Interest rate arbitrage. The transfer of funds from one financial asset and currency to another to take advantage of higher interest rates. *See also* Covered interest arbitrage.

Interindustry trade. Trade that involves exports and imports of goods that are produced in different industries, for example, when the United States exports cars and imports sugar cane.

Intermediate inputs. Parts and materials that are incorporated into a final good such as a consumer good or investment good.

Intermediation. The role of banks as institutions that concentrate savings from many sources and lend the money to investors.

Internal economies of scale. The idea that an individual firm experiences a decline in its average cost of production as it increases the number of units produced.

International financial architecture. The complex of institutions, international organizations, governments, and private economic agents that make up the international financial system.

International investment position. The value of all foreign assets owned by a nation's residents, businesses, and government, minus the value of all domestic assets owned by foreigners.

International Labor Organization (ILO). The international organization charged with responsibilities for researching international labor conditions and providing technical assistance in the area of labor conditions and standards.

International Monetary Fund (IMF). One of the original Bretton Woods institutions, IMF responsibilities include helping member countries that suffer from instability or problems with their balance of payments. It also provides technical expertise in international financial relations.

Intrafirm trade. International trade between two or more divisions of the same company that are located in different countries.

Intraindustry trade. Exports and imports of the same category of goods and/or services.

Investment income. A subcomponent of the current account; income received or paid abroad.

J-curve. A currency depreciation often results in a worsening of the trade deficit in the short run and an improvement in the long run.

Labor argument. The argument for trade protection based on the false belief that high-wage countries will be harmed by imports from low-wage countries.

Labor productivity. The amount of output per unit of labor input.

Large country case. A country that purchases a significant share of the world's output of a particular good may improve its welfare by imposing a tariff that causes import prices to fall.

Lender of last resort. In international economics, a place where nations can borrow after all sources of commercial lending have dried up. Today, the IMF (International Monetary Fund) fills this role.

Lost Decade. The period of recession in Latin America brought on by the region-wide debt crisis beginning in August 1982. There is no official date ending the Lost Decade, but 1989 is a useful benchmark, since it coincided with a new strategy for handling the crisis.

Maastricht Treaty. Sometimes called the Treaty on Economic and Monetary Union. Ratified in 1991 by the members of the European Union, its most visible provision includes the single currency program that began in 1999. It creates an economic union among the members of the European Union.

Magnification effect. The idea that a rise or decline in goods prices has a larger effect in the same direction on the income of the factor used intensively in its production.

Manmohan Singh. Indian leader responsible for initiating economic reforms in 1991.

Managed float. A floating exchange rate in which the monetary authority occasionally intervenes to cause a rise or fall in the value of the country's currency.

Maquiladora. Mexican manufacturing firms, mostly along the U.S.-Mexico border, that receive special tax breaks.

Market failure. A situation in which markets do not produce the most beneficial economic outcome. Market failure has numerous causes, including externalities and monopolistic or oligopolistic market structures.

Mercantilism. The economic system that arose in western Europe in the 1500s, during the period in which modern nation states were emerging from feudal monarchies. Mercantilism has been called the politics and economics of nation building because it stressed the need for nations to run trade surpluses to obtain revenues for armies and national construction projects. Mercantilists favored granting monopoly rights to individuals and companies, they shunned competition, and they viewed exports as positive and imports as negative. Today, the term *mercantilism* is sometimes used to describe the policies of nations that promote their exports while keeping their markets relatively closed to imports.

Merchandise trade balance. Exports of goods minus imports of goods.

MERCOSUR. The Mercado Común del Sur, or Common Market of the South, is the largest regional trade grouping in South America. It includes four countries: Brazil, Argentina, Uruguay, and Paraguay.

Monetary policy. National macroeconomic policies related to the money supply and interest.

Monopolistic competition. Competition between differentiated products, combining elements of perfect competition and monopoly.

Moral hazard. A financial incentive to withhold information, take on excessive risk, or behave in a manner that generates significant social costs.

Most-favored nation (MFN). The idea that every member of the World Trade Organization (WTO) is required to treat each of its trading partners as well as it treats its most favored trading partner. In effect, MFN prohibits one country from discriminating against another.

Multilateralism. An approach to trade and investment issues that involves large numbers of countries. Multilateralism stands for the belief that market openings should benefit all nations. Multilateral institutions include the World Trade Organization, the World Bank, and the International Monetary Fund.

Multiplier effect. The macroeconomic concept that a change in spending has an impact on the national product, which is ultimately larger than the original spending change.

Mutual recognition of standards. An alternative to the harmonization of standards. Under a mutual recognition system, countries keep different standards while agreeing to recognize and accept each other's standards within their national jurisdictions.

National income and product accounts (NIPA). A set of accounts for a nation showing the components of GDP. These have both an income view and a product view. In theory, they are equivalent as total income in an economy must equal the total value of output produced.

National treatment. The idea that foreign firms operating inside a nation should not be treated differently than domestic firms.

Neoliberalism. Market fundamentalism that became common throughout Latin America in the late 1980s and 1990s.

Newly industrializing economies (NIEs). The most recent wave of rapidly growing and industrializing developing nations. There are a number of these economies in Latin America (e.g., Argentina, Brazil, Chile, and Mexico) as well as in East Asia (the HPAE, Indonesia, Malaysia, and Thailand).

Nominal exchange rate. The price of a unit of foreign exchange. *See also* Real exchange rate.

Nominal rates of protection. The amount of a tariff (or the tariff equivalent of a quota) expressed as a percentage of the good's price. *See also* Effective rates of protection.

Nominal tariff. The tax on imports of a particular good, expressed in either percentages or absolute amounts. *See also* Effective rates of protection.

Nondiminishable. A good or service that is not reduced by consumption. For example, listening to a radio broadcast does not reduce its availability to others.

Nondiscrimination. The notion that national laws should not treat foreign firms differently than domestic firms.

Nonexcludable. When people who do not pay for a good or service cannot be excluded from its consumption. National defense is an example.

Nonrival. *See* Nondiminishable.

Nontariff barrier (NTB). Any trade barrier that is not a tariff. Most important are quotas, which are physical limits on the quantity of permitted imports. Nontariff barriers include red tape and regulations, rules requiring governments to purchase from domestic producers, and a large number of other practices that indirectly limit imports.

Nontariff measure. Nontariff measures are nontariff barriers that are not quotas. They include red tape or cumbersome and unevenly applied rules. In general, the term refers to any regulatory or policy rules other than tariffs and quotas that reduce the physical quantity of imports or exports.

Nontransparent. Not easily interpreted or understood. For example, some countries use red tape and bureaucratic rules to block imports.

North American Agreement on Environmental Cooperation. The environmental "side agreement" to the NAFTA.

North American Agreement on Labor Cooperation. The labor "side agreement" to the NAFTA.

North American Development Bank (NADBank). A financial institution responsible for raising private funds and providing its financing for development projects along the U.S.-Mexico border.

North American Free-Trade Agreement (NAFTA). The free-trade area formed by Canada, Mexico, and the United States. NAFTA began in 1994.

Odious debt. Debt that is contracted by a country with an unrepresentative government and that is used in ways that do not benefit the people of the nation.

Official reserve assets. Assets held by governments for use in settling international debts. Official resource assets consist primarily of key foreign currencies.

Off-shoring. The movement of some or all of a firm's activities to a foreign country.

OLI theory. A model of the determinants of foreign direct investment that is based on the key variables Ownership-Location-Internalization.

Oligopoly. A market with so few producers that each firm can influence the market price.

Open market operations. The main tool of monetary policy, consisting of the buying and selling of government debt (bills, notes, and bonds) in order to influence bank reserves and interest rates.

Openness. *See* Index of openness.

Opportunity cost. The value of the best forgone alternative to the activity actually chosen.

Optimal currency area. A region of fixed exchange rates or a single currency. A currency area is optimal in the sense that it is precisely the right geographical size to capture the benefits of fixed rates without incurring the costs.

Orthodox. An orthodox stabilization policy is designed to cure inflation by the following: cutting government spending, limiting the creation of new money, and reforming the tax system. *See also* Heterodox.

Outsourcing. Outsourcing is the shifting of procurement from within a firm to outside a firm. It is often used to refer to services that are purchased abroad, such as the procurement of business services in India by a firm based in Europe or the United States.

Partial trade agreement. An agreement that covers only some goods and/or services and is less than a free-trade agreement.

Pegged exchange rate. A form of fixed exchange rate. *See* Crawling peg.

Pollution havens. Countries that compete for investment by advertising their low environmental standards.

Price line. The rate at which one good trades for another in a two-good model; the slope of the price line is the relative price. The same as a trade line.

Private returns. The value of all private benefits minus all private costs, properly adjusted to take into account that some costs and benefits are in the future and must be discounted to show their value in today's dollars. *See also* Social returns.

Producer surplus. The difference between the minimum price a producer would accept to produce a given quantity and the price it actually receives. Graphically it is the area under the price line and above the supply curve. *See also* Consumer surplus.

Product cycle. The idea that manufactured goods go through a cycle of heavy research and development requiring experimentation in the product and the manufacturing process, followed by stabilization of design and production, and a final stage of complete standardization.

Product differentiation. Two products that serve similar purposes but that are different in one or more dimensions. Most consumer goods are differentiated products.

Production possibilities curve (PPC). This curve shows the maximum amount of output possible, given the available supply of inputs. It also shows the trade-off that a country must make if it wishes to increase the output of one of its goods.

Public goods. Goods that share two characteristics: nonexcludability and nonrivalry or nondiminishability. If they are excludable but nondiminishable goods, they are sometimes called collective goods.

Purchasing power parity. An adjustment to exchange rates or incomes designed to keep constant the real purchasing power of money when converted from one currency to another.

Qualified majority. Most EU legislation passed by the European Union Council of Ministers requires a qualified majority, equivalent to about 72 percent of the total votes cast.

Quota. A numerical limit on the volume of imports.

Quota rents. The excess profits earned by foreign producers (and sometimes domestic distributors of foreign products) in an export market. Quota rents occur whenever a quota causes a price increase in the market receiving the exports.

Race to the bottom. Downward pressure on labor, environmental, or other standards that comes about through price competition.

Real exchange rate. The inflation-adjusted nominal rate. The real rate is useful for examining changes in the relative purchasing power of foreign currencies over time.

Regional trade agreement (RTA). Agreements between two or more countries, each offering the others preferential access to its markets. RTAs provide varying degrees of access and variable amounts of deep integration.

Relative price. The price of one good in terms of another good. It is similar to a money price, which expresses the price in terms of dollars and cents, but relative price is in terms of the quantity of the first good that must be given up in order to buy a second good.

Rent seeking. Any activity by firms, individuals, or special interests that is designed to alter the distribution of income to their favor. Political lobbying, legal challenges, and bribery are common forms of rent-seeking behaviors, which use resources (labor and capital) but do not add to national output. For this reason, rent seeking is a net loss to the nation.

Resource curse. The economic and/or political problems caused by an abundance of one valuable natural resource such as petroleum.

Revaluation. An increase in the value of a currency under a fixed exchange rate system. *See also* Appreciation.

Rules of origin. Trade rules within a free-trade area or other agreement requiring that a set percentage of the value of a good must originate in the countries engaged in the trade agreement in order for the good to qualify for free-trade treatment. The percentage is negotiated when the trade agreement is created.

Section 301. A clause in U.S. trade legislation that requires the United States Trade Representative to take action against any nation that persistently engages in what the United States considers unfair trade practices. *See also* Special 301.

Securitization. The bundling of a group of assets so as to sell shares in the bundle.

Separate standards. Environmental, labor, or other standards that are unique to each country.

Shallow integration. The elimination or reduction of tariffs, quotas, and other border-related barriers (such as customs procedures) that restrict the flow of goods across borders. *See also* Deep integration.

Single European Act (SEA). The act that created a common market among the members of the European Community. The SEA was implemented in 1993.

Smithsonian Agreement. This 1971 agreement by major industrialized countries to devalue the gold content of the dollar was the beginning of the end for the Bretton Woods exchange rate system.

Social networks. Members of a migrant's family or village that provide support in the migrant's new location.

Social returns. Social returns include private returns, but they add costs and benefits to the elements of society that are not taken into consideration in the private returns. For example, a firm that generates pollution that it does not have to clean up imposes costs on society, which causes social returns to be lower than private returns.

Sovereign wealth funds. Assets held by a central government that are available for settlement of international claims.

Sovereignty. Free from outside intervention, or self-determining.

Special 301. A part of U.S. trade law requiring the United States Trade Representative to monitor property rights enforcement around the globe.

Special drawing right (SDR). The unit of account and artificial currency used by the International Monetary Fund (IMF). The SDR is a weighted average of several currencies and serves as an official reserve asset.

Special economic zone (SEZ). A special region in China in which local officials are encouraged to experiment with new economic policies. SEZs are designed to encourage foreign investment and exports.

Specific factors model. A trade model that allows for mobile and immobile factors of production.

Spot markets. Market transactions that are concluded at the same time the price is agreed upon. In the currency spot market there is usually a day's lag before the currency is actually delivered. *See also* Forward markets.

Stabilization policies. National macroeconomic policies designed to cure inflation and reduce a government deficit. Stabilization policies are usually a first step in compliance with IMF conditionality during a macroeconomic crisis. *See*

also Structural adjustment policies, Orthodox stabilization policies, and Heterodox.

Standstills. An agreement between international creditors and debtors to allow a temporary halt to the payment of interest and principal on previous loans.

Statistical discrepancy. The sum of the current, capital, and financial accounts (multiplied by minus one).

Sterilization. Sterilization refers to the actions by a central bank to counteract the money supply effects of an inflow of foreign currency. Without sterilization, foreign currency inflows will expand the domestic money supply as recipients of foreign funds convert them to domestic money. With sterilization, the central bank removes excess money from the economy with open market operations.

Stolper-Samuelson theorem. A corollary of the Heckscher-Ohlin Theory stating that changes in import or export prices lead to a change in the same direction of the income of factors used intensively in its production.

Strategic trade policy. The use of trade barriers, subsidies, or other industrial support policies designed to capture the profits of foreign firms for domestic firms.

Structural adjustment policies. Policies that are designed to increase the role of market forces in a national economy. Structural adjustment policies are mainly microeconomic in nature and include privatization, deregulation, and trade reform. *See also* Stabilization policies.

Structural reform policies. A set of reform policies designed to make economies more efficient. These usually include the freeing of prices (ending of price subsidies), liberalization of trade, privatization, and the removal of interest rate controls, among others.

Subsidiarity. The principle that the authority of the European Union to involve itself in individual national affairs is limited to those issues that are transnational in scope. In current practice, this includes environmental policies, regional policies, research and technology development, and economic and monetary union.

Subsidy. Government assistance for industry. The Uruguay Round of the GATT defined subsidies as direct loans or transfers, preferential tax treatments, a direct supply of goods, or income and price supports.

Sudden stop. The sudden cessation of capital inflows that had been used to finance a current account deficit.

Supervisory review. One of the areas of reform emphasized by the Basel Accord, dealing with the supervision of risk management and standards for daily business practices for banks engaged in international borrowing.

Supply-push. *See* supply-push factors.

Supply-push factors. The factors that "push" migrants out of their home country. *See also* Demand-pull factors.

Swap agreements. Also called swaps, useful tools for short-term borrowing when a central bank encounters a shortage in international reserves. For example, the Chiang Mai Initiative among the ASEAN+3 countries allows Thailand to borrow dollar reserves from China. China, or another lending country, plays a role similar to the IMF, but with greater flexibility and a faster response.

Tariffs. Taxes imposed on imports. Tarrifs raise the price to the domestic consumer and reduce the quantity demanded.

Technology transfer. The spread of technological information and capacity from one country to another.

Terms of trade (TOT). The average price of a country's exports divided by the average price of imports: TOT = (index of export prices)/(index of import prices). A decline in the terms of trade means that each unit of exports buys a smaller amount of imports.

Total factor productivity (TFP). A measurement of the quantity of output per unit of input. Increases in TFP mean that overall productivity has improved and that a given level of inputs will create more output; hence, technology or enterprise organization must have improved.

Township and village enterprises (TVE). Chinese enterprises outside major cities that are owned and operated by local governments, or, in many cases, privately owned and operated.

Trade adjustment assistance (TAA). Government programs that offer temporary assistance to workers who lose jobs because of foreign trade or their firms moving abroad.

Trade balance. Net exports, that is, the difference between exports of goods and services and imports of goods and services.

Trade bloc. A preferential trade area; a group of nations that reduces or eliminates barriers between themselves while maintaining higher tariffs and other barriers to trade against nonmember, third party countries.

Trade creation. The opposite of trade diversion. Trade creation occurs when trade policies cause a shift in production from a higher cost producer (often a domestic one) to a lower cost producer.

Trade deficit. A negative merchandise trade balance; the deficit may or may not include measurement of services trade.

Trade diversion. The opposite of trade creation. Trade diversion occurs when trade policies cause a shift in production and imports from a lower cost producer to a higher cost producer.

Trade line. *See* Price line.

Trade Related Aspects of Intellectual Property Rights (TRIPS). An agreement that emerged from the Uruguay Round of the GATT. It requires increased enforcement of intellectual property.

Trade rounds. Multilateral negotiating rounds under the auspices of the GATT or the WTO.

Tranches. Parts of an IMF loan that are made in several installments.

Transaction costs. The costs of gathering market information, arranging a market agreement, and enforcing the agreement. Transaction costs include legal, marketing, and insurance costs, as well as quality checks, advertising, distribution, and after-sales service costs.

Transboundary and non-transboundary environmental impacts. Environmental externalities that do or do not cross international borders.

Transition economies. Countries that are in the process of moving from bureaucratically controlled economies to market-based economies. Transition economies include most of the countries that adopted socialist or communist ideologies during the twentieth century.

Transparency. Any trade barrier that is clearly defined as a barrier. Tariffs have the most transparency (are the most transparent) because they are usually clearly specified and published in each country's tariff code. Any disguised or hidden trade barriers cause a country's trade policy to be nontransparent.

Treaty of Lisbon. An EU treaty awaiting adoption by all EU members. The Lisbon Treaty will reorganize the voting shares in EU bodies and provide for a common foreign policy, among other things.

Treaty of Rome. The funding document of the European Economic Community (EEC), the Treaty of Rome was signed by six nations in 1957 and went into force in 1958. The EEC has since become the European Union and includes fifteen members, but the Treaty of Rome remains its core legal document.

Treaty on European Union. Also known as the Maastricht Treaty, it is the agreement that deepened EU integration from a common market to an economic union.

Unilateral transfers. A component of the current account that measures the grants from one country to another.

Uruguay Round. The latest round of tariff negotiations within the GATT framework, the Uruguay Round began in 1986 in Punta del Este, Uruguay, concluded in 1993, and was ratified in 1994. Among other accomplishments, it created the World Trade Organization.

Value added. The price of a good minus the value of intermediate inputs used to produce it. Value added measures the contribution of capital and labor at a given stage of production.

Voluntary export restraint (VER). An agreement between nations in which the exporting nation voluntarily agrees to limit its exports in order to reduce competition in the importing country.

Washington Consensus. A set of policies prescribed for developing countries by the U.S. government, the International Monetary Fund and World Bank, and the unofficial community of think tanks centered in Washington, D.C. In general, the policies favor the use of market forces over government direction as an allocative mechanism.

World Bank. A Bretton Woods institution, originally charged with the responsibility for providing financial and technical assistance to the war-torn economies of Europe. In the 1950s, the World Bank began to shift its focus to developing countries.

World Trade Organization (WTO). An umbrella organization created by the Uruguay Round of the GATT talks, the WTO houses the GATT and many other agreements. It is the main international body through which multilateral trade talks take place.

Zero sum. The costs and benefits of an activity cancel each other (equal zero).

INDEX